THE ROUTLEDGE COMPANION TO REWARD MANAGEMENT

T0341264

The Routledge Companion to Reward Management provides a prestige reference work and a state-of-the-art compilation, mapping contemporary developments and debates on rewarding people in employment, and how they relate to business, corporate governance and management.

Reward management stands at the interdisciplinary interface between economics, industrial relations and HRM, industrial psychology and organizational sociology, and increasingly corporate governance incorporating debates around equity and fairness in and around the employment relationship and wider capital–labour relations. In recent years, trade union decline and widening differentials between those employed at the top of organizations have generated critical commentary in the popular media which can negatively impact on social cohesion.

Theoretically underpinned but practically oriented, this Companion will synthesize these trends and controversies around issues while tracing conceptual and empirical provenance, currency and future prospects. It will be an invaluable resource for policy makers, practitioners, students and researchers in reward management, corporate governance, management and HRM seeking convenient access to an area which is highly complex and controversial in application.

Stephen J. Perkins JP DPhil (Oxon) is Emeritus Professor, London Metropolitan University and a Senior Research Fellow with the Global Policy Institute, London. His doctoral thesis at the University of Oxford analysed strategies for managing senior management activity under the rubric of Anglo-American corporate governance principles. He is a Chartered Manager and Fellow of the Chartered Management Institute, a Chartered Fellow of the Chartered Institute of Personnel and Development, and a Fellow of the Higher Education Academy. Immediate past Chair of the Corporate Governance Special Interest Group of the British Academy of Management, he has occupied a series of senior management posts in industry during privatization and internationalization initiatives, served as secretary to a FTSE top-30 board remuneration committee, as a board non-executive director, and as an advisor to an array of state-owned and stock market-listed companies transnationally. With over 100 publications, Professor Perkins' research focuses, in particular, on the interplay of corporate governance, strategy, performance and reward – connecting theory with practice. He has for several years held a commission from the CIPD to conduct the widely consulted annual survey of reward management across UK organizations, as well as co-authoring that institution's core text *Reward Management* for students completing their professional education.

Routledge Companions in Business, Management and Accounting

Routledge Companions in Business, Management and Accounting are prestige reference works providing an overview of a whole subject area or sub-discipline. These books survey the state of the discipline including emerging and cutting edge areas. Providing a comprehensive, up to date, definitive work of reference, Routledge Companions can be cited as an authoritative source on the subject.

A key aspect of these Routledge Companions is their international scope and relevance. Edited by an array of highly regarded scholars, these volumes also benefit from teams of contributors which reflect an international range of perspectives.

Individually, Routledge Companions in Business, Management and Accounting provide an impactful one-stop-shop resource for each theme covered. Collectively, they represent a comprehensive learning and research resource for researchers, postgraduate students and practitioners.

Published titles in this series include:

The Routledge Companion to Risk, Crisis and Security in Business
Edited by Kurt J. Engemann

The Routledge Companion to Fair Value in Accounting
Edited by Gilad Livne and Garen Markarian

The Routledge Companion to European Business
Edited by Gabriele Suder, Monica Riviere and Johan Lindeque

The Routledge Companion to Management Buyouts
Edited by Mike Wright, Kevin Amess, Nick Bacon and Donald Siegel

The Routledge Companion to Co-opetition Strategies
Edited by Anne-Sophie Fernandez, Paul Chiambaretto. Frédéric Le Roy and Wojciech Czakon

The Routledge Companion to Reward Management
Edited by Stephen J. Perkins

The Routledge Companion to Accounting in China
Edited by Haiyan Zhou

The Routledge Companion to Critical Marketing
Edited by Mark Tadajewski, Matthew Higgins, Janice Denegri Knott and Rohit Varman

The Routledge Companion to the History of Retailing
Edited by Jon Stobart and Vicki Howard

For more information about this series, please visit: www.routledge.com/Routledge-Companions-in-Business-Management-and-Accounting/book-series/RCBMA

THE ROUTLEDGE COMPANION TO REWARD MANAGEMENT

Edited by Stephen J. Perkins

Routledge
Taylor & Francis Group

LONDON AND NEW YORK

First published 2019 by Routledge
2 Park Square, Milton Park, Abingdon, Oxon OX14 4RN
605 Third Avenue, New York, NY 10017

Routledge is an imprint of the Taylor & Francis Group, an informa business

First issued in paperback 2022

Publisher's Note
The publisher has gone to great lengths to ensure the quality of this reprint but points out that some imperfections in the original copies may be apparent.

British Library Cataloguing-in-Publication Data
A catalogue record for this book is available from the British Library

Library of Congress Cataloging-in-Publication Data
A catalog record has been requested for this book

ISBN: 978-1-138-29426-4 (hbk)
ISBN: 978-1-03-233873-6 (pbk)
DOI: 10.4324/9781315231709

Typeset in Bembo
by Sunrise Setting Ltd, Brixham, UK

CONTENTS

FIGURES

Figures

TABLES

CONTRIBUTORS

James Allan is Managing Director, Head of Corporate Banking FX, Barclays International, responsible for delivering FX payments and risk management solutions to corporate clients in the UK and internationally. James has an Executive MBA (Distinction) from Cass Business School, City, University of London. A passionate advocate of diversity, James plays a key role in promoting inclusion with clients, and in the broader community. He featured in the OUTStanding Top 50 LGBT Future Leaders List published in the *Financial Times*.

Conny Herbert Antoni is Professor of Work and Organizational Psychology at the University of Trier and President of the German Psychological Society. His current research interests include reward management, psychological contracts, (virtual) leadership and teamwork, stress and work–life balance. In his applied work, he helps management to design and change work and reward systems.

Alexandra Arnold is senior research associate and lecturer at the Center for Human Resource Management (CEHRM) at the University of Lucerne (Switzerland). She received her PhD in work and organizational psychology from the University of Zurich (Switzerland). She further spent two years as a visiting scholar at the School of Management and Labor Relations (SMLR) at Rutgers University (USA). Her primary research interest evolves around pay transparency and employees' attitudes and behaviours. Her current research examines the drivers and outcomes of pay transparency in different countries around the world.

Marie Bailey, PhD, is a practitioner and academic in HRM, currently resident in Paris, France. She is the founder of an evidence-based consultancy firm, *Promise in People*. Marie has previously worked in both the public and private sector and, in particular, in the pharmaceutical, financial services and engineering sectors.

Ewa J. Beck-Krala is an assistant professor of human resources at the Faculty of Management, AGH University of Science and Technology, Krakow. She has been teaching, conducting research and consulting in human resources management in Poland and has produced more than 80 publications based on her research and experience which include her book: Evaluation of the Effectiveness of Rewards.

Magdalena Bielenia-Grajewska, PhD habil, is an Associate Professor in the Department of Translation Studies and a head of the Intercultural Communication and Neurolinguistics Laboratory at the Faculty of Languages, University of Gdansk. She is a linguist (MA in English Studies, PhD and Venia Legendi in Humanities, University of Gdansk), an economist (MA in Economics, Gdansk University of Technology), a specialist in managing scientific projects (postgraduate studies, Gdansk University of Technology) and a specialist in the mechanisms of the Eurozone (postgraduate studies, University of Gdansk). Her scientific interests include organizational discourse, neuromanagement, online social networks, intercultural communication, sociolinguistics, ANT and symbolism in management studies.

Duncan Brown, PhD, is the Head of HR Consultancy and Research at the Institute for Employment Studies and a Visiting Professor at the University of Greenwich. He has more than 25 years' experience in rewards consulting and research with firms, including Aon Hewitt, PricewaterhouseCoopers and Towers Perrin. Duncan has an MA from Cambridge University, and an MBA from the London Business School. He is a Chartered Fellow of the Chartered Institute of Personnel and Development.

Andrea Ceschi, PhD, is currently a Post-Doctoral researcher in Work and Organizational Psychology at Verona University, Department of Human Sciences, Italy. His field of work deals with organizational dynamics related to decision-making processes in the workplace.

Jonathan Chapman, PhD, is Chief Operating Officer, Group Internal Audit, Lloyds Banking Group and a visiting fellow at Cranfield School of Management. He has an MBA plus 25 years' financial service experience covering time in regulation at the Bank of England/Financial Services Authority and commercially at Aviva, PWC and Lloyds Banking Group. Roles have included banking regulator, private secretary, HR Director, Change Consultant and Chief Operating Officer.

Arianna Costantini is currently a PhD Candidate in Work and Organizational Psychology at Verona University, Department of Human Sciences, Italy. Her field of work is workplace innovation, reward management, and organizational behaviour.

Charles Cotton is the CIPD's performance and reward specialist. He directs the institute's reward research agenda and also leads its public policy work in the area of pay and benefits. Charles frequently appears in the media, commentating on reward, and is often invited to present on his research at events. He has a degree in economics and economics and social history from Aberystwyth University and a master's degree in HR from the London School of Economics. He is also a fellow of the CIPD.

Romain Daste has operated in the reward management field as an external special consultant on mergers and acquisition, job evaluation, long-term incentive plans, specific reward teambuilding and Initial Public Offerings transition in the UK for the past 15 years. Romain has lived and worked in France, Spain the UK and the USA, and published in the *Journal of European Industrial Training*.

Stephan Dickert is currently a Senior Lecturer in Marketing at the School of Business and Management at Queen Mary University of London. His research interests include judgement and decision making, information processing, risk perception and emotions.

Brian J. Dive has worked across 70 countries in over 100 organizations. He previously chaired the New York Conference Board's International Council on Organization. He is widely experienced in strategic HR, focusing now on organization design and leadership development. He developed and has written three books on the Decision Making Accountability Solution Set. His contribution was recognised with an honorary DBA from London Metropolitan University.

Marion Festing is a Professor of Human Resource Management and Intercultural Leadership and the Academic Director of the ESCP Europe Talent Management Institute. Former responsibilities at ESCP Europe include her work as the European Research Dean and the Dean of the Berlin Campus. She is the incoming editor-in-chief of the *German Journal of HRM* and was an Associate Editor of the *International Journal of Human Resource Management*. Marion Festing is also the German Ambassador to the HR Division of the Academy of Management. Her current research interests are concerned with International Human Resource Management with a special emphasis on strategies, talent management, (female) careers, rewards, performance management as well as diversity and inclusion in various institutional and cultural contexts.

Alan Fish, PhD, has been involved in Human Resource Management in both professional and academic roles for over 40 years; and retired from full-time academic involvement in 2012, as Professor of Human Resource Management at Charles Sturt University, Wagga Wagga. Alan's PhD, awarded by The University of Sydney, is in International Human Resource Management. Since becoming an Emeritus Professor, Alan has held various international honorary appointments in England, China and Malaysia as well as in Australia. Alan has published over one hundred refereed articles and conference papers, as well as working papers and white papers.

Ingrid S. Fulmer is Professor of Human Resource Management and Director of the Centre for Workplace Excellence (CWeX) at the University of South Australia Business School in Adelaide, Australia. She received her PhD in Organization Studies at Vanderbilt University (USA). In her research, she studies human resource management practices and systems and their effects on worker and organizational outcomes, with particular interest in and ongoing research projects examining the effects of compensation systems on these outcomes. She also studies interpersonal interactions in organizations and how those interactions are shaped by social processes such as social comparisons and communication.

Adebabay Abay Gebrekidan received his MA in International HRM, from London Metropolitan University and Postgraduate Certificate in Public Sector Reform from Bradford University, UK. A Certified Management Training Consultant, with a Masters-level Professional Certificate in the Balanced Scorecard, he has served in the Ethiopian Public Civil Service for more than 28 years, including as Advisor to the Minister of Capacity Building in Public Sector Reform.

Howard Gospel is Professor of Management at King's Business School, King's College London and at the Libera Università Internazionale degli Studi Sociali (LUISS) Rome. He is also a Visiting Fellow of the Said Business School, University of Oxford. He has a long-term interest in the management of human resource and corporate governance, with a historical and comparative perspective.

Jian Han is an associate professor of Management at China Europe International Business School (CEIBS), Shanghai. He researches management control systems vested in platform-oriented organizational strategy.

Ian Kessler joined King's College, London as Professor of Public Policy and Management in 2014 after more than twenty years at Oxford University. He has researched many aspects of human resource management in the public services, with a particular focus on performance pay and work organization in health and social care. He has written two books: *The Modernisation of Public Service Employment Relations* (with Stephen Bach) and *The Restructuring of the Nursing Workforce* (with Paul Heron); acted as a commissioner on the Local Government Pay Commission; and undertaken research work for the National Audit, the Audit Commission, the Royal College of Nursing and the Royal College of Midwives.

Katarzyna Klimkiewicz is assistant professor at the AGH University of Science and Technology in Cracow. She graduated in Management Science in 2013 completed a PhD focused on Corporate Social Responsibility and Employer Branding. Dr. Klimkiewicz's research combines the Business Ethics/CSR and Human Capital Approach, especially in the field of employee motivation and responsible supply chain management. Her teaching focuses on developing critical thinking skills and encouraging students to apply these skills in strategic human capital management and sustainability.

Andreas Kornelakis, PhD is Senior Lecturer in International Management at King's Business School, King's College London and Visiting Senior Research Fellow at the University of Sussex. His research interests dwell on the changing political-economic environment in Europe with a focus on comparative employment relations and HRM. He is an Editorial Board member of the journal *Work, Employment and Society*. He has published in a wide range of journals including: *Work, Employment & Society*; *British Journal of Industrial Relations*; *Business History*; and *The International Journal of Human Resource Management*.

Sergio M. Madero-Gómez, PhD, is a Research Professor in the Management and Human Talent Department at Tecnologico de Monterrey, Campus Monterrey,Mexico.A member of the National System of Researchers CONACYT (SNI Level I), his research deals with human resources management, compensation and rewards systems, career development, workplace environment, and Latin American studies.

Almuth McDowall is Professor of Organisational Psychology at Birkbeck University of London. As an Assistant Dean, she heads up her department and is committed to bringing the science of psychology to work. Her research areas comprise professional development, rewards and performance, work–life balance and occupational health and coaching. She has delivered large-scale projects for a range of funders and is committed to dissemination in academic and practitioner outlets. Her research regularly features in the press and has won awards for its impact and relevance to organizational practice.

Miguel R. Olivas-Luján is a Professor at Clarion University of Pennsylvania, serving as Chairperson for the Management Education & Development (MED) division of the AOM (2014–2019). His research areas include: Human Resources, Diversity, Ethical Decision Making, and Information Technologies. His work has appeared in four languages and has been presented in all inhabited continents; he is also an editor for the Advanced Series in Management.

Andrew Pendleton is Professor of Human Resource Management at Durham University Business School, and is a Fellow and Mentor on the Beyster Program at Rutgers University in the USA. His main research interests are employee ownership, employee share ownership, and corporate ownership and governance. He has written extensively on these topics.

Stephen J. Perkins, DPhil (Oxon) is a Senior Research Fellow, Global Policy Institute, London and Emeritus Professor, London Metropolitan University, UK. His research and publications engage with the interaction of corporate governance and reward management.

Nicholas R. Prince is an Assistant Professor in the Department of Marketing & Management at the University of Wyoming, where he helps to lead the HR concentration within the Management Major. His research focuses on international HR, high-performance work systems, and small business HR and culture. He received his PhD from the University of Illinois at Urbana-Champaign.

J. Bruce Prince is Full Professor in the Department of Management at Kansas State University where he leads the HR major. His research focuses on high-performance work systems, and international comparative systems. He received his PhD from the University of Southern California.

Vicky Pryce is on the board of the Centre for Economics and Business Research (CEBR), a former joint Head of the UK Government Economic Service and author, amongst others, of *It's the Economy, Stupid, Economics for Voters* with Andy Ross and Peter Urwin. She holds a number of visiting professorships, including most recently at Aston University and Birmingham City University.

Catherine Rickard is a Senior Research Fellow at the Institute for Employment Studies. Catherine has been involved in a range of research and consultancy projects for both private and public sector clients, including the House of Commons, the Prince's Trust and the Department for Work and Pensions. In prior roles, Catherine was Assistant Editor of the Incomes Data Services (IDS) *Pay Report* journal before moving to the Executive Compensation and Reward division of Towers Perrin.

Ihar Sahakiants is a Professor of International Human Resource Management at the Cologne Business School (CBS), Germany. He received his PhD from ESCP Europe in Berlin and conducts research on a variety of topics, such as international comparative and executive compensation, corporate governance, organizational practices in European transition states and socially responsible human resource management. His work comprises publications in a number of academic and practitioner-oriented outlets, including journals such as *The International Journal of Human Resource Management, European Management Journal, Management International Review, Journal for East European Management Studies* and *Thunderbird International Business Review*.

Daria Sarti is Assistant Professor of Organization and Human Resource Management at the University of Florence, Department of Economics and Business Studies, School of Economics and Management. She received her PhD in Economics and Management of firms and local systems from the University of Florence in January 2005. Her current research interest is currently focused on the study of organizational factors and forms for enabling knowledge exploitation; the impact of information and communication technologies in the workplace; and engaging workforce through effective rewarding practices. Her studies mainly concentrate on SMEs, company belonging to the service industry and non-profit enterprises.

Riccardo Sartori is Associate Professor in Work and Organizational Psychology at Verona University, Department of Human Sciences, Italy. His main research interests include psychological assessment and organizational innovation.

Dow Scott, PhD, is a Professor of Human Resources and Employment Relations at Loyola University Chicago, and President of Performance Development International, LLC. Dr. Scott's applied research is frequently featured at Chicago Compensation Association programs, WorldatWork Annual Conferences and in the WorldatWork Journal. His over 120 publications include his book *Incentive Pay: Creating a Competitive Advantage*. His most recent research and management consultancy focus on how rewards drive innovation, employee pay preferences, pay transparency, future of work and rewards, and the evaluation of pay programmes.

Jason D. Shaw, PhD, is Shaw Foundation Chair of Business, Division of Strategy, Management and Organisation College of Business (Nanyang Business School), Nanyang Technical University, Singapore, and Editor-in-Chief at the Academy of Management Journal.

John Shields is Deputy Dean and Professor of Human Resource Management and Organizational Studies at The University of Sydney Business School. His principal areas of research, publication and teaching include performance management, reward management, executive remuneration and corporate governance, leadership, and business and labour history.

Susan Shortland, PhD, is a Senior Lecturer in HRM at the University of Westminster. She also holds Professor Emerita status at London Metropolitan University. She is a Senior Fellow of the Higher Education Academy and a Chartered Fellow of the Chartered Institute of Personnel & Development, and holds Masters degrees in Geography and in Higher Education from Cambridge and Westminster Universities respectively. She is the author of a series of peer reviewed journal articles and book chapters, and of five books in the field of HRM. Prior to working in Higher Education, Susan held a managerial consultancy role in international HRM at KPMG, managed The Confederation of British Industry's (CBI) Employee Relocation Council, and carried out reward research and writing for Incomes Data Services and Industrial Relations Services.

Charlotte Lucy Smith, PhD, is Senior Lecturer in Organizational Behaviour and Management at Lincoln International Business School, University of Lincoln. Her research mainly focuses on employee reward (particularly non-cash forms), with recent projects exploring individuals' experiences of recognition in organizations and higher education institutions. She also has an interest in workplace stress and is currently developing The Actor Well-being Project with Dr Christopher Hogg (University of Westminster), which investigates the factors affecting the psychological well-being of actors working in the UK television industry.

Natarajan Sundar is a Senior Research Fellow at the Global Policy Institute, London. His career began in India initially working at one of the country's top three banks, Punjab National Bank, where his succession of managerial roles included Head of the Management Training College. Later appointments in Finance, HR and General Management were with Unilever in India (including being Hindustan Unilever's first head of remuneration and Finance and HR Director of a Unilever subsidiary) and the UK, and then with BG Group as the Global Head of Remuneration and Performance Management. He is now a consultant to entrepreneur-led Indian companies and multinationals in the UK and India – including over the years, the BG Group, ECA International, Aditya Birla Group, Murugappa Group and Tata Steel.

Michael Tekieli is a doctoral candidate and research assistant at the Chair of Human Resource Management and Intercultural Leadership at ESCP Europe Business School, Berlin. His research interest is in the field of reward management of multinational enterprises. Michael holds a degree in Psychology (Diplom-Psychologe) and a Bachelor of Science in Business Administration from his studies at the University of Tuebingen, the University of Trier and the Warsaw School of Economics. Before working for ESCP Europe, Michael gained international experience during a one-year assignment at Kienbaum Consultants International in Warsaw.

Teresina Torre is full professor of Organization Studies and Humana Resource Management at the University of Genoa, Department of Economics and Business, School of Social Science She is co-editor of *Impresa Progetto Electronic Journal of Management* and director of the International MBA – University of Lima and of Genoa. She is vice-president of the Association of Italian Organization Studies Academics. Her current research interests focus on the practices of reward management and engagement strategies, the evolution of work in digital context, its organization and assessment. Her studies mainly concentrate on SMEs, companies belonging to the service industry and non-profit enterprises.

Jonathan Trevor, PhD, is Associate Professor of Management Practice at Saïd Business School, University of Oxford. He is a management researcher, author, adviser, speaker and teacher on the subject of Strategic Alignment – how all elements of a business, including market strategy and the way the company itself is organized, are arranged in such a way as to best support the fulfilment of its long-term purpose.

Matti Vartiainen is Professor of Work and Organizational Psychology in the Department of Industrial Engineering and Management, Aalto University, Finland. His research focuses on the nature of collaborative working environments in distributed, often global contexts, and includes organizational innovations, digital work and organizations, and new ways of working in e-learning settings.

Qi (Jean) Wei is a Senior Lecturer in HRM at Kingston Business, Kingston University, London. She received her PhD from Cass Business School, City University of London and is an Academic Member of Chartered Institute of Personnel and Development (CIPD). Her specialist areas of interest include rewards, performance management and international HRM.

Mark Wickham is a Senior Lecturer in Management at the University of Tasmania. His teaching and research interests include sustainability and its role in the strategic management process, the role of ethics in business decision-making and has a particular interest in qualitative methodologies.

Tommy Wong is a Lecturer in Management at the University of Tasmania, Australia, teaching post-graduate Business Management and Retail Marketing. His research interests focus on business strategy in the retail and hospitality sectors in emerging markets.

Geoff White is Professor of Human Resource Management at the University of Greenwich Business School and a Visiting Professor at Hong Kong Baptist University. Prior to becoming an academic in 1991, Geoff was head of research at the employment relations research company, IDS. He has written widely about reward management, especially minimum wages and public sector pay, as well as having interests in construction employment relations. He has acted as an advisor to the Low Pay Commission, the Local Government Pay Commission, the NHS Staff Council, the Office for Manpower Economics and the Universities and Colleges Employers Association. His most recent research has covered the impact of the National Living Wage on employee terms and conditions.

Zara Whysall, PhD, is a Chartered Psychologist and Associate Fellow of the British Psychological Society, with over 15 years' experience in research, consulting and training roles in public and private sector organisations. Zara splits her time between academia and practice. She is both a Senior Lecturer in Business and Management in the Corporate and Executive Education team at Nottingham Business School, Nottingham Trent University, and Head of Research at Kiddy & Partners, a London-based human capital consultancy firm specialising in talent assessment and development.

Angela Wright, PhD, has spent most of her career working in reward as a pay researcher, reward consultant and academic. Her recent research is in reward and organization culture, in employee benefits and in equality and diversity. She is a Chartered Fellow of the Chartered Institute of Personnel and Development.

Clive Wright has spent his entire career helping organizations improve their employee environment. He is widely recognised as an expert in reward, has worked in the private sector and in consultancy for leading organizations in their field. He has also had the pleasure to support London Metropolitan University where he is a visiting professor.

ACKNOWLEDGEMENTS

Contributions to the volume from our distinguished team of authors are greatly appreciated. And particular thanks too, go to the editorial advisory board formed two years prior to publication, comprising the following leading scholars and practitioners in the reward management field, some of whom are also authors of chapters in the volume:

Prof. Dr. Conny Herbert Antoni, University of Trier, Germany
Prof. Xavier Baeton, Vlerick Business School, Ghent, Belgium
Prof. Jaime Bonache, ESADE Business School, Madrid, Spain
Dr Duncan Brown, Institute for Employment Studies, UK
Charles Cotton, Chartered Institute of Personnel and Development, UK
Prof. Dr. Marion Festing ESCP, Berlin, Germany
Prof. Ian Kessler, Kings College London, UK
Vicky Pryce, Centre for Economics and Business Research, UK
Prof. Chris Rowley, Kellogg College, University of Oxford, UK
Prof. Jason Shaw, The Hong Kong Polytechnic University, HK, PRC
Prof. Dow Scott, Loyola University, Chicago, USA
Prof. John Shields, University of Sydney, Sydney, Australia
Dr Susan Shortland, University of Westminster, UK
Jock Simpson, Executive Chair, National Joint Council for Engineering Construction, UK
Prof. Matti Vartiainen, Aalto University School of Science, Finland
Prof. Geoff White, University of Greenwich, UK

The advisory board and indeed the author base was assembled drawing on a network which at its core is the organising committee for the biennial Reward Management Conference series held under the auspices of the European Institute for Advanced Studies in Management (EIASM), based in Brussels, the seventh of which is scheduled for December 2019.

Our capacity to reach out to the widest based for contributing authors was greatly enhanced thanks not only to the EIASM leadership, paying particular tribute to Graziella Michelante. Additionally, colleagues within the British Academy of Management and the Chartered Association of Business Schools, who promulgated the call for papers across the memberships of their institutions.

The editor-in-chief wishes particularly to acknowledge Jacqueline Curthoys as commissioning editor of the volume, supporting the project from conception to publication.

PART I

Conceptualizing and theorizing reward management

The eight chapters making up this segment of the volume offer ways of thinking about its field of enquiry and concomitant action. While starting from various alternative disciplinary roots, it is striking how the direction of travel intellectually to make sense of reward management choices and outcomes from decision-making intertwine, looking at these contributions holistically. While a variety of tools are thoughtfully brought to bear, all demand critical reflection on the complex and multifaceted sociopolitical contexts within which reward management is constituted by the social actors involved.

After the editor's thematic introduction, in the first of our analyses of ways of 'coming at' reward management conceptually, **Vicky Pryce** offers an economist's perspective. Calling for attention to questions at the heart of valuing work in its various forms, mediated through the sociopolitical prism of employer willingness to pay judgements. The call to action for employers facing uncertainties across jurisdictions and trading economies worldwide is to reflect carefully on how working for their organizations will be attractive to diverse workforce members whose talents are necessary and working cooperatively, if the perennial productivity puzzle is to be successfully tackled.

Conny Antoni introduces a range of frames of reference psychologists bring to bear to unpack the interactions taking place in managing reward within the employment relationship. He calls for researchers to enhance the contribution to understanding in the area by engaging with more longitudinal investigation, enabling a better grasp of what's taking place at the psychological interface between words and action at individual and workgroup level, balancing unwritten as well as formal contractual undertakings with considerations of socially just outcomes in mind and how they are perceived.

Arianna Costantini and her colleagues further develop critical thinking around psychological conceptualizations of reward management, delving into the specifics of risk for organizational leaders if perceptions around the balance between corporate support and the effort–reward bargain are ignored or overlooked. Informed by ideas from industrial and organizational psychology, a better grasp is proposed of the dynamic, ever-shifting contexts as the stakeholders in organizational performance work continuously through the process of securing cooperation and its recognition in tangible and intangible ways.

Risks for those attempting to manage reward, informed only by normative assumptions, are foregrounded by **Angela Wright** – shining a light on the 'dark side' of the volume's topic, relatively silenced in mainstream literature. She adopts a 'back to the future' frame of reference, surfacing not only problems for the unwary manager, but also sources of corrective understanding – in particular, from classic organizational sociology conceptualizations and related methodologically immersive empirical investigations.

The organizational landscape and actions taken by those inhabiting it is mediated through language. And language in its various forms – including non-verbal forms of communication – is a product of social construction, culturally and value-laden as it becomes institutionalized. **Magdalena Bielenia-Grajewska** considers the way language formed into particular reward management discourses may be unpacked to help analysts, practising managers and regulators alike better comprehend and thus consciously communicate and respond to perceived intentions in reward management interactions. In this context, the potential contribution of neurolinguists is flagged up.

Duncan Brown engages critically with the impetus given initially by American theorizing, informed by management science perspectives, soon embraced across the Atlantic, over at least the past quarter-century to make reward management *strategic*. He uses empirical evidence to weigh the merits of the case, arguing that while managerial choices around the direction of travel can be traced, as well as findings suggesting that caution is needed before simply embracing 'best-practice' norms, in practice the more significant development is the reconceptualization of what 'being strategic' means in approaching the management of employee reward investment given the dynamics of political economy surrounding it.

Alan Fish brings this segment of the volume to a conclusion with a discussion of one of the seminal approaches to thinking and practice in approaching the employment relationship and its reward components – Maslow's motivation theory, which reached its 75th anniversary in 2018. We learn that, despite celebrity influence, Maslow has been presented in ways that leave his message incomplete in a manner rather similar to the misappropriation of Adam Smith's classic *The Wealth of Nations*, bereft of its partner, contextualizing volume *The Theory of Moral Sentiments*. Presenting Maslow holistically opens scope for reward strategies and practices that move from unidirectional manipulation to enabling managers to lay the ground more sustainably for organizational effectiveness by paying attention to workforce well-being.

1

WHITHER REWARD MANAGEMENT THEORY RESEARCH AND PRACTICE? THE ESSENTIAL COMPANION

Introduction to the volume and its themes

Stephen J. Perkins

A rewarding companion

A companion is someone or something that *accompanies* another – often on a journey. An *accompaniment* complements, for example, a soloist performing a piece of music, or maybe something tangible being consumed such as food. The connotation generally being that this is pleasant, something the interlocutor would welcome and benefit from. A companion can provide a match to its partner, and we hope that each reader of this volume will receive and use it in that spirit. Finding in the Companion a match to their interests – and questions – on the topic and practise of reward management; one that will complement their intentions and linked intellectual and practical steps to increase and enhance knowledge, and informed action, encompassed by this aspect of the management discipline.

Reward management is something that as contributors and editors of the Companion we perceive less as a 'thing' and more as an activity, a dynamic process that contributes to, and is contextualized by, the employment relationship. A relationship that due to its indeterminacy (Marsden 1999) needs continuous reproduction through an interactive set of moves between the multiplicity of participating socio-economic actors. Moves that can be difficult to predict with accuracy, although being prepared is better than leaving to chance ramifications from what for some employers may be their largest cost – or at least the largest 'controllable' cost for most, if not all organizations.

The inverted commas around *controllable* are necessary given the preceding comment about the indeterminacy of the relationship within which (employee) reward management is central. Despite that, managers have choices to make, once they have weighed up the alternative possible actions they could take, in how they determine reward outcomes for those in respect of whom they have accountability. And the steps preceding these choices. The process of weighing the alternatives can be assisted by reference to consequences that are likely to flow – likely, but not certain due to the indeterminacy caveat – that may be clarified by reference to relevant theories or by evidence from systematic research – whether experimental or 'real world'. In surfacing and assessing the issues around choices and consequences in reward management, it helps to take into account the circumstances or 'contexts' within which the interaction between manager and subordinate, individually or in groups, takes place (Perkins et al. 2016). Circumstances that, while the parameters may have similarities with other settings broadly defined (e.g. time, scale of operation, character of workforce and organization), in respect of the choices a manager will make, in practice, will have features that are unique, and hence consequences may be equally nuanced.

Ideas around reward management, drawing on a multiplicity of scholarly perspectives, and evidence from rigorously conducted investigation while not giving 'right answers' none the less can help those engaged in the processes surrounding reward management in working methodically with the aim of achieving particular goals they and their organizational sponsors wish to see satisfied. Not forgetting the variety of other stakeholders in these dynamic interrelationships. And placing into the open the assumptions underlying actions taken and criteria applied to judge outcomes.

In the readings that follow in the 39 subsequent chapters, 'reward' embedded in the employment relationship – between employer (or managerial representative) and employee – is variously defined by the authors. As is the idea of 'reward management'. The notion of reward can range from a very instrumental and tangible sum of cash to a sense an employee may have of being 'at one' with their employing organization. From value then to values, if you will. And the act of managing reward – deciding how much, how, when, where and why a reward, as opposed to some form of punishment (Kohn 1993) should apply – is not taken for granted.

Classical economists may argue that no one determines (*or should* determine) reward allocation: it is no more than a function of the supply and demand curve in the market for 'labour' or for people willing to exchange their leisure, instead to work under the control of an employer. The problem with such a limited conceptualization is that it overlooks the psychological and social aspects that industrial relations-oriented economists termed the effort–reward bargain (Behrend 1957). Something that, as we noted at the outset, is not readily determined, given the institutional setting in which it is enacted. Employees as sentient beings with free will *interpret* the exchange relationship into which they are entering. While perhaps not having the theoretical leisure to surrender in order to undertake labour – given the need for those without alternative access to material resources to provide for their basic needs and, in turn, for those who may depend on them in a family-type setting – they are not automatons. Employees hired on the 'open' market can be expected to think about the extent to which they will lend their cooperation to the employer or organizational manager's project. And, of course, employees drawn from settings domestically and across the world are likely to bring a diverse set of characteristics (including skill sets) and expectations to the relationship around work that is formally rewarded in some combination of ways.

Reward management: 'cheques (sic) and balances'?

Given these factors, a raft of approaches has evolved over time and been studied, recorded and analysed, by commentators whose academic orientation is towards an institutional view of economic and social relations. Where it is in the hands of those who wish to extract value from the employment relationship to induce the employee working singly or more often as a member of an organizational group of employees to harmonize their actions while at work in ways intended to achieve managerial goals. But – again – however sophisticated the approach, for the reason already offered, that outcome cannot be assumed as assured in every particular instance, if at all. Especially due to the scope for employer intention and employee action to fall foul of the 'interpretative gap' (Knights and McCabe 2000) whereby people interpret the signals others give to them intent on conveying meaning in socio-economic settings. And, however well explained or intentioned, these can be open to misinterpretation, with the scope for disappointment on both sides if the investment in the employment relationship fails to meet the criteria either party attaches to its realisation.

Thus, as former reward specialist John Brannigan, at the time an executive with Hewlett-Packard, once observed to me: 'reward is more often likely to do harm than good', as defined in terms of attempts to match expectations and outcomes in diverse organizational settings. A good – preferably essential – companion to reward management will, we hope, in setting this volume before our readership illuminate complexity and the risky nature of the effort–reward bargaining process. And will go one step further, in suggesting ways in which those who wish to investigate, set policies for, and/or enact the managerial process may approach the task in a systematic manner. Informed by an array of international scholarly and reflexive practitioner commentary that should help identify what the choices are, what consequences flow from deciding to jump one way or another in managing reward in organizational settings taking full account of the specificity of contextual conditions that prevail.

Volume purpose and rationale, and intended distinctive contribution

The overarching objective for this theoretically underpinned, but practically oriented volume is to provide students and researchers, and also policy makers and practitioners, with a state-of-the-art compilation. One that maps out ways of thinking about, discusses contemporary developments and debates in, and illustrates through 'real world' evidence about rewarding people in employment. And how these phenomena relate to the business, corporate governance and management contexts where they play out. While, to an extent inevitably given our English-language medium for its compilation, coverage draws on published debates within 'Anglo-American' or at least 'Western' literature, we have sought out contributions from academic and practitioner sources reflecting the wider geo-ethnic environment, including developing and emerging economies. It is hoped that this lifts a veil on perspectives in formation and transition as well as those that are well-established.

Reward management has emerged conceptually and practically from a variety of disciplines: it stands at the interdisciplinary interface between economics, industrial relations and HRM, industrial psychology and organizational sociology, with an increasing interest being taken via a corporate governance lens. The latter incorporates debates around equity and fairness in and around the employment relationship and wider capital–labour relations. The more prescriptive writing in the field, especially from among transatlantic consultants, that emerged in the early 1990s has somewhat disappointed in terms of aligning rewards for employment with business strategy generating space for the 'high performance organization'. Equally over the same period the widening differentials between those employed at the top of organizations, especially but not exclusively those operating for-profit, have generated hyperbolic commentary in the popular media with analysts not necessarily being able to offer evidence to support the trend, other than notions of greed and unequal treatment negatively impacting on social cohesion. The interplay of reward disparity and demography is also to the forefront of popular and regulatory consciousness. Contributions to the volume synthesize – in an accessible way – these trends and controversies and explore the basis to theorize around issues while tracing conceptual and empirical provenance, currency and future prospects for outcomes acceptable among all reward management stakeholders.

In summary, compared with other books that relate to reward management, *The Routledge Companion to Reward Management* has been designed to:

- Bring a more balanced approach to the understanding and application of theoretical approaches, informed equally across the range of disciplinary sources. This means not privileging one or two disciplines such as economics and psychology but, given the interactive and politicised nature of reward management, including political-scientific and sociological sources and, reaching further, disciplines such as sociolinguistics to help understand and interpret the way the field of study may be framed.
- Avoid an overemphasis on Western, particularly Anglo-American sources, opening up the field to a more diverse portfolio of thinking that reflects the international landscape within which reward management may be interpreted and enacted informed by varying cultural and institutional path dependencies.
- Move beyond the prescriptive character of some commentary in the field, as well as remaining sensitive to the fact that management activities and ideas behind them do not call exclusively for approaches that may be characterized as 'managerialist'. Instead applying critical reasoning, to make sense of factors impacting on the ways in which reward management is practised and consequences flowing from it.
- Remain aware that, while the past three decades have witnessed economic 'deregulation' and 'disintermediation', where the 'contract' between employee and employer mediated by reward has become less collectively determined in a formal sense, institutions such as professional bodies and trade unions still exercise an influence. Even if one practised differently to that under the traditional 'system of industrial relations' that characterised the mid- to late twentieth century. The volume is mindful that attention to 'employee voices' exercised in different ways, individually and in groups remains fundamental to engaging with reward management debates.
- Draw out not only agendas for future research, but also seek to inform ethically, or socially informed, as well as rationally based managerial action; something that is especially significant given ongoing and amplifying controversies about fairness in pay dispersion within and between organizations, groups of people employed in them, and across geographies.

Chapters have been written by an international selection of authors drawn from Africa, Asia Pacific (incorporating Australasia), mainland Europe, the Americas, and the UK. The authors comprise experts in the relevant subject. Some are seasoned opinion formers. Others are up-and-coming names in the field – encompassing academia and practice.

Content and structure

The volume is made up of chapters of varying length: from short to extended essays, written following a call to those specializing in the field, organized in three broad thematic parts. These reflect the intention behind the volume to offer readers a basis on which to understand, first, from where in all its conceptual diversity the reward management field of inquiry has developed. Secondly, to have access to clearly described and evaluated contemporary problems under academic investigation and challenging practising managers mindful of influences on organizational interactions around the employment and reward relationship, and how it is being managed. And with what recorded outcomes. Influences both external *and* internal to organizations and business systems within which they are located – nationally, regionally and trans-continentally. And, thirdly, to examine current thinking and evidence about practice in the field observable across the world's major continents. Chapters situate their coverage in the array of literature around reward management, thus serving as a companion to theory building and empirical research, as well as serving educational purposes. In addition, content offers a guide to crafting and evaluating managerial practice.

Part I: Theoretical and disciplinary provenance

Here the chapters concentrate attention on the source of commentary and practice relevant to managing reward associated with the employment relationship. Contributions variously grounded in economics, industrial and organizational psychology, organizational sociology, industrial relations, strategic management and corporate governance along with wider socio-political commentary and linguistics are presented, enabling readers to compare and contrast ideas informing reward management interpretation and action.

Part II: Current debates

Here the articles take up analytically the ways academic and practitioner literature has sought to capture and interpret current issues in reward management, and trends in terms of outcomes informed by choices being made by key actors – both employees and employers as well as other stakeholders, such as government regulators, investors and their representatives and the voice(s) of organized labour (e.g., trade unions). Particular subthemes will pay attention to issues around diversity, efforts to combine corporate strategy, HRM and reward management, and the changing context for managing the indeterminate employment relationship: the role of organizational development in terms of scale, sector, and geography; concerns regarding fairness in reward outcomes, processes and inter-relational dynamics; relative positioning of executives and others; and the corporate governance agenda.

Part III: Locating reward management in (multiple) contexts

Here the articles draw strength from the foregoing analysis to situate reward management across a range of contexts – with particular attention to business systems and sectors internationally. As with the contributions in Part II efforts are directed to charting prospects for thematic development in how reward management may be theorized, described, analysed and interpreted over the coming decade.

A summary of the focus of each chapter is offered in the short introduction situated at the beginning of each part of the volume introducing its coverage, enabling the reader at a glance to pinpoint where they may usefully move between the volume's various forms of content, depending on a specific interest they wish to pursue or problem to engage with.

Conclusion

So whither reward management in its various incarnations? Two thoughts to ponder.

First it is striking engaging with the contributions to this volume how, irrespective of 'home' discipline, attention is repeatedly drawn to the importance of *interaction* between the various stakeholders in the effort–reward bargain, at all levels from large-scale economic landscape to small-scale setting. From the point of view of relevant theory building repeatedly the call is for more integration of ways of framing the issues; how they can be interpreted by individuals and groups of human beings with an interest in effective organization. It seems to me that enhanced understanding of the possibilities and risks in managing employee reward emerges when we recognise its complex and contested nature, with battle enjoined most prominently between elite groups seeking to shape the agenda. One that, by definition, is socially constructed; its manifestations open to be traced, for example, through documented claims to a regulatory mandate that have emerged over at least the past quarter-century and continue to evolve in forms such as the UK Corporate Governance Code (Perkins 2017).

Secondly, and underscored by the preceding observation, *social justice* in its various forms, and with the struggles to 'own' its definition and consequent criteria for regulation, stands out as a foundational principle influencing the extent to which reward management approaches and their outcomes will find acceptance, let alone result in the kinds of organizational effectiveness (itself dependent on who's asking?) to which interest groups aspire. Unpacking this a little we have questions around the value of contributions to organizational activity – what and how – on the basis of hierarchy, sector or 'job family' domain, as well as diverse factors characterizing demographically stratified groups across society. And regarding time and expectations around the overarching 'deal' in the short, medium and long term: guaranteed reward when an *employment* relationship itself has become increasingly precarious in the so-called 'gig' economy, 'at risk' pay, and then deferred reward as well as 'fringe' benefits. Within the latter, the struggles around tensions in financing retirement income promises, set against the 'psychological contract' groups of employees believe they have entered into, and the reaction when employers are perceived to renege on the deal.

The landscape has thus altered and continues to develop dynamically since a 'New Pay' discourse came to prominence, with commentators and then policy makers encouraging a move from the post-war consensus around collectively regulated employment relations and job-focused pay and benefits determination to ideas emphasizing communication and individualized dynamism. The preceding 'consensus' phase had ushered in a shift from day- or piece-rate working to the extension of salaried status and the shelter of employment within internalized labour markets to significant parts of the employed population. Tenure that had a sense of permanency – a career-long involvement with one or at most a few employers accompanied by an understanding between the parties that recognition for contribution could be progressive (e.g., annual advances along incremental scales) and deferred (e.g., defined benefit pensions).

Deregulated, normative reward management principles and a pay for performance orientation came to the fore in the final quarter of the twentieth century: the New Pay era. Managers were expected to use pay (less so fringe benefits, given fiscal neutralization efforts by taxation authorities) proactively as an incentive with the expectation that 'paying people right' (Zingheim and Schuster 2000), a declaration itself provoking contestation – see Heery 1996, would additively result in the attract, retain and motivate outcomes a 'war for talent' zeitgeist demanded. Contradictions in these aspirations and assumptions have come to the fore, however, and are currently being played out among regulators, investors, media commentators as well as in workplaces.

As the contributions in what follows illustrate, paying people justly as well as efficiently and opening up the frames of reference to determine exactly how such outcomes should be defined and assessed in meaningful social interaction perhaps represents the direction of travel in the field. We hope that readers will find immediate and longer-term value from engaging with the volume, across its varied but thematically assembled parts, with recurring and interconnecting themes as well as variability in the ways authors specify ideas on priorities for future research, regulatory policy development and managerial action.

On behalf of my distinguished colleagues making up the editorial advisory board, we hope to provide you with a friendly, lively and engaging companion for your excursions along the highways and byways of managing employee reward.

References

Behrend, H. (1957). The effort bargain. *The ILR Review*. 10(4), 503–515.

Heery, E. (1996). Risk, representation and the new pay. *Personnel Review*. 25(6), 54–65.

Knights, D. and McCabe, D. (2000). 'Ain't Misbehavin'? opportunities for resistance under new forms of 'Quality' Management'. *Sociology*. 34(3), 421–436.

Kohn, A. (1993). *Punished by Rewards: The Trouble with Gold Stars, Incentive Plans, A's, Praise and Other Bribes*. Boston, MA: Houghton Mifflin.

Marsden, D. (1999). *A Theory of Employment Systems*. Oxford: Oxford University Press.

Perkins, S.J. (2017). The social construction of executive remuneration in the UK: elite competition around codification and legitimation. *Journal of Organizational Effectiveness: People and Performance*. 4(1), 76–88.

Perkins, S.J., White, G. and Jones, S. (2016). *Reward Management: Alternatives, Consequences and Contexts*. London: CIPD-Kogan Page.

Zingheim, P. and Schuster, J.R. (2000). *Pay People Right!* San Francisco, CA: Jossey Bass.

2

REWARD MANAGEMENT AND THE ECONOMY[1]

Vicky Pryce

Introduction

This contribution has been prepared at a time of considerable uncertainty in the UK. The country is going through the paces of attempting to exit the European Union (EU), although not perhaps in as smoothly and as frictionless a way as those who voted to leave the EU in the referendum of June 2016 had perhaps hoped. And behind it is a population divided, not just between EU 'remainers' and 'leavers' but also, and perhaps connected with this, between the vast majority of people whose incomes are stagnating and a clutch of highly paid individuals, be they university vice chancellors, local authority chief executives, heads of school academy groups, bankers or CEOs of big companies, who appear to earn vastly inflated salaries by comparison to the average wage. Of course, the UK is not unique in this – much of the industrialized world has seen similar trends, particularly since the financial crisis which began in 2008. But the problem is more intense – and perhaps more transparent – in places like the UK which has, in recent decades, adopted the US tradition of equating financial success with value to society.

Across the developed world people with intermediate skills are the ones to have seen most pressure on their wages – in jobs where technology can more easily take over. It seems that both low-skilled labour and high-skilled labour have done better comparatively. With the middle classes particularly squeezed, there has been an intensification of the rumblings against the current reward management system. In the last couple of decades, the share of GDP going to profits, rather than declining as had been forecast has in fact been increasing. The share of wages in the economy, despite the rise of the 'knowledge worker', has been decreasing. How else, for example, do we explain the record employment rate in the UK and an unemployment rate of 4.3%, the lowest since 1975, at the same time as one of the slowest periods of real wage increases in recent history? Government and businesses finally have to take some action, as the implications of these trends, should they continue, can be destabilizing.

The social division created by big differences in pay is well documented. In economics, there is not just Piketty (2014), with his focus on capital and inequality, but also Krugman's analysis (e.g. Eggertsson and Krugman 2012), which argues that, though an unequal society can still be doing comparatively well in terms of GDP growth, for a while at least, as savings may be being created that could be reinvested, the social divisions it creates ultimately lead to less investment, particularly inward investment, than would otherwise be the case and to a downward effect on both productivity and growth. And here we are in the UK with a level of productivity that has now fallen back to pre-crisis levels – effectively suggesting no progress at all in the underlying dynamism of the economy in the past decade. Demand is being met by extra hiring rather than by investment. On the other hand, the fall in the pound has improved share values as some 80% of the FTSE 100 companies' earnings are from overseas and profits (as measured in sterling terms) have gone up. This has been of benefit to those CEOs awarded share options, as well as to those whose bonus is linked to share prices. And while, as Kay (2016) argues, people in general are less concerned about the likes of Wayne Rooney in football and Bill Gates in business as they believe their exceptional talents should be rewarded, they don't have the same view of finance sector employees being at all exceptional and therefore resent their level of earnings. And, as he says, 'inequality which seems unconnected to deserts is particularly corrosive'.

Never before has it been so important, therefore, to look again at reward management systems and whether or not they are currently fit for purpose. How one rewards employees – in both the private and the public sectors – can affect performance and therefore productivity in the economy, and not always for the better. And yet the system clearly needs fixing, as it is full of distortions. During the financial crisis and for a period thereafter equality in living standards, at least in the UK, perversely improved. This was mainly because the tax and benefit system protected the incomes of those at the bottom of the income distribution. During this period the wages of those in employment fell in real terms for a while, worsened by a serious decline in average earnings for the millions who joined the army of the self-employed, whose real average earnings have declined by 22% between 2009 and 2014. Following some recovery in 2015, inflation has risen and wage growth has failed to accelerate, leading to a squeeze on incomes which have now been falling in real terms for a number of quarters. But share prices were doing fine. Increased disgruntlement with top pay, and the resultant moves to increase transparency, women's groups campaigning for pay equality and the abuses of the system that have come to prominence in both the private sector and public institutions like the BBC have all posed the question: 'What is a fair reward system?' Can we in fact justify average pay for an FT chief executive of 140-160 times average workers' pay? And what about university vice chancellors – have the remuneration committees worked together, albeit perhaps unintentionally, to drive up top pay?

Government interventions on pay

Unfortunately, the UK government's overall stance remains confused. Pronouncements so far seem to have been knee-jerk reactions to populist pressures rather than a well-thought-out evidence-based rethink. As a result, policy responses have been inconsistent. The current government had earlier expressed the intent to tighten up governance of companies and, in particular, to tackle issues of excessive pay. Suggestions of workers sitting on boards of companies have been watered down to a proposal that a person on the board 'represents' workers rather than being a worker in the company themselves. At the same time the legal framework for increasing shareholder involvement in remuneration has been moving very slowly. They have had a vote for some time on policy, but on remuneration it remains advisory rather than binding, although there have recently been some cases of top pay being scaled back because of worries regarding concerns about the possibility of a shareholder revolt. But institutional shareholders have been forcing more pay transparency and a requirement to publish and explain if the pay gaps and excesses that materialize cannot be explained. Universities, for example, will now have to explain why their vice chancellors get paid more than the prime minister!

By law, big firms are now obliged to publish information on the gender pay gap in their organizations between male and female employees. But a requirement to have more women on boards remains a target rather than a quota. The system still discriminates against female senior executives, where they remain in the minority, especially in the private sector, with average pay at the top some 15% below that of men – with bonuses also lagging behind. That is no way to incentivize women to stay in work and use the skills they have gained at large expense to the country and themselves in a way that improves firm profitability and productivity across the economy as a whole (Pryce 2015). A report by the High Pay Centre and the Chartered Institute of Personnel and Development (2017) found that, in 2016 among FTSE 100 firms in the UK, the male chief executives were earning an average of £4.7 million, which was some 77 per cent more than their female counterparts. Admittedly, the sample of females was small as there were just six female CEOs out of a sample of one hundred!

New challenges

How much do we actually value work of different kinds in society? The test is what we are prepared to pay for it. The Taylor Review of modern working practices published in mid-2017 found that the way we are rewarding some classes of workers undervalues the contributions made (Taylor et al. 2017). As Matthew Taylor himself wrote, the issue to tackle is that 'bad work – insecure, exploitative, controlling – is bad for health and wellbeing, something that generates cost for vulnerable individuals but also for wider society'. His worry was also that the way new employment practices are being applied in the UK, such as for UBER-type services, but also for those working more generally under zero hour contracts or those that get paid for only the amount spent caring for an elderly patient at their home, and not the in-between travelling, in fact seem to make whatever contract may exist very one sided as it transfers the risk over to employees and adds to insecurity and of course to low pay.

The Chartered Institute of Personnel and Development have found that many people working on short hours were among the most satisfied with their situation and with the flexibility that they allowed, and that zero hour contracts worked well for many (CIPD 2015). But they were not right for everyone. As the Taylor report highlights, while there is nothing wrong with zero and low hours contracts what is worrying is that employers in this market are in effect seeking through those practices to transfer all risk on to the shoulders of workers . This tends to add to financial insecurity and restrict the ability to manage one's life, and can result in being denied loans or mortgages because of the lack of guaranteed hours from week to week. Taylor has therefore asked the Low Pay Commission to explore how one can be properly rewarded, perhaps through a higher minimum wage, for the hours one is asked to work but may in fact not get paid for if they don't materialize. His commission also called for the 'right for people to request fixed hours and permanent contracts along with a requirement that companies disclose how they have responded to such requests'. And, of course, from a business perspective it stands to reason that, as the report stresses, 'low quality work and weak management is implicated in our productivity challenge. Improving the quality of work should be an important part of our productivity strategy.' If we are not prepared to have a pay system that improves and properly rewards that quality then we end up with a chronically poor productivity record. In turn, if the state has to supplement that low income to ensure a decent standard of living, then the risk is in fact transferred to the taxpayer.

But we could take this even further. The relevant test is not just the value we attribute and the reward mechanisms we set up for the jobs done by those we choose to employ to perform various tasks, but how as a society we view unpaid work currently done by, for example, 'stay at home' mums and dads, charity workers and those who currently care for an elderly relative. The person doing it for nothing would have had to be substituted by a paid worker who would have had to do that in their place. And there is an opportunity cost too for society as the unpaid carer could instead be using their skills to full effect to contribute to the economy. Yet we value that at zero.

Consideration of this situation has led to talk of a national guaranteed basic income irrespective of whether one works – a debate that has also been informed by the fear that increased automation take over performing most of our present tasks and jobs in the future!

The truth is that we generally undervalue work that isn't directly linked to profit making. The renewed concern about the pay cap for public sector workers, for example, where morale is fading and recruitment difficulties are intensifying, is a case in point. It is true that raw data from the New Earnings Survey and the Annual Survey of Hours and Earnings suggested that public sector workers in general had an average pay advantage over private sector workers of some 15% for men and 22% for women back in 2005–2006 (Bozio and Johnson 2010). But this has traditionally been partly a reflection that, on balance, public sector workers, such as those in the civil service, were more highly educationally qualified, so the comparison is not on a like-for-like basis. In any case in recent years that premium has now been eroded and effectively disappeared through the imposition of a pay freeze and then a pay cap since the financial crisis, in an effort to constrain public sector spending. This pay cap is finally lifting, though only marginally. And it may take some time to make a real difference.

Not only do we need nurses, teachers and care workers, but we also need civil servants to be properly motivated to deal with the huge and difficult requirements of Brexit. The nation, including our public services, seems at present unprepared for the impact of Brexit – any slowdown in the economy from a potential loss of markets in the EU, and the consequent extra costs involved in moving away from the frictionless trade in both goods and services that it enabled has made this a priority. The danger now is that it may now become much more difficult to hire extra staff with the right skills from across Europe to meet the increased demand. Easy access to EU skills may be harder in the future and the government is increasing the amount firms must pay the authorities for every non-UK worker they employ. We await concrete proposals but there may be quotas for particular jobs, that will also apply to EU workers in the future, and firms may well end up being responsible for applying for, and administering, work visas for their new EU employees, adding to uncertainty, delay and cost.

Workers from other European countries have already start to finding the UK less of an attractive place in which to live and work, and not just because of the weakness of sterling. The vote to leave the EU has intensified worries about the productivity of the economy and how the economy as a whole will cope with an exodus of staff – or certainly a lower level of net immigration than we have experienced for a while. The independent Office for Budget Responsibility (OBR) has warned that net migration of under 200,000 or so a year would have a negative impact on growth and productivity and would increase the deficit to GDP ratio; as well as the debt to GDP ratio. Indeed, in the first half of 2017 productivity fell back to levels not seen since before the crisis. The 'productivity puzzle' has numerous competing explanations: mis-measurement of output in the digital economy; changes in the sectoral mix, such as the decreased share of total output from the oil and gas and the financial sectors; weak investment; the shift to self-employment and a lack of innovation and economic dynamism. All may have a role to play, but economists are unsure of their relative importance. But in a sense it has not mattered. Increased demand has been met mostly by rising employment, much of this from the EU, rather than extra capital spending as this has allowed greater flexibility in the face of uncertainty.

For the UK to prosper after Brexit in a world where both the demand for, and the supply of, labour is negatively affected it will need to raise levels of productivity. And this needs to be done at both the economy level and at the company level. In future, the minds of business leaders and HR professionals should be focusing on how to attract and retain labour. Keeping workers engaged will be necessary and will probably become costlier. And competitiveness will need to be preserved, particularly if one has to start diverting efforts away from Europe and towards markets that are further afield and more difficult to access and service. This will be a particular problem for small and medium-sized firms.

Reward management from here on will have to be looked at from that viewpoint. Much of the recent focus has been on 'fat cat' pay where the 'principal-agent' problem (see Cuevas-Rodríguez et al. 2012) is both most obvious and is often the greatest and where work from the High Pay Centre has demonstrated that the gap between pay at the top and the average pay of employees (now some 150-fold for FTSE 100 companies) can lead to demotivation among lower paid employees, absenteeism and also worsen staff retention problems.

The contribution of firms

With the spotlight now falling increasingly on people practices within firms and organisations, particularly the big players, the pressure is intensifying to introduce effective employee reward systems. Not only is the gap between the highest- and lower-paid members now the focus of government attention and legislation, but it is also looking at the gender gap between male and female employees. The reputational damage can be severe and could also endanger a firm's contracts within the supply chain in which it operates, preventing it from preserving its preferred suppliers and losing customers. Successive Edelman Trust Barometer surveys show that how a firm treats its employees is one of the most important factors influencing public perceptions of the reputation of a business. What is less clear is how much it alters their purchasing decisions.

A proper reward system and treatment of its employees forms part of a firm's attractiveness as a place to work. Much of that reward system could in fact be non-monetary (to the employee). It could be access to training, time off (such as sabbaticals or time off for volunteering), enhanced maternity, parental or other forms of family leave, help with travel – even in some cases access to subsidized accommodation near the office (see Cotton, this volume for a discussion of 'fringe benefits'). We know of a firm that fired its HR director when it first failed to make it into the then new *Sunday Times* '100 Best Firms to Work For' list.

For large organizations one of the main principles for reward management, affecting people at the top but also further down as it filters through performance management systems, is to attempt to align the objectives of the individual with those of the organization itself. And even wider than that, ensuring that the organization's own objectives align with that of its owners' as this isn't always the case. Witness a major publicly listed firm which is paying its CEO much more that its owners, the shareholders, would consider to be appropriate. Or the case where a share option scheme which forms a substantial part of the reward package encourages the CEO and possibly the entire board to embark on actions that lead to short- or medium-term hikes in share prices but do little for, or even destroy, the long-term sustainability of the company and the livelihood of their employees. Witness also the fallout from the overexuberance and doubtful practices of some financial sector firms before the 2008/2009 financial crisis.

Forms of ownership that limit the principal/agent problem include employee share ownership schemes of the John Lewis type or partnerships, where there is a collective coming together, at least by the people at the top, to agree the organization's objectives (see Pendleton, this volume, for a discussion of 'employee financial participation').

In many firms reward mechanisms take into account what goes on elsewhere and are often influenced by pressure exercised by other organizations with which the firm is dealing. One example could be worker conditions imposed on a subcontractor by a prime contractor, in terms of what is expected in relation to, say, skills and training and/or diversity and behaviour. Governments also intervene to constrain organizations' decisions, requiring minimum levels of some benefits (not just minimum wages but also redundancy payments, annual leave and so on). All employers will soon be compelled to contribute to an employees' pension – adding an intertemporal dimension to reward.

What works best for firms and the economy? The interesting finding is that in fact we are not really sure! The problem remains that most firms do very little evaluation of the effectiveness of their reward programmes, or indeed of any of their people management practices; indeed, many firms are unclear about the very objectives of their reward management practices.

Another difficulty is that there can be a difference between the value of reward packages as seen by firms (and their accountants) and the value as perceived by employees, who do not possess the information or mindsets predicted by economic theory. For example, individuals seem to exhibit higher time preference discount rates than is predicted by theory or indeed by observed interest rates, which implies insufficient saving and leads them to undervalue those elements of reward that accrue in the future rather than the present (such as pension income). Many firms do not help their employees by failing to provide information about the value of their total reward package or its elements (cf. Cotton, this volume).

There is also still little evidence on what combination of variable versus fixed pay may lead to the best results, in part because it is often unclear what counts as 'results'. Experimental evidence provides insights regarding how people respond to incentives, but does it reflect behaviour in a far less controlled environment such as the workplace? Contingency seems to be important: a reward management system needs to incentivize desired behaviours and discourage deleterious behaviour; and fit with the ethos and culture of the organization and the workforce, with practices that fail these tests, producing unanticipated and possibly unwelcome consequences (e.g., see Prince, this volume). It seems that companies embark on different pay reward structures on very little evidence or because others do them. Following fashion may normally be a rational, if conservative, strategy for organisations.

But the impact on the economy could be severe when circumstances are tougher. How to reward people at a time of uncertainty is always tough. More flexible performance-related pay may be the answer, but then one needs very good systems to enforce it. Do we have the skills and the systems – and a supporting and engaged government and public sector – to achieve this? This remains to be seen.

Note

1 Mark Beatson's assistance in developing this chapter is acknowledged.

References

Bozio, A. and Johnson, P. (2010). *Public Sector Pay and Pensions*. London: Institute for Fiscal Studies.

CIPD in Partnership with High Pay Centre. (2017). *Research Report: Review of FTSE 100 Executive Pay Packages*. London: Chartered Institute of Personnel and Development.

CIPD. (2015) *Employer/employee Views of Zero-hours Contracts* Available at: https://www.cipd.co.uk/knowledge/fundamentals/emp-law/terms-conditions/zero-hours-views-report, accessed on September 5, 2017.

Cuevas-Rodríguez, G., Gomez-Mejia, L.R., and Wisem, R.M. (2012). Has agency theory run its course?: making the theory more flexible to inform the management of reward systems. *Corporate Governance: An International Review*. 20(6), 526–546.

Eggertsson, G.B. and Krugman, P.R. (2012). Debt, deleveraging, and the liquidity trap: a Fisher–Minsky–Koo approach. *The Quarterly Journal of Economics*. 127(3), 1469–1513.

Kay, J. (2016). *Other People's Money: Masters of the Universe or Servants of the People?* London: Profile Books.

Piketty, T. trans. Goldhammer, A. (2014). *Capital in the Twenty-First Century*. Boston, MA: HBS Press.

Pryce, V. (2015). *Why Women Need Quotas*. London: Biteback.

Taylor, M., Marsh, G., Nicol, D., and Broadbent, P. (2017). *Good Work: The Taylor Review of Modern Working Practices*. London: Royal Society for the Encouragement of Arts, Manufactures and Commerce.

3

PSYCHOLOGICAL PERSPECTIVES ON REWARD MANAGEMENT

Conny Herbert Antoni

Introduction

Psychology tries to explain and predict human experience and behaviour to develop evidence-based interventions that support people, organizations, and the society as a whole. Psychological knowledge about how people perceive and react to reward systems and practices in different contexts and cultures can therefore inform reward management to attract, retain, and motivate those employees needed for the achievement of company goals and sustainable company development within and across different labour markets and societies.

This chapter begins by examining the psychological concepts of work motivation and work behaviour from a simplified recursive model of action phases (Heckhausen and Gollwitzer 1987), which is related to reward management and leadership behaviour. In so doing, we first describe valence–instrumentality–expectancy theory and discuss its implications for reward management, particularly for attracting and retaining employees. Next, we examine goal-setting theory, which is focused on stimulating high individual and team performance. Then, we discuss organizational justice theory and psychological contract theory and their implications for pay system design to achieve pay satisfaction, and reduce employee turnover.

Linking motivation theories to reward management based on an action phase model

Work motivation theories try to explain the direction, the intensity, and the persistence of work behaviour as an interaction of employee motives and situational characteristics; so-called incentives. Why does a person accept an offer to work as a HR manager in an IT start-up company, and reject the alternative offer to work in a hospital? Is it because the person needs money to buy a house for his family, and the IT company pays more than the hospital and offers additional stock options, or is it because the IT company offers flexible working hours and sabbaticals allowing a better work–life balance? Valence–instrumentality–expectancy theory (Vroom 1964) explains these deliberative processes and predicts such decisions between action alternatives better than it predicts the degree of intensity and persistence the person will show later on the job (Ambrose and Kulik 1999).

Heckhausen and Gollwitzer (1987) have highlighted in their Rubicon model of action phases that different psychological processes characterize the deliberative pre-decision and evaluative post-action phase compared to the pre-action phase and action phase, where one commits oneself to goals and tries to implement them. Based on this action phase model, motivational processes in the pre-decision and evaluative post-action phase, and volitional processes in the pre-action phase and action phase, can thus be differentiated within a broader sense of the concept of motivation.

Pre-action phase and action phase questions are for example: Why does an employee commit himself to work on difficult goals? Why does an employee work hard trying to achieve milestones despite unforeseen difficulties, while other employees leave work on time, although they will then not meet their goals? Goal setting (Locke and Latham 1990) and self-regulation theory (Latham and Locke 1991) provide answers to these types of questions. They also have clear implications for the design of reward systems and practices to support goal implementation and achievement, such as how to design variable bonus systems contingent on the degree of goal achievement.

However, none of these theories can explain why a person is dissatisfied despite receiving the bonus as promised upon goal attainment. A person might even decide to look for another job, when noticing that a colleague gets paid more for a comparable performance. The social comparison process between one's own input and reward, and another person's input and reward relationship, is explained by equity and organizational justice theories (Adams 1963; Colquitt 2012). Social comparison is not only a retrospective evaluation process, but also feeds forward to the negotiation of future goals and rewards, or to the next job contract decision.

Evaluative processes might not only be based on social comparison, but also on the reciprocity of social exchange. Social contract theory (Rousseau 1989, 1995) explains what happens if an employee perceives that an organization breaks a psychological contract based on mutually given explicit or implicit promises; for example, if a supervisor does not appreciate the extra effort he or she has invested to finish a project in time.

To sum up, in the next sections of the chapter the Rubicon model is used as a framework to explain pre-decision processes by valence–instrumentality–expectancy theory, pre-action and action processes by goal setting and regulation theory, and post-action processes by organizational justice and psychological contract theory, and to draw conclusions for reward management.

Valence–instrumentality–expectancy theory

Valence–instrumentality–expectancy (VIE) theory explains the preference for an action alternative based on a rational choice model that maximizes subjective utility (Vroom 1964). Similar to expectancy-value theories it assumes that people assess the probability (from 0% to 100%) to act successfully for each alternative to reach the desired outcome. For example, one person might be 100% sure that one can accomplish a task, while another person perceives a 50% chance of succeeding or might see no chance at all. The anticipated value of the outcome of each action alternative defines its valence. The valence of an outcome is assessed subjectively and weighted by the perceived expectancy to reach it in order to determine the motivational force to go for the outcome. This assumption implies for reward management that rewards might not only have different valences for different employees, but might also be weighted differently due to differing expectations to reach them. Furthermore, Vroom (1964) points out that the valence of an action outcome depends on its perceived positive or negative potential consequences and their respective valences, which an employee perceives to be more or less strongly linked to an outcome. The perceived linkage or cause–effect relationship between an outcome and a consequence is called instrumentality. An outcome can be seen as strongly furthering or hindering a consequence, and the perceived instrumentality can therefore vary between +1 and −1. For example, an employee who wants more time to care for his or her family might rather accept a job with stable income, allowing for reduced and flexible working hours, than a higher-paid job requiring overtime work on a regular basis. The employee accepts a lower-paid job, because he or she expects to be unable to regularly work overtime, and perceives overtime work negatively linked to family care. The combination of the valence of caring for one's family, and having a decent and stable income, might lead to a stronger motivational force than the prospect of earning more money, but not being able to care for one's family, particularly if the expectancy is low that one will be able to fulfil one's job requirements.

The major contribution of VIE theory to reward management is that people perceive different valences, instrumentalities, and expectancies for given action alternatives and decide between them based on a subjective comparison process. Offering the same rewards for everybody will not suffice. VIE theory describes a within-person decision model, which implies for reward management systems that supervisors have to find out about employees' intra-individual preferences to be able to offer attractive rewards. Depending on the employee's preferences financial rewards or non-financial rewards might be more effective. Financial rewards could be fixed and variable pay, and shared ownership. Alternative indirect and/or deferred forms of financial rewards could be benefits, e.g., pension plans or health programmes, or perquisites, such as onsite fitness centres, medical care or health facilities, and company cars. However, employees might also prefer non-financial rewards, such as appreciation, job security, and assigning interesting tasks. Given the multitude of potentially motivating financial rewards a cafeteria system allowing employees to choose between reward alternatives might be helpful (see also Cotton; Smith, this volume). Another implication of VIE theory is that clear and reliable contingencies between work outcomes and rewards are needed, and that supervisors have to care whether employees perceive these contingencies. Last, but not least, supervisors have to find out whether their employees feel able to fulfil their task requirements, and if they feel able to attain intended outcomes. Therefore, supervisors should strengthen behaviour–outcome expectancies by training, and/or by supporting employees' self-efficacy, so that they have the belief that they are able to be successful in their job.

Qualitative reviews (Gerhart and Fang 2014; Shaw and Gupta 2015) and meta-analytic studies (Cerasoli et al. 2014; Jenkins et al. 1998) have shown that extrinsic rewards, such as financial incentives, can improve employee motivation and performance, and shape employee health (Giles et al. 2014) and safety behaviour (Mattson et al. 2014). But also, intrinsic rewards, such as offering an interesting task, can be motivating (Hackman and Oldham 1976). Although VIE theory is mainly focused on extrinsic rewards, intrinsic rewards can be integrated. An interesting task can be perceived as a valence of an action in itself, which might be perceived as instrumental for attaining other valenced intrinsic outcomes, such as increasing one's expertise, and feelings of competence and control.

By focusing on expectancies, instrumentalities and valances, VIE theory highlights the importance of individual human cognition and anticipation for an informed behavioural choice between action alternatives. It informs reward management to design incentive and reward systems that allow supervisors to respond to individual preferences and to strengthen perceived instrumentalities and expectancies. In contrast, a behaviouristic approach relies on objective reinforcement contingencies to shape employee behaviour by rewards (see also Fish, this volume). VIE theory has the anticipative and cognitive approach in common with goal setting and self-regulation theory, which are described in the next section.

Goal-setting theory

Goal-setting theory (Locke and Latham 1990, 2002) takes goals as immediate regulators of human behaviour. With respect to the Rubicon model (Heckhausen and Gollwitzer 1987), goal-setting theory describes pre-action and action processes. Goal-setting theory states that, given adequate ability and commitment to the goal, difficult and specific goals will lead to higher performance than easy or 'do best' goals. This linear relation between performance and goal difficulty has been confirmed by hundreds of studies, which have shown that performance only levels out at high levels of goal difficulty if goal commitment drops and when the limits of an employee's ability are reached (Latham and Locke 1991).

Besides ability and goal commitment, feedback is a necessary precondition moderating the effects of goals on performance. Setting a high goal creates a discrepancy between the status quo and the desired state, and mobilizes the person in a feed-forward process to reach this goal. Feedback helps to regulate the effort to attain the goal. Assigned or participatively set goals, as well as feedback and rewards, are therefore key elements of performance management (Latham and Locke 1991). Even though goal setting works on the individual, group, and organizational level, the majority of research has focused on the individual level. At the meso and macro level processes get even more complex, as additional variables come into play influencing performance, such as intragroup and intergroup cooperation, and information exchange (Locke and Latham 1990).

Rewards linked to the degree of individual, group, or company goal attainment, such as variable contingent pay systems, e.g. piece-rate pay, bonus systems or profit sharing, can strengthen goal commitment via increasing goal attractiveness. In contrast, bonus payments for attaining difficult goals might lead to goal rejection, as people perceive that they may not be able to reach the bonus (Locke and Latham 1990). Besides strengthening goal commitment, financial rewards induce persons to set higher goals and thus increase goal difficulty leading to higher performance. People offered financial rewards performed better than those being offered only recognition, even when goal difficulty and commitment were controlled for (Locke and Latham 1990; Wright 1992). Even within financial rewards direct cash rewards lead to better performance via goal difficulty, as people selected more difficult goals, than non-cash incentives, such as earned points with an equivalent retail monetary value (Presslee et al. 2013).

To sum up, goal-setting research informs reward management that linking rewards to the degree of goal attainment can improve performance, particularly, if cash rewards are used. Rewarding the degree of goal attainment works better than rewarding just goal attainment, as difficult and specific goals might be rejected if people believe they won't be able to attain the rewards. Rewards seem to work as they make goals more attractive, stimulate people to choose more difficult goals and strengthen goal commitment. However, the effects of rewards might differ depending on employees' fairness perceptions, which are discussed in the next section.

Equity theory and organizational justice

Equity or inequity theory (Adams 1963) proposes that employees respond with dissonance or tension, such as pay and job dissatisfaction, when they perceive to be treated more or less favourably than a referent other. They try to reduce this tension, e.g., by improving or lowering their performance to achieve equity or by leaving the situation causing inequity. Perceptions of inequity or distributive justice are based on social comparison processes of exchange relationships. Inequity is perceived if one's ratio of outcomes to inputs is unequal to the ratio of outcomes to inputs of the referent other. Perceived outcomes can be financial or non-financial rewards, such as pay or status. The propositions of the theory are well supported regarding the effects of undercompensation, but not regarding overpayment (Ambrose and Kulik 1999).

Lawler (1971, 1973) suggested that social comparison processes influence employees' perception, about what they should receive, compared to what they actually receive, and that this discrepancy influences their pay satisfaction. A meta-analysis (Williams et al. 2006) testing key assumptions of Lawler's discrepancy theory (1973) shows that increasing pay discrepancy is associated with decreasing pay satisfaction. Also, internal and external pay comparisons, i.e., with employees within the same or with employees of other companies, were strongly associated with pay satisfaction. Unfortunately, the design of the primary studies did not allow for testing the assumed mediating role of pay discrepancy regarding the relation between equity perceptions and pay satisfaction.

Organizational justice research has shown that employees do not only rely on social comparisons between themselves and other employees, but also reflect on what has happened and could have happened to them or others, and thus develop referent cognitions by mental simulations, which influence their fairness perception (Folger 1986). Cognitive referent theory explains that people experience fairness or unfairness not only in situations affecting themselves, but also when they perceive how others are treated. Whether reward management is perceived as fair or unfair is therefore also dependent on how employees perceive how other employees are rewarded, even if they are not affected by these decisions (Greenberg et al. 2007).

Besides the distribution of outcomes, which is focused by equity theory, employees also assess the fairness of reward management, with respect to how they or others are treated in the exchange relationship (see Shortland and Perkins, this volume, on expatriate reward). Procedural justice has been further differentiated in interactional and informational justice (Colquitt 2012). Although the different aspects of justice are correlated, they show differential relationships with outcome variables (Colquitt 2001). For example, pay satisfaction seems have a stronger correlation with distributive justice than with procedural justice. In addition, pay satisfaction is negatively correlated with turnover intentions and voluntary turnover (Williams et al. 2006).

Research on the different aspects of organizational justice informs reward management not only about how people react to fair or unfair conditions, but also about criteria that can be used to design, implement, and practice reward systems that are perceived as fair. Employees typically perceive organizational practices as fair if they have control over the process, e.g., can directly or indirectly participate in pay system design and decisions, if it is possible to correct decisions, and if unbiased and accurate procedures are applied consistently in a way that people are treated with dignity, respect, and truthfulness (Greenberg et al. 2007; Colquitt 2012).

People also differ in their tolerance to inequity and consequently evaluate and respond to pay system characteristics differently. For example, in situations where information exchange about what people get paid is restricted, persons with a lower level of tolerance to inequity show lower task performance, while persons with a higher level of tolerance to inequity show higher task performance. These negative effects of pay secrecy on individual task performance can be explained in part by reduced perceived performance-pay contingencies, i.e., weaker instrumentality perceptions (Bamberger and Belogolovsky 2010). See also Arnold and Fulmer (this volume) on pay transparency.

Another example of how individual differences influence pay fairness perceptions shows the concept of promotion focus, i.e., whether people believe they have the opportunity to get better pay. Research shows that pay dispersion increases pay fairness perceptions when employees have a strong focus on promotion (Park et al. 2017).

To sum, equity and organizational justice theory informs reward management about how social comparison processes of exchange processes influence the perception of fairness and how reward systems should be designed and used to be perceived as fair. Exchange processes are also the core of psychological contract theory, which is described in the next section.

Psychological contract theory

Rousseau (1989, p. 123) defines a psychological contract as "an individual's belief regarding the terms and conditions of a reciprocal exchange agreement between the focal person and another party". Thus, the concept of psychological contract describes an individual's belief that mutual obligations exist between employer and employee. Within the psychological contract literature there is a strong agreement that contracts can be categorized into two types: relational and transactional (Conway and Briner 2005). Relational psychological contracts emphasize long-term personal, socio-emotional, and value-based mutual obligations, e.g., that job security is reciprocated with loyalty. Transactional psychological contracts are based on more specific, monetary, and economic short-term elements of exchange, e.g., pay increases in return for high performance. The challenge is to measure these types (Coyle-Shapiro and Parzefall 2008).

The concept of psychological contracts is theoretically based on the ideas of exchange theory (Blau 1964) and the norm of reciprocity (Gouldner 1960). According to exchange theory (Blau 1964), individuals seek for balance in exchange relationships. Therefore, a promise made by one party obligates the other party to reciprocate. Rousseau and Ho (2000) underline the importance of psychological contracts within the context of employee reward systems. They expect psychological contracts to be mainly influenced by reward strategies and argue that the fulfilment of psychological contracts might influence employees' satisfaction.

A person believes that a promise has been made either explicitly or implicitly and that both parties are bound to a set of mutual obligations (Robinson and Rousseau 1994). Obligations based on promises are much more specific beliefs about what, when, and why something will happen than general beliefs about whether something will or should happen (e.g., general expectations or group norms), and therefore much more psychologically engaging (Conway and Briner 2005; Guest and Conway 2002). Hence, psychological contract breach, i.e. if an employee believes that the company or the supervisor has not fulfilled its promised obligations, he or she might have a negative affective reaction (Morrison and Robinson 1997). A meta-analysis confirmed a direct relationship between contract breach and negative affective reactions such as mistrust and violation, which in turn negatively influence attitudes such as organisational commitment and job satisfaction, as well as behaviour such as in-role and extra-role performance (Zhao et al. 2007).

Psychological contract theory focuses on the employer–employee relationship (Morrison and Robinson 1997). Since supervisors are the key agents of employers, employees may perceive them as responsible for establishing and fulfilling psychological contracts. Therefore, employees may equate their supervisor with the organization and personify explicit promises made by their supervisor as reflecting promises by the organization (Rousseau 1995). Indeed, several studies suggest that leaders might influence employees' perception of psychological contracts (e.g. Brown and Moshavi 2002).

Particularly, transactional and transformational leadership behaviour seems to be relevant for establishing and fulfilling transactional and relational psychological contracts. The major aspect of *transactional leadership* is *contingent reward*, i.e., emphasizing clear relationships between performance and rewards (Bass and Riggio 2006). Transformational leaders communicate an attractive vision, provide meaning, and respond to an employee's values, needs, and goals (Bass and Riggio 2006). A plethora of studies have shown substantial positive and unique relationships between both contingent reward and transformational leadership, and employee job satisfaction and motivation (Judge and Piccolo 2004). Transformational leadership behaviour also influences employees' pay satisfaction by providing meaning to and understanding of the pay and wider reward system (Salimäki et al. 2009).

Research findings indicate that transformational leadership is related to pay satisfaction via the fulfilment of transactional psychological contracts, while the fulfilment of relational psychological contracts mediates the relationship between transformational leadership and job satisfaction and affective organizational commitment (Antoni and Syrek 2012). When pay systems are changed, the fulfilment of relational psychological contracts supporting long-term personal, socio-emotional, as well as value-based, and thus trustworthy employee–employer relationships, seem to play an even more important role. Research analysing the introduction of a performance-based bonus system (with the risk to earn even less) shows that the fulfilment of relational psychological contracts mediates not only the effects of transformational leadership on job satisfaction, but also on bonus satisfaction. In contrast, transactional psychological contract fulfilment mediates the influence of transformational leadership on general pay satisfaction, but not bonus satisfaction. These findings indicate that a trustworthy relationship is needed to accept pay based on risk (Syrek and Antoni 2017).

To sum up, psychological contract theory informs reward management about the implications of perceived mutual relational and transactional obligations for pay satisfaction and employee behaviour. Research has shown the key role of leadership behaviour for the development and fulfilment or breach of psychological contracts, and consequently for the effects of reward management systems.

Conclusions

In the last decades reward management research has seen significant progress, and studies based on psychological theories have contributed to these findings (Antoni et al. 2017; Cerasoli et al. 2014; Gerhart and Fang 2014; Shaw and Gupta 2015). Nevertheless, reward management remains an under-researched area (Gupta and Shaw 2015). The financial crisis has highlighted the potential detrimental effect of rewards systems for individuals, companies, and the society as a whole (see Kornelakis and Gospel; A. Wright, this volume). Therefore, more research has to be done analysing under which conditions particular rewards are most effective or under which they lead to unintended consequences. To fully understand the underlying mediating and moderating mechanisms, linking reward practices to individual, team, and organizational behaviour and outcomes, more longitudinal and multi-level research is needed (e.g., Trevor and Wazeter 2006). Specifically, research on how team- and organizational-level variables, such as work structure, leadership behaviour, organizational culture, and corporate strategy influence the relation between different rewards and outcomes is missing. Conceptual papers on multi-level effects of pay variation or team pay-for-performance (Conroy and Gupta 2016) could stimulate future empirical studies. When looking at the enormous financial resources companies invest in reward systems and their potential detrimental effects, both more funding and support for empirical reward management research seems to be justified.

References

Adams, S.J. (1963). Towards an understanding of inequity. *Journal of Abnormal and Social Psychology.* 67(5), 422–436.

Ambrose, M.L. and Kulik, C.T. (1999). Old friends, new faces: Motivation research in the 1990s. *Journal of Management.* 25(3), 231–292.

Antoni, C.H., Baeten, X., Perkins, S.J., Shaw, J.D. and Vartiainen, M. (2017). Reward management-linking employee motivation and organizational performance: a special issue of the Journal of personnel psychology. *Journal of Personnel Psychology*. 16(2), 57–60.

Antoni, C.H. and Syrek, C.J. (2012). Leadership and pay satisfaction: the mediating role of psychological contracts. *International Studies of Management and Organization*. 42(1), 88–106.

Bamberger, P. and Belogolovsky, E. (2010). The impact of pay secrecy on individual task performance. *Personnel Psychology*. 63(4), 965–996.

Bass, B.M. and Riggio, R.E. (2006). *Transformational Leadership* (2nd ed.). Mahwah, NJ: Lawrence Erlbaum Associates.

Blau, P. (1964). *Exchange and Power in Social Life*. New York: Wiley.

Brown, F.W. and Moshavi, D. (2002). Herding academic cats: Faculty reactions to transformational and contingent reward leadership. *Journal of Leadership and Organizational Studies*. 8, 79–93.

Cerasoli, C.P., Nicklin, J.M. and Ford, M.T. (2014). Intrinsic motivation and extrinsic incentives jointly predict performance: a 40-year meta-analysis. *Psychological Bulletin*. 140, 980–1008.

Colquitt, J.A. (2001). On the dimensionality of organizational justice: a construct validation of a measure. *Journal of Applied Psychology*. 86(3), 386–400.

Colquitt, J.A. (2012). Organizational justice. In Kozlowski, S.W. (ed.). *The Oxford Handbook of Organizational Psychology* (Vol. 1, pp. 526–547). Oxford University Press.

Conway, N. and Briner, R.B. (2005). *Understanding Psychological Contracts at Work. A Critical Evaluation of Theory and Research*. Oxford: University Press.

Conroy, S.A. and Gupta, N. (2016). Team pay-for-performance: the devil is in the details. *Group and Organization Management*. 41, 32–65.

Coyle-Shapiro, J.A.-M. and Parzefall, M. (2008). Psychological contracts. In Cooper, Cary L. and Barling, Julian, (eds.) *The SAGE Handbook of Organizational Behavior* (pp. 17–34). London, UK: SAGE Publications.

Folger, R. (1986). Rethinking equity theory: A referent cognitions model. In Bierhoff, H.W. Cohen, R.L. and Greenberg, J. (eds.). *Justice in Social Relations* (pp. 145–162). New York: Plenum Press.

Gerhart, B. and Fang, M. (2014). Pay for (individual) performance: Issues, claims, evidence and the role of sorting effects. *Human Resource Management Review*. 24, 41–52.

Giles, E.L., Robalino, S., McColl, E., Sniehotta, F.F. and Adams, J. (2014). The effectiveness of financial incentives for health behaviour change: systematic review and meta-analysis. *PLoS ONE*. 9(3), e90347.

Guest, D.E. and Conway, N. (2002). Communicating the psychological contract: an employer perspective. *Human Resource Management Journal*. 12(2), 22–38.

Gouldner, A.W. (1960). The norm of reciprocity. *American Sociological Review*. 25, 161–178.

Greenberg, J., Ashton-James, C.E. and Ashkanasy, N.M. (2007). Social comparison processes in organizations. *Organizational Behavior and Human Decision Processes*. 102(1), 22–41.

Gupta, N. and Shaw, J.D. (2015). Employee compensation: the neglected area of HRM research. *Human Resource Management Review*. 24, 1–4.

Hackman, J. R. and Oldham, G. R. (1976). Motivation through the design of work: Test of a theory. Organizational behavior and human performance, 16(2), 250–279.

Heckhausen, H. and Gollwitzer, P.M. (1987) Thought contents and cognitive functioning in motivational versus volitional states of mind. *Motivation and Emotion*. 17, 101–120.

Jenkins Jr, G.D., Mitra, A., Gupta, N. and Shaw, J.D. (1998). Are financial incentives related to performance? A meta-analytic review of empirical research. *Journal of Applied Psychology*. 83, 777–787.

Judge, T.A. and Piccolo, R.F. (2004). Transformational and transactional leadership: a meta-analytic test of their relative validity. *Journal of Applied Psychology*. 89, 755–768.

Lawler, E.E. III (1971). *Pay and Organization Effectiveness: A Psychological View*. NY: McGraw Hill.

Lawler, E.E. III (1973). Motivation in work organizations. In Taylor and Tetrick, L. E. (eds.). *The Employment Relationship: Examining Psychological and Contextual Perspectives* (pp. 226–253). Oxford: University Press.

Latham, G.P. and Locke, E.A. (1991). Self-regulation through goal setting. *Organizational Behavior and Human Decision Processes*. 50(2), 212–247.

Locke, E.A. and Latham, G.P. (1990). *A Theory of Goal Setting and Task Performance*. Englewood Cliffs, NJ: Prentice Hall.

Locke, E.A. and Latham, G.P. (2002). Building a practically useful theory of goal setting and task motivation: a 35-year odyssey. *American Psychologist*. 57(9), 705.

Mattson, M., Torbiörn, I. and Hellgren, J. (2014). Effects of staff bonus systems on safety behaviors. *Human Resource Management Review*. 24, 17–30.

Morrison, E.W. and Robinson, S.L. (1997). When employees feel betrayed: a model of how psychological contract violation develops. *Academy of Management Review*. 22(1), 226–256.

Park, T. Y., Kim, S. and Sung, L. K. (2017). Fair pay dispersion: a regulatory focus theory view. *Organizational Behavior and Human Decision Processes*. 142, 1–11.

Presslee, A., Vance, T.W. and Webb, R.A. (2013). The effects of reward type on employee goal setting, goal commitment, and performance. *The Accounting Review*. 88(5), 1805–1831.

Robinson, S.L. and Rousseau, D.M. (1994). Violating the psychological contract: not the exception but the norm. *Journal of Organizational Behavior*. 15, 245–259.

Rousseau, D.M. (1989). Psychological and implied contracts in organizations. *Employee Responsibilities and Rights Journal*. 2(2), 121–139.

Rousseau, D.M. (1995). *Psychological Contracts in Organizations: Understanding Written and Unwritten Agreements*. Thousand Oaks, CA: Sage.

Rousseau, D.M. and Ho, V.T (2000). Psychological contract issues in compensation. In Rynes, S.L. and Gerhart, B. (eds.). *Compensation in Organizations: Current Research and Practice* (pp. 273–310). San Francisco: Jossey Bass.

Salimäki, A., Hakonen, A. and Heneman, R.L. (2009). Managers generating meaning for pay: a test for reflection theory. *Journal of Managerial Psychology*. 21, 161–177.

Syrek, C.J. and Antoni, C.H. (2017). Psychological contract fulfillment and employee responses to pay system change: the effects of transformational leadership. *Journal of Personnel Psychology*. 16(4), 172–185.

Trevor, C.O. and Wazeter, D.L. (2006). A contingent view of reactions to objective pay conditions: Interdependence among pay structure characteristics and pay relative to internal and external referents. *Journal of Applied Psychology*. 91, 1260–1275.

Vroom, V.H. (1964). *Work and Motivation*. Oxford, England: Wiley.

Williams, M.L., McDaniel, M.A. and Nguyen, N.T. (2006). A meta-analysis of the antecedents and consequences of pay level satisfaction. *Journal of Applied Psychology*. 91(2), 392–413.

Wright, P.M. (1992). An examination of the relationships among monetary incentives, goal level, goal commitment, and performance. *Journal of Management*. 18(4), 677–693.

Zhao, H., Wayne, S. J., Glibkowski, B. C. and Bravo, J. (2007). The impact of psychological contract breach on work-related outcomes: a meta-analysis. *Personnel Psychology*. 60(3), 647–680.

4

PSYCHOLOGICAL PROCESSES UNDERLYING ORGANIZATIONAL REWARD MANAGEMENT

The role of perceived organizational support and effort–reward management

Arianna Costantini, Stephan Dickert, Andrea Ceschi and Riccardo Sartori

Introduction

Good organizational reward management is often critical in boosting employee commitment, motivating behavioural changes and promoting competence which, in turn, influence the attainment of organizational goals (Beer et al. 2015). To this end, organizational reward management is comprised of strategies, policies and processes required to ensure that the contribution of people to the organization is recognized by both financial and non-financial means (Armstrong 2007). To stimulate behaviour helping to achieve the organization's goals and reward employees fairly and consistently in accordance with their value to the organization, reward systems have to be carefully designed, implemented and maintained (Armstrong 2003, 2007).

In this chapter we argue that it is critical to identify and recognize the role of psychological processes underlying the dynamics of reward management, an issue that has not been fully examined in previous research. We believe it is important not only to focus on the introduction and monitoring of reward policies, but also to investigate the role of employees' attitudes over time in influencing the effectiveness of reward policies themselves. The literature on reward management has had a tendency to consider individual psychological facets of rewards mainly as static non-financial aspects of the implemented reward management policies. Yet current research in the industrial/organizational (I/O) psychology domain underlines the importance of adopting a multi-level approach to the study of the work environment which accounts for the effects of malleable individual psychological perceptions.

By showing the connection between two main psychological constructs (i.e., *perceived organizational support* and *effort–reward imbalance*) developed in the field of I/O psychology, we seek to encourage future scholarship and practice that examines and scrutinizes the dynamic role of individual psychological factors for the introduction and evaluation of reward policies. Such an approach will lead to a clearer definition of the behavioural outcomes of reward policies and a deeper understanding of the dynamics involved in the effectiveness of reward management.

Before exploring how psychological factors may be linked to the effectiveness of reward policies, we will review how reward management currently considers employees' psychological factors as part of static non-financial rewards.

Psychological processes in the context of reward management: Current conceptualizations and the need for a dynamic perspective

The study of reward management has acknowledged the importance of complementing financial and non-financial reward types in order to include any valued outcome an employee receives from the employer in exchange for the employee's effort and contribution (Armstrong 2010; Milkovich and Newman 2008; Henderson 2003). The current conceptualization of psychological factors in reward management, while important for understanding how different rewards influence different outcomes, does not entirely answer the need for unpacking the mechanisms through which psychological perceptions influence the effectiveness of implemented organizational reward policies (Takeuchi et al. 2009). In turn, the effectiveness of such policies is crucial to foster the performance and well-being of both individuals and organizations (Shaw and Gupta 2001). We now briefly discuss current conceptualizations of psychological factors within the reward management literature and give insights into a possible framework to examine the dynamic role of psychological factors.

How attitudes and psychological aspects are conceived in reward management

Along with pay and employee benefits, reward management is equally concerned with non-financial rewards such as recognition, learning and development opportunities, and increased job responsibility (Armstrong 2007). While financial rewards include fixed (i.e., salary and benefits) and variable rewards (i.e., incentives contingent upon individual, group, or organization performance), non-financial ones also consist of intangible rewards provided and controlled by firms (Kanungo and Hartwick 1987; see also Cotton, this volume). Examples include public recognition and alternate work arrangements, as well as training and development opportunities (Chiang and Birtch 2011). Organizations can use these rewards in order to develop, motivate and increase the performance of their employees. In turn, from the point of view of the employee, receiving recognition is reflected in perceived organizational support, which represents employees' "global beliefs concerning the extent to which the organization values their contributions and cares about their well-being" (Eisenberger et al. 1986: p. 501; see also Smith, this volume).

In the domain of reward management, research to date has focused mainly on financial rather than non-financial rewards (de Gieter and Hofmans 2015; Fay and Thompson 2001), while the study of the psychological facets behind such rewards has received only limited attention. Against this background, both human resource (HR) practitioners and scholars have highlighted the added value of focusing on non-financial rewards in order to deepen our understanding of how organizational and employee implications are related (de Gieter and Hofmans 2015; Chiang and Birtch 2011; Milkovich and Newman 2008). Despite this, there is little research focusing on the psychological implications related to rewards. Accordingly, the study of reward management needs to acknowledge the importance of complementing financial and other reward types, encompassing a fuller and representative set of rewards (Armstrong 2010; Milkovich and Newman 2008). Additionally, it also needs to acknowledge the dynamic effects of psychological factors on behavioural outcomes of reward policies.

Within such a framework of combined rewards, several categorizations have been proposed in order to reflect the multidimensional nature of reward satisfaction (de Gieter and Hofmans 2015;

Hofmans et al. 2013; Williams et al. 2008). Indeed, research conducted to account for the psychological aspects involved in reward management has shown that it is not only the rewards themselves that influence employees' behaviours and attitudes; the attitude towards the rewards (i.e., the satisfaction with them) also influences job-relevant outcomes (de Gieter et al. 2008). That is, based on the satisfaction with rewards, employees adapt their work behaviour and attitudes in either a favourable or an unfavourable way (Porter and Lawler 1968; Vroom 1964). Although useful for acknowledging the role of employee attitudes in influencing the effectiveness of rewards, satisfaction with rewards represents only one of the possible viewpoints an employee could develop towards reward policies, meaning that more research is needed to gain a fuller and more comprehensive understanding of how individual perceptions influence reward-policy outcomes, at both the organizational and the individual level.

The dynamic interplay between psychological factors and the context of reward management

In order to foster the success of reward policies in the workplace, it is necessary to consider how the pattern of multiple actions is linked to the achievement of the desired outcomes (Delery and Doty 1996). This perspective highlights the need for considering how the range of already present organizational factors impacts on the effectiveness of an introduced policy (Costantini et al. 2017). Also, given that implemented policies shape employees' reward expectations, and that individual reward attitudes can influence the effectiveness of these policies, it is important to consider cognitive and affective processes underlying individuals' reward sensitivities. Whether strategies and policies are considered as rewarding or not depends on the subjective perceptions of the employee him-/herself, which are likely to depend on previous reward actions.

Given that the main referent of reward management are employees, reciprocal effects between them and reward strategies should be considered, including the analysis of how implemented reward policies relate to individual employee perceptions. Such an ecological and dynamic perspective underlines the reciprocal interaction between individuals and their contexts, arguing that individuals both act *in* contexts and *upon* the context (Bronfenbrenner 1994; Cleveland et al. 2015). That is, individual perceptions of rewards not only represent an outcome of implemented policies but also actually exert an influence on the context, meaning that a reciprocal influence occurs between the individual and the organization (Katz and Kahn 1978; Klein and Kozlowski 2000) when reward policies are implemented. In this vein, it has been argued that reward strategy and policies cannot be considered, designed and operated independently of their setting (Armstrong 2007; see also Wright, this volume). For this reason, there are no universally effective or ineffective reward practices because the diversity of people working in highly varied organizations and settings is likely to affect the success of reward policies (Armstrong 2007). Hence, reward management in organizations should be modelled based on the principle of the best fit rather than best practice, because the former allows a consideration of the dynamic interplay between individual and organizational factors.

Organizational reward management can be effective only if structural support is provided through the implementation of practices contemplating a fit between individual needs, culture and characteristics, and rewards (Verwaeren et al. 2017; Chiang and Birch 2011). Since organizations are embedded in culture and individuals are embedded in both culture and organizations, the effectiveness of rewards is grounded in values and norms, which are elements of the organizational culture (Costantini et al. 2017). Such an awareness of the reciprocal influence between organizational factors and the effectiveness of rewards contributes to a better understanding of the causal processes linking organizational outcomes to employee behaviours through policies alignment (Christina et al. 2017). That is, a better understanding of culture and change processes, including those originating from individual perceptions, is at least as important as the technical design of reward plans if improvements are to be put into practice (Armstrong et al. 2011).

Building a link between individual psychological factors and reward management

After highlighting the need for considering the interplay between psychological factors and the context of reward policy implementation, we discuss the conceptual integration between two main constructs developed within the field of I/O psychology, i.e., perceived organizational support and effort–reward imbalance, and reward management. By suggesting possible mechanisms linking rewards to behavioural and attitudinal outcomes, and the extent to which individual psychological perceptions of rewards are connected to such mechanisms, we provide a possible framework to investigate how psychological perceptions are related to the effectiveness of reward policies.

How perceived organizational support is linked to reward management

It has been argued that non-financial rewards such as recognition for good work, opportunities for promotion and job security nurture perceived organizational support in that they meet employees' needs for approval, esteem and affiliation (Eisenberger et al. 2016). That is, such kinds of rewards are likely to represent antecedents of perceived organizational support, especially if the employee believes that these rewards are given voluntarily by the organization (Rhoades and Eisenberger 2002). Against this background, perceived organizational support is expected to represent a key element of reward management approaches, because evidence shows that high perceived organizational support positively relates to performance (Kurtessis et al. 2015), occupational well-being (Rhoades and Eisenberger 2002; Kinnunen et al. 2008), and signals that the organization is ready to reward increased performance (Eisenberger et al. 2016). Figure 4.1 illustrates this assumption, depicting that perceived organizational support acts as a mediator between non-financial rewards and work outcomes.

Such a relationship can be explained based on social exchange theory and the principle of reciprocity (Cropanzano and Mitchell 2005; Gouldner 1960). Social exchange involves a series of interactions generating obligations (Emerson 1976). Employees who experience perceived organizational support are more inclined to care about and further organizational goals (Eisenberger et al. 2001). Accordingly, one possible explanation for the proposed mediating role of perceived organizational support can be the elicitation of increased obligation, trust, and expectations that effort will be rewarded by the organization (Kurtessis et al. 2015).

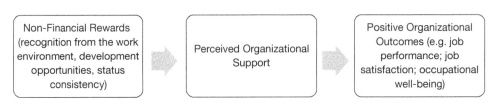

Figure 4.1 Proposed relationship between non-financial rewards and work-related outcomes mediated by perceived organizational support

The interplay between occupational rewards and efforts at work

The conceptualization of work-related benefits as a reciprocal and equitable relationship between effort and rewards has been developed in the effort–reward imbalance model (ERI; Siegrist 1996). This model assumes occupational rewards as encompassing *esteem*, i.e., the extent to which one perceives to be respected, supported and accepted by supervisors and colleagues, *job promotion*, which refers to the perception of career opportunities, and *job security*, which includes perceptions related to status consistency and to stability (Siegrist 1996).

The model assumes that a lack of balance in the relationship between effort and rewards may cause emotional distress and other negative organizational and individual outcomes (e.g., emotional exhaustion: Bakker et al. 2000; de Jonge et al. 2000; job dissatisfaction: Calnan et al. 2000; de Jonge et al. 2000; van Vegchel et al. 2001). Research has expanded on this model and evidence exists that perceived occupational rewards as put forth in the ERI model, but not efforts, exert a buffering role on the positive relationship between cognitive antecedents and counter-productive work behaviours (Costantini et al. under review). This means that psychological perceptions of being rewarded make the link between intentions and counterproductive work behaviours weaker. Also, some of the occupational rewards conceived within the ERI model have been found to partially mediate the relationship between age and risk-taking tendencies among managers (Ceschi et al. 2017). This suggests that perceived psychological rewards may also be influenced by individual differences, which in turn relate to differences in organizational behaviours.

In sum, along with findings showing the relationship between satisfaction with psychological rewards and job satisfaction (Hofmans et al. 2013; de Gieter et al. 2010), this reviewed literature suggests that perceived occupational rewards and efforts differently interact with individual and organizational factors, influencing both positive and unfavourable organizational behaviours.

Assessing individual psychological factors underneath the effectiveness of reward policies

Even though both perceived organizational support and effort–reward imbalance are based on social exchange theory (Kinnunen et al. 2008), these models refer to different elements within the organizational reward framework. It has been argued that organizational rewards such as those included in the ERI model (i.e., esteem, perceived job promotion opportunities and job security) positively relate to perceived organizational support, while job stressors (i.e., efforts) negatively predict it (Rhoades and Eisenberger 2002). This is consistent with a causal pattern between the elements of the ERI model and perceived organizational support. However, such distinct, linear patterns between perceived organizational rewards/efforts and support fail to consider the extent to which concomitant, individual perceptions of both gains and losses at work might be related to perceived organizational support (Siegrist 1996).

This reasoning becomes important when considering that perceived efforts and rewards, rather than representing two opposite sides of a single continuum, constitute two separate dimensions. That is, a reward policy aiming at promoting higher perceived organizational rewards may have no effects on efforts or, on the contrary, prompt individual perceptions of higher introduced efforts, which could render the policy ineffective. Also, without considering the interplay between perceived rewards and efforts, the risk might be to invest in only one of the two dimensions, failing to consider possible benefits related to any investment in the other one.

For these reasons, it is fundamental to capture the perceived level of imbalance between efforts and perceived occupational rewards when approaching the design of organizational reward strategies. Especially for non-financial rewards, which are rooted in individual psychological perceptions, an analysis of this imbalance would allow for the identification of a cut-off point required for reward policies to be effective. Furthermore, the quantification of this imbalance at the individual level provides important additional information with a single indicator, which permits assessing how individuals perceive their efforts to (not) be equally balanced by provided rewards (Siegrist et al. 2014). Indeed, policy makers would benefit from the assessment of the overall level of effort–reward imbalance within their organization prior to the design or the introduction of a policy, so as to identify not only the most suitable reward strategy to be introduced but also the investment needed to make it work.

Such organizational analyses can efficiently help in the design of non-financial reward policies, considering not only structural changes, but also the underlying psychological aspects involved. In this case, assuming that the relationship between efforts and rewards is likely to influence perceived organizational support, it is possible to conceptualize the following model, where rewards (R) are put in the numerator and efforts (E) in the denominator:

$$POS = \frac{Rk_r}{Ek_e}$$

Moreover, since organizational support is perceived, and its sensitivity is not equal for all individuals, we introduce a k_r correction factor that accounts for individual differences related to the importance attached to organizational rewards, and efforts (k_e). To this extent, relevant individual differences may include gender, age and culture. As far as gender is concerned, previous studies showed that women and men tend to differ in their perceptions of efforts and rewards. Even though findings on this topic are mixed (e.g. Li et al. 2005, 2006), recent studies show that men are likely to perceive more efforts than women (Omansky et al. 2016), and that they tend to expose themselves more often to high job demands and react by high intrinsic effort (Li et al. 2005). On the other side, women tend to perceive and be more attracted by higher rewards from work than men (Schlechter et al. 2015; Li et al. 2005), as well as to have significantly higher preference for non-financial rewards compared to men (von Bonsdorff 2011). As for age, research shows that the oldest age groups have the highest preference for non-financial rewards, with older employees tending to value recognition at work, opportunities for sharing knowledge and to use skills diversely (von Bonsdorff 2011; Loi and Shultz 2007). This may be explained by the desire of older employees to keep their employability high regardless of age. It is important to note, however, that these differences should be considered within a cultural perspective, given that changes in the interpretation and meaning of traditional gender roles, working conditions and relevant laws and regulations are likely to shape the perceptions of balance between efforts and rewards (von Bonsdorff 2011; Chiang and Birch 2007; Li et al. 2005, 2006).

Overall, the proposal to capture perceived organizational support as originating from individual psychological factors related to efforts and rewards represents a tool to improve the understanding of the processes underlying the implementation of rewards policies. By doing so, it is possible to enhance contextual and empirical analysis capabilities, and to ensure that employees directly involved and affected both appreciate and understand any new reward arrangements (Armstrong et al. 2011).

Conclusions

With the changes occurring in today's work environment and leading to a growth in high flexibility and mobility, short-term contracts and increasing job insecurity, rewards play a significant role in current job content, especially those linked to perceptions of esteem, promotion prospects, or job insecurity (Li et al. 2006). While financial rewards seek to promote high results and productivity, the use of non-financial rewards aim at strengthening employees' commitment to their organization (Gomez-Mejia et al. 2015). However, while much research has been conducted to investigate how rewards in work settings are indeed effective with regards to the quantity and quality of employees' performance and to intrinsic motivation (Cerasoli et al. 2014), little is known about the role of individual perceptions within such relationships.

Drawing on the importance of investigating how individual perceptions of rewards other than satisfaction can influence the effectiveness of reward policies, we proposed that perceived organizational support and effort–reward imbalance are two mechanisms underlying the effectiveness of implemented reward strategies. Rather than focusing exclusively on the outcomes of the reward strategies, it is important to explore how individual and organizational factors may represent antecedents and mediators implied in reward management implementations. In doing so, a broader approach is needed which includes both the role of individual perceptions (i.e., effort–reward imbalance) and organizational attitudes (i.e., perceived organizational support) as variables influencing the effectiveness of financial and non-financial rewards.

This reasoning is aligned with an ecological perspective on reward management, where organizational cultures and individuals are intertwined and reciprocally influence each other. This perspective suggests that higher performance and well-being are simultaneously achievable when all the factors influencing reward policies are included in the mix (Costantini et al. 2017). Such a framework leads to a holistic vision of reward management inside organizations, which gives insights into how HR practices influence employee attitudes and improve workers' performance in ways that are beneficial to the employing organization (Purcell and Hutchinson 2007).

Practitioners and policy makers inside organizations would benefit from the adoption of reward-strategy approaches based on the assessment of both the individual and organizational balance between employees' psychological perceptions and the values of the organization. Reward policies designed to recognize the contribution of people to the organization should include a preliminary analysis of individual perceptions of balance between effort and rewards. Research is needed to investigate whether work environments that account for the existing levels of perceived rewards and efforts answer to the need for considering the dynamic interplay between individual and contextual factors, eventually influencing the effectiveness of reward policies through perceived organizational support.

References

Armstrong, M. (2003). *Employee Reward* (3rd ed.). London: CIPD.

Armstrong, M. (2007). *A Handbook of Employee Reward Management and Practice* (2nd ed.). London: Kogan Page.

Armstrong, M. (2010). *Armstrong's Handbook of Reward Management Practice: Improving Performance through Reward*. Philadelphia, PA: Kogan Page Limited.

Armstrong, M., Brown, D. and Reilly, P. (2011). Increasing the effectiveness of reward management: an evidence-based approach. *Employee Relations.* 33, 106–120.

Bakker, A. B., Killmer, C. H., Siegrist, J. and Schaufeli, W. B. (2000). Effort–reward imbalance and burnout among nurses. *Journal of Advanced Nursing.* 31, 884–891.

Beer, M., Boselie, P. and Brewster, C. (2015). Back to the future: implications for the field of HRM of the multistakeholder perspective proposed 30 years ago. *Human Resource Management.* 54, 427–438.

Bronfenbrenner, U. (1994). Ecological models of human development. In Bronfenbrenner, U. (ed.) *International Encyclopedia of Education* (2nd ed., Vol. 3, pp. 1643–1647). Oxford: Elsevier.

Calnan, M., Wainwright, D. and Almond, S. (2000). Job strain, effort-reward imbalance and mental distress: a study of occupations in general medical practice. *Work and Stress.* 14, 297–311.

Cerasoli, C. P., Nicklin, J. M. and Ford, M. T. (2014). Intrinsic motivation and extrinsic incentives jointly predict performance: a 40-year meta-analysis. *Psychological Bulletin.* 140, 980–1008.

Ceschi, A., Costantini, A., Dickert, S. and Sartori, R. (2017). The impact of occupational rewards on risk taking among managers. *Journal of Personnel Psychology.* 16, 105–112.

Chiang, F. F. and Birtch, T. A. (2011). The performance implications of financial and non-financial rewards: an Asian Nordic comparison. *Journal of Management Studies.* 49, 538–570.

Chiang, F.F. and Birch, T. A. (2007). The transferability of management practices: examining cross-national differences in reward preferences. *Human Relations.* 60, 1293–1330.

Christina, S., Dainty, A., Daniels, K., Tregaskis, O. and Waterson, P. (2017). Shut the fridge door! HRM alignment, job redesign and energy performance. *Human Resource Management Journal.* 27, 382–402.

Cleveland, J. N., Byrne, Z. S. and Cavanagh, T. M. (2015). The future of HR is RH: respect for humanity at work. *Human Resource Management Review.* 25, 146–161.

Costantini, A., Ceschi, A. and Sartori, R. (under review). The moderation effect of rewards on the relationship between the behavioral intention of CWB and actual behavior: a study based on three preeminent theories of OB.

Costantini, A., Sartori, R. and Ceschi, A. (2017). Framing Workplace Innovation through an organizational psychology perspective: A review of current WPI studies. In Oeij, P.R.A., Rus, D. and Pot, F.D. (eds.) *Workplace Innovation. Aligning Perspectives on Health, Safety and Well-Being* (pp. 131–147). Cham: Springer.

Cropanzano, R. and Mitchell, M. S. (2005). Social exchange theory: an interdisciplinary review. *Journal of Management.* 31, 874–900.

de Gieter, S., and Hofmans, J. (2015). How reward satisfaction affects employees' turnover intentions and performance: an individual differences approach. *Human Resource Management Journal.* 25, 200–216.

de Jonge, J., Bosma, H., Peter, R. and Siegrist, J. (2000). Job strain, effort-reward imbalance and employee well-being: a large-scale cross-sectional study. *Social Science and Medicine.* 50, 1317–1327.

de Gieter, S., de Cooman, R., Pepermans, R. and Jegers, M. (2008). Manage through rewards, not only through pay: Establishing the Psychological Reward Satisfaction Scale (PReSS). In Vartiainen, M., Antoni, C., Baeten, X., Hakonen, N., Lucas, R. and Thierry, H. (eds.). *Reward Management: Facts and Trends in Europe* (pp. 97–117).

de Gieter, S., de Cooman, R., Pepermans, R. and Jegers, M. (2010). The psychological reward satisfaction scale: developing and psychometric testing two refined subscales for nurses. *Journal of Advanced Nursing.* 66, 911–922.

Delery, J. E. and Doty, D. H. (1996). Modes of theorizing in strategic human resource management: tests of universalistic, contingency, and configurational performance predictions. *Academy of Management Journal.* 39, 802–835.

Eisenberger, R., Armeli, S., Rexwinkel, B., Lynch, P. D. and Rhoades, L. (2001). Reciprocation of perceived organizational support. *Journal of Applied Psychology.* 86, 42–51.

Eisenberger, R., Huntington, R., Hutchison, S. and Sowa, D. (1986). Perceived organizational support. *Journal of Applied Psychology.* 71, 500–507.

Eisenberger, R., Malone, G. P. and Presson, W. D. (2016). *Optimizing Perceived Organizational Support to Enhance Employee Engagement.* Alexandria, VA: SHRM-SIOP Science of HR Series.

Emerson, R. M. (1976). Social exchange theory. *Annual Review of Sociology.* 2, 335–362.

Fay, C. H. and Thompson, M. A. (2001). Contextual determinants of reward systems' success: an exploratory study. *Human Resource Management.* 40, 213–226.

Gomez-Mejia, L.R., Balkin, D.B. and Cardy, R.L. (2015). *Managing Human Resources* (8th ed.). Upper Saddle River, NJ: Pearson Prentice Hall.

Gouldner, A. W. (1960). The norm of reciprocity: a preliminary statement. *American Sociological Review.* 25, 161–178.

Henderson, R. I. (2003). *Compensation Management in a Knowledge based World.* Englewood Cliffs, NJ: Prentice-Hall.

Hofmans, J., de Gieter, S. and Pepermans, R. (2013). Individual differences in the relationship between satisfaction with job rewards and job satisfaction. *Journal of Vocational Behavior.* 82, 1–9.

Kanungo, R. N. and Hartwick, J. (1987). An alternative to the intrinsic-extrinsic dichotomy of work rewards. *Journal of Management.* 13, 751–766.

Katz, D. and Kahn, R. L. (1978). *The Social Psychology of Organizations.* New York, NY: Wiley.

Kinnunen, U., Feldt, T. and Mäkikangas, A. (2008). Testing the effort-reward imbalance model among Finnish managers: the role of perceived organizational support. *Journal of Occupational Health Psychology.* 13, 114–127.

Klein, K. J. and Kozlowski S. W. J. (2000). *Multilevel Theory, Research and Methods in Organizations: Foundations, Extensions, and New Directions*. San Francisco, CA: Jossey-Bass.

Kurtessis, J. N., Eisenberger, R., Ford, M. T., Buffardi, L. C., Stewart, K. A. and Adis, C. S. (2015). Perceived organizational support a meta-analytic evaluation of organizational support theory. *Journal of Management*. 43(6), 1854–1884.

Li, J., Yang, W. and Cho, S. I. (2006). Gender differences in job strain, effort-reward imbalance, and health functioning among Chinese physicians. *Social Science and Medicine*. 62, 1066–1077.

Li, J., Yang, W., Cheng, Y., Siegrist, J. and Cho, S. I. (2005). Effort–reward imbalance at work and job dissatisfaction in Chinese healthcare workers: a validation study. *International Archives of Occupational and Environmental Health*. 78, 198–204.

Loi, J. L. P. and Shultz, K. S. (2007). Why older adults seek employment: differing motivations among subgroups. *Journal of Applied Gerontology*. 26, 274–289.

Milkovich, G. T. and Newman, M. J. (2008). *Compensation*. New York: McGraw-Hill.

Omansky, R., Eatough, E. M. and Fila, M. J. (2016). Illegitimate tasks as an impediment to job satisfaction and intrinsic motivation: moderated mediation effects of gender and effort-reward imbalance. *Frontiers in Psychology*. 7.

Porter, L. W. and Lawler, E. E. (1968). *Managerial Attitudes and Performance*. Illinois: Richard Irwin Inc.

Purcell, J. and Hutchinson, S. (2007). Front-line managers as agents in the HRM-performance causal chain: theory, analysis and evidence. *Human Resource Management Journal*. 17, 3–20.

Rhoades, L. and Eisenberger, R. (2002). Perceived organizational support: a review of the literature. *Journal of Applied Psychology*. 87, 698–714.

Schlechter, A., Thompson, N. C. and Bussin, M. (2015). Attractiveness of non-financial rewards for prospective knowledge workers: an experimental investigation. *Employee Relations*. 37, 274–295.

Shaw, J. D. and Gupta, N. (2001). Pay fairness and employee outcomes: exacerbation and attenuation effects of financial need. *Journal of Occupational and Organizational Psychology*. 74, 299–320.

Siegrist, J. (1996). Adverse health effects of high-effort/low reward conditions. *Journal of Occupational Health Psychology*. 1, 27–41.

Siegrist, J., Li, J. and Montano, D. (2014). *Psychometric properties of the effort-reward imbalance questionnaire*. Department of Medical Sociology, Faculty of Medicine, Düsseldorf University, Germany. Available at:: www.uniklinik-suesseldorf.de/fileadmin/Datenpool/einrichtungen/institut_fuer_medizinische_soziologie_id54/ERI/Psychometrie.pdf

Takeuchi, R., Chen, G. and Lepak, D. P. (2009). Through the looking glass of a social system: cross-level effects of high-performance work systems on employees' attitudes. *Personnel Psychology*. 62, 1–30.

van Vegchel, N., de Jonge, J., Meijer, T. and Hamers, J. P. (2001). Different effort constructs and effort–reward imbalance: effects on employee well-being in ancillary health care workers. *Journal of Advanced Nursing*. 34, 128–136.

Verwaeren, B., van Hoye, G. and Baeten, X. (2017). Getting bang for your buck: the specificity of compensation and benefits information in job advertisements. *The International Journal of Human Resource Management*. 28(19), 2811–2830.

von Bonsdorff, M. E. (2011). Age-related differences in reward preferences. *The International Journal of Human Resource Management*. 22, 1262–1276.

Vroom, V. H. (1964). *Work and Motivation*. New York: Wiley.

Williams, M. L., Brower, H. H., Ford, L.R, Williams, L. J. and Carraher, S. M. (2008). A comprehensive model and measure of compensation satisfaction. *Journal of Occupational and Organizational Psychology*. 81, 639–669.

5

THE DARK SIDE OF REWARD MANAGEMENT FRAMED IN THE SOCIOLOGICAL TRADITION

Angela Wright

Introduction

Linstead et al. (2014: 166) say use of the term 'dark side' in organizational behaviour literature signals a focus on issues that have "traditionally been overlooked, ignored, or suppressed". This is a view shared by Donaldson and Philby (1985), who argue that 'partial theories' in the literature covering employee pay and benefits management, which describe and predict a limited class of observations, lead to a lack of attention to certain kinds of evidence. The central argument developed in the chapter is that conceptual as well as empirical limitations prevent the dark side of reward management from being fully examined in systematic research. One of the consequences of conceptual weakness is that 'dark' areas concerning the unintended, and sometimes disastrous, consequences of reward management do not feature as prominently as propositions, for example, about the motivational power of pay. Much of the literature concentrates on arguing about what reward practices will achieve for organizations on the positive side rather than on exposing the dark side. And a survey of reward practitioners' views about reward risks (CIPD 2012) found little evidence of an appreciation of risks beyond immediate legal vulnerabilities. Whilst dark-side evidence may be hidden, some emerges via media reports, and in older relevant research. Some 'dark-side' concepts that have been developed in sociological and sociopsychological literatures, as well as elements of management science commentary such as business ethics, have relevance in guiding future reward management research.

Unforeseen consequences or unexpected outcomes from reward management might be classed as either optimal (serendipity) or suboptimal (disaster) for individuals or organizations. On the dark side, they tend to be suboptimal for the organizations, according to Vaughan (1999:274), who argues that this is "a predictable and recurring product of all social systems". In examining how things go wrong in organizations, Vaughan (1999) proposes that there is a progression from mistake through misconduct to disaster. Hence, those organizations facing a disaster are likely to have previously experienced instances of mistake and misconduct, which accumulate and culminate in disaster. Dealing with the question of how dark-side phenomena arise, Vaughan (1999) argues that these mistakes, instances of misconduct and disasters are systematically produced by the interconnection between environment, organizational processes, cognition and choice. Thus, in studying the dark side, contextualization is vital; an aspect often absent in reward management writing.

To begin to address this gap, using Vaughan's (1999) categorization of the dark side as including *mistake*, *misconduct* and *disaster*, set alongside other concepts potentially relevant to a study of reward's dark side, the chapter examines evidence from a range of sources, mindful that some reward settings may be more vulnerable to the dark side than others. It then turns to what future research might usefully examine, accounting for methodological considerations, if dark-side reward management is to be addressed.

The dark side is variously defined, depending on the theoretical tradition of the subject studied. Vaughan's (1999) review shows that, although not necessarily referred to specifically as the dark side, there is published commentary which refers to things going wrong within organizational boundaries and producing harmful results. In some writing, the dark side is portrayed in dysfunctional or abnormal terms, whilst other scholars argue that it is a normal and expected condition in organizations. Academic literature on the dark side of organizational behaviour informed by psychology tends to focus on deviant behaviour and/or psychotic personality disorders (Linstead et al. 2014). For instance, Furnham and Taylor (2004) focus on the vengefulness of individuals who are angry with their organization and engage in consequential dark-side behaviours such as fraud, sabotage and theft. In other cases, these individuals may simply leave their employer, creating unplanned transactional costs.

In contrast, broadly-defined sociological perspectives tend to focus on social structure as well as individual human agency (and their interrelationship); the collective as well as the individual. The themes of both order and disorder in organizations have pervaded sociological theory and research since at least the first third of the twentieth century. Vaughan's seminal review traces dark-side work on organizations back to the writing of Merton in the 1930s as "the foundation of any consideration of the dark side of organizations" (1999:273). Under this conceptualization, secondary consequences are inevitably generated within all organizations as they seek to achieve their objectives, and these secondary consequences may run counter to primary managerial objectives. Routine non-conformity, unforeseen consequences and unexpected outcomes are considered to be naturally occurring social phenomena.

In the next section, Vaughan's (1999) dark-side tripartite model – positing a progression from mistake through misconduct to disaster within organizational settings – is applied to shape a review of prominent strands in reward management writing, in an attempt to illustrate dark-side shortcomings and identify the scope for more contextualized research. Relevant questions associated with the contexts for dark-side factors play out in relation to practical considerations in managing employee reward: viz., the risks of triggering adverse behaviour, monitoring and control considerations, and the interplay of these within particular organizational cultures. Table 5.1 summarizes issues for attention.

In the final section of the chapter some propositions are outlined, along with their methodological implications, which may inform future empirical research as well as being taken into consideration by practitioners weighing the reward management choices before them. It will be argued that benefits may flow from re-engaging with published analyses from several decades ago that have been neglected in more recent contributions to the literature. On closer inspection, these earlier ways of conceptualizing work, organization and reward management provide promising avenues to advance understanding under the dark-side rubric.

Framing investigation of reward management's dark side

In what follows, Vaughan's (1999) three dark-side categories of mistake, misconduct and disaster are applied to group potential dark-side effects in reward management that could be focal points for future systematic research. These are complemented in each case by concepts featuring in

Table 5.1 Summary of 'dark-side' reward issues needing to be investigated using Vaughan's (1999) categories

Dark-side issue	Reward system risks	Monitoring and control factors	Organizational cultural factors
Mistake:			
Additional costs	Potentially any reward system	Extent of monitoring of reward system for mistakes	Self-organization and the informal organization
Tunnel vision	Performance pay: short- and long-term		Organization cultures within the organization including sub-cultures
Morale effects	Potentially any reward system	Risk assessment of variable pay systems	
Misconduct:			
Gaming	Target-based rewards: short- and long-term	Analysis of potential moral hazards	Language and development by employees of special words covering reward misconduct
Active neglect	Work quantity bonuses		
Falsification	Financial equity-based reward	Oversight of share or stock price and effect on executive equity-based rewards	Condoning of potential executive actions to manipulate share or stock price
Disaster:			
Cumulative mistake and misconduct effects	High amount of performance contingent pay at stake	Weak monitoring and control systems	Mistake and misconduct condoned by senior/top management
	Vulnerability of short-term rewards		No challenge environments
			Tournament environments
			Single-minded sales focus

published reward management commentary, derived from economics, organizational behaviour and other social and management science literatures. Heuristically, the process may assist in more holistic theoretical analysis of reward management, balancing reward research to include dark-side considerations.

Mistake

Vaughan defines 'mistake' broadly to cover any violation of formal organizational goals, normative standards and expectations which leads to 'routine non-conformity' or unintended negative consequences. Although the academic and practitioner literature is very limited, there are some sources and examples which show the vulnerability of reward systems in this regard.

Risk of unexpected additional costs or unrealized benefits: Often hidden, such risk may result from additional unanticipated pressures on managerial time in operating reward policies, increasing management costs. Cox (2007) reports significant unanticipated costs in management time, administration, staff recruitment and training resulting from pay system change. Understandably, new pay systems might be planned to increase performance or productivity. A case in point is skills-based pay systems which give additional reward for skills acquisition. Research (e.g., Shaw et al. 2005) shows that these systems can be effective in encouraging investment in training by employers, and can encourage flexibility through self-directed employee learning. But published research covers darker-side risks only lightly: these systems not only require substantial investment in training; they are also costly to administer because of the need to develop *as well as to assess* skills. Without changes in management processes and styles, the potential of productivity gains may be unrealized, resulting in substantial costs without the proposed business benefits, a concern surfaced in the CIPD's 2017 annual reward survey report (Bailey et al. 2017).

A related question is whether or not advocates for reward management innovation sufficiently distinguish between competing approaches, to illustrate the potential for some to be disproportionately open to risk than others. For example, performance pay takes a variety of forms, as a reward or incentive. Employers may provide incentives to their employees intended to enhance their performance, and there is some evidence of achievement (e.g., Shaw and Gupta 2015; Gerhart and Fang 2014). However, what might equally systematic studies of the darker side of performance pay reveal about potentially inherent riskiness, such as allegedly opening organizations to the threat posed by cultural milieu like those brought to public attention during the 2008–2009 financial crisis? In the finance sector reward practices had institutionalized "excessive risk-taking that did not consider the long-term risks created for banks and, ultimately, wider society" (Angeli and Gita 2015: 322)? Relatedly, the notion of 'moral hazard', with conceptual roots in the insurance business and developed in the economics literature, posits that people may get involved in a risky undertaking knowing that they are protected and that someone else will pick up the cost. A key assumption is that both parties have incomplete information about the risk and its consequences (Holmström 1999). The concept has not been used much in the investigation of reward management despite explicitly featuring in a 2009 warning by governor of the Bank of England, Mervyn King, that government bailouts of banks in the wake of the financial crisis had "created possibly the biggest moral hazard in history . . . Bankers were given incentives to behave the way they did" (Conway 2009).

Larkin et al. (2012) stress the psychological costs of incentive systems, where they argue the efficacy of paying for performance is reduced when it engenders misplaced overconfidence among recipients. Additional costs might not be immediately obvious and might stem from different reward systems. The darker side of traditional shopfloor pay systems has been scrutinized in earlier academic studies; attention now could focus on unexplored or misplaced assumptions that may undermine intended outcomes from equity-based incentives at corporate executive level. What are the hidden costs, for example, in the degree to which government interventions give rise to the need for institutional investors to increase the resources they invest in monitoring and control systems?

Monitoring and control issues – or what is rewarded is what you get: Contemporary organizations are complex and what determines their performance is also complex and potentially difficult to measure (Park and Sturman 2012). Prentice et al. (2007) give examples of this from the UK public services, which have numerous performance targets set for them. If incentives can only be linked to easy-to-measure outcomes one consequence may be an excessive focus on these at the expense of other tasks; a managerial problem conceptualized as 'tunnel vision' syndrome (Kessler and Purcell 1992). For example, hospitals which receive financial incentives linked to cost reduction may have incentives to compromise on quality; while teachers monitored on student pass rates may choose to reduce the effort they put into less able students. The problem may be compounded for managers administering individual performance-related pay: employees are in effect encouraged to achieve what is necessary to earn the performance payment and not on activities that are not incentivized (Kessler and Purcell 1992). Managerial use of 'SMART' objectives underpinned by goal theory may be regarded positively (e.g. MacLeod 2012), but the possible negatives of 'tunnel vision' are less discussed, including the risk that collective endeavour to sustain an organization over the longer term is subordinated to individual short-term results.

The economics-based literature tends to support the use of reward as a check on potential employee misbehaviour but provides patchy evidence on its effectiveness. Principal–agent theory (hereafter agency theory) has been promoted as a positive basis by which it is proposed to secure alignment between corporate interests (in particular, financial investor interests) and those of organization executives mediated through reward management. The argument is that a 'principal' (business owner or shareholder) has imperfect information about the contribution of 'agents' employed to manage the organization's operations; potentially problematic if heterogeneity is assumed between the economic interests of the parties (Jensen and Meckling 1976). Agents are assumed to be risk averse and so unwilling to risk their security of tenure in pursuit of supernormal levels of profitability for principals (Eisenhardt 1989). Bosse and Philips (2016) argue that this divergence results in significant costs and inefficiencies for both businesses and society as a whole.

Agency theory posits that incentivizing executives will align owner and executive interests. If agency theory is unmistaken there should be a clear relationship between levels of executive reward and corporate performance. But, as Pepper and Campbell's (2014) review of a multiplicity of largely econometric studies seeking statistical correlation between these variables concludes, evidence points to a weak relationship between executive pay and performance and a stronger relationship between pay and corporate size. This indicates deficiencies in the explanatory power of agency theory to assess what many might regard as a currently prominent feature of the dark side of reward – excesses in executive pay. Ghosal (2005: 85) goes further, arguing that "instead of controlling the opportunistic behaviour of people [agency theory] is likely to create and enhance such behaviour"; and Sanders and Hambrick (2007) draw on empirical findings to argue that executive incentive plans lead to losses rather than gains for firms. For Pffefer (2005), it is not just agency theory but all economists' assumptions about the 'bleak' self-seeking of people that leads businesses to operate in ways, including planning reward systems, that can prove counterproductive.

'Social exchange' is a concept that may serve as a counterweight to contemporary ideas in the HRM literature about reward as an instrument of managerial control of employees (e.g., 'strategic pay' writers like Lawler, 1990, and Schuster and Zingheim 1992). Mid-twentieth-century strands of theory and research examined in depth the broader organizational effects of reward systems, revealing the limits to managerial control of employee behaviour using reward interventions. But such studies have stalled somewhat since then (Thorpe and Homan 2000). This earlier research tended to deploy sociological perspectives to look at the interaction between pay systems, employees as agents and social and organizational structures. Findings underlined the social exchange at the heart of the employment relationship described in terms of a 'wage-effort bargain' (Behrend 1957), a process containing the potential for employees, as active agents, as well as managers to shape it and consequent outcomes.

Negative cultural influences on employee relations: In 1957, Sayles showed that the incentive schemes used by employers for one section of the workforce could have strong negative effects on employee relations in others. Sayles' work is a rare example of research in organizations that attempts to gauge employee morale effects; in his case showing the negative consequences when managers do not take account of how people in one part of a business feel about the equitability of incentive pay applied to others. More recent examples include the unintended effects of the forced ranking of individual performance pay. Rather unusually, a public debate surfaced (mainly in sections of the US media) from 2013 to 2015 about the negative cultural consequences of such a reward practice and the changes that major companies (e.g., Microsoft) were making (Cohan 2013; Colvin 2015; Rock and Jones 2015).

Once promoted by major remuneration consultancies (which used the approach for their own staff), 'stack ranking' of performance awards became popular after it was adopted by GE in the 1980s. CEO Jack Welch referred to it as 'rank and yank'. In essence, these systems translated performance ratings directly into percentage salary raises for the annual round of performance-based pay awards with set rating categories each year and an enforced distribution of payments (Stewart et al. 2010). Ensuring the distribution of resultant pay awards conformed to a 'bell curve' rather than a skewed distribution. This meant that some employees each year were performance managed out of the business even if their performance was not actually poor, engendering a culture of competitive behaviour between employees, undermining teamwork, collaboration and innovation. These issues first surfaced on social media (Cohan 2013) before the business press reported on companies abandoning the practice (Rock and Jones 2015).

Misconduct

Vaughan (1999:288) distinguishes misconduct from mistake as: "acts of omission or commission by individuals or groups of individuals acting in their organizational roles who violate internal rules, laws, or administrative regulations on behalf of organization goals". Conceptually, 'organizational misbehaviour' can refer to agency on the part of employees that does not conform to managerial expectations and which, whilst discouraged, is not entirely prevented (Ackroyd and Thompson 1999).

Risks arising from employee capacity to frustrate corporate management influence: Early studies in the sociology of work literature undermine the wisdom of assuming employee compliance with managerial intentions when using reward interventions, with employees emerging as active agents in resisting managerial plans – possibly in covert ways. Again, putting the spotlight on particular reward management approaches to judge the degree of risk involved, one could assume that behaviour described in studies by Ditton, Roy and others from the 1950s to the 1970s might be thought to be limited to factory-based workplaces of the past, or only to restrictions of output when time-rated or piecework pay systems are used. But there is evidence (Fleming and Spicer 2007) that comparable misbehaviour is present in the modern workplace – up to and including the 'white collar crime' included in Vaughan's (1999) specification, evidenced most prominently in notorious cases such as Enron (Bratton 2002).

Roethlisberger and Dickson (1964) surface the influence and workings of what they term 'the informal organization' in limiting managerial control of the workplace and workers, extended in the work of Ackroyd and Thompson (1999), covering several aspects relevant to reward systems from work limitation to pilfering. Ackroyd and Thompson (1999) argue that self-organization by workers enables their engaging in misbehaviour to be largely concealed from managers.

The notion of 'goldbricking', or output quota restriction within the effort–reward bargain was a term used in studies surfacing evidence of industrial rate fixing (and busting) during the period when piecework pay systems were in vogue. Goldbricking constitutes a form of alchemy, used in the workplace to describe how workers can portray their performance as good, or good enough to pass scrutiny and gain bonuses, but without being as high as it could be (Roy 1952). A collection of mainly participant observation studies (e.g., Dalton 1948; Ditton 1979; Roy 1952) showed the subtle ways in which workers manipulated their output to make the most of their pay for the least work. They did not do this in obvious ways, hiding the full extent of their restricted effort from managers (or any other workers assumed not to be in sympathy such as 'rate busters'; Dalton 1948). Some of the tactics used were "arranging" machine breakdowns (Ditton 1979), controlling breaks (Roy 1952), and not putting in full effort. As Lupton and Gowler (1969:9) put it:

> If a payment by results scheme does not meet [employees'] idea of a fair and proper bargain between effort and reward, they might well choose to adjust the bargain, by controlling, either individually or jointly with their mates, the effort or the reward.

This might perhaps be categorized as less than misconduct. However, the research draws attention to the tendency of workers to add informally to their pay in subtle ways, which sometimes does stray into misconduct or 'gross misconduct'. For example, Ditton (1977) finds evidence that pilfering is used tactically by some workers to make up for wage deficiencies.

Perverse effects of monitoring and control systems combining into dark-side cultures: Analytically, distinguishing between low- and higher-level misconduct recognises that the term covers a range of phenomena, from minor misdemeanours to the verges of criminality. Low-level misconduct may be illustrated using the concept of 'gaming', a term defined by Bevan and Hood (2006: 521) as: "reactive subversion . . . hitting the target and missing the point . . . or reducing performance where targets do not apply". Individuals or groups seeking to game processes attempt either to manipulate performance measures or to persuade managers not to raise performance requirements that are typically used to determine pay. In the economics literature, three main types of gaming are identified with respect to the use of targets and performance measures: "ratchet effects, threshold effects and opportunistic output distortions" (Bevan and Hood 2006). *Ratchet effects* describe the tendency to base next year's targets on last year's performance, meaning that established employees may have a perverse incentive not to exceed targets even if they could easily do so. *Threshold effects* also produce a perverse incentive, putting pressure on those performing below the target level to do better but also providing a perverse incentive for those doing better than the target to allow their performance to deteriorate to the standard level. *Opportunistic output distortions* refer to the cost of significant, but unmeasured aspects of performance.

Much of the literature on gaming covers the problem in using targets and budgets in organizations, not necessarily specifically related to reward. Jensen's (2003) analysis of gaming and fraud suggests that the central problem leading to gaming is that incentive or performance bonuses tend to be based on targets, often linked to the budgeting process. He contends that, when managers receive a bonus once targets are realized, they will attempt to set targets that are easily reachable. When targets are set they will do their best to see that they are met even if it is damaging to the company (cf. 'what is rewarded is what you get' in the previous section). He gives an example from an American heavy equipment manufacturer whose managers met their budget targets and gained their consequent bonuses in one quarter by shipping unfinished industrial products from their plant in England to the Netherlands so they could realize the sales revenues early. This tactic incurred greater costs for the company and lowered overall corporate profits, but the sales were registered at the right time for managers to earn their bonus. Gaming such as this is considered 'part of business life', Jensen (2003) argues, and the root cause is that, beyond their use as management information, budgets and targets are mechanisms that determines bonuses in many organizations. While it might be thought that sales-based and production environments are more prone to gaming, Prentice et al.'s (2007) research on performance pay in public services shows evidence of gaming at the same time as making only minor productivity improvements.

From a cultural perspective misbehaving has been identified as manifesting in forms of language used by employees. Roy (1952), Ditton (1979) and Ackroyd and Thompson (1999) all report that those engaged in dark-side activities developed their own words for describing what they were doing. Since this happens in a way that is largely hidden from management in a mode of self-organization, research designs need to help get beneath the managerial veneer to study this in action in contemporary contexts.

Higher levels of misconduct related to reward management bifurcate into active neglect and falsification/misrepresentation. In terms of the former, trade unions have argued that bonus schemes in manufacturing or mining environments which encourage workers to accelerate work can compromise safety or health. One example of this occurred in the Alton Towers theme park accident in 2016. Engineers working to maintain the rides were incentivized by a bonus scheme which reduced payouts if 'downtime' was above a certain level. The *Smiler* ride crashed, severely injuring several people, because an engineer "felt pressure" (The Telegraph 2016) to get the ride back into service after it developed a fault shortly beforehand.

The following examples of falsification and financial misrepresentation illustrate the range of misconduct under this subcategory linked with reward management:

1 The pensions mis-selling scandal during the 1980s, when incentivized sales people sold pensions to people who already had secure occupational pension arrangements, persuading their clients to take up private pensions providing benefits of lesser value (Jenkins 2016).
2 Executives in Wells Fargo, incentivized by profit-based bonuses, created around 1.5 million phantom bank accounts and credit cards for clients without their knowledge with the intention of inflating sales numbers, hitting targets and boosting bonuses (Tett 2016; United States Senate, 2016).
3 Ambitious young members of the legal profession overcharged clients when, pressed by their performance system to bill as many hours as possible (Callahan 2004).

Exemplifying types of reward arrangements that may contain the greatest potential risk in encouraging serious misconduct, Harris and Bromiley (2007) provide data showing that increasing the proportion of executive reward in the form of stock options increases the probability of accounting misrepresentation of company financial positions. Likewise, Denis et al. (2006) assess the likelihood of fraud allegations against companies based on their reward structures, focusing on executive reward. Their data suggest that stock options increase the incentive to engage in fraudulent activity; and Johnson et al. (2005) examined 43 cases of corporate fraud in the US finding that firms engaged in fraudulent activity were significantly more likely to use equity-based reward for executives than a control group of firms.

Disaster

Vaughan (1999) applies the term to categorize a progression from mistake and misconduct, with these elements forming building blocks leading to instances of organizational disaster. She says that disaster is a type of routine non-conformity that is significantly different from what may be thought normal at the relevant time and/or place. It often has a dramatic quality and it damages the fabric of social and organizational life. Two corporate disasters – Wells Fargo and Enron – together with the 2008 financial crisis – are examples that seem to fall within this definition.

Wells Fargo escalated from misconduct to a full-blown disaster (Tett 2016). According to the United States Senate (2016), this agency was "not the work of a few rogue employees over the course of a few weeks", but a "long-standing, systemic problem created by stringent sales quotas and incentives imposed by senior management". The US Consumer Financial Protection Bureau Director, Richard Cordray, noted: "Wells Fargo built an incentive-compensation program that made it possible for its employees to pursue underhanded sales". Consequences were fines reported by the US Senate to reach $185 million, plus the loss of their jobs by the bank's chief executive and other senior executives, along with hundreds of employees. There were lawsuits and the bank, while surviving, lost future business from large city councils and other clients (Li and Dugan 2017).

In the case of Enron, Callahan (2004) reports action taken by top executives, who received significant compensation in the form of stock options, as active share price manipulation incentivized through these incentives reached fraudulent levels. Both corporate cultural and personal values may increase susceptibility to fraudulent and ultimately disastrous agency: "Option holding dulls the actor's sensitivity to degrees of distress on the downside . . . Enron's managers, with a belief system biased toward winning, lost touch with both hard economic constraints and the rules of the game" (Bratton 2002:1327).

So-called 'toxic bonus cultures' in the 2008–9 financial crisis have been hotly debated. In his review, Lord Turner (2009:81) says:

> There is a strong prima facie case that inappropriate incentive structures played a role in encouraging behaviour which contributed to the financial crisis. . . . [It is] likely that past remuneration policies, acting in combination with capital requirements and accounting rules, have created incentives for some executives and traders to take excessive risks and have resulted in large payments in reward for activities which seemed profit making at the time but subsequently proved harmful to the institution, and in some cases to the entire system.

Inadequacies in formal communication from managers on reward may foster the development of subcultural values among workforce communities (Wright 2013). If these subcultural values run counter to the values of corporate principles then darker-side consequences can emerge from their agents' behaviours. Of course, in some of the examples of disasters described above, misconduct was instigated or condoned by senior managers. These instances indicate that some corporate-level cultures may support dark-side values. In other words, it is not a case of groups of workers forming counter-cultural groupings that challenge corporate cultural values, but rather of malpractice becoming an accepted cultural norm. Analyses of both formal and informal communications within organizations on reward could yield some useful evidence of how misconduct becomes an acceptable way of behaving.

Building on seminal work by writers such as Lupton and Gowler (1969) and Cox (2007) illustrates how organizational context influences reward outcomes at a systemic level. From a sociological perspective, the expectation is that all organizations are potentially vulnerable to dark-size mistake and misbehaviour, sometimes culminating in disaster. Anecdotally, to date, more evidence has surfaced in some organizational contexts than others as vulnerable to the promulgation of darker-side practices. While research is needed to expand the picture, three settings stand out as potential disasters in the making:

- *No challenge environment* as was evident at Wells Fargo and Enron in which employees felt unable to challenge the dark- side practices they were witnessing (Bratton 2002).
- *Tournament workplace environment* with characteristics identified as highly competitive internally; e.g., as engendered by the forced ranking performance system at GE and Microsoft (Callahan 2004).
- *Single-minded sales environment* in which individuals had to achieve sales at all costs, is viewed as leading in part to the 2008–9 financial crisis (Turner 2009).

Propositions for practice and research to shed some light on the dark side

For practitioners, key messages from the analysis sketched in this chapter are that they should become sensitized to possible dark-side activities and *expect* – not be surprised – to find mistakes and misconduct related to reward management in their organizations. They should investigate the way that target-setting and budgeting processes operate in practice where these are linked to a reward system. They should monitor decision-making processes and their outturn, consider more formal communications on reward and how they link to expected corporate value systems, and informally 'listen' to the language people use when talking about aspects that might be the subject of routine non-conformity. Literature aimed at practitioners also has a role. Rather than being persuaded by all-positive 'learnings', more balanced investigation would be beneficial for practitioners as to dark-side risks, regulatory limitations and organization cultural factors.

For researchers, currently, the dark side of reward management – how it manifests, what causes it, and what can be done to mitigate its effects – seem marginalized in specialist peer-reviewed literature. There is anecdotal and policy-based evidence of the dark side in several forms of performance pay that need to be researched more systematically. Evidence that incentive systems can yield unintended results has tended to be published in work from financial management, legal or governance disciplinary perspectives or in journalism.

To enable reward researchers to engage systematically, the theoretical foundation for the dark side needs to be developed, given that the "socially organized circumstances that produce harmful outcomes remain obscure" (Vaughan 1999:272). There are useful concepts within the literature, such as gaming, moral hazard, tunnel vision, subculture formation, or goldbricking; but their use in reward management research has been limited. It is particularly the dynamic relationship between organizational processes (as social structures) and employees as agents that could fruitfully be developed in the reward field, drawing on heritage studies such as those cited above. Theoretically, dark-side work might build on social constructionist analyses, as in Perkins' (2017) discussion of legitimation issues concerning executive pay, while field studies could draw on work operationalizing the concepts of structuration theory (Giddens 1987) as in Neu Morén's (2013) study of communications between managers and employees on performance appraisal.

The following seven propositions are put forward for investigation:

1 There will be evidence of routine non-conformity and mistakes in all organizations' reward systems overlooked or ignored in normative design assumptions.
2 Reward systems linked to target setting or budgeting processes will lead to mistakes and misconduct, including systemic gaming.
3 Performance pay systems contain both positive and negative motivational effects, particularly taking into account issues around forced distribution rankings.
4 Equity-based reward for top managers will be vulnerable to misconduct, when these managers have the capability to manipulate corporate stock values.
5 Short-term bonuses are more vulnerable to mistake and misconduct than properly regulated long-term bonuses (clarifying what 'long-term' means in practice).
6 Corporate cultures are vulnerable to misconduct when they include values manifested in reward management practices that celebrate high levels of competition between individuals, or single-minded privileging of short-term revenue growth above sustaining the organization as a going concern and/or collective workforce morale.
7 Reward mistakes and misconduct will be socially constructed in a dynamic process between structure (organizational policy and practice) and agency (employee cognition and choice), within the constraints of the relevant business environment.

Factors summarized in Table 5.1 may be used to guide investigation of the above propositions.

Methodologically, because the disciplinary background of contemporary reward management studies has tended to stem from economics or psychology, much of the research literature seems uncompromisingly positivist. Methods adopted in reward research are also in part influenced by practical considerations such as the availability of data for empirical research and there may be few data sets readily available for dark side studies.

To address this, because research on disasters and misconduct is likely to be retrospective, content analysis of secondary company data could offer a way forward. The unit of analysis also is worthy of revisiting to mount organizational-level studies that draw on a sampling frame that includes, e.g., more managers outside the potentially vested interests among HRM and reward specialists. And as some of the mistakes and misconduct described above first came to public view on social media, one starting point for empirical inquiry may be examining social media outlets.

Given the hidden nature of much dark-side activity, more up-to-date reward management research is needed to examine the workings of the informal organization or informal practices. Ackroyd and Thompson (1999) argue that ethnography is appropriate for the study of misbehaviour and the informal organization. Undertaking in-depth qualitative research, in the vein of Roy's classic (1952) participant observer study of the manipulation of a factory payment system, would fit with the need to contextualize the study of dark-side activities.

Conclusion

Analysis in this chapter reveals that, despite evidence on dark-side reward management practices, since the 1970s there has been very little systematic investigation of the contribution by reward researchers. This gap seems to stem from the subject's reliance on ideas from economics and psychology as its principal theoretical foundations. The chapter argues for studies drawing on more sociological traditions; in particular, from the premise of routine non-conformity in organizations. The chapter builds on Vaughan's (1999) review, illustrating how her dark side categories of mistake, misconduct and disaster can be used in describing and analysing the dark side of reward management. Given that vintage academic commentary using dark-side evidence has contemporary relevance, it stresses, in particular, the value of examining in detail the working of reward systems in their social contexts.

References

Ackroyd, S. and Thompson, P. (1999). *Organizational Misbehaviour*. London: Sage Publications.

Angeli, M. and Gita, S. (2015). Bonus regulation: aligning reward with risk in the banking sector. *Bank of England Quarterly Bulletin*. Q4 2015, 322–333.

Bailey, M., Mariott L. and Perkins, S. J. (2017). *Annual Reward Survey*. London: CIPD.

Behrend, H. (1957). The effort bargain. *Industrial and Labor Relations Review*. 10(4), 503–515.

Bevan, G. and Hood, C. (2006). What's measured is what matters: targets and gaming in the English public health care system. *Public Administration*. 84(3), 517–538.

Bosse, D. and Philips, R. (2016). Agency theory and bounded self-interest. *Academy of Management Review*. 41(2), 276–297.

Bratton, W. (2002). Enron and the dark side of shareholder value. *Tulsa Law Review*. 76, 1275.

Callahan, D. (2004). *The Cheating Culture: Why More Americans Are Doing Wrong to Get Ahead*. New York: Harcourt.

CIPD. (2012). *Reward Risks Survey*. London: Chartered Institute of Personnel and Development.

Cohan, P. (2013). *Adobe's stock up since it dumped stack ranking*. Available at: https://www.forbes.com/sites/petercohan/2013/11/29/adobes-stock-up-68-since-it-dumped-stack-ranking-will-microsofts-follow/#291d60961bab.

Colvin, G. (2015). Microsoft and Dell are ditching employee performance reviews. *Fortune*, October 29, 2015, Available at: http://fortune.com/2015/10/29/microsoft-dell-performance-reviews, accessed on January 6, 2018.

Conway, E. (2009). Mervyn King: bail-outs created "biggest moral hazard in history". *The Telegraph*, 20 October, Available at: http://www.telegraph.co.uk/finance/economics/6389906/Mervyn-King-bail-outs-created-biggest-moral-hazard-in-history.html, accessed on December 20, 2017.

Cox, A. (2007). The outcomes of variable pay systems: tales of multiple costs and unforeseen consequences. *International Journal of Human Resource Management*. 16(8), 1475–1497.

Dalton, M. (1948). *The industrial 'rate-buster': a characterization, applied anthropology*, Winter 1948, pp. 5–18, reprinted in Lupton, T. (ed.). (1972) *Payment Systems* (pp. 64–91). Harmondsworth: Penguin Books.

Denis, D., Hanouna, P. and Sarin. (2006). Is there a dark side to incentive compensation? *Journal of Corporate Finance.* 12(3), 467–488.

Ditton, J. (1977). Perks, pilferage, and the fiddle: the historical structure of invisible wages. *Theory and Society.* 4(1), 39–71.

Ditton, J. (1979). Baking time. *The Sociological Review.* 27(1), 157–167.

Donaldson, J. and Philby, P. (1985). *Pay Differentials.* Aldershot: Gower Publishing Co. Ltd.

Eisenhardt, K. (1989). Agency theory: an assessment and review. *Academy of Management Review.* 14, 57–74.

Fleming, P. and Spicer, A. (2007). *Contesting the Corporation: Struggle, Power and Resistance in Organisations.* Cambridge: Cambridge University Press.

Furnham, A. and Taylor, J. (2004). *The Dark Side of Behaviour at Work: Understanding and Avoiding Employees Leaving, Thieving and Deceiving.* Basingstoke: Palgrave Macmillan.

Gerhart, B. and Fang, M. (2014). Pay for (individual) performance: Issues, claims, evidence and the role of sorting effects. *Human Resource Management Review.* 24(1), 41–52.

Giddens, A. (1987). *Social Theory and Modern Sociology.* Oxford: Blackwell Publishers.

Ghosal, S. (2005). Bad management theories are destroying good management practices. *Academy of Management Learning & Education.* 4(1), 75–91.

Harris, J. D. and Bromiley, P. (2007). Incentives to cheat: the influence of executive compensation and firm performance on financial misrepresentation. *Organization Science.* 18(3), 350–367.

Holmström, B. (1999). Managerial incentive problems: a dynamic perspective. *The Review of Economic Studies.* 66(1), 169–182.

Jenkins, P. (2016). Crimes, misdemeanours and cross-selling, *Financial Times* September 19, 2016, Available at: https://www.ft.com/content/9681aa7e-7e53-11e6-bc52-0c7211ef3198, accessed on October 6, 2017.

Jensen, M. (2003). Paying people to lie: the truth about the budgeting process, professional forum. *European Financial Management.* 9(3), 379–406.

Jensen M. and Meckling, W. (1976). Theory of the firm: managerial behavior, agency costs and ownership structure. *Journal of Financial Economics.* 3, 305–360.

Johnson, S., Ryan, H. and Tian, Y. (2005) Executive compensation and corporate fraud. *SSRN Electronic Journal,* May 2005.

Kessler, I. and Purcell, J. (1992). Performance-related pay: objectives and application. *Human Resource Management Journal.* 2(3), 16–33.

Larkin, I., Pierce, L., and Gino, F. (2012). The psychological costs of pay-for-performance: implications for the strategic compensation of employees. *Strategic Management Review,* 33, 1194–1214.

Lawler, E. E. III (1990). *Strategic Pay: Aligning Organizational Strategies and Pay Systems.* San Francisco, CA: Jossey-Bass.

Li, D. and Dugan, K. (2017). City to cut ties with Wells Fargo after fake-accountscandal. *New York Post,* 31 May 2017.

Linstead, S., Maréchal, G. and Griffin, R. (2014). Theorizing and researching the dark side of organization. *Organization Studies.* 35(2), 165–188.

Lupton, T. and Gowler, D. (1969) *Selecting a wage payment system.* Reprinted in Lupton, T. (ed.) (1972) *Payment Systems: Selected Readings* (pp. 239–276). Harmondsworth, UK, Penguin Books.

MacLeod, L. (2012). "Making SMART goals smarter." *Physician Executive,* March–April, p. 68+. *Academic OneFile,* accessed on January 2, 2018.

Neu Morén, E. (2013). The negotiated character of performance appraisal: how interrelations between managers matters. *The International Journal of Human Resource Management.* 24(4), 853–870.

Park, S. and Sturman, M. (2012). How and what you pay matters: the relative effectiveness of merit pay, bonuses and long-term incentives on future job performance. *Compensation & Benefits Review.* 44(2), 80–85.

Pepper, A. and Campbell, R. (2014). *Executive Reward: a Review of the Drivers and Consequences,* Research report – summary, April 2014, CIPD.

Perkins, S. J. (2017). The social construction of executive remuneration in the UK – elite competition around codification and legitimation. *Journal of Organizational Effectiveness: People and Performance.* 4(1), 76–88.

Pffefer, J. (2005). Why do bad management theories persist? A comment on Ghoshal. *Academy of Management Learning and Education.* Published Online November 30, 2017. Available at https://doi.org/10.5465/amle.2005.16132570.

Prentice, G., Burgess, S. and Propper, C. (2007). *Performance Pay in the Public Sector: a Review of the Issues and Evidence*, a paper commissioned by the Office of Manpower Economics. Available at: http://www.ome.uk.com/Search/Default.aspx?q=performance%20pay, accessed on October 9, 2009.

Rock, D. and Jones, B. (2015). Why more and more companies are ditching performance ratings. *Harvard Business Review*. 9. Online reference: https://hbr.org/2015/09, accessed April 9, 2016.

Roethlisberger, F. and Dickson, W. (1964). *Management and the Worker* (pp. 517–535). New York: Wiley, reprinted in Lupton, T. (ed.). (1972) *Payment Systems: Selected Readings* (pp. 21–34). Harmondsworth, UK: Penguin Books.

Roy, D. (1952). *Quota Restriction and Goldbricking in a Machine Shop*, reprinted in Lupton, T (ed.). (1972) *Payment Systems: Selected Readings* (pp. 35–63). Harmondsworth, UK: Penguin Books.

Sanders, W. and Hambrick, D. (2007). Swinging for the fences: the effects of CEO stock options on company risk taking and performance. *Academy of Management Journal*. 50(5), 1055–1078.

Sayles, L. (1957). The impact of incentives on inter-group work relations. In Lupton, T. (ed.). (1972) *Payment Systems: Selected Readings* (pp. 92–102). Harmondsworth, UK: Penguin Books.

Schuster, J. R. and Zingheim, P. K. (1992). *The New Pay: Linking Employee and Organizational Performance*. San Francisco: Jossey-Bass.

Shaw, J. and Gupta, N. (2015). Let the evidence speak again! Financial incentives are more effective than we thought. *Human Resource Management Journal*. 25(3), 281–293.

Shaw, J., Gupta, N., Mitra, A. and Ledford, G. (2005) Success and survival of skill-based Pay plans. *Journal of Management*. 3(1), 28–49.

Stewart, S., Gruys, M. and Storm, M. (2010). Forced distribution performance evaluation systems: advantages, disadvantages and keys to implementation. *Journal of Management & Organization*. 16, 168–179.

Tett, G. (2016). Why Wells Fargo is a watershed moment for clawbacks. *Financial Times*, 29 September 2016, Available at: https://www.ft.com/content/33a8e0ae-856d-11e6-8897-2359a58ac7a5, accessed on January 6, 2018.

The Telegraph. (2016). *Alton Towers crash: Owner Merlin fined £5m for health and safety breach leading to accident.* Available at: http://www.telegraph.co.uk/news/2016/09/27/alton-towers-crash-owner-merlin-fined-5m-for-health-and-safety-b/, accessed on October 6, 2017.

Thorpe, R. and Homan, G. (2000). *Strategic Reward Systems*. Harlow: Pearson Educational.

Turner, A. (2009) The Turner Review: A Regulatory Response to the Global Banking Crisis, Financial Services Authority, March 2009, posted at http://www.fsa.gov.uk/pubs/other/turner_review.pdf. Accessed June 6, 2009.

United States Senate. (2016). Letter to John Strumpf, September 15.

Vaughan, D. (1999). The dark side of organizations: mistake, misconduct, and disaster. *Annual Review of Sociology*. 25, 271–305.

Wright, A. (2013). *Reward systems and organisation culture – An analysis drawing on three perspectives of culture*. University of Greenwich: unpublished doctoral thesis.

6

THE DISCURSIVE SIDE OF REWARD MANAGEMENT

Magdalena Bielenia-Grajewska

Introduction

Reward management can be studied from different perspectives, depending on what is supposed to be analysed. For example, Perkins (2015) groups various frames of reference for analysing managers' remuneration, heuristically: 'agency', 'tournaments', 'power', and 'upper echelon', having economic or sociological orientations. In this chapter the discursive prism is adopted to view how reward management vocabulary shapes the way remuneration is perceived by the broadly understood stakeholders. By using this perspective, reward management discourse is studied in greater detail, drawing attention to how text and talk on remuneration are created and perceived.

HRM and reward management

Discussion of rewards is visibly present in the HRM discourse (e.g., Armstrong and Taylor 2014; Banfield et al. 2018; Lussier and Hendon 2018; Syed and Kramar 2017). As Syed and Kramar (2017: 215) state, "a reward may be anything tangible (for example, pay), or intangible (for example, praise) that an organization offers to its employees in exchange for their belonging to the organization and for contributing work behaviours and results of the type that the organization needs from its people in order to meet its strategic objectives, however these might be defined". Pocztowski (2017) argues that rewards have a key role in international companies since they increase the effectiveness of individuals, groups, teams and the whole company. In addition, they attract and retain talented workers. Moreover, they build organizational engagement and stimulate the mobility of workers. It should also be mentioned that they create relations within organizational units and communicate values, influencing the perception of 'company brand' in the working environment.

Syed and Kramar (2017) stress that reward, and, within reward, pay structure depends on several factors, such as the characteristics of an organization's product and labour market, socio-cultural rules, type of government intervention and regulation as well as systems of employee relations such as institutional-level union and employer interaction as well as national and industry-level bargaining systems. In addition, Podmoroff (2005) discusses two types of motivators: internal and external. Internal motivators include those aspects of a working environment that make a person look for a particular type of employer. They are not influenced by external factors. External motivators include the quality of work and the possibility of using skills while performing tasks. Rewards allow workers to possess consumer staples and some extra aspects of the employment offer, such as trips, housing and possibilities of gathering funds within a pension scheme, medical treatments, good relations with co-workers, and the possibility of being promoted.

Moreover, there are several factors which influence salary and wage levels. Firstly, job 'size' has traditionally been the main determinant of pay. It includes such factors as responsibility, level in the organizational hierarchy, required knowledge, skills or competencies, external contacts, complexity and decision-making. Hence, the individual's hierarchical position in large organizations has been central to the design of internal pay structures, with performance rewarded by promotion. However, job size is now seen as less important than individual contribution. In other words, having many subordinates and/or control of larger budgets do not in themselves indicate a significant contribution that merits extra reward. Secondly, individual characteristics – such as age, experience, qualifications, and special skills, contribution and performance – are also significant factors. Thirdly, labour market factors – such as the supply and demand of particular skills both locally and the 'going rate' in the market – are important. Fourthly, product market conditions and the employer's cost structure – such as its position in the market, profitability and market ambitions and strategies – have a major influence on pay strategy. Finally, the remuneration philosophy of the organization also has an influence on wage and salary levels. An organization with the reputation for being a 'good employer', and wishing to attract the most able staff, "is likely to offer higher wages than one where staff are valued less positively" (Loudon et al. 2009:203). Additionally, Taylor (2015) draws attention to how workers respond to the organization's performance management system, taking into account the design of the performance *measurement* system, the types of rewards on offer and how they are implemented. Discussion on reward management may also focus on specific types of reward by taking into account the group that benefits from them. An example includes executive reward management, with an executive "defined as someone in an organization's senior management group employed at corporate level" (Perkins 2009:149). The executive reward framework may include salary, the annual incentive plan, the voluntary bonus/share investment/retention plan and the long-term incentive plan (Perkins 2009).

Strużyna et al. (2008) state that today there is the tendency to rely on social issues in analysing rewards, paying attention to the natural scenery of conducting an analysis. Perkins et al. (2016) stress that reward strategies do not exist in a vacuum, but are shaped by the environment in which they operate. Thus, national regulatory frameworks or the labour market environment are crucial in designing reward systems. Beer and Eisenstat (2000) list 'six silent killers' that influence companies in a negative way. Silent killer four is poor vertical communication. This is the situation in which employees who notice a problem are not eager to discuss it with senior managers who prefer avoiding negative issues and they decide to keep their remarks to themselves. Blocked vertical communication affects the possibilities of implementing and refining strategies in a negative way, just one driver for paying detailed attention to the linguistic aspect of reward management.

The linguistic side of reward management

Behrend (2016) stresses that serious communication problems may take place when politicians, economists and ordinary citizens interact. Not everyone understands government statements and newspaper reports. Thus, only motivated individuals will search and understand data.

Moreover, economic issues and governmental policies are often written in forms that are difficult for an average person to understand. Balance of trade deficits or economic crises should be explained in simple language. Understanding economic interdependence will lead to reducing the communication gap that often exists in the light of economic resource constraints. Taking all the aspects into account, the performance of organizations in the twenty-first century is determined by the language itself and this relation can be investigated in different ways.

One of the key notions in considering the linguistic side of organizations is to treat language as the crucial determinant for companies' performance on both the internal and external levels. This dimension encompasses aspects resulting from the increasing complexity in terms of languages used in organizations, as well as professional sublanguages, dialects and genres. This linguistic complexity results in artefacts such as organizational strategies that aim to respect corporate linguistic rights, to exercise effective linguistic policy and thus to facilitate organizational performance. Language is also an important factor mediating cooperation between the company and its broadly understood operating environment, including customers (Bielenia-Grajewska 2013a). The expansion of global trading markets has removed restrictions on geographical distance, so that organizations may operate across a number of distant countries which differ, among other aspects, in terms of languages and codes of communication used by diversified stakeholders. Such complexity in the use of language in contemporary organizations, even taking matters at face value, is thus of direct interest to students and practitioners of reward management.

Reward management ideas shape thinking about other areas of life (both private and professional) and it is shaped, at the same time, by other disciplines. Building on that premise, communication and language may be understood, therefore, as key aspects of reward management. First, reward management (and even the lack of it) is communicated in organizations, in verbal and non-verbal forms. Secondly, language is indispensable in showing one's understanding about reward management and its reaction to a given tangible or intangible offer. Moreover, language can be studied as a factor determining one's possibilities of gaining access to rewards: for example, the employee category of 'expatriate' designated linguistically as eligible for certain forms of reward (cf. Shortland and Perkins, this volume). Bielenia-Grajewska (2010) discusses linguistic aspects connected with expatriation, investigating factors that determine the acquisition of a host language. Expatriate linguistic performance is shaped by the 'individual corporate linguistic dimension' and 'societal corporate linguistic dimension'. Individual corporate linguistic dimension incorporates the following notions: attitude to host culture; assignment factors (phase, place, time and culture as well as occupation); and language-related benefits. Societal corporate linguistic dimension includes in-company linguistic issues, language policy in companies, corporate communication and hierarchy (Bielenia-Grajewska 2010). In addition, the linguistic side of reward management, and HRM in general, may be studied through the prism of gender (cf. Shortland, this volume specifically in relation to female expatriation and reward issues).

Language is also discussed as a crucial factor determining the position of employees in a given organization. For example, Lawler (2008) discusses the need to limit the social distance and work on communication not only between managers but also workers. And different specialists argue about labelling used to designate professions and their male and female equivalents, including foregrounding skills that are stereotypically associated with a given gender. For example, many so-called caring professions have titles that are perceived by users as rather female-oriented. With representatives of both genders now performing jobs that were associated with just one gender in the past, there is also a growing need to change the names for occupational groupings across organizational settings, or at least to mitigate against a lack of gender neutrality. The discussion may be extended to reward management. It concerns the offer of benefits that will meet the needs and expectations of both genders.

Attention may be directed towards terms that are used in professional literature which colour reward management practice discourse. For example, Marasi and Bennett define "pay communication" as "the organizational practice that determines if, when, how, and which pay information (such as pay ranges, pay raises, pay averages, individual pay levels, and/or the entire pay structure) is communicated to employees and possibly outsiders" (2016:51). Marasi and Bennett (2016) draw our attention to the fact that in the early literature pay communication was associated with pay secrecy. And the notion of 'pay administration' has been previously in common usage, especially in older literature on the topic. Perkins et al. (2016) argue, when engaging with 'The New Pay' normative writing, that the term reward management is itself significant since it denotes an active role for employers, not the passive (administrative) reaction to economic forces.

Reward Management Discourse

Reward Management Discourse (RMD) is defined by the current author as the type of communication that takes place between people involved in reward distribution for some reason. Thus, the stakeholders of RMD include managers, supervisors, workers, customers and users of services/products offering rewards. It can be analysed in an individual and group way, examining the attitude to rewards of a single person or the institutional policy in its entirety.

While of particular interest to HRM specialists the interest of the broadly understood external stakeholders in the reward management system is especially visible in the public sector since rewards are financed by public money. For example, rewards to teachers and those working in publicly owned enterprises are a hotly discussed topic in Poland. Such elements of their reward system as '13th month' pay and extra money for holidays are discussed in the press.

Another important aspect of rewards is the relation between what is said and what is really distributed.

> Reward carries strong messages. If you want to see what an organization values, look at what it pays for, not what it says. Words are cheap and it is easy to make statements about what is important in an organization. However, if you say one thing, but pay for something quite different you can guess which message will have the greater effect on what people actually do.
>
> *(Rose 2014:15)*

In addition, Knights and McCabe draw attention to the gap between 'rhetoric' and 'reality' of innovation (Knights and McCabe 2003:97). The same can be applied to discourse and rewards; in some companies the communicative side of reward management is stronger than its practical implementation. In other words, the promises made on paper are never implemented in real organizational life. The discussion on reward management discourse should also take into account the way information is shared among stakeholders. It happens that what is written differs from what is really meant. The rhetoric–reality gap is exemplified by Rose (2014:17):

Rhetoric	Reality
We pay for performance	Only as a tiny % of total cash
We are customer-focused	We incentivize sales
Contribution to team success is key	Pay reviews are based on individual objectives
We value contribution and performance	We have service-based benefits and pensions
We push down decision-making to all	There is no choice in any parts of reward

In addition to the already mentioned discrepancy, some organizations do not cater for the informative needs of their employees. "Many organizations give their employees too little information about the reward/pay/benefits that apply to them. A new pay system that makes a miraculous appearance as a conjuror produces a rabbit from a hat may not fulfil its potential" (Wright 2004:9). It should be pointed out that consulting with employees increases understanding as to why changes have to be implemented. Moreover, employee surveys provide information on staff opinions (Armstrong and Brown 2006). Syed and Kramar (2017) stress that not disclosing information on salaries to other workers may explain their lack of demands for higher pay levels. To put it differently, when they learn that their colleagues earn more for doing the same job, they may ask for a salary increase. It is also stressed by some that pay secrecy is connected with the violation of workers' rights. In addition, Perkins et al. (2016) stress the role of 'toxic bonus culture', notoriously represented in the reported pre-global financial crisis banking sector practice of allocating trading profits more to employees than to shareholders.

Communicating reward management is often associated with pay openness. Marasi and Bennett (2016) stress that nowadays pay openness (also called pay transparency) in companies can be observed. They offer the following reasons for this situation. First, data on pay are easily available online. Secondly, in some countries pay openness is regulated (e.g., the Executive Order signed in 2014 in the US). The third reason is connected with the current employment market entrants – 'Millennials' – who prefer open culture and social media.

Robertson (2007) discusses reward communication from the perspective of consequences for employees. "I understand" is connected with employees' understanding the content and purpose of reward communication. This may include information on how they are rewarded, taking into account such notions as performance, skills or the financial situation of a company. "I believe" includes employees' belief that the elements of reward communication are fair and they meet their expectations and needs. It reflects their trust in the given type of reward. "I do" reflects the engagement of workers in their daily routines because the rewards offered (e.g. discounted retail vouchers) are beneficial for them. Armstrong and Murlis (1988) discuss what should be communicated regarding reward management at workforce and individual levels. At the workforce level, the following topics should be discussed. The first one is the company salary policy, representing rules of pay and benefits level. The next item is the pay and benefits structure, encompassing salary brackets and fringe benefits. The third notion is called methods of grading and re-grading jobs, focusing on a job evaluation scheme. The fourth aspect is called salary progression that concentrates on how salaries are progressed, taking into account grades or a salary curve system. The last element – the incentive/bonus scheme – involves information on bonuses or profit shares. Commentators argue that information to individual employees should also be distributed. Job grade entails information on how a given grade is determined. Salary progression, on the other hand, encompasses the possible growth of salaries. Similarly, potential is connected with how higher salaries can be achieved, taking into account performance criteria and the availability of adequate positions. Performance appraisal is linked with methods of assessing performance and potential. Salary levels, in contrast, explain why such rewards are offered to workers. A benefit statement, in turn, is connected with the worth of benefits the employee receives, corresponding to his/her job satisfaction (Armstrong and Murlis 1988).

Methods of studying reward communication

Reward communication can be researched in different ways. One option is to use methods and tools that look at the unit of investigation from different angles at the same time. For example, different discourse theories, e.g., Critical Discourse Analysis, are applied to examine how communication on reward management is conducted. Discourse is understood in the broad sense, observing the selection of words and phrases, pictures, drawings (pictorial metaphors), textual features (the division into chunks and text types) and their implication for communicating rewards. Discourse analysis is planned to involve different types of reward management, not necessarily only those which are positive for employees, but also the rather negative ones, such as cutting salaries or limiting perks. To observe differences in reward systems from the discourse perspective in different countries, approaches such as Cross-Cultural Discourse Analysis (CCDA) can be used. This "concerns descriptive an interpretive comparison of discourse genres (television news programs, literature textbooks, internet newsgroups, parental guidebooks, etc.) in two or more different ethnolinguistic communities" (Münchow 2012). To observe how employees describe their job and the reward system they have in place, one may apply Action-Implicative Discourse Analysis (Tracy 2003): "AIDA takes the commitment to study everyday interaction and the practice of repeatedly listening to exchanges that researchers have transcribed where they attend to many particulars, including intonation, abrupt word or phrase cut-offs, and repetition and vocalized sounds (uh, um, eh)" (Tracy 2003: 221).

It should be noted that HRM discourse is not limited to literal communication. Metaphors constitute important tools in discussing human resources and the overall job market. For example, Taylor (2015) presents the metaphor of an hourglass to discuss the labour market in the UK. This metaphor is used to stress the polarization of jobs into high-skilled and well-paid ones and those that are low-skilled and low-paid (Taylor and Woodhams 2016). Discussing the role of symbolism in HRM, the focus is on such metaphorical names as golden parachutes, golden umbrellas, golden handcuffs, golden hellos, etc. to stress the positive and negative aspects of using metaphors in reward management. The domain of gold is often used to create names connected with economics, taking into account their value for business. They can be perceived through the prism of possessed funds or qualifications, paid taxes or the represented social position. 'Gold collars' are professionals in a given domain, having unique and demanded skills and those performing innovative jobs. The term 'golden collars' is also used to denote the representatives of the young generation, spending a relative part of their income on luxurious products (Bielenia-Grajewska 2015). Apart from the discussed dichotomy between literal and figurative terms, words and phrases with a similar meaning can be analysed to observe the meaning they connote. This can be found in the use of phrases such as 'pay progression' and 'variable pay' as well as 'merit pay' or 'incentive pay'. These names can be studied by taking into account how emotionally loaded they are and what their perception among the users is.

There are different texts that can be used as source materials for studying rewards. Letters written by CEOs and their implications for the workers constitute some of these examples. Armstrong and Murlis (1988) present the ways of informing employees about their rewards. One of these is a staff handbook that is distributed among all new workers when they join the company. Pension schemes, profit sharing and share ownership schemes are discussed in brochures. The aim of such publications is to present the possible benefits for employees for their performance and loyalty to the company. In addition to written forms of reward communication, face-to-face contacts should not be avoided. Performance, promotion and pay progression possibilities should be discussed by managers or supervisors with workers on a regular basis.

It should be noted that the discussion on reward management discourse can also take into account presenting neuroscientific tools and their usage in neurolinguistics, neuromarketing and neuromanagement. This perspective acts by focusing on such neuroscientific tools as functional magnetic resonance imaging (fMRI), galvanic skin response (GSR) or electroencephalography (EEG), which are used not only in medical examinations (Bielenia-Grajewska 2013b).

Conclusion

The aim of this chapter has been to stress the importance of discourse in creating and disseminating rewards. Since it is a very broad topic the author has selected some methodologies and notions that, according to her, best exemplify the complexities of reward management discourse. Reward management discourse can be studied at different levels and using diversified methodologies, focusing on words, phrases and texts. Taking into account the growing role of technology in the twenty-first century it can be predicted that research directed at technological aspects will be even more important in the future.

References

Armstrong, M. and Brown, D. (2006). *Strategic Reward: Implementing More Effective Reward Management. Making it Happen*. London: Kogan Page.

Armstrong, M. and Taylor, S. (2014). *Armstrong's Handbook of Human Resource Management Practice*. London: Kogan Page.

Armstrong, M. and Murlis, H. (1988). *Reward Management. A Handbook of Salary Administration*. London: Kogan Page.

Banfield, P., Kay, R. and Royles, D. (2018). *Introduction to Human Resource Management*. Oxford: Oxford University Press.

Beer, M., Eisenstat, R. A. (2000). The silent killers of strategy implementation and learning. *Sloan Management Review*. 41/4, 29–40.

Behrend, H. (2016). *Problems of Labour and Inflation*. Abingdon: Routledge.

Bielenia-Grajewska, M. (2010). The linguistic dimension of expatriatism-hybrid environment, hybrid linguistic identity. *European Journal of Cross-Cultural Competence and Management*. 2/3, 212–231.

Bielenia-Grajewska, M. (2013a). The heteroglossic linguistic identity of modern companies. Management and Business Administration. *Central Europe*. 21/4(123), 120–131.

Bielenia-Grajewska, M. (2013b). International neuromanagement: deconstructing international management education with neuroscience. In Tsang, D., Kazeroony, H. H. and Ellis, G. (eds.). *The Routledge Companion to International Management Education* (pp. 358–373). Abingdon: Routledge.

Bielenia-Grajewska, M. (2015). Rola języka symbolicznego w edukacji ekonomicznej na przykładzie nazw metaforycznych wykorzystujących domenę złota. *Edukacja Ekonomistów i Menedżerów: problemy, innowacje, projekty*. 3(37), 57–70.

Knights, D. and McCabe, D. (2003). *Organization and Innovation*. Maidenhead: Open University Press.

Lawler, E. E. IIII (2008) Talent: *Making People Your Competitive Advantage*. San Francisco: Jossey-Bass.

Loudon, R., McPhail, R. and Wilkinson, A. (2009) *Introduction to Employment Relations*. Frenchs Forest: Pearson.

Lussier, R. N. and Hendon, J. R. (2018). *Human Resource Management: Functions, Applications, Skill Development*. Thousand Oaks, CA: SAGE Publications.

Marasi, S. and Bennett R.J. (2016). Pay communication: Where do we go from here? *Human Resource Management Review*. 26/1, 50–58.

Münchow, P. (2012). Cross-cultural discourse analysis and intercultural education in foreign language teaching and learning. *Journal of Intercultural Communication*. 29.

Perkins, S. J. (2009). Executive reward. In White, G. and Druker, J. (eds.). *Reward Management: A Critical Text* (pp. 148–173). London: Routledge.

Perkins, S. J. (2015). Perspectives on problems in managing managers' remuneration. In Wilkinson, A., Townsend, K. and Suder, G. (eds.). *Handbook of Research on Managing Managers* (pp. 36–61). Cheltenham: Edward Elgar Publishing Company.

Perkins, S. J., White, G. and Jones, S. (2016). *Reward Management: Alternatives, Consequences and Contexts*. London: CIPD Publishing.

Pocztowski, A. (2017). Zarządzanie zasobami ludzkimi w przedsiębiorstwach międzynarodowych. In Wiktor, J. (ed.). *Zarządzanie przedsiębiorstwem międzynarodowym: integracja różnorodności* (pp. 195–228). Warsaw: Wydawnictwo C.H. Beck.

Podmoroff, D. (2005). *365 Ways to Motivate and Reward Your Employees Every Day – With Little or No Money*. London: Atlantic Publishing Group.

Robertson, R. (2007). *The Together Company: Rewarding What Matters Most to People and Organizations.* Wakefield: Cogent.

Rose, M. (2014). *Reward Management (HR Fundamentals).* London: Kogan Page.

Syed, J. and Kramar. R. (2017). *Human Resource Management: a Global and Critical Perspective.* London: Palgrave.

Strużyna, J., Bratnicki, M., Majowska, M. and Ingram T. (2008). *Rozwój zarządzania zasobami ludzkimi.* Katowice Wydawnictwo Akademii Ekonomicznej w Katowicach.

Taylor, S. and Woodhams, C. (2016). *Human Resource Management: People and Organisations.* London: Chartered Institute of Personnel and Development.

Taylor, J. (2015). Closing the rhetoric-reality gap? Employees' perspective of performance management in the Australian Public Service. *Australian Journal of Public Administration.* 74(3), 336–353.

Tracy, K. (2003). Action-implicative discourse analysis: a communication approach to analyzing talk. *Texas Linguistic Forum* 47, 219–237, *Proceedings of the Eleventh Annual Symposium about Language and Society*, Austin, April 11–13.

Wright, A. (2004). *Reward Management in Context.* London: Chartered Institute of Personnel and Development.

7

NEW REALISM IN 'STRATEGIC' REWARD MANAGEMENT

Bringing together research and practice

Duncan Brown

Introduction

Despite often being under-researched (Perkins and White 2016; Rose 2014), the idea of reward strategy has been much debated, both in academic and practitioner circles and in-between the two communities. The remarkable uncertainties and unpredictability of events in 2016, with the victory of the Brexit campaign in the UK followed by Donald Trump's presidential triumph, has restimulated the debate over the effectiveness of strategy and planning in such rapidly changing environments. ', In the words of an article published by Reeves (2016): 'The world just got more uncertain and your strategy needs to adjust'. At the start of 2016 the reward director of a FTSE 100 company told the REBA reward conference that after the surprise announcement of the National Living Wage the previous year, he wasn't even setting out an annual reward plan, never mind any longer-term strategy, until after the Chancellor's Budget in April.

I believe the debate leaves four questions to answer in terms of the continuing role, if any, for reward strategy thinking and practice:

- What does reward strategy mean and what is its value?
- How can reward strategies be applied and implemented in practice?
- How can you measure the effectiveness and improve the impact of a reward strategy?
- What is the relationship in concept and practice between reward strategy and total rewards?

Reward strategy, I will argue, has been redefined and the concept is now characterized by a less unitarist, multi-stakeholder, more employee-engaging and evidence-based approach, with a stronger emphasis on employee communication and line manager buy-in. By further bridging the gap between academics and practitioners we can improve the rigour and the relevance of the concept.

The origins and evolution of reward strategy

Reward strategy is a broad, often ill-specified concept, which helps to explain some of the controversy it has occasioned. Rose (2014) notes at least half a dozen different definitions of the term. As Pfeffer (1998) observes, there is surprisingly little evidence on how and how well rewards work in reinforcing business strategy, although "there is much evidence that pay and pay plan designs loom large in management attention".

The term 'reward strategy' has its origins in a number of strands of thinking, most notably American research in the emerging field of strategic human resource management in the early 1980s (Beer et al. 1984; Fombrun et al. 1984). A related strand of thinking, resource dependency theory, emerged, emphasizing the importance of employers acquiring control over the key 'talent' and human resources that minimize their dependence on other organizations, in which reward practices were held to play an important part (Ulrich and Barney 1984; Pfeffer 1982). This contrasted with a more pluralistic role for traditional personnel departments, as essentially the mediators between management and workers and, pay and rewards-wise, as the interpreters and administrators of internal procedures and external legislation (Heery 1996; Guest and Bryson 2009).

In the UK in the 1980s and 1990s, a series of environmental changes were seen to give employers much greater freedom in determining the levels and composition of remuneration (Brown and Walsh 1994) following the more prescriptive and regulated era of the 1970s (Brown and Sissons 1975). These included: the shift to a more service-based economy (Porter and Ketels 2003); the decline of trade union membership and collective bargaining (Kessler and Bayliss 1998; Wood and Bryson 2009); and government promotion and incentives for particular initiatives, such as employee share plans and profit-related pay (White 1996).

A more forward-looking, change-oriented approach seeking improved business alignment is therefore usually referred to in most definitions of reward strategy (Perkins and White 2016). Early ideas of strategic Human Resources Management (HRM) were taken up and applied more explicitly to the rewards field (Lawler 1986, 1990, 1995). Lawler defined reward strategy as an integrated approach linking company strategy, pay systems and employee behaviours, describing it as a simple linear model in his highly influential book on consulting and practitioners, *Strategic Pay* (Lawler 1990), illustrated in Figure 7.1. Research studies in the years following demonstrated the increasing numbers of employers claiming to adopt written reward strategies and a strategic approach, involving higher levels of pay change to support business alignment (Vernon 2006; Watson Wyatt Worldwide 2007).

Supporting Lawler's concept, one strand of strategic HRM research describes the positive associations found in the private sector between the use of a 'bundle' of HRM practices, including performance-related pay and employee shareholding, and the financial performance of these

Figure 7.1 Lawler's Model of Strategic Reward

employers (Huselid 1995; Guest et al. 2003). Studies also found associations between strategic business typologies and patterns of pay practice. Perkins, for example, using Miles and Snow's business strategy typology, found that employers pursuing a 'Prospector' strategy of innovation and change were more likely to set pay levels in the top 10% of the market and use competencies and skills as pay progression criteria than 'Defender' firms with a cost and low price-driven strategy (CIPD 2012). This research therefore supported Lawler's concept, suggested it was being practised by employers, and that it was associated with certain performance outcomes.

Criticisms of the original concept

Since this time, however, research studies and practitioner experiences have cast increasing doubts on these original strategic reward ideas.

First, academic critics point to the definitional imprecision and confusion with the original concept, leading to the doubt as expressed by Guest (2001) as to whether reward strategy theory is sufficiently precise to point to the kind of empirical testing that results in convincing support or refutation. In particular, Guest (2001) and other researchers (Chadwick et al. 2015) highlight the confusion as to whether HR and reward practices should be tailored to suit the characteristics, culture and business strategy of an organization; or if there is a common basket of HR and reward plans that are associated with high performance in all contexts – the so-called "best fit versus best practice" debate (Purcell 1999). White (1996) notes the theoretical confusion as to the degree to which employers align with their own business strategies or with the practices of competing employers. And in terms of the claimed impact of business-aligned reward practices on performance, summarizing the literature on the links between pay and performance, Gerhardt and Rynes (2003) note that "it is difficult to identify characteristics of either pay design or context that contribute to performance variance".

Second has been the growing evidence that written reward strategies were not actually very common and, more importantly, not only were not being applied in practice by employers but reward and line managers were struggling to implement the concept (CIPD 2007). This created what Bevan (2006:13–14) refers to as a "rhetoric/reality gap" in rewards management, which has led to him questioning the validity and practical existence of the concept.

Reviewing 25 years of the Workplace Employment Relations Survey research, Guest and Bryson's (2009) conclusion is that far from being Ulrich's (1997) leading-edge, human resource champions implementing radical, change-oriented reward and HR practice innovations, personnel specialists are in the main "traditionalists, bringing up the rear, their time engaged in a variety of operational activities". Bach et al. (2009) similarly conclude "these uneven patterns of change signal transition rather than transformation in the process of pay determination".

One key criticism, which has become ever louder over the few decades, has been the issue of implementation. Trevor and Brown (2014) note strategic intent "often may be implemented in ways that differ from the initial intention", replicating findings on the limitations of rationalist accounts of strategic management (Pfeffer and Sutton 2006). And Trevor (2009) argues on the basis of research in seven multinational employers that, because of institutional pressures for conformity, the risks involved and difficulties of change such as staff and line manager resistance (see also Abay, this volume) pay cannot, in reality, provide competitive advantage. Reward strategy is therefore "a largely unattainable ideal in practice". Pay and rewards should therefore largely be reactively managed to limit risk (Chapman and Cotton 2010).

Kessler (2001) points to the relevance of new institutional theory in explaining real-life reward-setting decisions, with its emphasis on institutional pressures encouraging conformity, and isomorphism of practice between organizations, supported, for example, through the extensive use of pay surveys and benchmarking (Meyer and Rowan 1991; Oliver 1997). Oliver points to the influence of unwritten but powerful industry norms of practice, encouraging what Arrowsmith and Sissons (1999) termed "sectoral convoys".

So rather than proactively aligning rewards with the strategic and performance requirements of the organization, this research suggests that tweaking historic practices only when necessary, and copying what competitors do, better reflects contemporary models and patterns of reward management in practice.

Two related issues predominate in the research on practical implementation: employee understanding and support; and line management competence and commitment to delivering strategic reward policies as intended (Becker and Huselid 2006; Banks and Kepes 2015). More generally across all HR policies (McGovern et al. 1997) and in other European countries (Larsen and Brewster 2003) similar implementation issues appear to be commonly evident in reward and HR strategy delivery. Rather than fulfilling Lawler's ambition of bringing written reward strategy intentions to life, these line manager and employee dimensions appear to be commonly rendering them lifeless.

For Lawler's concept to operate, employees need to understand the reward strategy in order that it influences their behaviour and performance; and line managers need to practise it as intended. As far as employee communications is concerned, despite the long history of research that shows that even limited employee consultation on reward system designs and implementation makes a major difference to the success of outcomes (Bowey and Thorpe 1983; Cox 2005); and the emphasis on motivating key employees in the resource dependency and talent management literature (Ulrich and Barney 1984; Michaels et al 2001), as Cox argues, employee views generally seem to be neglected by employers in making reward decisions. Research also confirms the generally poor perceptions of reward communications and resulting low levels of employee understanding of reward strategies, practices and processes (Scott et al. 2008; EHRC 2010).

Given the research evidence on the challenges of reward strategy implementation, one might anticipate that the literature on the measurement of effectiveness of rewards would be extensive. Researching into aerospace companies, for example, Thompson (2000) discerned higher profit per employee levels in companies with various pay practices such as performance pay and flatter pay structures. In another study, Guest et al. (2003) found performance-related pay, share ownership and profit sharing amongst a group of 18 high-performance work practices associated with higher added value per employee. While there are definitional and research issues with some of these studies, such as the varied contents of the HR 'bundle' of practices, and problems identifying the direction of causation, nonetheless there are a compelling number now in existence, from different parts of the world and different sectors. Combs et al. (2006), in their meta-analysis report on over 90 studies of this type, finding positive associations between reward and HR practices and performance outcomes, a foundation of reward strategy concepts.

But there are also studies (Lewis 1998; Cox 2005) documenting the difficulties in implementing specific reward practices generally associated with strategic reward approaches, particularly performance-related pay (Marsden and Richardson 1994; Suff and Reilly 2004); and the general disappointment of managers with pay outcomes (Brown and Nolan 1988). Werner and Ward (2004), Burgess and Metcalf (1999) and Jenkins et al. (1998) all conclude from extensive literature reviews that pay incentives can influence employee behaviour and performance, but that this impact is often exaggerated.

These research findings emphasize the need for individual employers to be able to accurately measure the effects of their reward practices in order to achieve a "best fit" impact. Yet researchers point to this lack of evaluation of the effectiveness of reward strategies as a key reason for what Pfeffer and Sutton (2006) call the 'knowing–doing gap' in reward. Milsome (2006) similarly concludes that merit pay became popular for reasons of ideology and fashion, with the evidence that it may not work, she claims, largely ignored.

The *CIPD Annual Reward Management Survey* (2009) confirmed few systematic attempts to evaluate the impact and effectiveness of reward practices. Less than a quarter of the almost 500 participants used any sort of business data to assess reward practices. In pioneering research work for the Department of Health amongst 15 large employers, Corby et al. (2005) found that only two made any real attempt to assess the effects of the pay structure changes implemented. Again this suggests an inertia-driven and reactive approach to reward management rather than Lawler's proactive, business strategy-driven and performance-impacting model.

Total rewards? From their origins, ideas of reward and HRM strategy have incorporated the dimension of "lateral integration" of reward and HR policies with each other, in order to create consistency in people management, as well as vertical integration with business strategy (Beer et al. 1984). As Armstrong and Murlis (2007) explain, "the total reward concept emphasises the importance of all aspects of the rewards package as a coherent whole . . . account is taken of all the ways in which people can be rewarded and obtain satisfaction through their work, linking financial and non-financial aspects". And, theoretically, to influence and engage employees to implement the business strategy successfully.

Benkhoff (1997) applies social identity theory to explain that employee engagement requires an integrated strategy congruent with the employee's own values, with varied rewards to suit the different needs of employees. The total rewards literature, like that on employee engagement, generally emphasizes non-financial methods of motivating staff, harking back to Herzberg's two-factor theory of motivation (Herzberg, 1966). Bloom and Milkovich (1995) point out, in a more knowledge and service-based, human-capital-driven economy, financial rewards alone cannot extract the behaviours that distinguish outstanding from ordinary performance, so "a broad bundle of valued rewards" needs to be offered in return for the "valuable cluster of employee contributions" to the delivery of the business's strategy. In addition, O'Neal (1998) argues that an increasingly diverse workforce also gives the opportunity to individualize packages to suit the differing needs of employees.

Some studies do suggest that employees like to be offered a choice in their package. Barber et al. (1992), for example, found that in a financial services company flexible benefits choices increased employee satisfaction with their rewards. Another study indicated that the pay premium required to recruit was halved if an employer possessed an attractive total rewards package (Conference Board 2001). And some studies have used quantitative techniques to demonstrate associations between the use of particular employee benefits and positive outcomes (Baughman et al. 2003; Tsai and Wang 2005).

The concept of 'total reward' represents a number of challenges, however, to Lawler's original concept of reward strategy. First, as indicated by its early 'New Pay' nomenclature (Lawler 1995), there has been a historical focus on pay and incentives as the strongest means of influencing employee behaviour and performance in support of the business strategy, rather than non-pay motivations. Indeed, some of the early reward strategy proponents are strongly critical of total rewards approaches for encouraging the spread of expensive benefits packages with no relationship to organization or individual performance (Zingheim and Schuster 2000; Torre and Sarti 2013). Wright (2009) finds little impact of total rewards on recruitment and retention and believes that the high transaction costs will restrict the further spread of flexible benefits in the UK.

Holbeche (2014) goes further and notes that it could be argued that the balance of power and benefit in the employment relationship has shifted to the advantage of employers at the expense of employees since the financial crash of 2008–9, with some employers regarding employee engagement and total rewards, however achieved, as a "luxury for the good times". Rewards are a cost to be minimized rather than invested in to engage employees behind the strategic goals of the organization. Tahmincioglu (2004) contends that total reward approaches risk demotivating many employees and being interpreted as a cynical attempt to appease them in times of low or no pay increases, restructuring and downsizing.

Redefining reward strategy grounded in UK contexts

All of this research might suggest, therefore, that Lawler's reward strategy concept can not be implemented in practice and that in any case there is no evidence it impacts on performance and the delivery of business strategy. Fortunately, there are strong signs now that the reward strategy 'baby' is not getting thrown out with the 'bathwater' so to speak, and a newer, more realistic and workable variant of the concept is emerging, characterized by a multidimensional and more process-focused approach: One that takes more account of line manager and employee needs and genuine total reward perspectives, and with more attention to evaluation.

An increasing amount of research highlights that strategic, longer-term thinking and tactical reaction both characterize reward management in the UK. Although business alignment and performance reinforcement were the overwhelmingly predominant goals of their reward policies, only 35% of the 466 employers in the *CIPD Annual Reward Management Survey* (2007) actually possessed explicit, written reward strategies, a slight decline from two years previously. The survey's conclusion was of a still "tactically-focused, piecemeal scene".

Larger employers (62% of those with over 5,000 employees) in the CIPD survey did claim to have an articulated rewards strategy. However, a follow-up investigation (Brown and Perkins 2007) involving a survey of 63 large multinationals and qualitative interviews with their reward functions, contrasted a short-term, externally-driven, reactive approach with the claimed longer-term, business-driven and strategic approach to reward management. The more reactive approach, the research found, was being applied more strongly (on the X axis) by more of the organizations (on the Y axis) than the strategic one, but interestingly, both were being applied simultaneously in all of these employers – see Figure 7.2.

This mixed pattern was found in a similar US study (Bloom et al. 2003).

In business strategy research, in response to a faster-moving, more knowledge- and human capital-driven economy, we have seen just such a shift summarized by Ghoshal and Bartlett (1998) as moving from concerns with strategy, structure and systems to purpose, process and people. Mintzberg perhaps most radically defines this, writing of the reality of emergent as well as planned strategies, describing strategy as a pattern in a stream of decisions, sometimes only discernible after the event, rather than the top-down implementation of business plans. These ideas have been applied to HRM and reward strategies, termed "living (HR) strategy" (Grattan 2000) and "new HRM" (Bach 2005). Rather than implementing top-down, supposedly rational, "best practice" HR policies derived directly from the business strategy in a unitarist way or copied from competitors, HR strategy is presented as a social construction, influenced by multiple stakeholders and the wider context, inside and outside of the organization (Grint 2005; Perkins 2017).

Reward work is characterized under this perspective as being of a blended nature, having clear business and reward goals, but open-minded and with flexibility in the 'best fit' between business needs and reward practices at any particular time (Brown 2012). And this emerging process rather than top-down strategy perspective highlights three further ways in which the term needed to and is evolving.

First, reward strategy is not just the intended *goals* of reward policies, but also the *processes* such as line management and communications used to put those policies into practice, as well as the

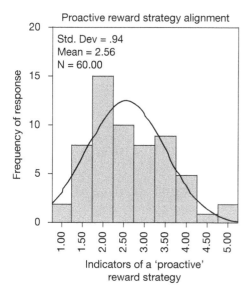
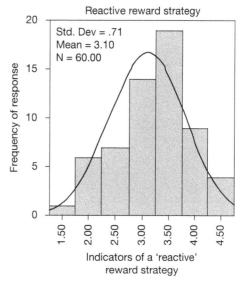

Figure 7.2 Results from study of reward strategy in multinational companies (n = 63)

Source: Brown and Perkins 2007.

effectiveness of their delivery (Armstrong and Brown 2006). Employers can not just have a reward strategy plan, they also need to influence the process and practice.

Second, the concept needs to reflect a multiple stakeholder agenda and, in particular, to reassert the primacy of aligning rewards with employee needs and culture alongside business requirements (Armstrong and Brown 2006; Brown and Reilly 2013; Brown 2012). Banks and Kepes (2015) note that positive employee perceptions of practices such as merit pay are critical to delivering the intended alignment between business strategy and employee behaviour. Employees have to understand and 'buy into' the business goals and purpose for rewards to be able to influence how and how powerfully they pursue those goals.

Third, the idea of reward strategy needed to expand, beyond the monetary pay focus of the early advocates and obsession with performance pay techniques, to encompass the full range of financial and non-financial factors that engage employees to perform – a true "total rewards" perspective (Cox et al. 2010).

This *new realism in reward strategy* as a pattern and a process of continuous improvement, rather than an end-point plan (Armstrong and Brown 2006), can be represented as a more balanced, two-way employer/employee model of reward strategy in comparison to the linearity of Lawler's original theory (1990). This 'rebalanced' model is illustrated in Figure 7.3 (Brown 2001). It highlights the need to align rewards with employee characteristics and needs on the right-hand side as well as business goals and needs on the left; and it encompasses four dimensions of total rewards in the design criteria in the centre of the model, rather than just the singular Lawler focus on pay.

But what about the key issue of effectiveness and difficulties in making the model work in practice? One recent study (Aon Hewitt 2012) found that while 87% of respondents believed that their pay and other reward policies reflected business needs and priorities, the lowest ratings of effectiveness were in the areas of employee communications and involvement, line manager application, and the delivery of an integrated total reward offer. Addressing these areas comprised three of the most commonly mentioned top five reward priorities for the future across the whole survey sample (Brown 2012).

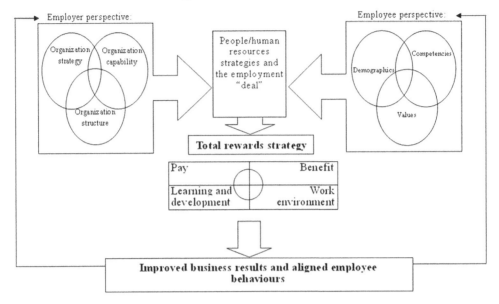

Balanced reward strategy model

Figure 7.3   A balanced reward strategy model

Fixing the practice: employee engagement and communications

Advocates of so-called "new HRM" (Bach 2005), and the emergence of an open systems approach to HR strategy in more complex, fast-changing organizations, highlight the importance of employees and line managers in turning the HR strategy concept into reality, the policy into practice (Purcell et al. 2003). Similarly, research showing that effective two-way communications and trust in the design and ongoing operation of pay practices are essential, if they are to succeed, has been around for many years. Bowey and Thorpe's (1983) research, for example, found the degree of employee involvement and communication was more important than the design of bonus plans in explaining successful outcomes.

The research and theoretical frameworks for employee engagement (Brown and Reilly 2013) can play a key role in helping to define and specify the broadening of Lawler's original reward strategy concept which we have seen occurring. And they can also specify how reward and other HR practices are associated with organizational performance, opening up Guest's (2011) 'black box' as to just how associations between these practices and performance outcomes actually operate. IES research in the NHS, for example, demonstrated that staff perceptions of pay and benefits correlated with them feeling valued and involved, which was in turn the most important determinant of employee engagement levels (Robinson et al. 2004).

Research in individual employers has produced some of the best evidence on linkages between reward policies, employee engagement and employer performance, the ultimate aim of any reward strategy. The Sears study (Rucci et al. 1998), which found positive associations between employee engagement, customer satisfaction and sales growth across their North American stores, has been highly influential and replicated in the UK. At the Nationwide Building Society, research in their branch network found that a 3% improvement in employee perceptions of five HR practices, including pay transparency and fairness, was associated with positive customer perceptions and a 1% increase in sales growth.

Notwithstanding such developments, it is true that the most negative ratings of reward effectiveness made in contemporary research studies still tend to be in respect of employee communications (Trevor and Brown 2014; Brown 2012). But, while 'weak communications' appears to be a persistent and critical 'Achilles' Heel' in the effective implementation of intended reward strategies (Brown 2008), we are seeing far more information on the researched case for improved reward communications and also evidence-based frameworks, tools and case studies to help employers to communicate rewards more effectively in practice. The CIPD Reward Strategy Toolkit (2005), for example, majors on this area and has been downloaded over 27,000 times since it was launched. More recently, the NHS equivalent developed with an advisory group of NHS managers has also proved highly popular (NHS Employers 2014), illustrating the more solution-focused research approach which Gas and Gillis suggest would be beneficial (1995).

Fixing the practice: line managers and reward strategy

The failings of line managers in delivering on strategic reward intentions in the workplace is similarly an area of continuing difficulties, but also an increasing volume of helpful research and practical progress (see Hutchinson and Purcell 2007; Brown and Purcell 2007). The folly of HR professionals focusing on strategy-aligned reward designs rather than delivery was highlighted by the CIPD's survey of 535 of them (CIPD 2006; Hutchinson and Purcell 2007). Although 80% of the HR group had consulted board executives in developing their reward strategies, just 40% had spoken in advance with line managers (and fewer than 10% with the employees themselves). Yet there is now far better evidence too that the role of "warm, supportive and enabling" line managers is critical to encouraging high levels of employee engagement and customer service (Brown and West 2005) and that "the role of front line leaders in bringing [HR and reward] policies to life can be crucial in making the difference between low-performing and high-performing organizations" (Hutchinson and Purcell 2007).

This research programme's conclusion was that "where reward professionals understand, support, skill and enable line managers to create a totally rewarding environment for their staff, then this alignment of reward policy and practice is far more likely to result in a highly engaged and high performance workforce" (Brown and Purcell 2007). Business and reward strategies have therefore to be concerned with financial and non-financial means of engaging managers and employees, not just pay; and they have to worry at least as much about implementation and practice as they do about planning. Moreover, this research highlighted a number of practical actions to investigate and address the identified issues, including better training and support for line managers and the simplification of reward management processes (cf. Bailey et al. 2017).

One of the case studies profiled was John Lewis (Brown and Purcell 2007) where a new competency framework and pay structure was developed with extensive management and employee involvement. Another was the retailer Selfridges, where two-thirds of staff in an initial survey said that they had never been asked their views by their manager and some employees had never had an appraisal. The second survey 12 months later after a range of initiatives to improve reward communications revealed significant improvements in employee satisfaction and engagement levels.

Delivering the outcomes: measuring the effectiveness, improving the impact of reward strategy

We have already discussed the surprising lack of measurement of the effectiveness of reward strategy and need for more academic research in the field and more evidence-based reward

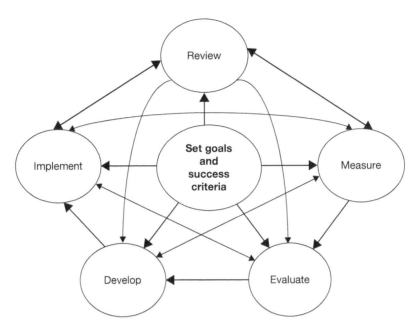

Figure 7.4 The process model for evidence-based reward management

Source: Armstrong, Brown and Reilly (2010).

practice. But more and more employers now seem to be addressing this lacuna. IES's research study (Armstrong et al. 2010, 2011) found that almost half of employers did make some attempt to review the effectiveness of their reward practices. However, just 54% of these were satisfied with the results and the survey confirmed that employers on the whole conducted limited, piecemeal evaluation of their reward practices and any changes designed to improve them.

The six case study organizations featured in the research described reward evaluation as a journey, a continuous process of improvement, rather than a measurement dashboard and one-off review. As the head of reward at a regulatory body told the researchers, engage key stakeholders such as senior line managers and trade unions and build a consensus on the strengths and weaknesses of current rewards and possible improvements; use quantitative data, but always in context; and "include and interpret the 'grey' as well as the 'black and white' areas".

A reward effectiveness model developed from the research is shown in Figure 7.4. As well as a conceptual and research framework, it is designed to be a practical process so as to encourage practitioners to use the model. Evaluating the effectiveness of reward practices has to be a key component of any strategic reward approach. But this needs to be a continuous and multidirectional process, linking reward goals and intended outcomes, as well as reward programme designs intended to deliver these outcomes, with ongoing evaluation, monitoring and adjustment, based not just on performance results but also line management and employee feedback.

Delivering the outcomes: total rewards and its relationship with reward strategy

A CIPD study carried out with an Aston University team amongst a sample of 15 service sector organizations found that the five highest performers made greater use of bonuses and non-financial recognition than the remainder. In similar fashion to Guest (2003), however, the study found that a variety of other management practices and HR policies – regarding career development, employee involvement, performance management and work–life balance – were vital in creating the supportive context for employees to commit to serve the customer, and created a strong sense that the entire organization "practices what it preaches" (Brown and West 2005). Anyone interested in using rewards proactively to help reinforce the delivery of their business strategy therefore needs to pay at least as much attention to non-financial as to financial rewards.

However, following the onset of economic recession in 2008, evidence has been emerging that more and more UK organizations were not 'practising what they preach' in respect of total rewards. The familiar say/do, policy/practice, rhetoric/reality gap (Bevan 2006) in reward strategy appeared to be particularly evident in respect of total rewards (Brown 2012, 2014). While attractive total rewards language remained on company recruitment sites and intranets, 40% of UK employers froze pay in 2009/10 and many reduced employee pensions benefits, as well as placing increasing numbers of staff on significantly inferior 'zero hours' contracts. This low-investment, total rewards rhetoric, with its uniform flexible benefits plans, does no more to support the delivery of business strategy in practice than the totally pay-focused approach of the early reward strategy proponents (Brown 2014). It can also be seen to have played a role in the launch of the current UK government's agenda of what the prime minister called a "fairer economy that works for everyone" (May 2016).

Based on case study observations, recent research has identified the components of a more genuinely strategic total rewards concept, again more to do with the process and practice of reward management in an employer (Brown 2014). This comprises:

- a simpler and more flexible focus on a few core values and reward principles;
- a more evidence-based approach, with clearer measures of success and more use of them;
- a stronger emphasis on employee communications and engagement;
- less focus on 'desire and design' and more emphasis on 'communications and delivery', particularly important given the growing range of flexibility and choices being offered to employees.

One commentator describes this shift in the application of the total rewards concept as being "about having a much simpler, clearer, more open, realistic and, crucially, evidence-based approach" (Paton 2014). Increasingly, we are seeing research studies addressing this latter gap, with the Money Advisory Service, for example, recently launching a fund of over £7 million to encourage research into evaluating initiatives supporting workplace financial wellbeing (MAS 2016).

Conclusions and future research agenda

With its theoretical underpinning in the work of the Harvard School researchers on strategic human resource management and the desire for newly-christened HR functions to demonstrate their impact, supported by changes in the economy towards a more market-oriented philosophy and individualized social and employee relations context, Lawler's original reward strategy ideas achieved widespread popularity in UK practitioner circles from the early 1990s.

Research does lend some support to the contention that typologies of business strategy are likely to be associated with particular pay and reward policies, and that certain reward practices are more likely to be used by higher-performing organizations. Despite limited research in some areas, however, particularly reward evaluation and total rewards, and despite reported difficulties in being able to test the concept, studies since then have cast serious doubts as to the applicability and validity of the original reward strategy concept, centring on four issues.

First are the doubts as to whether reward strategies exist in practice and if organizations, as many of them claim, really are designing tailored reward policies to suit their strategy, rather than simply copying general market and sector practice and responding to external legislation (Trevor 2009). Second are the problems of reward strategy implementation (Trevor and Brown 2014), based on a common lack of employee understanding and engagement, and the widespread failure of line managers to implement pay and other reward practices in the intended manner. Third are the absence and difficulties of evaluating the effectiveness of reward management practices and their impact at both national/macro, and individual organization/micro levels. This lack of theory, frameworks and methods and tools for evaluation helps to explain the continuing controversy over the reward strategy concept (see also Wright, this volume).

Fourth are the challenges presented by total reward approaches, both in terms of challenging the original focus of reward strategy theory, research and practice on pay and incentives, but also because of the relative paucity of evidence as to the positive impact of reward management on employee engagement and behaviour and the seeming gap between the rhetoric and reality of total rewards strategies from an employee perspective. Total reward has become a stated component of, particularly large, employer reward strategies. But here again, while there are studies demonstrating the effectiveness of certain practices and links with employee engagement and organization performance, "there is little systematic research in this area" (Wright 2009) and a lack of validated research frameworks, methods and practitioner tools (Torre and Sarti 2013). This has led some to argue that the concept has in reality been used to support a low pay and employee exploiting management agenda (Holbeche 2014).

We have, however, seen a more broadly-based, multi-stakeholder and process-oriented model of reward strategy emerge, with greater attention being paid to these highlighted areas of implementation and enactment, measurement and improvement, and non-financial as well as financial rewards, integrating with thinking and research into employee engagement. But there is still considerable room for improvement in evidence-based practice and implementation. Demonstrated linkages between aspects of organization performance, employee engagement and reward practice, the intended outcome of any reward strategy, remain tantalisingly elusive and almost certainly support a 'best fit' not 'best practice' model. Yet the potential to improve remains large and these potential performance benefits surely make the continuing reward strategy effort worthwhile, both for practitioners and academics.

A divorce between reward practitioners unwilling to produce evidence as to the effectiveness of their methods, and business academics "failing to answer the questions that managers need answering" (Davis 2015; see also Bailey, this volume), has led to continuing controversy and debate in these areas, and a focus on the problems of reward strategy delivery rather than more relevant and "solutions focused" work (Gas and Gillis 1995). Bloom and Milkovich (1995) believe that, given the lack of research evidence for much actual reward management practice, "a better blend of theory, research and practice holds the promise of expanding knowledge about the forces and processes that shape compensation systems", resulting in more evidence-based rather than "faddish" practice in employers (Milsome 2006). Over 20 years later this wish remains to be fulfilled but surely should motivate us all to persist in our reward strategy work.

In terms of future research, this shift in the prevailing concept of reward strategy indicates a rich agenda to explore in the following areas:

- More multi-stakeholder studies comparing the views of employees and line managers on financial and non-financial rewards. Torre and Sarti (2013) note that rather than the adoption of a "top-down model" there is a need for more employee-centred "bottom-up analyses". Bruce and Skovoroda (2015) argue that we need a richer understanding of the idiosyncrasies of process, the organizational politics which help to explain reward outcomes. Werner and Ward (2004) note the paucity of research on how organizational culture affects reward systems.

- Given that the reality of reward strategy appears to be that it is a long-term and at least partly emergent process, more time-series case studies following the progress of specific reward strategies and changes in individual employers would be valuable. Guest (2011) believes we are still unable to answer core questions about the relationship between reward and HR systems and performance due to the limited amount of longitudinal research.

- This would also help in addressing the need to produce more studies which assess the effectiveness of reward strategies and changes, still a relatively under-researched area, testing out conceptual models in the area, for example (Armstrong et al. 2010, 2011).

- The nature and forms of reward communications which employees perceive to be most effective; how these perceptions vary according to type of employer and employee demographics; and whether employees are interested in the wider strategic objectives of reward practices, or primarily just about their own rewards.

- Studies into the effects of external variables such as the National Minimum Wage on the reward strategies that employers adopt and the effectiveness with which they are managed, as well as on the relationships between rewards in the employer and employee engagement.

References

Aon Hewitt. (2012). *Reward Fundamentals 2012: European research report*. Aon Hewitt, London. Available at: http://www.aon.com/unitedkingdom/attachments/thought-leadership/reward-fundamentals-full-report2012.pdf

Armstrong, M., Brown, D. and Reilly, P. (2010). *Evidence-based Reward Management: Creating Measurable Business Impact from Your Pay and Reward Practices*. London: Kogan Page.

Armstrong, M., Brown, D. and Reilly, P. (2011). Increasing the effectiveness of reward management: an evidence-based approach. *Employee Relations*. 33(2), 106–120.

Armstrong, M. and Murlis, H. (2007). *Reward Management: A Handbook of Remuneration Strategy and Practice*. London: Kogan Page.

Armstrong, M. and Brown, D. (2006). *Strategic Reward: Making it Happen*. London: Kogan Page.

Arrowsmith, J. and Sissons, K. (1999). Pay and working time: towards organisation-based systems. *British Journal of Industrial Relations*. 37(1), 51–75.

Bach, S. (2005). *Managing Human Resources: Personnel in Transition*. Oxford: Blackwell.

Bach, S., Kolins Givan, R. and Forth, J. (2009). The public sector in transition. In Brown, W., Bryson, A., Forth, J. and Whitfield, K. (eds.). *The Evolution of the Modern Workplace*. Cambridge: Cambridge University Press.

Bailey, M., Mariott, L. and Perkins, S. J. (2017). *Annual Reward Survey*. London: CIPD.

Banks, G. and Kepes, S. (2015). The influence of internal HRM activity on the dynamics within the black box. *Human Resource Management Review*. 25(4), 352–367.

Barber, A., Randall, B., Dunham, A. and Formisano, R. (1992). The impact of employee benefits on employee satisfaction: a field study. *Personnel Psychology*. 45(4), 55–75.

Baughman, P., DiNardi, D. and Holtz-Eakin, D. (2003). Productivity and wage effects of family-friendly fringe benefits. *International Journal of Manpower*. 24(3), 247–259.

Becker, B. and Huselid, M. (2006) Strategic HRM: where do we go from here? *Journal of Management*. 32(6), 898–925.

Beer, M., Spector, B., Lawrence, P., Mills, D. and Walton, R. (1984). *Managing Human Assets*. New York: Free Press.

Benkhoff, B. (1997). A test of the HRM model: good for employers and employees? *Human Resource Management Journal*. 7(4), 44–60.

Bevan, S. (2006). *New Realism in Reward Strategy*, Report 49, E-reward, Stockport, pp. 13–14.

Bloom, M., Milkovich, G. and Mitra, A. (2003). International compensation: learning from how managers respond to variations in local host contexts. *International Journal of Human Resource Management*. 14(8), 1350–1367.

Bloom, M. and Milkovich, G. (1995). *Issues in Managerial Compensation Research*, Cornell University Centre for Advanced Human Studies, Working Paper No 95 – 24, Ithaca, NY. Available at: http://digitalcommons.ilr.cornell.edu/cgi/viewcontent.cgi?article=1213&context=cahrswp

Bowey, A. and Thorpe, R. (1983). *The Effectiveness of Incentive Pay Systems*. London: Department of Employment Research Paper, 36, HMSO.

Brown, D. (2001). Using competencies and rewards to enhance business performance and customer service at the standard life assurance company. *Compensation and Benefits Review*. 33(4), 14–24.

Brown, D. (2014). The future of reward management: from total reward strategies to smart rewards. *Compensation and Benefits Review*. 46(3), 147–155.

Brown, D. (2008). Measuring the effectiveness of pay and rewards: the Achilles heel of contemporary reward professionals? *Compensation and Benefits Review*. 40(5), 23–41.

Brown, D. (2012). European rewards in an era of austerity: shifting the balance from the past to the future. *Compensation and Benefits Review*. 44(3), 131–144.

Brown, D. and Reilly, P. (2013). Reward and engagement: the new realities. *Compensation and Benefits Review*. 45(3), 145–157.

Brown, D. and Purcell, J. (2007). Reward management: on the line. *Compensation and Benefits Review*. 39(3), 28–34.

Brown, D. and Perkins, S. (2007). Reward strategy: the reality of making it happen. *WorldatWork Journal*. 16(2), 82–93.

Brown, D. and West, M. (2005). Rewarding Service? Using reward policies to deliver your customer service strategy. *WorldatWork Journal*. 14(4), 22–31.

Brown, W. and Walsh, J. (1994). Managing pay in Britain. In Sisson, K. (ed.) *Personnel Management: A Comprehensive Guide to Theory and Practice*. (2nd ed.). Oxford: Blackwell.

Brown, W. and Nolan, P. (1988). Wages and labour productivity. *British Journal of Industrial Relations*. 26(3), 339–361.

Brown, W. and Sisson, K. (1975). The use of comparisons in workplace wage determination. *British Journal of Industrial Relations*. 13(1), 23–53.

Bruce, A. and Skovoroda, R. (2015). *The Empirical Literature on Executive Pay: Context, the Pay-Performance Issue and Future Directions*. High Pay Centre Report, London, May.

Burgess, S. and Metcalf, D. (1999). *Incentives in Organisations: A Selective Overview of the Literature with Application to the Public Sector*, CMPO Working Paper 99/016, Bristol University.

Chadwick, C., Super, J. and Kwon, K. (2015). Resource orchestration in practice: CEO emphasis on SHRM, commitment-based HRM, and firm performance. *Strategic Management Journal*. 36(3), 360–376.

Chapman, J. and Cotton, C. (2010). A systematic approach to reward risk identification. *Strategic HR Review*. 9(2).

CIPD. (2005). *Reward Strategy Toolkit*. Available at: http://www.cipd.co.uk/hr-resources/practical-tools/reward-strategy.aspx.

CIPD. (2006). *Annual Reward Management Survey*. London: CIPD. Available at: http://www.cipd.co.uk/research/reward-management-survey.aspx.

CIPD. (2007). *Annual Reward Management Survey*. London: CIPD. Available at: http://www.cipd.co.uk/research/reward-management-survey.aspx.

CIPD. (2009). *Annual Reward Management Survey*. London: CIPD. Available at: http://www.cipd.co.uk/research/reward-management-survey.aspx.

CIPD. (2012). *Annual Reward Management Survey Supplement: Aligning Strategy and Pay*. London: CIPD.

Combs, J., Liu, Y., Hall, A. and Ketchen, D. (2006). How much do High Performance Work Practices Matter? A meta-analysis of their effects on organisational performance. *Personnel Psychology*. 59(3), 501–528.

Conference Board. (2001). *Engaging Your Employees Through Your Brand*. New York: Conference Board.

Corby, S., White, G. and Stanworth, C. (2005). No news is good news? Evaluating new pay systems. *Human Resource Management Journal*. 15(1), 4–24.

Cox, A. (2005). The outcomes of variable pay systems: tales of multiple costs and unforeseen consequences. *International Journal of Human Resource Management*. 16(8), 357–375.

Cox, A., Brown, D. and Reilly, P. (2010). Reward strategy: time for a more realistic reconceptualization and reinterpretation? *Thunderbird International Business Review*. 52(3), 249–260.

Davis, G. (2015). What is management research actually good for? *Harvard Business Review.*

EHRC. (2010). *Proposals for Measuring and Publishing Information on the Gender Pay Gap.* Equality and Human Rights Commission Report. Available at: http://www.equalityhumanrights.com/sites/default/files/documents/research/gender_pay_gap_proposals_final.pdf.

Fombrun, C., Tichy, N. and Devanna, M. (1984). *Strategic Human Resource Management.* New York: Wiley.

Gas, M. and Gillis, H. (1995). Focusing on the solution rather than the problem: empowering client change in adventure experiences. *Journal of Experiential Education.* 18(2), 63–89.

Gerhardt, B. and Rynes, S. (2003). *Compensation: Theory, Evidence and Strategic Implications.* Thousand Oaks, CA: Sage.

Ghoshal, S. and Bartlett, C. (1998). *The Individualized Corporation: A Fundamentally New Approach to Management.* London: Heinemann.

Grattan, L. (2000). *Living Strategies: Putting People at the Heart of Corporate Purpose.* Harlow: Pearson Education.

Grint, K. (2005). Problems, problems, problems: the social construction of leadership. *Human Relations.* 58(11), 1467–1494.

Guest, D. (2001). Human resource management: when research confronts theory. *International Journal of Human Resource Management.* 12(7), 1092–1116.

Guest, D. (2011). Human resource management and performance: still searching for some answers. *Human Resource Management Journal.* 21(1), 3–13.

Guest, D. and Bryson, A. (2009). From industrial relations to human resource management: the changing role of the personnel function. In Brown, W., Bryson, A., Forth, J. and Whitfield, K. (eds.). *The Evolution of the Modern Workplace.* Cambridge: Cambridge University Press.

Guest, D., Michie, D., Conway, N. and Sheehan, M. (2003). Human resource management and corporate performance in the UK. *British Journal of Industrial Relations.* 41(2), 291–314.

Heery, E. (1996). Risk, representation and the new pay. *Personnel Review.* 25(6), 54–65.

Herzberg, F. (1966). Work and the Nature of Man. Cleveland, OH: World.

Holbeche, L. (2014). Is it right to expect employees to be permanently engaged? In Gifford, J. and Robinson, D. (eds.). *The Future of Engagement: Thought-piece Collection*, Engaging for Success Report. Available at: http://www.cipd.co.uk/binaries/the-future-of-engagement_2014-thought-piece-collection.pdf.

Huselid, M. (1995). The impact of human resource management practices on turnover, productivity, and corporate financial performance. *Academy of Management Journal.* 38, 635–672.

Hutchinson, S. and Purcell, J. (2007). *Line Managers' Role in Reward and Learning and Development.* Research Report. London: CIPD.

Jenkins, D., Mitra, A., Gupta, N. and Shaw, J. (1998). Are financial incentives related to performance? A meta-analytic review of empirical research. *Journal of Applied Psychology.* 3, 777–787.

Kessler, I. (2001). Reward system choices. In Storey, J. (ed.). *Human Resource Management: A Critical Text* (pp. 159–76). London: Thomson Learning.

Kessler, I. and Bayliss, F. (1998). *Contemporary British Industrial Relations.* Basingstoke: Macmillan.

Larsen, H. and Brewster, C. (2003) Line manager responsibility for HRM: what is happening in Europe? *Employee Relations.* 25(3), 228–244.

Lawler, E. (1986). *The New Pay.* Los Angeles, CA: Centre for Effective Organizations, University of Southern California.

Lawler, E. (1990). *Strategic Pay: Aligning Organizational Strategies and Pay Systems.* San Francisco, CA: Jossey Bass.

Lawler, E. (1995). *The New Pay: a Strategic Approach.* Centre for Effective Organizations Publications, Paper G 95 – 3 (279). March. University of Southern California, Los Angeles, CA.

Lewis, P. (1998). Managing performance-related pay based on evidence from the financial services sector. *Human Resource Management Journal.* 8(2), 66–77.

Marsden, D. and Richardson, R. (1994). Performing for pay? The effects of 'merit pay' on motivation in a public service. *British Journal of Industrial Relations.* 32(2), 243–261.

MAS. (2016). *Money Advice Service launch new £7 million fund to support financial capability projects.* Available at: https://www.fincap.org.uk/what_works_funding

May, T. (2016). *A Country that Works for Everyone.* Conservative Party conference speech. Available at: http://www.independent.co.uk/news/uk/politics/theresa-may-speech-tory-conference-2016-in-full-transcript-a7346171.html

McGovern, F., Grattan, L., Hope-Hailey, V., Stiles, P. and Truss, C. (1997). Human resource management on the line? *Human Resource Management Journal.* 7(1), 12–29.

Meyer, J. and Rowan, B. (1991). Institutionalized organizations: formal structure as myth and ceremony. In Powell, W. and DiMaggio, P. (eds.). *The New Institutionalism in Organizational Analysis* (pp. 41–62). Chicago, IL: University of Chicago Press.

Michaels, H., Handfield-Jones, E. and Axelrod, B. (2001). *The War for Talent.* Boston, MA: Harvard Business Press.

Milsome, S. (2006). Evidence-based management: the knowing–doing gap. *IRS Employment Review.* 861, 14–15.

NHS Employers. (2014). *Reward Strategy Toolkit.* Available at: http://www.nhsemployers.org/your-workforce/pay-and-reward/reward/reward-strategy-toolkit/

Oliver, C. (1997). Sustaining competitive advantage: combining institutional and resource-based views. *Strategic Management Journal.* 18(9), 697–713.

O'Neal, S. (1998). The phenomenon of total rewards. *ACA Journal.* 7(3), 8–12.

Paton, N. (2014). Is total reward dead? *Employee Benefits Magazine*, December 10. Available at: http://www.employeebenefits.co.uk/benefits/total-reward/is-total-reward-dead/105861.article

Perkins, S. J. (2017). The social construction of executive remuneration in the UK: elite competition around codification and legitimation. *Journal of Organizational Effectiveness: People and Performance.* 4(1), 76–88.

Perkins, S. J. and White, G. (2016). *Reward Management: Alternatives, Consequences and Contexts.* London: CIPD.

Pfeffer, J. (1982). *Organizations and Organization Theory.* Marshfield, MA: Pitman.

Pfeffer, J. (1998). *The Human Equation: Building Profits by Putting People First.* Boston, MA: HBS Press.

Pfeffer, J. and Sutton, R. (2006). Evidence-based management. *Harvard Business Review.* 84(1), 62–74.

Porter, M. and Ketels, H. (2003). *Competitiveness: Moving to the Next Stage.* Economics Paper No 3, DTI, London.

Purcell, J. (1999). Best practice and best fit: chimera or cul-de-sac? *Human Resource Management Journal.* 9(3), 26–41.

Purcell, J., Kinnie, N., Hutchinson, S., Rayton, B. and Swart, J. (2003). *Understanding the People and Performance Link: Opening the Black Box.* Research Report, London: CIPD.

Reeves, M. (2016). The world just got more uncertain and your strategy needs to adjust. *Harvard Business Review* online. Available at: https://hbr.org/product/the-world-just-got-more-uncertain-and-your-strategy-needs-to-adjust/H039II-PDF-ENG

Robinson, D., Perryman, S. and Hayday, S. (2004). *The Drivers of Employee Engagement.* IES Research Report 408, Institute for Employment Studies, Brighton, Sussex.

Rose, M. (2014). *Reward Management.* London: Kogan Page.

Rucci, A., Kirn, S. and Quinn, R. (1998). The employee–customer–profit chain at Sears. *Harvard Business Review.* 76(1), 82–97.

Scott, D., McMullen, T. and Sperling, R. (2008). *Reward communications and pay secrecy: a survey of policies, practices and effectiveness.* WorldatWork Report. Scottsdale, Arizona, USA. Available at http://www.worldatwork.org/waw/adimLink?id=25110.

Suff, P. and Reilly, P. (2004). *Flexing your Remuneration: Variable Pay at Work.* HR Network Paper MP39 November, Institute for Employment Studies, Brighton.

Tahmincioglu, E. (2004). Gifts that Gall. *Workforce Magazine*, April, pp. 43–46.

Thompson, M. (2000). *The Competitiveness Challenge: The Bottom-Line Benefits of Strategic Human Resources.* London: Society of British Aerospace Companies and DTI.

Torre, T. and Sarti, D. (2013). *Total Rewards Systems: Towards an Operational Model.* Paper presented at the Fourth European Rewards Management Conference: What can we learn from a comparative approach? Brussels, December 2–3.

Trevor, J. (2009). Can pay be strategic? In Corby S., Palmer, S. and Lindop, E. (eds.). *Rethinking Reward.* Basingstoke: Palgrave Macmillan.

Trevor, J. and Brown, W. (2014). The limits on pay as a strategic tool: obstacles to alignment in non-union environments. *British Journal of Industrial Relations.* 52(3), 553–578.

Tsai, K. and Wang, J. (2005). Benefits offer no advantage on firm productivity? *Personnel Review.* 39(4), 393–405.

Ulrich, D. (1997) *Human Resource Champions: The Next Agenda for Adding Value and Delivering Results.* Boston, MA: HBS Press.

Ulrich, D. and Barney, J. (1984). Perspectives in organizations: resource dependence, efficiency, and population. *Academy of Management Review.* 9(3), 471–490.

Vernon, G. (2006). International pay and reward. In Edwards, T. and Rees, C. (eds.). *International Human Resource Management: Globalisation, National Systems and Multinational Companies* (pp. 217–241). Harlow, UK: Financial Times/Prentice Hall.

Watson Wyatt Worldwide. (2007). *Effectively Managing Global Compensation and Benefits*, September. Available at: https://www.worldatwork.org/waw/adimLink?id=17181

Werner, S. and Ward, S. (2004). Recent compensation research: an eclectic review. *Human Resource Management Review*. 14(2), 201–227.

White, G. (1996). The New Pay: Losing sight of reality? *Management Research News*, Vol. 19 (4/5), pp 56–58.

Wood, S. and Bryson, A. (2009). High involvement management. In Brown, W., Bryson, A., Forth, J. and Whitfield, K. (eds.). *The Evolution of the Modern Workplace*. Cambridge: Cambridge University Press.

Wright, A. (2009). Flexible benefits: shaping the way ahead? In Corby S., Palmer, S. and Lindop, E. (eds.). *Rethinking Reward* (pp. 206–223). Basingstoke: Palgrave Macmillan.

Zingheim, P. and Schuster, J. (2000). *Pay People Right! Breakthrough Reward Strategies to Create Great Companies*. San Francisco, CA: Jossey Bass.

8

REVISITING MASLOW

Enhancing staff psychological health for staff engagement through eupsychic reward management

Alan Fish

Introduction

The year 2018 marks the 75th anniversary of Abraham Maslow's (1943a, 1943b) seminal work on human motivation. Maslow identified five drives in 'prepotent', hierarchical order: physiological, safety, love, esteem and self-actualization. The principle is that *prepotency* – i.e., the greatest need influencing action – drives the movement of human need from level to level. Maslow was a behavioural psychologist who, when originally presenting his *human motivation* theory, had no experience in linking this theory to business, management or work circumstances. This chapter overviews Maslow, and identifies three issues linked to misunderstandings of his theory with consequences for reward management.

First, by treating Maslow's hierarchy as a *content theory* of motivation (i.e., internal factors, rather than contextual processes that may affect behaviour), Maslow's contribution to motivation generally, and reward management specifically, has been misunderstood and misappropriated. Secondly, *organizational culture* and *strategic human resource management* (SHRM) prescriptions (of which reward management is a key component – see Lawler 2000) lack balance; contributing to problematic outcomes tied to *staff psychological health* to support staff engagement. Thirdly, *balance and synergy* amongst reward management strategies and practices are rarely found; with *extrinsic* overemphasised to the detriment of *intrinsic* factors.

Originally, Maslow identified these five drives as underpinning human motivation associated with *life's* needs and experiences; *not* (in 1943 at any rate) as what underpinned *work* motivation. In the process, Maslow (1943b) identified 13 principles (see Table 8.1), as a foundation for human motivation. Some 22 years later, Maslow (1965) presented *Eupsychia*: a concept tied to what he believed represented *manager effectiveness*, operationalized as 36 integrated assumptions (see Table 8.2).

Typically, Maslow's 13 principles and 36 assumptions and, critically, their interdependence, are ignored, when employee motivational strategies are designed and applied. However, treated interdependently, Maslow's principles and assumptions are necessary to appreciate his contribution to work motivation and reward management. And, more generally, to debunk treating Maslow's hierarchy of needs as a content theory of human motivation.

Table 8.1 Maslow's 13 propositions for human motivation*

1	Integrated wholeness of the organism.
2	Any drive which is somatically based and localizable, e.g., physiological, is atypical, rather than typical.
3	Any theory should centre on ultimate goals, rather than partial, upon ends rather than means. Hence one's unconscious motivators, play a stronger role than conscious motivations.
4	There are usually various cultural paths to the same goal.
5	Any motivated behaviour must be understood to be a channel through which many basic needs may be simultaneously satisfied.
6	Practically all organic states are understood as motivated and as motivating.
7	Human needs arrange themselves in hierarchies of prepotency. The appearance of one usually rests on the satisfaction of a more prepotent need.
8	Lists of drives will get us nowhere. Any classification must deal with the problem of levels of specificity or generalization of the motives to be classified.
9	Classifications must be based upon goals rather than instigating drives or motivated behaviour.
10	Motivation theory should be human-centred not animal-centred.
11	The situation where reaction occurs must be considered, but the situation alone rarely serves as an exclusive explanation of behaviour.
12	The integrated whole is insufficient, the possibility of isolated, specific, partial or segmented reactions, must also be addressed.
	Maslow later added #13
13	Motivation theory is not synonymous with behaviour theory. Motivators are only one determinant of behaviour. Whilst behaviour is almost always motivated, it is also almost always biologically, culturally and situationally determined.

Source: **Maslow (1943a)* 'A preface to motivation theory', *Psychosomatic Medicine*. 5, 85–92.

Maslow's interdependent frameworks, SHRM and reward management

To support effective design and application, Maslow argued: (i) all human motivation theories should address the 13 principles; whilst (ii) manager effectiveness should reflect the 36 assumptions. The implications of failing fully to address what Maslow argued are highlighted by Meyer et al. (2004:991): "theorists and researchers interested in employee commitment and motivation have not made optimal use of each other's work". Also by Jung (1942/1948:170), who uses Maslow as a point of comparison for his own work: "we sit on treasures of information, whereby years of misinterpretation has prevented awareness and understanding of the knowledge which might otherwise have supported greater expertise; creating 'sacrosanct unintelligibility'". Reward management is compromised by misinformed interpretations and use of such theories.

Notwithstanding calls for improvements to *organizational justice,* the *psychological contract, job design, self-determination* and *meaningful management practices*, academic research outcomes have made minimal inroads into professional practice (e.g. Rousseau 2006). Maslow's work is no exception; in the face of Maslow's own (1965) critique, a *rules–process-control* mentality exists in organizations, represented by dysfunctional organization cultures, and toxic management practices. Little attention is given in SHRM to what Maslow (1965) saw as *staff's psychological health,* to enhance employee engagement. Contemporary demands for innovative and creative behaviour have also proven problematic, while achieving balance between extrinsics and intrinsics, is largely ignored.

Explanations for such circumstances are, first, organizational cultures not establishing the appropriate focus to support SHRM prescriptions. Secondly, because treating extrinsics and intrinsics equally is considered uncontrollable, or too esoteric, and thus irrelevant to what

Table 8.2 Matching Maslow's 36 eupsychian management assumptions*

Maslow's 36 assumptions	Matching
1 Everyone is to be trusted	1 Equity Theory
2 Everyone to be informed as fully as possible	2 Goal Theory
3 All staff want to achieve	3 Job Design/Redesign
4 No dominance-subordination hierarchy	4 Service Leadership
5 Everyone tied to common origin objectives	5 Organization Commitment
6 Good will come for all	6 Shared Value
6a Resolving synergy between selfishness and unselfishness	6a Shared Value
7 All staff have a healthy outlook on life	7 ERG Theory
8 Organization is healthy	8 Organization/Job Design
9 Everyone has the ability and willingness to be objective	9 Self-Determination Theory
10 There is no fixation on safety needs for staff	10 Self-Efficacy/Personal Growth
11 Staff tend towards self-actualization	11 Goal Theory
12 Everyone enjoys teamwork, friendship, harmony	12 Esprit de Corps
13 Hostility is reactionary, rather than innate in staff	13 Attribution Theory?
14 Staff are capable of looking after themselves	14 Self-Determination Theory
15 Staff are improvable [not perfect]	15 Goal Theory
16 Staff desire to feel important, needed, useful, respected	16 Job Design/Redesign/Equity Theory
17 People prefer to respect their boss	17 Esprit de Corps
18 People dislike fearing others	18 Self-Efficacy
19 Staff prefer to be a prime mover, rather than passive	19 Self-Efficacy
20 Staff want to improve things	20 Job Design/Redesign/Goal Theory
21 Growth occurs through all experiences	21 Goal Theory & Learning Theory
22 Staff prefer to employ all their capabilities	22 Job Design/Redesign
23 Staff prefer work to idleness	23 Self-Efficacy/Goal Theory
24 Staff prefer meaningful activity to meaningless activity	24 Job Design/Redesign & Self-Determination Theory
25 Staff prefer having a personal uniqueness/identity	25 Job Design/Redesign
26 Staff can tolerate stressful situations, endure anxiety, know creative insecurity	26 Self-Efficacy
27 Staff have a social conscience	27 Equity Theory
28 Staff value self-choice	28 Self-Efficacy
29 Staff like to be treated fairly and appreciated, preferably in public	29 Equity Theory
30 Staff can balance the good / bad duality	30 Self-Efficacy
31 Staff prefer responsibility	31 Job Design/Redesign
32 Staff receive more pleasure from loving something than hating something	32 Organization Commitment
33 Staff prefer to create rather than to destroy	33 Job Design/Redesign
34 Staff prefer to be interested, rather than bored	34 Job Design/Redesign
35 Staff prefer to identify with more and more of the world	35 ERG Theory
36 Need to understand the metamotives and metapathologies of the yearning for B-values – truth, beauty, justice, perfection, etc.	36 Goal Theory & Self-Determination Theory

*Maslow (1965) *Eupsychian Management: A Journal.* Homewood, IL: Richard D. Irwin, Inc. Dorsey Press. Matching prepared by author of this chapter, Alan Fish.

supports *organizational effectiveness*. Maslow (1965:188) argued that it is an overreliance on extrinsics, including the dominance of "obsessional neurotic behaviour from Theory X managers" (i.e., authoritarian management grounded in belief that management must counteract an inherent tendency among humans to avoid work). Managerial behaviour which has led to inappropriate responses to cognitive psychological factors which seek to improve person/organization fit, enhanced staff psychological health and effective staff engagement.

Problems have emerged, which arise from the failure to acknowledge two *dualities*. First, *the staff psychological health/organizational health duality*. Secondly, the *duality* between what key leadership teams value and what staff value. Evans (1999:328 and 332–333) explains dualities,

> (where) opposites are not viewed as 'either/or' choices, the appropriateness of which depends on a particular context, but dualities that must be reconciled or dynamically balanced . . . further arguing: duality theory leads us to focus on the tensions that are involved in any attempt to achieve fit, or to match tensions, which are also the key to understanding development.

Both need appropriate attention, if reward management strategies and practices are to achieve their intended outcomes.

In supporting close attention to dualities, Biloslavo et al. (2013:423–442) argue: ". . . organizations able to transcend dualities, will enhance their effectiveness and efficiency". Whilst Kets de Vries (2000) notes that organizations regularly performing above the norm have a set of corporate values which create the appropriate culture to support and sustain high performance; and where rewards are identified, known and distributed in line with the expectations of all stakeholders, leaving them better placed to support and sustain the outcomes which all stakeholders expect. Consequently, negative staff performance issues, e.g., poor organizational commitment, intention to quit, problematic psychological contracts, and workplace disharmony, have become all too common and they reflect absence of synergy between reward management strategies and practices designed to enhance staff psychological health and staff engagement.

Notwithstanding contemporary ideas on reward management and staff engagement/staff psychological health, e.g., self-determination theory (Ryan and Deci 2000; Gagne and Deci 2005), inherent in Maslow's *Eupsychia*, Kenrick et al. (2010) represent a lonely voice supporting staff psychological health, as a key issue impacting employee engagement. The implications of this are highlighted by Coplestone (2003), who finds it absurd that people may inform themselves of recent events, but remain ignorant of ideas that informed them.

Critically, however, Maslow (1965) also tied his analysis to theoretical psychologists, i.e., Freud, Adler and Skinner, amongst others, to support the application of psychological principles to enhance staff psychological health and ultimately engagement, treating contextual and processual factors interdependently. An argument central to Maslow's framework, but ignored in the literature; moreover, one which further debunks any idea that Maslow's contribution simply offered a content theory of motivation. Within this context, for Maslow, understanding *why* people work, work in a particular role, employ particular skills, and share and transfer their knowledge, and seek particular outcomes were also key issues to understand if transferring his ideas on *human* motivation to a *work* motivation context.

By ignoring the totality of Maslow, the foundation for *ineffective* reward management was laid. Maslow (1965) clearly highlights the *interdependence* of his five drives, his 13 principles, and his 36 assumptions; and, critically, highlights potential differences within and between various organizational levels, different ages, different genders, different cultural backgrounds, different family circumstances, and different socio-economic circumstances. Contemporary issues surrounding generational differences (e.g., Millennials) could easily be added to this list.

Reward management strategies and practices, however, reflect not simply imbalance, but the inability to address competing agendas. First, *what* organizational cultures value and support, and *how* SHRM prescriptions operate to support staff psychological health and staff engagement. Secondly, *what* organizational cultures reward (or sanction) versus *how* staff seek intrinsic value. An intrinsic outcome, e.g., happiness, is a derivative of *how* people work, more than *what* they actually do. Implications for job design, tied to the work of Hackman and Oldham (1976), are palpable. Coplestone (2003) comments on the imbalance resulting from how work practices and outcomes (by being reduced to quantifiable units) creates an illogical life; to wit, the imbalance, found in the opportunity cost of pursuing material X at the expense of failing to address emotional Y. Negative outcomes result that compromise staff psychological health and staff engagement.

In exploring how staff psychological health may be enhanced through a Eupsychic approach, Maslow (1965) analysed the work of high-profile management luminaries, such as Drucker, McGregor, Likert and Argyris. Significantly, Maslow notes how contributions from such authors muddied the waters regarding the effective application of *human* motivation theory to *work* motivation circumstances, including the effectiveness of managerial practice more specifically.

> It's really fantastic that one book after another will make a pious statement about this new development, and about organization theory and management theory, all resting on a knowledge and a new conception of human nature, and especially of motivation, and then proceed to say nothing whatsoever about values and purposes.
>
> *(1965:40)*

Maslow (1965:40 and 41) notes: "organizations which best care for the development of people, will win in the end". But "managers may feel they are being hard-headed if they use as the criteria . . . increased profits etc.". In so doing, the Eupsychian growth and personal development side of enlightened enterprises are neglected. An issue also highlighted by Csikszentmihalyi (1999:824) when commenting on questionable business and management practices:

> the connection between work activity and desired outcomes has become so dysfunctional, it is now almost impossible to label something a work goal, then provide a suitable reward, unless it can be matched by a metric.

A process supporting short-term agendas, in the hope of achieving long-term value.

Notwithstanding the ebb and flow of short-term investments, especially their perceived value, long-term stability and positive returns are usually valued. However, attempting to achieve long-term benefit from short-term practice is problematic unless short-term positive returns are re-invested immediately. A potential analogy can be found transferring in this to a work motivation context: offering short-term feedback (possibly a simple *thank you*) may be all that is needed by way of a valued reward; and goes to *how* short-term returns can be re-invested, to achieve positive long-term gain, e.g., staff engagement. It is ironic, therefore, that so-called *staff investments*, designed to positively impact staff engagement and organizational effectiveness, usually reflect short-term thinking, and an immediate gratification metric. This observation emphasising that *extrinsics* are overemployed; with potentially positive returns from *intrinsics* ignored. A contradiction which ignores Maslow's (1965:15) key theme – "human beings are born with a desire to achieve their maximum potential". Reward management strategies and practices reflecting short-term agendas (*extrinsics*), creating imbalance with long-term connections (*intrinsics*), risk ignoring staff psychological health and engagement.

Csikszentmihalyi (1999:824) also identifies where excessive attention to *extrinsics* has created what is a lack of investment in the wherewithal of employees to achieve value, and support their own well-being, thereby contributing to their psychological health. Absence of a focus which supports attention to valued *intrinsics* contributes to frustrations, lower performance, and potential psychological problems; with sanctions rather than rewards employed, raises questions as to the professional practise of reward management. Organizational cultures and SHRM prescriptions generally, and reward management strategies and practices in particular, which neglect *balance* usually fail to support effective long-term positive outcomes.

Such situations become more evident and problematic as one moves down an organization hierarchy. Consequently, staff psychological health is generally unacknowledged; moreover, it is compromised as having no connection with organizational effectiveness. With the exception of writers like Wahba and Bridwell (1976), Meyer et al. (2004) and Kenrick et al. (2010), little credence is given to the impact of failing to address staff psychological health.

The psychological literature on work motivation has been sidelined, save for findings on lists of drives to explain: (i) what motivates individual behaviour, and (ii) how? A focus which Maslow (1965) debunks. Under *Eupsychian* conditions, Maslow (1965:206–207) argued people can, more often than not, be influenced more by non-monetary than by monetary rewards. However, existing reward management practices, predominantly based in extrinsics, treat staff as inter-changeable parts, with staff psychological health compromised, thereby failing to consider how supporting staff engagement can redress problematic performance issues. However, new age commentary, e.g., *shared value* (Porter and Kramer 2011) and *self-determination* (Ryan and Deci 2000), highlight attempts to counter the overuse of extrinsics, to redress staff psychological health/staff engagement issues (or intrinsics) raised by Maslow.

Maslow has been criticized regarding the absence of an explanation as to how each element of his hierarchy applies to the day-to-day realities of reward management. These are unfair criticisms, for two reasons. First, Maslow (1965: 55) clearly questions how his theory of *human* motivation operates without change in a *work* context, versus his original application regarding the management of *neuroses*.

> The carry-over of this theory to the industrial situation has some support from industrial studies; but I would like to see a lot more studies of this kind before feeling finally convinced that this carry-over from the study of neuroses to the study of work is legitimate.

Secondly, no critique identified by this author acknowledges Maslow's 13 principles, or the 36 assumptions.

Supporting effective reward management

In supporting a Eupsychic approach, Maslow made a critical point: as communities become more affluent, as people become better educated, etc., people, and their societies, develop higher expectations regarding the value they seek, and the benefits they are prepared to accept. This goes to expectations from life's experiences; and, more importantly for our purposes here, from work experiences – i.e., the management practices, organizational life and value sought and received from work and employment. Highlighting the search for effective work/life balance, which Stum (2001:7) identifies as central to Maslow's framework: "at this level, the drive is to achieve a sense of fulfilment in balancing work and life responsibilities". Moreover, the balance and synergy needed to satisfy two expectations. First, achieving a balance between what extrinsics *and* intrinsics employees actually value, derived from their work, to then contribute to organization heath. Secondly, by seeking synergy between how intrinsics and extrinsics are delivered through organizational cultures to support staff psychological health and staff engagement.

Reward management needs to respond in more sophisticated ways to contemporary human and organizational contexts. Maslow's perspective that as one satisfies lower-order needs, higher-order needs become more important, needs renewed attention. With intrinsics usurping extrinsics as the dominant focus as people's life circumstances change they seek to satisfy higher-order needs, complemented by managerial styles, which are dismissive of control mindsets.

Maslow (1965) highlighted where two interdependent areas – organization cultures and SHRM prescriptions – need to impact. First, staff must have the capabilities to support their work roles/careers, including to achieve their own expectations of self-esteem, self-actualization and, ultimately, psychological health. Csikszentmihalyi (1999) supports this argument, whereby knowledge provides a point of measuring the required action, or the challenge. Capabilities permit intrinsic feedback. Experiences permit opportunities to 'test' ourselves. Attributes support balanced awareness. Promoting such a focus requires change to SHRM prescriptions; and a supportive organization culture must exist, whereby performance expectations are believed as achievable, and rewarded (or sanctioned) appropriately. This thereby reflects Hackman and Oldham (1976) on job design, Porter and Lawler's (1968) expectancy theory of motivation and Locke's (1997) theories on goals and incentives.

Person–environment fit and person–organization fit also highlight where balance and synergy between organizational cultures and SHRM prescriptions are likely to assist the design and application of reward management strategies and practices. Latham and Pinder (2005:496) note: "a limitation of. . . research is that interactions between the person and characteristics of the job or organization are usually treated as stable, rather than dynamic". Thus, any attempt at *fit* raises conflicts between what individuals value, and how organizations meet expectations (if at all). Prescriptions to enhance capabilities or rewards, especially a person's belief in their own self-esteem, to achieve staff psychological health and engagement, become clear.

However, remedying problems does not simply mean organizations should engage a particular skill, and then hope for positive outcomes. Fish (2012:6) notes the key importance of balance and synergy between organization cultures and SHRM prescriptions, to support a diversity of organizational needs; whereby linking (i) job design – staff selection – job redesign, (ii) role/organization/environment fit, (iii) role and career enhancement, and (iv) reward management strategies and practices is likely to positively inform the staff psychological health/organization health duality (see Figure 8.1).

Expectations of value for and by all staff from their work is increasing, a focus which key leadership teams need to address in managing the organization culture/SHRM interface; such that what (i) attracts and retains staff in the first place, e.g. perceptions of a good career, job satisfaction, self-actualization, etc., and (ii) what contributes to attrition, etc., in their absence, are known and responded to appropriately. Anything less contributes to frustrations and commitment problems, highlighting what Ryan and Deci (2000:68–71) note under the rubric of Self-Determination Theory:

> . . . that overuse of extrinsics, can compromise effective staff engagement, because how individuals acquire the motivation to carry out tasks, and how this motivation affects ongoing persistence, behavioral quality, and well-being . . . and the performance of an activity in order to attain some separable outcome, need to be understood.

Fostering intrinsics, even on an equal basis with extrinsics, appears anathema to orthodox organizational cultures. Critically, however, Meyer et al. (2004:999) note that "the effects of

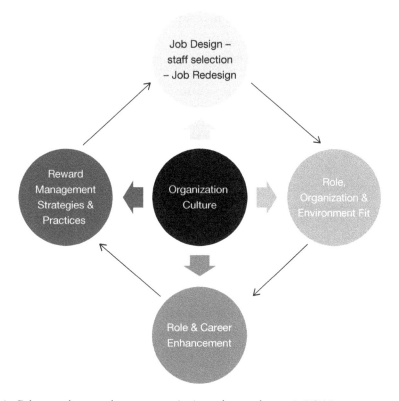

Figure 8.1 Balance and synergy between organization culture and strategic HRM

Source: Adapted from Fish, A. J. (2012) A Renewed Business Leadership Culture through a Refocused Mindset, White Paper, Guildhall Faculty of Business & Law, London Metropolitan University, p. 6: ISSN – 2396–8591.

personal needs, values, personality, incentives, self-efficacy, and outcome expectancies on goal choice [intrinsics] are mediated by their effects on goal regulation". This highlights that intrinsics are being negatively impacted by how organizational cultures are fostered. By supporting extrinsics, and ignoring intrinsics, organizations fail to consider how staff psychological health impacts staff engagement, and ultimately organization health. As Neal et al. (2005:505) highlight: "perceptions of organizational environment moderate the relationship between productivity and HRM, negatively".

Refocusing on intrinsics, the potential positive impact of shared value and self-determination theory on staff psychological health, and, ultimately, staff engagement, is highlighted. Such a focus also requires manager effectiveness and managerial styles to be redressed, which is a perspective supported by Ryan and Deci (2000:68):

> factors have been examined that enhance versus undermine intrinsic motivation, self-regulation, and well-being. The findings have led to the postulate of three innate psychological needs - competence, autonomy, and relatedness - which when satisfied, yield enhanced self-motivation and mental health, and when thwarted lead to diminished motivation and well-being.

A perspective which Maslow (1965:73) highlights through *Eupsychia*: "realistic perceiving is prerequisite to realistic behaving; and realistic behaving is prerequisite to good results".

Conclusions

As outdated as Maslow may seem, correctly interpreted and appropriately applied, his analysis offers important insights, regarding the *what*, and the *how*, of reward management, whilst in the process, enhancing staff psychological health, staff engagement and organizational effectiveness. Such a focus goes to how Maslow's *Eupsychia* identifies ways to redress problems through re-engineering organizational cultures and refocusing SHRM prescriptions. Facilitating more enlightened management strategies and practices and, in turn, acknowledging the need to treat the extrinsics and intrinsics of reward management interdependently.

It is more than a century since Parsons (1909) identified employee/work role fit; soon afterwards Woodworth (1918) noted the futility of *not* addressing psychology, when seeking improved workplaces. Critically, Parsons (1909:3) notes:

> an occupation out of harmony with its workers' aptitudes and capacities, means inefficiency, unenthusiastic and perhaps distasteful labor, and low pay; while an occupation in harmony with the nature of man, means enthusiasm, love of work and high economic value, superior products, efficient service and good pay.

Thus, synergy between organizational culture intentions and SHRM prescriptions is needed to achieve staff psychological health and staff engagement.

Integrating Maslow's three dimensions – drives, principles and assumptions – take us comfortably beyond what has traditionally been called a *content* theory of motivation to address what *process* theories, e.g., goal theory, job design and expectancy theories, and self-determination theory and shared value offer motivation and reward management.

Together, Maslow, Csikszentmihalyi and Kets de Vries highlight where staff psychological health and staff engagement can be achieved, especially where the interdependence of organizational cultures and SHRM prescriptions support three key interdependent challenges:

(i)   organizational goals and expectations are clarified for all employees,
(ii)   the roles of, and careers for, employees, support meaningful outcomes for all; and especially,
(iii) where valued opportunities are provided and supported for employees to enhance their self-worth and psychological health.

By not redressing Maslow's stress on the interdependence of his five drives, 13 principles and 36 assumptions, improved reward management strategies, and, subsequently, improvements to staff psychological health, organization health and staff engagement, have been compromised. Maslow's (1965) message, though, goes to his argument that the proper management of the working lives of human beings, of the way in which they earn their living, can improve them, and improve the world; and in this sense it can be a utopian or revolutionary technique. Maslow's overall framework, with its interdependent elements containing implications for reward management, may yet provide the focus to renew attention to employee well-being and engagement and thence organizational effectiveness; not by manipulative and coercive business and management, but through approaches which value what employees have to offer and how they may be helped to do their best.

References

Biloslavo, R., Bagnoli, C. and Figelz, R. (2013). Managing dualities for efficiency and effectiveness of organizations. *Industrial Management & Data Systems*. 113(3), 423–442.

Coplestone, F (2003). *A History of Philosophy: Greece and Rome* (Vol. 1). London: Continuum.

Csikszentmihalyi, M. (1999). If We Are So Rich, Why Aren't We Happy? *American Psychologist.* 54(10), 821–827.

Evans, P. L. (1999). HRM on the edge: a duality perspective. *Organization.* 6(2), 325–338.

Fish, A. J. (2012). *A Renewed Business Leadership Culture through a Refocused Mindset*, White Paper, Guildhall Faculty of Business & Law. London: London Metropolitan University.

Gagne, M. and Deci, E. L. (2005). Self-determination theory and work motivation. *Journal of Organizational Behaviour.* 26(4), 331–362.

Hackman, J. R. and Oldham, G. R. (1976). Motivation through the design of work: test of a theory. *Organizational Behaviour and Human Performance.* 16(2), 250–279.

Jung, C. G. (1942/48). *A Psychological Approach to the Dogma of the Trinity: Psychology and Religion - Collected Works*, vol. 11. Princeton, NJ: Princeton University Press.

Kenrick, D. T., Griskevicius, V., Neuberg, S. L. and Schaller. (2010). Renovating the pyramid of needs: contemporary extensions built on ancient foundations. *Perspectives on Psychological Science.* 5(3), 292–314.

Kets de Vries, M. (2000). Beyond Sloan: trust is at the core of corporate values. in Pickford, J. (ed.). *Financial Times Mastering Management*, Financial Times, 2 October: 10.

Lawler, E. E. III (2000). *From the Ground Up: Six Principles for Building the New Logic Corporation.* San Francisco, CA: Jossey-Bass.

Latham, G. P. and Pinder, C. C. (2005). Work motivation theory and research at the dawn of the twenty-first century. *Annual Review of Psychology.* 56, 485–516.

Locke, E. A. (1997). The motivation to work: what we know. *Advances in Motivation and Achievement.* 10, 375–412.

Maslow, A. H. (1943a). A preface to motivation theory. *Psychosomatic Medicine.* 5, 85–92.

Maslow, A. H. (1943b). A theory of human motivation. *Psychological Review*, 50(4), 370–396.

Maslow, A. H. (1965). *Eupsychian Management: a Journal.* Homewood, IL: Richard D. Irwin, Inc. Dorsey Press.

Meyer, J. P., Becker, T. E. and Vandenberghe, C. (2004). Employee commitment and motivation: a conceptual analysis and integrative model. *Journal of Applied Psychology.* 89(6), 991–1007.

Neal, A., West, M. and Patterson, M. (2005). Do organizational climate and competitive strategy moderate the relationship between human resource management and productivity? *Journal of Management.* 31(4), 492–512.

Parsons, F. (1909). *Choosing a Vocation.* Boston, MA: Houghton Mifflin.

Porter, L. W. and Lawler, E. E. (1968). *Managerial Attitudes and Performance.* Homewood, IL: Irwin.

Porter, M. E. and Kramer, M. R. (2011). Shared value: how to reinvent capitalism and unleash a wave of innovation and growth. *Harvard Business Review.* 89(12), 62–77.

Rousseau, D. M. (2006). Academy of Management 2005 Presidential Address: is there such a thing as "evidence-based management"? *Academy of Management Review.* 31(2), 256–269.

Ryan, R. and Deci, E. (2000). Self-determination theory and the facilitation of intrinsic motivation, social development, and well-being. *American Psychologist.* 55(1), 68–78.

Stum, D. L. (2001). Maslow revisited: building the employee commitment pyramid. *Strategy and Leadership.* 29(4), 4–9.

Wahba, M. A. and Bridwell, L. G. (1976). Maslow reconsidered: a review of research on the need hierarchy theory. *Organizational Behaviour and Human Performance.* 15(2), 212–240.

Woodworth, R. (1918). *The Dynamics of Behaviour.* New York: Columbia University Press.

PART II

Contemporary themes in reward management

The second segment of the volume casts an eye across the various issues – frequently controversial and contested – to the fore in contemporary reward management thinking, policy development and practice.

Greater transparency around employee reward determination – between levels of the workforce and in relation to demographic characteristics – has become increasingly prominent due to public and, in turn, regulatory pressure on organizational leaderships. **Alexandra Arnold and Ingrid Fulmer** argue for widening the lens to inform scrutiny around managing pay, illustrating the multidimensionality of transparency as a construct and the multiple levels at which it operates. Drawing on organizational justice theory, an assessment is provided of ways to evaluate transparency – in terms of processes, interpersonal communication and comparative outcomes.

Another question that has attracted considerable notice within current corporate governance debates has been the extent to which managerial actions are socially responsible and enable or inhibit sustainable organizational evolution. **Ewa Beck-Krala** and her colleagues offer an analytical focus on socially responsible reward programmes, exploring, in turn, the implications of both salaries and incentive payment plans for corporate social responsibility and sustainability, and how rewards may be designed to encourage employees to recognise their interdependency with multiple stakeholders in organizational life and beyond, through socially responsible and environmentally sustainable agency.

Evaluating investment in reward management practices is a topic of interest to all organizations, with a focus on securing the effective application of scarce resources. **Dow Scott and Ewa Beck-Krala** set out a proposed, multidimensional, framework with which reward programmes may be evaluated systematically; each element of the framework offers employers the means by which to assemble and review valuable information about the effects on the major stakeholders in their reward management activities.

The gender pay gap is a focus of significant popular and regulatory concern, intertwined with a far-reaching set of issues that have surfaced illustrating the use and abuse of power in the workplace. Using their recent research findings, **Duncan Brown and Catherine Rickard** analyse the stubborn persistence of gender pay gaps some four decades after legislation outlawing discrimination between men and women employed to undertake work of equal value. They compare and contrast action taken over the years by employers and government and argue that for a corrective outcome to be sustainable, a more integrated approach needs to be taken by multiple stakeholders over a significant time period.

Jonathan Chapman uses his direct experience as well as results from a programme of rigorous research to build and specify a more unified basis for theorizing the reward mix, i.e., the various elements that make up what employers offer to the financial services sector workforce in return for their contribution to desired business outcomes. Shifting attention from concentrating primarily on fixed and variable pay, the relative importance of the various components in 'the mix' is weighed enabling a more systematic basis for scrutiny of reward management practices in this sector, with potential wider application across the economy.

Executive remuneration is a contentious area within both academic and popular reward management literature. **Zara Whysall and Almuth McDowall** adopt a psychological perspective to assess reward–performance associations applicable to business leaders and an apparent disconnect with more nuanced behaviours necessary to secure sustainable organizations as evaluated by stakeholders beyond exclusively those holding financial shares. Informed by their recent research, questions are posed and addressed as to an appropriate direction for research, theory building and its practical application if the judgement that current levels of executive reward are unsubstantiated is to be reversed by more 'fit-for-purpose' corporate governance stipulations.

Clive Wright engages with an emergent understanding about the diverse nature of organizational workforce members, and scope to engage them, locating reward management as part of wider human capital strategies. In turn, he holds out the prospect of enhanced sustainable performance at all levels and across employee configurations internationally. His call is for corporate leaders to get better at listening to, and acting on, what employees themselves say motivates them in the broadest sense within the effort–reward bargain. Putting current and emerging technology to good use as a means of tapping 'employee voice'. Failure to respond to this managerial challenge implies willingness to continue in effect to waste what for most organizations is the largest single controllable investment.

The digital economy is a significant factor impacting on organizations and those who work in them, and **Matti Vartiainen** summarizes observable trends as these interact with choices faced in approaching contemporary reward management. New demands are evident on managers to respond to as yet still unspecified implications for the design of work roles at the human–digital interface, understanding the capabilities necessary to support organizational effectiveness under competitive market conditions where 'first-movers' may secure advantages over the less technologically developed, while balancing these with generational shifts in employee expectations around autonomous working and socially just reward determination.

Deploying employees to work as expatriates has long been a staple of work for HR specialists in traditional multinational organizations. In recent years, competitive pressures and changes to the composition of what counts as transnational operations and overseas work deployment, as well as growing pressures leading traditional MNEs to offer less generous terms to international assignees, have changed the landscape of expatriate reward management. **Susan Shortland and Stephen J. Perkins** apply equalizing differences theory to discuss the heterogeneity of expatriation types and questions around continued validity of *the* 'expat package', taking into account questions of organizational justice.

Despite the pressures on expatriate reward management, **Nicholas R. Prince and J. Bruce Prince** point to the increasing number of multinational employers as well as labour force mobility under conditions of economic globalization. With these changes, they argue, innovation is required to ways of offering incentives to diverse individuals and groups making up the global workforce to secure their willing cooperation with managerial priorities. Not only is a research agenda sketched, but ideas are also put forward as to how businesses may successfully use incentive elements within reward management investments in ways relevant to the composition and expectations of globally mobile working populations.

Marion Festing and Michael Tekieli review considerations influencing the balance multinational employers strike between standardized (i.e., irrespective of geography) and localized reward management practices. Their analysis goes further than firm-external and firm-internal considerations featuring in the published literature, surfacing ways in which the two thematic aspects may be theorized as interacting with one other when units of analysis are adjusted to encompass wider sets of reward practices and target employee groups within organizational role hierarchies. The resultant call is to pay attention to multi-level approaches, including psychological, social power and decision-making to enhance insights to be reached.

Drawing reflexively on extended participant observation across a number of case settings, **Romain Daste** tackles a question with which contemporary organizations seem to struggle: the effective valuation of work and, by extension, those employed to perform it. His conclusion draws attention to the interplay of espoused managerial intentions to conduct their reward management by the application of objective criteria and enacted practice coloured by political considerations – which may result in simply muddling along, with the consequent inefficiency comparing aims to outcomes this entails.

The rhetoric–reality gap observable in some contemporary reward management situations is explored further by **Marie Bailey**, with illustrations from the transport sector, standing at the interface between public and private sector employment. Further illustrating the risk of a reward management and wider HRM 'dark side' prevailing, evidence is presented of ways in which through ignoring or overlooking the possibilities inherent in taking an evidence-based approach to policy making and its practical implementation employee engagement with managerial intentions is put at risk, with the outcome that anticipated outcomes are sacrificed. Lessons are also drawn for academics if they are to secure positive impact from their theory-building and research endeavours, necessitating greater empathy with practitioners.

Reward management as *risk management* is delineated by **Jonathan Trevor**. Rewarding for performance is at the core of narratives describing contemporary managerial aspirations. But for the unwary, or for managements unwilling to embrace its full connotations as a form of social interaction around the psychological contract reflected in the employment relationship, more harm than good may be expected for those in search of organizational effectiveness. Based on empirical findings that control for industry effects and embrace a range of employee levels, a proposal is advanced for employers to shift away from the dominant *unitarist* logic of mainstream reward management, fundamentally to revise what they say and what they do to recognise the roles employees individually and in groups play in value creation.

9

PAY TRANSPARENCY

Alexandra Arnold and Ingrid S. Fulmer

Introduction

Pay transparency, the information that employees have about the pay of other employees in an organization (Colella et al. 2007), is currently a hot topic among scholars, professionals, employers, employees, politicians and the wider public. The volume of articles on pay transparency (and its opposite, pay secrecy) in newspapers, professional magazines and top scholarly journals has increased in the last few years, and professional HR associations such as the Chartered Institute of Personnel and Development (CIPD) in the United Kingdom or WorldatWork in the United States have started to address pay transparency issues in their compensation survey reports (e.g., CIPD 2015; WorldatWork 2016). The movement within organizations to adopt policies that promote greater transparency has been triggered to some extent by the increasing amount of pay information easily accessible to workers on the Internet. Online wage calculators together with platforms such as Glassdoor.com, Payscale.com or Salary.com, where employees share their own pay data publicly, are enjoying increasing popularity with workers. In addition, politicians have started to participate in discussions about pay transparency as a potential tool to reduce the gender pay gap.

Despite the growing interest, different parties still have mixed opinions about the effects of pay transparency (Colella et al. 2007). Supporters of pay transparency argue that it will increase employees' performance (Bamberger and Belogolovsky 2010) while reducing the gender and racial pay gap (Castilla 2015). Opponents of pay transparency argue that disclosing everyone's salary could cause envy and conflicts among employees (Bamberger and Belogolovsky 2017) and would equalize pay and thereby generate weak incentives for high performers and hard-to-find talent (Bartol and Martin 1989).

However, pay transparency is a multidimensional construct that can take many different forms, operate at many different levels, and be influenced by different types of organizational policies. In order to understand how organizational pay transparency policies affect employees and organizations, we first define organizational pay transparency and look at data describing the prevalence of different aspects of pay transparency. We then look at governmental regulations that might impact pay transparency policies, and follow this with a section where we consider the effects of pay transparency on employees and organizations. We will conclude with recommendations for practitioners, policy makers and scholars.

Definition and occurrence of organizational pay transparency

Broadly speaking, pay transparency policies refer to the extent to which an organization voluntarily discloses pay-related information to its employees and allows employees to discuss pay-related information with other employees inside the organization (Marasi and Bennett 2016). More specifically, we distinguish among three different aspects of pay transparency policies:

1 Pay outcome transparency (disclosure of pay amount)
2 Pay process transparency (disclosure of information on *how* pay is determined)
3 Pay communication restriction

In the following we will discuss each of these aspects in more detail.

Pay outcome transparency

Pay outcome transparency policies refer to the extent to which an organization voluntarily discloses information about the amount of pay to its employees. Such pay information can be released in many different forms, ranging from exact individual pay information to aggregated pay information (e.g., pay bands, ranges, averages) to minimal to no pay information. Companies like Buffer and Whole Foods Market and many state and local governments in the United States, as well as Alternative Bank in Switzerland, for example, share individual-level pay information with all their employees. However, companies that are fully transparent about pay outcome are the exception. In a recent survey by WorldatWork, a US-based association for compensation practitioners, only about 4% of responding organizations provide actual pay levels for all employees (WorldatWork 2016). In addition, some 37% indicated that they report base salary range for that employee's pay grade and 15% report ranges for all pay grades and jobs. For example, some government agencies publish aggregated pay information in the form of pay bands for different ranks and experience levels. In comparison, nearly half of the organizations surveyed in the WorldatWork survey indicate that they only disclose minimal pay-related information to their employees (WorldatWork 2016).

In addition, according to a recent CIPD survey with 715 organizations across private, public and third sectors in the United Kingdom, the amount of disclosed individual pay outcome differs among pay components (CIPD 2017). Organizations are the most likely to display exact individual respectively aggregated pay information for benefits (70%), followed by information on pay increase (59%), base pay (54%) and team-level variable pay (47%). The least amount of exact either individual or aggregated pay information (41%) is displayed for individual variable pay.

Glassdoor's Global Salary Transparency Survey, with responses from over 8000 employees from seven countries, shows that organizations' disclosure of individual salaries within the company also varies across countries (Glassdoor 2016). Employees report that organizations in the Netherlands are most likely to disclose salary (50%), followed by Canada (45%), the United Kingdom (45%), France (33%), the United States (31%), Germany (28%) and Switzerland (25%).

Individuals also differ in terms of pay outcome transparency preferences. This preference suggests that individuals differ in term of how much they value personal privacy over knowing what their co-workers earn (Smit and Smit 2017). Early research shows that about three-quarters of managerial employees preferred managerial compensation to be confidential (Lawler 1966), while Schuster and Colletti (1973) show that the preferences for pay secrecy (44%) were slightly higher than preferences for pay transparency (39%) among professional employees. However, a recent representative study conducted with about 1000 employees in Switzerland shows that preferences for pay outcome transparency might have changed (XING 2017). According to the study, 71% of the surveyed employees are in favour of publishing all incomes. More detailed results reveal distinct results for high- versus low-income earners. Employees with higher incomes (those with a yearly income of over 110,000 Swiss Francs) are more sceptical about publishing all incomes (55% are in favour) while employees with lower incomes (those with a yearly income of under 70,000 Swiss Francs) are more in favour of publishing all incomes (79% are in favour).

Pay process transparency

Pay process transparency policies reflect the extent to which an organization voluntarily discloses *how* pay is determined. Such procedural pay information can include information on the processes and criteria by which base pay, pay increases, variable pay and benefits are determined. Buffer, a social media management tool provider, for example, provides a standardized formula for calculating pay, where employees can fill in all the components of the formula and estimate pay outcomes (Gascoigne 2013). Being fully transparent about the processes and criteria by which pay is determined and distributed among employees does not necessarily mean that organizations disclose any individual's specific pay outcome.

The abovementioned WorldatWork survey (2016) conducted in the United States reveals that about 41% of organizations share information regarding the design of the pay programme with their employees. However, the number of respondents sharing such information decreased significantly from 49% in a 2010 wave of the survey to 41% in 2016.

Recent surveys conducted with HR professionals in the United Kingdom (CIPD 2017) also shows that the level of procedural transparency varies by the specific pay component. Organizations are most transparent about how benefits are determined and managed (51%), followed by base pay (31%) and pay increases (31%). Organizations are least transparent about how team-based variable pay (21%) and individual variable pay (20%) are determined and managed. In addition, results show that public sector and larger organizations are significantly more transparent about how pay is determined than private sector and smaller organizations (CIPD 2017).

Glassdoor's Global Salary Transparency Survey (2016), with responses from over 8000 employees, shows that employee-reported transparency, i.e., their understanding of how people are compensated at all levels in their company, varies from country to country. Pay understanding is highest in Canada (71%), followed by the United Kingdom (61%), the United States (60%), Netherlands (56%), France (52%), Switzerland (49%) and Germany (43%).

Pay communication restriction

Pay communication restriction policies reflect whether or not an organization allows employees to disclose and discuss pay-related information with other employees inside the organization (Marasi and Bennett 2016). Organizational policies can vary widely from informal discouragement (e.g., verbally transmitted at the job interview or by the supervisor) to formal discouragement (e.g., written codes of conduct) or even formal obligation (e.g., employment clauses). In addition, there might be specific pay discussion restriction policies for specific employee groups that have access to company-wide pay data, such as, for example, employees working in the HR department or employees with a supervisory function.

A survey among private sector organizations in 2001 shows that one-third of companies in the United States had policies forbidding pay-related discussions at work (Gely and Bierman 2003) despite its potential illegality. However, according to the Institute for Women's Policy Research

(IWPR)/Rockefeller Survey of Economic Security, the percentage of employees who perceive that there is some kind of pay communication restriction in the United States is much higher. The results reveal that about half of the surveyed employees in the United States indicated that they were either discouraged or prohibited from discussing pay-related information at work (Hayes and Hartmann 2011).

A representative employee survey conducted with about 1000 employees in Switzerland shows that only about one in every five employees discusses pay with their work colleagues (XING 2017) and that employees seem to have different preferences when it comes to organizational pay communication restriction practices (Smit and Smit 2017).

Examples of governmental regulations

In the following section, we will discuss examples of governmental regulations for the three forms of pay transparency policies: (1) pay outcome transparency policies; (2) pay procedure transparency policies; and (3) pay communication restriction policies.

Pay outcome transparency. In countries such as the United States, many state and local governmental entities have been required for years to publicly disclose public sector employees' pay information, in keeping with a general duty of accountability to the public and taxpayers. However, private companies' disclosure requirements in the United States have related primarily to executive pay (Gerhart et al. 2009). Organizations being investigated for gender-based pay disparities are, of course, obliged to turn over pay information to investigators (e.g., Nicas and Koh 2017), but since the Obama-era efforts to require reporting of pay by race and gender have been subsequently halted by the Trump Administration (Mann 2017), general disclosure of employee pay information by gender in the United States continues to not currently be required by law.

However, driven by concerns about the gender pay gap, recent initiatives that force organizations to disclose such pay information have been more successful in other countries. For example, under the new German Pay Transparency Act, employees in organizations with more than 200 employees have the right to request the pay information of work colleagues. Specifically, organizations have to display the average monthly gross salary of at least six colleagues of the other gender in similar positions and employees are allowed to ask for pay information on up to two pay components (Borgmann 2017). Beginning in 2018, under the Equality Pay (Transparency) Act in the United Kingdom, organizations with more than 250 employees will have to publish pay information, including bonuses, that show potential pay inequalities between male and female employees (Mason 2016), while the Swiss Federal Council is preparing a draft bill in which organizations with more than 50 employees will be forced to conduct an equal pay analysis every four years. After an external evaluation, employers need to inform employees about the extent of any potential pay discrimination (Wozny 2017). In Australia, the Workplace Gender Equality Act of 2012 requires non-public sector employers with 100 or more employees to report average earnings by gender within occupational category, together with other company profile information. Furthermore, organizations with 500 or more employees must have policies or strategies in place that support gender equality considerations (Workplace Gender Equality Agency, 2017).

Pay process transparency. There also has been a movement that aims to increase pay process transparency. In 2017, the German parliament passed a new Act on Pay Transparency, which will give employees working in organizations with more than 200 employees the individual right to inform themselves about the *criteria and procedures* used in determining pay (Borgmann 2017).

Pay communication restriction. In 2015 the Office of Federal Contract Compliance Programs in United States published a Final Rule that prohibits federal contractors or subcontractors from discriminating against employees and job applicants who discuss, disclose or inquire about compensation (OFCCP 2016), and the United States Court of Appeals has affirmed that pay secrecy policies violate workers' rights to discuss their working conditions as protected by law (Fulmer and Chen 2014). Similar to the United States, restricting pay communication in Switzerland is not based on legal grounds. In 2010, the Swiss Federal Court decided that compensation is not a business secret (Swiss Federal Court, 2010) and that, therefore, employees are free to talk about pay-related issues at work.

Consequences of organizational pay transparency

In the following, we will shed light on the consequences of organizational pay transparency. We will distinguish, therefore, between the three forms of pay transparency policies: (1) pay outcome transparency policies; (2) pay procedure transparency policies; and (3) pay communication restriction policies.

Pay outcome transparency

Pay knowledge. Theoretically, much of what we think we know about how pay motivates people is based on the assumption that individuals are able to evaluate their salary as competitive and fair or not. This implies that employees are aware of what others make, that they have the full information, and that their knowledge is sufficiently accurate to be used plausibly for social comparison purposes (e.g., to compare workplace inputs and outcomes/rewards with those of other employees; Adam 1965). In general, pay outcome transparency should increase employees' knowledge of other employees pay. However, studies indicate that employees' pay knowledge is moderate at best. A study of more than 6000 managers and employees across 26 US and Canadian organizations shows that about half of the employees surveyed know the grades/bands/levels of other jobs in the organization and that they are also aware of the average annual base pay increase awarded to employees in that organization (Mulvey et al. 2002). This is in line with the results from a representative survey of 1370 employees in Switzerland. Nearly half of the employees have a very low or low pay knowledge perception of other jobs within the organization (Grote and Staffelbach 2008).

Wage gap. According to the OECD (2017), the average gender wage gap is 14.5%, ranging from 4% in Costa Rica, 17% in the United Kingdom, 19% in the United States to 37% in South Korea. Politicians and scholars have long argued that pay outcome transparency would help reveal pay inequalities based on demographics such as gender, race or nationality (Burkus 2016; Castilla 2015; Lytle 2014). Addressing such pay differences would help to reduce both the intentional and unintentional pay discrimination still existing in many countries (OECD 2017). Research indeed shows that pay outcome transparency helps to reduce pay inequity. For example, in settings with higher levels of pay outcome transparency (e.g., state government and unionized workplaces) pay differences based on gender and race are smaller than in non-unionized private companies (Ramachandran 2012). In line with that finding, a recent longitudinal field experiment supports the notion that transparency in pay decisions reduces the pay gap (Castilla 2015). Specifically, introducing accountability and transparency procedures into the organization's pay for performance scheme reduced the gap for women, ethnic minorities and non-US-born employees after controlling for factors like performance evaluation, turnover and part-time status.

Pay for performance. Employees covered by performance plans at the individual, group, business or organizational levels has increased between 1987 and 2002 in Fortune 1000 Corporations (Lawler and Mohrman 2003). In fact, surveys have found that nearly 90% of responding US organizations use variable pay (WorldatWork 2016) and that about half of the surveyed organizations across private, public and third sectors in the United Kingdom offered a performance-related reward scheme (CIPD 2015). Thus, variable pay seems to be a prevalent HR practice to increase employees' performance.

Under individual pay for performance plans, pay will inevitably vary among employees. If organizations are transparent about their variable pay outcomes, employees are able to compare their variable pay outcome with relevant others. Employees are not necessarily unsettled by pay differences since they take into consideration both the inputs (performance) and the outputs (pay) to draw conclusions about fairness (Adam 1965). Pay differences should have less harmful effects if these pay differences can be explained by exclusively objective and easily observable performance differences (Larkin et al. 2012). Research has indeed shown that employees perform better under the condition of high pay outcome transparency if performance is measured objectively (Belogolovsky and Bamberger 2014; Futrell and Jenkins 1978; Huet-Vaughn 2013).

Yet pay comparisons can cause distress due to perceived inequity if performance is either not observable or biased (Larkin et al. 2012). For example, subjective performance measures are error-prone. The meta-analysis of Viswesvaran et al. (1996) shows that the mean inter-rater reliability for performance ratings was only 0.52. Thus, justifying differences in variable pay based on rather unreliable subjective performance measures is more difficult for organizations and could lead to never-ending discussions. Also, individuals consistently overestimate their own performance relative to others. For example, a study with engineers showed that nearly 40% assessed their own performance within the top 5% of their peers and 92% had the feeling that they performed in the top 25% (Zenger 2017). In addition, individuals also underestimate how much they are paid compared to the going market rate (Smith 2015). A PayScale study of 71,000 employees shows that two-thirds of employees who are being paid the market rate believe that they are actually underpaid. Such biases can cause inequity feelings as perceptions of input (performance) or output levels (pay) are inaccurate.

Pay process transparency

Letting employees know how pay is determined should increase their level of pay understanding. In general, employees' understanding of pay seems to be moderate. A recent study of HR professionals in the United States reveals that more than half of them believe that most or all employees do not understand their compensation philosophy (WorldatWork 2016). In line with this finding, nearly 400 compensation professionals shows that about half of these professionals believe that less than 40% of the employees understand how base pay, variable pay and the benefit programme are set up (Scott et al. 2008) and that only 36% of the employees understand how their pay range is determined and 41% of the employees how their base pay increase is determined (Mulvey et al. 2002).

There might be several reasons why organizations are not transparent about the processes and criteria that determine pay. For example, some organizations have not elaborated a clear pay strategy and therefore might not be able to explain the processes and criteria by which pay is determined and managed. This may be the case, in particular, for small and medium-sized organizations where the processes by which employees are rewarded have not yet been formalized. Another reason might be that organizations choose to be secretive because they want to hide certain inconsistencies.

In fact, especially for pay components that should increase employee motivation such as variable pay and merit pay raises, employees should know why they are paid in the way that they are and what they have to do to increase their pay outcome. In general, research has shown that employees' understanding of the pay system is positively related to employee satisfaction (Brown and Huber 1992; Judge 1993) and retention (Smith 2015), while employees' understanding of their work group pay plan increases their perceptions of procedural fairness (Dulebohn and Martocchio 1998). Such procedural fairness perceptions have been shown to be a crucial part of employees' attitudes towards and reactions to pay decisions. Folger and Konovsky (1989), for example, found that perceptions about the procedures used in determining pay raises were related to employees' trust in their supervisor and organizational commitment while Greenberg (1990) showed that employees' theft rate was significantly lowered when the reasons for a pay cut were thoroughly explained to employees.

Pay communication restriction

Organizations impose restrictions on pay communication to prevent employees from talking about pay-related issues at work. Employees who engage in internal pay information-seeking behaviour would violate organizational norms, and therefore likely face high social costs for doing so (not to mention the threat of real monetary costs if they were to be caught and terminated). Interestingly, communication restriction policies continue to be a prevalent phenomenon in the current work environment despite its potential illegality.

However, recent research shows that such pay restriction practices do not seem to hinder employees from talking about pay at work and might even backfire. Results from a longitudinal survey of employees in the United States showed that, contrary to predictions, neither formal nor informal communication restrictions were associated with lower pay discussion at work (Day 2012). Thus, employees who have pay restriction policies in place are just as likely to seek pay information as employees who do not have such restrictions in place. Thus, pay communication restrictions seem ineffective and could even lead to unintended effects. Restricting employees from talking about pay-related issues at work may raise suspicion and employees might question whether an organization's pay policies are fair or whether they want to hide unfavourable pay practices. To reduce uncertainty about the intentions and motives of an organization's pay practices, employees might be tempted to talk about pay-related issues even under the condition of extensive restrictions on pay communication.

Conclusions and recommendations

Pay transparency is a highly debated topic and opinions about it differ widely. In order to get a common understanding on the nature of pay transparency and how it affects employees and organizations, a clear definition is necessary. In this chapter we distinguish between three different aspects of pay transparency: (1) pay outcome transparency; (2) pay process transparency; and (3) pay communication restriction policies. Empirical research and policy makers have focused mainly on pay outcome transparency while pay process transparency and pay communication restriction policies play only a secondary role. Thus, future research should look at all three forms of pay transparency simultaneously to understand how these forms interrelate and whether different forms of pay transparency have different employee- and organization-level effects.

Organizations not only have to decide how to compensate their employees, but also how transparent they want to be about individual pay outcomes and about how pay is determined. While many public organizations have to share individual pay outcomes, private companies mostly do so on a voluntary basis. However, politicians across the globe put more pressure on public organizations to increase pay transparency in order to address the gender pay gap. Especially for larger organizations, new pay outcome and pay process transparency policies have been introduced recently. However, the majority of employees are employed by small and medium-sized organizations. For example, in Switzerland only 31%, in Germany 38% and in the

United Kingdom 47% of the employees are employed by large organizations with more than 250 employees (BFS 2017). Thus, in order to reduce the gender pay gap it might also be necessary to introduce pay transparency policies for smaller organizations.

If individual pay outcome is disclosed, some employees will inevitably compare their income with that of others and draw conclusions about whether or not pay is fairly distributed. Employees will be more likely to accept pay differences if they can be explained. For example, differences in performance pay that is based on objective performance measures such as piece-rate or sales is easier to explain than pay differences that stem, for example, from subjective performance evaluations. However, variable pay will only unfold its full potential if employees have a clear understanding of how variable pay is determined and what they have to do to increase their pay outcome, Thus, if organizations are reluctant to share individual pay outcomes with their employees, they should at least consider sharing the criteria and processes by which individual variable pay is determined.

Organizations that choose to be secretive about individual pay outcomes might think about displaying aggregate pay information (e.g., means, bands). That employees know where they are standing and have at least an idea of how much more they might be able to make in the future. Displaying aggregate pay information might help shaping more realistic assessments of how much other employees are making without displaying any individual pay outcome information.

Finally, organizations should think twice when it comes to pay communication restriction policies. About half of the surveyed employees in the US perceive some kind of pay communication restriction (Hayes and Hartmann 2011). Even though such policies have the intention to reduce pay discussion at work, evidence suggest that pay communication restriction policies do not hinder employees from talking about pay at work (Day 2012). On the contrary, such policies might backfire as they raise suspicions and could lead to lower levels of trust in the organization.

References

Adam, J. S. (1965). Toward an understanding of inequity. *Journal of Abnormal and Social Psychology*. 67, 422–436.

Bamberger, P. and Belogolovsky, E. (2010). The impact of pay secrecy on individual task performance. *Personnel Psychology*. 63(4), 965–996.

Bamberger, P., and Belogolovsky, E. (2017). The dark side of transparency: how and when pay administration practices affect employee helping. *Journal of Applied Psychology*. 102(4), 658–671.

Bartol, K. M. and Martin, D. C. (1989). Effects of dependence, dependency threats, and pay secrecy on managerial pay allocations. *Journal of Applied Psychology*. 74(1), 105–113.

Belogolovsky, E. and Bamberger, P. A. (2014). Signaling in secret: pay for performance and the incentive and sorting effects of pay secrecy. *Academy of Management Journal*. 57(6), 1706–1733.

BFS. (2017). *Struktur der Schweizer KMU 2014*. Neuchâtel: BFS.

Borgmann, B. (2017). *Germany: New act on pay transparency*. Available at: https://www.shrm.org/resourcesandtools/legal-and-compliance/employment-law/pages/germany-pay-transparency.aspx, accessed on September 8, 2017.

Brown, K. A. and Huber, V. L. (1992). Lowering floors and raising ceilings: A longitudinal assessment of the effects of an earnings-at-risk plan on pay satisfaction. *Personnel Psychology*. 45(2), 279–311.

Burkus, D. (2016). Why being transparent about pay is good for business. *Wall Street Journal*. Available at: http://www.wsj.com/articles/why-being-transparent-about-pay-is-good-for-business-1464660062

Castilla, E. J. (2015). Accounting for the gap: a firm study manipulating organizational accountability and transparency in pay decisions. *Organization Science*. 26(2), 311–333.

CIPD. (2015). *Reward Management 2014–15*. London: CIPD.

CIPD. (2017). *Reward Management: Annual Survey Report 2017*. London: CIPD.

Colella, A., Paetzold, R. L., Zardkoohi, A. and Wesson, M. J. (2007). Exposing pay secrecy. *Academy of Management Review*. 32(1), 55–71.

Day, N. E. (2012). Pay equity as a mediator of the relationships among attitudes and communication about pay level determination and pay secrecy. *Journal of Leadership & Organizational Studies*. 19(4), 462–476.

Dulebohn, J. H. and Martocchio, J. J. (1998). Employee perceptions of the fairness of work group incentive pay plans. *Journal of Management*. 24(4), 469–488.

Folger, R. and Konovsky, M. A. (1989). Effects of procedural and distributive justice on reactions to pay raise decisions. *Academy of Management Journal*. 32(1), 115–130.

Fulmer, I. S. and Chen, Y. (2014). How communication affects employee knowledge of and reactions to compensation systems. In Miller, V. and Gordeno, M. (eds.). *Meeting the Challenge of Human Resource Management: A Cperspective* (pp. 167–178). New York: Routledge/Taylor & Francis.

Futrell, C. M. and Jenkins, O. C. (1978). Pay secrecy versus pay disclosure for salesmen: a longitudinal study. *Journal of Marketing Research*. 15(2), 214–219.

Gascoigne, J. (2013). Transparency introducing open salaries at Buffer: our transparent formula and all individual salaries. Available at: https://open.buffer.com/introducing-open-salaries-at-buffer-including-our-transparent-formula-and-all-individual-salaries/, accessed on September 26, 2017.

Gely, R. and Bierman, L. (2003). Pay secrecy/confidentiality rules and the National Labor Relations Act. *Journal of Labor and Employment Law*. 6, 120–156.

Gerhart, B., Rynes, S. L. and Fulmer, I. S. (2009). Pay and performance: individuals, groups, and executives. *The Academy of Management Annals*. 3(1), 251–315.

Glassdoor. (2016). *Global Salary Transparency Survey*. Available at www.glassdoor.com.

Greenberg, J. (1990). Employee theft as a reaction to underpayment inequity: the hidden cost of pay cuts. *Journal of Applied Psychology*. 75(6), 661–668.

Grote, G. and Staffelbach, B. (2008). *Schweizer HR-Barometer 2008: Lohnzufriedenheit und psychologischer Vertrag*. (G. Grote and B. Staffelbach, Eds.). Zürich: NZZ Verlag.

Hayes, J. and Hartmann, H. (2011). *Women and Men Living on the Edge: Economic Insecurity after the Great Recession*. Washington: IWPR/Rockefeller Survey of Economic Security.

Huet-Vaughn, E. (2013). *Striving for Status: A Field Experiment on Relative Earnings and Labor Supply for Their Consistently Fruitful Feedback*. Available at: http://econgrads.berkeley.edu/emilianohuet-vaughn/jobmarket/

Judge, T. A. (1993). Validity of the dimensions of the pay satisfaction questionnaire: evidence of differential prediction. *Personnel Psychology*. 46(2), 331–355.

Larkin, I., Pierce, L. and Gino, F. (2012). The psychological costs of pay-for-performance: Implications for the strategic compensation of employees. *Strategic Management Journal*. 33, 1194–1214.

Lawler III, E. E. (1966). The mythology of management compensation. *California Management Review*. 9, 11–22.

Lawler, E. E. and Mohrman, S. A. (2003). *Pay Practices in Fortune 1000 Corporations* (vol. 6).

Lytle, T. (2014). Making pay public. *HR Magazine*. Available at: https://www.shrm.org/hr-today/news/hr-magazine/Pages/0914-salary-transparency.aspx

Mann, T. (2017). White House won't require firms to report pay by gender, race. Available at t-require-firms-to-report-pay-by-gender-race-1504047656 accessed September 26, 2017.

Marasi, S. and Bennett, R. J. (2016). Pay communication: where do we go from here? *Human Resource Management Review*. 26(1), 50–58.

Mason, R. (2016). Gender pay gap reporting for big firms to start in 2018. *The Guardian*.

Mulvey, P. W., LeBlanc, P. V., Heneman, R. L. and McInerney, M. (2002). Study finds that knowledge of pay process can beat out amount of pay in employee retention, organizational effectiveness. *Journal of Organizational Excellence*. 21(4), 29–42.

Nicas, J., and Koh, Y. (2017). Google's "trust us" approach doesn't satisfy pay gap skeptics. Available at: https://www.wsj.com/articles/googles-trust-us-approach-doesnt-satisfy-pay-gap-skeptics-1498302004 accessed on September 26, 2017.

OECD. (2017). *Gender Wage Gap*. Available at: https://data.oecd.org/earnwage/gender-wage-gap.htm, accessed on September 26, 2017.

OFCCP. (2016). *Frequently asked questions: Pay transparency regulations*. Available at: https://www.dol.gov/ofccp/regs/compliance/faqs/PayTransparencyFAQs.html, accessed on September 8, 2017.

Ramachandran, G. (2012). Pay transparency. *Penn State Law Review*. 116(4), 1043–1079.

Schuster, J. R. and Colletti, J. A. (1973). Pay secrecy: who is for and against it? *Academy of Management Journal*. 16(1), 35–40.

Scott, D., Sperling, R. S., Mcmullen, T. and Bowbin, B. (2008). A study on reward communications: methods for improvement of employee understanding. *WorldatWork Journal*. 17(3), 6–20.

Smit, B., and Smit, T. (2017). Aligning organizational pay secrecy policies and employee preferences: a person–environment fit perspective. *Forthcoming in Human Resource Management Journal*.

Smith, D. (2015). Most people have no idea whether they're paid fairly. *Harvard Business Review*.

Viswesvaran, C., Ones, D. S. and Schmidt, F. L. (1996). Comparative analysis of the reliability of job performance ratings. *Journal of Applied Psychology*. 81(5), 557–574.

WorldatWork. (2016). *Compensation Programs and Practices Survey*. Available at: http://www.worldatwork. org/waw/adimLink?id=65522.

Wozny, N. (2017). Sommaruga macht Ernst mit Lohntransparenz. *Tages Anzeiger*.

XING. (2017). *Repräsentative Studie zu Einkommen und Lohn-Fairness*. Zürich.

Zenger, B. T. (2017). The downside of full pay transparency. *Wall Street Journal*.

10

SOCIALLY RESPONSIBLE AND SUSTAINABLE REWARDS PROGRAMMES

The new frontier

Ewa Beck-Krala, Dow Scott and Katarzyna Klimkiewicz

Introduction

Human resources comprises an essential component of an organization, and since Human Resource Management (HRM) deals with people, it follows logically that each strategic decision made is, in essence, a moral one, as Freeman and Gilbert (1988) have noted. According to Armstrong (2010), HRM is "a strategic and coherent approach to the management of an organization's most valued assets: the people working there who individually and collectively contribute to the achievement of its objectives". However, achieving organizational success requires more than just managing the employees of an organization; it must also incorporate the values of multiple stakeholders, those individuals (or groups of individuals) who affect or may be affected by the organization: stockholders, employees, customers, suppliers, local communities, governmental administration, as well as the environment, that is described as a *silent stakeholder* (Freeman 1984).

Organizations should identify their key stakeholders when designing a strategic plan and a coherent HRM approach that achieves organizational goals and supports people without compromising their integrity. However, in practice, strategies most often only focus on achieving the objectives of the owners or stockholders. That is why some researchers use the terms *human resource consumption* or *exploitation* instead of HRM or HR development (e.g., Ehnert 2008). Work-related stress, work–family conflicts, health problems, and burnout are only some of the examples of the consequences of modern workplace practices. Other researchers posit that treating employees solely as resources or assets violates their humanity (Crane and Matten 2010). Consequently, we may ask how HRM sees employees: is it purely an instrumental view, where the organization uses all available resources to achieve its ends (i.e., the cost of doing business) or is it a holistic view that recognizes the intrinsic value of the people working within the organization as a justifiable end in and of itself? The Harvard HRM model, considered best practices, explains that the interests of various stakeholders must be fused in HRM and business strategies in order to build high levels of employee commitment (Beer and Eisenstat 2009).

Thus, even if people are viewed as organizational assets, we must recognize their needs, individual goals and expectations in order to obtain their commitment and best efforts. This requires a broader look at how people are managed within organizations; it requires an assessment of HR policies and procedures, according to their contributions across the triple bottom line of economic, societal and environmental issues (Elkington 1998). It is important that organizations not only avoid practices that may injure or limit chances for development in terms of the triple bottom line, but also fulfil promises given to multiple stakeholders. This holistic approach to management provides the rationale for Corporate Social Responsibility (CSR), which underlines the importance of sustainability of the value creation process (Laszlo 2008). Therefore, CSR is recognized as a business strategy focused on both improving corporate performance in a wide sense via economic, environmental and societal outputs, as well as preventing possible negative societal impacts of business operations and practices (European Commission 2011).

CSR can be integrated with a business strategy to varying degrees and for different purposes (Carroll, 1999). For some organizations, CSR may become a central strategy (e.g., providing social and environmental innovations, social entrepreneurship) or may encourage initiatives that are socially and environmentally responsible (e.g., customer and employee education, work–life balance, and a reduction in the use of natural resources). Organizations can also carry out CSR initiatives that support their business strategy (e.g., organizations that operate in the environmental sector can undertake pro-ecological investments to limit and/or to compensate for any potential negative environmental impact). Finally, organizations can use their resources to handle stakeholder expectations and challenges occurring in the environment (e.g., an IT company may develop an application that helps solve certain social issues).

In this chapter, we identify the linkage between CSR and rewards and explain how rewards support socially responsible business outcomes for both internal and external stakeholders. Rewards are examined in terms of philosophy, strategy, policies and programmes as they relate to pay level, pay structure, pay system and benefits.

Corporate Social Responsibility and sustainability within the context of rewards

Corporate Social Responsibility (CSR) and sustainability begin with the beliefs and values that organizational strategies and goals incorporate social justice, are responsive to multiple stakeholders, and meet the needs of the present without compromising the ability of future generations to meet their own needs (Brundtland Commission 1987). HRM, in large part, defines the relationship between the organization and the employees who work there (Becker and Huselid, 2009). Working with senior management, HRM determines who will be employed and under what conditions, the commitment of the organization to diversity and equal opportunities, and the extent to which information will be shared with employees and the rewards employees will receive as contributors to the organization's success (Barrena-Martínez et al. 2016; Ehnert 2008; Thom and Zaugg 2002). All of these aspects of HRM, when incorporating CSR and the sustainability perspective, are part of the Sustainable Work System (SWS), which is aimed to prevent negative outcomes of intense HR practices (e.g., high workload, stress, and the lack of a work–life balance), providing a supportive work environment (e.g., training, constructive employment relations, cooperation, trust), employability, motivation, and allowing for regeneration and development of HR, as well as providing balance between the quality of work life and organizational performance (Docherty et al. 2002; Ehnert 2008).

It has been argued that among the many functions of rewards systems, aligning employee interests with the goals of the organization and encouraging CSR and sustainability are core elements (Thom 2002; Thom and Zaugg 2002). Responsible rewards integrate the interests of all stakeholders (especially owners, employees, and customers) and motivate employees towards the adoption of socially responsible behaviours. Klimkiewicz and Beck-Krala (2015) assert (p. 75) that responsible rewarding should "recognize the role of human subjectivity in organizational and employee matters and create favourable conditions for further sustainable development of the organization and its employees (and all other stakeholders of the organization)". Here lies the challenge, as the role of HRM is to provide a rewards system that supports the organization's business strategy, which most often involves generating profits or earnings, gaining market share, and increasing the value of the organization (Freeman 1984; Freeman et al. 1991; Gross and Friedman 2004; Armstrong and Brown 2005, Brown 2014), as well as promoting an organization with cultural values linked to CSR and sustainability (Klimkiewicz 2011; Wheeler et al. 2003). Research indicates that organizations in which sustainability and CSR are a central part of the managerial culture are more attractive to potential employees (Jones and Willness 2013; Albinger and Freeman 2000). When management shares similar values with employees, it sends a strong message to employees that management will take care of them and, as a result, employees will be proud to work for the organization (Jones and Willness 2013). Recent research shows that 76% of employees (mostly Millennials) consider a company's social and environmental commitments when deciding where to work, and 64% will not accept a job with a potential employer that does not have a strong CSR (Cone Communications Millennial Employee Engagement Study 2016).

Although CSR and sustainability are popular topics in the management and human resource literature, few researchers have explored this issue in the context of rewards (Linder and Mottis 2013; Sahakiants et al. 2015). When one does consider CSR and sustainability within the context of rewards, two perspectives emerge (as shown in Figure 10.1). First, one can consider whether salary levels, incentives, employee benefits, and the work environment support CSR and sustainability and how these programmes may influence employee decisions with CSR and sustainability implications. The second perspective is how rewards encourage employees to take socially responsible and environmentally sustainable actions, which could include making charitable donations and volunteering to support community programmes. The second

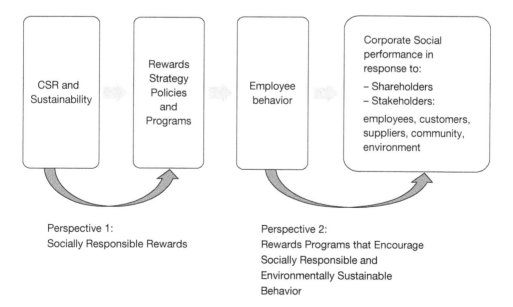

Figure 10.1 The influence of CSR and Sustainability on rewards programs – two perspectives

perspective is often referred to as Corporate Social Performance (CSP), which means evaluating corporate performance in terms of the triple bottom line. CSP is linked to the degree to which CSR motivates actions on behalf of a company and delivers outcomes of societal benefit (Blowfield and Murray 2014).

This chapter examines both perspectives in terms of rewards design and implementation and if and how these programmes promote an organizational culture of social responsibility and sustainability.

Perspective 1: Socially responsible and sustainable rewards

The first perspective of assuring sustainability and socially responsible rewards within an organization focuses on ensuring the consistency of the rewards strategy, processes, and programmes with the core values and principles of social responsibility and sustainability. Practices within rewards may vary, depending on how deeply the organization is committed to CSR and how seriously it treats its core values (Carroll 1999). The challenges of creating socially responsible rewards become pronounced in a global perspective, as companies integrate rewards strategies across countries with differing laws, traditions, and cultures (Scott et al. 2011).

This perspective helps managers consider the possible weaknesses of rewards systems. Taking this point of view, organizations may try to avoid any harm that the rewards system may create when it does not ensure compliance with applicable social norms and laws or by intentionally or unintentionally motivating employees to unethical behaviours. When the organization is strongly committed to CSR, its rewards will create a socially responsible and sustainable environment and employee well-being.

The **Principles of Socially Responsible Rewards** include:

- Legal and liveable
- Safe
- Equitable
- Transparent
- Economically sustainable
- Creates employee well-being
- Does not harm other stakeholders.

Legal rewards means that rewards must be compliant with the specific labour standards of the country in which the organization operates. Many global companies have been accused of being irresponsible to their employees through providing poor working conditions, abusing child labour laws, forcing overtime, or abusing human rights (Crane et al. 2008:229). A global organization is compliant with international directives and the law in the particular countries where it operates (in the EU, for example, companies follow both national and international directives). Rewards can support human rights or at least not harm (the stakeholders). Specific issues most often concerned with legalities include minimum wages that are set in each country, working hours, obligatory wage costs, equal pay opportunities, taxes, leave options, obligatory bonuses, advancement opportunities, termination pay, unionization, and so on. Annually auditing this compliance with legislation is critical to the sustainability of the organization.

A living wage is defined as the minimum income necessary for a worker to meet basic needs. Although most would agree that a living wage is an essential element of a socially responsible rewards system, establishing what this means in reality is challenging. Given that cultural norms and living conditions vary across countries, a living wage may differ accordingly. Should a living wage cover just the worker or the family? Should it include two wage earners? How many dependents should it support? Is the assertion that "a low-paid job is better than no job" ever justifiable?

Safe rewards involve providing safe and healthy working conditions and reducing workplace-related injuries and illnesses. Similarly, in this case, rewards should be compliant with national laws and collective agreements on Occupational Safety and Health (OSH) issues. For example, incentive programmes may put too much pressure on employees who will work excessively long hours, not report accidents, or will take on too much risk associated with dangerous conditions. All rewards programmes must be systematically reviewed to fulfill changing legal requirements in this regard.

Equitable rewards are consistent with societal norms (social justice) and do not encourage employees to participate in unethical or illegal behaviour. Unfortunately, fairness is difficult to define and is often to be in the eye of the beholder. Therefore, we distinguish between objective fairness (equity) and perceived fairness (Johnson 2012). The first construct covers whether an outside observer, unaffected by compensation decisions, would view a compensation programme as fair (Johnson 2012:1), whereas perceived fairness considers whether individual employees in an organization view their compensation as fair.

The context of equitable rewards usually considers equal pay (usually fair pay grades, fair bonuses) and equal opportunity for promotions and raises (proper promotion and raise criteria). In many regions (as, for example, the US and the EU) employees are expected to receive equal pay for equal work, regardless of gender, race, national origin, religion, or age.

When designing their rewards systems in the context of equitable rewards, organizations need to attend to four forms of equity: external, internal, individual and procedural (Folger and Konovsky 1989; Simons and Roberson 2003). This is not easy, as they may be in conflict with one another (Milkovich and Newman 2002).

External equity refers to the fairness of the rewards for specific jobs in an organization compared with similar jobs in the labour market. By contrast, internal equity refers to the fairness of the pay for different types of jobs within one organization. Individual equity refers to the fairness of pay based on the relative performance contributions of individuals working on the same type of job in the same organization. Finally, procedural equity refers to the perceived fairness and procedures used to make decisions regarding the allocation of pay (Terpstra and Honoree 2003).

Research indicates that CEOs in firms considered to be socially responsible may accept a lower level of compensation in order to avoid or alleviate agency conflicts with other stakeholders (mostly employees) and to assure wealth distribution between the firm and other stakeholders (Cai et al. 2011; Collett Miles and Miles 2013). This presents a particularly difficult issue. At minimum, a CSR employer must ensure that the process of establishing pay is rigorous and follows acceptable standards dictated by law as well as sound compensation methods. In some industrial countries, these standards are monitored, and penalties are assessed for non-compliance. The question then becomes: will global companies set standards that are higher than the minimums set by law or expectations established by the culture?

When designing base pay structure, the job-valuing process (market pricing and job evaluation) is crucial in terms of both internal and external equity. Employee perceptions of rewards fairness is only one aspect of equal pay; therefore, according to the law of many countries, it is important to ensure that equal opportunities will counteract any discriminatory pay practices. In addition, the issue of overpaying employees at any level can jeopardize the sustainability of the firm.

One of the most important values of CSR is **transparency**. Rewards transparency opens the pay system to scrutiny by all stakeholders and may demonstrate to employees that their pay is fair, at least within the context of company policies and government regulations. However, determining what rewards transparency means exactly and what information the employer should provide is a real challenge. It may be understood only in terms of transparent pay for specific employee positions (which is written in a legal contract as it is in Eastern European countries, e.g., Ukraine). In many countries, it means transparent grades and rules of remuneration (as it is in many EU countries, e.g., Poland). Sometimes rewards transparency means sharing information on every individual's pay, as is done in Finland and in the case of US government employees. Answering the question of how far socially responsible rewards may be transparent depends on the organizational culture, societal values or pay traditions in a particular country, as the scope of shared information on rewards may vary significantly across organizations.

When considering transparency from the *do not harm* rule – pay ranges and midpoints in the range, performance criteria, and variable pay rules are supposed to be transparent. Research suggests that increased transparency in executive compensation has a positive influence on employee understanding of pay policies and practices (Ben-Amar et al. 2014; Gelb and Strawser 2001). However, if actual levels of management pay are shared and these levels cannot be justified, this may create perceptions of unfairness, since the vertical disparity in pay levels for senior management is very high, as evidenced by the US corporate financial scandals at corporations such as Enron, WorldCom, Arthur Andersen, and the Northern Rock Bank (Somelofske and Padgett 2008), which drew attention to the problem of executive compensation and corporate governance. As a result, some countries, such as the US, have specific regulations that demand clarity and greater disclosure of executive compensation plans (Somelofske and Padgett 2008). Transparency of executive compensation is a particularly important issue because of the critical role of executives in the decision-making process within the organization, as well as the significant costs of executive compensation (Gomez-Mejia and Balkin 1992).

Socially responsible rewards mean they are **economically sustainable.** Rewards, or what are often termed labour costs, are often the largest employer expense. As a result, organizations that do not control these costs can endanger employee jobs, stockholder investments and community tax revenues. Economically sustainable rewards means that organizations take the strategic perspective and recognize the role of rewards not only as cost-generating, but also as investments. Rewards policies that strive for short-term profit may cause the exploitation of workers and may reduce their satisfaction and engagement (Werbel and Balkin 2010). Economically sustainable rewards do not mean aggressive pay strategies. Economically sustainable rewards are based on the assumption that economic value depends on non-economic factors, such as employee engagement and the willingness to perform given tasks. This is closely connected with the next principle, which is employee well-being.

Socially responsible rewards are oriented towards **employee well-being**. Therefore, many organizations tend to focus on total rewards strategies that underline the importance of both financial and non-financial rewards and help build a supportive environment and development opportunities for employees. Health and well-being programmes (HWP) are interventions put in place by employers to improve the lifestyle choices and health of workers, as a way of preventing illness or injury. In socially responsible organizations, HWPs may also target organizational and environmental practices to improve overall health and safety in the workplace.

The employer may provide employee benefits, especially health and welfare benefits and retirement plans, if these are not provided by the government. A healthy and safe work environment might be extended to work-life programs, such as paid time off (e.g., maternity/paternity leave, sabbaticals), workplace flexibility (flexible work schedules, teleworking, job sharing, etc.) health and wellness benefits (e.g., employee assistance programmes, outcomes-based wellness programmes, stress management programmes, health coaching), caring for dependents programs (resources and referrals for child care/elder care, child-care spending accounts, subsidies and vouchers, special needs care, etc.). Organizations are also investing in improving the work environment with innovations such as flexible work options, unlimited vacation days, and multiple office space options. Research shows that for the majority of workers (59 percent), ethical behaviour consistent with social norms and principles of mutual respect has the greatest impact on happiness in the workplace (Preston 2015). Ethical and transparent behaviour, respect for others, open communication, and employee engagement with possibilities for participation are all important aspects of a high-quality work life.

Finally, socially responsible rewards **do not harm** other stakeholders. Research shows that some rewards programmes, particularly short-term incentives, may lead to unethical employee behaviour or incidences of employee misconduct (Greenberg 1987; Werbel and Balkin 2010). These unethical behaviours can be directed against both the organization (destruction and misuse of organizational property), as well as against other stakeholders, e.g., physical violence and milder forms of aggressive behaviour, such as harassment, verbal abuse, and bullying (Spector et al. 2006).

When considering external stakeholders such as clients, the problem of mis-selling is often invoked in the context of financial institutions that pay huge penalties for this unethical employee behaviour (NAO Report, 2016). Gomez-Mejia and Balkin (1992) suggest that certain rewards systems, such as sales commission plans and large cash bonuses, might encourage employees to engage in misconduct. According to Werbel and Balkin (2010), the greater the proportion of performance contingent on individual incentive compensation in relation to base pay, the greater the likelihood of misconduct. Discontinuous incentives are also likely to convey the legitimacy of misconduct, increasing the perceived acceptability of misconduct (Bosse and Phillips 2016; Werbel and Balkin 2010). For example, Wells Fargo's infamous incentive plans are attributed to a culture where employees created accounts for customers without their knowledge. Other incentive plans may promote risky decisions that harm the environment, such as the case of the BP and Transocean Gulf of Mexico oil spill in 2010.

Again, harm to other stakeholders may be understood differently, depending on the culture and societal norms; however, this can be costly for an organization in the long term. To avoid the risk of employee misbehaviour, the authors suggest using a mix of pay incentives across organizational levels that balance individual incentives with group pay incentives. Moreover, using reliable measures of both performance outcomes and behaviour performance, as it provides the *balanced scorecard* would be important in preventing employee misconduct. New incentive programmes should be scrutinized for potential unintended consequences, and incentive pay plans should be systematically monitored to ensure they are driving expected employee behaviours.

The first perspective described above refers to the way rewards can be structured to meet the core values and requirements that come from the sustainability and CSR approach. We can understand this as a normative approach that seeks to provide support for managers and the organization who want to improve rewards according to the triple bottom line associated with CSR and sustainability. Each one of these issues is fraught with potential problems and different challenges across countries and cultures. The main aspect, when discussing corporate social responsibilities in relation to rewarding, is to distinguish between the fulfilment of basic employer responsibilities, which are named by law, and voluntary activities, which are expected by employees and society. The nature and understanding of socially responsible rewards in national and international institutions, as well as in socio-economic structures, will vary across different countries and societies. In a global environment, companies who often benefit from cooperation with partners from developing countries are expected to take responsibility for the workplaces of their suppliers. A strong influence on promoting sustainable rewards may have large companies as key groups that are seeking to change current institutional agreements (Whitley 2008). Therefore, it is important to raise awareness of benefits and the necessity of creating socially responsible rewards programs through associations of local firms, such as the UN Global Compact that promotes CSR and integrates organizations from various countries.

Perspective 2: Rewards programmes that encourage socially responsible and environmentally sustainable behaviour

The second perspective shown in Figure 10.1 demonstrates how rewards can encourage employees to exhibit socially responsible behaviour. In the past, corporate performance was evaluated only in terms of economic goals, such as profits, earnings, or stock prices, and calls for including social criteria in compensation schemes have been criticized (Berrone and Gomez-Mejia 2009). Recent studies, however, attempt to evaluate the linkage and possible impact of promoting socially responsible behaviour with incentive schemes. Most existing studies explore the effect of executive compensation on corporate social performance (Maas 2018; Mahoney and Thorn 2006). While Mahoney and Thorn (2006) point to the importance of the structure of executive compensation for encouraging socially responsible actions, other studies provide mixed findings (Maas 2018; Deckop et al. 2006). A range of researchers report on the negative relationship between CSR and executive salaries (Cai et al. 2011), CSR and short-term bonuses (Deckop et al. 2006), or the inefficiency of financial incentives for socially responsible behaviour (Linder and Mottis 2013). Other contributions show, however, that long-term CEO incentives are positively related to CSP (Deckop et al. 2006) as the strategic perspective seems the only appropriate one for evaluating CSP. Short-term incentives may unleash activities whose positive effects will only be visible years later.

While there are several studies in the literature on the interrelation between executive pay and CSP, only a few studies explore the effect of pay on CSR behaviours of lower-level managers and employees (Crilly et al. 2008). Here findings are also mixed, as some researchers express doubts about the sense of rewarding pro-social behaviour (Bénabou and Tirole 2006). Others find that while CSR engagement positively moderates the association between non-executive compensation and firm performance, at the same time it negatively moderates the association between executive compensation and firm performance (Feng et al. 2015). Faleye and Trahan (2011) found that while top management does not benefit from labour-friendly practices, the shareholders do, as the benefits gained from labour-friendly practices significantly outweigh the costs. Albright and Burgess (2013) found that, in the context of balance scorecard systems, high-performing banking employees behaved in a socially responsible manner by helping clients and exhibited more commitment to the culture of the bank than did employees performing at lower levels. According to the researchers, high-performing employees retain a long-term focus and their decisions are consistent with the strategic mission of the firm, as well as with the best interests of the customers (Albright and Burgess 2013).

There are a number of ways organizations have incentivized employees to support CSR/S. These include (Renwick et al. 2012):

- Rewarding staff suggestions to improve the firm's CSR/S.
- Rewards schemes linked to staff gaining CSR skills via skill-based pay (e.g., for competency-based rewards for acquiring knowledge on environmental legislation, etc.).
- Green benefits (transport/travel; e.g., free bus tickets, car sharing).
- Financial or tax-reduction incentives; e.g., mass transportation, bicycle loan services, and the use of less-polluting cars.

- Monthly managerial bonuses for socially responsible behaviour (bonuses for ethical behaviours, such as reduced energy consumption).
- Economic, social and green goals/targets as part of pay for performance for senior staff.
- Incentives to achieve social and environmental goals.
- Executive compensation for managers based partly on socially responsible stewardship.
- Recognition-type rewards for achieving social and environmental goals, such as public recognition, awards, paid vacations, time off, gift certificates.

Initiatives directed towards social and environmental goals seem to be important to employees. One example of successful green initiatives at GlaxoSmithKline involved an employee bonus that reduced energy consumption by 11% (Brammer et al. 2015). Research also shows that employers can incentivize environmental activities via a range of green benefits and recognition devices rather than simply using pay (Renwick et al. 2012).

Another socially responsible rewards practice that has become extremely popular is paid time off work in order to become involved in community events or committees. Employers usually offer unpaid or paid days off for volunteer work or incentives and recognition for such activities. For example, there are incentives for volunteer work in public schools, orphanages, hospitals and environmental (planting trees) or other community projects or activities important to employees. Many *Fortune 100 Best Companies to Work* offer philanthropic programmes, especially those companies from high-tech industries (Snyder 2015). According to the CIPD survey (2015), half of all HR professionals report that employees within their organizations are able to participate in either paid or unpaid volunteer activities during work time. Of the organizations that allow employees to use work time for volunteer activities, four-fifths (84%) are entitled to up to five days per year (Rudiger 2015). Effective employee volunteering generates broad-based employee enthusiasm, support and stewardship for employee volunteering and an enriched employee work-related experience, as demonstrated by increased morale, productivity, retention, workplace skills and/or other indicators of engaged employment (Renwick et al. 2012).

Finally, many employers contribute to or sponsor events to raise money or awareness for special causes, such as walks to raise money and awareness for breast cancer or local bicycling events that encourage exercise and wellness. Given the numerous national and local organizations attempting to raise money or awareness for their causes, the big challenge may be setting criteria to prioritize which organizations will be supported.

Evaluating and monitoring corporate social performance

In the past, evaluation of rewards programmes referred mostly to compliance with organizational goals or employee satisfaction (Beck-Krala and Scott 2013). Incorporating the CSR approach requires a more comprehensive view, including both shareholder and stakeholder views (Klimkiewicz and Beck-Krala 2015).

CSR may be evaluated according to external standards and norms, such as SA 8000, AA 1000, Global Reporting Initiative, or ISO 26000; however, a range of organizations also use auto-evaluation tools to help them monitor the social impact of CSR. Organizations attempt to incorporate CSR issues into their management system by providing analysis, such as Life Cycle Assessment or Social Accounting methods, using environmental, social and governance (ESG) criteria in the balance scorecard (Epstein and Wisner 2001) or calculating the Social Return of Investment (Hall et al. 2015). For sustaining the impact that rewards have towards the broad range of stakeholders, it is necessary to align the remuneration evaluation system with the monitoring of CSP. According to a CIPD rewards report (Cotton 2008), 40% of UK employers reported reviewing their rewards and employment conditions policies and practices to see if they supported their environmental objectives. However, this has largely been concerned with benefits such as transport and travel rather than pay itself. In so doing, organizations get a comprehensive view of the impact of CSP on the stakeholders, gather the necessary information on stakeholder expectations, and avoid any adverse impact that may cause conflicts and pressures. Rewards program evaluation is examined in more detail in another chapter.

Practical applications of CSR and sustainability

It is a major challenge to design rewards systems that work as intended, avoid distorted outcomes and encourage sustainability and socially responsible employee behaviour.

As shown in Figure 10.2, the process of designing and managing sustainable and responsible rewards strategies, policies, and programmes begins with ensuring a strong, sustainable CSR culture and values, through designing and risk assessment and finally embedding and continuous monitoring.

Phase 1: Build strong cultural Values consistent with CSR/S. To successfully build a CSR/S programme, the employer must first have a strong commitment to an open and ethical organizational culture which is communicated and reinforced by top management and integrated

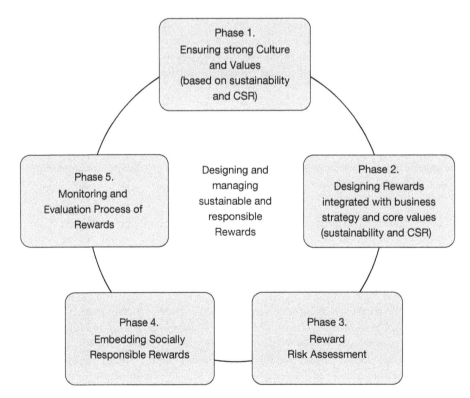

Figure 10.2 The process of designing and managing sustainable and responsible rewards

Source: Adapted from Moxey, 2016, p.13.

with the business strategy, company values, code of ethics and compliance programmes (Freeman 1984; Freeman et al. 1991; Armstrong and Brown 2005; Scott et al. 2008; Greene 2010; Klimkiewicz 2011; Moxey 2016). At this stage, it is important that top and senior management understand and demonstrate a strong commitment to those values, communicate those values, and make decisions and take actions consistent with those values. This is crucial, since employees will respond not only to what is communicated but also to how senior management behaves.

Phase 2: Design and integrate rewards systems. The design of the rewards programmes must comply with the organization's core values and support its business strategy in a sustainable and socially responsible manner according to the two perspectives discussed above. First, rewards systems are designed according to CSR/S, and, second, rewards for CSR/S behaviour are included. If the business strategy is oriented towards creation of shareholder value, the rewards system should be long-term-oriented and reflect the understanding of all main stakeholder interests. For example, when designing incentive programmes, the targets must be achievable without resorting to unethical behaviour and the evaluation criteria must include multiple measures reflecting the interests of multiple stakeholders in the organization's success. There may be programmes that reward employees for desired socially responsible behaviour, such as the CEO 'thank you' letter or any award or prize. Finally, employees should not be rewarded or receive promotions if they breach core values and principles. To avoid employee misbehaviour or misconduct, some experts suggest that the company focus on long-term incentive and intrinsic rewards rather than short-term incentives (Cox et al. 2010; Mahoney and Thorn 2006; Moxey 2016).

Phase 3: Risk assessment. As discussed previously, rewards systems, particularly incentive plans, may have unintended consequences that negatively impact other stakeholders. To ensure that rewards policies and programmes function as intended, it is important to identify and understand potential problems and assess policy and program risk. The risk arises from the way employees respond to particular rewards programmes (mostly individual incentives) and how they perceive and respond to particular targets, goals and evaluation criteria. For example, an incentive plan that encourages increased sales may encourage salespeople to oversell customers, so they have a larger inventory of the vendors' product than necessary, thus potentially damaging the relationship with the customer. Moreover, the pressure to meet targets may led to unethical employee behaviour, which may result in the mis-selling of products. Such employee behaviour may consequently lead to huge penalties and damage the reputation of an organization (Report of NAO 2016).

Phase 4: Embedding sustainable and responsible rewards: The effectiveness of rewards programmes requires that employees understand the purpose, criteria and target for which they will be rewarded and the means by which they can earn those rewards. Thus, the firm must invest in training and communications both for the employee that is eligible for the rewards programme as well as for the supervisors who will be managing these employees. Effective communication and training enhances awareness of the sustainable and responsible culture and shows employees how they contribute to these goals. Some guides can be found in books and journals for human resource professionals. Additionally, employees must know where to find resources that offer help in determining proper courses of action to resolve moral and ethical problems.

Phase 5: Monitor and evaluate: Business strategies and markets change, as do the values and rewards preferences of employees. Furthermore, where there are rewards, there are employees who may attempt to obtain the payoffs with methods that were never intended by the designers of rewards policies and programmes. Therefore, rewards programmes need to be monitored systematically and evaluated to ensure they, in fact, are achieving their goals efficiently. This process for monitoring and evaluating rewards programmes must be built into their design. In Chapter 11 of this volume, Scott and Beck-Karla discuss the design of rewards evaluation in detail. They highlight how rewards policies and programmes should be evaluated from the CSR/S perspective. This process should help the organization ensure that the rewards work effectively, not only in terms of financial profits and cost optimizing, but also in supporting an organizational culture based on strong ethical values. From this perspective, the transparency of CEO rewards and corporate governance plays an important role, as ethical behaviour at the top strengthens the values culture and communicates to employees that top management is committed to the core values of the organization. This will build a sustainable and socially responsible culture among other employees. Rewards policies and programmes may also be evaluated according their contributions to corporate social performance, as described above.

Future directions of research

Sahakiants et al. (2015) predicts research on the integration of CSR and HRM (including, in particular, rewards) will be one of the most important areas for future study. First, it is important to test how socially responsible rewards practices influence organizational outcomes and what kind of benefits the organization might experience from a long-term perspective. There also needs to be an initial focus on theorizing how and why rewards connect to Corporate Social Performance. Furthermore, future studies should explore the influence of rewards on Corporate Social Performance, including the influence on both internal stakeholders, such as employees, managers, and executives, as well as the impact of their behaviour and performance on external stakeholders from a long-term perspective.

It would be desirable to develop a comprehensive approach for an evaluation of rewards programmes that would include not only economic, but also social, ethical and environmental performance criteria from the perspective of all stakeholder interests (Armstrong et al. 2011; Beck-Krala and Klimkiewicz 2016). A number of studies contribute to the fields of strategic rewards and corporate social responsibility by providing specific CSR criteria by which those rewards might be evaluated (Beck-Krala and Klimkiewicz 2016; Sahakiants et al. 2015; Scott et al. 2006). However, it would be important to develop and incorporate new measures that focus on sustainability and social impact from a long-term perspective. Development of such specific measures, such as the Blended Value Proposition, a measure that integrates social and financial returns (Emerson 2003), the Social Return on Investment (SROI), or Workplace Well-Being Index would be useful.

Finally, it would be interesting to take a broader view as to how and why particular rewards instruments and programmes, e.g., LTI, bonuses, etc., promote or discourage employee social behaviours. Thus, the effects of personality variables on reactions to different kinds of rewards contingencies also need to be studied, along with the specific conditions under which reinforcement might have positive or negative effects. Furthermore, this stream of research should also be tested in the light of various theories, e.g., social agency theory, and even other theoretical perspectives (Bosse and Phillips 2016). Such analysis would shed light into a better understanding of unethical employee or executive behaviours, such as mis-selling. Extremely important would be the situational context under which reinforcement might have detrimental effects or no effects at all (Eisenberger and Cameron 1996).

References

Albinger, H. and Freeman, S. (2000). Corporate social performance and attractiveness as an employer to different job-seeking populations. *Journal of Business Ethics*. 28(3), 243–253.

Albright, T. L. and Burgess, C. M. (2013). Best practices of high-performing employees: rewards and performance in a balanced scorecard environment. *The Journal of Corporate Accounting & Finance*. 24(6), 59–65.

Armstrong, M. (2010). *A Handbook of Human Resource Management Practice* (10th ed.). London, Philadelphia: Kogan Page Publishers.

Armstrong, M. and Brown, D. (2005). Reward strategies and trends in the United Kingdom: the land of diverse and pragmatic dreams. *Compensation & Benefits Review*. 37(4), 41–53.

Armstrong, M., Brown, D. and Reilly, P. (2011). Increasing the effectiveness of reward management: an evidence-based approach. *Employee Relations*. 33(2), 106–120.

Barrena-Martínez, J., López-Fernández, M. and Romero-Fernández, P. M. (2016). Socially responsible human resource policies and practices: academic and professional validation. *European Research on Management and Business Economics*, 23(1), 55–61.

Becker, B. and Huselid, M. (2009). Strategic human resources management: where do we go from here? *Journal of Management*. 32(6), 898–925.

Beck-Krala, E. and Klimkiewicz, K. (2016). Occupational safety and health as an element of a complex compensation system evaluation within an organization. *International Journal of Occupational Safety and Ergonomics*. 22(4), 523–531.

Beck-Krala, E. and Scott, D. (2013). Research design for compensation systems evaluation. In *4th European Reward Management Conference*. Presented at the 4th European Reward Management Conference, Brussels: European Institute for Advanced Studies in Management.

Beer M. and Eisenstat M., (2009). *High Commitment, High Performance: How to Build a Resilient Organization for Sustained Advantage*. San Francisco, CA: Jossey-Bass.

Ben-Amar, W., Smaili, N. and Wa Manzili, E. (2014). Corporate social responsibility and the quality of executive compensation disclosures. *The Journal of Applied Business Research*. 30(2), 625–632.

Bénabou, R. and Tirole, J. (2006). Incentives and prosocial behavior. *American Economic Review*. 96(5), 1652–1678.

Berrone, P. and Gomez-Mejia, L. R. (2009). The PROS and CONS of rewarding social responsibility at the top (PDF Download Available). *Human Resource Management*. 48(6), 959–971.

Blowfield, M. and Murray, A. (2014). *Corporate Responsibility*. Oxford: Oxford University Press.

Bosse, D. A. and Phillips, R. A. (2016). Agency theory and bounded self-interest. *Academy of Management Review*. 41(2), 276–297.

Brammer, S., Hoejmose, S. and Millington, A. (2015). Managing sustainable global supply chains: Framework and best practices. Network for business sustainability nbs.net: Canada.

Brown, D. (2014). The future of reward management. *Compensation & Benefits Review*. 46(3), 147–151.

Brundtland Commission. (1987). *Our Common Future*. Oxford, UK: World Commission on Environment and Development, Oxford University Press.

Cai, Y., Jo, H. and Pan, C. (2011). *Vice or Virtue? The Impact of Corporate Social Responsibility on Executive Compensation Journal of Business Ethics*, 104(2), 159–173.

Carroll, A. B. (1999). Corporate social responsibility: Evolution of a definitional construct. *Business and Society*. 38(3), 268–295.

Collett Miles, P. and Miles, G. (2013). Corporate social responsibility and executive compensation: exploring the link. *Social Responsibility Journal*. 9(1), 76–90.

Cone Communications Millennial Employee Engagement Study. (2016). When It Comes to Work, Social Responsibility Trumps Pay for Millennials. *Work Span – a publication of WorldatWork Association*. Available at: https://www.worldatwork.org/adimLink?id=80928, accessed on February 2, 2017.

Cotton, Ch. (2008). Reward Management Survey Report. CIPD. Available at: http://www2.cipd.co.uk/NR/rdonlyres/A0A6B058-0433-4099-948D-0669ACE2F95C/0/rewmansr0108.pdf.

Cox, A., Brown, D. and Reilly, P. (2010). Reward strategy: Time for a more realistic reconceptualization and reinterpretation? *Thunderbird International Business Review*. 52(3), 249–260.

Crane, A. and Matten, D. (2010). *Business Ethics: Managing Corporate Citizenship and Sustainability in the Age of Globalization*. Oxford, New York: Oxford University Press.

Crane, A., Matten, D. and Spence, L. J. (2008). *Corporate Social Responsibility. Readings and Cases in a Global Context* (pp. 7–9). London and New York: Routledge.

Crilly, D., Schneider, S. and Zollo, M. (2008). Psychological antecedents to socially responsible behavior. *European Management Review*. 5(3), 175–190.

Deckop, J. R., Merriman, K. K. and Gupta, S. (2006). The effects of CEO pay structure on corporate social performance. *Journal of Management*. 32(3), 329–342.

Docherty, P., Forslin, J. and Shani, A. B. (2002). *Creating Sustainable Work Systems: Emerging Perspectives and Practice*. London: Routledge.

Ehnert, I. (2008). *Sustainable Human Resource Management – A Conceptual and Exploratory Analysis from a Paradox*. Bremen: Physica-Verlag, Springer.

Eisenberger, R. and Cameron, J. (1996). Detrimental effects of reward: reality or myth? *American Psychologist*. 51(11), 1153–1166.

Elkington, J. (1998). *Cannibals with Forks: The Triple Bottom Line of 21st Century Business*. Gabriola Island, BC; Stony Creek, CT: New Society Publishers.

Emerson, J. (2003). The blended value proposition: integrating social and financial returns. *California Management Review*. 45(95), 35–54.

Epstein, M. and Wisner, P. (2001). *Balanced scorecard report: Good neighbors: Implementing social and environmental strategies with the BSC* (No. Article Reprint No. B0105C).

European Commission. (2011). Communication from the Commission to the European Parliament, the Council, the European Economic and Social Committee and the Committee of Regions. A renewed EU strategy 2011-14 for Corporate Social Responsibility. COM (2011) 681.

Faleye, O. and Trahan, E. (2011). Labor-friendly corporate practices: Is what is good for employees good for shareholders? *Journal of Business Ethics*. 101(1), 1–27.

Feng, M., Wang, A. X. and Saini, J. S. (2015). Monetary compensation, workforce-oriented corporate social responsibility, and firm performance. *American Journal of Business*. 30(3), 196–215.

Folger, R. and Konovsky, M. A. (1989). Effects of procedural and distributive justice on reactions to pay raise decisions. *Academy of Management Journal* 32(1), 115–130.

Freeman, R. E. (1984). *Strategic Management: A Stakeholder Approach*. New York: Cambridge University Press.

Freeman, R. E., Gilbert, D. L. and Gilbert, D. R. (1991). *Unternehmensstrategie, Ethik und persönliche Verantwortung*. Frankfurt: Campus Verlag.

Freeman, R. E. and Gilbert, D. R. (1988). *Corporate Strategy and the Search for Ethics*. Englewood Cliffs, NJ: Prentice Hall.

Gelb, D. S. and Strawser, J. A. (2001). Corporate social responsibility and financial disclosure: an alternative explanation for increased disclosure. *Journal of Business Ethics*. 33(1), 1–13.

Gomez-Mejia, L. R. and Balkin, D. B. (1992). *Compensation, Organization Strategy, and Firm Performance*. Mason, OH: South-Western Series in Human Resource Management.

Greene, R. J. (2010). Evaluating the ongoing effectiveness of rewards strategies and programs, *WorldatWork Journal, Second Quarter* 2010, 50–66.

Greenberg, J. (1987). A taxonomy of organizational justice theories. *Academy of Management Review*. 12(1), 9–22.

Gross, S. E. and Friedman, H. M. (2004). Creating an effective total reward strategy: holistic approach better supports business. *Benefits Quarterly*. 20(3), 7–12.

Hall, M., Millo, Y. and Barman, E. (2015). Who and what really counts? Stakeholder prioritization and accounting for social value. *Journal of Management Studies*. 52(7), 907–934.

Johnson, J. (2012). *Perceived Fairness in Compensation*. Redmont, WA: Economic Research Institute.

Jones, D. A. and Willness, C. R. (2013). Corporate Social Performance, Organizational Reputation and Recruitment.

Klimkiewicz, K. (2011). Społeczna Odpowiedzialność Przedsiębiorstw jako Wyraz Kultury Organizacyjnej. *Prace Naukowe UE we Wrodawiu*. 156, 136–146.

Klimkiewicz, K. and Beck-Krala, E. (2015). Responsible rewarding systems – the first step to explore the research area. *Research Papers of Wrocław University of Economics*.

Laszlo, C. (2008). *Firma zrównoważonego rozwoju*. Warszawa: Wydawnictwo Studio EMKA.

Linder, S. and Mottis, N. (2013). Incentives for socially responsible behavior (SRB): Is 'bribing' managers a promising way to foster SRB? Presented at the ERMC Conference, Belgium: EAISM.

Maas, K. (2018). Do corporate social performance targets in executive compensation contribute to corporate social performance? *Journal of Business Ethics*. 148 (3), 573–585.

Mahoney, L. and Thorn, L. (2006). An examination of the structure of executive compensation and corporate social responsibility: a Canadian investigation. *Journal of Business Ethics*. 69(2), 149–162.

Milkovich, G. T. and Newman, J. M. (2002). *Compensation*. Boston: McGraw-Hill Irwin.

Moxey, P. (2016). *Incentivizing Ethics: Managing Incentives to Encourage Good and Deter Bad Behavior. Editors*. Available at: http://www.transparency.org.uk/publications/incentivising-ethics-managing-incentives-to-encourage-good-and-deter-bad-behaviour/, accessed on February 2, 2017.

Preston, M. (2015). *The Well-being Pulse Survey*. Deloitte. Available at: https://www2.deloitte.com/us/en/pages/about-deloitte/articles/press-releases/deloitte-well-being-survey-press-release.html.

Renwick, D., Redman, T. and Maguire, S. (2012). Green human resource management, a review and research agenda. *International Journal of Management Reviews*. 15(10), 1–14.

Report of NAO. (2016). Financial services mis-selling: regulation and redress, UK, Available at: https://www.nao.org.uk/wp-content/uploads/2016/02/Financial-services-mis-selling-regulation-and-redress.a.pdf.

Rudiger, K. (2015). From big society to the big organisation? The role of organisations in supporting employee volunteering, CIPD Report, GB.

Sahakiants, I., Festing, M. and Steger, T. (2015). Paying your employee right: exploring the concept of socially responsible rewards. In *Uncertainty is a great opportunity*. Presented at the EURAM 2015, Warsaw: Kozminski Academy.

Scott, D., Marajda, D. and McMullen, T. (2006). Evaluating pay program effectiveness. *WorldatWork Journal*. 2, 50–59.

Scott, D., Sperling, R. S., McMullen, T. D. and Bowbin, B. (2008). A study of pay communications: methods for improvement of employee understanding. *WorldatWork Journal*. 17(3), 6–20.

Scott, D., McMullen, T. and Royal, M. (2011). Reward fairness: slippery slope or manageable terrain? *WorldatWork Journal, Fourth Quarter*, 20(4), 50–64.

Simons, T. and Roberson, Q. (2003). Why managers should care about fairness: the effects of aggregate justice perceptions on organizational outcomes. *Journal of Applied Psychology*. 88(3), 432–443.

Somelofske, M. and Padgett, S. (2008). Internal pay equity: A compensation committee tool for effective corporate governance. *WorldatWork Journal, Fourth Quarter*.

Spector, P. E., Fox, S., and Domagalski, T. (2006). Emotions, violence and counterproductive work behavior. In Kelloway, E. K., Barling, J. and Hurrell, J. J. (eds.). *Handbook of Workplace Violence* (pp. 29–46). Thousand Oaks, CA: SAGE.

Snyder B. (2015). 100 best companies to work for, Fortune. Available at: http://fortune.com/2015/03/21/companies-offer-incentives-for-volunteering.

Terpstra, D. E. and Honoree, A. L. (2003). The relative importance of external, internal, individual and procedural equity to pay satisfaction. *Compensation & Benefits Review*. 35(6), 67–74.

Thom, N. (2002). *Personal Management: Mehr Nachhaltigkeit*. Bern: Universität Bern.

Thom, N. and Zaugg, R. (2002). Das Prinzip Nachhaltigkeit im Personalmanagement. *Personalfuehrung*. 35(7), 52–55.

Werbel, J. and Balkin, D. B. (2010). Are human resource practices linked to employee misconduct?: A rational choice perspective. *Human Resource Management Review*. 20(4), 317–326.

Wheeler, D., Colbert, B. and Freeman, R. E. (2003). Focusing on value: reconciling corporate social responsibility, sustainability and a stakeholder approach in a network world. *Journal of General Management*. 28(3), 1–28.

Whitley, R. (2008). *Business Systems and Organizational Capabilities. The Institutional Structuring of Competitive Competences*. Oxford and New York: Oxford University Press.

11

EVALUATING REWARD STRATEGIES, PROGRAMMES AND POLICIES

Research and practice

Dow Scott and Ewa Beck-Krala

Introduction

Systematically evaluating reward strategies, programmes and policies (RSPP) is important for several reasons. First, labour costs represent the largest single cost of doing business for most employers, especially for those in the human services industry and government. Since most major investments receive careful scrutiny, it is troubling that reward decisions are often not held to the same standard as other investitures (e.g., Scott and McMullen 2014; Scott et al. 2006b). Second, since employees can represent an important competitive advantage, employers attempt to develop RSPP that align employee goals with the business strategy, offer reward packages desired by employees, and establish reward strategies and polices to control labour costs. Third, reward programmes are vulnerable to changes in external and internal environments, and therefore require modification and new approaches in line with changes in consumer demands, employee preferences and labour market conditions. Fourth, RSPP can encourage unethical behaviours and employee misconduct, such as selling customers products they do not need or overlooking quality problems in the production process (Werbel and Balkin 2010). Finally, RSPP can severely damage organizational effectiveness by failing to attract and retain talent or by misdirecting employee efforts (Scott et al. 2008).

Programme evaluation has long been an important issue among human resource (HR) professionals, as is evident by the nearly universal use of Kirkpatrick's training evaluation model developed in the 1950s (Kirkpatrick 1959, 1994). However, interest in systematically evaluating reward strategies, policies and programmes (RSPP) is a relatively recent development, occurring only over the last two decades. For the most part, RSPP evaluation has been limited to identification of methods used to evaluate reward programmes (Beck-Krala 2014; Balkin and Gomez-Mejia 1990; Brown 2008; Greene 2010; Ritcher 2002: Scott et al. 2006b), and a few surveys of reward professionals to determine the degree to which reward evaluation occurs within organizations (Armstrong et al. 2011; Corby et al. 2005; Kearns 1995; Scott et al. 2006b). To a lesser extent, reward professionals are asked if the evaluation methods used are effective (Armstrong et al. 2011; Brown 2008; Corby et al. 2005; Scott et al. 2006b). Although survey evidence indicates increased interest in reward programme evaluation, we found no consistent approach to evaluation or rigorous empirical evidence for the effectiveness of RSPP evaluation.

The intent for this chapter is to address this gap and provide guidance for practitioners. Specifically, our goals are to:

1   Review reward evaluation methodologies and models articulated in the literature and used in practice.
2   Propose an integrative, more systematic and rigorous approach for evaluating RSPP.
3   Suggest research opportunities to further develop and test reward evaluation perspectives and methodologies.

Evaluating reward strategies, programmes and policies (RSPP)

The literature suggests a variety of approaches for evaluating RSPP (Armstrong et al. 2011; Beck-Krala 2014; Brown 2008; Greene 2010; Scott et al. 2006b). Initially, RSPP evaluation focused primarily upon the alignment of rewards with competitive business strategies (Balkin and Gomez-Mejia 1990; Ritcher 2002). Reward evaluation next emphasized organizational outputs (mostly financial performance) and economic efficiency (Kearns 1995; Corby et al. 2005). Finally, the most recent RSPP evaluation literature has incorporated employee perceptions and behaviours and the administrative efficiency of the reward programme (Armstrong et al. 2011; Beck-Krala 2014; Brown 2008; Scott et al. 2006b). Over time, researchers recognized that RSPP evaluation was more complex than originally thought and that more systematic and rigorous evaluation methods were needed.

Figure 11.1 is a framework we developed to group disparate methods into four categories, based upon the evaluation perspective: (1) employee perceptions, understanding, and behaviour; (2) financial and operational impact (e.g., benchmarking, cost, ROI); (3) administrative efficiency and effectiveness; and (4) social responsibility and sustainability consideration. Each perspective provides important information about the effect RSPP are having on important employer stakeholders.

Evaluation methods for the first three categories have been discussed in a variety of articles, but the social responsibility and sustainability perspective is a new and relatively unexplored perspective for evaluating RSPP. We recognize that the insight offered by each perspective is, in

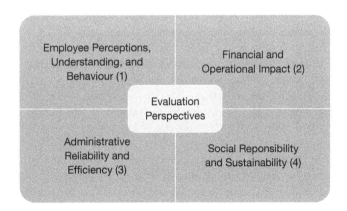

Figure 11.1   Integrated reward evaluation perspectives

large part, dependent on the rigour of the collection and analysis of data. It is equally important to recognize the importance of engaging other stakeholders and integrating their input as appropriate. Obtaining rigour and engagement from the multiple perspectives is discussed in a subsequent section of this chapter.

1. Employee perceptions, understanding and behavior

Based on an adaption of Kirkpatrick's model for evaluating training programmes developed in the 1950s (Kirkpatrick 1994), Scott et al. (2006a) proposed that employee perspective be included in RSPP evaluation.

There are a variety of motivational theories that can help explain how employee perceptions, understanding and behaviour influence RSPP effectiveness. Skinnerian Reinforcement Theory (Festinger 1957; Skinner 1969) offers insight into how linking reward to behaviour and reward timing and frequency shape behaviour. Vroom's Expectancy Theory (1964) reveals the importance of linking employee effort to performance and performance to valued rewards in motivating employee choice or direction of behaviour, effort levels and persistence. Adam's Equity Theory (1963) and Lawler's Discrepancy Theory (1971) indicate how perceptions of fairness based on perceived inputs and outcomes shape employee behaviour, particularly as they relate to reward programmes. Agency and Tournament Theories offer insight for aligning employee rewards with the goals of the firm, and the amount of rewards required to motivate competition among employees for scarce senior positions in organizations, respectively (Connelly et al. 2014).

Although it is beyond the scope of this chapter to revisit motivational theory, these theories, and the accumulated research supporting them, suggest how perceptions, knowledge and behaviours are associated with RPSS and identify measures for conducting the evaluation. For example, equity theory shows how employees are motivated by reward fairness, as perceived in the context of social comparisons (Festinger 1957). Employees evaluate reward fairness in the context of the amount they receive compared to others (i.e., distributive justice) and by the way the amount of pay was determined by their employer (i.e., procedural justice). Those conducting research in this area have developed several attitudinal measures for each of these measures of fairness (e.g., Folger and Konovsky 1989).

Expectancy Theory offers another example of how employee perceptions of RSPP can be evaluated (Vroom 1964). Employee perceptions of expectancy (the relationship between effort and performance), instrumentality (the relationship between performance and outcomes) and valence or the perceived value of the rewards, are all important ways to assess incentive pay programmes. If employees do not believe the rewards are obtainable or if the rewards are not valued by employees, then the incentive programme is compromised.

Employee perspective can be examined in three ways, as suggested by Scott et al. (2006a): (1) employee perceptions; (2) employee understanding; and (3) how employee behaviour may be influenced by RSPP. These are described below.

Employee perceptions (i.e., reaction). This perspective assesses employee perceptions of the fairness, ability or likelihood of obtaining the promised rewards, and the degree to which employees value those rewards. If these perceptions are negative, it is unlikely that RSPP will effectively elicit the desired behaviours or outcomes and it may, in fact, damage the employee–employer relationship. Employee perceptions can be accessed via opinion surveys, individual interviews, or group feedback sessions. Perceptions of those who manage eligible employees should also be collected, since manager influence can enhance or undermine employee commitment to RSPP. Note that care must be used when collecting employee reward perceptions, as these questions may suggest employer commitment to resolve perceptions of underpayment; whereas pay surveys may indicate that employee is competitively paid or that the employees pay is in line with the employer's pay structure. Thus, opinion survey questions may be better directed at procedural issues (how rewards are chosen and allocated) and framed as choices to better ascertain employee preferences (e.g., does the employee prefer a pay mix that has more variable pay, or is the employee willing to accept a more personally costly healthcare plan in return for receiving a larger company contribution to his or her retirement programme). Examining employee pay preferences by forcing employees to select their most preferred options can be accomplished through conjoint analysis. Lopez (2014) provides an excellent description of MaxDiff Scaling, which is an efficient form of conjoint analysis for evaluating employee preferences for reward programmes.

Employee understanding. Many RSPP, particularly incentive pay programmes, are designed to invoke certain behaviours or to communicate specific messages or priorities to employees; however, if managers or employees do not understand the reward policy or programme, they may not direct their efforts or behaviours in the appropriate direction. The result may be thwarted programme goals and frustration among employees who, as a consequence, do not obtain the promised rewards.

Testing the knowledge of eligible employees and their managers can help determine the success of efforts to communicate the policy or programme and identify complexities or flaws inherent in the RSPP. Testing RSPP knowledge can also be an effective tool for teaching employees about programme goals, performance criteria, targets and other programme features. Thus, it is suggested that periodic tests of employee knowledge of RSPP for which they are eligible be performed.

Employee behaviour. In many cases, the RSPP is expected to influence employee behaviour. If employee behaviour is unaffected, then it is unlikely the organization will achieve the desired outcome for which the RSPP was designed. For example, it is not uncommon for sales incentive programmes to reward employees for calling on new customers to increase market share. If the incentive does not invoke that desired behaviour (in this case, calling on new customers) then the desired outcome, increased sales to new customers, is unlikely to occur. If the behaviour is not elicited, this result may indicate that the reward was of insufficient value to motivate the employee, or that other factors blocking the desired behaviour are at work (for example, travel restrictions that prevent sales people from visiting new customers). Another example of the importance of a behavioural metric is demonstrated by a company offering a large incentive to employees for sales to new customers during an economic downturn. New sales may increase temporarily, but the practice of aggressively pushing excessive stock to customers is generally unsustainable in the long term and may annoy customers. Monitoring how new sales were achieved can indicate flaws in the incentive programme or reveal any possible prospect that employees may "game" the incentive plan.

2. Financial and operational impact

Benchmarking with pay surveys and affordability (cost) analysis are two of the most frequently used assessments which give an indication of the financial feasibility of RSPP. The first, benchmarking, reveals the frequency of RSPP use among competitors for customers or employees, along with some of the features of those programmes. For example, short-term or annual cash incentives are often included in pay surveys. A company can usually learn the frequency with which this incentive is offered to employees, the levels in the organization that offer this incentive, and the average percentage of base pay targeted for eligible employees. A knowledge of the reward programmes offered by competitors is often important to senior management and this knowledge is frequently referenced when adding new programmes or adjusting reward programme features.

Since reward programmes represent a major expenditure, the Chief Executive Officer (CEO) or the Chief Financial Officer (CFO) typically demand a programme budget before approving the expenditure and an annual accounting of the actual programme costs. In recent years, CFOs have also started asking for return-on-investment (ROI) analyses, recognizing that investments in reward programmes should be compared with other ways in which the employer might invest capital (Fitz-enz 2001; Scott and McMullen 2014). Although calculating ROI might be feasible for some reward programmes, particularly sales incentives, calculating ROI may be particularly challenging, given the indirect linkage of these programmes to desired outcomes, such as individual employee performance, company performance, attracting desired talent, and the cost of turnover. Furthermore, while ROI may indicate the value of the investment, it provides little information as to why the RSPP works or fails to meet ROI expectations. Thus, ROI represents a potentially important measure for evaluating rewards on offer, but it is unlikely to be helpful in suggesting ways to improve a reward programme.

There are a variety of ways to measure the operational impact of an incentive pay programme, such as units produced, productivity levels, waste and materials used in a process. Often these operational measures can be more clearly specified if developed for specific operations, work units or functional areas. For example, the operational measures used to evaluate quality are specific to an operation, but can also be excellent measures as to how well an operation or process performs. Obtaining the perspective of the CFO, vice president of operations and other key executives in relation to these measures will prove substantial insight as to how to interpret these data.

Gain-sharing incentive programmes usually focus on operational measures, recognizing that most employees cannot directly impact profits, earnings or other corporate financial results. These programmes have developed numerous operational measures and methods for establishing obtainable payout targets. The effectiveness of Scanlon Plans (a form of gain-sharing) is often attributed to the fact that such plans provide a robust method of giving employees actionable information for influencing operational decisions and for educating employees as to the effect they can have on these operational outcomes (Scott 2016; Scott et al. 2007).

Financial measures, such as profit and earnings, are considered the gold standard for evaluating RSPP, especially from the perspective of senior management and stockholders. Such measures are considered *self-funding*, since payouts to employees are generated by increased funds or reduced costs received by the organization. Unfortunately, the line of sight for most employees is limited as to how employees are affecting performance or employee attitudes towards the RSPP programmes. Furthermore, the state of the economy can have a substantial impact on achievement of performance goals, such as earning or profits and, in turn, the incentive payout.

3. Administrative reliability and efficiency

Armstrong et al. (2011) emphasize the importance of examining RSPP reward designs and processes to be sure they are consistent with the programme's goals, integrated with management/HR systems, and efficiently administered. Their suggestions for reward evaluation also include programme communications and the ability to make changes in the programme, based on external and internal conditions.

Considerable emphasis has been placed on the reliability of reward programmes. Employees expect (and will complain) if they do not receive the promised rewards. Additionally, there is a legal obligation for employers to provide the rewards that are indeed earned and submitted as a cost of doing business (i.e., tax and organizational governance implications). Given these high expectations for accuracy and timeliness, accounting routinely audits reward payments, and most reward programmes are indeed reliable. That said, now that many reward programmes are self-serve (that is, they require employees to enter data) and handled by outside vendors, the routine audit of these software platforms, accounts and systems is a must.

Efficiency of collecting the data, processing it and producing the required rewards usually receives less attention than does reliability. The process by which employees are enrolled in the programme, as well as update requirements, can be examined in terms of the time required to complete these tasks, questions or problems associated with processing the reward programme, and the reliability of the inputted data.

4. Social responsibility and sustainability

The obligations that employers have to multiple stakeholders and the communities in which they are located has taken on increased importance in recent years. Society is holding management more responsible for how they treat customers, employees, stockholders and even the environment (Ackermann and Eden 2011; Jo and Harjoto 2011; Mahoney and Thorne 2005). Wells Fargo (opening unrequested customer accounts), Volkswagen (tampering with emission controls) and other ethical lapses among employers have been blamed, in part, on poorly designed incentive plans that may (even inadvertently) encourage employee misconduct. Employers are being punished by consumers, potential employees and government agencies for these failures of judgement. Thus, we propose that RSPP evaluation incorporate social responsibility and environmental sustainability criteria.

In addition to considering unintended consequences associated with RSPP, employers can engender goodwill by incorporating reward programmes that encourage employees to exhibit socially responsible and environmentally sustainable behaviour (Mahoney and Thorne 2005). For example, employers can match charitable contributions and provide paid days off for employees to volunteer their time to perform good works. Research demonstrates that there are numerous benefits to employers who support social responsibility and sustainability, including attracting talent (particularly younger employees), demonstrating a commitment to customers, local communities, employees and other stakeholders, and reducing costs (Albinger and Freeman 2000; Jones and Willness 2013).

However, it is difficult to evaluate the impact of RSPP on social responsibility and sustainability. Identifying how RSPP may create detrimental effects on stakeholders is one challenge. Another involves the voluntary nature of employee participation in programmes that support social responsibility and environmental sustainability. Some employees will consider such encouragement by their employer to be an infringement on their personal freedom. Furthermore, some stockholders and employees believe that these reward programmes and policies divert resources and attention from the central mission of the organization which is to serve the owners (i.e., stockholders).

Incorporating social responsibility and sustainability into RSPP is complicated by the relationship of executive reward programmes and the governance of the organization. Laws regulating how pay decisions are made and the degree to which those decisions are transparent certainly affect employer efforts to become more socially responsible and environmentally sustainable (Somelofske and Padgett 2008). In some countries, there are regulations or there have been court decisions require certain minimum standards related to pay transparency (e.g. the European Union (EU), the US, Canada and Australia). Thus, one of the priorities in EU policy concerning CSR and rewards is "Equal pay for equal work and work of equal value". EU countries must eradicate all discrimination from their national rules and laws and inform workers that they have done so and how. There are also international regulations that are aimed to counteract the gender pay gap (e.g., *Directive 2006/54/EC* of the European Parliament and of the Council of 5 July 2006 on the implementation of the principle of equal opportunities and equal treatment of men and women in matters of employment and occupation; and Article 157 of the Treaty on the Functioning of the European Union (TFEU), which entered into force on 1 December 2009). One of the important tools that supports the RSPP evaluation process from the socially responsible perspective is Corporate Governance. It is a form of control which is designed to protect the interests of shareholders and stakeholders in a systemic and integrated way, and ensure that the organization takes opportunities to improve its processes and performance. A corporate governance is often a combination of various mechanisms: internal (e.g., a performance measurement system) and external mechanisms (governments, trade unions, etc.) as well as independent audits. For example, in the United States, public corporations are required to publish salaries of the highest-paid employees. However, since these laws vary widely it behoves the evaluators of reward programmes to understand the laws specific to each country in terms of what is required and accepted practice.

A threefold approach is the most straightforward way to evaluate the impact of RSPP on social responsibility. The first part involves reviewing programme designs, modifying them for potential unintended consequences, and then monitoring these programmes to ensure that violations of employer commitment to socially responsible behaviour and environmental sustainability do not occur. Issues of equity and fairness should be considered, at least as defined by the organization's pay philosophy and societal norms. The second part is to simply tally the percentage of employees who participate in programmes that encourage socially responsible and environmentally sustainable behaviours, e.g., the number of employees who participate in company programmes that match charitable gifts or use days off to participate in volunteer programmes. Attempting to determine the impact these programmes have on society or the environment is commendable but far more difficult. The third part creates as much transparency as possible, concerning the design and administration of RSPP, especially as it relates to programme goals and administration.

Rigorous evaluation design, data collection and analysis

Although a variety of perspectives for evaluating RSPP are outlined above, without a rigorous and continuous process for conducting an evaluation the findings will at best be vague and inconclusive and, at worst, misleading.

The process for creating rigorous evaluation is not new. The scientific method, a structured form of evaluation, has been in place for hundreds of years. A recent spate of articles and conference presentations on evidence-based management shows that it is still alive and well in the twenty-first century (e.g., Pfeffer and Sutton 2006; Rousseau 2006).

Based on a rich evaluation of the research literature, Scott et al. (2006b) articulated a systematic and continuous process for conducting an evaluation summarized in Figure 11.2. The steps include:

1 Establish specific goals for each RSPP – preferably goals indicating the metrics required to evaluate their attainment.
2 Identify at least one measurable criteria for each RSPP goal and the target associated with achieving that reward goal.
3 Create an evaluation methodology (i.e., research design) that will indicate the degree to which the goal(s) were accomplished; this involves decisions about what and how data will be collected.
4 Collect and analyse data appropriately, given the evaluation design and information desired.
5 Interpret and report evaluation results in a format that is both efficient and understandable to management and other interested employees.
6 Use the feedback to re-establish goals and develop appropriate criteria for the subsequent evaluation of the RSPP.

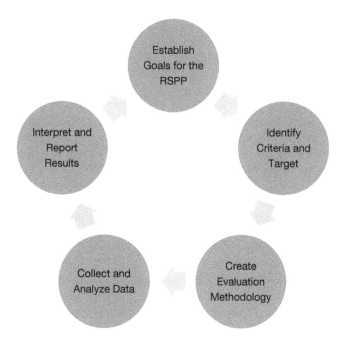

Figure 11.2   Steps in a rigorous evaluation process

Following these steps substantially increases the likelihood that the findings will indicate the value, or lack thereof, of the RSPP and suggest ways to improve it. Although these steps are relatively straightforward, there are technical decisions requiring expertise in developing valid and reliable measures and methodologies that can test the robustness of the RSPP. For example, one can evaluate the RSPP by comparing similar business units where the reward programme was implemented in one but not the other. Of course, creating comparison groups is often not feasible in functioning organizations, which is why time-series analysis is often used for data evaluation. Time-series analysis involves comparing metrics before and after the implementation of the RSPP and, as such, requires that different and more robust statistical models (e.g., vs. ANOVA) be used to compare groups and interpret findings. Ultimately, the design of the study will determine which analytical methods are appropriate and what insights that evaluation will provide.

To ensure rigour, evaluation should be incorporated in the design by making sure the goals are clear and the expectations for the RSPP are accurately reflected in the evaluation metrics. A major benefit in formulating the evaluation when designing the programme is that this process will help clarify the intent of the programme and also engender commitment to RSPP success. In addition, this provides a tool for monitoring programme success and can alert management to potential problems. While not directly related to rigour, sharing information about the success or challenges of RSPP contributes to perceptions that management and RSPP can be trusted, and that if problems arise they will be corrected.

Opportunities and challenges of evaluating RSPP

Our experience suggests that the approach taken to evaluate reward programmes is based upon assumptions or values held by senior management. If management views employees as a cost of doing business, then they may be satisfied with simply knowing if their competitors are offering a particular reward programme (i.e., benchmarking) and assessing affordability, and possibly the ROI, of the reward programme. However, if management considers employees to be an investment, then a more multifaceted and nuanced evaluation process to optimize this investment becomes a priority.

The assumptions or values held by senior management may be driven, in part, by the context in which they operate. For example, programme evaluation traditions vary considerably among different countries and cultures when it comes to priority, methods used, and reliance upon findings (Jacob et al. 2015). Research shows that there is a strong awareness of the need for compensation system evaluation among US employers, as 81% of studied companies in the US provide some form of evaluation of their RSPP (Scott et al. 2006b). In European countries, the practice of regular evaluation occurs in only approximately 20% of studied employers (Armstrong et al. 2011; Corby et al. 2005).

Beck-Krala and Scott (2013) found that US employers are more likely to use qualitative measures than employers in Poland, where financial measures predominate. In this context, there appears to be a completely different perception of the RSPP, which seems to be connected with cultural and economic differences between these countries. Other factors, such as access to trained staff (frequently more present in larger organizations) and organizations in industries more reliant on technology and measurement, may influence RSPP. As such, the introduction of RSPP evaluation will be more challenging for some employers than for others.

It is unclear how other regions of the world will react to, and subsequently structure, RSPP. For example, in Asian culture, where feedback is seldom direct, obtaining an accurate assessment of employee perceptions may not be feasible. We can only speculate as to how evaluation efforts will be received in countries located in the Middle East, Africa or South/Latin America.

To optimize a RSPP one must learn how the programme achieves the desired goals of the organization and where the RSPP is deficient in achieving those goals. A variety of factors can contribute to or impede achievement of RSPP goals, including employee perceptions of fairness, value and likelihood of benefiting from the programme. Furthermore, if the programme is not understood or the nature of working conditions prevents employees from performing as desired, the programme will fail, if these issues are not discovered and corrected.

In this chapter, we have articulated the compelling reasons for the evaluation of RSPP and summarized a variety of evaluation methods and requirements for a rigorous evaluation. A 2006 survey of reward professionals (Scott et al. 2006b) showed that, according to those surveyed, 66% of companies evaluated base-pay programmes, 53% evaluated variable-pay programmes, and 47% evaluated both. However, as indicated by this research and our experience, most RSPP evaluation is largely superficial, with most employers using informal methods, less than a third attempting to determine ROI for reward programmes, and few conducting an evaluation that incorporates multiple perspectives.

A subsequent study by Scott and McMullen (2014) indicated that little had changed with regard to evaluating RSPP. Although human resource and reward professionals and senior executives more clearly acknowledged the value of evaluating pay programmes, most respondents reported that they relied on informal feedback from both managers and employees, exit interviews of departing employees, pay surveys and feedback from engagement surveys. The least-used methods for evaluating reward programmes reported by this survey were ROI calculations, formal managerial and employee feedback from surveys, focus groups and interviews, and the assessed value of human capital, such as the replacement cost of talent.

Brown (2008) shares insights into why RSPP evaluation is not better utilized by reward and HR professionals. First, resources are not available, either in terms of staff time or for hiring consultants to design and implement formal methods to evaluate RSPP. Second, reward professionals often do not have the competencies to evaluate RSPP. In our experience, reward and HR professionals may be reluctant to evaluate the success or effectiveness of reward policies and programmes, fearing they will be held responsible for problems over which they have limited control.

However, even when resources are scarce, we can suggest ways to more effectively and rigorously evaluate RSPP. First, and foremost, one must make a strong case to senior management for evaluating reward programmes, calculating the costs associated with the proposed or existing RSPP and the comparative cost of evaluating the programme. The cost of even the most extensive evaluation will likely be small; i.e., less than 1 or 2% of the total cost of offering a reward programme.

Second, stakeholders should recognize that good evaluation requires sophisticated design and analytical skills. Internally, these skills may be available in the human resource development area, which has a long history of evaluating training programmes, or in the marketing department, which has also become very data-driven in recent years. Management consultants and academicians often have the necessary competencies for conducting these evaluations.

Although there is an initial investment, once in place most evaluation programmes can be maintained or replicated for other RSPP for only a modest additional investment. This is consistent with Figure 11.2, which suggests continuous monitoring of RSPP. Again, a poorly administered or ineffective programme can drain resources, create dissatisfaction among employees, and thwart programme goals.

Third, in any type of evaluation, particular RSPP, a rigorous methodology should be followed. An evaluation that is not accurate or cannot provide the desired answers concerning the efficiency and effectiveness of the programme will erode confidence in this investment. Developing specific goals and the criteria/targets with which to evaluate a RSPP will not only insure that the evaluation occurs efficiently, but should also result in a better designed RSPP and one that is more likely to meet management expectations. When identifying or creating criteria for evaluating reward programmes, it is necessary that these data are reliable. How the data might be affected by other factors, such as the economy, changes in employee demographics, or shifts in markets must also be considered.

Fourth, those evaluating RSPP must anticipate that information management will need to make actionable decisions about reward strategies or policies, increase the investment in a reward programme, or replace it. For example, if management decides to pay employees 10% above the market, with the expectation they will be able to attract and retain better talent, how will management know if, in fact, this goal is achieved? It is valuable to determine in advance how data will be collected on variables, such as acceptance of job offers or rate of turnover among more qualified and high-performance employees, compared with good or average performers.

Fifth, because reward programmes benefit organizational stakeholders in different ways, one should expect differences as in how reward data is interpreted and what actions different stakeholders would take to improve the reward programmes from their perspective. However, given the nature of most organizations, board members and senior management are the ones who must make these decisions. We argue that collecting feedback from multiple stakeholders or sources will better inform key decision-makers as to the effect of their decisions and suggest ways that can improve the rewards programmes for all stakeholders.

Finally, it is important to monitor the evaluation process to be sure that data are being collected correctly and that evaluation reports are generated as scheduled. Demonstrating that the RSPP evaluation can inform judgement about the value of the programme and ways to improve the quality of the programme will lend considerable credibility to evaluation efforts.

Future RSPP evaluation research

Academicians have conducted numerous studies examining the effectiveness of specific reward programmes, primarily incentives, and have attempted to understand the underlying motives that people associate with rewards and why these programmes are effective. These typically one-off studies most often examine a programme unique to a particular company or compare a category of incentive programmes (e.g., profit sharing or merit pay) tried in multiple organizations. However, systematic and rigorous RSPP evaluation by an employer attempting to improve programme quality has only lately become of interest to HR and reward professionals. Currently, RSPP evaluation literature is limited to articles about its importance and largely confined to descriptive studies of methods used by HR and reward professionals' evaluations of reward programmes. This chapter advocates for the importance of evaluating RSPP, taking the divergent reward evaluation methodologies suggested in literature and integrating them into two models. The first model sorts evaluation methodologies into four perspectives (Figure 11.1). The second model outlines a process for conducting a rigorous evaluation of RSPP (Figure 11.2). What follows are suggested research strategies to increase our knowledge of reward evaluation and improve our capability to efficiently evaluate reward programmes.

Advocate and conduct descriptive research: Since there are compelling reasons for evaluating RSPP and few HR or reward professionals actually conduct comprehensive and systematic evaluations, it is important to continue conducting research that demonstrates the value associated with their use. Developing empirically-based RSPP evaluation is consistent with evidence-based management practices and supports this nascent movement in the field towards more rigorous decision-making.

Conduct global descriptive research: Most reward evaluation research has been conducted in the US and, to a lesser extent, in European countries (e.g., England and Poland). Reward evaluation advocacy and descriptive research are needed in other countries to determine the extent to which reward programmes are evaluated, what methods are used, and the effectiveness of those methods. Given that countries differ in their economic and employment relationships, it follows logically that reward evaluation may also be perceived differently and be subject to different challenges.

Extend evaluation to include total rewards: Reward evaluation has focused primarily on base pay and incentive pay (e.g., Scott et al. 2015). Employers recognize that employees make judgements about their total pay package or the rewards they receive. Thus, this research needs to be extended to the broader definition of total rewards that includes employee benefits, employee development opportunities, the work environment itself and promotional opportunity.

Develop reward evaluation measures: Adding evaluation perspectives requires additional measures or criteria. For example, employee perceptions of pay fairness have been measured frequently for academic research purposes and also by consultants to assess employee engagement. However, the reliability and validity of these measures are inconsistent and not necessarily available for scrutiny (e.g., methods promoted by consulting firms that market opinion surveys). This is particularly true in terms of measuring social impact of the RSPP in a long-term perspective. New measures, such as the Social Return on Investment or the Blended Value Proposition (which integrates social and financial returns (Emerson 2003)), need to be explored and incorporated in reward evaluation.

Conduct case studies: Although surveys of HR and reward professionals to determine what reward evaluation methods are used and their effectiveness provides overall insight, case studies can offer a much richer examination of an employer's experience with reward evaluation. This type of research can provide a much more compelling story as to why reward evaluation was undertaken, what was involved in the evaluation effort, and thereby encourage a more nuanced discussion of the effectiveness of the reward evaluation. The rich detail provided by case studies can uncover substantially more information than a survey and provides a concrete example for other employers to follow when developing reward programme evaluation. Gomez-Mejia and Balkin (1989) provide a case study example in which the pay effectiveness criteria included payment satisfaction, propensity to leave, team performance and individual performance.

Conduct theory-driven empirical research: Without a doubt, HR and reward professionals have substantial insight into the effectiveness of reward programmes; however, reward programmes are complex in terms of their goals, metrics, targets, and eligible populations and it is difficult, therefore, to determine which elements of these programmes actually drive employee behaviour or performance and which elements are a hindrance. As such, evaluation methods and processes must receive much closer scrutiny. Does the monitoring of employee perceptions and understanding of a pay programme result in desired outcomes? Can we determine how reward evaluation affects ability of the RSPP to attract, retain and motivate employees? The answers to these questions will be much more compelling if the research that produces them is longitudinal, rather than simply a snapshot of existing employee perceptions of RSPP. Longitudinal research will require more extensive data collection and sophisticated analytical techniques than current procedures can provide.

References

Ackermann, F. and Eden, C. (2011). Strategic management of stakeholders: theory and practice. *Long Range Planning.* 44(2011), 179–196.

Albinger, H. and Freeman, S. (2000). Corporate social performance and attractiveness as an employer to different job seeking populations. *Journal of Business Ethics.* 28(3), 243–253.

Armstrong, M., Brown, D. and Reilly, P. (2011). Increasing the effectiveness of reward management: an evidence-based approach. *Employee Relations.* 2, 106–120.

Balkin, D. and Gomez-Mejia, L. (1990). Matching compensation and organizational strategies. *Strategic Management Journal.* 11, 153–190.

Beck-Krala, E. (2014). Implementation of the methodology for compensation system evaluation. *Organization and Management Quarterly.* 4(28), 5–18,

Beck-Krala, E. and Scott, D. (2013). Research design for compensation systems evaluation. 4th European Reward Management Conference (RMC 2013): Brussels, European Institute for Advanced Studies in Management. December 2–3.

Brown, D. (2008). Measuring the effectiveness of pay and rewards: the Achilles' heel of contemporary reward professionals. *Compensation and Benefits Review.* 5, 23–41.

Connelly, B. L., Tihanyi, L., Crook, T. R. and Gangloff, K. A. (2014). Tournament theory: thirty years of contests and competitions. *Journal of Management.* 40(1), 16–47.

Corby, S., White, G. and Stanworth, C. (2005). No news in good news? Evaluating new pay systems, *Human Resources Management Journal.* 1, 4–24.

Emerson, J. (2003). The blended value proposition: integrating social and financial return. *California Management Review.* 45(4), 35–51.

Festinger, L. (1957). *A Theory of Cognitive Dissonance.* Stanford, CA: Stanford University Press.

Fitz-enz, J. (2001). *How to Measure Human Resources Management?* New York: McGraw-Hill.

Folger, R. and Konovsky, M. A. (1989). Effects of procedural and distributive justice on reactions to pay raise decisions. *Academy of Management.* 32(1), 115–130.

Gomez-Mejia, L. R. and Balkin, D. B. (1989). Effectiveness of individual and aggregate compensation strategies. *Industrial Relations Journal.* 28(3), 431–445.

Greene, R. (2010). Evaluating the ongoing effectiveness of rewards strategies and programs, *WorldatWork Journal.* 18(2), 59–66.

Jacob, S., Speer, S. and Furubo, J. E. (2015). The institutionalization of evaluation matters: up-dating the international atlas of evaluation 10 years later. *Evaluation.* 21(1), 6–31.

Jo, H. and Harjoto, M. A. (2011). Corporate governance and firm value: the impact of corporate social responsibility. *Journal of Business Ethics*. 103(3), 351–383.

Jones, D. A. and Willness, C. R. (2013). Corporate social performance, organizational reputation, and recruitment. In Yu, K. Y. T. and Cable, D. M. (eds.). *The Oxford Handbook of Recruitment* (pp. 298–313). Oxford, England: Oxford University Press.

Kearns, P. (1995). *Measuring Human Resources and the Impact on Bottom Line Improvements*. Hitchin: Technical Communication (Publishing), Ltd.

Kirkpatrick, D. L. (1959). Techniques for evaluating training programs. *Journal of American Society of Training Directors*. 13(3), 21–26.

Kirkpatrick, D. L. (1994). *Evaluating Training Programs*. San Francisco: Berrett-Koehler Publishers, Inc.

Lawler, E. E. (1971). *Pay and Organizational Effectiveness: A Psychological View*. New York: McGraw-Hill.

Lopez, F. (2014). Measuring total rewards: conjoint analysis versus MaxDiff scaling. *WorldatWork Journal*. 23(4), 31–58.

Mahoney, L. S. and Thorne, L. (2005). Corporate social responsibility and long-term compensation: evidence from Canada. *Journal of Business Ethics*. 57, 241–253.

Pfeffer, J. and Sutton, R. I. (2006). Evidence-based management. *Harvard Business Review*. 84(1) 1–11.

Ritcher, A. S. (2002). How does your compensation strategy measure up? *Journal of Strategic HR Review*. 3, 2–40.

Rousseau, D. M. (2006). Is there such a thing as "evidence-based management"? *Academy of Management Review*. 31(2), 256–269.

Scott, D. (2016). A "tried and true" method for encouraging innovation. *WorldatWork Journal*. 25(4), 30–35.

Scott, D., Brown, M., Shields, J., Long, R., Antoni, C., Beck-Krala, E., Casademunt, A. M. L., and Perkins, S. (2015). A global study of pay preferences and employee characteristics. *Compensation and Benefits Review*. 47(2), 60–70.

Scott, K. D., Davis, P. and Cockburn, C. (2007). Scanlon principles and processes: building excellence at Watermark Credit Union. *WorldatWork Journal*. 16(1), 29–37.

Scott, K. D. and McMullen, T. (2014). Assessing reward effectiveness: a survey of reward, HR and line executives. *WorldatWork Journal*. 23(4), 7–19.

Scott, K. D., Morajda, D. and McMullen, T. D. (2006a). Evaluating pay program effectiveness. *WorldatWork Journal*. 15(2), 50–59.

Scott, D., McMullen, T. and Sperling, R. (2006b). Evaluating pay program effectiveness: a national survey of compensation professionals. *WorldatWork Journal*. 15(3), 47–53.

Scott, D., Sperling, R. S., McMullen, T. D. and Bowbin, B. (2008). A study of pay communications: methods for improvement of employee understanding. *WorldatWork Journal*. 17(3), 6–20.

Skinner, B. F. (1969). *Contingencies of Reinforcement: A Theoretical Analysis*, Englewood Cliffs, NJ: Prentice Hall.

Somelofske, M. and Padgett, S. (2008). Internal pay equity: a compensation committee tool for effective corporate governance. *WorldatWork Journal*. 17(4), 6–15.

Vroom, V. H. (1964). *Work and Motivation*. New York: Wiley.

Werbel, J. and Balkin, D. B. (2010). Are human resource practices linked to employee misconduct: a rational choice perspective. *Human Resource Management Review*. 20(4), 317–326.

12

GENDER PAY GAPS AND SOLUTIONS

What can governments and employers do to deliver equal pay – what works?

Duncan Brown and Catherine Rickard

Introduction: *Mind the Gap*

With female premiers in both the UK and Scotland and approximately twenty other countries globally (Christensen 2016), the issue of gender pay is once again high on political and boardroom agendas. We saw millions of women involved in the feminist protests globally at the inauguration of President Trump in early 2017 (Booth and Topping 2017): the first legislation enacted by Trump's predecessor had been the Lily Ledbetter Fair Pay Act, 2009, strengthening women's rights to pursue claims for equal pay.

Theresa May (2016) set out in her first speech as prime minister her "mission to make Britain a country that works for everyone . . . fighting against the burning injustice that . . . if you're a woman, you will earn less than a man". The UK median earnings gap for all male and female employees is currently 18%, compared to the EU average of 16.4% (European Commission 2014).

Her predecessor David Cameron had vowed to "end the gender pay gap in a generation" and we are seeing legislative threats and action increasingly evident in the UK and internationally in pursuit of this aim. For example, the UK's mandatory gender pay reporting requirements were introduced for all employers with more than 250 employees in April 2017. And Germany is currently in the process of implementing the European Commission's drive for a 40% female target with this statutory representation quota of women on large company boards required by 2018 (European Commission 2015).

Based on a research review the authors carried out in 2015/16 for the UK's Equality and Human Rights Commission (Brown et al. 2017), as well as other contemporary research, this chapter summarizes the evidence on the scale and causation of gaps and the effectiveness of policy and employer actions designed to address them. For this research project we carried out a UK and international literature review using academic and 'grey' sources. We also held five structured workshop discussions in London, Edinburgh and Cardiff with almost 50 employers and key stakeholders, to discuss the research evidence on the effectiveness of interventions to close pay gaps and their own personal experiences. Participants are listed in the Appendix at the end of this chapter. We conclude that there is no 'silver bullet' solution and that only multiple actions over sustained periods of time involving all key stakeholders can be effective in addressing such a complex, deep-rooted and intractable social, cultural and economic phenomenon.

Gender pay: interest grows as progress slows

This re-emergence of interest and legislative action on gender pay has been driven by a range of factors: the stubborn persistence of these pay gaps and general reductions in the rate of closure; the apparent failure of voluntary initiatives such as the UK government's 'Think, Act, Report' programme; and the economic benefits in a tightening UK labour market of increased female participation (Brown et al. 2017).

According to the World Economic Forum (2015), women take home one-tenth of global income yet they account for two-thirds of global working hours. Big inequality but also big economic opportunity. The McKinsey Global Institute (2015) estimates that as much as $28 trillion could be added to global GDP if women could replicate male levels of labour market participation and earnings, with Europe standing to gain some 21% of GDP or $5.1 trillion. PwC estimates gains to the UK economy of £170 billion if it could match Sweden in terms of rates of female employment and earnings. The annual report on gender equality progress from the European Commission (2014) finds that at the current rate of change, it will take almost thirty years to reach the EU's target of 75% of women in employment; over seventy years to make equal pay a reality; over twenty years to achieve gender balance on the boards of Europe's largest companies; and almost forty years to ensure that housework is equally shared between women and men.

The 40th anniversary in 2015 of the original UK Equal Pay Act, which had led to a virtual halving of the gender pay gaps as obviously discriminatory structures were outlawed, stimulated a significant amount of research on the issue. But much of it has highlighted the complex 'moving target' (O'Reilly et al. 2015) and the difficulties in attempting to close the gap, supporting the European Commission's estimate rather than David Cameron's single generation.

Progress in closing the pay gap continues to be slow (see Figure 12.1). Office for National Statistics (2017) figures on the gender pay gap in the UK showed that the gap for all staff actually rose from 18.2% in 2016 to 18.4% in 2017, although it decreased marginally for full-time employees. The ONS figures highlight that the gender gap among the top 10% of earners (full-time employees) has remained largely constant, fluctuating at around 20% (18.2% in 2017). Hence the significance of the senior representation agenda and increasing the proportion of women in higher-paying roles. However, for the bottom 10%, the gap has narrowed over the long term, to a median of 5.0% by April 2017, partly influenced by Minimum and National Living Wage legislation. Lower-paid groups such as carers have much higher proportions of female employees.

In the private sector, the UK's gender pay gap for full-time employees fell from 17.6% in 2014 to 15.9% in 2017, continuing a long-term downward trend. However, the narrower gap in the public sector, where there is a statutory equality duty on employers, greater use of job evaluation and higher trade union density increased for the third consecutive year, from 11.1% to 13.1% – the figure had been fluctuating at around 10% since 2000. The gender pay gap is also shown to vary significantly by occupation and reflects the heavy concentration of female employment in generally low-paying sectors and occupational groupings; so-called horizontal and vertical segregation.

Progress in closing the gender pay gap in recent years has therefore, unarguably, been slow. Some commentators believe it is now far more difficult to take interventions that have such a large effect as the introduction of equal pay legislation (Gow and Middlemiss 2011). Rubery and Grimshaw (2014) explain that because pay is influenced by such a variety of pressures, progress in

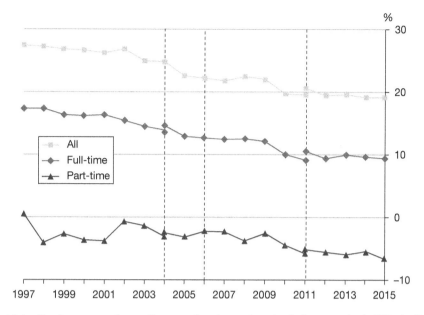

Figure 12.1 Gender pay gap for median gross hourly earnings (excluding overtime), UK, April 1997 to 2017

Source: Annual Survey of Hours and Earnings – Office for National Statistics.

one pay dimension can be counteracted by declines in other dimensions and therefore "equal pay becomes a constantly moving target" (Rubery and Grimshaw 2014:2). They attribute the failures of "key levers" (ibid.) in closing the gap to the emergence of new causes, such as technological change, linked in some cases to changing conditions in employment, or to a failure to accurately identify the exact reasons for the gap (ibid.).

Gender pay gaps: causation and controversy

Addressing the UK's persistent gender pay gap is therefore far from easy, for both governments and individual employers. Our research and consulting experience at IES points to the complex, deeply-rooted historical, cultural and social causes of gender pay gaps (O'Reilly et al. 2015). These range from continuing patterns of schools' and parental career guidance, channelling girls towards traditional, female-dominated, low-paying occupations; to the lack of affordable childcare provision, the continuance of maternal-dominated shared parental leave (despite the more flexible, in theory, government provisions); and what one delegate in our Scottish research meeting referred to as 'inflexible flexible working provisions' and effectively a 'glass ceiling' applied in practice in many employers.

The UK's gender pay reporting requirements have taken more than five years to implement, having originally been set out in the consolidated Equal Pay Act in 2010. Business groups such as the CBI initially described the required statistics as 'misleading' and a 'red tape' burden for small business to deal with for little, if any return (GEO 2015). The parliamentary Women and Equalities Committee (2016), however, has attacked the UK government's action for its timidity and failure to address the scale of the difficulties experienced by women, particularly those over 40 years old. The vertical segregation of the UK labour market means that two-thirds of the UK's low-paid employees are female while over 80% of high-earning executives are men.

Their own enquiry advocated addressing these structural factors with co-ordinated action in low-paying sectors such as catering and cleaning and more widespread legislation to support women with childcare and in working flexibly.

Wild (2016) similarly points to the failure of voluntarism, the general decline in private-sector pay transparency and government advice and enforcement activity, alongside the watering down of the public-sector equality duty in England. She believes that a much more fundamental reform of the equality legislative framework is required. The Government Equality Office's own survey (IFF 2015) found just a quarter of employers carrying out equal pay audits, mostly in the public sector. The majority did not plan to undertake one either. To illustrate the scale of the problems in tackling gender pay gaps, the Halifax's annual pocket-money survey reveals, rather depressingly, that a 12% gender gap exists for those under 12 years old. As the *Financial Times* noted wryly, "boys force a better deal, just like their dads in the workplace" (Barrett 2016).

Actions and reactions

As politicians in more and more countries have apparently become frustrated at the lack of voluntary progress in closing gaps – the UK government's 'Think, Act, Report' initiative was a dismal failure, with just five employers actually publishing their pay gaps – we have seen more extensive legislative action of this type and beyond. Germany, for example, is also requiring more extensive employer reporting and countries such as Denmark and Austria are employing mandatory equal pay auditing and publishing of plans to close gaps (as is required in the public sector in Wales). In the US, Philadelphia's Wage Equity Bill is set to follow Massachusetts in banning employers from asking job applicants about their prior earnings (Maher and Keon 2016).

Many of the participants in our EHRC research consultation groups also believed that stronger and additional action is required beyond mandatory reporting. Partly this was because of recalcitrance and also the ability of employers to disguise and manipulate their gaps under headline reported figures, as illustrated by Metcalfe and Woodhams' research in one employer (2012); see also findings in the CIPD's 2017 annual reward survey report (Bailey et al. 2017). Some participants favoured stronger and more wide-ranging government intervention. But as delegates in our Cardiff EHRC group pointed out, there is a limit as to how far even the most interventionist legislation can actually impact on employer practice. In Wales, the public-sector equality duty has been extended, requiring not just reporting of gender, ethnic and disability pay gaps, but also action plans to address them. Delegates felt that this requirement, however, was almost impossible to police. They also pointed out that many willing employers simply do not know how best to close their gaps in an effective and affordable way – they need to be supported to change and address these gaps, rather than being threatened and cajoled by legislation and fines.

PERC's latest research, which takes in the views of more than 120 UK employers, suggested why the government has felt compelled to legislate, but also indicates a more positive shift in employer views. The prevailing employer attitude was perhaps best summed up by a private-sector company which told the researchers, with no sense of irony whatsoever, that "gender is an invisible thing for us . . . we go where the talent is and pay everyone their market worth". The general reaction to the regulations they found has moved on from opposition to a cautious but sceptical welcome, but, as Professor Woodhams described it, employers seem to think that gender pay gaps "are everyone else's problem", and that the reporting legislation will lead to little change.

Some employers have taken steps already to address their gender gap. Computer giant Intel's annual report (McGregor 2016) entitled 'Strong Progress and More to Do', and anticipating the California state's impending reporting requirement, revealed that employees with the same role at the same level achieved identical 100% equal pay rates. The firm announced a range of initiatives to promote higher rates of female representation at senior levels, including enhancing its parental and sabbatical leave programmes, setting itself the goal of becoming the first technology business to reach full representation of women and minorities throughout the US. Following the complaints of two female employees, the chief executive of Salesforce, Marc Bienoff, was amazed at the scale of the gender pay gap revealed by an audit he ordered of their 17,000 employees. Since then, he has invested $3 million in addressing these inequities (Bellstrom 2015). We have seen similar direct action to increase female professors' pay recently at Essex University (BBC News 2016).

As well as responding to legislation, employers more widely have been implementing a range of diversity initiatives designed to address gender and other target groups under-represented and underpaid compared to white males, ranging from setting representation targets and carrying out equal pay audits, to unconscious bias training, more widespread promotion of job sharing and part-time working at senior levels, and even encouraging the Nordic practice of including breaks for childcare as a positive experience on CVs.

But the impact of these actions has been much debated and is highly questionable. In the UK, for example, unconscious bias training (UBT) has enjoyed some popularity. Yet recent research at Harvard University by Professor Iris Bohnet highlights how difficult changing individual attitudes is through such techniques and supports the view that enforced 'organizational designs' are much more effective (Morse 2016). In the UK, Warmington and Klein's research (2016) in the NHS found that UBT and other 'softer' initiatives such as mentoring did not help to increase diversity levels subsequently.

On the other hand, the research found that approaches which established management support and accountability, where leadership expected change, were more effective and were associated with increases in diversity. One approach, for example, was to oblige interview panels to make their decisions more transparent and accountable. Dobbin and Kalev (2016) argue on the basis of their research that "you can't outlaw bias" and mandatory selection testing and monitoring programmes generally fail due to management opposition. They instead emphasize the need to engage managers in supporting initiatives and encouraging social accountability for change, rather than trying to force or control it.

We review below evidence on these various government and employer interventions to consider their effectiveness of in closing gender pay gaps, drawing on our research as summarised in Table 12.1.

Government actions

The Equality Act

As indicated above, the size of the gender pay gap differs significantly between the public and private sectors and one clear difference is that the gender equality duty was introduced for the public sector in 2007 (Gow and Middlemiss 2011). This duty was replaced by a more general duty under the Equality Act 2010 (ibid.). The Equality Act also allowed for the creation of specific duties which are devolved to the Scottish and Welsh Assembly governments, resulting in differing obligations on public bodies relating to equal pay.

For example, in Scotland, the specific duties include a requirement for public bodies with 150 or more employees to publish gender pay gap information every two years and to publish a statement on equal pay every four years, specifying their equal pay policy and the occupational segregation of men and women in particular grades and occupations (Close the Gap 2012; Gow and Middlemiss

Table 12.1 Summary of research evidence on potential actions for closing gender pay gaps

Action	Responsibility	Interventions	Sources of evidence
Equality reporting	Government	– Mandatory reporting, with reporting requirements relating to gender, disability and ethnicity – Lower the Section 78 requirement to organizations with fewer than 250 employees.	– Gow and Middlemiss (2011) – Dewson et al (2011) – IFF Research (2015) – EHRC Workshops
	Government/ EHRC	– Educate employers to overcome wrongful assumptions that equal pay issues are not relevant where there is job evaluation and other formalised HR processes in place.	
	Employers	– Emphasis on action points following equal pay reviews and inclusion of metrics/ evaluation methods to determine effectiveness of actions.	
Shared Parental Leave	Government/ Employer	– Raise level of Shared Parental Pay (consider statutory and employer top ups) – Attempt to mitigate the perceived negative career impact of an extended period of time off for fathers	– Plantenga and Remery (2005, cited in BIS, 2013) – Moss, 2011, cited in BIS, (2013) – Manning and Petrongolo (2008)
National Minimum Wage	Government	– Raise level of NMW appropriately and progressively	
Flexible working	Employers	– Re-organization of work to provide opportunities for flexible working at all grades, particularly at senior levels and in high paying functions	– EHRC Workshops
	EHRC	– Educate all employees on right to request flexible working arrangements at all grades.	
Performance management and the provision of training	Employers	– Pooled ad moderated evaluation of employees against the same criteria – Use of clear, established and bias-free criteria for performance assessments; and with a defined and robust link to pay – Checking of performance ratings by groupings eg part time vs full time employees – Standardised promotion cycles – Greater training opportunities for those working flexibly – Unconscious bias training for those who make appraisal and promotion decisions – Monitor and review promotions and training by equality strand and use this data to inform HR strategy	– Menino (2013) – Olsen et al (2010)

Table 12.1. (continued)

Action	Responsibility	Interventions	Sources of evidence
Maternity	Employers	– Enhanced support for maternity returners; flexible working opportunities; mentoring and confidence building activities, networks etc – Unconscious bias training for managers dealing with maternity returners	– Workshops – Best practice examples
Recruitment	Employers/ EHRC/ Government	– Promote use of blind applications and a move away from CV applications in the private sector – Evaluate job applicants as a common pool	– Menino (2013) – National Centre for Social Research (2009) – Heath and Cheung (2006) – Best practice examples
	Employers	– Ensure diverse evaluators for recruitment – Central control and monitoring of starting salaries for new recruits on a regular basis – Monitor recruitment and selection by equality strand – Review equality policies and their impact regularly – Target-setting around the recruitment of protected characteristic groups to benchmark against for recruitment development purposes.	
Senior representation	Employer/ EHRC/ Government	– Attention to the talent pipeline eg. formal leadership programmes or senior mentors who sponsor diverse talent – Promotion of the business case for diversity in the senior team and risks of ignoring the pay gaps agenda. – Setting and monitoring of targets at employer, sector and national levels	– EHRC Workshops – Menino (2013)

(Continued)

Table 12.1. (continued)

Action	Responsibility	Interventions	Sources of evidence
Practical support	Government/ Employer/ EHRC	– Focus on provision of support for those with mental health difficulties – Promote awareness of existing support packages among employers and employ-ees/applicants and employer awareness of adjustment needs – Attention to the importance of working hour's flexibility (at all grades) as a means of accommodating disability. – Promote best practice with reference to ensuring there are written adjustment agreements in place – Attention to SMEs recruitment and retention of disabled employees – Ensure disabled employees have access to a committed mentor/sponsor and visible senior staff support – Promote the visibility of disability within an organization eg. staff networks etc. – Focus on building the skills and confidence of line managers in managing employees with disabilities; and ensuring consistency in the application of related policies.	– Workshops – RADAR/ Sayce (2010) – Law et al (2007, cited in Riddell et al, 2010) – Savenera & Whippy (2015)
Early years education intervention	Government, EHRC	– Attention to educational inequalities/stereotypes – Focus on the careers services in schools, further education and universities, as well as relevant charities and employer bodies involved	– Workshops – London Economics (2015) – Heath and Cheung (2006)
Active labour market policies	Government	– Sustained active labour market policies in deprived areas	– Heath and Cheung (2006) – NAO (2008)

Source: Brown et al. 2017.

2011). In respect of the duties relevant to pay, the Equality and Human Rights Commission Scotland found that the publishing rate for gender pay gaps was 95%; for equal pay policies, it was 96% and for occupational segregation it was lower, at 75% (EHRC Scotland, 2013).

But what was the quality of these reports? Progress made since 2013 was assessed in a report published by Close the Gap (2015) and found that proportion undertaking gender pay gap reporting remained poor, with many public bodies publishing incorrect calculations, flawed analysis and few subsequent action points (Close the Gap 2015). A third of organizations required to publish a gender pay gap had failed to publish a single figure and some organizations published pay gaps that excluded groups of staff, most commonly senior management, with "organizations citing the negative impact of a small number of typically male-dominated roles on their gender pay gap". Also, "many public bodies viewed publishing their gender pay gap, or undertaking an equal pay review, as an end in itself. There were few examples given of specific actions to tackle the causes of the pay gap" (ibid.). Based on this indicative evidence, public bodies' response to the duty appears to have been slow (ibid.) and its impact on the gender pay gap minimal.

Equal pay audits

The Equality Act 2010 (Equal Pay Audits) Regulations 2014 was a further UK government intervention linked to closing the gender pay gap. This act requires an organization which loses an equal pay case to carry out an equal pay audit. Whilst it is too soon to assess the effectiveness of the legislation, qualitative research found that there was good reason to think that an equal pay audit would be appropriate to minimise the risk of future discrimination (IDS 2012).

Some measures directly targeting the reduction of the gender pay gap through equal pay audit tools have been undertaken in a number of European countries. For example, an online tool, Logib, has been developed in Austria, Germany, Luxembourg and Switzerland to enable companies to voluntarily analyse their pay systems to reveal any gender pay gaps (European Commission 2013). Similarly, in The Netherlands the 'Wage Indicator' (Loonwijzer) project attempts to share and compare pay information and the 'Equal Pay Quick Scan' software, also from the Netherlands, allows organizational pay data to be analysed (Eurofound 2010).

One view from the workshops conducted as part of our EHRC review was that the quality of equal pay reviews is typically poor and the proportion of organizations conducting them in the UK private sector is very low. The focus on analysing and reporting on a single pay gap figure many felt was misleading, so a more in-depth audit internally was preferable, but there were concerns about the risks of making any of the findings public. The focus in all our discussion groups was rather on how to move from analysis to action.

Gender pay reporting

Following detailed consultation, compulsory gender pay reporting regulations were introduced in the UK in April 2017 for all employers with more than 250 employees. They are now required to provide a snapshot of differences in the pay of male and female employees as of April each year, including: the percentage difference in mean and median hourly pay; the percentage difference in mean and median bonus pay as well as the percentage of male and female employees who received bonus pay; and the distribution of men and women in each pay quartile ordered lowest to highest. Narrative explanation is also encouraged by the official guidance on the regulations produce by ACAS.

The Fawcett Society, however, has identified that around 59% of UK employees are unaffected as, of the 4.7 million businesses in the UK, only about 6,000 have more than

250 employees (cited in Gow and Middlemiss 2011). The minimum size requirement was designed to reduce the burden of administration on small businesses.

The view generally expressed by employers present in our EHRC workshops was supportive; and that equality reporting can be an onerous task for employers, is considered a major undertaking for most organizations and not possible for smaller organizations, which do not have the required resources. However, some thought that the requirement should be lowered to 150 employees, as is reflected in other parts of Europe. In Sweden, businesses with 25 or more employees have to conduct an equality action plan every three years, which has contributed to a gender pay gap of only 3% for women working in male-dominated occupations (Gow and Middlemiss 2011; GEO 2015).

In Austria, companies with more than 150 employees must provide gender pay gap information every other year to employees (GEO 2015). And in Finland, the Equality Act requires employers with more than thirty staff to produce an equality plan to share with employees every other year (ibid.).

But, irrespective of size, the employers we consulted felt that the bigger issue is what the reported data show and the effort needed and potential financial costs to remedy any pay gaps revealed. There were concerns that a single figure would present a misleading picture and "attract the wrong kind of publicity", opening up a 'Pandora's Box' with a fear of equal pay claims if the pay gap is disclosed, and so there was a desire to include a narrative alongside any statistics.

The UK government's actions on compulsory reporting followed continuing evidence of non-compliance on the equal pay requirement (GEO 2012) and the failure of voluntary gender pay gap reporting; with the most recent research from IFF Research (2015) examining the extent to which private and non-profit employers with 150 or more staff collect, report and publish data on pay by gender. Dewson et al. (2011) investigated the same with employers of 150–249 staff; and Adams et al. (2010) undertook similar research with employers of 250 staff or more. Interestingly, all of these studies identified that the most common reason for not conducting a gender pay gap review was not a lack of data, knowledge or skills to undertake an analysis. But that organizations considered that they already provided equal pay (89% for those with 150 or more staff; 80% for medium-sized employers; and 85% for large employers). And therefore measurement of the gender pay gap was not necessary. Such assumptions encouraged the government to implement the compulsory requirement.

National Minimum Wage

The introduction of the UK's National Minimum Wage (NMW), followed by the more rapidly escalating National Living Wage in 2015, benefited low-paid workers, and, in particular, women, as they hold the majority of minimum wage jobs (59% – LPC, 2014). Furthermore, 41% of these minimum wage jobs are held by female part-time workers (LPC 2015). Women have been cited as one of the primary direct beneficiaries of the NMW (Low Pay Commission, 2008, cited in Phimister and Theodossiou 2009). Therefore, it should follow that the introduction of the NMW in 1999 would go some way to closing the gender pay gap at the bottom of the earnings distribution and, in particular, the position of part-time women (Azmat 2015).

When the NMW was first introduced, the average pay increase for workers in the bottom decile of the earnings distribution (April 1998 to April 1999) was about 10%, or double the growth in median earnings over the same period. This improvement in relative pay was greater for part-time than full-time workers (Metcalf 2008). Recent evidence from the Low Pay

Commission also shows that the gap has almost halved at the lowest decile – from 12.9% in 1998 to 5.5% in 2014 (LPC 2015).

The NMW has had a larger impact on the pay of part-time women than full-time women (Manning and Petrongolo 2008). However, Manning and Petrongolo's analysis of the impact of the introduction of the NMW showed that its effect was in fact only small – at about 1%. This small impact is attributed to the NMW being set at a 'modest level' and Manning and Petrongolo argue that "unless the NMW is set at a considerably higher level it is not going to have a large effect on the part-time pay penalty" (ibid.).

However, indicative research has shown that even if the minimum wage was raised to the level of the higher real Living Wage level (using the following figures: £7.65 outside London, £8.80 in London), the gender pay gap would only reduce by 0.8% (Fawcett Society 2014). This research, conducted by Landmann Economics, found that this measure would raise the pay of almost one million more women (2.96 million) than men (2.03 million). The reduction in the gender pay gap is, however, still small despite the large number of women impacted, due to the majority of women affected working part-time (1.8 million); whereas the majority of men affected are full-time (1.36 million).

These calculations highlight the importance of interventions tackling barriers to women's pay and career progression and the Fawcett Society argue that whilst interventions addressing low pay can be effective, these need to be supported by changes to increase the quality of part-time work and remove barriers to career progression for part-time workers (Fawcett Society 2014).

Since this research the higher National Living Wage was introduced in the UK, with the aim of increasing the minimum wage to close to two-thirds of average earnings by 2021. The latest forecasts from the Institute for Fiscal Studies (2017) suggest that this will continue to narrow both wage differentials in the economy, and the gender pay gap, with pay escalating most rapidly in its forecasts for the lowest-paid, majority female group and least for the highest paid, largely male decile (see Figure 12.2).

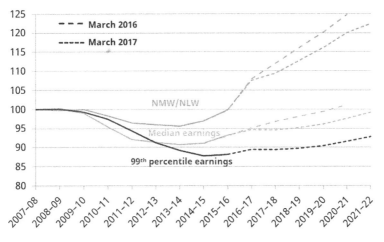

Figure 12.2   Path of real earnings since 2007–2008

Sources: OBR Economic and Fiscal Outlook (various years) and IFS calculations using Annual Survey of Hours and Earnings.

Shared parental leave

A UK government intervention aimed at improving women's position in the labour market is the recent legislation concerning shared parental leave. This is designed to give parents more flexibility over childcare arrangements in the first year, by increasing the share of leave fathers can take (BIS 2013).

Despite this new legislation offering more flexibility, it has not yet delivered substantial change. Indeed, practitioner research by legal firm Hogan Lovells and My Family Care (2014) based on a sample of 70 organizations, suggested that only 2% of these companies had seen a significant uptake of shared parental leave since it came into effect in April 2015.

This albeit small survey found the biggest barrier to take up (41%) was a cultural perception that an extended period of time off for a father would be career-limiting. Furthermore, some qualitative research by the National Childbirth Trust, based on interviews with 2,112 men and women, found that almost a third of the men interviewed (30%) would not consider sharing parental leave with their partner, with almost half (45%) stating that the poor remuneration of parental leave was the key barrier (NCT 2014). While many employers provide maternity leave and payments at least at or above the statutory requirement, few have enhanced payments above the statutory rate for paternity pay, making for a common financial penalty in sharing the childcare more equally.

Drawing some broad conclusions from these indicative studies, without significant change to the pay and structure of the arrangements, the effectiveness of the new legislation may be limited. Germany is moving to harmonize maternity and paternity pay rates at 75% of earnings, so it will be interesting to monitor the effects of this on male take-up rates.

Plantenga and Remery (2005) found that there are four main determinants of take-up rates of paternity/parental leave by fathers, based on an analysis of 30 European and Canadian paternity/parental leave arrangements. These were: the payment level; the organizational and social culture; programme flexibility; and the labour market (in terms of employer attitudes and perceived career advancement) (cited in BIS 2013). It was found that "the highest take-up rates are apparent in the countries that have a high rate of income replacement, shown to be the Scandinavian countries of Sweden, Norway, Iceland and Denmark. Conversely those countries with low rates of income replacement tend to show much lower take-up rates by fathers where generous amounts of leave are available" (BIS 2013).

Some international evidence does find positive change occurring from the provision of statutory leave for fathers. For example, in Norway, the proportion of men taking some parental leave increased from 4% to 89% since the introduction of a one-month father's leave quota (Moss, 2011, cited in BIS 2013). In Sweden, the proportion of leave days taken by men doubled between 1997 and 2004 with the introduction and extension of a father's leave quota (ibid.). In Quebec, the proportion of fathers taking paternity/parental leave increased from 56% (in 2006) to 82% (in 2008), following reform which provided a longer period of time-off for fathers and higher wage replacement (ibid.). This compares to 12% of fathers taking leave across the rest of Canada where there is no paid paternity leave and a poorer parental leave offering (ibid.).

In Germany, in 2007, the federal government introduced a monthly parental leave allowance ('Elterngeld') (Eurofound 2010). As a result, the proportion of fathers taking leave rose from 3.3% in 2006 to 20% in 2010 (Moss, 2011, cited in BIS 2013). An evaluation of the Elterngeld conducted in 2008 found that 1.5 years after birth, mothers who received parental allowance were more likely to be employed than before the Elterngeld was introduced (43% vs. 38%) (Vogler-Ludwig and Giernalczyk 2009). Therefore, it could be concluded that this parental allowance is facilitating re-entry into the labour market for mothers and also encouraging fathers to take on a greater share of child care (ibid.).

In the workshops conducted for our EHRC review, participants raised the fairness of shared parental leave pay being significantly lower than maternity leave pay in the UK, agreeing that this is a significant barrier to greater sharing of this leave in practice. Reference was also made to 'inflexible flexible working policies' and a 'glass ceiling' policy in practice, whereby, at least tacitly, some employers refuse to agree flexible or part-time working arrangements for more senior and higher-paid positions.

Education policy

Various education policy approaches have intended to remove obstacles and encourage young women to pursue study which does not conform to typical gender stereotypes and therefore increase women's earning power (European Commission 2013). A major policy focus has been on increasing young women's entry into STEM (Science, Engineering, Technology and Maths) and ICT subjects. For example, following a report published by the Women's Business Council, an independent panel of experts commissioned by the UK Government Equalities Office, in 2013, the government committed to creating a greater partnership between schools, business and parents to broaden young women's aspirations and career choices and in particular to study STEM subjects at all levels.

Quantitative research by London Economics (2015) highlighted the importance of encouraging female pupils to take STEM subjects as a means of closing the gender pay gap. The report found that wage returns are greater when a STEM A-Level is undertaken and girls taking one STEM A-Level can expect wages to rise by £4,500 a year on average; while those who take two STEM A-Levels can expect a wage return of 33.1% (London Economics 2015). The research also found that for men, the grade of A-Level is important; but for women, the grade of A-Level is less important than the choice of subject in determining earnings (ibid.).

In the workshops conducted for our EHRC research, there was a common view that greater intervention is required in early years' education, for example, in primary schools. It was thought that non-traditional role models also need to be promoted, like at BAE Systems UK which named a Female Apprentice of the Year in 2015.

Employer interventions

Evidence on the effectiveness of employer interventions which impact on the gender pay gap is harder to locate and we must consider more descriptive evidence about what interventions employers are implementing. However, Women Adding Value to the Economy (WAVE) research has found that that even where employers are operating good practices in job evaluation and pay systems "the gender segregation in society and economy can be pulled into and reproduced within employment structures within organizations" (Parken 2015). Observations from this and our workshop findings follow below.

Working hours flexibility

More than 20 million UK employees can now request flexible working according to the latest government statistics, due to the statutory right to request flexible working being extended in June 2014 to all employees (after 26 weeks' service), regardless of parental or caring responsibilities. Before the right to request was extended, CIPD research found that out of 218,100 employment tribunal claims in 2010/11, just 277 alleged that employers had failed to observe flexible working regulations (CIPD 2012). The majority of these claims were successfully conciliated or settled out of court and, of the 48 that reached tribunal, just 10 were successful (cited by Woods 2011). These figures may suggest that the right to request is an effective intervention which has not placed undue burdens on employers (ibid.).

However, generally working hours flexibility is also associated with lower earnings (Olsen et al. 2010). Part-time workers (both men and women) earn less, on average, per hour than their full-time counterparts, but a much higher proportion of women work part-time (41%) compared with men (11%) (ONS, 2015). Goldin (2014) observes that "the gender gap in pay would be considerably reduced and might even vanish if firms did not have an incentive to disproportionately reward individuals who worked long hours and who worked particular hours".

WAVE research also identified that part-time work is associated both with working patterns in feminized occupations and with low pay. For example, some three-quarters of all women's part-time work (in Wales) is undertaken in administration, personal services, sales and elementary occupations (Parken et al. 2014). The impact of part-time working on earnings has also been found to be negative and cumulative (ibid.). However, Olsen et al. (2010) found that other forms of working hours' flexibility did not contribute much to causing lower wages, with term-time working being the only form of working hours that had much effect on wages; a small, but statistically significant negative effect (–7%). These findings highlight the need to further address the pattern of caring responsibilities to help women with young children stay in work (Olsen et al. 2010).

A wide range of organizations display good practice in flexible working programmes, although the impact on pay and career gaps is much less well-documented (GEO 2011). For example, Eversheds LLP, an international law firm represented in our research, employing about 3,000 people in the UK, has an award-winning flexible working programme called "Lifestyle", which has seen strong take-up rates, with over 400 employees having flexible working arrangements in 2011 (GEO 2011).

Support for maternity returners

Women taking time out of the labour market for children also has a significant impact on the gender pay gap (GEO 2015). Government policy initiatives such as shared parental leave, the extension of the right to request flexible working, tax-free childcare and free early education places for three- and four-year-olds have attempted to support women's return to work after having children (GEO 2015). But some employers are enhancing provisions further for maternity returners in order to increase the retention rates of these women.

For example, Eversheds also offers an enhanced maternity package, including greater support for returners in the form of a transition period of return, with shorter hours, reduced days and mentoring and unconscious bias training across the business to support managers as they support maternity returners. The investment bank Goldman Sachs is another example: it has offered a paid, ten-week return-to-work programme since 2008, aimed at women who have been out of the workforce for two or more years, providing training, mentoring and networking. Since its introduction, over 120 people have attended and more than half have returned to work full-time (Sullivan 2015).

There was a view from our EHRC workshops that managers often lack the confidence and knowledge to communicate with those away on maternity leave and, as a result, 12-month maternity leavers can feel very isolated. An example was also cited where a private sector organization observed that a number of its senior female staff left on maternity leave and did not return. It therefore introduced the concept of the 'Mum Internship', which helps maternity returners understand any changes that have occurred whilst they have been away from work. As a result, return rates improved.

Training and performance management

The provision of training as an intervention to close the gender pay gap can be viewed from two perspectives. Firstly, undertaking training whilst employed is known to help facilitate career progression (Olsen et al. 2010). Secondly, training for those who make appraisal and promotion decisions can contribute to the closing of the gap if it makes them aware of the biases which place women at a disadvantage in the performance management process.

Olsen et al. (2010) found that training (formal study, on-site training and other training paid for by employers) was more common among women than men and was associated with 6% higher hourly wages. Olsen et al. conclude that in the light of the impact of part-time working on hourly earnings, encouraging training within part-time jobs may go some way to offsetting the negative impact of part-time work on pay (ibid.)

Some organizations also provide unconscious bias training to managers who have a role in the performance management process, which has the potential to improve the pay gap across all equality strands. For example, a key element of the professional services firm EY's diversity policy is to monitor staff appraisals and promotions by gender to ensure fairness. After analysing the results of staff appraisals they have offered 'unconscious bias' training to ensure that managers making appraisal and promotion decisions are aware of the biases which can place some people at a disadvantage (GEO 2011).

It is also suggested that collective evaluations of employees can reduce unconscious bias by ensuring that staff are evaluated against the same criteria and also against one another (Menino 2013). Conducting comparative promotion reviews, through which promotion cycles are standardized and promotion candidates are collectively evaluated, has been shown to reduce gender bias and stereotyping by ensuring men and women are evaluated against the same criteria (ibid.).

In the workshops conducted for the EHRC review, there was a strong and near-unanimous view that better careers advice was vital, with observations that women are commonly still directed into low-paid or part-time work. Lower levels of confidence amongst women were also cited as contributing to the gender pay gap, since it meant that women were less likely to seek promotion. It was also felt that the unconscious bias of line managers contributes to the gender pay gap and many of the participants ran such training in their organization.

Recruitment processes

The WAVE programme identified that the uneven distribution of jobs between men and women is key to the "maintenance of gender disparities" (Parken 2015). In some occupations and industries, such gender bias against women limits those short-listed for interview and impacts on recruitment decisions (Menino 2013) which, in turn, impacts on the gender pay gap. The use of gender-blind screening – whereby the applicant name is removed during the initial screening process – has been found to have a significant positive impact on the number of women recruited (Menino 2013).

Within the EHRC workshops, one private-sector employer commented that in a male-dominated industry, getting women onto the short list in an organization is a challenge as senior managers will typically recruit people who 'look like us'. One organization has tried to recruit more senior women and provided training on stereotyping and coaching on what it is like to work in a male-dominated environment. However, the key actions that will get more women into the sector were considered to be long-term actions, such as addressing gender stereotyping and the provision of better careers advice in schools.

The literature suggests that the use of diverse evaluators in the recruitment process has also been found to help address unconscious bias and therefore a gender-balanced recruitment panel may be more effective in reducing bias than one which includes only one gender (Menino 2013). A comparative review of candidates, where candidates are collectively evaluated, has also been shown to reduce the influence of stereotypes in the recruitment process (ibid.).

It is also at the point of recruitment that interventions around controlling starting salaries for new recruits (Menino 2013) and limiting line manager discretion in this area will also, in turn, affect the size of the gender pay gap. For example, through regular analysis of starting salaries it is possible to identify whether female recruits are paid less than male recruits at the same grade (ibid.).

In April 2015, Reddit, a small US-based Internet news company, announced it would prohibit salary negotiations for new recruits and existing employees in an attempt to close the gender pay gap and ensure fair and consistent salaries. It stated that women tended not to negotiate their starting salaries, leaving them at a disadvantage (Sammer 2015). Some US states, such as Massachusetts, are now making it illegal to ask questions about existing salaries in the course of the recruitment process (New York Times 2016).

Senior representation

On the basis of all the available evidence, it would be sensible to predict that interventions aimed at increasing the representation of women at senior levels and in higher-paid roles and occupations could go a significant way to closing the gender pay gap. Organizations providing support to move women up the 'talent pipeline', for example through formal leadership programmes or senior mentors who sponsor female talent, or those who actively recruit women to executive or board-level positions, are taking positive actions towards reducing the gender pay gap (Menino 2013).

A UK government report conducted by Lord Davies in 2011 found that the growth in numbers of females on boards was very slow and recommended that FTSE 100 companies should aim for a minimum of 25% female representation by 2015 (Davies 2011). Sealy and Vinnicombe (2013; cited in IES 2014) found the overall percentage of female-held board directorships in FTSE 100 companies to be 17.3%, with only seven all-male boards and two-thirds of boards having more than one female director. Davies's target was achieved in 2015, although this was heavily focused on growth in part-time and lower-paid non-executive roles.

Research has also found that women on FTSE boards had worked in 1.3 functional areas in their careers, so they had generally focused in one function in order to progress their career, rather than moving across general management roles (Davies 2011). A new five-year plan was agreed in 2016, focusing on building the talent pool below board level and achieving greater representation in executive as opposed to non-executive roles. Although a voluntary initiative rooted in individual corporate actions, the tacit threat of legislation has undoubtedly also encouraged progress.

Cardoso and Winter-Ebmer (2010; cited in Hensvik 2014) found using a large representative sample from Portugal that female earnings increased when organizations appointed a female manager; and Bell (2005; cited in Hensvik 2014) found that the earnings of female executives were higher and women were more likely to be among the highest-paid executives in female-led firms.

In all our EHRC research groups examples were cited of organizations paying equally for work of equal value, but that there was an overall gender pay gap being driven up by the lack of female representation in senior posts. It was generally felt that the focus of work on female representation should be on achieving equality across the whole pipeline feeding senior managerial appointments, not just at board level. At middle-management level, gender representation was generally closer to 50:50 in these employers but declined rapidly thereafter, except in some corporate functions such as HR.

Conclusion: the need for integrated solutions

Gender pay gaps, in conclusion, are the result of a complex and multifaceted set of issues and therefore a difficult area: for academics to research; for policy makers and governments to legislate and support; and for employers and practitioners to act. Employer bodies have argued for many years that there is a strong business case for equality and so employers have sufficient motivation to address the issue of senior-level female representation, which they regard as the primary driver of gaps (GEO responses, 2016). Yet nothing has had, or is likely to ever have, the effect in closing the national gap of the original Equal Pay Act and, as the gap has persisted and voluntary action disappointed, governments in the UK, Europe and the US more than 40 years later have become impatient and are once again encouraging or requiring action.

As we have seen, and as summarised in Table 12.1, many individual actions by individual employers and governments have the potential to impact on gaps. Yet in almost all cases the effect is small and highly context-dependent. It is also clear that, just as factors of causation interact, with older women in their forties suffering, for example, from having the main childcare costs and responsibilities, inflexible working policies and norms and so on (WEC 2016), so supporting actions can exert a positive upwards effect on female pay, with the legislative right to request flexible working, for example, encouraging more employers to follow the example of the leading firms and to apply their policies at more senior levels (IES 2016).

Ultimately, therefore, it appears that the only really effective way to continue to reduce and even eventually remove gender pay gaps is for multi-stakeholder groups to co-operate in working together to address this complex web of causation with multiple and sustained initiatives. This can be seen in the progress made in Boston in analysing and starting to reduce the city's overall gap (Boston City 2013) A similar example in the UK is the already-cited Women Adding Value to the Economy (WAVE) Programme in Wales, funded by the European Social Fund, through the Welsh Government and with key partners including the universities of South Wales and Cardiff, The Women's Workshop and trade unions. The first phase of WAVE ran between 2012 and 2015 with the aim of understanding and 'interrupting' the ways in which gender pay disparities are consistently reproduced through occupational segregation, through the ways in which 'women's work' is valued and contracted and through the operation of pay systems. The second phase of WAVE is continuing in 2016 and 2017.

Another example is in UK higher education (HE), where we can see the progress that effective data analysis and advice can produce in a sector that, perhaps surprisingly, has one of the widest gender pay gaps. Employers, represented by the Universities and Colleges Employers Association, and the HE trade unions undertook joint work researching information on gender pay interventions, with a view to identifying and actively promoting effective practice. Their report (UCEA 2015) highlights 43 actions which their research suggests can have a positive impact, ranging from advertising all jobs as open to flexible working, to equal pay audits, fully representative promotion and appointment panels and female networking groups.

Partly through UCEA's work, more than 90% of HE institutions now carry out gender pay audits and, based on this knowledge, we are seeing a wide range of interventions adopted. These range from Kings College's 'positive discrimination', to unconscious bias training, to more widespread promotion of job sharing and part-time working at senior levels, as well as encouraging the Nordic practice of including breaks for childcare as a positive experience on CVs. And that data leading to analysis and action is already having an impact. The November 2015 national earnings data published by the Office for National Statistics revealed that the HE gender pay gap is narrowing, with a significant fall of 2.4 percentage points for full-time staff working in the sector (from 13.5% in April 2014 to 11.1% in April 2015). The 2015–16 pay settlement commits employers and trade unions to further work in this area.

IES's research in Lewisham Council, which is characterized by what is referred to as a 'negative pay gap', i.e., women earn more than men, highlights the importance of sustained focus and example-setting by senior leaders, effective HR monitoring and support measures, and a 'promote-from-within talent' strategy (IES 2016).

The new gender pay reporting requirements in the UK should help to encourage a more transparent pay environment which we know is conducive to smaller gender pay gaps. But researchers and HR practitioners would almost certainly agree on the basis of the evidence we have reviewed with Professor Caroline Gattrell (2015) that "while it is a good thing to encourage more transparency around levels of average pay and to expose the discrepancies between what men and women in the same roles earn, it is important not to think that the task ends there".

Appendix: List of participant organizations in the EHRC research

Workshop 1 (Edinburgh)	Workshop 2 (Edinburgh)	Workshop 3 (London)	Workshop 4 (London)	Workshop 5 (Cardiff)
NHS Fife	Close the Gap	Aon Hewitt	Christian Aid	Welsh Local Government
Scottish Government	Engender	NHS Employers	Fox Williams	Fairer Futures Division/Welsh Government
NHS Education for Scotland	Edinburgh Napier University	University of Sheffield	University of Brighton/ PayCompare	Burges Salmon LLP
Dumfries and Galloway College	Highlands and Islands Enterprise/ Iomairt na Gàidhealtachd's nan Eilean	Guys and St Thomas NHS Foundation Trust	Together: For Mental Wellbeing	Women Adding Value to the Economy (WAVE), Cardiff University
Thirteen Group	Queen Margaret University	University of Cambridge	Financial Ombudsman Service	University of South Wales
University of Strathclyde	The State Hospital	EY	Jacky Hilary – HR Consultant	Women Connect First
	Scottish Government	Pearl Meyer		RCTCBC
	NHS National Services Scotland	Addleshaw Goddard		Unite Wales
		Surrey Police Sainsbury's		Chwarae Teg Eversheds

(Continued)

Appendix (continued)

Workshop 1 (Edinburgh)	Workshop 2 (Edinburgh)	Workshop 3 (London)	Workshop 4 (London)	Workshop 5 (Cardiff)
		ISG		Cardiff University
				Blaenau Gwent County Borough Council
				Thompsons Solicitors
				University Health Board
				Welsh Government
				Adele Baumgardt
				Dr Kath Atkinson

Source: Brown et al. 2017.

References

Adams, L., Gore, K. and Shury, J. (2010). *Gender Pay Gap Reporting Survey 2009*, Research Report 55. Equality and Human Rights Commission. Available at: www.equalityhumanrights.com/sites/default/files/research-report-55-gender-pay-gap-reporting-survey-2009.pdf

Azmat, G. (2015). *Gender Gaps in the UK Labour Market: Jobs, Pay and Family-friendly policies*, CEP 2015 Election Analyses Series, Paper EA027. Centre for Economic Performance, London School of Economics. Available at: www.cep.lse.ac.uk/pubs/download/ea027.pdf

Bailey, M., Mariott. L. and Perkins, S. J. (2017). *Annual Reward Survey*. London: CIPD.

Barrett, C. (2016). Gender pay gap emerges in children's pocket money. *The Financial Times* June 3rd. Available at: www.ft.com/content/e25f55a6-28c5-11e6-8b18-91555f2f4fde

BBC News. (2016). *University Wipes out Gender Pay Gap*. June 3rd. Available at: www.bbc.co.uk/news/education-36444063

Bellstrom, K. (2015). Salesforce spent $3million to close the gender pay gap. *Fortune Magazine*. November 7th. Available at: www.fortune.com/2015/11/07/salesforce-3-million-close-pay-gap/

BIS/Department for Business Innovation and Skills. (2013). *Modern Workplaces: Shared Parental Leave and Pay Administration Consultation – Impact Assessment*. Department for Business Innovation and Skills. BIS/13/651. Available at: www.gov.uk/government/uploads/system/uploads/attachment_data/file/110692/13-651-modern-workplaces-shared-parental-leave-and-pay-impact-assessment2.pdf

Booth, R. and Topping, A. (2017). Two million protest against Trump's inauguration worldwide. *The Guardian*. January 22nd. Available at: www.theguardian.com/lifeandstyle/2017/jan/22/two-million-protest-against-trumps-inauguration-worldwide

Boston City. (2013). *Closing the Wage Gap*. Available at: www.cityofboston.gov/images_documents/Boston_Closing%20the%20Wage%20Gap_Interventions%20Report_tcm3-41353.pdf

Brown, D., Rickard, C. and Broughton, A. (2017). *Tackling Gender, Disability and Ethnicity Pay Gaps: A Progress Review*. London: EHRC.

Close the Gap. (2012). *Public Sector Equality Duty: Guidance for Publishing Information on Gender and Employment, Equal Pay, and Occupational Segregation*. Close the Gap. Available at: www.closethegap.org.uk/content/resources/CTG-PSED-guidance-for-employers-August-2012.pdf

Close the Gap. (2015). *Making Progress? An Assessment of Public Sector Employers' Compliance with the Public Sector Equality Duty*, Close the Gap Working Paper 15. Available at: www.closethegap.org.uk/content/resources/Making-Progress—An-assessment-of-employers-compliance-with-PSED-November-2015.pdf

Christensen, M. (2016). *Worldwide Guide to Women in Leadership*. Available at: www.guide2womenleaders.com/index.html

CIPD. (2012). *Flexible Working*. May. London: CIPD. Available at: www.cipd.co.uk/hr-resources/survey-reports/flexible-working-provision-uptake.aspx

Davies, M. (2011). *Women on Boards*. Department for Business Innovation and Skills. Available at: www.gov.uk/government/uploads/system/uploads/attachment_data/file/31710/11-745-women-on-boards.pdf

Dewson, S., Gloster, R., Chubb, C., Carter, M. and Reilly, P. (2011). *Voluntary Gender Equality Reporting in Organisations with 150 to 249 Employees*. Government Equalities Office. Available at: www.gov.uk/government/uploads/system/uploads/attachment_data/file/85541/gender-equality-reporting.pdf

Dobbin and Kalev. (2016). Why Diversity Programmes Fail, *Harvard Business Review*, July–August. Available at: www.hbr.org/2016/07/why-diversity-programs-fail

Eurofound. (2010). *Addressing the Gender Pay Gap: Government and Social Partner Actions*. European Foundation for the Improvement of Living and Working Conditions. Available at: www.eurofound.europa.eu/sites/default/files/ef_publication/field_ef_document/ef1018en.pdf

European Commission. (2013). *Tackling the Gender Pay Gap in the European Union*. European Commission. Luxembourg: Publications Office of the European Union. Available at: www.ec.europa.eu/justice/gender-equality/files/gender_pay_gap/140227_gpg_brochure_web_en.pdf

European Commission. (2014). *The Situation in the EU*, European Commission [Online]. Available at: www.ec.europa.eu/justice/gender-equality/gender-pay-gap/situationeurope/index_en.htm

European Commission. (2015). *Gender Balance on Corporate Boards: Europe is Cracking the Glass Ceiling*. October. Available at: www.ec.europa.eu/justice/gender-equality/files/womenonboards/factsheet_women_on_boards_web_2015-10_en.pdf

Fawcett Society. (2014). *The Time to Act is Now: Fawcett's Gender Pay Gap Briefing*. Fawcett Society. Available at: www.fawcettsociety.org.uk/wp-content/uploads/2014/11/Fawcett-Equal-Pay-Day-report-November-2014.pdf

Gattrell, C. (2015). *Opinion: Why is Society Sustaining Our Gender Pay Gap?*, CIPD [Online]. Available at: www.cipd.co.uk/pm/peoplemanagement/b/weblog/archive/2015/07/16/opinionwhy-is-society-sustaining-our-gender-pay-gap.aspx

GEO. (2012). *Legislative Proposals to Promote Equal Pay: Impact Assessment*. Government Equalities Office. Available at: www.gov.uk/government/uploads/system/uploads/attachment_data/file/85571/impact-assessment.pdf

GEO. (2015). *Closing the Gender Pay Gap: Government Consultation*. Government Equalities Office. Available at: www.gov.uk/government/consultations/closing-the-gender-pay-gap

GEO. (2011). *Legislative Proposals to Promote Equal Pay: Impact Assessment*. Government Equalities Office. Available at: www.gov.uk/government/uploads/system/uploads/attachment_data/file/85571/impact-assessment.pdf

Goldin, C. (2014). A grand gender convergence: its last chapter. *American Economic Review*. 104(4), 1091–1119.

Gow, L. and Middlemiss, S. (2011). Equal pay legislation and its impact on the gender pay gap, *International Journal of Discrimination and the Law*. 11(4), 164–186.

Heath, A. and Cheung, S. Y. (2006). *Ethnic Penalties in the Labour Market: Employers and Discrimination*, Research Report 341. Department for Work and Pensions. London: CDS. Available at: www.webarchive.nationalarchives.gov.uk/20130128102031/http://statistics.dwp.gov.uk/asd/asd5/rports2005-2006/rrep341.pdf

Hensvik, L. (2014). Manager impartiality: worker-firm matching and the gender wage gap, *Industrial and Labor Relations Review*. 67(2), 395–421.

Hogan Lovells, My Family Care. (2014). *Shared Parental Leave Survey*. Copy available on request. Details Available at: www.hoganlovells.com/en/news/shared-parental-leave-getting-managers-on-board-is-the-key-concern-for-employers-says-survey

IDS. (2012). *Equal Pay Cases and Pay Audits: A Report for the Government Equalities Office*. Incomes Data Services. Available at: www.gov.uk/government/uploads/system/uploads/attachment_data/file/85572/equal-pay-audit-report.pdf

IES. (2014). *IES Perspectives on HR 2014*, Report 504. Brighton: Institute for Employment Studies. ISBN: 978 1 85184 452 4. Available at: www.employment-studies.co.uk/system/files/resources/files/504.pdf

IES. (2016). *The Power of Parity*. Available at: www.employment-studies.co.uk/resource/power-parity

IFF Research. (2015). *Company Reporting: Gender Pay Data, Prepared for Government Equalities Office*. IFF Research. Available at: www.gov.uk/government/uploads/system/uploads/attachment_data/file/445458/Company_Reporting_GPG_research.pdf

London Economics. (2015). *The Earnings and Employment Returns to A levels: A Report to the Department for Education.* London Economics. Available at: www.londoneconomics.co.uk/blog/publication/the-earnings-and-employment-returns-to-a-levels/

LPC [Low Pay Commission]. (2015). *National Minimum Wage: Low Pay Commission Report 2015.* Available at: www.gov.uk/government/uploads/system/uploads/attachment_data/file/520052/National_Minimum_Wage_LPC_report_2015.pdf

Maher, D. and Keon, M. (2016) *The Philadelphia Wage Equity Bill.* December 14th. Available at: www.littler.com/publication-press/publication/philadelphia-wage-equity-bill-will-ban-employers-asking-prospective

Manning, A. and Petrongolo, B. (2008). The part-time pay penalty for women in Britain. *The Economic Journal.* 118(526), 28–51.

May, T. (2016). *Statement from the New Prime Minister.* July 13th. Available at: www.gov.uk/government/speeches/statement-from-the-new-prime-minister-theresa-may

McGregor, J. (2016). Intel finds no pay gap between men and women. *Washington Post.* February 3rd Available at: www.washingtonpost.com/news/on-leadership/wp/2016/02/03/intel-says-there-is-no-pay-gap-between-men-and-women-at-the-chipmaker/?utm_term=.d3e51e24bf37

McKinsey Global Institute. (2015). *How Advancing Women's Equality Can Add $12 Trillion to Global Growth* [Online]. Accessed: 22 January 2016]. Available at: www.mckinsey.com/insights/growth/how_advancing_womens_equality_can_add_12_trillion_to_global_growth

Menino, T. (2013). *Boston – Closing the Wage Gap: Becoming the Best City in America for Working Women.* City of Boston, Office of the Mayor. Available at: www.cityofboston.gov/images_documents/Boston_Closing%20the%20Wage%20Gap_Interventions%20Report_tcm3-41353.pdf

Metcalf, D. (2008). Why has the British National Minimum Wage had Little or No Impact on Employment? *Journal of Industrial Relations.* 50(3), 489–512.

Metcalfe, B. D. and Woodhams, C. (2012). Introduction: new directions in gender, diversity and organization theorizing – re-imagining feminist post-colonialism, transnationalism and geographies of power. *International Journal of Management Reviews.* 14(2).

Morse, G. (2016) Designing a Bias Free Organization. *Harvard Business Review.* Available at: www.hbr.org/2016/07/designing-a-bias-free-organization

NCT. (2014). *Shared Parental Leave Survey.* Copy available on request. Details Available at: www.nct.org.uk/press-release/new-research-finds-13-dads-wouldnt-use-shared-parental-leave-because-low-paternity-pay

New York Times. (2016). *Illegal in Massachussets: Asking Your Salary in a Job Interview.* August 3rd. Available at: www.nytimes.com/2016/08/03/business/dealbook/wage-gap-massachusetts-law-salary-history.html?_r=0

Olsen, W., Heuvelman, H., Gash, V. and Vandecasteele, L. (2010). *The Gender Pay Gap in the UK 1995–2007: Part 2 – Policy-related Factors Offsetting Women's Low Pay in the UK, 2004–07.* Government Equalities Office, February 2010. Available at: www.webarchive.nationalarchives.gov.uk/20100505211508/http://www.equalities.gov.uk/pdf/301113_GEO_GenderPayGap_Part2_acc.pdf

ONS. (2015). *Occupational Pension Schemes Survey 2014.* London: Office for National Statistics.

O'Reilly, J., Smith, M., Deakin, S. and Burchell, B. (2015). Equal pay as a moving target: international perspectives on forty-years of addressing the gender pay gap, *Cambridge Journal of Economics.* 39(2), 299–317.

Parken, A., Pocher, E. and Davies, R. (2014). *Working Patterns in Wales: Gender Occupations and Pay.* Women Adding Value to the Economy. Cardiff University. Available at: www.wavewales.co.uk/uploads/STRAND1/Working_Patterns_In_Wales.pdf

Parken, A. (2015). *The WAVE Employer Case Studies: From Evidence to Action on Gender Pay Gaps.* Women Adding Value to the Economy. Cardiff University. Available at: www.cardiff.ac.uk/__data/assets/pdf_file/0008/112796/CU-WAVE-Research-Review-Employer-Workforce-and-Pay-Case-Studies.pdf

Phimister, E. and Theodossiou, I. (2009). Gender Differences in Low Pay Labour Mobility and the National Minimum Wage, *Oxford Economic Papers New Series,* Vol. 61, Supplement: Women and Wages, pp. i122–i146.

Plantenga, J. and Remery, C. (2005). *Reconciliation of Work and Private Life: a Comparative Review of Thirty European Countries.* DG for Employment, Social Affairs and Equal Opportunities, European Commission. Office for Official Publications of the European Communities. Available at: www.research.mbs.ac.uk/ewerc/Portals/0/docs/ReconciliationofWorkandPrivateLife.pdf

Rubery, J. and Grimshaw, D. (2014). The 40-year pursuit of equal pay: a case of constantly moving goalposts, *Cambridge Journal of Economics.* 39(2), 319–343.

Sammer, J. (2015). Take it or leave it: Should salary discussions be a one way street?, *HR Magazine*. 60(7), 34 www.members.businessdisabilityforum.org.uk/media_manager/public/86/State%20of%20the%20 Nation%20Report%20-%20Retaining%20disabled%20talent.pdf

Sullivan, R. (2015). Return-to-work schemes: support for women, *Financial Times*, 5 March. Available at: www.ft.com/content/91635c3e-b83b-11e4-86bb-00144feab7de

UCEA. (2015). *New JNCHES Gender Pay Working Group Report*, Universities and Colleges Employers Association. Available at: www.ucea.ac.uk/en/publications/index.cfm/njgender

Vogler-Ludwig, K. and Giernalczyk, H. (2009). *Parental Allowance (Elterngeld) – An Innovative Policy*, Discussion paper. European Employment Observatory Germany. Economix Research and Consulting. Available at: www.economix.org/Parental%20allowance.pdf

Warmington, J. and Klein, R. (2016). *Unconscious Bias – Silver Bullet or Just a Useful Tool?* Available at: www. brap.org.uk/about-us/blog/550-joy-warmington-and-roger-kline-unconscious-bias-silver-bullet-or-just-a-useful-tool

Wild, S. (2016). *Where to Start*. Available at: www.equalpayportal.co.uk/where-to-start-2/

Women and Equalities Committee. (2016). *Gender Pay Gap: Second Report*. Available at: www.publications. parliament.uk/pa/cm201516/cmselect/cmwomeq/584/584.pdf

Woods, D. (2011). CIPD: Freedom of Information request proves flexible working "carries no red tape" for business, *HR Magazine*, 7 November. [ONLINE]. Available at: www.hrmagazine.co.uk/article-details/ cipd-freedom-of-information-request-proves-flexible-working-carries-no-red-tape-for-business

World Economic Forum. (2015). *The Global Gender Gap Report 2015*. Available at: www.reports.weforum. org/global-gender-gap-report-2015/

13

INFLUENCES ON REWARD MIX DETERMINATION

Evidence from UK financial services

Jonathan Chapman

Introduction

Since the economic disruptions centred on financial services that began in 2007 reward mix determination (RMD) in the financial services sector has been the subject of significant scrutiny and comment by government, regulators, media and the wider public. The sector is strategically important, contributing around 8.5% to UK GDP; it comprises over 34,000 firms employing more than 900,000 people (FSSC 2010).

This chapter examines what influences 'reward mix', defined as "the combination of the elements making up overall reward" (Balkin and Bannister 1993), in UK financial services organizations, and why these influences are significant. To address criticism of the concentration of research at the reward level of top executives, the material presented is not limited to executives. It extends to all employees based on the premise that the success of an organization depends on all contributions.

Combining findings from critically examining relevant literature with evidence collected through a series of interviews with senior reward specialists in 30 financial services firms (hereafter, RSs) along with perspectives gathered from 10 reward consultants (RCs), the chapter offers both an account of the pressures facing reward mix determination in the contemporary financial services sector, and a theoretically informed approach to understanding those pressures through the presentation of a unified theory of reward mix determination. RCs were selected for interview due to their access and integration into the process of reward mix determination through their work with clients (Chapman and Kelliher 2011a); RSs were able to talk directly about the influences on reward mix determination.

The focus of the academic reward literature has largely been on pay, both fixed, in the form of salaries and wages, and variable, through a range of schemes such as incentives, bonuses and stock-related schemes (Gerhart and Rynes 2003). This is unsurprising given the amount that organizations spend on pay as a proportion of their overall costs (Lawler 1971) and its importance to individuals (Milkovich and Newman 2008), but it does neglect the wider approach to reward management choices in organizations that incorporate non-wage compensation elements.

Significant quantitative research has been carried out analysing the relationships between a range of both firm and environmental items to reward decisions, including reward mix (e.g., Eisenhardt 1988; Boyd and Salamin 2001; Tremblay et al. 2003). However, while the statistical nature of this work may have identified causality, it has only been able to infer why these items might be showing these statistical relationships. Whilst helpful, these lists of variables and their relationships give no insight into the relative importance of factors in the actual organizational reward decisions taken (Perkins et al. 2016).

Therefore, despite the amount of research carried out, we know little about how reward mix is actually determined – the 'why' as much as 'what'. In this chapter, it is argued that convergence around a smaller number of theoretical perspectives might prove helpful in directing future research (Pfeffer 1993) and informing managerial practice.

Reward mix within financial services is distinctive when compared with other industry sectors. It is typically weighted towards variable reward, with employee benefits also playing a significant role. Whilst there are notable differences in the reward mix between the retail and wholesale businesses that make up the financial services sector, both subsectors are characterized by relatively high levels of variable pay and benefits (PriceWaterhouseCoopers 2010).

Theoretical perspectives on reward mix

Over thirty years ago, Mahoney stated that no "comprehensive theory of employee compensation exists at present. Rather, there exists a number of segmented theories or models of compensation" (Mahoney 1979). In the last thirty years, we have added further to this collection of 'segmented' theories (e.g., Bloom and Milkovich 1996; Baeten 2008). Therefore, although research has been carried out, we know little about why reward strategy decisions are taken as there is no consensus emerging from all the work (Gerhart and Rynes 2003). This may be an accurate reflection of the reality with the area of reward mix decision-making being particularly complex, and as a result each theory adding insight to this complex issue. Alternatively, it may be that despite published commentary, we actually know very little.

In the interests of building convergence around a smaller number of theoretical perspectives, following a review of this extensive literature three theoretical frameworks have been adopted for the research reported in this chapter: resource dependency (Pfeffer and Davis-Blake 1987); neo-institutional theory (DiMaggio and Powell 1991); and agency theory (Jensen and Meckling 1976). Each of these perspectives offers a different explanation about how reward mix is determined. Agency theory gives insight into how to align an organization's objectives to those of the individual and specifically what reward mix will best achieve this alignment (Jensen and Meckling 1976). Neo-institutional theory helps to understand the pressures organizations are under to conform and, specifically, to mimic the reward mix of other firms (Eisenhardt 1988; Conlon and Parks 1990; Crystal 1991). Resource dependency theory helps predict who may have most power in influencing the reward mix decision. It contends that some jobs exercise control over the resources critical to the success of the organization. Individuals or groups holding those jobs are consequently able to exercise higher levels of power and therefore can use this to influence both the level and mix of the overall reward package (Tremblay et al. 2003; Pfeffer and Davis-Blake 1987; Balkin and Bannister 1993). Space considerations prohibit detailed description of the three theoretical domains; an extended discussion appears in Chapman (2011b).

Whilst most research has adopted agency theory to explain the mix decision, the other theoretical viewpoints have been shown to potentially have further explanatory power (Miller et al. 2001; Festing and Sahakiants 2010). The trend appears to be towards using complementary theoretical perspectives to deepen our knowledge of reward mix, and in particular to counter some of the criticisms that have been made of agency theory alone in explaining the phenomenon (Eisenhardt 1989; Fernandez-Alles et al. 2006; Berrone and Gomez-Mejia 2009). A summary of the three theoretical perspectives is given in Table 13.1.

Table 13.1 Summary of agency, resource dependence and institutional theories

	Agency	Resource dependence	Institutional
Purpose of reward mix decisions	To control and direct behaviour towards the objectives of the principal, especially when monitoring is difficult/costly	Acquisition of business-critical resources	Conformity with other organizations and market practice to gain legitimacy
Main assumptions	Rational decisions People are self-interested, risk-averse Goal conflict exists between owners and employees Information asymmetry	Rational decision Control of critical resources leads to power	Organizations seek legitimacy Organizations conform to norms Process of satisficing behaviour
Organizational reaction	Rational active management	Rational active management	Passive conformity or rational legitimacy seeking
Implications for reward mix	Relative weight of incentives versus fixed reward will be managed to optimize the alignment of agents' and principals' interests	Reward mix will be influenced by the relative strength of employee groups determined by their criticality to organization success	Reward mix will be influenced by institutional norms and the extent to which operating within them confers legitimacy

Each of the theoretical perspectives offers a slightly different explanation about what factors influence RMD in organizations.

If agency theory is to be accepted, then we might expect RCs and RSs to discuss how monitoring of employees, efficiency considerations around this monitoring and the span of controls of managers has determined the mix of at least fixed and variable pay. However, it has little to say about the benefits or relational elements of the reward mix. Resource dependency meanwhile focuses on the relative power between the actors involved in the employment exchange. Organizational success will be controlled by those individuals, groups of individuals or influential organizations who control access to critical resources needed for that success. Consequently, reward mix, including the benefit component, will be developed with the acquisition and retention of those critical resources in mind. Institutional theory questions these more economic and resource efficiency-based approaches, identifying a societal dimension to RMD as organizations seek to gain wider legitimacy. Reward mix is therefore largely driven by fixed constraints, both legal and tax regulations, as well as pressure to conform to the practice of other successful organizations or prescribed best practice.

The conceptual framework in Figure 13.1 presents interests, forces, practices and resources as theoretical drivers of RMDs.

Primary attention in what follows is given to what has been learned empirically through this research which has contributed an understanding of the complexity of RMD in financial services, informed by evidence on the practices and responses of financial services firms in the post-financial crisis environment showing how they have been reacting to regulatory and market-based pressures. Specifically, we now have empirical evidence of how the combination of both a

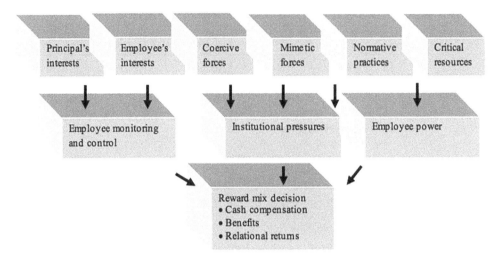

Figure 13.1 Conceptual framework

firm's desire and capability to differentiate their reward mix informs their judgement of whether to 'break free' from the established institutional norm.

An integrated model to understand influences on the determination of reward mix

Whetten's process of theory building helps build an integrated, descriptive model of RMD (Figure 13.2) informed by the findings from the interviews with 10 RCs and 30 RSs (see Chapman 2011b for a detailed report). Informed by Sutton and Shaw (1995:378), theory building here identifies "connections among phenomena, a story about why acts, events, structure and thoughts occur". One that may be complemented by positioning within the context of the reward mix literature discussed in summary above.

The integrated model is an amalgam of underlying models informed by the research being reported here that, first, inductively theorizes industry norm reward mix development and firm-specific RMD. Secondly, the model development is informed by the agency, institutional and resource dependency literatures complemented by two other relevant theoretical perspectives that have been articulated in the literature: namely, path dependency and strategic compensation. An appropriate combination of all these theoretical positions provides the foundation of an overall theory of RMD. The object is not to offer an analytical model showing definite causality, but rather a diagrammatic representation of the author's interpretation of what was heard during the research presented in a logical manner to support wider understanding and focused discussion of this area.

Whetten notes that diagrams of this nature are useful "as visual aid(s) that helps storytellers highlight the main features of their explanations". In this context, the lines and directional arrows shown in the model indicate relationships believed to exist by the actors themselves with the interrelationships shown being drawn from the author's interpretation of their accounts. The model provides a resource to others to test some of the hypotheses that the model suggests.

Industry norms significantly influence the final reward mix position taken by financial services employers. Data from RC interviews emphasized, in particular, what were described as labour market influences on the overall industry norm position, moderated only by specific legal, tax and

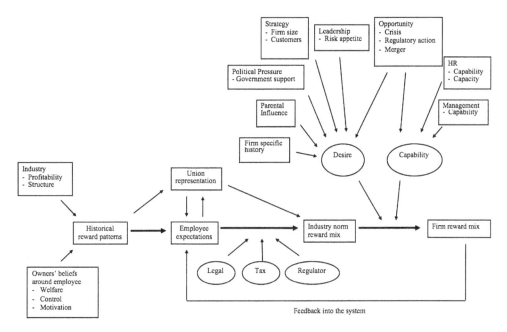

Figure 13.2   A model of reward mix determination

regulatory requirements that may be present. The data from the interviews with the RSs served to clarify what, at least in the sector, is meant by market forces and the importance of employee expectations as the primary influence on the industry norm reward mix. Employee expectations were seen by both RSs and RCs as being the reason why benchmarking of the market reward mix was so significant as there was a general belief that adopting a reward mix position away from the established norm would not be consistent with employees' expectations and therefore would cause problems with regard to attraction and retention.

Employee expectations are seen to both influence, and be influenced by, union representation, when this is present in firms. Employee expectations (and those of their unions where present) were believed to be driven by strong historical reward patterns formed over several decades which were strongly engrained in employees' expectations and therefore were seen as being particularly difficult to change. These patterns were seen to have been formed by a combination of two factors. First, the interviews identified that the general structure and profitability of the financial services sector builds a sense of entitlement among employees with respect to the sharing of wealth created in the industry between the owners of the firms and employees. Second, owner beliefs about the role of reward structures were significant in forming historical reward patterns and, through this, influencing employee expectations over time – in particular, the role played by incentive and bonus schemes in motivating employee behaviour and benefits, and the responsibility firms felt for the welfare of their employees both for paternalistic reasons, and with respect to their search for productivity and engagement effects. Interviewees identified, however, that employee expectations were not acting unfettered on the benchmark position. Three key moderating variables were present, affecting the transmission of these strong employee expectations through to the final industry norm: the influence of legal, taxation and regulatory requirements on remuneration structures.

This industry norm reward mix was seen by the interviewees as the starting point for firms' RMD. The research found that not all firms adopted the benchmark position. Other factors identified by the interviews influence the propensity of firms to follow the norm position or operate an alternative reward mix.

The interviews with both RCs and RSs identified that, despite risks associated with diverging from the industry norm reward mix, there is employer willingness to operate outside the perceived 'safe harbour' of the industry norm position through the interplay of two variables. First, the firm's desire to resist the industry norm and differentiate its reward mix which was seen as being influenced by the following five dimensions:

- Leadership – The appetite of the leadership to adopt reward mix positions that differentiated the reward offering to employees from firms competing for the same labour.
- Business strategy – Specific and unique positioning with respect to each firm's product and customer management strategies.
- Political pressure – Exerted on the specific firm rather than the market as a whole. The strength of this influence was further dependent on the extent to which the firm in question was subject to state control through participation in some form of government support following the financial crisis.
- Parental influence – For those operating as subsidiaries of overseas firms, specific parental requirements with regard to the reward mix that were not necessarily in line with the industry norm reward mix in the UK.
- Firm-specific history – The influence of enduring historical, but firm-specific, positions and precedents.

These five dimensions could be further categorized into desires driven from within the firm through leadership, business strategy formation and firm-specific history, and coercive externally driven desires generated for the firm by others, shown by either direct political pressure or parental dictum. This distinction is significant in that it helps identify what actions the firm itself can take to manipulate the dimensions (i.e., those from within) and which it was simply a matter of reacting to (i.e., external pressures).

Second, operating alongside the firm's desire to operate to some degree away from the established industry norm was the firm's capability to resist the institutional pressures formed in the industry norm. This was influenced by two dimensions:

- HR capability and capacity – To manage any change from the industry norm position and the potential implications this may have for attraction and retention of employees holding industry norm expectations with respect to their reward mix.
- Line management capability – Managing employee expectations could not come solely from the HR function, but was dependent on line management understanding and supporting the messages in their daily interaction within their teams. Therefore, the capability of line management to work with HR in managing and communicating differences to the industry norm to their teams, and managing any implications, was important in adopting a non-conforming reward mix position.

In addition, one further dimension was seen in the findings to influence both the firm's desire to resist the institutional pressure to conform to the industry norm, and also the firm's capability to resist this pressure – opportunity.

- Opportunity – The presence of an opportunity, both to act as a catalyst for change and therefore influence the firm's desire, and also a justification, largely to employees, of the need for a differentiated approach relative to the norm and therefore influence the firm's capability to change. These events were found to be firm-specific financial crises, regulatory pressure and mergers/takeovers.

What emerged from the interviews was that the model was not a static one and so the complete model, displayed in Figure 13.2, also incorporates a feedback loop. This was found to be present between the individual firm reward mix and employee expectations. Where firms did diverge from industry practice, this would eventually be communicated back into the wider labour market. The extent to which this feedback loop was influential was seen as being affected by the size of the firm, with larger employers being seen as more significant in moving general employee expectations when they did diverge from the industry norm position.

Implications for the theoretical understanding of RMD

One of the criticisms made of the reward mix research to date is that, despite the large amount of research carried out, we know little about RMD as there is no dominating paradigm explaining the process (Gerhart and Rynes 2003). It may be that the list of factors statistical work has identified as being related to RMD has muddied the waters and that we need to develop a framework to better understand what's really going on. The research informing this chapter set out with the aim of providing greater clarity on how reward mix is determined accounting for these multiple influences. Gerhart and Milkovich (1992) note that we should be looking to adapt the range of theories that have emerged to improve our knowledge of reward systems. In this context, the literature suggested that our three theoretical explanations for how firms determine their reward mix merit further examination. The analysis is set out in Table 13.2, drawing on a 'shopping list' of inputs to RMD suggested by the largely deductive research carried out previously. The 'shopping list' has been rationalized and ordered by applying the RMD model. The variables listed are complemented by observation on the extent to which they were significant in the findings from RC and RE interviews.

An integrated approach

Analysis of the three theoretical approaches used to examine RMD, summarized in Table 13.1 – agency, institutional and resource dependency – appeared similar in that they all examine managerial decisions from a perspective of those decisions being influenced by external factors, i.e., ownership structure, critical resource holders, institutional norms. Each of the approaches also operates with similar dependent and independent variables. Where the differences between the theoretical approaches lie is in the assumptions they make about both firms' and employees' behaviour and the outcome of this behaviour on final RMD. Through adopting multiple perspectives to assess the problem, the research presented in this chapter has enabled a review and challenge to those assumptions. A unified and practitioner-led theory of RMD coming through the RCs' and RSs' voices on the issue has thus been developed, standing in contrast to abstract assessment through reviewing statistical data. Building on the commentary in Table 13.2, this unified theory is sketched out in Table 13.3. It presents the main premises, assumptions, organizational reactions and their implications for reward mix highlighted by this research.

This unified explanation identifies the strength of institutional pressures on firms to conform to an agreed norm with the aim of gaining legitimacy with both current and prospective employees. Firms still have room for manoeuvre in the form of strategic choice influenced by the strength of their desire and capability to differentiate their mix from this strong, institutionally

Table 13.2 Significance of 'shopping list' factors in this research

Theoretical perspective	Decision driver	Significance in this research
Agency	Alignment of employee effort	Not as perceived by agency theory as solely a means to reduce or manage employee shirking. Alignment of effort was also about looking for ways to build reward packages that both meet the desires of employees whilst managing costs for employers.
	Managing monitoring costs (spans of control and contract type)	Not as perceived by agency theory in an analytical approach to RMD. Cost control was important, but was not seen as a trade-off between monitoring and spans of control, but rather optimizing reward such that it met employee desires whilst keeping costs as low as possible for the employer.
	Business risk	Not raised.
Institutional	Legal requirements	A moderating influence on the transmission of employee expectations as to their reward mix through to the industry norm position.
	Political and societal pressure	Was an influence over the regulatory change that was occurring in reward in the sector. This exhibited itself as a moderating influence on the transmission of employee expectations to the industry norm position.
	Taxation and other regulations	A moderating influence on the transmission of employee expectations to the industry norm position.
	For subsidiaries of multinationals, parent group policies	An influence on firms' desire to differentiate their position from the industry norm reward mix.
	Union pressures	An influence on the transmission of employee expectations to the overall industry reward mix norm.
	Historical precedents	Strong influence on both the employee expectations of an appropriate reward mix, but also individual firms' propensity to follow the industry norm reward mix.
	Benchmarking others' practice	Strong element. Central construct in RMD being the industry norm mix which is ascertained largely through separate benchmarking of the components making up reward mix.
	Consultants' advice	Less prevalent than suggested in the literature, although they perform a key role in collation and provision of the industry benchmarks.
	Professional networks	Play an important role in the communication of the industry norm reward mix to RSs across the sector through groups and conferences.
	Codification of practice in reward qualifications	Not raised.

Table 13.2. (continued)

Theoretical perspective	Decision driver	Significance in this research
	Organizational exposure to other institutional settings	Not raised.
	CEO and board members' business education and experience	Not raised as an influence although the CEO was seen as significant in influencing the firm's risk appetite for differentiation from the industry norm mix.
	Cost of loss of legitimacy against benefit of differentiation	An influence in the firm's decision as to whether to differentiate its reward mix from the industry norm or take the safer route of adopting this position.
Resource dependency	Attraction and retention of critical employees/ employee groups	Employee expectations were significant. However, it is not solely about key groups but also concerns a wider understanding of the generality of expectations and through this a strong influence on the industry norm reward mix developed.
	Union dominance	An influence on the transmission of employee expectations to the overall industry reward norm mix.
	Task complexity and the need for specialist skills	Not raised.
	Ease of employee monitoring and performance visibility	Not raised.
	Substitutability of skills	Not raised.
	Task centrality	Not raised.
	Organizational connections	Not raised.

Table 13.3 Summary unified theory of reward mix determination

	Research findings
Purpose of reward mix decisions	Conformity with market practice in order to gain legitimacy with current and prospective employees.
Main assumptions	Strong employee expectations of receiving the industry norm reward mix.
	Goal alignment often exists between employee needs and firms' requirements.
	Employees are not always acting rationally, often resisting change to a potentially non-optimal historical norm.
	Firms are typically risk-averse, seeking out the safe harbour position of the industry norm.
	Process of satisficing behaviour by employers.
	Firms follow the industry norm unless both the desire and capability to differentiate their position are present.
Organizational reaction	Both rational legitimacy seeking, with respect to employees, and passively conforming to industry norm position, depending on firms' specific circumstances.
Implications for reward mix	Reward mix will be influenced by institutional norms and the extent to which operating within these norms confers legitimacy with current and prospective employees.

reinforced position as they look to reach an economically satisficing position. This, alongside employees potentially irrationally resisting change, can mean that a suboptimal reward mix may be in place for both employer and employee.

Conclusion

This chapter is positioned in the reward mix literature and the explanations provided to date for RMD through the lenses of agency, institutional and resource dependency theories. A framework for understanding RMD in financial services is offered and assessed using evidence from interviews with key actors in the field of RMD.

Much of what we know about RMD is through a positivist research approach. However, an emerging body of work has developed, taking a more constructionist approach to reward determination, albeit largely at an executive level, as a potential means to establish not only what is driving reward decisions but significantly why (e.g., Bender 2004; Perkins and Hendry 2005; Bender and Moir 2006). Methodologically, the approach taken in this research adds further weight to this emerging body of work, being qualitative in a largely quantitative field.

So what influences RMD in financial services organizations? Following analysis of the data, the simple 'answer' to this question is, in line with Eisenhardt's (1988) earlier conclusion, the need to conform with market practice in order to gain legitimacy. However, legitimacy is found to be with respect to employees' expectations of the reward mix that should be provided in the financial services sector. This conformity is both a position of passive conformity for some firms, as suggested by DiMaggio and Powell (1991), but for others it is much more a rational assessment of the risks associated with differentiation, in line with the work of Norman et al. (2007). Beyond this simple explanation, the findings show that the RSs identify that a small number of firms have adopted a differentiated position (10 RSs spoke of their firms in this way). These firms had either moderately moved their reward mix away from the industry norm position or in more limited cases radically adopted a significantly different reward mix position from the industry norm practice (Chapman 2011b).

The propensity of firms to differentiate their reward mix from the dominant industry norm was a function of both their desire to differentiate and their capability to make desired change happen. The desire to change was seen to be influenced by coercive pressures from their parent organization, government intervention in their operation and strategic reasons with respect to leadership beliefs, customers or suppliers, whereas the capability to move away from the industry norm, where change is considered desirable, was seen to be a function of both HR and management capabilities. Additionally, both the desire and capability to differentiate the reward mix were influenced by opportunities for change being presented in the form of mergers or acquisitions, or firm-specific financial crises which provided the 'excuse' to make the change happen.

To the best of the author's knowledge, this is only the second study (the first being Barringer and Milkovich's (1998) theoretical assessment of these three areas plus transaction cost theory) that has combined these three perspectives, and the first that has involved empirical research with practitioners in developing knowledge of RMD. In practical terms, the research prompts organizational decision-takers to think more consciously about the influences on their firms' reward mix, to ensure that these influences are genuinely in line with business need, however this may be defined. Development of a stronger theoretical base for understanding the determinants of reward mix choices also assists policy makers in furthering their understanding of the extent to which organizational free choice and institutionally determined choice influence final reward choices when discussing policy options and, consequently, the level at which any regulatory intervention should occur. If labour markets and institutional factors dominate, as the research proposes, and therefore operate as a significant constraint on firm choice, this may suggest the need for macro-level regulatory policy intervention to change reward practice (if this is felt desirable for social or political reasons).

References

Baeten, X. (2008). Executive remuneration: towards a structured multi-theory approach. 5th Research Workshop on Corporate Governance, 26–28 November 2008, EIASM, Brussels, EIASM.

Balkin, D. B. and Bannister, B. D. (1993). Explaining pay forms for strategic employee groups in organizations: a resource dependence perspective. *Journal of Occupational and Organizational Psychology*. 66(2), 139–151.

Barringer, M. W. and Milkovich, G. T. (1998). A theoretical exploration of the adoption and design of flexible benefit plans: A case of human resource innovation. *The Academy of Management Review*. 23(2), 305–324.

Bender, R. (2004). Why do companies use performance-related pay for their executive directors? *Corporate Governance: An International Review*. 12(4), 521–533.

Bender, R. and Moir, L. (2006). Does 'Best Practice' in setting executive pay in the UK encourage 'good' behaviour? *Journal of Business Ethics*. 67(1), 75–91.

Berrone, P. and Gomez-Mejia, L. R. (2009). Environmental performance and executive compensation: an integrated agency-institutional perspective. *Academy of Management Journal*. 52(1), 103–126.

Bloom, M. C. and Milkovich, G. T. (1996). Issues in management compensation research. In Rousseau, D. M. and Cooper, D. M. (eds.). *Trends in Organizational Behavior* (pp. 23–47). New York: Wiley.

Boyd, B. K. and Salamin, A. (2001). Strategic reward systems: A contingency model of pay system design. *Strategic Management Journal*. 22(8), 777–792.

Chapman, J. and Kelliher, C. (2011a). Influences on reward mix determination: reward consultants' perspectives. *Employee Relations*. 33(2), 121–139.

Chapman, J. (2011b). An Examination of the Influences on Reward Mix. Observations from the UK Financial Services Industry. Unpublished PhD thesis. Cranfield University School of Management.

Conlon, E. J. and Parks, J. M. (1990). Effects of monitoring and tradition on compensation arrangements: an experiment with principal–agent dyads. *Academy of Management Journal*. 33(3), 603–622.

Crystal, G. S. (1991). *In Search of Excess: The Overcompensation of American Executives*. New York: Norton.

DiMaggio, D. P. and Powell, W. W. (eds.) (1991). *The New Institutionalism in Organizational Analysis*. Chicago: University of Chicago Press.

Eisenhardt, K. M. (1988). Agency – and institutional – theory explanations: the case of retail sales compensation. *Academy of Management Review*. 31, 1153–1166.

Eisenhardt, K. M. (1989). Agency theory: an assessment and review. *Academy of Management Review*. 14(1), 57–74.

Fernandez-Alles, M., Cuevas-Rodríguez, G. and Valle-Cabrera, R. (2006). How symbolic remuneration contributes to the legitimacy of the company: an institutional explanation. *Human Relations*. 59(7), 961–992.

Festing, M. and Sahakiants, I. (2010). Compensation practices in Central and Eastern European member states – an analytical framework based on institutional perspectives, path dependencies and efficiency considerations. *Thunderbird International Business Review*. 52(3), 203–216.

FSSC. (2010). *UK Skills Assessment: The Financial Services Industry, the Accountancy Sector and Finance Function*. London: Financial Services Skills Council.

Gerhart, B. and Milkovich, G. T. (1992). Employee compensation: Research and practice. In Dunnette, M. D. and Hough, L. M. (eds.). *Handbook of Industrial and Organizational Psychology* (2nd ed., pp. 481–569). Palo Alto, CA: Consulting Psychologists Press.

Gerhart, B. and Rynes, S. L. (2003). *Compensation: Theory, Evidence, and Strategic Implications*. Thousand Oaks, CA: Sage Publications Inc.

Jensen, M. C. and Meckling, W. H. (1976). Theory of the firm: managerial behavior, agency costs, and ownership structure. *Journal of Financial Economics*. 3, 305–360.

Lawler, E., L. (1971). *Pay and Organizational Effectiveness: A Psychological View*. New York: McGraw-Hill.

Mahoney, T. A. (1979). *Compensation and Reward Perspectives*. Homewood, IL: Irwin.

Milkovich, G. T. and Newman, C. (2008). *Compensation* (9th ed.). Boston: McGraw-Hill/Irwin.

Miller, J. S., Hom, P. W. and Gomez-Mejia, L. R. (2001). The high cost of low wages: Does Maquiladora compensation reduce turnover? *Journal of International Business Studies.* 32(3), 585–595.

Norman, P. M., Artz, K. W. and Martinez, R. J. (2007). Does it pay to be different? Competitive non-conformity under different regulatory regimes. *Journal of Business Research.* 60(11), 1135–1143.

Perkins, S. J., White, G. and Jones, S. (2016). *Reward Management Alternatives, Consequences and Contexts.* London: Chartered Institute of Personnel and Development.

Perkins, S. J. and Hendry, C. (2005). Ordering top pay: interpreting the signals. *Journal of Management Studies.* 42(7), 1443–1468.

Pfeffer, J. (1993). Barriers to the advance of organizational science: paradigm. *The Academy of Management Review.* 18(4), 599–620.

Pfeffer, J. and Davis-Blake, A. (1987). Understanding organizational wage structures: a resource dependence approach. *Academy of Management Journal.* 30(3), 437–455.

PriceWaterhouseCoopers. (2010). *Financial Services Remuneration – Design, Structure and Recent Industry Developments.* London: PwC.

Sutton, R. I. and Shaw, B. M. (1995). What theory is not. *Administrative Science Quarterly.* 40, 371–384.

Tremblay, M., Cote, J. and Balkin, D. B. (2003). Explaining sales pay strategy using agency, transaction cost and resource dependence theories. *The Journal of Management Studies.* 40(7), 1651–1682.

14

BEHAVIOURAL PERSPECTIVE FOR A CHANGE AGENDA FOR EXECUTIVE REWARDS

Almuth McDowall and Zara Whysall

The rise of executive rewards

The magnitude of Chief Executive Officer (CEO) rewards and their disproportionate rise relative to the salaries of more junior employees continues to receive much criticism in the public domain, particularly in the aftermath of the recent global financial crisis (Farmer et al. 2013). A European comparison of over 700 listed companies across a number of European countries showed that CEOs in the UK earn 50% more than their German counterparts, and one and a half times as much as CEOs in Sweden (Financial Times 2016). Between 2000 and 2014 the median total earnings for UK FTSE 100 CEOs increased by 278%, while the corresponding rise in total earnings for full-time employees was only 48% (Income Data Services 2015). Analysis of the 'single figure' for CEO pay declared by companies in their annual reports suggests that the average UK FTSE 100 CEO was paid almost £5 million in 2014 – amounting to approximately a fivefold increase since the late 1990s (High Pay Centre 2015). Trends show that inflation-adjusted CEO compensation in the US increased about 941% from 1978 to 2015, a rise roughly 70% faster than stock market growth and substantially greater than the 10.3% growth in the compensation paid to a typical worker over the same period (Mishel and Schieder 2016).

In the UK, there is tentative evidence of a reversal in trends, as the average FTSE 100 CEO has seen their overall package drop by 17% from 2015 to 2016 (CIPD and High Pay Centre 2017). Nevertheless, international data trends show that CEO compensation continues to rise, even during times of economic recession (e.g. Mishel and Schieder 2016).

Despite attempts to tie a greater percentage of executives' pay to company performance, for instance by increasing the percentage of pay directly linked to performance indicators, many CEOs continue to receive reward packages which appear disproportionate to any returns delivered to company shareholders. Only one of the 10 highest-paid CEOs in the 2014 Wall Street Journal's annual pay survey ranked among the top 10% by investor performance (WSJ 2015). Bebchuk and Fried (2005) noted over a decade ago, ". . there is now recognition that many boards have employed compensation arrangements that do not serve shareholders' interests" (p. 6). We contend that the lack of alignment with shareholder interests is only one side of the coin, however, as executive compensation also needs to be considered by taking a wider stakeholder perspective, which is a thread which we return to at various points in this chapter.

Organizations use a range of financial, accounting and market-based measures to benchmark CEO performance (for a recent overview, see Li and Young 2016) such as Earnings per Share (EPS) and Total Shareholder Return (TSR). Such measures are then linked to what is usually a complex set up of short-term (e.g., cash bonus) and long-term incentives (e.g., based on share performance); Li and Young highlight that an increasing proportion of CEO compensation is linked to performance, but that the constitution of CEO pay is now so complex that the metrics and their constitution are difficult to disentangle, even for those with financial acumen. Indeed, recent research examining UK-listed firms' remuneration reports revealed that in cases of high CEO pay, a less readable remuneration report was associated with reduced 'say-on-pay' voting dissent (Hooghiemstra et al. 2017). The authors suggest, therefore, that reducing 'readability' could be an effective obfuscation strategy to influence the level of shareholder say-on-pay voting dissent in firms with excessive CEO pay.

Li and Young found that firm size, industry, and levels of compensation set in the previous year are the most consistent predictors of CEO remuneration, and question if there is any link between levels of compensation and performance. Indeed, an analysis using US financial firm data (Yang et al. 2014) showed that incentive-based CEO contracts did not have the intended effects in the aftermath of the financial crisis given that CEO compensation continued to raise whilst there was a decline in stock-based performance.

Much dissatisfaction has been voiced regarding resulting pay inequity; there appears far less evidence about potential alternatives or solutions (see also Pepper 2015, Dorff 2014). As Dorff (2014) noted cogently, the growth in CEO compensation has effectively been an experiment, where organizations have manipulated reward size and structure without much or indeed any proof for the effectiveness of their strategies and processes. Against this backdrop of a disputed association between pay and performance, an absence of evidence for suitable alternatives or solutions, and a need for greater recognition of broader stakeholder perspectives and considerations, we focus our chapter on: (a) how organizational stakeholders perceive current and future reward structures and processes; (b) the current research evidence with consideration of governance and corporate responsibility, behavioural agency theory, and CEO characteristics; and (c) implications for research, theory, and practice.

UK research on the "power and pitfalls" of executive rewards

The research we draw upon used a sequential mixed methods design (Creswell 2013) to investigate executive rewards from an explicitly behavioural perspective; the full report and technical supplement can be found online (CIPD research report by McDowall et al. 2015). The focus of this investigation was to explore what kind of leaders and leadership behaviours are needed at the top of contemporary organizations, the types of behaviours encouraged by current rewards, how rewards are and should be decided, and what the barriers might be to any reforms. For the purpose of this chapter, we integrate the survey findings from 52 practitioners, comprising senior leaders, HR directors, and reward specialists, and qualitative data from 14 individuals via focus groups. A diverse sample of leaders, HR directors, and reward specialists also inform our synthesis and critique of literature in the domain.

The survey juxtaposed the CEO behaviours that are valued now against those needed in the future, using semantic differential items. Respondents were asked to rate on a scale from 1 (not important) to 4 (very important) which contrasting behaviours are more important now, or should be important in the future (for example, for the item set "Inspire, energise, engage versus Drive, direct and control" the mean of 3.25 indicates that currently a more directive approach is observed. However, the mean of 2.02 for future behavior reflects the stakeholder perception that CEOs need to shift more towards an inspirational rather than directive approach).

Table 14.1 Descriptive statistics (n = 52): the qualities needed in CEOs

Item	Current behaviours		Future behaviours		Difference score
	M	SD	M	SD	
Inspire, energize, engage versus Drive, direct and control	3.25	1.25	2.02	.98	− 1.23
Develop resources long-term versus Resources for short-term results	2.65	1.28	1.61	.66	− 1.04
Focus on results versus Focus on behaviour	2.23	.88	3.10	.89	.87
Organize and manage versus Nurture and support	2.48	1.20	3.25	1.06	.77
Focus on create and innovate versus Focus on efficiency and performance	3.29	1.19	2.71	.87	− .58
Shareholder value versus Stakeholder value	2.56	1.30	3.11	1.20	.55
Personal strength and confidence versus Humility and seeking understanding	2.28	1.05	2.79	.75	.51
What's in it for me – versus What's in it for us	3.98	1.20	4.42	.78	.44
Focus on profit versus Focus on meaning and purpose	2.40	1.29	2.87	.85	.38
Analysis of numbers and information versus Intuition and Feeling	2.27	1.17	2.44	.75	.17

Table 14.2 Factors determining CEO rewards now and in the future (N = 52)

Item	Current		Future		Difference
	M	SD	M	SD	
Encouraging required CEO behaviours and ethics	2.20	0.73	2.67	0.55	0.47
Aligning package with shareholder interests	2.27	0.67	2.64	0.56	0.37
Consideration of predecessor's reward package	1.47	0.58	1.17	0.38	− 0.30
Fostering CEO motivation to achieve business goals	2.31	0.62	2.52	0.50	0.21
Attraction and retention (of CEO talent)	2.27	0.60	2.37	0.63	0.10
Aligning package to industry standards	2.06	0.57	2.00	0.69	− 0.06

Overall, the findings indicate that respondents rate a shift towards a more engaging, long-term and nurturing perspective as important, as shown in Table 14.1, which ranks the items in order of magnitude for the biggest differences between current and future behaviours.

The survey also explored how CEO reward packages are determined at present, and how they should be determined in the future, using a similar scale as in the previous set, which ranged from 1 to 3. As shown in Table 14.2 (items are also ranked here by magnitude for the greatest differences between what is important now and what should be important in the future), there was some agreement that consideration of the past (e.g., the magnitude of the predecessor's reward package) should become less important and, in turn, that a wider stakeholder focus, motivating CEOs to achieve business goals paired with a greater focus on ethics, should grow in importance.

We then used Cluster Analysis to determine patterns and to explore potential subgroups of individuals based on item-response patterns using a range of statistical techniques. These include Ward's method of clustering together with squared Euclidean distances among clusters, which was used in order to maximize within-subgroup homogeneity and between-subgroup heterogeneity (Everitt et al. 2011). We inspected Agglomeration schedules and dendrogram plots visually, both of which offer suggestions about the number of emergent clusters within the larger group (see Hair et al. 1998 for a comprehensive discussion of these approaches). Guided by this information, three distinct clusters were identified and the analysis was re-run with a forced three-cluster solution. A new dataset was saved that matched each participant to one of the three identified subgroups. A one-way ANOVA revealed that significant ($p < .05$) differences were observed across all items used in the clustering process, providing initial evidence for the validity of the cluster solution.

Three clusters were identified, taking into consideration items with the largest variance in mean ratings, and inspections of dendrograms as well as analysis of variance, all of which pertained to views on rewards rather than respondents' organizational role (we had also collected data on organization size, respondents' role, and other basic characteristics). Cluster 1 (n = 28) was termed "Profit-driven transactors" because these respondents agreed that profit, strength, and power, paired with a short-term and organizationally focused perspective, are important. Cluster 2 (N = 14) was termed "Long-term nurturers" as they focused on future results, paired with a more nurturing approach on the part of the CEO. Cluster 3 (N = 9) was termed "Person-focused" as group members had strong views that CEO rewards are being driven by the need to compete for talent; and that fostering CEO motivation through rewards and a focus on ethics are important.

It was also notable that all three clusters converged on certain views, including that a more strategic focus on innovation and creation (as opposed to efficiency and performance) is needed for the future; also that a 'What's in it for us' rather than 'What's in it for the CEO' mentality should take prominence. All groups also agreed that CEO packages should be aligned to the complexity of the role, but did not express positive views about the role of regulation in any changes in CEO pay.

Qualitative data analysis

Narrative comments were received from 28 respondents in relation to challenges or resistance experienced with regards to CEO reward practice (and any changes they had made); these were content-analysed, as shown in Table 14.3, which illustrates the barriers identified with concrete examples from the data.

Shareholder views were considered one of the greatest obstacles to any changes in CEO rewards, including open pressure to align with their interests. Fear of not being competitive in the international market and being unable to attract the best CEOs also featured strongly in participants' comments. Two people described CEOs who are 'thinking outside the box' and had instigated a real change in reward perceptions by instigating a more equitable and fair reward scheme. The increasing complexity of rewards was stressed as a factor in leaving all stakeholders unhappy, and that it was reported that a shift towards rewards based on group and shared, rather than silo, performance was needed.

Last, we consider the data from the one-day workshop with 14 senior participants including reward, and HR directors, as well as a CEO and reward consultants which comprised a series of focus group discussions in which each group was asked to seek agreement on, and outline, what ideal reward practice looks like and how practice needs to evolve to achieve it. Participants underlined the counterproductive effects of quarterly reporting (for listed companies) and overly dominating shareholder influence which fuel a predominantly short-term perspective, but also the focus on a ranking perspective ("Is my reward larger than yours?"). Participants stressed the prevailing 'myth' of the CEO as 'saviours' and 'heroes', alleging a lack of internal and strategic

Table 14.3 Content analysis of challenges and barriers

Barriers identified	Examples
Governance	
The influence of shareholder views (n = 8)	Over-involvement in reward criteria and selection criteria
Role of Remuneration committee (n = 2)	"Nervous" about change, need to be realistic about what is "fair"; Fear of "bad press"
The market	
Comparisons to other organizations affecting pay (e.g. international, n = 6)	Competing organizations offer larger rewards
Sector-specific challenges (n = 2)	Constrained financial incentives
The rewards	
Constitution of rewards and how these are applied across people (n = 6)	LTips need to balance short-term rewards, short-term rewards often ineffective
	Too complex
	Too little emphasis on non-financial metrics
Alignment to business performance and goals (n = 5)	Short-term rewards do not align to business coals "hard to be competitive and ethical"
The CEOs	
Attracting/ retaining talent (n = 4)	Not enough strategic business focus on personnel planning at the top
The influence of personal characteristics (n = 3)	CEOs can completely shape strategic direction
	Deliberately ethical stance as refreshing, but also constraining

succession planning for top teams. Overall, consensus was that CEOs of the future need to: (a) exhibit mindful and authentic leadership by bringing an emotionally intelligent and reflective approach to their role; (b) focus on long-term business sustainability to facilitate organizational learning and growth; and (c) remain being responsible and responsive to the wider stakeholder community. This tallied with the data from the survey, which also indicated a necessity for a wider stakeholder perspective, and for the influence of prevailing parameters, for the setting of rewards such as the size of previous packages, to diminish in importance.

Mapping of the literature – corporate governance, corporate social responsibility, and CEO characteristics

Informed by these themes, we then synthesized the relevant literature, using systematic mapping to categorize relevant papers under the headings of: (a) corporate and governance perspectives; (b) corporate social responsibility; (c) the limitations of financial perspectives and behavioural agency theory; and (d) CEO characteristics. US data continue to dominate the available evidence which needs to be acknowledged as a limitation from the outset, given that legal requirements differ but only few publications even acknowledge national idiosyncrasies and differences. For instance, CEO duality (the chief executive officer also chairs the board, e.g., see Jizi et al. 2014) is not permissible due to company law in the UK.

Corporate and governance perspectives. There is a long history to instigate regulatory reviews and policy which go back to the Cadbury Report (1992) and the more extensive Greenberg Report (1994) in the early 1990s. As a result, levels and constitutions of executive pay are now made public. Yet there continues to be resistance to further calls for greater government intervention and the instigation of regulatory policy surrounding this issue. When Theresa May was elected prime minister in 2016, she made executive pay a key focus and called for the publication of executive pay/employee pay ratios to stop 'careless' behaviour (Swinford 2016), yet her calls for a detailed and bespoke code of practice have not yet materialized to the extent promised; as other political concerns have taken centre stage (CIPD 2017) At the time of writing, certain 'compromise policies' are being instigated, such as a register of dissenting votes by shareholders on pay decisions.

Studies considering CEO compensation from a corporate governance perspective provide a wider organizational and legislative context. Cohen et al. (2013) found that, in general, legislation has some moderating effect on CEO pay, but cautioned that a causal link cannot be inferred. Black (2014) provides an interesting angle on diversification, showing that CEO compensation is higher where organizational tasks are more complex and international.

In order to provide shareholders with greater power over executive pay, a number of countries have introduced 'say-on-pay' initiatives (the role of organizational monitoring). In the UK, for instance, the Enterprise and Regulatory Reform Act (ERRA) 2013 requires listed companies to hold a binding shareholder vote on executive remuneration at least every three years, on top of the annual advisory vote on the remuneration report detailing pay over the previous year. Although the average vote against FTSE 100 remuneration reports in 2014 was just 6.5% (High Pay Centre 2015), 2016/17 saw a number of high-profile votes going against board recommendations. For example, almost two-thirds opposed a rise in pay for the Pearson CEO, 40% voting against remuneration proposals at AstraZeneca, and 58% at the housebuilding company Crest Nicholson.

Say on pay has been considered in several papers. Cai and Walkling (2011) discovered that 'say on pay' initiatives appear to be beneficial for organizations with inefficient compensation systems, in other words 'abnormally' high CEO pay and low pay-for-performance sensitivity, but can be counterproductive for others. They found that the positive impact was stronger for firms with weak, but not the weakest, governance. While a shareholder vote may benefit firms with overpaid CEOs, it is up to the board of directors to make these changes. The authors emphasize that legislation is unlikely to affect deeply entrenched managers. Furthermore, evidence from other countries where some progress has been achieved on the composition of boards and remuneration committees (in the UK remuneration committees have to be composed of non-executive directors) suggests that boards with 'best practice' structural arrangements – those chaired and dominated by non-executive directors at the board and compensation committee – are no more adept at enforcing CEO pay-for-firm-performance than are executive-dominated boards (Capezio et al. 2011). Another analysis (Gregory-Smith et al. 2013) found that the effects of corporate voting dissent are small, and most pronounced for higher quartiles of rewards. Mobbs (2013) also considered board composition, finding that greater competition between respective members on boards results in more aligned compensation contracts.

A rare experiment on shareholder voting which simulated realistic scenarios using vignettes (Krause et al. 2014) indicated that shareholders value a strong link between pay and performance in line with agency theory (Jensen and Meckling 1976), which predicts symmetrical assessments of gains and losses, but are also more concerned about losses than gains, which is in line with prospect theory (which holds that that individuals are loss-averse). These results suggest that it is important to understand shareholders' 'frame of reference' In other words, we should understand which factors guide decision-making, an important issue given the complexity of current executive reward structures. Overall, the evidence suggests that corporate governance and imposed regulation appears in itself insufficient to regulate and optimize CEO reward practice, as human biases and heuristics will also influence how rewards are allocated and evaluated.

Corporate social responsibility. An alternative to a focus on regulation and market and investor reactions is the 'ethos' of any firms – corporate social responsibility (CSR). CSR refers to the proactive actions taken to "further some social good, beyond the interests of the firm" (McWilliams and Siegel 2001:117), for instance, with respect to environmental activities, community involvement, product qualities, employee relations and diversity policies (McCarthy et al. 2017). In this context, it is also important to consider the role of monetary versus non-monetary incentives – do organizations dispense too much of the former and too little of the latter, and what is the role of the CEO in fostering a more altruistic organizational orientation? A robust US study considered monetary (bonuses) and non-monetary incentives (power, career concerns, etc.) for nearly 600 organizations over a four-year period (Fabrizi et al. 2014). The results outlined that monetary incentives had a negative effect on CSR, and that non-monetary incentives had a positive effect on CSR. It follows that executive compensation decisions should look far beyond salaries and incentives.

Rekker et al. (2014) offer one of the few studies to take a differentiated look at executive rewards and the varied aspects of CSR (see also Beck-Krala, Scott and Klimkiewicz, this volume). Firstly, consistent with Fabrizi et al. (2014), they identified a significant negative relationship between CSR and size of salaries as well as long-term compensation. This finding, consistent with their expectation that CEOs who are employed in CSR firms tend to accept a lower level of compensation, suggests that intrinsically motivated CEOs do not require long-term financial incentives to engage in CSR. Their further differentiated analysis; a "disaggregation of CSR into its components matters" (p. 100); suggests that employee relations, environmental, and diversity elements of CSR all have an important impact on CEO compensation, whilst community and product quality elements do not. Finally, and perhaps rather sobering, they also find that once the effects of the financial crisis and efforts to further gender equality (through the size of rewards for female CEOs) are accounted for in the model, a CSR orientation makes little difference.

However, rather than concluding that CSR is irrelevant in the context of rewards, future research would do well to disentangle further the potentially reciprocal effects between CSR and the influence of CEOs. Perhaps too little research has concerned itself with the reverse side of the coin; rather than asking "are reward sizes and constitutions set appropriately?", researchers and policy makers should ask "What actually motivates CEOs?", and in particular what is the role of financial versus non-financial performance measures. Current practice and policy are dominated by financial and market considerations, which, in turn, fuels the focus on financial benchmarks and measures.

The limitations of financial perspectives and behavioural agency theory

As mentioned, much of the existing research on executive reward remains dominated by economic and financial perspectives, exploring monetary incentives in the context of market-based explanations (e.g. Murphy and Zábojník 2004). However, academics outside of the economic and financial fields have criticized these rational, market-based explanations for overlooking other influences such as managerial power (Bebchuk and Fried 2003, 2004, 2005), social-psychological processes (O'Reilly and Main 2010; Pepper and Gore 2014; Pepper 2015) and the institutional environment (DiPrete et al. 2010).

A meta-analysis of 219 US-based studies to investigate the links between executive power, pay, and performance noted "a lack of interdisciplinary consensus" (Van Essen et al. 2012:165) regarding the factors that drive executive rewards; this offered mixed support for Managerial Power Theory (MPT; Bebchuk and Fried 2003, 2004), which broadly holds that CEOs exert power over corporate boards which influences compensation. The results indicated that where boards have more power over the pay-setting process, CEOs tend to receive lower rewards; results were mixed, however, for performance-pay sensitivities, as only one indicator of CEO power (tenure) had an impact. Without explicit consideration of behavioral factors and social-psychological processes, organizational understanding of the full range of influences on executive reward is likely to remain underdeveloped (Lupton et al. 2015; Main 2011; Pepper and Gore 2014), which should encompass better primary data from executives (Devers et al. 2007). Capezio et al. (2011) argued that greater attention should be paid to the "deeper social, institutional, cognitive, and behavioural processes in play that will influence executive pay above and beyond board structural characteristics per se" (p. 506).

Pepper (2015) proposed revised behavioural agency theory as a lens for executive reward research which explicitly acknowledges that executives, and indeed other organizational decision-makers, do not think or act entirely rationally. Rather, they are subject to cognitive information processing biases and are motivated by a range of intrinsic and extrinsic factors rather than solely financial incentives; these include risk aversion (loss aversion below a threshold) and inequity aversion. In brief, the theory proposes that rewards that are complex and delayed are less valued by individuals than simple immediate rewards, thereby contributing to observed inflations in pay. Yet current executive rewards remain complex as they typically comprise a base salary, short-term incentives such as yearly cash bonuses, and long-term incentives (LTIPs) usually based on a delayed receipt of company stock, contingent on time or performance conditions, or both.

Pepper (p. 133) articulates new design principles for executive pay, which range from the actual selection of CEOs and the redesign of their roles through to the streamlining and simplification of executive reward systems to inform reforms in the context of appropriate legal frameworks. He also challenged academics to advance better theories. We concur, and advance that in order to do so further attention must be paid to the role, influence, and characteristics of CEOs, in addition to the mechanics of remuneration arrangements and a wider corporate perspective.

CEO characteristics. The evidence suggests that nuanced understanding of CEO performance over time is needed to inform reward decisions. Fitza (2013) used observations from over 250 CEOs and 2,400 US companies to show that random effects (positive trends in financial and market performance) are regularly and overly attributed to CEO influence, as two CEOs whose individual performance is exactly equal may nevertheless lead organizations with different performance metrics. It is yet another matter, however, to ascertain how to remedy such misconceptions and biases, given the almost mythical quality attributed to the high-profile contemporary CEO, an issue to which we return in our series of recommendations.

Given the cautionary findings on the limited influence of corporate governance and performance-compensation ratios over time, a behavioural perspective is needed to allow a more finely grained understanding of the influence of CEO on their organizations. There is no unique theory or framework for CEO or executive leadership to frame relevant research; rather, studies have drawn on an array of leadership concepts and theories. Indeed, it can be contended that CEOs should be considered against similar parameters as other organizational leaders. The complex interplay between CEO leadership and organizational culture suggests a reciprocal effect, where CEOs use a 'repertoire' of leadership behaviours to respond to social norms putting emphasis on aspects valued by shareholders and actively manage impressions, presumably to retain their position and the trust of the organizations (Densten and Sarro 2010). In order words, CEOs respond to their environment, adapting their leadership behaviour to what is valued in the environment. Another analysis using a high-technology sample (O'Reilly et al. 2014a) indicates that CEO personality is linked to organizational culture, which in turn influences organizational performance outcomes. Given the relative stability of personality as a construct, it is unlikely that a CEO's personality is influenced by the organizational culture, but more likely that CEOs are selected based on their fit with the pre-existing culture, and/or that the personality of a CEO influences the culture of the organization they lead. Likewise, although the nature of rewards is unlikely to change an individual's personality, rewards and incentives can and do differentially encourage or discourage certain behaviours. Thus, when appointing CEOs, organizations should assess for personality characteristics which complement their corporate values, mission and objectives, then design reward and incentive packages to encourage or reinforce behaviours consistent with this.

A US study with an unusual sample of baseball league CEOs, explored the relationships between CEO characteristics and the organizational performance of Major League Baseball organizations over a 100-year period. They identified that CEO 'bright-side' personality characteristics were positively related to transformational leadership, whereas 'dark-side' CEO personality characteristics (e.g., narcissism) were negatively related to contingent reward leadership. In turn, CEO transformational and contingent reward leadership were related to four different strategic outcomes, including manager turnover, team winning percentage, fan attendance, and an independent rating of influence. CEO transformational leadership was positively related to ratings of influence, team winning percentage, and fan attendance, whereas contingent reward leadership was negatively related to manager turnover and ratings of influence (Resick et al. 2009). In other words, the type of personality at the top may fundamentally influence organizational success.

Other studies have shown that CEO personality characteristics may not always be altruistic or beneficial; as more narcissistic CEOs tend to negotiate higher rewards (O'Reilly et al. 2014b), they may hence may put their own interests before the firm. In summary, there is no question that the personal characteristics of senior leaders have a profound impact on organizations. Not only are CEO characteristics linked to organizational culture and performance, but these characteristics also influence the size and negotiation of reward packages themselves.

Implications for executive reward structures and governance

CEOs' contributions to their organizations are insufficiently linked to performance measures. Our analysis showed that a "Profit-driven transactor" model prevails which frames the size of executive rewards as a result of legitimate market forces. There is an alternative view, however, that motivating CEOs to focus on responsible and sustainable business goals should underpin future reward practice. Yet regulation may not be the most effective way of instigating any changes in isolation, as CEO compensation does not exist in a vacuum. As our review of the literature demonstrated, CEOs influence their organisations but are also liable to social influences around them in turn. Whilst previous authors have highlighted the growing misalignment between CEO pay and shareholders' interests (e.g., Bebchuk and Fried 2005), the importance of broadening this consideration to include non-shareholder interests is now also recognised. It is important to understand the perspectives of broader key stakeholders and how these both influence and are influenced by the context in which reward decisions are made. The qualitative data we presented above underlines the need for a wider perspective as current parameters such as the need for quarterly reporting for listed companies, and a purported lack of effective talent strategies for senior teams, may constitute barriers to changes in the size and constitution of executive rewards. Whilst unravelling the diversity angle is beyond the scope of the current chapter, CEOs and boards remain predominantly male, and female senior leaders are still likely to earn less than their male counterparts (CIPD 2017; Li and Young 2016). Despite various reforms, diversity at senior levels in organizations needs to better reflect our society.

Where do research, theory, and practice need to go next?

Executive rewards are a complex issue. Does their size matter? UK data would suggest that yes, it does, as 60% of employees report that the size of CEO rewards is demotivating (CIPD 2015). Would workers be more engaged and happy if the rewards were more fairly distributed, and what kind of CEOs do we need to make this happen? A decade ago, Devers et al. (2007) noted that there is insufficient primary data on senior executives, and we find that little has changed in the literature since then. The same needs to be noted about primary data from other stakeholders involved in reward decisions, such as HR and reward specialists, a gap we endeavoured to start addressing with the present chapter. We need a better understanding of the characteristics and motivations of CEOs, top teams and relevant others, to supplement the more general theories of leadership, power, and agency in order to fully develop theoretical understanding and inform executive reward practice. It follows from the analysis offered here that researchers and practitioners stand to benefit from undertaking wider-scale research to understand the CEO characteristics needed now and for the future, and the interaction between the person and any compensation system in question. As we argued above, more consideration should be given to the personality and attributes of the CEO, and arguably also their top teams in selection, to ensure that they align with the values and mission of the organization to ensure a wider CSR, rather than a shareholder perspective. Researchers would do well to gather such primary data and then use this to refine our understanding through a more considered analysis of the 'seasons' of a CEO's tenure. Data show that the effectiveness of incentive plans varies across CEO tenure (Hou et al. 2014) as CEO performance varies over time as tenure is positively associated with the strength of the relationship between the firm and the employee, but inverted with firm-customer relationship strengths (Luo et al. 2013). These data suggest that CEOs are more concerned with external factors when they first take tenure, but more concerned with internal matters further on in their role. This observation in itself is not necessarily good or bad, but, as our review of the literature shows, the interaction between top-level leadership and corporate success is complex. This matter needs more careful unpacking than financial data alone, which is the subject of much existing research.

Conclusion

Taken together, the analysis offered here suggests that current levels of CEO rewards are unsubstantiated given that compensation is rarely aligned with performance measures, and when it is the performance measures rarely consider a sufficient range of valid outcomes. Governance initiatives, such as 'say on pay', do not appear to have regulating effects, leaving powerful and self-focused CEOs to negotiate 'their deal'. Our analysis showed that a shift towards more ethical and sustainable CEO behaviours is needed, but that ranked reward comparison, the perceived 'war for CEO talent' and short-term perspectives fuelled by mandates for reporting (for listed companies) constitute barriers to change. It remains a reality that too little research concerns itself with primary data on CEOs (Devers et al. 2007) but also wider stakeholders. Our taxonomy showed that stakeholder views may differ, for instance by either subscribing to the regulating effects of market forces, or to the need to take a more behavioural perspective. Longitudinal research into the compensation–performance relationship is also needed given that CEO performance is likely to vary over tenure. Without the latter, research and practice in the domain risk stagnation, continuing what is arguably one of the biggest, but ill-controlled corporate experiments.

Acknowledgements

The authors wish to gratefully acknowledge the work of Paul Hajduk and Duncan Jackson which was instrumental for shaping the CIPD report which fed into this chapter; and the input of Charles Cotton and Jonny Gifford for shaping this report.

References

Bebchuk, L. A. and Fried, J. M. (2003). Executive compensation as an agency problem. *Journal of Economic Perspectives*. 17, 71–92.

Bebchuk, L. A. and Fried, J. M. (2004). *Pay without Performance: The Unfulfilled Promise of Executive Compensation*. Cambridge, MA: Harvard University Press.

Bebchuk, L. A. and Fried, J. M. (2005). Pay without performance: overview of the issues. *Journal of Applied Corporate Finance*. 17(4), 8–23.

Black, D. E. (2014). CEO Pay-for-complexity and the risk of managerial diversion from multinational diversification. *Contemporary Accounting Research*. 31(1), 103–135.

Cai, J. and Walkling, R. A. (2011). Shareholders' say on pay: does it create value? *Journal of Financial and Quantitative Analysis*. 46(2), 299–339.

Capezio, A., Shields, J. and O'Donnell, M. (2011). Too good to be true: board structural independence as a moderator of CEO pay-for-firm-performance. *Journal of Management Studies*. 48(3), 487–513.

Chartered Institute for Personnel and Development (CIPD) and High Pay Centre (2017). Executive Pay. Review of FTSE100 Executive Pay packages, published August 2017.

CIPD. (2015). Available at: http://www2.cipd.co.uk/pm/peoplemanagement/b/weblog/archive/2015/12/18/dramatic-rethink-needed-on-demotivating-ceo-pay-levels-warns-cipd.aspx.

Cohen, D. A., Dey, A. and Thomas, Z. L. (2013). Corporate governance reform and executive incentives: implications for investments and risk taking. *Contemporary Accounting Research*. 30(4), 1296–1332.

Creswell, J. W. (2013). *Research Design: Qualitative, Quantitative, and Mixed Methods Approaches*. Thousand Oaks, CA: Sage Publications.

Densten, I. L. and Sarro, J. C. (2010). The impact of organizational culture and social desirability on Australian CEO leadership. *Leadership and Organization Development Journal*. 33(4), 342–368.

Devers, C., Canella, A., Reilly, G. and Yoder, M. (2007). Executive compensation: a multidisciplinary review of recent developments. *Journal of Management*, 33(6), 1016–1072.

DiPrete, T. A., Eirich, G. M. and Pittinsky, M. (2010). Compensation benchmarking, leapfrogs, and the surge in executive pay 1. *American Journal of Sociology*. 115(6), 1671–1712.

Dorff, M. (2014). *Indispensable and Other Myths: Why the CEO Pay Experiment Failed and How to Fix It*. Berkeley/Los Angeles, CA: University of California Press.

Everitt, B. S., Landau, S., Leese, M. & Stahl, D. (2011). *Cluster Analysis* (5th Ed.). Chichester: John Wiley and Sons.

Fabrizi, M., Mallin, C. and Michelon, G. (2014). The role of CEO's personal incentives in driving corporate social responsibility. *Journal of Business Ethics*. 124, 311–326.

Farmer, M., Brown, D., Hewitt, A. Reilly, P. and Bevan, S. (2013). Executive remuneration in the United Kingdom: will the coalition government's latest reforms secure improvement and what else is required? *Compensation and Benefits Review*. 45(1), 26–33.

Financial Times. (2016). UK chief executives earn much more than European peers. Published online, Available at: https://www.ft.com/content/585f41d4-c778-11e6-9043-7e34c07b46ef

Fitza, M. (2013). The use of variance decomposition in the investigation of CEO effects: how large must the CEO effect e to rule out chance? *Journal of Strategic Management*. 35, 1839–1852.

Gregory-Smith, I., Thompson, S. and Wright, P.W. (2013). CEO pay and voting dissent before and after the Crisis. *The Economic Journal*. 124, 22–39.

Hair, J., Anderson, R., Tatham, R. and Black, W. (1998). *Multivariate Data Analysis with Readings* (5th ed.). Upper Saddle River, NJ: Prentice-Hall International, Inc.

High Pay Centre. (2015). No Routine Riches. Report. Available at: www.highpaycentre.org/files/No_Routine_Riches_FINAL.pdf.

Hooghiemstra, R., Kuang, Y. and Qin. (2017). Does obfuscating excessive CEO pay work? The influence of remuneration report readability on say-on-pay votes. *Accounting and Business Research*. 47, 695–729.

Hou, W. and Priem, R.L. (2014). Does one size fit all? Investigating pay–future performance relationships over the "seasons" of CEO tenure. *Journal of Management*, 20(10). 1–28.

Income Data Services. (2015). Executive compensation review 2014–15. Available at: www.incomesdata. co.uk/books/view/directors-pay-report/

Jensen, M. C. and Meckling, W. H. (1976). Theory of the firm: managerial behavior, agency costs and ownership structure. *Journal of Financial Economics*. 3(4), 305–360.

Jizi, M. I., Salama, A., Dixon, R. and Stratling, R. (2014). Corporate governance and corporate social responsibility disclosure: evidence from the US banking sector. *Journal of Business Ethics*. 125(4), 601–615.

Krause, R., Whitler, K.A. and Semadeni, M. (2014). Power to the principals! An experimental look at shareholder say-on-pay voting. *Academy of Management Journal*. 57(1), 94–115.

Li, W. and Young, S. (2016). An analysis of pay arrangements and value creation for FTSE-350 Companies. Report published by the Chartered Financial Analysts Society, UK.

Luo, X., Kanuri, V. K. and Andrews, M. (2013). How does CEO tenure matter? The mediating role of firm–employee and firm–customer relationships. *Strategic Management Journal*.

Lupton, B., Rowe, A. and Whittle, R. (2015). *Show me the Money! Report Published by the Chartered Institute of Personnel and Development (CIPD)*, London. Available at: www.cipd.co.uk/binaries/show-me-the-money_2015-behavioural-science-of-reward.pdf.

Main, B. (2011). Career shares – a proposed long-term incentive arrangement: implementation considerations relating to proposal in 'Executive Pay – a career perspective'. *Hume Occasional Paper*. June, No 89. University of Edinburgh Business School.

McCarthy, S., Oliver, B. and Song, S. (2017). Corporate social responsibility and CEO confidence. *Journal of Banking and Finance*. 75, 280–291.

McDowall, A., Whysall, Z., Hajduk, P. and Jackson, D. (2015). *Taking Stock. What the Behavioural Science has to Say about Executive Rewards*. London: The Chartered Institute for Personnel and Development.

McWilliams, A., and Siegel, D. (2001). Corporate social responsibility: a theory of the firm perspective. *Academy of Management Review*. 26, 117–127.

Mishel, L. and Schieder, J. (2016). Stock market headwinds meant less generous year for some CEOs CEO pay remains up 46.5% since 2009. Economic Policy Institute Report. Available at: www.epi.org/files/pdf/109799.pdf

Mobbs, S. (2013). CEOs under fire: the effects of competition from inside directors on forced CEO turnover and CEO compensation. *Journal of Financial and Quantitative Analysis*. 48(3), 669–698.

Murphy, K. J. and Zábojník, J. (2004). CEO pay and appointments: a market-based explanation for recent trends. *The American Economic Review*. 94(2), 192–196.

O'Reilly, C. A., Caldwell, D. F., Chatman, J. A. and Doerr, B. (2014a). The promise and problems of organizational culture: CEO personality, culture and firm performance. *Group and Organization Management*. 39(6), 595–625.

O'Reilly, C. A., Doerr, B, Caldwell, D. F. and Chatman, J. A. (2014b). Narcissistic CEOs and executive compensation. *The Leadership Quarterly*. 25, 218–231.

O'Reilly, C. A. and Main, B. G. M. (2010). Economic and psychological perspectives on CEO compensation: a review and synthesis. *Industrial and Corporate Change*. 19(3), 675–712.

Pepper, A. A. and Gore, J. (2014). Behavioral agency theory: new foundations for theorizing about executive compensation. *Journal of Management*, 41(4), 1045–1068.

Pepper, A. (2015). *The Economic Psychology of Incentives*. Basingstoke: Palgrave Macmillan.

Rekker, S. A., Benson, K. L., and Faff, R. W. (2014). Corporate social responsibility and CEO compensation revisited: do disaggregation, market stress, gender matter? *Journal of Economics and Business*. 72, 84–103.

Resick, C. J., Whitman, D. S., Weingarden, S. M. and Hiller, N. J. (2009). The bright-side and dark-side of CEO personality: examining core self-evaluations, Narcissism, transformational leadership, and strategic influence. *Journal of Applied Psychology*. 94(6), 1365–1381.

Swinford, S. (2016). Theresa May unveils crackdown on executive pay and announces new plans to protect pensions. *The Telegraph*, 29 November 2016 published at www.telegraph.co.uk/news/2016/11/29/theresa-may-unveils-crackdown-executive-pay-announces-new-plans/.

Van Essen, M., Jordan, O. and Carberry, E. J. (2012). Assessing managerial power theory: a meta-analytic approach to understanding the determinants of CEO compensation. *Journal of Management*. 41(1), 164–202.

Wall Street Journal (WSJ, 25 June 2015) How much the best-performance and worst-performance CEOs got paid. Available at: www.wsj.com/articles/how-much-the-best-and-worst-ceos-got-paid-1435104565.

Yang, F., Dolar, B. and Mo, L. (2014). CEO compensation and firm performance: did the 2007–2008 financial crisis matter? *Journal of Accounting and Finance*. 14(1), 137.

15

REWARD MANAGEMENT DESIGNED FOR A DIGITALLY EMPOWERED AGE

Clive Wright

The problem

We need to improve the way we view and manage reward in organizations very soon or we will continue to squander money on programmes only suitable for the middle of the twentieth century. The reward strategies, policies and programmes generally in use today are already obsolete and no longer fit for the effective motivation and engagement of today's workforce, let alone tomorrow's. Businesses and organizations are moving on rapidly, the employee environment is changing dramatically with better-educated and informed workers who are used to using technology as part of their daily lives and have a new perspective on employment. Organizational design and social media means that command and control structures no longer work in most environments. Employees expect to be listened to; they have a view on what they would like from their employer and expect it to be fair, equitable and appropriate for them. Technology has given us the opportunity to manage and work in new ways with personally derived work schedules and societal changes are driving demands for new thinking on organizational responsibilities.

Traditionally, reward has been determined and delivered by the organization to drive directly the business objectives and results. Salaries are determined by closely defined job responsibilities, incentives linked directly to business output and employment contracts to organizational needs. The executive team, at whatever level this might be in the organization, determines what rewards are appropriate, what they want to achieve with reward and what programmes they think will motivate employees to deliver their predetermined objectives and, therefore, the overall business results of the organization. All, of course, with the advice, direction and guidance of the HR team.

Over the last fifty years, reward structures have developed slowly – job evaluation, detailed grading, broadbanding, flexible benefits, pension changes and, more recently, wellness programmes have changed very slowly, more as a factor of fads or technical improvement than any innovative design. These have all been driven from an organizational perspective of what will motivate employees and drive up productivity. 'The company knows best': very much the relationship is that between an adult and a child. This was probably fine when the company *did* know best, but as today's employees have been better educated, know more about what is going on inside and outside their own organization through the use of technology and the media and have information available to them with a click on a tablet, smartphone or laptop we can no longer make such a broad assumption of the company's omniscience.

Key actor misperceptions of what's needed of them

But executives still see it as their sole prerogative to make these decisions. They are paid to run the organization and an essential element of this is the management of reward. If they are a director of a UK listed company they are legally responsible for "the success of the company for the benefit of its members as a whole" but only have "regard for" the "interests of the company's employees" (Companies Act 2006), so they are driven towards maximum financial success achieved through high productivity and the lowest possible costs. This, quite understandably, drives an executive team to consider the organization from a strategic viewpoint based upon their view of what is needed to achieve success. And this applies to reward as much as any other aspect of the organization. They tend to see reward as an economic, transactional deal.

Within the area of HR every time that they or the reward professional are asked to review one of the reward programmes, design something new or just build an additional plan to help improve productivity, retention, motivation or whatever the problem is that needs to be resolved they use their experience or what they have learned works from conferences or professional publications. They probably discuss it with the business leader, check costs and affordability, ensure legal compliance and then announce it to the unsuspecting population of employees that it is supposed to motivate. There are two problems here: firstly, they build on what they have tried before or what someone else has done successfully in another organization with a very different history, culture, environment, etc.; secondly, they have taken no account of the employee views – are they interested in the reward (valence), is there a strong correlation between performance, outcomes and reward (instrumentality) and do they trust the manager/leader/company to provide the rewards when the results are delivered.

For reward to be effective it must be based on the organization's business objectives and these are currently changing like never before (this also includes the public sector and the 'third' sector, where 'business objectives' may not be quite so clear, but are changing just as quickly). These objectives are changing massively for just about every organization. In the 1920s the average life for an S&P 500 company was 67 years; in the 2010s it is 15 years (Dr Richard Foster, Yale University; Foster 2012). Just think about the implications of this finding for the company, its employees and their families. And as well as the product, service, financial and customer changes the business objectives need to be linked to the people challenges of the organization – culture, skills requirements, labour supply, management capability, knowledge development and dissemination, changing demographics, etc.

Unless there is a clear link between the reward strategy and programmes and the business objectives, why are you doing it? If the programme is not there to increase income, save costs, drive productivity, improve service or limit risk, what is it for? Just because it has worked somewhere else does not mean that it is right for your organization. At one of my previous companies we were working with a leading business strategy consultancy. I was introduced to their 'reward expert' and told that the way leading companies were developing reward was along a particular line and that we should follow this approach to be just as successful. I asked which companies she was talking about and was shown a list of young, high-tech companies who were experiencing massive growth and significant increases in their share price. Apparently, if we took the same approach it would drive our share price higher too. She seemed surprised when I pointed out that we were a 114-year-old chemicals/engineering company, that our growth had been steady at 5–10% for the last 40 years and that the share price had increased broadly in line with the FTSE100, and that, consequently, our approach needed to be something that was appropriate for us and not just something we had copied from someone else, however successful it had been for them!

Building towards a sustainable response

So organizations should be revisiting their reward strategy to take into account the organization's objectives over the next few years, including consideration of the people issues that will be arising, align reward with other HR programmes and changes and develop a strategy that they can honestly say links reward to successful business outcomes. To be successful, however, this needs to include the views of the employees on what will work, what will motivate them and what is needed to engage them fully in the success of the organization.

In most organizations, wages, salaries, incentives, benefits and perquisites account for more than half of the operating costs. In some companies, especially in the knowledge, creative or high-tech sector, this figure could be more than three-quarters of the operating costs. So the executives should be involved and responsible for rewards. The problem is that the members of an executive team are generally, at a personal level, remote from the employees. They have different personal experiences, are driven by different motivations, have different economic needs, have a different perspective on the world and have a different social environment. The executives occupy a different communal space to most employees and so there is generally a 'values disconnect'. They wouldn't be leading the organization if they weren't exceptional people, which makes them different to the average employee. As they have risen through the ranks, their own rewards, personal needs and expectations have changed dramatically.

During my time as a consultant working with some of the bigger global companies there was always a reluctance in client companies to include employees in the consultation for the new strategy or programme design. There was a consistent fear that including employees would start the rumour mill, would only result in a list of employee demands, would set unrealistic expectations or would provide no useful input. But this is to overlook the views of the very people that the new strategy is designed to engage and motivate.

But before I go any further I should explain what I mean by reward. I view reward from the employee perspective – anything that the employee likes, appreciates, values or needs from the employer is reward. This means that reward includes not only the traditional pay and benefits (the extrinsic rewards), but also the learning and development opportunities (building for the future); the working environment including flexibility, line manager capability, being listened to, recognition, and then finally the values and reputation of the employer and the quality of the leadership team (taken all together these make up the intrinsic rewards). If the pay and benefits are fair, equitable and market-aligned the employee is motivated by extrinsic rewards to perform adequately; if the employee appreciates the future opportunities and the immediate working environment then he or she will perform highly; and if, in addition, the values of the two parties are aligned, intrinsic rewards, the employee is truly engaged. As Matthew Taylor and his team say in the 2017 report *Good Work: The Taylor Review of Modern Working Practices*, 'Pay is only one aspect in determining quality work; for many people fulfilment, personal development, work life balance or flexibility are just as important.'

Getting the balance right between extrinsic and intrinsic rewards is essential when designing reward systems. Organizations can successfully manage with lower than market rate pay and benefits if the intrinsic rewards are at such a high level that employees actually want to work for the organization. It can be a waste of money to pay higher than the market if the intrinsic rewards are at such a high level that the employees feel motivated and engaged to achieve the organization's objectives.

In addition, almost all organizations benchmark with their competitors for levels of pay and provision of benefits or perks, the extrinsic rewards, so they know what other organizations are doing compared to their own levels. They can measure their position relative to the market and determine whether they need to increase or decrease their pay levels based upon the competitive position they want to establish. However, measuring the level of intrinsic rewards against the competition is impossible, so we really don't know how much the competition might be enjoying an advantage through higher levels of intrinsic rewards which might enable them to provide lower levels of extrinsic rewards. If an organization can increase its level of intrinsic rewards, it can gain not only a financial advantage but also a competitive advantage through higher levels of employee engagement.

Increasing extrinsic rewards through pay or benefits is an expensive exercise. A 1% increase in pay will have little effect on motivation over the medium or longer term, and this is a significant cost that is built into the reward package over a long period. Increasing the level of intrinsic rewards is much cheaper and if carried out in the right way could even lower costs, thereby giving a competitive advantage.

The final aspect is that if you have a high level of intrinsic rewards where employees feel valued and listened to, enjoy their work, buy in to the company values, have career and development opportunities and feel that they are achieving something worthwhile you have an environment where employees are motivated and engaged and which is impossible for the competition to copy. The reasoning is consistent with Jay Barney's (1991) resource-based view of strategy: combining people and organizational characteristics successfully is inimitable and non-substitutable by others; and it may be rare and valuable to boot. This competitive business advantage can be extremely valuable when compared with the cost of increasing pay and benefits to achieve the same results.

The significance of context and employee characteristics

So, employees join an organization based upon the deal of intrinsic and extrinsic rewards that is acceptable to them. Whilst that deal remains in balance and is still perceived as fair the employee remains motivated, but if any aspect of the deal changes the whole balance needs to be reviewed and revisited if employee motivation is to be maintained. With the end of the traditional system of industrial relations (via trade unions 'recognised' for collective bargaining purposes), the potential has been for more direct engagement between workers and managers. But the issue has foundered on the rocks of the breakdown in trust and a greater transactional employment relationship (now manifested in the 'gig' economy). If people don't trust the processes (i.e., if it fails to provide 'processual justice') then its premise fails to achieve the intended outcome. This reinforces the grievances being generally expressed in terms of poor distributional justice when the executive minority benefits from unfairly high (or excessive) reward packages than the majority (see Shortland and Perkins, this volume).

Reward is typically designed for the "average" employee. But if you consider in more detail the desired reward balance and the motivation of employees you will see that there are as many combinations as you have employees. Everyone at all levels of the organization has their own personal priorities and needs as far as rewards are concerned. It may depend on whether they are single, married or have a family, their age, whether they are a single parent, whether the children are still at school, university or have left home, their own economic situation, their interests outside work that may require specific times to follow. The combinations are endless.

All reward is contextual. Employees with different circumstances, different beliefs, different backgrounds, different life and work experiences and different visions desire different reward packages. The societal context is also important; if the job is seen as being valuable to society, e.g., a teacher, a nurse, police officer, the whole of society confers an intrinsic reward for the employee.

So, consider reward as four boxes: financial rewards (cash and incentives); benefits and perks; learning, development and opportunities; and the quality of the working environment (including leadership and organization values). Every employee at every level and in every role will have a view of what the balance might be of these four boxes. For example:

> For an **executive,** the primacy might be financial (specifically long-term incentives) and the benefits (especially a final salary 'defined benefit' pension plan). They set their working environment and as an executive there is little the company can offer in development opportunities, so these areas are of little importance in their total reward package.

> For a **single parent** in an administrative position, the priorities might be financial (I need the salary to pay for food and rent) and work environment (I appreciate an understanding and flexible boss and work colleagues when family priorities occur in working time). The person receives few benefits and development is probably not a priority for them at the moment.

> For a **R&D engineer**, the priority is probably learning and development (I need to keep up with the latest research, theories and techniques) and the working environment (I need some freedom to follow my research path and good equipment to help me get there). They appreciate the pay and understand that they've got some benefits, but these are not overriding priorities.

The list could be endless and within each category there will be differences – an unmarried R&D engineer might have a different view to one with a family and different to one whose children have left home. And the motivation of each individual is driven by a series of factors, including personality, upbringing, education and previous life and work experiences. So while some may be motivated by targets and competition, others will be motivated by teamwork or social contribution and still others by personal status or power. In the classic text *The Achieving Society* (2010 [1961]) David McClelland describes three types of motivational needs – achievement, authority/power and affiliation). Not everyone, even in the same team or department, will be motivated by the same factors.

So how do we find out what motivates employees, what they value and what will get them truly engaged? Well, the simple answer is to ask them, perhaps through the traditional approach of an opinion or engagement questionnaire, but paper or web-based surveys are not effective in gaining a good view of employee opinions on reward; there are many other questions that need to be answered, so the number on reward is limited and employees game-play their answers. The better approach is to use focus groups, but the design of the questions needs to be considered carefully. It's not about using direct questions such as 'Would you like more salary?'; but open questions such as 'What works for you in your reward package and relationship with the organization?'; 'How could the employer make the package more effective for you'; 'Would your manager be able to operate a new process effectively, would they have the skills, information, tools and techniques needed?' Organizations can also use web-based 'pulse' surveys to get a comprehensive view from employees. Social media and internal web tools also now give organizations additional opportunities to really involve employees in a non-threatening and collaborative way. Current techniques in use by some forward-looking organizations are:

- **Yelpification:** a process where employees are asked to rate aspects such as the culture, management, people processes, etc. of the organization to give their views on what's working and what isn't working.

- **Design thinking:** a social invitation to employees who have expressed an interest in participating and contributing to the solution.
- **Sentiment analysis:** measurement of employee sentiment through social site analysis; for example, looking for the frequency of key words or phrases on the organization's internal social media facilities.
- **Hackathons:** a process where proposals are submitted on social media for general review, analysis and comment by interested employees to determine whether the proposal will be effective, have the appropriate impact, be feasible and provide a level of innovation which would not have been possible through any other practical means.

This development of social media is now opening up new avenues for organizations to research not only the views of employees, but also to positively engage them in the review and development of reward strategies, policies and programmes.

Whichever avenue is chosen to garner employee input and involve them in the process, the benefit to the organization is enormous. There is plenty of research (e.g., Purcell 2014; Rees et al. 2013; Marsden 2013) which demonstrates the increase in employee engagement and productivity if employees are involved in, and listened to, in discussions. And indeed, in the 2017 Taylor Review, referred to previously, states that 'People are most likely to enjoy what they do when they have a meaningful say at work'.

When companies undertake traditional employee opinion or engagement surveys one of the aspects that falls in the most negative responses is 'not being listened to or involved in decisions impacting me'. The implication is for organizations to undertake comprehensive programmes to educate line managers on their role of engaging in (two-way) communication with employees. And for HR and the Executive team, it is important that they understand that they need the views, input and opinions of employees on reward programmes and changes if they are to be successful in motivating and engaging them. In some recent work that I was doing with one organization about the reward packages for lorry drivers the client said they have two types of drivers: one has multiple stops in a day offloading the delivery themselves and the other made one or two deliveries a day, where it was the customer who did the unloading. The immediate assumption of the company was that the driver who made multiple deliveries worked harder and therefore deserved higher levels of pay. They were just about to implement their changes when they asked for the views of the drivers and found most of the multiple delivery drivers liked their job and would not want to swap. They liked the interaction with customers and the physical activity between driving. They saw themselves not as working harder, but as simply enjoying their job more. It is not enough to make assumptions that 'parent' knows best.

So, it is not good enough to assume that you know what employees like or dislike, what they would like to see happen or not happen. Managers need to engage with them in a meaningful way to ensure that they really understand employee preferences and listen to their views.

Building on research-informed understanding of commitment and engagement

This is not a new proposal, but the environment in which it can be effective has developed over the past few years and it is applicable now in most organizations. In reward terms, over the past thirty years, while the emphasis on local collective bargaining (or local application of sector-wide detailed agreements) and the 'rate for the job' has given way to individual packages, there is still discontent on both sides of the employment relationship. The communication process has lagged behind in this environment, with communication shifting from collective to individual bargaining (albeit often on standardized terms). It has yet to move to a collaborative discussion of the pros and cons of the various approaches to, and the balance of factors in, reward matched to individual circumstances.

In the past, the basis for 'continuance commitment' to the employer was being part of an internal labour market which offered security of employment. But the environment has changed to reflect a set of common values which may form the basis for employees to feel rewarded; categorized as 'affective commitment' (Meyer and Allen 1991). And 'Millennials' are said to value organizational values more highly that align with their own. 'Normative commitment' – sense of obligation – is the third in the 'three-component model of commitment' articulated by John Meyer and Natalie Allen. The model relates to the psychological basis of engagement. It compares and contrasts with earlier analysis going back to the Hawthorne studies in the 1920s (Economist 2008), which surfaced the idea of employees as *social* not simply economic actors – having a need for a sense of belonging and involvement in their work organizations. A shift over the past three decades for employees to seek to define themselves as consumers, not just producers may have diluted these sentiments as well as the greater insecurity (or flexibility) of the contemporary work situation. The environment of change has been developing for some time.

But as most in HR, and especially reward, will know one of the issues is getting corporate management to grasp that these factors are important. What are the mechanisms involved in this process? Four decades ago, the Bullock Committee undertook a UK government inquiry in response to the European Commission's Draft Fifth Company Law Directive (Bullock 1977), which sought to harmonize worker participation in management of companies across Europe. The inquiry talked about employee engagement and the need for industrial democracy. In response to the report, the City Company Law Committee wrote:

> The more people are able to influence decisions which closely affect their work the more effective will that involvement be; the more effective the involvement the greater the commitment to the company's objectives which, in the final analysis, will be concerned with generating wealth or services for the community as a whole.
>
> *(1977:3)*

In 1979 at the EU level there was the proposed Vredling Directive, followed later by the Information and Consultation (or 'voice and value') Directive for European Works Councils, which aimed to embrace consultation and involvement of employees across national borders. In some companies this has given rise to employee works councils under 'The Information and Consultation of Employees Regulations 2004'.

Gallie et al. (1998) point to 1980s-style, Japanese-inspired continuous improvement management alongside HRM, emphasizing the supervisor–employee relationship. This has involved supervisors replacing the union as employment relations intermediaries. But with the more recent delayering and reduction of traditional supervisors, requiring those in leadership and coordination roles to do a lot of other things than supervising or overseeing the work of others, this means that time to play such a role has been limited. So here too, at this level, a conduit to policy management at the senior levels is lacking. In the collective bargaining era, there were opportunities for leaders to engage directly with worker representatives to appreciate how the workers were characterized as feeling. In my view the shift from partnership-oriented unions to 'organizing' (more 'politically') oriented unions as part of the change from the traditional system of industrial relations has created a sense among many managers that they are getting little more than a politicized version of the employee viewpoint.

Conclusions and implications for management

Looking to the future there is much debate about the future of work, the diverse nature of the workforce and the changing employment relationship. In a report on the 'Future of Work and Rewards' (Scott et al. 2017), the expectation is that the employment relationship will become increasingly diverse with more workers who are not employees (contractors, zero hours, 'gig' workers), bringing the need for more openness and transparency. With the result that reward will be far more customised to the individual 'contractor', in turn, introducing complexity and an even greater need for effective communication as to the nature of the 'effort–reward bargain'.

Managerial implications are to give even more importance to 'employee voice', and for organizations to communicate more effectively with employees and include their views on what is needed to engage them. The answers will be individual, diverse and complex and will be even more challenging when the solutions need to comply with legislative requirements for equality. Unfortunately, there is no simple solution to the dichotomy, but unless we really engage and listen to employees we will continue to design strategies and programmes for the many that satisfy the few.

References

Barney, J. (1991). Firm resources and sustained competitive advantage. *Journal of Management*. 17(1), 99–120.

Bullock, A. (1977). *A Report of the Committee of Inquiry on Industrial Democracy*. London: HMSO.

City Company Law Committee. (1977). *A Reply to Bullock*. London: City Law Committee.

Companies Act. (2006). Accessible from legislation.gov.uk.

Economist. (2008). 'Idea: The Hawthorne Effect', published in *online extra*, November 3, Available at: www.economist.com/node/12510632, accessed on July 27, 2017.

Foster, R. (2012). *Executive Briefing: Creative Destruction Whips through Corporate America*. Innosight, Winter edition, Available at: www.innosight.com/wp-content/uploads/2016/08/creative-destruction-whips-through-corporate-america_final2015.pdf, accessed on July 27, 2017.

Gallie, D., White, M., Cheng, Y. and Tomlinson, M. (1998). *Restructuring the Employment Relationship*. Oxford: Oxford University Press.

Marsden, D. (2013). Individual voice in employment relationships: a comparison under different forms of workplace representation. *Industrial Relations: A Journal of Economy and Society*. 52(1), 221–258.

McClelland, D. (2010 [1961]). *The Achieving Society*. Eastford, CT: Martino Fine Books.

Meyer, J. and Allen, N. (1991). A three-component conceptualization of organizational commitment. *Human Resource Management Review*. 1(1), 61–89.

Purcell, J. (2014). Employee engagement. In Truss, C., Delbridge, R., Alfes, K., Shantz, A. and Soane, E. (eds.). *Employee Engagement in Theory and Practice*. London: Taylor & Francis.

Rees, C., Alfes, K. and Gatenby, M. (2013). Employee voice and engagement: connections and consequences. *The International Journal of Human Resource Management*. 24(14), 2780–2798.

Scott, D., McMullen, T. and Larson, E. (2017). The future of work and rewards: forward thinking from the C-suite and total rewards leaders. *World at Work Journal*. 26(1).

Taylor, M. (2017). *Good Work: The Taylor Review of Modern Working Practices*. Available at: www.gov.uk/government/publications/good-work-the-taylor-review-of-modern-working-practices, accessed on July 11, 2017.

16

CONSEQUENCES OF DIGITALIZED WORKING LIFE FOR REWARD MANAGEMENT IN THEORY AND PRACTICE

Matti Vartiainen

Work motivation and reward practices in the grip of change?

The working life contexts and expectations for employees' skills and competencies are changing constantly. The changes not only affect the division of work and employment relationships in societies, but also the structures, contents and organizing work and the ways in which people become motivated and get rewarded. One material driver of change in working life is technological innovation, which is dynamically implemented and used in almost any field of working life. Technological innovation in organizations is often the trigger for change also to other aspects of the systemic whole such as reward management (RM). Finally, the changes show as employees' altered valuations, attitudes, expectations and changes in their resources as well as in the desire to utilize voluntarily their talent, expertise and competences to act in a goal-oriented manner and be rewarded for doing so. This chapter describes technology-related working life trends and how they are connected to work itself, its organizing, the desire to act and, lastly, the fluency of work as an outcome. The interaction between these observable trends and possible implications for employee motivation and RM are explored. In RM, the internal balance of the total reward paradigm is challenged as the expected changes are so great.

Trends of change in working life

Working life changes continuously. As do the threats and dreams associated with change. During the past few years, discussion has been dominated by the computerization of occupations (Frey and Osborne 2013) by replacing them and possibilities of new work such as 'crowdwork' (Meil and Kirov 2017) or 'online work' in digital platforms renewing occupations. It is evident that these changes in jobs, tasks and their organization are brought about by the digitalization of tasks. Digitalization means the intruding of digital technologies into everyday activities and communication; a phenomenon which started in the 1980s with the introduction of desktop computers (see, for example, Hertel et al. 2017). In addition to the development of technology and the generalization of its use, working life environment and demands are being changed by many other global factors: population growth and migration, creating increased demand for natural resources and immigration; limits of natural resources and the environment, such as the sufficiency of raw materials and climatic changes; economic factors, such as the deregulation of world trade and the polarization of income; social factors, such as ageing, urbanization and gaps in living standards; political factors, such as wars, terrorism and extremist movements. Ultimately, changes are potentially influenced and regulated by psychological factors.

Questions arise such as: what basic needs do people have and are they changing? What do people want from their life and work? What do they want to do; and are they ready to change? The changes in increasingly digitalized work and environments generally have opened work and organizational psychology academics try to interpret future prospects for motivation of people at work and the role played by a reward system and its management. In addition, management professionals need to consider new practices in designing and applying reward approaches to their workforce members with the intention of serving changing organizational requirements.

Digital impacts on work

Of the general, global trends the most immediate material factor affecting people's work activities and resources at the organizational level is the extensive utilization of digitalization and mobile access to the Internet. This chapter is written from this perspective, although it tries to avoid technological determinism. It is seen, however, that key applications in communications, working platforms and the automation of work processes affect work and leisure and their relationship – and organization practices – in many ways. Digital platforms and the transition to online virtual work, the analysis and 'algorithmization' of large bulk data into intelligent cloud services, 'artificial intelligence', the 'Internet of Things' and 'mobile Internet', machine learning and robotization are particularly associated with changes in the structure and contents of work. And possibly work motivation and ways of rewarding employees.

The challenge of computerization and digitalization for occupations (Frey and Osborne 2013) is global. In their seminal work, Frey and Osborne (2013), providing numerous examples, estimate the probability of computerization for 702 occupations in the USA. They focus on technological advancements in Machine Learning (ML), including Data Mining, Machine Vision, Computational Statistics and other subfields of Artificial Intelligence (AI). In AI especially, algorithms are developed that allow cognitive tasks to be automated. In addition, they examine the application of ML technologies in Mobile Robotics (MR), and computerization in manual tasks. According to their estimates, around 47% of total US employment over the next decade or two is in the high-risk category to be replaced: for example, most workers in transportation and logistics occupations, together with office and administrative support workers, and labour in production occupations. They also find that a substantial share of employment in service occupations is highly susceptible to computerization because of an increasing number of service robots. They conclude that as technology races ahead, low-skill workers will reallocate to tasks that are non-susceptible to computerization, i.e., tasks requiring creative and social intelligence.

For workers to win the race, however, they will have to acquire creative and social skills. Pajarinen et al. (2015) repeated the study and also analysed data from Finland and Norway. Their replication of Frey and Osborne, using data for 2012 rather than 2010, suggests that 49% of US employment is in the high-risk category. The corresponding share for Finland is 35% and for Norway 33%, i.e., 14–16% less than in the US. Low-wage and low-skill occupations appear to be most under threat, whereas service and public sector jobs are relatively more sheltered than those in manufacturing and the private sector. Decreasing occupational groups include, for example, shop assistants, secretaries, bank employees and office workers. On the other hand, the change is estimated to have a lesser effect on nursing staff, social workers and counselling professionals. However, 'social robotics', for example, robotic nurses, is predicted also to affect the tasks of nursing staff (Jesuthasan 2017). Previously, mostly manual and routine information work tasks have decreased, but in future, thanks to cognitive robotics, the impact is expected to spread to more demanding and more complex information work. Creative tasks requiring social intelligence are thought to remain to a large extent outside this development. In all, these changes create a need to develop new know-how.

Digitalization of work has multiple faces. With digital technologies, it is possible to replace some tasks traditionally performed by people, such as robots replacing an assembly worker in car manufacturing. However, new, partly more demanding knowledge-intensive jobs can be created such as a programmer in 3D printing, or hybridized in some others, such as a physician's job using artificial intelligence as help in medical diagnosis. Robots can not only perform a routine worker's tasks in production, but also, for example, replace customer counselling delivered by a bank clerk by providing intelligent programmed services. The most familiar digital services are bank services, which have already become online services for the majority of the population. With the 'Internet of Things', digitalization penetrates more deeply and closely into everyday life by means of sensors in objects and goods and the feedback given by digital identifiers; for example, well-being wristbands. Objects and goods are connected to the Internet and through it to each other and other people, forming a new kind of sociomaterial working and living environment. With means for interaction based on mobile Internet and augmented reality, access to information and communication is possible from different places at different times. This brings consequences for the interdependence of workers, creating flexible work structures with consequences such as sharing rewards for people's contributions individually and in teams, and for management to be mindful of the requirements for organizationally just outcomes and processes for arriving at the outcomes.

Digital working platforms, or crowdsourcing platforms, as new working environments are varied, from those based on volunteer work (e.g., Wikipedia) and those exploiting it (e.g., Facebook, Google, YouTube) to global platforms providing employment services (e.g., Amazon Mechanical Turk) and enterprises using internal social media. Routine micro-tasks (e.g., translating an advertising slogan from Finnish to English) as well as large innovation projects are carried out on the digital platforms. Perhaps the best example of a knowledge community exploiting voluntary work is Wikipedia, which provides a free-of-charge information pool for all with access to the Internet. Facebook, Google and YouTube, in turn, exploit voluntary peer production effectively to promote their own businesses. An example of a Finnish working platform based on common interests is Solved, which provides a working environment to 1,500 'cleantech' experts and consultation services involved in new and experimental design projects.

What makes people use digital work platforms and social media environments? Why do many experts, professionals and amateurs want to participate in crowdsourcing and peer production? The motives are both extrinsic and intrinsic (Deci and Ryan 2012). In global employment service environments like Mechanical Turk, the motive is subsistence, because in producing use value, digital work is a medium of exchange like a traditionally produced service and product. Thus, a part of digital work is paid labour both within an enterprise and on the global market. The so-called intrinsic motivating factors are seen, for example, in Wikipedia, where immaterial rewards, such as the possibility of using knowledge and skills autonomously, the esteem of others, fame and glory, and belonging to a community of the like-minded, motivate content production. These developments bring with them likely implications for how individual, group and organization-wide performance, against purposive goals, is envisaged, tracked, appraised and rewarded.

Job structures and ways of working change

Digitalization and changes in work and working environments influence professions and employment relationships by making organizational structures, working times, places of work and collaboration more flexible. All the more often, work is organized within and between workplaces into temporary projects. Point in time varies a lot. Work is also more often done in many places outside the main workplace, supported by mobile information technology. Virtual teams are used as a way of co-operating as are digital platforms to arrange global online work. All in all, information technology enables a flexible choice of time and place but simultaneously create reward management and societal challenges such as on what bases (job-, person- or performance-based) to compensate work and taxation. The flexible structures of working life involve the 'projectization' of assignments into temporary projects for which a team of workers is assembled as necessary to realize the project at hand. Both within and between organizations, the participation of different players in common projects creates challenges at the interfaces between organizations: how to make co-operation and common projects run and how to agree on the distribution of the commonly produced benefit?

Flexible organizing also involves temporal flexibility; that is, a worker can, or is expected to, begin and end his or her work according to the situation and the need. One essential question for work motivation is to what extent the choice of working place and time is autonomous. Worker-oriented flexibility can help facilitate the co-ordination of work and other life, and coping in one's work. On the other hand, the border between working time and leisure is obscured, when work spills to leisure and vice versa. Colleagues, superiors and customers contact workers ever more easily also outside official working hours. The choice of working hours is also affected by international co-operation, which requires, for example, arranging online meetings requiring some participants to be available unusually early in the morning and late in the evening.

Mobile Internet and cloud services enable mobile, multilocational work (Koroma et al. 2014). Co-operation with others is done in local meetings, online and periodically at the main workplace, if it exists. Eurofound (2016), in its recent survey study, describes telework in Europe though not directly specifying how much digital technology is used while working. The vast majority of workers in the EU (70%) have still a single regular workplace (particularly employees), while 30% carry out their work in multiple locations. The proportion of workers with multiple workplaces varies substantially between countries: from a low of 17% in Turkey to over 40% in the Nordic countries.

Due to the technological change, there is a reason to presume that this development will gain strength. In Europe, the proportion of workers reporting working in multiple workplaces is larger for men than for women and increases with age. It is also larger for self-employed workers (with and without employees), agricultural workers and managers, and is particularly prevalent in the construction, transport and agriculture sectors. A majority of the self-employed with employees report working daily at their own premises (72% doing so), but are also more likely to work on a daily basis at the client's premises (13%), in a car or vehicle (14%), outdoors (13%) or from home (16%). Self-employed workers without employees are less likely to work at their own premises (only 48% doing so), but are more likely to work daily at the client's premises (18%) or from home (23%). In general, a small proportion of workers report working in public spaces such as coffee shops and airports: 3% daily, 3% several times a week, and 4% several times a month.

Virtual teams and collaboration are one of the now-traditional working types utilizing digitalization (Gilson et al. 2015). They operate in a geographically distributed manner and, as necessary, also at different times, supported by information technology. The virtual teams of a project organization form and disperse in accordance with the assignment cycle. The virtual teams are not formed only of the people working in the enterprises participating in the cooperation, but they also encompass customers and more loosely involved subcontractors. Online work is a type of virtual collaboration. Digital platforms increasingly serve as crowdsourced dispersed workplaces for online workers. One such platform, Amazon Mechanical Turk, acts as an employment agency. An employer somewhere in the globe posts digital tasks for the site's users to complete. A worker enters the site using an owned or borrowed device, selects a task, completes it, is credited with the proceeds, and selects the next task. Each completed task earns the worker a form of remuneration.

A whole 'digital working class' has emerged worldwide, working for international employers (Scholz 2013). Lehdonvirta (2016) characterizes digital delocalized labour as two types: work as partly relocalized elsewhere and delocalized work that is dispersed. Relocalization is exemplified by offshored work and dispersed work by globally crowdsourced microwork. Virtual or digital work indicates, for example, working as a freelancer on the Internet doing micro-tasks from a remote place utilizing digitalized working environments. A major difference versus conventional jobs is the fact that this kind of work is entrepreneurial freelancing, and often without any kind of social protection. Lehdonvirta (2016) states that the key feature of these platforms is that they provide employers with an application programming interface: a codified interface through which the employer's software can issue inputs to and receive outputs from the workforce as if it was a software module. Employees doing microwork may be detached from interaction with other employees and from national legal frameworks and contracts.

Changing employment relationships

The changes in work structures, flexible schedules and ways of working are challenging from the viewpoint of a single company and its management, including human resource management. As a consequence of the replacement of work tasks and the creation of new ones, workforce supply and demand of will be polarized: there will be an oversupply of some skilled workers and a shortage of others. Luckily, new jobs with new types of competences are also created. Unpredictability will, however, increase both in organizations and on the personal level. The ways of working will change within and between organizations. Organizations will adapt their operations to the demands of the market and to seasonal variations by means of flexible employment relationships mediated through digitalized locales.

Figure 16.1 illustrates the types of employment relationships from the perspectives of an individual worker's work life cycle and the organization: as the core and contingent types of workforce such as temporary external workers and freelancers from whom labour input is purchased. One might argue that what is being witnessed here is a digitalization of the classic core–periphery workforce model articulated by Atkinson (1984).

Contingent and autonomous types of job are sometimes called 'flexible' (see, for example, Eurofound 2015). Demands for increased flexibility have resulted in the emergence of new forms of employment across the world. These have transformed the traditional one-to-one relationship between employer and employee. This development was anticipated in an early study on virtual workplace (Crandall & Wallace 1997), where its blended workforce was divided into the full-time regular, temporary and contract-based employees.

From the organization perspective, the core workforce consists of workers indispensable to the organization and in a permanent, full-time employment relationship, with the expertise, know-how and professional competences. The core workforce is supplemented by the contingent workforce in a looser relationship with the organization, performing routine wage work of lesser value to the work organization. Contingent workforce participants are more often than those in the core workforce in so-called atypical, temporary employment relationships, characterized, for

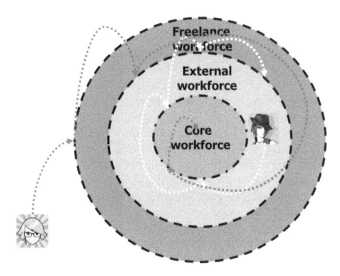

Figure 16.1 Types of employment relationships from an individual worker's and an organization's perspectives

Source: Based on Atkinson 1984, p.4.

example, by part-time employment and zero-hour contracts. The freelance workforce is characterized by an occasional, result-based relationship with the contracting organization. The workers are not the organization's own workforce, but, for example, employed by a subcontractor or a work lease enterprise. They also include freelancers, consultants and contract workers. A fixed-term contractual nature applies to almost all occupations. Many tasks are seasonal (peak periods and seasons, night and weekend work, substitutions, etc.).

Lehdonvirta from the Oxford Internet Institute states that what is crucial for the online business model is that labour is detached from local organizational and institutional structures, so that it may be sold as an on-demand 'cloud' service. In his study on microwork (2016), he found that it is seldom 'a full-time job'. In the study, a group of Nepalese workers mainly depended on their parents for their subsistence and used microwork to earn additional income. Filipino workers were 'precariats', combining microwork and other irregular income sources. American workers were a mix of precariats, typically housewives economically dependent on their spouses, and salary earners, who did microwork as a hobby as much as to earn additional income. Lehdonvirta also reports (2017) about the location of the online workforce. The largest overall supplier of online labour according to the Institute's data is India, home to 24% of the workers observed, followed by Bangladesh (16%) and the United States (12%). Different countries' workers focus on different occupations. The software development and technology category is dominated by workers from the Indian subcontinent, who command a 55% market share. The professional services category, which consists of services such as accounting, legal services, and business consulting, is led by UK-based workers with a 22% market share.

Will the values and personal objectives change along with new ways of working?

In addition to technologies, new generations entering their working lives challenge managerial and reward practices. They may bring along 'a subjective factor', underlining the importance a social actor places on a good for the achievement of the individual's desired end. New generations either adapt to the changed circumstances or try to change them to correspond with their needs and objectives. But what kinds of needs and personal objectives do different generations have today and in the future? The average person of the early last century lived and worked to satisfy her or his physiological basic needs and to renew chances of survival. The prevailing culture and turbulent living conditions as well as locally varying circumstances may, however, change the things people hold important – and therefore their motivations – in ways difficult to foresee. The assumption is that people are motivated by job content and the results they value. This has implications for expectations employees bring to what their rewards will be and how they are set and managed.

Changing values and motives have been studied, for example, by means of intergenerational research. A 'generation' consists of (e.g., Twenge et al. 2010) a group of people born at broadly the same time and who are interconnected by the social and historical events distinctive of the time during their socialization. Each generation is influenced by a set of factors, such as parents, peers, the media, the social and economic events of the time period, and culture, which create common value systems for the group, distinguishing them from others who have grown up at a different time. The 'silent generation' was born in 1925–45. The 'Baby Boomers' were born between the years 1945 and 1964, entered working life in the 1970s and exit it in the 2010s. 'Generation X' was born in the years 1965–1981, lived its childhood and youth in the 1980s and reached maturity in the 1990s. The 'Y' or 'Millennial' generation was born in 1982–1999. They have formed the new worker and manager group of the 2010s. The majority of the 'Z generation', born in the late 1990s and the first decade of the twenty-first century, will enter their working life only in the 2020s.

It appears that different generations partly value different things. Twenge and partners (2010) studied the work values associated with work and personal objectives by analysing data (N = 16,507) collected in the United States in the years 1976 ('big age group'), 1991 (the X generation) and 2006 (the Y generation). They studied the significance of leisure, extrinsically motivating factors, such as salary, ownership and influence, and intrinsically motivating factors, such as the attractiveness of work. The gratification obtained from altruistic rewards, such as the desire to help others and society as well as sociability, was also examined.

According to the study, leisure values increased steadily while the centrality of work declined from one generation to the next. Extrinsic values, such as status, money and influence, were more important to the X and Y generations than to the Baby Boomers; however, for the Y generation, the significance of external rewards was smaller than for the X generation. Millennials did not favour altruistic work values (e.g., helping, societal worth) more than previous generations. Social values (e.g., making friends) and intrinsic values (e.g., an interesting, results-oriented job) were rated lower by Millennials than by Boomers (Twenge et al. 2012). Barkhuizen's (2014) study confirms that representatives of the Y generation value basic pay (salary), equilibrium of work and leisure and career development opportunities as remuneration methods. Intrinsic motivating factors, such as valuation of interesting work targeting objectives, were lesser in the Y generation than among Baby Boomers. There were no differences between the generations with regard to altruistic rewards. The gratification from social relationships was smaller with the Y generation than with the other two. So, according to these studies, the generations born in different time periods have some differences in values, which should be taken into account, for example, in recruitment and the development of remuneration systems now and in the future (Cogin 2012).

Little is known so far of the values and modes of operation of the Z generation. They grow in an environment permeated by information and digital technology. Thus, they utilize these technologies naturally, using, for example, social media, leading to them being called 'digital natives'. The new forms of work enabled by digitalization make working more independent, and controlling micromanagement is no longer possible or necessary with the Z generation. Thus, it may be predicted that the need for autonomy in work will increase in the future. Ever more power and responsibility is transferred to individual workers and their co-operation partners.

The general views of HR professionals and business management on the significant value differences between generations have been criticized (Parry and Urwin 2011, Cadiz et al. 2015) for the simplification of matters, because there is some variation in terms of the empirical research results on value differences. According to Parry and Urwin, when differences have been found, 'generation' or cohort has been approximated too closely with 'age'. If the differences in value attitudes are due to age, it would be expected, they argue, that they change with age. On the other hand, if the cohort explains the differences, the differences between age cohorts should remain the same. Many surveys have been cross-sectional rather than longitudinal. Therefore, the time effects have rarely been reported.

Also, other factors, such as the operating environment, gender and ethnic background, can influence valuations. In the debate on generational differences, it has also often been assumed that single events important in one country (or a continent) affect the values of all those born in the same time period. Earlier research on socialization also demonstrates that the individual often adopts and internalizes the prevailing value system and the accepted operations model when entering an established organization. However, new operating cultures and remuneration practices may emerge when the actors themselves get to shape their operating environment either along with an increased freedom of action in an established organization or in a completely new and open situations; for example, in a start-up company.

On the whole, we can conclude that the digitalization of working life influences working generations and the ways of motivating them in different ways through structural – and possible value – changes. And at the end of the day, to cover the costs of living individuals need to earn an income – in the immediate and for the longer term – with market economy principles putting more emphasis on the person to satisfy their 'hygiene needs' within the classic motivational hierarchy. In addition, if new generations' basic needs for competence, autonomy and relatedness (Deci and Ryan 2012) hold, the emphasis shifts perhaps to 'reward mix' (see Chapman, this volume) of total rewards in the digital economy and the processes of arriving at it, linked with demographic and other socializing factors impacting on digital working life.

Motivators in digital working life

In order to operate in a complex environment, an employee needs personal resources, including competences and motivation. Personal motivation is a state of alertness which produces action spurred by personal objectives related to work, defining its form, direction, strength and duration. Where, then, does the desire come from to work in an enthusiastic, committed and engaged manner in such a way that activity flows smoothly and accomplishments are made in an increasingly digital work and working environment? As described above, digitalization affects the individual's actions and accomplishments by changing both the job demands and the resources needed in work. According to the sociomaterial approach (Carlile et al. 2013), human goal-oriented activity is built in a multi-factor operating environment, in which technology is, in many ways, merged and absorbed into the physical structures of work, tools, work processes and communication by augmenting their smartness (Vartiainen 2014). Changes in these factors further influence the character and content of tasks and the division of work and by extension the context for RM.

The Job Demands-Resources Model (JD-R) (Bakker and Demerouti 2007; Demerouti et al. 2001) aptly describes the demands of fluency and productivity of activities and of work engagement, which can be influenced by management, work design and crafting, also in digital work. In the JD-R model, personal resources are formed of positive self-assessments, resilience and the feeling that one can successfully control and influence one's operating environment. Resources associated with work include the physical, social and organizational factors of work, such as the support, feedback and opportunity to use knowledge and skills, obtained from the social environment. As digitalization intrudes more and more deeply into our life, it has an increasing role as a job demand. By means of his or her personal resources, the worker is able to face the changing demands of the individual's operating environment, change them autonomously and to achieve personal objectives and those set by the job. The same need for autonomy and the same motivation type are also found in the theory of self-determination (Deci and Ryan 2000, 2012), in which motivation types are divided according to the causes or objectives of activity. According to the theory, activity is energized by three universal psychological needs for competence, autonomy, and relatedness. Exactly the same values have emerged in the studies of new generations described earlier.

The fluency of work is helped by an experience of work engagement (Bakker 2011). Work engagement means a relatively permanent, positive emotional and motivational state. It manifests itself as vigour and dedication to and absorption in work. Vigour appears as exuberance, devotion to work and persistence. Dedication, in turn, appears as zeal, being inspired by work and pride in one's own work. The state of absorption is described by the passage of time as if on wings. According to Bakker, work engagement has many positive consequences, such as good work performance and better business results, such as productivity and customer satisfaction. Work engagement is born from intrinsic motivation.

So, the experience of autonomy is the foremost prerequisite of motivation in digital work.

The motivation types are situated on a continuum according to the quantity of self-determination or autonomy. In one end of the continuum is 'amotivation', or a total lack of the will to act, and in the other an intrinsic motivation spurred by the content of the work. Between these are situated the four types of extrinsic motivation, which differ from each other in terms of the quantity of autonomy. With the extrinsically motivated person, activity is guided by an instrumental objective, such as monetary rewards, acknowledgement or the avoidance of punishment. According to self-determination theory, the other forms of extrinsic motivation are associated with controlled motivation. External control is described by a person experiencing external pressure to perform a task. The greatest sense of autonomy, in turn, is associated with activity felt to be an essential part of oneself. For example, one accepts the values and operating principles of the enterprise. This motivation type is called motivation by integrated regulation, which, together with intrinsic motivation, forms autonomous motivation, according to the theory. Autonomous motivation is described by spontaneity and a feeling that one is acting voluntarily.

Many of the traditional work motivation models can be fitted into these two theories: the JD-R model and the self-determination theory. The motivation models of working life have traditionally been divided into content and process theories. The former tries to answer the question "What motivates?" and the latter "How are we motivated?" The best known of content theories is Maslow's description of the hierarchy of needs, according to which physiological needs and needs related to safety are on the lowest levels of the hierarchy (but see the critique in Fish, this volume). Once these needs have been met, people strive for things higher up the hierarchy, such as self-fulfilment. Process theories focus on a person's individual choices made on the basis of knowledge and own preferences. Essential in process theories is the endeavour to elucidate the thought and assessment process based on human knowledge. Examples of these theories include expectancy-value theory, goal-setting theory and equity theory. According to expectancy-value theory, a person considers three things: is achieving the goal possible, what is the consequence of achieving it, and is the consequence sufficiently attractive? According to goal-setting theory, an individual's work performance is improved by challenging, clear and comprehensible goals accepted by him or her. Equity theory, in turn, is based on the individual's desire to achieve equilibrium between his or her inputs and outputs and to see that they are in the same proportion as the inputs and outputs of other persons.

Motivating new ways of working

Most essential for the fluency of the future digital work is to create intrinsic work motivation and work engagement among employees by increasing autonomy and self-determination and supporting the growth of personal resources. This indicates the use of 'non-monetary' reward elements of the total reward model for motivation purposes. However, monetary compensation as a means of exchange is still a necessary mechanism. The mix of non-financial and financial rewards should attract, motivate and engage different groups of workers, for example, belonging to different generations, having flexible employment relationships and different needs which change along with the progress of life and career. Remuneration should support new flexible and autonomous ways of working, such as project-like and digital work. It must promote the central processes for achieving objectives, such as co-operation, learning and development. Financial remuneration should also work flexibly in economic fluctuations, as it is in the interest both of the economy of the organization and of the employment capacity of the workforce.

Deci's and Ryan's self-determination theory (2012) with its description of motivation and needs clearly crystallizes the probable future bases of motivation: people have needs for autonomy, fostering and using their competences and being related to others in their activities. These bases are designable features in work and therefore influenced by reward management. Based on the contents of total reward system, company management can design jobs and their environments in such a manner that it leaves room for self-initiated design of jobs – that is, job crafting by incumbents themselves. Autonomy is increased by providing access to knowledge, enhanced responsibility and decision-making, possibilities to influence – i.e., providing conditions to job crafting at work. Job crafting means the modification of work originating from the worker to match his or her own objectives and motivation (Bakker 2011). The pivotal idea of job crafting is thus the modification of the current task from one's own, individual bases or a group's common bases by influencing physical, digital and social factors in work. According to this idea, work can be modified in the direction preferred by quite small and commonplace practical matters. In practice, this can mean, for example, doing things in the order that makes sense to one, or the flexible choice of one's place of work. Enabling job crafting by increasing autonomy is one way of immaterial remuneration in an organization.

Creating on-the-job learning opportunities brought about by the digitalization of tasks add to the feeling of competence. Positive relationships between people improve cohesion. Put simply, self-determination theory and related studies represent the idea that, when a person is given the freedom to make personal decisions, it leads to empowerment and the feeling of autonomy, and thereby increases interest and work engagement. This, in turn, leads to the person devoting him- or herself more to the performance of the task and taking more responsibility for it.

Developing context-sensitive RM practices

Given the observable technologically-driven trends outlined in this chapter, reward management in both existing and emerging organizations needs to consider ways of rewarding core, external and freelance workforces in a well-justified and consistent manner by focusing on increasing human potential. Additionally, in traditional organizations there are well-known and old challenges concerning job- and person-based reward structures and gender differences in the allocation of base pay. New generations may encourage consideration of more value-based rewarding. The adoption of total reward systems, combining material and non-material remuneration methods that are sensitive to external changes, offer one avenue for strategic action. However, the total reward strategy concept has been criticized (for example, Brown 2014) being too complicated to maintain and update demanding flexible 'smart rewards'. In addition, Dulebohn and Werling (2007) note that much past research conducted on compensation reflected organizational characteristics and personnel practices that had an internal rather than an external focus. This included a focus on issues and practices such as job evaluation, internal equity, pay level, and individual reactions to pay. The change trends described at the beginning of this chapter have shifted the focus onto external labour markets, market pricing and concern with issues such as external competitiveness and stakeholder interests.

But perhaps revisiting earlier reward management practice and conceptual influences on it may, with adaptation to changing contexts, offer possible sources to inform contemporary initiatives. Latham and partners (2006) claimed at the beginning of the millennium, before the economic crisis of 2008, that many of the principles of earlier motivation research are still valid. According to them, people's needs, working conditions and the rewards and punishments contingent on the operating environment influence motivation in the future as well as the present time. They also highlighted attainable goals, experiencing the results of activities as valuable, and their equitable assessment as factors influencing work motivation. Latham and Ernst (2006) also emphasize that it is important for the worker to know what results others expect from their activities. According to the researchers, the efficiency of operations is influenced by the part played by significant others important to the worker in question creating a sense of empowerment through acting as a model to, and encouraging, him or her. The immediate manager, for example, can be such an influencer. It is also important in the future that workers experience the organization's procedures and interaction as fair. As digitalization will influence work structures, content and ways of working, it is increasingly relevant to evaluate what is more or less useful in traditional reward management strategies and practices in these changing work contexts.

References

Atkinson, J. (1984). Manpower strategies for flexible organizations. *Personnel Management*. 16, 28–31.

Bakker, A. B. (2011). An evidence-based model of work engagement. *Current Directions in Psychological Science*. 20, 265–269.

Bakker, A. B. and Demerouti, E. (2007). The Job Demands-Resources Model: state of the art. *Journal of Managerial Psychology*. 22, 309–328.

Barkhuizen, N. (2014). Exploring the importance of rewards as a talent management tool for Generation Y employees. *Mediterranean Journal of Social Sciences*. 5, 1100–1105.

Brown, D. (2014). The future of reward management: From total reward strategies to smart rewards. *Compensation & Benefits Review*. 46, 147–151.

Cadiz, D. M. and Truxillo, D. M. and Fraccaroli, F. (2015). What are the benefits of focusing on generation-based differences and at what cost? *Industrial and Organizational Psychology*. 8, 3.

Carlile, P. R., Nicolini, D., Langley, A. and Tsoukas, H. (2013). How matter matters: objects, artifacts, and materiality in organization studies. In Carlile, P. R., Nicolini, D., Langley, A. and Tsoukas, H. (eds.) *How Matter Matters: Objects, Artifacts, and Materiality in Organization Studies* (pp. 1–15). Oxford, UK: Oxford University Press.

Crandall, N. F. and Wallace, M. J. (1997). Inside the virtual workplace: forging a new deal for work and rewards. *Compensation and Benefits Review*. 27, 27–36.

Cogin, J. (2012). Are generational differences in work values fact or fiction? Multi-country evidence and implications. *The International Journal of Human Resource Management.* 23, 2268–2294.

Deci, E. and Ryan, R. (2000), The 'what' and 'why' of goal pursuits: human needs and the self-determination of behavior. *Psychological Inquiry.* 11, 227–268.

Deci, E. L. and Ryan, R. M. (2012). Self-determination theory. In Van Lange, P. A. M., Kruglanski, A. W. and Higgins, E. T. (eds.). *Handbook of Theories of Social Psychology* (Vol. 1, pp. 416–437). Thousand Oaks, CA: Sage Development, and Health.

Demerouti, E., Bakker, A., Nackreiner, F. and Schaufeli, W. B. (2001). The job demands–resources model of burnout. *Journal of Applied Psychology.* 86, 499–512.

Dulebohn, J. H. and Werling, S. E. (2007). Compensation research past, present, and future. *Human Resource Management Review.* 17, 191–207.

Eurofound. (2015). *New Forms of Employment.* Luxembourg: Publications Office of the European Union.

Eurofound. (2016). *Sixth European Working Conditions Survey – Overview Report.* Luxembourg: Publications Office of the European Union.

Frey, C. B. and Osborne, M. A. (2013). The future of employment: how susceptible are jobs to computerisation? *OMS Working Papers*, September 18. Available at: www.futuretech.ox.ac.uk/sites/futuretech.ox.ac.uk/files/The_Future_of_Employment_OMS_ Working_Paper_0.pdf

Gilson, L. L., Maynard, M. T., Jones Young, N. C., Vartiainen, M. and Hakonen, M. (2015). Virtual teams research: ten years, ten themes, and ten opportunities. *Journal of Management.* 41(5), 1313–1337.

Hertel, G., Stone, D. L., Johnson, R. D., Johnson, R. D. and Passmore, J. (2017). The psychology of the Internet @ Work. In Hertel, G., Stone, D. L., Johnson, R. D. and Passmore, J. (eds.). *The Wiley Handbook of the Psychology of the Internet at Work* (pp. 1–18). Chichester, UK: Wiley Blackwell.

Jesuthasan, R. (2017). How to manage a new work ecosystem. From free agents to automation. *Workspan.* 3, 25–29.

Koroma, J., Hyrkkänen, U. and Vartiainen, M. (2014). Looking for people, places and connections: hindrances when working in multiple locations - a review. *New Technology, Work and Employment.* 29(2), 139–159.

Latham, G. P. and Ernst, C. T. (2006). Keys to motivating tomorrow's workforce. *Human Resource Management Review.* 16, 181–198.

Lehdonvirta, V. (2016). Algorithms that divide and unite: delocalisation, identity and collective action in 'microwork'. In Flecker, J. (ed.) *Space, Place and Global Digital Work* (pp. 53–80). UK: Palgrave Macmillan.

Lehdonvirta, V. (2017). Where are online workers located? The international division of digital gig work. Available at: www.oii.ox.ac.uk/blog/where-are-online-workers-located-the-international-division-of-digital-gig-work/, accessed on October 8, 2017.

Meil, P. and Kirov, V. (eds.) (2017) *Policy Implications of Virtual Work.* Switzerland: Palgrave Macmillan.

Parry, E. and Urwin, P. (2011). Generational differences in work values: A review of theory and evidence. *International Journal of Management Reviews.* 13, 79–96.

Pajarinen, M., Rouvinen, P. and Ekeland, A. (2015) Computerization threatens one-third of Finnish and Norwegian employment. ETLA Brief No 34. Available at: www.pub.etla.fi/ETLA-Muistio-Brief-34.pdf

Scholz, T. (ed.) (2013). *Digital Labor: The Internet as Playground and Factory.* New York: Routledge.

Twenge, J. M., Campbell, S. M., Hoffman, B. J. and Lance, C. E. (2010). Generational differences in work values: leisure and extrinsic values increasing, social and intrinsic values decreasing. *Journal of Management.* 36, 1117–1142.

Twenge, J. M., Freeman, E. C. and Campbell, W. K. (2012). Generational differences in young adults' life goals, concern for others, and civic orientation, 1966–2009. *Journal of Personality and Social Psychology.* 102, 1045–1062.

Vartiainen, M. (2014). Hindrances and enablers of fluent actions in knowledge work. In Sachse, P. and Ulich, E. (eds.). *Psychologie menschlichen Handelns: Wissen und Denken – Wollen und Tun* (pp. 95–111). Langerich: Pabst Science Publishers.

17

SEGMENTING INTERNATIONAL ASSIGNMENTS

Theorizing expatriate reward

Susan Shortland and Stephen J. Perkins

Introduction

When designed and implemented effectively, international assignment reward policies support the acceptance of expatriation, employee satisfaction and motivation outcomes (Shortland and Perkins 2016). But when poorly constructed, costs can increase and barriers to current and future mobility can be created (Air Inc. 2016). The role of theory is to help human resource (HR) and Global Mobility professionals predict how expatriate reward policy design can best support and deliver organizational goals in relation to international mobility. However, there is relatively little theory to guide effective design of expatriate rewards (Harvey and Moeller 2009). As multinational companies (MNCs) increasingly segment their international assignment policy portfolio (Air Inc. 2016, 2017), unintended consequences can result in potentially detrimental assignee perceptions of inequity and organizational justice. These can lead to unwelcome return on investment outcomes such as assignment refusal, poor performance or early return.

This chapter begins by briefly examining the typical content of expatriate reward policy. Following on from this, it addresses the trend to segment international assignment policies to reflect different assignment types and provide flexibility to organizations, while simultaneously attempting to reduce costs and maximize expatriate return on investment. It then takes as its focus theoretical frameworks that can help expatriate reward professionals to predict outcomes of their policy design choices. In so doing, it first examines the role of equalizing differences or compensating differentials theory (Rosen 1986) as a basis to justify differential treatment in expatriate reward within a segmented international assignment policy suite. Next, it reviews the impact of equity (and perceived inequity) (Adams 1963) within a segmented policy approach on assignees' potential willingness to accept assignments and remain satisfied with – and motivated by – reward policy while on assignment.

Finally, the chapter draws upon the organizational justice literature to consider the reasonableness of procedures, the context surrounding these and the (unintended?) consequences of policy outcomes (Byrne and Cropanzano 2001; Colquitt et al. 2005; Hansen et al. 2013). 'Distributive' justice (Chory and Kingsley Westerman 2009; Homans 1961) is proposed as an appropriate theoretical framework to help predict assignees' evaluation of what they receive compared to others; 'procedural' justice is set out as a frame to assist policy implementers to determine how outcomes are allocated (Palaiologos et al. 2011); and 'interactional' justice is presented to address how decisions are communicated and implemented (Brown et al. 2010; Gilliland et al. 2014).

Expatriate reward policy content and segmentation

Expatriate reward policy is most usually linked to home-based pay with additional elements included as allowances and benefits to ensure that expatriates are no worse off (and, theoretically, no better off) by undertaking an international assignment. Known as the 'balance sheet', this home-based pay approach creates equity between those individuals from the same sending home country (Perkins et al. 2016). The additions to basic salary paid to keep assignees 'whole' include housing and utilities, cost of living, and education allowances, their aim being to ensure that the assignee and family are not disadvantaged financially. In addition, compensatory payments to address issues such as disruption to family life include foreign service, mobility, relocation, disturbance, hardship and danger premiums, and spousal allowances. Rest and relaxation leave from designated hardship/danger areas, home leave flights, transport costs to and from the host location, emergency assistance, medical insurance, pension continuity, temporary accommodation, household goods shipments, tax and visa advice/support and an array of other benefits are also typically included in the package (Kroeck and Von Glinow 2016). While the aim is to ensure there is no financial detriment, the outcome is usually highly financially beneficial to assignees (Perkins and Shortland 2006).

Cost control has become increasingly significant to organizations, and thus the use of the balance sheet is giving way to international assignment reward policy alternatives (Brookfield 2016). These include approaches such as host-based pay (the assignees receive local terms and conditions in the host country) or host-plus arrangements (local terms, but with some recognition of the additional costs faced by assignees). Under such arrangements, reward equity lies within the host country, with expatriates being treated similarly to local nationals (Perkins and Shortland 2006). Globalist reward systems are also in evidence, although these are applied less commonly (Air Inc. 2017), whereby equity in relation to other individuals rests within the globally mobile assignee population (Perkins and Shortland 2006).

To design and implement an expatriate reward policy requires taking into account that international assignments are not all the same. Thus, reward policies need to address differing situations, but ensure cost effectiveness and equity as far as possible (Kroeck and Von Glinow 2016). Indeed, according to current practitioner research, 17% of organizations segment their policy by business reason, 7% by employee level, and 4% by region/geography (Brookfield 2016). Air Inc. (2017) reports that HR and Global Mobility professionals manage an average of 4.5 different international assignment policies in their organizations (4.9 in North America; 4.4 in Europe; and 3.0 in Asia Pacific). And the trend is for greater differentiation between policy types (for example, by length and/or purpose) as organizations strive to contain expatriate costs and reduce assignment administration. Thus, while the majority of organizations operate both long-term and short-term assignment policies, additional policy types are increasingly being developed and implemented. These include: commuter assignments; developmental/graduate assignments; globally mobile cadres; rotators; and volunteer assignments. In addition, policies are being designed specifically for locally hired non-nationals, business travellers and international one-way transfers (Air Inc. 2016, 2017). As these forms of international mobility become used more frequently, so the need for a segmented international assignment policy to address expatriate reward by assignment type becomes ever more desirable or necessary. To determine the appropriate reward elements and their emphasis in policy and practice therefore requires consideration of necessary differentials and justification of their emphasis for particular assignment types. This leads us to review relevant theory in this regard.

Equalizing differences/compensating differentials

Rosen's (1986) theory of equalizing differences or compensating differentials provides a relevant framework for analysis of both the content of expatriate reward policies and the differences in compensation and benefits applied to different purposes, lengths and patterns of international mobility. He argues that favourable employment and working conditions are attractive to workers and thus individuals are willing to undertake these jobs at wages lower than average. In contrast, jobs with unfavourable working conditions require the payment of differentials or premiums to provide additional compensation so as to be attractive to workers. Rosen (1986:641) states that compensating differentials aim to equalize "the total monetary and nonmonetary advantages or disadvantages among work activities and among workers themselves". At first glance, the offer of expatriate employment appears an attractive proposition, particularly given the literature that highlights its role in providing career advantage (Dickmann and Baruch 2011; Orser and Leck 2010). The provision of additional monetary and non-monetary rewards therefore seems unnecessary to support an expatriate workforce. Yet we know that unless the reward package is enhanced to be considered suitable by prospective expatriates, especially with regard to particular elements such as salary, housing, cost of living payments, and healthcare, the assignment is likely to be refused (Sims and Schraeder 2005; Warneke and Schneider 2011).

Rosen (1986) draws attention to a variety of factors which he proposes require compensating differentials. These include: working conditions that pose a risk to life and health, such as pollution exposure; differences in the weather/climate, crime and crowding; working hours and the scheduling of working time; and job insecurity. In addition, he suggests that jobs that might lead to potential failure linked to unpredictable outcomes from the work environment and/or alternative career choices will need to be addressed in terms of equalizing differences. Work that requires investment in on- and/or off-the-job training might also lead to the requirement for compensating differentials. These factors all have a bearing on expatriate reward. For example, hardship or location premiums are designed to address geographical differences that present a challenge to employees living outside of their home countries (Perkins and Shortland 2006). Expatriates are typically reported as working long hours with a high degree of encroachment of working time into their family lives, particularly as their roles can involve significant business travel and communications across time zones (Fischlmayr and Kollinger 2010; Shortland 2015; Shortland and Cummins 2007). While expatriation is considered to provide career growth, this is by no means certain and insecurity and uncertainty with regard to job opportunities on repatriation have been well documented over the decades (Forster 1992; Kroeck and Von Glinow 2016; Tung 1988).

Working in a different culture and language requires adjustment to overcome culture shock before full productivity can be achieved and even then there is no guarantee of assignment success. Although employers typically provide necessary training to address cultural and language differences so that expatriates can manage effectively in the foreign environment, personal investment in time spent undertaking training programmes (such as culture and language training) is needed to reduce the risk of assignment failure (Perkins and Shortland 2006).

Given these factors, it is typical to see the application of premiums, allowances and non-cash benefits to address the specifics that differentiate an organizationally-assigned expatriate worker from a home-country-based employee. Expatriate reward policies do not, however, apply a 'one-size-fits-all' approach in relation to the provision of compensating differentials. Different types of assignments are typically rewarded differentially, i.e., a suite of reward policies will contain specific components reflecting the nature of the differences between assignments (Perkins et al. 2016). Thus, developmental assignments such as those designed for graduate trainees and trainee executives are expected to be less 'rich' in content as the 'reward' for the individual from undertaking them comes from the employer investment in their training and development (Perkins and Shortland 2006). Commuter assignments can be relatively poorly supported in reward policy (often aligned to business travel rather than expatriate assignments); short-term assignments are typically less well-provisioned in policy compared to long-term assignments (Kroeck and Von Glinow 2016; Perkins et al. 2016). Yet although short-term, commuter and other types of 'flexpatriate' assignments, such as rotational working, all involve relatively limited periods of time abroad, they are usually unaccompanied and thus involve family separation, and are disruptive to the individual in terms of travel requirements (Shortland 2015).

Long-term assignments (typically accompanied) are usually the best rewarded financially. The most common approach used to determining reward components is the home-based balance sheet under which a comprehensive range of allowances and fringe benefits are provided to the employee to equalize or compensate for the various factors involved in expatriation. The design of the balance sheet, underpinned by tax equalization, aims to expedite mobility between and among high- and low-cost destinations (Perkins et al. 2016).

Host-based pay may not achieve the same outcomes in relation to the facilitation of geographic mobility, but it is regarded as a less expensive method of expatriate reward and it does provide equity in the host country regardless of expatriates' home country origin. However, the use of this approach may serve to increase total remuneration for those expatriates moving from countries where lower salaries and benefits apply, or provide broadly equivalent remuneration for those moving from higher salary/benefit home countries. A pay supplement may be required if the assignee is asked to move from a high-paying to a lower-paying country under the host-based approach (Kroeck and Von Glinow 2016).

Different approaches to expatriate reward with adjustments to pay made as necessary to achieve the desired end-point might seem logical to employers, but to assignees undertaking expatriation, the rationale for different groups receiving different levels of compensation and benefits and/or additions or deductions to pay for working in similar environments with common challenges can seem inequitable. Thus, perceived inequities can flow from the use of home- or host-based or other pay systems, as well as from different approaches used to managing different lengths and patterns of mobility even if a single home- or host-based philosophy is held for all assignment types. As organizations increasingly apply segmented or tiered arrangements to provide appropriate compensation from an organizational viewpoint, this results in further differences in terms of levels of support, benefits, premiums and so on linked to assignment purpose, pattern, length, etc. (Air Inc. 2017), suggesting that perceptions of equity/inequity require theoretical examination.

Equity theory

In determining the content of expatriate policies and especially in applying a segmented approach, employers need to consider assignee perceptions of inequity. Equity theory (Adams 1963) is therefore of particular value to employers in helping to regulate the outcomes of expatriate reward policy design and its implementation. Equity theory predicts that reward will only result in assignee satisfaction if it is considered to be equitable and fair. However, perceptions of equity are related to imperfectly correlated inputs and outcomes within the effort–reward exchange relationship.

Assignees invest their contribution to the exchange, bringing as inputs their skills, knowledge and behaviours to the expatriate position. Competencies, as inputs to the exchange relationship, may be recognised and valued in terms of their relevance differently by the individual and the employing organization. If this is the case then this can lead to a source of perceived inequity. Outcomes, such as pay and benefits, provided to the assignee in exchange for their inputs may or may not be delivered and/or valued as expected, again potentially contributing to perceived inequity. Adams (1963) also indicates that individuals make comparisons between themselves and their colleagues in respect of inputs and outcomes in the exchange relationship. These too can lead to perceptions of inequity. For example, single expatriates may have no requirement for allowances that address children's education, spousal support or provide larger family-sized accommodation. If all (singles and accompanied) perform the same duties, then rewards that reflect family status may be viewed by solo assignees as privileging their colleagues with accompanying family members. Solo assignees may thus seek alternative, additional rewards to boost their package, such that its monetary equivalent equals that given to their accompanied assignee colleagues, thereby matching perceived equity in job inputs to a common level of monetary outcome commensurate with the expatriate role.

As employers increasingly segment international reward policy and introduce approaches that relate ever more closely to the host location's reward philosophy, typically in order to reduce costs, so the potential for an even greater variety of referents occurs. Policies that specify different reward components for expatriates on host-based or host-plus arrangements, for volunteer assignees and for locally hired non-nationals, and differentiate these from those terms given to local national hires present a case in point: any variation from local terms applied to these different groups could suggest favourable treatment for some and less favourable treatment for others. As Bonache (2006) suggests, with so many referents, there is inevitability of inequity and reward package dissatisfaction flowing from this perception.

The aim of theory is to predict and, as a consequence, we use it to determine the most appropriate course of action. In relation to international assignment reward policy design, we need to understand when and how assignees will perceive inequity in relation to a mix of inputs and outcomes. Clearly, this is very difficult as each individual will have different values, referents and perceptions of inequity. Nonetheless, HR and Global Mobility professionals do need to consider how international assignment reward policy design can influence assignees' perceptions of fair treatment and set out to avoid negative effects as these can result in assignment refusal, poor performance or early return. In addition, they need to consider the influence of the compensation packages offered to expatriates in relation to the effect that these can have on local employees and, in turn, how locals will respond in terms of their working relationships with expatriates. This is particularly notable in newly emerging economies where expatriate compensation can significantly exceed that of locals. This can lead to negative attitudes by locals towards expatriates with consequent adverse effects on the support that they provide, such as willingness to share knowledge (Leung et al. 2014). How locals support expatriates is, of course, crucial for assignees' successful assignment outcomes (Kang and Shen 2017). Explanation of compensating differentials is necessary to build trust, and demonstrate equity and fair management practices to local employees (Leung et al. 2014).

Guzzo et al. (1994) point out that the application of assignment policy to expatriates is a sensitive matter. International mobility affects not only workers, but also their families. Hence, employee satisfaction and productive employment relationships may be jeopardized if assignees believe that they have not received appropriate policy application in return for their efforts (and family sacrifices) in undertaking expatriation (Bonache 2006). Thus, besides the determination of policy content, HR and Global Mobility professionals also need to understand how assignees might evaluate what they receive, the effects of how assignment rewards are allocated, and how reward policy outcomes are communicated as all of these factors influence assignees' views of organizational justice.

Organizational justice

Organizational justice considerations help HR and Global Mobility professionals to consider the impact of the 'how' – rather than simply the 'what' – of designing and applying international assignment policies, in the context of employee segmentation decisions. Applying organizational justice theory places attention on socio-economic interactions in determining expatriate assignment terms and conditions: how will an individual's socially informed reflections on the distribution of rewards, on the organizational processes leading to such distributions, and related interpersonal experiences, impact on perceived equity or inequity when comparing themselves with other employees? How can we gain a sense of how reasonable individuals consider expatriate reward management to be as an interactive experience in particular contexts? These conclusions may impact directly and/or indirectly on the degree to which expatriates choose to cooperate with MNC managerial intentions; a material consideration given the indeterminacy of the employment relationship (Marsden 1999). Organizational justice theorists highlight three interconnected elements: distributional justice; procedural justice; and interpersonal justice.

'Distributive' justice (Chory and Kingsley Westerman 2009; Homans 1961) is proposed as an appropriate theoretical framework to help predict assignees' evaluation of what they receive compared to others. Gilliland et al. (2014) argue that this means three elements need to be satisfied. First, that individuals in an employment relationship secure their 'fair share' when being hired, developed, promoted and rewarded. Referents are selected not by management but by the individual employees – so, in the case of expatriates, attention needs to focus on the segment of the population an individual may choose to identify with. This does not mean offering that individual the same terms and conditions as their chosen comparator (whether a fellow international assignee or a local peer). It does require management to offer a credible rationale for their expatriation offer by reference to the context (e.g., the capabilities an individual brings matched to the organization's needs at the time and the outcomes from applying these capabilities matched to performance expectations and achievement levels by comparable others). Explanations drawing upon distributive justice can thereby aid trust building between locals and expatriates (Leung et al. 2014) and among expatriates. Second, and this may form part of the explanation for the reward distribution, Gilliland et al. (2014) argue that organizationally just outcomes enable an individual to feel valued as more than a collective mass 'labourer'. Instead, individuals see themselves as recognised as having value to the organization within the group to which they belong, thus satisfying a sense of being a repository of human capital invested in a particular organizational setting, and hence, in turn, securing a commensurate return on that investment. Third, the authors point to a moral imperative: rather than being the butt of instrumental compliance, as social beings, individuals need to be treated with dignity and respect – reflected in a just distribution of reward among all 'organizational citizens'. While this may encourage employees to behave reciprocally above and beyond the status of 'hired hands', the argument is that employees themselves may judge managerial actions towards them not only narrowly in making a personal gain, but also by offering or withholding trust in management to 'do the right thing' more broadly (Cugueró-Escofet and Fortin 2014).

The core notion of procedural justice (Palaiologos et al. 2011) refers to conditions within the organization that ensure all members have a 'voice' and are enabled to exercise it, with scope to reflect within that exercising of their voice their own particular characteristics. This means that individuals are not merely regarded as indistinct atoms within a homogeneous group; rather, their diversity and demographic status (including age, gender, disabilities, sexual orientation, ethnicity, etc.) are taken into account and, in the case of expatriation processes, being mindful that there are consequences more directly salient than in the course of regular employment. In addition, factors such as the individual's family and wider social interconnections must be considered. Relatedly, organizational communications – how policies and their application are explained – and their timing become important in establishing the sense in which organizational management are treating justly those they employ and deploy. Within this conceptualization, just procedures tend to reference consistency of treatment, ability/willingness to rectify mistakes, absence of bias, and a sense that the manager acted in the only way they reasonably could in the circumstances (Cugueró-Escofet and Fortin 2014).

Interpersonal justice considerations reflect on the ways an organizational member is treated as they interact with formal organizational agents who control decision-making processes when policies are being implemented, such as determining expatriation terms and conditions. Here one may engage with aspects of the employment relationship that go beyond the purely contractual, involving social exchange, which, in turn, give rise to perceptions of the extent to which the parties are acting in good faith (Wang et al. 2010). In particular, consideration is required when arriving at managerial judgments about how an employee has performed relative to others, and the possible recognition of that performance. As Brown et al. (2010) point out in this context, a policy and related procedures may be – and be viewed as – just; but if the actions of those interpreting the policy in action are inappropriate, then the risk for the organization is that the target of the policy application may regard the outcome as unjust. For example, remarks made by a manager when dealing with an expatriate that might appear to overlook or denigrate the circumstances of the performance they are required to give, or the explanation they give is sensed as falling short of a full appreciation of the individual's circumstances when called on to perform in culturally and institutionally unfamiliar settings.

Finally, in considering questions around organizational justice as this applies to expatriation management within MNCs, policy makers and implementation decision-makers face potential risks when considering the social interaction between expatriates and locally employed members of the organization. Here again, attention is necessary to understand the implications of the context for those interactions and the consequences flowing in terms of organizational commitment in the sense of supporting enactment of managerial priorities and in respect of intention to quit the firm. Space considerations prohibit a detailed discussion of this matter but, if it is assumed that local capabilities are valuable to an employer, perhaps specific knowledge of local market conditions will be needed (for example, working alongside and/or under the direction of assignees from the MNC's parent organization). Managers would be wise to be informed by organizational justice theory to reflect on the effects of any degree of starkness in compensating differentials between expatriate and local workforce members. Corporate managements may be well advised to think carefully through the ways in which local employees interpret and act on their perceptions of the justice between the comparative distribution of rewards. Will they regard scope for apparently enhanced lifestyles on the part of expatriates and their families as justified in terms of the capacity to enhance the operation to which they belong with consequential positive implications for their own ongoing employment and scope to be recognised? In what ways can procedures for determining reward outcomes between expatriates and locals be demonstrated as reasonable, and what role is there for transparency of how reward is managed comparatively? How too can organizations ensure that the interactions between expatriates and locals are successful in a specific geographical setting – including when expatriates are accountable themselves for applying corporate reward policy through interactions with the locals on whom they may depend to secure cultural and institutional engagement? Some evidence for the importance of attention by corporate policy makers to this aspect of MNC reward management is supplied in a study of a China-based international joint venture – findings from which suggested that local employees attribute disparities between expatriate and local reward allocations entirely to their employer's overall (i.e., corporate) reward management framework (Choi and Chen 2007). While the policies and their application may be wholly legitimate, it behoves MNC managements to demonstrate that all employees are treated with dignity and respect. In addition, it must be shown that the reward management policy will operate so as to be judged by all as consistent, unbiased, corrected as necessary and with reasonable actions taken by decision-makers appropriate to circumstances (Cugueró-Escofet and Fortin 2014).

Concluding remarks

Expatriates are typically well-rewarded. Compensating differentials are applied to address aspects of international mobility that are usually considered to be unfavourable – either in relation to working conditions or from being disruptive to family life. Organizations are mindful of cost constraints and, as a result, are engaging in policy segmentation such that a range of different policy content applies to different assignment types. By tailoring international reward policy content to different assignment lengths, patterns and purposes, some elements can be reduced and unnecessary payments and benefits stripped out to the employer's advantage. As the plethora of differing expatriate reward policy types increases, so variations in reward outcomes experienced by the assignee population becomes greater. This opens the way for comparison between and among different assignee groups with the potential for perceived inequity. Organizations will require very clear communication approaches to explain the variance in base pay and compensatory additions if employees are to fully understand why their rewards differ from those of others in seemingly similar expatriate circumstances. To assist with this, relevant theory can help to guide approaches to policy development and its communication. Under that rubric, organizational justice considerations provide a series of checks and balances that MNC managers may draw on when establishing expatriate rewards, mindful that individuals may be expected to calibrate their cooperation with organizational priorities related not only to the sense of fairness in reward distribution outcomes, but also by reference to the procedures via which these are enacted. Taking account of the specific circumstances in which expatriates are expected to operate, as well as their demographic characteristics, and the quality of social interaction between the expatriate and formal organizational agents who specifically determine policy and procedural application to them by reference to others, it is important to remember that referents are not necessarily mandated organizationally, but are selected subjectively by the expatriates themselves.

References

Adams, S. J. (1963). Towards an understanding of inequity. *Journal of Abnormal and Social Psychology*. 67(5), 422–436.

Air Inc. (2016). *Mobility Outlook Survey*. Cambridge, MA: Air Inc.

Air Inc. (2017). *Mobility Outlook Survey*. Cambridge, MA: Air Inc.

Bonache, J. (2006). The compensation of expatriates: a review and a future research agenda. In Stahl, G. K. and Björkman, I. (eds.). *Handbook of Research in International Human Resource Management* (pp. 158–175). Cheltenham, UK: Edward Elgar.

Brookfield. (2016). *Global Mobility Trends Survey*. Chicago, IL: Brookfield Global Relocation Services.

Brown, G., Bemmels, B. and Barclay, L. J. (2010). The importance of policy in perceptions of organizational justice. *Human Relations*. 63(10), 1587–1609.

Byrne, Z. S. and Cropanzano, R. (2001). History of organizational justice: the founders speak. In Cropanzano, R. (ed.). *Justice in the Workplace (Volume II): from Theory to Practice* (pp. 3–26). Mahwah, NJ: Lawrence Erlbaum Associates.

Choi, J. and Chen, C. C. (2007). The relationships of distributive justice and compensation system fairness to employee attitudes in international joint ventures. *Journal of Organizational Behavior*. 28(6), 687–703.

Chory, R. M. and Kingsley Westerman, C. Y. (2009). Feedback and fairness: the relationship between negative performance feedback and organizational justice. *Western Journal of Communication*. 73(2), 157–181.

Colquitt, J. A., Greenberg, J. and Zapata-Phelan, C. P. (2005). What is organizational justice? A historical overview. In Greenberg, J. and Colquitt, J. A. (eds.), *Handbook of Organizational Justice* (pp. 3–56). Mahwah, NJ: Lawrence Erlbaum Associates.

Cugueró-Escofet, N. and Fortin, M. (2014). One justice or two? A model of reconciliation of normative justice theories and empirical research on organizational justice. *Journal of Business Ethics*. 124(3), 435–451.

Dickmann, M. and Baruch, Y. (2011). *Global Careers*. Abingdon, UK: Routledge.

Fischlmayr, I. C. and Kollinger, I. (2010). Work–life balance – a neglected issue among Austrian female expatriates. *International Journal of Human Resource Management*. 21(4), 455–487.

Forster, N. (1992). International managers and mobile families: the professional and personal dynamics of trans-national career pathing and job mobility in the 1990s. *International Journal of Human Resource Management*. 3(3), 605–623.

Gilliland, S. W., Gross, M. A. and Hogler, R. L. (2014). Is organizational justice the new industrial relations? A debate on individual versus collective underpinnings of justice. *Negotiation and Conflict Management Research*. 7(3), 155–172.

Guzzo, R. A., Noonan, K. A. and Elron, E. (1994). Expatriate managers and the psychological contract. *Journal of Applied Psychology*. 79(4), 617–626.

Hansen, A. M., Byrne, Z. S. and Kiersch, C. E. (2013). Development and validation of an abridged measure of organizational justice. *The Journal of Psychology*. 147(3), 217–244.

Harvey, M. and Moeller, M. (2009). Expatriate managers: a historical review. *International Journal of Management Reviews*. 11(3), 275–296.

Homans, G. C. (1961). *Social Behavior: Its Elementary Forms*. New York, NY: Harcourt, Brace and World.

Kang, H. and Shen, J. (2017). Antecedents and consequences of host-country nationals' attitudes and behaviors toward expatriates: what we do and do not know. *Human Resource Management Review*. 28(2), 164–175.

Kroeck, K. G. and Von Glinow, M. A. (2016). Total rewards in the international context. In Harzing, A.-W. and Pinnington, A. H. (eds.). *International Human Resource Management* (pp. 429–467). London: Sage.

Leung, K., Lin, X. and Lu, L. (2014). Compensation disparity between locals and expatriates in China: a multilevel analysis of the influence of norms. *Management International Review*. 54(1), 107–128.

Marsden, D. (1999). *A Theory of Employment Systems*. Oxford: Oxford University Press.

Orser, B. and Leck, J. (2010). Gender influences on career success outcomes. *Gender in Management: An International Journal*. 25(5), 386–407.

Palaiologos, A., Papazekos, P. and Panayotopoulou, L. (2011). Organizational justice and employee satisfaction in performance appraisal. *Journal of European Industrial Training*. 35(8), 826–840.

Perkins, S. J. and Shortland, S. M. (2006). *Strategic International Human Resource Management: Choices and Consequences in Multinational People Management*. London: Kogan Page.

Perkins, S. J., White, G. and Jones, S. (2016). *Reward Management: Alternatives, Consequences and Contexts*. London: CIPD.

Rosen, S. (1986). The theory of equalizing differences. In Ashenfelter, O. and Layard, R. (eds.). *Handbook of Labor Economics*, Volume 1 (pp. 641–692). Amsterdam: Elsevier Science Publishers B.V.

Shortland, S. (2015). The 'expat factor': the influence of working time on women's decisions to undertake international assignments in the oil and gas industry. *The International Journal of Human Resource Management*. 26(11), 1452–1473.

Shortland, S. and Cummins, S. (2007). Work–life balance: expatriates reflect the international dimension. *Global Business and Organizational Excellence*. 26(6), 28–42.

Shortland, S. and Perkins, S. J. (2016). Long-term assignment reward (dis)satisfaction outcomes: hearing women's voices. *Journal of Global Mobility*. 4(2), 225–250.

Sims, R. H. and Schraeder, M. (2005). Expatriate compensation: an exploratory review of salient contextual factors and common practices. *Career Development International*. 10(2), 98–108.

Tung, R. L. (1988). Career issues in international assignments. *Academy of Management Executive*. 2(3), 241–244.

Wang, X., Liao, J., Xia, D. and Chang, T. (2010). The impact of organizational justice on work performance: mediating effects of organizational commitment and leader–member exchange. *International Journal of Manpower*. 31(6), 660–677.

Warneke, D. and Schneider, M. (2011). Expatriate compensation packages: what do employees prefer? *Cross Cultural Management: An International Journal*. 18(2), 236–256.

18

ADAPTING TO A GLOBAL WORLD
Rethinking incentive rewards

Nicholas R. Prince and J. Bruce Prince

Globally, rewards have long been used by organizations to attract and motivate employees. In organizations, these rewards are often delivered via incentive reward practices. Such practices used by organizations vary between countries (Prince et al. 2016; Schuler and Rogovsky 1998). These differences occur as a result of institutional differences (Kostova and Roth 2002). Organizations must adapt to changing competitive as well as institutional constraints. They must figure out the optimal approach to using rewards to motivate an increasingly diverse workforce and the nuances of how a different approach to incentive reward practices will affect their workforce.

> . . . employees each have their own mindset that is the result of contexts in which they have grown up and now currently live and work. These experiences shape employee perceptions, as well as employees being affected by what they believe others around them perceive.
>
> *(Farndale and Sanders 2017:5)*

With an increasingly global and mobile workforce, we can no longer assume that where people grow up is where they will live and work. This requires rethinking incentive rewards.

This chapter focuses on how the use of incentive reward practices in organizations differs across the globe. It revisits three institutional pillars (regulative, normative and cultural-cognitive) that influence the use of incentive reward practices and provides an assessment of the use of current practices. It ends by proposing a research agenda to further our understanding of incentive rewards in a global setting, and the practical implications globalization is having for the use of such rewards.

Incentive pay practices: organizational rewards

Incentives are a common reward used in organizations to align employee behaviours with desired organizational outcomes (Kerr 1975; Nyberg et al. 2013). There are a variety of different types of incentives that organizations have at their disposal. These generally come in the form of individual and group bonus rewards, where a reward is disbursed upon employee/s attainment of predefined criteria (i.e., pay-for-performance or individual bonuses) (Gerhart et al. 2009). They can also include the use of profit sharing, where organizations reward employees by giving them a percentage of quarterly or annual profits (Long and Fang 2012), as well as share schemes where stock distributions are determined by market reactions to organizational performance.

Traditionally, reward incentive practices have been seen as part of strategy implementation with consideration for job design factors such as workflow interdependence, and other key strategic factors such as their use as a tool for recruitment, retention, and their ability to influence other key employee-driven outcomes. This strategy-driven perspective sees incentives as the means for motivating employees to focus on important tasks and engage in behaviours necessary to effectively implement larger organizational strategies important for business success. From this view, the larger organizational context, such as geographic location and expectations that employees bring with them to work, is relatively unimportant. Organizations in different countries with very different workforce expectations facing similar strategic demands with similar work design would find similar reward incentives associated with success.

Theoretically, incentives serve two purposes in organizations. The first and most common is as a motivational tool to elicit desired employee behaviours (Gerhart et al. 2009; Kerr 1975). There is an underlying assumption that employee differences will lead them to be motivated rather than not motivated by rewards being offered. The second is to act as a sorting mechanism (Cadsby et al. 2007; Gerhart et al. 2009). Incentives act as a sorting mechanism in two ways. First, employees are drawn to those organizations that have incentives they like, and repulsed by those they don't like, or which they are uncomfortable with. Secondly, employees who find themselves in organizations that match their preferences tend to stay and those who do not leave. At a deeper level, incentives act as a signal of organizational norms and values. This attraction, selection and attrition sorting process (Schneider 1987) works with motivational influences of reward incentives to create a powerful managerial tool. Workforce norms and values are central to this logic and require further consideration about where they come from and the extent that other factors can be used to understand these preferences and how they evolve. Ignoring this suggests that workforce preferences are randomly distributed and that strategy–reward fit consideration is the only important logic in understanding how reward incentives and organizational effectiveness are related.

This chapter pursues the logic that organizations should adopt reward programmes that best fit workforce norms and values. These norms and values are an important factor that goes beyond strategy-based considerations. We see this development of workforce reward preferences and their underlying norms and values as substantially influenced by country-based institutional factors. This approach addresses the reality that incentive reward practices used vary significantly from country to country, going to an extent that goes well beyond any differences in business strategy. For example, French firms tend to rely on profit-sharing to reward their employees (Brown and Heywood 2002; Prince et al. 2016). Alternately, countries like Germany and Japan focus on contingent pay practices at the group or individual level, where rewards are dispersed upon attainment of prespecified levels of performance (Prince et al. 2016). Scandinavian firms (excluding Finland) present yet another incentive bundle preference, which reflects the minimal use of all incentive practices. Based upon the Prince et al. (2016) study, US firms appear to not have a strong incentive reward practice preference and use various incentive bundles, ranging from the minimal use of incentives to widespread use of individual-, group- and organizational performance-based incentive practices.

Institutional forces: why incentive rewards differ between countries

Why is it that countries differ in their use of incentive reward practices? One strong determinant of the values that employees and managers have is their country of origin. Within each country are a variety of institutional factors that influence what employees and managers expect and value in the organizations they work. These institutional factors have been organized into three separate pillars: cultural-cognitive, normative, and regulatory. These pillars are mutually reinforcing as cultural-cognitive schemas will influence the normative values that are present in an institution, and established schemas and values will influence regulations that evolve, formal and informal, in a country (North 1990; Scott 2008).

The cultural-cognitive pillar refers to the frames through which meanings are inferred (North 1990; Scott 2008). Hofstede and Hofstede (2005) refers to this as the programming of the mind; it is the schema through which employees and managers evaluate organizational action. These cognitive forces establish the way in which people encode, retain and recall information (Scott 2008) and through this process establish the taken-for-granted way that things are done (Meyer and Rowan 1977). The cultural-cognitive pillar is most evident in comparisons of national culture. For example, Asian countries are known for having high levels of collectivism. Although there are some exceptions, giving individual performance-based incentive rewards in these countries will conflict with the cultural-cognitive pillar and may act to undermine employee motivation, as being recognized and placed above one's peers will lead to feelings of discomfort. In arguing for a more nuanced contingency perspective rather than the dominate universalistic assumption where HRM practices are seen as having constant effects across cultures, Farndale and Sanders (2017) posit that the following societal cultures will have moderating effects in the employee-perceived HRM system strength and employee attitudinal/behavioural outcome relationship: (1) power distance; (2) uncertainty avoidance; (3) performance orientation; and (4) in-group collectivism.

The normative pillar refers to the common values and norms that exist in an institutional setting. These are the social expectations that dictate what is considered appropriate and inappropriate (North 1990; Scott 2008). Informal regulation of norms takes place in the form of social sanctioning when norms or values are broken or contradicted. In a reward setting, the normative pillar is a strong pillar that influences what is expected. For example, unless specified as a volunteer activity, everyone expects to get compensated for their work. Even the type of work performed can influence normative expectations that evolve (i.e., sales people getting paid a commission). Failure to follow these norms will result in social sanctioning that can come in a variety of ways such as reduced employee productivity, increased turnover, reduced hiring pool, etc.

The regulatory pillar refers to rule setting, monitoring and sanctioning behaviours within an institution. They can be formal, e.g., laws and regulations, or informal, e.g., the social sanctioning or coercion that takes place when normative expectations are not met (North 1990; Scott 2008). Regulations can also enable behaviour (i.e., licenses, permits, etc.) to take place in institutions. This creation of formal regulations acts as a sense-making activity to further understand the normative and cultural-cognitive pressures that exist in an organization. The regulatory pillar is most likely to exude pressure on incentive implementation in the form of legal regulations that organizations must follow (such as an equal pay act).

Employee-centric perspective

Historically, the institutional perspective has assumed that employees stay in the same organizational field. This reinforces the development of stronger institutional pressures for conformity but it is ans assumption that does not fully mesh with increasing levels of mobility. While many organizations have workforces that are largely made up of employees from within their country of origin, organizations increasingly have a multinational workforce that is not geographically bound to a single country. Following the logic that employee preferences, which are shaped by institutional forces, are an important determinant of how they respond to different reward incentives organizations will need to consider the rewards they are implementing from the perspective of their employees as their preferences are likely to differ based on the institutional forces to which they have been exposed. With a mobile global workforce, managing rewards becomes increasingly complex.

While not completely restricted to their country of origin, those institutional forces to which employees have been exposed, especially in their developmental years, will be a strong determinant of what they value. When rewards are discussed, an emphasis is placed on making sure there is an alignment between rewards and behaviours that the organization values (Kerr 1975). It is also essential that there is an alignment between rewards and what employees value. If there is no alignment between rewards and employee values' then incentive rewards will fail to align employee behaviours with organizations' desired outcomes. In sum, employees must value incentive rewards; otherwise rewards will no longer be an incentive and there will be no alignment between rewards and desired outcomes. In fact, a misalignment between employee values and rewards could motivate behaviours that are contradictory to desired organizational outcomes.

Manager-centric perspective

In addition to understanding that employees who have developed, grown up, in different institutional backgrounds will differ in what they value, it is also important to take into consideration how incentive rewards are implemented in organizations. Within every organization, there are managers, or owners, who determine how to incentivize their employees. Managers will determine the behaviours they want to incentivize, and will then assign rewards to incentivize the behaviours they deem necessary to accomplish the strategy and goals they have set forth.

An important reality to consider is that all managers themselves have been exposed to institutional pressures throughout their lives. These pressures have been present as managers have developed, both as children and throughout their careers. As a result, when managers evaluate incentive rewards and attempt to determine what will work best, they are biased by the institutional values and norms to which they have been exposed. We can return here, by way of illustration, to the example of differences between the Anglo-centric and Asian approaches to rewards. An Asian manager who is working as an expat in America is likely to have a negative view with regard to individual rewards and will, therefore, be more likely to implement group-level rewards. While group rewards will have some benefits, it is the use of individual incentive rewards that would be optimal.

The Complete Rewards Implementation Model

The model in Figure 18.1 utlines how the employee- and manager-centric perspectives relate to each other. First, it recognizes that both managers and employees are influenced by institutional pressures which evolve from the three pillars: cognitive-cultural, normative, and regulatory. Managers are responsible for the evaluation of different types of incentive rewards; this evaluation is influenced by their own institutional biases. Upon evaluating what they determine is best, they implement incentive/s or reward/s they deem fit best with the needs of their organization and which will evokc the desired employee behaviours and organizational outcomes. After a reward is implemented by their organization, employees will evaluate the reward. If the reward fits with employees' values, they will be motivated to perform desired behaviours and, assuming the organization's strategy was properly aligned, positive organizational outcomes will take place.

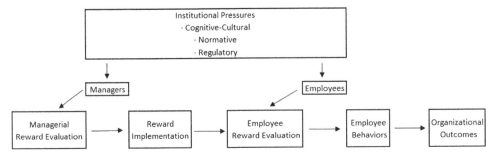

Figure 18.1 The complete rewards implementation model

If the reward does not align with employee values, then they will not perform desired behaviours. In the model, this is referred to as negative employee behaviours, and it is expected that negative organizational outcomes will ensue.

Adapting to a global world: rethinking incentive rewards – the road forward

The perspectives and model discussed above help to explain how incentive rewards will differ in their effectiveness based on the institutional environment that employees and managers have been exposed to throughout their lives. The key takeaways from understanding these influences on employees and managers are that different incentive rewards will be needed to influence employees from different institutional backgrounds. Additionally, managers need to be aware of their own institutional biases when they plan for and implement incentive rewards. While these takeaways are important, there is undoubtedly more that needs to be done by academics and practitioners alike to better understand and implement rewards in the complex global context.

Opportunities for academics

Oftentimes when incentive rewards are studied in organizations they are conceptualized and investigated as a single reward in isolation. For example, in their study on the effect of national culture on incentive rewards, Schuler and Rogovsky (1998) tested pay-for-performance and individual performance rewards, but they did not test how these rewards interacted with each other. The reality is that most organizations use more than one incentive reward in trying to motivate their employees. They might include or exclude a group or organizational-level incentives (i.e., profit-sharing, group or team bonuses) in conjunction with individual-level rewards (i.e., pay-for-performance, individual bonuses). To advance our understanding of how incentive rewards work in organizations as scholars, we need to theorize and test how the configuration of rewards influence employee behaviour (Delery and Doty 1996). The study of incentive reward configurations not only expands our understanding of how rewards work, but can also expand practitioners' ability to develop a reward programme that optimizes its impact and addresses institutional forces which enhance or diminish the legitimacy of a given bundle of incentive reward practices.

An understanding of the configuration of incentive rewards is increasingly important as the workforce becomes more global. The globalization of the workforce has led to two important trends that organizations need to consider as they design their incentive rewards programme. First, for companies across the globe, the workforce is becoming increasingly diverse (Toossi 2002). In developed countries, organizations' workforce is likely to be comprised of people from a variety of countries. Even when employees live in one country, if they are born and raised in another country their cultural-cognitive frameworks are likely to reflect their country of origin. These employees will have a different schema for evaluating if a set of management practices are legitimate or illegitimate, and will thus be motivated by a different configuration of rewards than what may be the taken-for-granted best practice that is prevalent in their country of residence. To maximize motivation and the alignment of employee behaviour, organizations will need to develop, and be ready to implement, a variety of incentive reward configurations that best fit with the needs, values and expectations of their increasingly diverse employee population. Practitioners need to have multiple incentive configurations for the same employee groups at their disposal, so that they can implement the configuration that best fits with the differing values of the employees in their organization.

In addition to the global workforce impacting the diversity of incentive reward configuration differences needed in an organization, multinational corporations (MNCs) bring an even greater need to diversify the set of incentive reward configurations that organizations provide managers and HR professionals to work with (Kostova and Roth 2002). While the same logic applies to the workforce within an MNC which was described above in relation to motivating a diverse workforce, institutional pressures that exist in the external environment will differ from country to country. Differences in institutional pressures will need to be taken into consideration if MNCs are to maintain their legitimacy with external stakeholders and motivate employees across the globe.

This confluence of pressures suggests that organizations will be best off if they craft an incentive rewards programme that adapts to the needs of individual employees. Developing a theoretical approach to determine which reward configuration to use with which employee and when to use it is essential for organizations to be successful in maximizing the productivity of their workforce. Scholars need to work towards developing a theory that can help lead practitioners to understand how to adapt and configure their incentive rewards programmes to meet individual employee needs.

This chapter has suggested that organizations should develop reward configurations that can be adapted to their employees' needs and to those of the external environment where they reside; however, having multiple reward configurations within an organization can cause design and implementation complications that need to be thought through. While there is merit in developing the capacity to configure rewards programmes that fit with individual employee needs, values and expectations, having multiple reward configurations can lead to problems with perceived equity differences (Adams 1963). Additionally, as rewards are used to signal organizational values (Stajkovic and Luthans 2001), the introduction of multiple reward configurations could send contradictory signals as to what the organization values, which can result in an unclear organizational identity and attendant potential problems. Researchers will need to investigate not only how rewards within a configuration will interact, but how the presence of multiple reward configurations in an organization will interact. The solution could be as simple as letting employees opt into the reward configuration that they prefer, but research on related conceptual and practical issues must be developed, organized and understood.

Finally, motivation theories, in general, advocate the use of incentive rewards as an important tool (Gerhart et al. 2009; Kerr 1975). With the concerns noted above, it is possible that there are situations where having a simplified rewards programme, or no rewards beyond the base compensation and benefits for employees is the optimal approach to motivating a workforce. Therefore, scholars should study not just the how (or the outcomes) of incentive reward configurations, but the when. When is it optimal to implement an incentive rewards programme, which members of the workforce should be rewarded, and which tasks should be incentivized by organizations. As theory on incentive rewards evolves to answer these questions, practitioners will be empowered to develop tools needed to deal with an ever-changing world.

Challenges for practitioners

While there are many opportunities for academics to study and develop new knowledge, these also represent challenges that practitioners must face as they operate in a global environment. Instead of repeating the list of opportunities for academics and labelling them as challenges for practitioners, this section will expand on some of the opportunities listed above and explain what practitioners must do to face these challenges.

The focus of this chapter has been to recognize that institutional forces shape how employees' and managers' values develop and subsequently has discussed how these values will influence the evaluations they make about incentive rewards that are offered in an organization. One of the suggestions for academics is to understand the impact of adapting an incentive reward programme to individual employee needs. Inherent in this idea is that employers will need to know what their employees value in order to maximize the effectiveness of the rewards they implement. There are several ways that employers can accomplish this.

The first approach is a simple suggestion: ask your employees what they prefer. This would seem to be easier for small businesses to achieve than for large ones. In a small business, owners or managers can ask employees what they value and then create individualized incentive reward programmes that optimize motivation. This can also be achieved by large organizations. The key in a large organization is to empower managers at the department or group levels with a variety of incentive rewards. This is similar to broadbanding in compensation; however, instead of giving managers some latitude on how much to pay employees in terms of base salary, in this instance the organization provides them with multiple incentive reward bundles from which to select. If managers have a variety of incentive rewards available to implement, they can adapt rewards they use to fit with values of their employees and thereby align rewards with values and maximize the benefit of using employee rewards.

If organizations are hesitant to empower managers with power over incentive rewards, then headquarters can design multiple equivalent incentive reward bundles and let employees opt into the bundle they prefer. Differences between bundles could be as simple as recognizing employees in departmental meetings and company newsletters, or not. Having multiple pre-designed reward options would simplify the process of collecting information that was discussed above. The key to this is having enough options that employees will find one that fits their values. Failure to have an adequate variety of options to choose from will result in employees being forced into a selection that does not fit their values and therefore fails to motivate them.

Having employees in the same role, or the same department, on different incentive reward programmes can lead to complications. Ideally, having a programme that is tailored to their values should result in increased motivation, and increased performance and productivity, it is important to make sure that alignment between incentivized behaviours and outcomes is consistent with organizations strategic objectives across all incentive programmes. For example, if an employee comes from a more collectivistic culture they might opt into a programme that focuses more on group-level rewards. This type of reward programme will motivate them and is also likely to encourage employees to perform organizational citizenship behaviours, behaviours where employees are not focused on their own work, but on helping their peers accomplish their goals. If they are working with several people, who chose a reward programme that is focused on individual rewards their peers will not be incentivized to reciprocate these same behaviours.

This might be acceptable and in line with the organization's goals, or it could create unwanted conflict and tension in the workplace that is counterproductive to the purposes of having an incentive rewards programme.

Management incentive reward training is another consideration that practitioners need to take into consideration. This applies to multiple aspects of incentive rewards and includes programmes designed to help managers understand their own institutional biases, the managerial evaluation of potential incentive rewards, and diversity training that helps managers to understand the institutional background of employees with which they work. Training in each area will increase managers' ability to develop incentive reward programmes that achieve their goals.

The last consideration that will be mentioned in this chapter is the idea that institutional force strength can be either tight or loose (Gelfand et al. 2006). When force strength is tight, there are negative consequences (i.e., social sanctioning, etc.) that take place when institutional norms and values are not followed. In countries with loose strength, by contrast, negative consequences are less likely to result when organizational practice deviates from institutional norms and values. As practitioners consider the incentive rewards they are using it will be helpful to understand the relative strength of the institutional forces in the country in which they are operating, and in the home countries of their employees.

Conclusion

When organizations implement incentive rewards, it is important for them to take into consideration their employees' institutional values. For US-centric organizations, however, there might only be a few differences between employees or between management and employees; organizations that span multiple countries are likely to employ people from a variety of countries, each with their own unique mindset or beliefs that are tied to their country of origin. To be successful, MNCs will need to take into account institutional differences when they implement an incentive rewards programme.

There are two key points that need to be made prior to ending this chapter. The first involves how we have conceptualized institutions. Throughout this chapter, we have looked at institutions as a country-level phenomenon. We have inferred that institutional values will differ between countries and that organizations need to understand how these values influence incentive rewards. It is possible for multiple institutional frameworks to exist in a country. For example, Germany was previously divided between East and West Germany and has been reunified for around three decades. Additionally, institutional differences can evolve from other sources such as the industry that an organization is embedded in, and the unions of which employees are members.

The next key point is the importance of maintaining alignment throughout the organization. The HR literature often refers to this as 'internal' and 'external' alignment. Internal alignment refers to the alignment of HR practices with each other in a coherent system. External alignment, by contrast, refers to the alignment of HR practices and the HR system with business strategy and non-HR practices. As noted above, HR practices do not operate in isolation; they are part of a larger system. It would be easy to focus so much on the alignment of employees' institutional values with incentive rewards, that practitioners neglect to ensure alignment with the rest of the HR system and business strategy. The alignment of the structure of incentive practices and business strategy remains paramount. The challenge for organizations is twofold: to address strategy implementation requirements while also understanding how the organization's increasingly diverse and global workforce will respond; and to craft incentive reward options that produce optimal business outcomes.

References

Adams, J. S. (1963). Wage inequities, productivity and work quality. *Industrial Relations.* 3(1), 9–16.

Brown, M. and Heywood, J. S. (2002). *Paying for Performance: an International Comparison.* Armonk, NY: M.E. Sharpe.

Cadsby, C. B., Song, F. and Tapon, F. (2007). Sorting and incentive effects of pay for performance: an experimental investigation. *Academy of Management Journal.* 50(2), 387–405.

Delery, J. E. and Doty, D. H. (1996). Modes of theorizing in strategic human resource management: tests of universalistic, contingency, and configurational performance predictions. *Academy of Management Journal.* 39(4), 802–835.

Farndale, E. and Sanders, K. (2017). Conceptualizing HRM system strength through a cross-cultural lens. *International Journal of Human Resource Management.* 28(1), 132–148.

Gelfand, M. J., Nishii, L. H. and Raver, J. L. (2006). On the nature and importance of cultural tightness–looseness. *Journal of Applied Psychology.* 91(6), 1225–1244.

Gerhart, B., Rynes, R. and Fulmer, I. (2009). Pay and performance: individuals, groups, and executives. *The Academy of Management Annals.* 3(1), 251–313.

Hofstede, G. and Hofstede, G. J. (2005). *Cultures and Organizations: Software of the Mind. Intercultural Cooperation and Its Importance for Survival* (2nd ed.). New York, NY: McGraw-Hill.

Kerr, S. (1975). On the folly of rewarding A, while hoping for B. *Academy of Management Journal.* 18(4), 769–783.

Kostova, T. and Roth, K. (2002). Adoption of an organizational practice by subsidiaries of multinational corporations: institutional and relational effects. *Academy of Management Journal.* 45(1), 215–233.

Long, R. J. and Fang, T. (2012). Do employees profit from profit sharing? Evidence from Canadian panel data. *Industrial & Labor Relations Review.* 65(4), 899–927.

Meyer, J. W. and Rowan, B. (1977). Institutionalized organizations: formal structure as myth and ceremony. *American Journal of Sociology.* 83(2), 340–363.

North, D. C. (1990). *Institutions, Institutional Change, and Economic Performance.* Cambridge: Cambridge University Press.

Nyberg, A. J., Pieper, J. R. and Trevor, C. O. (2013). Pay-for-performance's effect on future employee performance: integrating psychological and economic principles toward a contingency perspective. *Journal of Management.* 42(7): 1753–1783.

Prince, N., Prince, J., Skousen, B. and Kabst, R. (2016). Incentive pay configurations: bundle options and country-level adoption. *Evidence-based HRM: A Global Forum for Empirical Scholarship.* 4(1), 49–66.

Schneider, B. (1987). The people make the place. *Personnel Psychology.* 40, 437–453.

Schuler, R. S. and Rogovsky, N. (1998). Understanding compensation practice variations across firms: the impact of national culture. *Journal of International Business Studies.* 29(1), 159–177.

Scott, W. R. (2008). *Institutions and Organizations: Ideas and Interests.* Thousand Oaks, CA: Sage.

Stajkovic, A. D. and Luthans, F. (2001). Differential effects of incentive motivators on work performance. *Academy of Management Journal.* 44(3), 580–590.

Toossi, M. (2002). A century of change: the US labor force, 1950–2050. *Monthly Labor Review.* 125(5), 15–28.

19

GLOBAL REWARD MANAGEMENT

Marion Festing and Michael Tekieli

Introduction

Global reward management (GRM) is a critical issue for human resource managers in multinational enterprises (MNEs), as it influences and controls the behaviour of managers and employees worldwide and has a strong impact on global firm performance, since there is evidence that compensation systems are able to increase organizational effectiveness (Graham and Trevor 2000; Gross and Friedman 2004). While for many decades practitioners as well as scientists have defined rewards as everything provided by the firm that benefits employees in a monetary way, rewards today are defined as all "returns people receive from work" (Newman et al. 2016:13), including direct as well as indirect, and extrinsic as well intrinsic, types of rewards (Manas and Graham 2003) which can be categorized into monetary and non-monetary terms (Newman et al. 2016). According to the 'Total Returns' framework presented by Newman et al. (2016), monetary rewards consist of base pay, the merit/cost of living, performance-related pay (i.e., short-term and long-term incentives) and employee benefits such as income protection, work–life arrangements and allowances. Non-monetary rewards include aspects such as recognition and status, employment security, the work content itself and learning opportunities. With continuing globalization, MNEs are confronted with the challenges of managing rewards on a global level, i.e., they are concerned with differentiating and integrating their reward policies and practices according to the needs of their headquarters (HQ) as well as their subsidiaries on a global scale. As Sparrow (2004:102) states, "We see evidence both of international convergence around best practice coupled with an increasingly sophisticated awareness of the distinctive nature of rewards policies and behavior across countries."

Taking into account this convergence/divergence debate, and aiming at explaining these trends towards global standardization and local distinctiveness, involves the consideration of a variety of factors. The interplay between these factors has been captured by several frameworks (e.g., Bloom et al. 2003; Schuler and Jackson 2014); for instance, according to the meta-framework of global pay by Dowling et al. (2017), the investigation of global pay issues falls into two broad streams of literature, characterized by the universalist paradigm, assuming the worldwide convergence of human resource management (HRM) practices, and the contextualist paradigm, highlighting the constraints of such an approach (Brewster 1999). The stream following the universalist paradigm claims that (the same) HRM practices, including compensation and rewards, can be applied effectively in various cultural and institutional settings (Chênevert and Tremblay 2011;

Pfeffer 1994). This is often explained by theories that take a primarily firm-internal perspective, i.e., the resource-based view (Barney 1991), resource dependence theory (Pfeifer and Salancik 1978), behavioural theory (Larraza–Kintana et al. 2007; March and Simon 1958), new institutional economics (Eisenhardt 1989a; Zeckhauser and Pratt 1985) or knowledge-based perspectives (Fey and Furu 2008; Sveiby 1997). The second stream of literature focuses on the impact of the context of companies and claims that firms should take into account the external environment when designing HRM practices and policies. In particular, this approach draws from institutional theory, for example the national business system approach (e.g. Whitley 1992) and cultural perspectives (Hofstede 1980; House et al. 2004) or combinations of various factors in the sense of con-textualization (e.g., Michailova 2011). Localization and global alignment pressures antagonize each other, and the dominance of either localization or alignment in relation to global reward balance has an impact on MNEs' global reward approaches (Kang and Shen 2015).

The recent literature takes a more differentiated view and adds to the discussion on the simple dichotomy of convergence and divergence (Demirbag et al. 2016), suggesting explanations beyond the two major paradigms introduced above. For example, there is evidence that various reward practices, i.e., different elements of the reward mix, follow different patterns of localization and standardization and lead to greater complexity in the global reward picture (Ferner and Almond 2013; Rosenzweig and Nohria 1994; Yanadori 2011). Furthermore, pay level underlies stronger influences in the local context, resulting in a stronger local adaptation, though this is not necessarily the case for pay mix (ratio of cash bonus to base salary). In addition, as HRM has been perceived as a rather localized management function (McGraw 2015; Rosenzweig 2006; Rosenzweig and Nohria 1994) – a notion which is especially true for reward management (Ferner et al. 2001) – the organizational context is expected by some researchers to play a less important role than in past discussions (Gomez-Mejia and Welbourne 1991; Schuler and Rogovsky 1998). Overall, research has focused mainly on external constraints of HRM standardization and has actually neglected factors that emphasize and favour this approach (Brewster et al. 2016).

Taking into account all of these insights, this chapter is dedicated to providing insights into how various contextual factors affect the complexity of global rewards in MNEs. The main objective of the chapter is to provide an overview of the relevant factors influencing GRM and their impact on the complex balance between the global standardization and localization of reward practices across MNEs' HQs and subsidiaries. Therefore, in the remainder of this chapter, we shall first summarize major insights about the impact of the firm-external and firm-internal contexts on global rewards, before analysing and discussing the interplay between both aspects. In our discussion, we outline further influencing factors and explanatory approaches that go beyond the explanatory factors and approaches of the external and internal contexts which have dominated the discussion to date. Implications from this discussion for future research and managerial practice conclude this contribution.

Firm-external context

The firm-external context, i.e., the organization's cultural, social or political environment, is supposed to have an influence on variations in reward decision-making concerning certain pay elements (Armstrong and Murlis 1991; Bloom et al. 2003). The discussion on reward variation is dominated by the impact of the cultural context, the institutional environment (including industrial relations and labour market regulations), and the situation in the labour market and industry characteristics, as outlined below.

The *impact of the national culture on rewards* has been discussed intensively and is based on the cultural dimensions identified in cross-cultural management studies such as Hofstede (1980) or

GLOBE (House et al. 2004), understanding culture as the ". . . collective programming of the mind" (Hofstede 1980) that shapes perceptions and practices in all fields of HRM, including rewards (e.g., Grenness 2011; Rogovsky et al. 2000). Most of the literature analysing the impact of local culture on the design of compensation practices has focused on performance for pay (PFP). In this respect, Sparrow (2004) states that "different expectations of the manager–subordinate relationship and their impact on performance management and motivational processes influence the perceived validity and attractiveness of performance-related pay systems" (Sparrow 2004:105). For example, pay plans and bonus schemes based on individual performance (Schuler and Rogovsky 1998) as well as on organizational performance (Prince et al. 2016) have been found to be more prevalent in low-uncertainty avoidance countries. Furthermore, the cultural dimension of individualism is supposed to have an impact on performance criteria: while low-individualism countries prefer criteria based on group performance, high-individualism countries prefer rewards for individual achievement (Gomez-Mejia and Welbourne 1991). Interestingly, complex cultural adaptations occur in subsidiaries of MNEs: Ying Chang et al. (2007), for instance, found that UK subsidiaries of Taiwanese MNEs adapted to the highly individual values ascribed to UK society and shifted from home-based approaches of egalitarian and group-related pay to rewarding and promoting employees based on individual performance (see also Chang and Smale 2013). In addition, power distance has been related to PFP: Schuler and Rogovsky (1998) found that pay schemes based on organizational performance (i.e., employee share options, stock ownership) are less prevalent in high power distance cultures. Berber et al. (2017) indicate a positive impact of power distance (as well as individualism) on the usage of variable pay in Central and Eastern Europe. Furthermore, pay differentials between job levels tend to be higher in high-power-distance countries such as China (Tosi and Greckhamer 2004). Moreover, benefits have been related to various cultural dimensions. For example, social pensions have proven helpful in minimizing income differences in low-power-distance countries, while the masculinity dimension is related to whether a society prefers job or rather income protection (Hempel 1998). Benefits have been also related to the femininity dimension, predicting more important work–life arrangements such as maternity leave, workplace childcare or career-break schemes (Schuler and Rogovsky 1998).

The *impact of the institutional context on GRM* can, for example, be conceptualized by using the national business system approach (Whitley 1992), which identifies, amongst others, the industrial relations system, including labour law, and the education system as important features of the national business system (see also Festing 2012). Taking this perspective, it can be concluded, for example, that the importance societies place on industrial relations – and, more specifically, on labour unions – can have a significant impact on reward systems. It has been found that the influence of unions is the strongest – compared to other reward elements – where base pay is concerned (Newman et al. 2016). Another example would be that group-level performance measures are implemented more often in unionized firms (Heneman et al. 2002). Furthermore, in other studies, even a negative effect of unionization on the implementation of PFP has been found (Gunnigle et al. 1998; Long and Shields 2005). Concerning labour and employment laws, there is evidence of an important impact on global rewards (Allen et al. 2007; Traxler et al. 2008). For example, national minimum wages and equal pay legislation constrain a company's options when setting wages, especially base pay (Rubery and Grimshaw 2003). Additionally, performance-related pay elements such as stock options are regulated in many countries by the legal environment. Here, tax law plays a particularly important role (Bloom and Milkovich 1999; Gibson et al. 2002). With respect to financial participation in the European Union, "the incidence of. . . profit sharing and shared ownership differ[s] considerably among Member States, and this correlate[s] broadly with the extent of differences in legislative and fiscal support for them" (Pendleton et al. 2002:51). Earlier research by Festing et al. (1999) confirmed that due to the complexity of German law and the highly formal nature of German workplace industrial relations, financial participation schemes were not very commonplace in German firms. Furthermore, the execution of employee benefits (e.g., paid holiday) is greatly affected by local factors such as local laws and, in particular, tax laws (Newman et al. 2016; Tarique et al. 2015). The impact of the educational system on rewards can be illustrated by taking the example of German industries and German society, who value broad basic qualifications, displayed in the German dual vocational training system or the famous notion of the '*Facharbeiter*' (Festing 2012), which may explain the preference for skills-based pay systems in this country (Child et al. 2001).

Furthermore, the *impact of other host-country effects on rewards* has been discussed (Edwards 2015; Myloni et al. 2007). One central explanatory approach for this is based on the varieties-of-capitalism paradigm (Hall and Soskice 2001), comparing subsidiaries located in coordinated market economies (CMEs) and liberal market economies (LMEs). LMEs are countries in which firm behaviour is coordinated mainly through competitive markets, while firm behaviour in CMEs is more dependent on institutional actors such as unions (Hall and Soskice 2001). With respect to HRM, MNE subsidiaries are regulated more strongly in CMEs than in LMEs concerning their people management (Farndale et al. 2008), in that localization pressures are supposed to be stronger in CMEs than in LMEs. In line with these considerations, it has been found that MNEs standardize their practices in LMEs more than in CMEs (Farndale 2010).

The *impact of the labour market situation on rewards*, notably the supply and demand of employees, is also critical for determining rewards, as companies tend to adapt their base pay rates to the competitive situation (Rubery and Grimshaw 2003). Empirical studies have provided evidence that important deviations from market standards have a negative impact on the attraction and retention of employees, and therefore companies benchmark the market pay level for certain positions when setting the corporate pay level (Leonard 1987). Arrowsmith and Sisson (2001) confirmed this notion with respect to the UK market, finding that pay decisions were driven mainly by local concerns about the labour market, employee expectations and profitability, while pay comparisons with international competitors did not have particularly high importance. Conversely, pay costs were benchmarked using a global rather than a local approach. However, more recent studies (see, for example, the overviews by Fay (2008) and Yanadori (2014)) suggest that pay level might be adjusted on a global basis due to technical reasons (the Internet, global media and global recruitment and selection processes of firms), regional trade and employment blocks such as the EU, long-distance international commuting and the standardization of pay metrics via the use of the euro.

The *industry in which the firm primarily competes can also significantly affect reward choices*, including pay level and pay mix (Gerhart and Milkovich 1990; Newman et al. 2016; Richbell et al. 2011). The degree of competition and the level of product demand in the industry have a strong impact on (base) salary level, as both elements affect price elasticity and, consequently, determine organizational pay levels (Newman et al. 2016). Concerning PFP in a multinational context, Festing et al. (2007) consider market competitiveness and market size as important factors influencing the local adaptation of certain elements of the global reward system. Unfortunately, there is not much empirical evidence about the relationship between employee benefits and productivity on a general or industry level. Therefore, organizations should consider the industry as well as the specific socio-economic context and decide whether they would like to be in line with their major competitors, or below or above the market, when designing their offer. For example, if the public pension system does not provide sufficient resources for retirement, organizations could consider offering private pension funds and vice versa (Tarique et al. 2015) if the competitive situation in the industry indicates so.

Firm-internal context

The firm-internal context principally addresses the impact of organizational factors on rewards. Examples addressed in this chapter include organizational strategy and organizational culture.

There is evidence that *MNEs' strategies in global markets*, namely a differentiation, cost leadership or focused strategy (Porter 1980), have an *impact on the design of global reward systems* (see, for example, Gerhart and Milkovich 1990). As Balkin and Gomez-Mejia have pointed out, "management adjusts its pay strategies to fit with the organisational strategy" (1990:163), while Tsai et al. (2008) found that matching pay policy with strategic intent facilitates firm performance. Balkin and Gomez-Mejia (1990) illustrate this statement by pointing out that changes in the business strategy (e.g., focusing on stability instead of growth) may require adaptations in the pay mix, including, for example, a higher emphasis on incentives. In line with this notion, Yanadori and Marler (2006) found reward practice specificities related to an innovator strategy, albeit these focused mainly on target employees who were key to the innovative activity, e.g., people working in R&D, who had higher pay levels, a longer time horizon for long-term incentives and a shorter pension vesting period (as compared to employee groups working in other parts of the investigated firms). However, probably for consistency reasons, even other employees enjoyed some of the specific pay characteristics outlined above. Other studies emphasize the link between strategy and pay level. For example, Knouse (1995) outlined that a differentiation strategy with a high-quality focus is associated with the upward adaptation of base salaries. On the contrary, Arthur (1992) found that a cost leadership strategy might lead to a benefits offer that is below the market standard, while Mhatre (2012) confirmed that costs are the most important pressure where local employee benefits implementation is concerned. Taylor et al. (1996) highlighted the strategic role of a subsidiary as an impact factor for global rewards, outlining that the local innovator role is associated with the local adaptation of HRM practices and that the globally integrated player role is related rather to globally standardized HRM practices, including compensation. However, this fit between corporate strategy and the reward system also depends on other influencing factors such as the competence and experience of the HR actors themselves, i.e., "the level of technical insight into the mechanics of rewards systems, and the importance and degree of attention given to legislative, fairness and equity concerns in the operation of pay systems" (Sparrow 2004:104). Looking through the lens of agency theory (Eisenhardt 1989b), the subsidiary can be viewed as the agent and the headquarters as the principal (Doz and Prahalad 1991). Since the interests of the subsidiary might not be always consistent with those of the parent MNE, HQ managers might think of control mechanisms to reduce agency problems (O'Donnell 1999). Here, PFP can act as a central element in the execution of a company's business strategy, as it is supposed to support the alignment of individual behaviour with organizational goals (Jenkins et al. 1998; Montemayor 1996). Therefore, it can contribute to aligning subsidiary managers' goals with HQ's goals (O'Donnell 1999).

The *impact of organizational culture on rewards* attracts or repels a certain type of employees since compensation practices communicate the philosophy and values of an organization (Rynes 1987; Wright 2010) and is reflected, among others, in base pay practices, notably in the choices between the ratio of fix and variable pay or the relevance of seniority. The importance of variable pay and the underlying performance criteria signal how much emphasis is placed on individual performance and achievement within a specific corporate culture (Cable and Judge 1994). In line with this, Kuhn (2009) found that advertising bonuses based on team or organizational performance will lead to applicant perceptions of the organizational culture as being more collectivistic while bonuses based on individual performance result in an organization culture that is perceived as very individualistic. With respect to cross-cultural variations concerning preferences for equity and equality in reward systems (Fischer and Smith 2003) MNEs could consider a corresponding differentiation in their worldwide reward practices. Organizational culture is also related to the design of benefits and non-cash rewards; for example, in a family-friendly organization, longer paid maternity leave beyond national standards or childcare services could be offered. The non-cash reward dimension can also be related to organizational culture. The kind of leadership style as part of organizational culture, for instance, is linked directly to the quality and quantity of feedback and the recognition of employee performance as non-cash reward elements. Furthermore, organizational culture is reflected in other non-cash rewards such as the career and development opportunities in the organization (Jaeger 1983). Even though there are a few examples showing a relationship between organizational culture and reward management, empirical research is still scarce compared to other reward management aspects (Kuhn 2009; Wright 2010).

The complex balance of global reward management

We have seen that external and internal context factors have an impact on all elements of global rewards. The literature review has shown that the stronger the influence of local host contextual factors, the higher the responsiveness of MNEs to local reward practices (localization), while the strong influence of organizational factors results in an alignment of subsidiary reward management towards HQ practices (standardization) (Bloom et al. 2003; Yanadori 2011). The respective framework by Bloom et al. (2003) relies on the assumption that localization and global alignment pressures vary between different countries (Jackson and Schuler 1995), due to the interplay between various combinations of influencing factors (Myloni et al. 2007). In the following we discuss the specific challenges of the interplay between specific MNE home and host countries, the differentiation between the GRM balance with respect to various practices and also various hierarchical levels.

The interplay between specific home and host countries of the MNE and the GRM balance. We have discussed the host country as an external context variable more or less independent of the interplay between an MNE's home and host countries. However, this interplay dimension has also been identified as relevant for the discussion on global rewards, especially from an institutional perspective (Edwards et al. 2010; Ferner and Almond 2013). Several studies have found that the home-country context of the MNE also matters. For example, American MNEs often resist localization pressures and have the tendency to standardize their policies and practices in accordance with their HQ's standards (Almond and Ferner 2006; Fenton-O'Creevy et al. 2008; Gunnigle et al. 2001), commonly called the 'country-of-origin' effect (COO, Ferner 1997). However, some recent research was unable to identify 'country-of-origin' effects (Edwards et al. 2010; Ferner and Almond 2013; Poutsma et al. 2015). Looking closer, these studies were conducted in Europe, resulting in the interpretation that due to globalization pressures and the standardization of institutional parameters within Europe, MNEs tend to match practices in their European affiliates and apply them to a universal model (Poutsma et al. 2015), the so-called 'dominance' effect (Pudelko and Harzing 2007). However, McGraw (2015) concludes that global best-reward practices are used by MNEs as a reference, though these dominant effects do not automatically produce worldwide standardized reward practices.

Differentiation between reward practices and the GRM balance. The literature also suggests that some HRM practices are more susceptible to local constraints than others, resulting in a stronger localization of these practices (Chiang et al. 2017). A recent study by Yanadori (2011) showed that the pay mix (ratio of cash bonus to base salary) of an MNE was highly consistent across its subsidiaries, while the base pay level differed significantly across foreign subsidiaries, thereby suggesting that alignment logic plays a greater role when determining pay mix, while localization logic is better when determining base pay levels. Yanadori (2011) concludes from these results that MNEs distinguish between single reward practices when balancing the two sets of logic. Therefore, it is suggested that for each reward practice there is a distinct degree of localization pressure as well as of global alignment pressure. In an early study, Rosenzweig and Nohria (1994) showed, for subsidiaries located in the US, that executive bonus practices are transferred from HQs to subsidiaries to a greater extent than other rewards such as benefits, time off and training. Similarly, Sayım (2010) found a strict transfer of home-based policies with respect to performance-related pay and a high level of control by HQs of US MNEs located in Turkey, albeit with many local elements with respect to benefits. Even though the Turkish business system was acknowledged as highly permissive and with an enormous openness towards the application of US-originated reward management policies, the interviewed managers stated that it would be almost impossible to exchange traditional benefits without losing competitiveness in the local labour market.

Differentiation between various hierarchical levels and the GRM balance. The extent to which pressures affect MNEs' global reward approaches varies, not only between different reward elements, but also between different groups of reward recipients. Especially senior managers, who are identified as a "strategic employee group" (Milkovich 1988:266), are expected to be subject to alignment pressures (Yanadori 2011). However, while some scholars find differences in reward practices between various hierarchical levels (e.g., McGraw 2015), others suggest an increasing standardization of reward management for all hierarchical levels, which they explain through rising globalization pressures (Edwards and Kuruvilla 2005).

We can conclude that the GRM balance is determined strongly by external and internal context factors. However, the relationship is not deterministic, as complex 'country-of-origin' and host-country relationships and variations between the various reward elements and across hierarchical levels lead to a more complex maze of global rewards in MNEs.

Discussion and future research avenues

The literature review has shown that the design of GRM is not a simple, dichotomous choice between global standardization and local adaption (Pudelko and Harzing 2007; Yanadori 2011); rather, it is a more complex undertaking. This phenomenon is referred to as "hybridisation" (Chung et al. 2014) and means that each reward element has been found to be influenced by different localization and global alignment pressures, and this to varying degrees, as reflected in diverse sets of practice similarities between HQs and foreign subsidiaries in MNEs.

In the past, many studies have examined in a rather isolated way the impact of organizational and host-country factors as well as other contingent variables. According to Quintanilla and Ferner (2003), examining the HRM of multinationals should not be about one or the other influencing factor, but about the interplay between local, national, international and sectoral influences. For example, Budhwar and Khatri (2001) did not find any differences regarding compensation practices between Indian and British organizations related to the private sector; however, they established that public organizations from these countries differed in their compensation approaches. Accordingly, various scholars call for more multi-level analyses and a theoretical pluralism (see also Brewster et al. 2016). The micro-level, in particular, has been largely neglected in the past, though some qualitative studies suggest that individual decision-makers and the power distribution between HQ and foreign subsidiaries are relevant when analysing standardization (see also Brewster et al. 2016). For example, Zhu et al. (2014) and Zhu and Jack (2017) identified MNE managers' mindsets as a central factor in explaining MNEs' approaches to managing foreign subsidiaries. Thus, they *recommended a stronger focus on psychological processes* when examining the standardization/localization conundrum of MNEs' worldwide (reward) management practices. Another possibility in this respect could include taking a social identity perspective (Tajfel and Turner 1979) when looking at HQs and subsidiaries, thereby indicating the importance of HQs' "sense of superiority" (Chung 2014:229), and in consequence their in-group favouritism, as well as the influence of subsidiary managers' role identities (Kostova and Roth 2002; Vora and Kostova 2007) on reward management.

Furthermore, related to the individual level and power distribution between key individual and collective actors is the concept of *decision-making centralization*, which is often overlooked in GRM research. Most of the studies examining MNEs' global HRM approaches have focused on the degree of practice resemblance/similarity (Ahlvik et al. 2016), while the analysis of decision-making centralization has been limited to a few studies addressing the context of top management pay (Edwards et al. 1996) and salary expenditure (Martin and Beaumont 1999). Nonetheless, the approach of looking at practice resemblance/similarity does not allow for accurate interpretations regarding the extent to which a low degree of practice resemblance is due to local constraints or to conscious HQ intentions to allow their foreign subsidiaries greater autonomy (Ahlvik et al. 2016; Khilji and Wang 2006). Therefore, examining the degree of decision-making centralization – identified as a powerful determinant of the worldwide standardization of MNEs' practices (Ferner et al. 2011; Myloni et al. 2007) – allows for more accurate interpretations regarding corporate intentions in line with standardization and localization. Practice transfer, in most cases, may be the subject of transmutation, meaning that although the HQ has the decision-making power to transfer a practice to a subsidiary, modifications may be required due to local circumstances (Tayeb 2005). According to Al Ariss and Sidani (2016), MNEs would like to implement their own HR systems but are often "overpowered by institutional and cultural practices" (p. 353). Therefore, the examination of decision-making distribution instead of practice transfer reflects more precisely HQs' attempts to implement home-based practices in their subsidiaries (Al Ariss and Sidani 2016). Examining decision-making distribution might be relevant for explaining not only the transfer of practices, but also reverse transfers (Chung 2014). However, to date, research in the reward management field is lacking studies examining reverse and horizontal transfers (among subsidiaries). Additionally, Baeten (2014) emphasizes the need to put more research effort into examining benefits and non-financial rewards, since most of the research has looked at cash remuneration.

In summary, future research should consider multi-level research, including the individual and group level, in addition to local, national, international and sectoral influences. Theoretical pluralism is recommended in order to capture the complexity of the GRM dilemma, including not only the various levels, but also the perspectives chosen, namely the example of decision-making and the impact of power distribution and social identities. With respect to theory development, Singh et al. (2013) also point to the necessity of considering reward management from various cultural perspectives and going beyond traditional Westernized views.

References

Ahlvik, C., Smale, A. and Sumelius, J. (2016). Aligning corporate transfer intentions and subsidiary HRM practice implementation in multinational corporations. *Journal of World Business*. 51(3), 343–355.

Al Ariss, A. and Sidani, Y. (2016). Comparative international human resource management: future research directions. *Human Resource Management Review*. 26(4), 352–358.

Allen, M. M., Tüselmann, H.-J., El-Sa'id, H. and Windrum, P. (2007). Sectoral collective agreements: remuneration straitjackets for German workplaces? *Personnel Review*. 36(6), 963–977.

Almond, P. and Ferner, A. (2006). *American Multinationals in Europe: Managing Employment Relations Across National Borders*. Oxford: Oxford University Press.

Armstrong, M. and Murlis, H. (1991). *Reward Management: a Handbook of Remuneration Strategy and Practice* (2nd fully revised ed.). London: Kogan Page.

Arrowsmith, J. and Sisson, K. (2001). International competition and pay, working time and employment: exploring the processes of adjustment. *Industrial Relations Journal.* 32(2), 136–153.

Arthur, J. B. (1992). The link between business strategy and industrial relations systems in American steel minimills. *Industrial & Labor Relations Review.* 45(3), 488–506.

Baeten, X. (2014). Shaping the future research agenda for compensation and benefits management: Some thoughts based on a stakeholder inquiry. *International Human Resource Management Review.* 24(1), 31–40.

Balkin, D. B. and Gomez-Mejia, L. R. (1990). Matching compensation and organizational strategies. *Strategic Management Journal.* 11(2), 153–169.

Barney, J. (1991). Firm resources and sustained competitive advantage. *Journal of Management.* 17(1), 99–120.

Berber, N., Morley, M. J., Slavić, A. and Poór, J. (2017). Management compensation systems in Central and Eastern Europe: a comparative analysis. *The International Journal of Human Resource Management.* 28 (12), 1661–1689.

Bloom, M. and Milkovich, G. T. (1999). A SHRM perspective on international compensation and reward systems. *Research in Personnel and Human Resources Management, Supplement IV.* 283–303.

Bloom, M., Milkovich, G. T. and Mitra, A. (2003). International compensation: learning from how managers respond to variations in local host contexts. *International Journal of Human Resource Management.* 14(8), 1350–1367.

Brewster, C. (1999). Strategic human resource management: the value of different paradigms. *Management International Review.* 39, 45–64.

Brewster, C., Mayrhofer, W. and Smale, A. (2016). Crossing the streams: HRM in multinational enterprises and comparative HRM. *Human Resource Management Review.* 26(4), 285–297.

Budhwar, P. and Khatri, N. (2001). A comparative study of HR practices in Britain and India. *International Journal of Human Resource Management.* 12(5), 800–826.

Cable, D. M. and Judge, T. A. (1994). Pay preferences and job search decisions: a person–organization fit perspective. *Personnel Psychology.* 47(2), 317–348.

Chang, Y.-Y. and Smale, A. (2013). Expatriate characteristics and the stickiness of HRM knowledge transfers. *The International Journal of Human Resource Management.* 24(12), 2394–2410.

Chênevert, D. and Tremblay, M. (2011). Between universality and contingency. *International Journal of Manpower.* 32(8), 856–878.

Chiang, F. F., Lemański, M. K. and Birtch, T. A. (2017). The transfer and diffusion of HRM practices within MNCs: lessons learned and future research directions. *The International Journal of Human Resource Management.* 28(1), 234–258.

Child, J., Faulkner, D. and Pitkethly, R. (2001). *The Management of International Acquisitions.* New York: Oxford University Press.

Chung, C., Sparrow, P. and Bozkurt, Ö. (2014). South Korean MNEs' international HRM approach: hybridization of global standards and local practices. *Journal of World Business.* 49(4), 549–559.

Chung, L. (2014). Headquarters' managerial intentionality and reverse transfer of practices. *Management International Review.* 54(2), 225–252.

Demirbag, M., Tatoglu, E. and Wilkinson, A. (2016). Adoption of high-performance work systems by local subsidiaries of developed country and Turkish MNEs and indigenous firms in Turkey. *Human Resource Management.* 55(6), 1001–1024.

Dowling, P. J., Festing, M. and Engle, A. D. (2017). *International Human Resource Management* (7th ed.). London: Cengage.

Doz, Y. L. and Prahalad, C. K. (1991). Managing DMNCs: a search for a new paradigm. *Strategic Management Journal.* 12(1), 145–164.

Edwards, P., Ferner, A. and Sisson, K. (1996). The conditions for international human resource management: two case studies. *International Journal of Human Resource Management,* 7(1), 20–40.

Edwards, T. (2015). The transfer of employment practices across borders in multinational companies. In Pinnington, A. and Harzing, A.-W. (eds.). *International Human Resource Management* (pp. 429–467). London: Sage Publications Ltd.

Edwards, T., Edwards, P., Ferner, A., Marginson, P. and Tregaskis, O. (2010). Multinational companies and the diffusion of employment practices from outside the country of origin. *Management International Review (MIR).* 50(5), 613–634.

Edwards, T. and Kuruvilla, S. (2005). International HRM: national business systems, organizational politics and the international division of labour in MNCs. *The International Journal of Human Resource Management.* 16(1), 1–21.

Eisenhardt, K. M. (1989a). Agency theory: an assessment and review. *Academy of Management Review.* 14(1), 57–74.

Eisenhardt, K. M. (1989b). Building theories from case study research. *Academy of Management Review.* 14(4), 532–550.

Farndale, E. (2010). What is really driving differences and similarities in HRM practices across national boundaries in Europe? *European Journal of International Management.* 4(4), 362–381.

Farndale, E., Brewster, C. and Poutsma, E. (2008). Coordinated vs. liberal market HRM: the impact of institutionalization on multinational firms. *The International Journal of Human Resource Management.* 19(11), 2004–2023.

Fay, C. H. (2008). The global convergence of compensation practices. In Gomez-Mejia, L. and Werner, S. (eds.). *Global Compensation* (pp. 131–141). Oxford: Routledge.

Fenton-O'Creevy, M., Gooderham, P. and Nordhaug, O. (2008). Human resource management in US subsidiaries in Europe and Australia: centralisation or autonomy? *Journal of International Business Studies.* 39(1), 151–166.

Ferner, A. (1997). Country of origin effects and HRM in multinational companies. *Human Resource Management Journal.* 7(1), 19–37.

Ferner, A. and Almond, P. (2013). Performance and reward practices in foreign multinationals in the UK. *Human Resource Management Journal.* 23(3), 241–261.

Ferner, A., Quintanilla, J. and Varul, M. Z. (2001). Country-of-origin effects, host-country effects, and the management of HR in multinationals: German companies in Britain and Spain. *Journal of World Business.* 36(2), 107–127.

Ferner, A., Tregaskis, O., Edwards, P., Edwards, T., Marginson, P., Adam, D. and Meyer, M. (2011). HRM structures and subsidiary discretion in foreign multinationals in the UK. *The International Journal of Human Resource Management.* 22(03), 483–509.

Festing, M. (2012). Strategic human resource management in Germany: evidence of convergence to the US model, the European model, or a distinctive national model? *Academy of Management Perspectives.* 26(2), 37–54.

Festing, M., Eidems, J. and Royer, S. (2007). Strategic issues and local constraints in transnational compensation strategies: an analysis of cultural, institutional and political influences. *European Management Journal.* 25(2), 118–131.

Festing, M., Groening, Y., Kabst, R. and Weber, W. (1999). Financial participation in Europe – determinants and outcomes. *Economic and Industrial Democracy.* 20(2), 295–329.

Fey, C. F. and Furu, P. (2008). Top management incentive compensation and knowledge sharing in multinational corporations. *Strategic Management Journal.* 29(12), 1301–1323.

Fischer, R. and Smith, P. B. (2003). Reward allocation and culture: a meta-analysis. *Journal of Cross-cultural Psychology.* 34(3), 251–268.

Gerhart, B. and Milkovich, G. T. (1990). Organizational differences in managerial compensation and financial performance. *Academy of Management Journal.* 33(4), 663–691.

Gibson, V. L., Doyle, J. F. and Tanner, C. P. (2002). Tax and legal issues for global equity compensation plans. In Rodrick, S.S. (ed.). *Equity-based Compensation for Multinational Corporations* (4 ed., pp. 133–141). Oakland, CA: The National Center for Employee Ownership.

Gomez-Mejia, L. R. and Welbourne, T. (1991). Compensation strategies in a global context. *Human Resource Planning.* 14(1), 29–42.

Graham, M. E. and Trevor, C. O. (2000). Managing new pay program introductions to enhance the competitiveness of multinational corporations (MNCS). *Competitiveness Review: an International Business Journal.* 10(1), 136–154.

Grenness, T. (2011). The impact of national culture on CEO compensation and salary gaps between CEOs and manufacturing workers. *Compensation & Benefits Review.* 43(2), 100–108.

Gross, S. E. and Friedman, H. M. (2004). Creating an effective total reward strategy: holistic approach better supports business success. *Benefits Quarterly.* 20(3), 7–12.

Gunnigle, P., Murphy, K., Cleveland, J., Heraty, N. and Morley, M. J. (2001). Human resource management practices of US-owned multinational corporations in Europe: standardization versus localization? *Advances in International Management.* 14, 259–284.

Gunnigle, P., Turner, T. and d'Art, D. (1998). Counterpoising collectivism: performance-related pay and industrial relations in greenfield sites. *British Journal of Industrial Relations.* 36(4), 565–579.

Hall, P. A. and Soskice, D. (2001). *Varieties of Capitalism: the Institutional Foundations of Comparative Advantage*. Oxford, UK: Oxford University Press.

Hempel, P. S. (1998). Designing multinational benefits programs: the role of national culture. *Journal of World Business*. 33(3), 277–294.

Heneman, R. L., von Hippel, C., Eskew, D. E. and Greenberger, D. B. (2002). Alternative rewards in unionized environments. In Heneman, R. (ed.), *Strategic Reward Management* (pp. 131–152). Greenwich, CT: Information Age Publishing.

Hofstede, G. (1980). *Culture's Consequences: International Differences in Work-related Values*. Beverly Hills, CA: Sage.

House, R. J., Hanges, P. J., Javidan, M., Dorfman, P. W. and Gupta, V. (2004). *Culture, Leadership, and Organizations: the GLOBE Study of 62 Societies*. Thousand Oaks, London, New Delhi: Sage Publications.

Jackson, S. E. and Schuler, R. S. (1995). Understanding human resource management in the context of organizations and their environments. *Annual Review of Psychology*. 46(1), 237.

Jaeger, A. M. (1983). The transfer of organizational culture overseas: an approach to control in the multinational corporation. *Journal of International Business Studies*. 14(2), 91–114.

Jenkins, D., Mitra, A., Gupta, N. and Shaw, J. D. (1998). Are financial incentives related to performance? A meta-analytic review of empirical research. *Journal of Applied Psychology*. 83(5), 777–787.

Kang, H. and Shen, J. (2015). Transfer or localize? International reward and compensation practices of South Korean multinational enterprises in China. *Asia Pacific Business Review*. 21(2), 211–227.

Khilji, S. E. and Wang, X. (2006). 'Intended' and 'implemented' HRM: the missing linchpin in strategic human resource management research. *The International Journal of Human Resource Management*. 17(7), 1171–1189.

Knouse, S. B. (1995). *The Reward and Recognition Process in Total Quality Management*. Milwaukee, WI: Asq Press.

Kostova, T. and Roth, K. (2002). Adoption of an organizational practice by subsidiaries of multinational corporations: institutional and relational effects. *Academy of Management Journal*. 45(1), 215–233.

Kuhn, K. M. (2009). Compensation as a signal of organizational culture: the effects of advertising individual or collective incentives. *The International Journal of Human Resource Management*. 20(7), 1634–1648.

Larraza-Kintana, M., Wiseman, R. M., Gomez-Mejia, L. R. and Welbourne, T. M. (2007). Disentangling compensation and employment risks using the behavioral agency model. *Strategic Management Journal*. 28(10), 1001–1019.

Leonard, J. S. (1987). Carrots and sticks: pay, supervision and turnover. *Journal of Labor Economics*. 5(4), 136–152.

Long, R. J. and Shields, J. L. (2005). Performance pay in Canadian and Australian firms: a comparative study. *The International Journal of Human Resource Management*. 16(10), 1783–1811.

Manas, T. M. and Graham, M. D. (2003). *Creating a Total Rewards Strategy: a Toolkit for Designing Business-based Plans*. New York, NY: AMACOM.

March, J. G. and Simon, H. A. (1958). *Organizations*. New York: John Wiley and Sons, Inc.

Martin, G. and Beaumont, P. (1999). Co-ordination and control of human resource management in multinational firms: the case of CASHCO. *International Journal of Human Resource Management*. 10(1), 21–42.

McGraw, P. (2015). Changing patterns of compensation and benefits in multinational and Australian companies 1996–2009. *Asia Pacific Journal of Human Resources*. 53(1), 59–82.

Mhatre, A. (2012). Managing global employee benefits. *Pensions: An International Journal*. 17(4), 342–348.

Michailova, S. (2011). Contextualizing in international business research: why do we need more of it and how can we be better at it? *Scandinavian Journal of Management*. 27(1), 129–139.

Milkovich, G. T. (1988). A strategic perspective on compensation management. In Ferris, G. R. and Rowland, K. M. (eds.). *Research in Personnel and Human Resources Management* (Vol. 6, p. 444). Greenwich, CT: JAI Press.

Montemayor, E. F. (1996). Congruence between pay policy and competitive strategy in high-performing firms. *Journal of Management*. 22(6), 889–908.

Myloni, B., Harzing, A.-W. and Mirza, H. (2007). The effect of corporate-level organizational factors on the transfer of human resource management practices: European and US MNCs and their Greek subsidiaries. *The International Journal of Human Resource Management*. 18(12), 2057–2074.

Newman, J., Gerhart, B. and Milkovich, G. (2016). *Compensation* (12th ed.). New York, NY: McGraw-Hill Education.

O'Donnell, S. (1999). Compensation design as a tool for implementing foreign subsidiary strategy. *MIR: Management International Review*. 39(2), 149–165.

Pendleton, A., Poutsma, E., Brewster, C. and van Ommeren, J. (2002). Employee share ownership and profit-sharing in the European Union: incidence, company characteristics, and union representation. *Transfer: European Review of Labour and Research*, 8(1), 47–62.

Pfeffer, J. (1994). *Competitive Advantage Through People: Unleashing the Power of the Work Force*. Boston, MA: Harvard Business School Press.

Pfeifer, J. and Salancik, G. (1978). *The External Control of Companies: a Resource Dependence Perspective*. New York, NY: Harper & Row.

Porter, M. E. (1980). *Competitive Strategy: Techniques for Analyzing Industries and Competitors*. New York: Free Press.

Poutsma, E., Moerel, H. and Ligthart, P. E. (2015). Multinational enterprises: comparing performance-related pay between companies in Eastern and Western Europe. *Journal of Industrial Relations*. 57(2), 291–316.

Prince, N. R., Prince, J. B., Skousen, B. R. and Kabst, R. (2016). *Incentive pay configurations: bundle options and country-level adoption*. Paper presented at Evidence-based HRM: A Global Forum for Empirical Scholarship.

Pudelko, M. and Harzing, A. W. (2007). Country-of-origin, localization, or dominance effect? An empirical investigation of HRM practices in foreign subsidiaries. *Human Resource Management*. 46(4), 535–559.

Quintanilla, J. and Ferner, A. (2003). Multinationals and human resource management: between global convergence and national identity. *International Journal of Human Resource Management*. 14(3), 363–368.

Richbell, S., Brookes, M., Brewster, C. and Wood, G. (2011). Non-standard working time: an international and comparative analysis. *The International Journal of Human Resource Management*. 22(04), 945–962.

Rogovsky, N., Schuler, R. S. and Reynolds, C. (2000). How can national culture affect compensation practices of MNCs? *Global Focus*. 12(4), 35–42.

Rosenzweig, P. M. (2006). The dual logics behind international human resource management: pressures for global integration and local responsiveness. In Stahl, G. K. and Björkman, I. (eds.). *Handbook of Research in International Human Resource Management* (pp. 36–48). Northampton, MA: Edward Elgar Publishing.

Rosenzweig, P. M. and Nohria, N. (1994). Influences on human resource management practices In multinational corporations. *Journal of International Business Studies*. 25(2), 229–251.

Rubery, J. and Grimshaw, D. (2003). *The Organization of Employment: An International Perspective*. Basingstoke: Palgrave Macmillan.

Rynes, S. L. (1987). Compensation strategies for recruiting. *Topics in Total Compensation*. 2(2), 185.

Sayım, K. Z. (2010). Pushed or pulled? Transfer of reward management policies in MNCs. *The International Journal of Human Resource Management*. 21(14), 2631–2658.

Schuler, R. and Jackson, S. E. (2014). Human resource management and organizational effectiveness: yesterday and today. *Journal of Organizational Effectiveness: People and Performance*. 1(1), 35–55.

Schuler, R. and Rogovsky, N. (1998). Understanding compensation practice variations across firms: The impact of national culture. *Journal of International Business Studies*. 29(1), 159–177.

Singh, S., Mohamed, A. F. and Darwish, T. (2013). A comparative study of performance appraisals, incentives and rewards practices in domestic and multinational enterprises in the country of Brunei Darussalam. *The International Journal of Human Resource Management*. 24(19), 3577–3598.

Sparrow, P. (2004). International rewards systems: to converge or not to converge?. In Brewster, C. and Harris, H. (eds.). *International HRM: Contemporary Issues in Europe* (pp. 102–119). London, UK: Routledge.

Sveiby, K. E. (1997). *The New Organizational Wealth: Managing & Measuring Knowledge-based Assets*. San Francisco: Berrett-Koehler Publishers.

Tajfel, H. and Turner, J. C. (1979). An integrative theory of intergroup conflict. *The Social Psychology of Intergroup Relations*. 33(47).

Tarique, I., Briscoe, D. R. and Schuler, R. S. (2015). *International Human Resource Management: Policies and Practices for Multinational Enterprises*. New York, NY: Routledge.

Tayeb, M. H. (2005). *International Human Resource Management: a Multinational Company Perspective*. Oxford: Oxford University Press.

Taylor, S., Beechler, S. and Napier, N. (1996). Toward an integrative model of strategic international human resource management. *Academy of Management Review*. 21(4), 959–985.

Tosi, S. and Greckhamer, T. (2004). Culture and CEO compensation. *Organization Science*. 15, 657–670.

Traxler, F., Arrowsmith, J., Nergaard, K. and López-Rodó, J. M. M. (2008). Variable pay and collective bargaining: a cross-national comparison of the banking sector. *Economic & Industrial Democracy*. 29(3), 406–431.

Tsai, K.-H., Chou, C. and Chen, M.-Y. (2008). Does matching pay policy with innovation strategy really improve firm performance? An examination of technology-based service firms. *Personnel Review.* 37(3), 300–316.

Vora, D. and Kostova, T. (2007). A model of dual organizational identification in the context of the multinational enterprise. *Journal of Organizational Behavior.* 28(3), 327–350.

Whitley, R. (1992). *European Business Systems: Firms and Markets in Their National Contexts.* London, UK: Sage.

Wright, A. (2010). Culture and compensation – Unpicking the intricate relationship between reward and organizational culture. *Thunderbird International Business Review.* 52(3), 189–202.

Yanadori, Y. (2011). Paying both globally and locally: an examination of the compensation management of a US multinational finance firm in the Asia Pacific Region. *The International Journal of Human Resource Management.* 22(18), 3867–3887.

Yanadori, Y. (2014). Compensation and benefits in the global organisation. In Collings, D. Wood, G. and Caligiuri, P. M. (eds.). *The Routledge Companion to International Human Resource Management* (pp. 190–209). Abingdon, Oxon: Routledge.

Yanadori, Y. and Marler, J. H. (2006). Compensation strategy: does business strategy influence compensation in high-technology firms? *Strategic Management Journal.* 27(6), 559–570.

Ying Chang, Y., Wilkinson, A. J. and Mellahi, K. (2007). HRM strategies and MNCs from emerging economies in the UK. *European Business Review.* 19(5), 404–419.

Zeckhauser, R. J. and Pratt, J. W. (1985). *Principals and Agents: The Structure of Business.* Boston, MA: Harvard Business School Press.

Zhu, J. S. and Jack, R. (2017). Managerial mindset as the mechanism of the country-of-origin effect: evidence from Chinese multinational enterprises' approach to employer associations. *The International Journal of Human Resource Management.* 28(13), 1767–1785.

Zhu, J. S., Zhu, C. J. and De Cieri, H. (2014). Chinese MNCs' preparation for host-country labor relations: an exploration of country-of-origin effect. *Human Resource Management Journal.* 53(6), 947–965.

20

THE SOCIAL CONSTRUCTION OF VALUING WORK

Case cameos to inform practical understanding

Romain Daste

Introduction

At the core of reward management is evaluating work under an employment 'psychological' contract. This gives rise to the question of how to do so systematically in ways that will meet the expectations of parties to the employment relationship, including its external regulators.

In 1991, in their editorial for a special issue of *Human Resource Management Review*, Gupta and Jenkins (1991:91) state that job evaluation (hereafter JE) had been "accepted traditionally without question as the one right way to approach the design of compensation structures". And in the 2017 CIPD Reward Survey some 45% of respondents claim that JE continues to underpin their organizations' employment market-informed reward management arrangements. For the management consultant Alan Gibbons, JE constitutes "a 20th century millstone" that is "transforming itself into the 21st century's most powerful business tool" (Gibbons 2017).

> In the United States, decades of slavishly following market pay (and its 50th percentile holy grail) have now given way to a strong desire for structure and stability . . . In Europe, traditional equity-based internal reward structures can no longer ignore the real world's external pay market, characterised by a mobile, well-informed workforce who shun their parents' virtues of loyalty and patience. A pedestrian, myopic approach to rewards will not cut it with those whom we must engage with and motivate.
>
> *(Gibbons 2017)*

Back in 1991, Gupta and Jenkins offered their assessment of why JE had prevailed for so long: historically, JE approaches "fit well with the prevailing managerial styles" (op. cit.), and so empirical research concentrated on refining "mechanical and logistical details". But a 2017 survey of JE undertaken by eReward reports that high among concerns about the application of this approach to inform reward design is the 'poor understanding' among both employees and managers (eReward 2017). This appears to run contrary to increasing calls for reward management transparency – for example, proposals issued in 2017 by the UK government (BEIS 2017) related to overall corporate governance – and a need to ensure that outcomes from reward management and associated processes and interactions between participants are perceived as just, let alone compliant with the requirements of long-standing legislation requiring employees to receive 'equal pay for work of equal value' (HMSO 2010).

One conclusion that may be drawn from reflecting on these brief observations is that, to understand JE as a phenomenon in organizations, attention needs to be paid to the influence of *social construction*. In other words, it should be in accordance with the argument that everything known to human beings is formed through interaction in social settings. This should be the case even if its 'reality' becomes taken for granted, as though such knowledge has an existence independent from the circumstances including interaction between social actors in which it has been "developed, transmitted and maintained in social situations" (Berger and Luckmann 1966:15).

Gupta and Jenkins's (1991) observations that JE's longevity reflects its capacity to conform to managerial constructions of what legitimately should be the focus of work valuation procedures and outcomes serve as evidence in support of this contention. And even more starkly, even though separated by more than a quarter-century, the consultant's hyperbole about JE having shed its 'millstone' character to become a "powerful business tool" (Gibbons 2017). What do these forms of words say about the social agendas in play, and the interests in shaping the JE agenda on the part of key actors?

This chapter is informed by primary data assembled as a participant observer in three different organizations involved in programmes intended to revise and improve on the operation of their arrangements for valuing the work undertaken by their employees. The case studies presented below are analysed in accordance with the principles of social constructivist thinking, with the aim of distilling lessons to inform managerial practice in approaching and applying JE (and how academics study this aspect of reward management).

Allocating 'value' involves not only the technical process of 'sizing' jobs relative to one another within organizations, but also the 'politics' involved in the interplay between line managers, HRM specialists, employees and external interests such as shareholders in arriving at an evaluation. One that may be of a set of work tasks comprising a 'job', on the one hand, and, on the other hand, of the understandings intended to underpin evaluation – and concomitant reward determination – in respect of individuals and groups occupying the jobs being evaluated.

Three work valuation cases

The three cameo case studies described below (CC1, CC2 and CC3) have been selected experientially. In presenting them, there is no intention to suggest any empirical generalization, but the evidence may inform theoretical development in approaching JE as a socially constructed phenomenon. The purpose in presenting reflections from these three projects, in which the author has been a participant observer, is to explore some of the reward management 'choice and consequence' questions (Perkins et al. 2016) decision-makers encounter when considering a 'work value' – or JE – project to set (or re-set) their organization's reward management architecture. The reader is presented with a set of questions to bear in mind before implementing a JE programme, including mindfulness of the sociopolitical contexts within which JE and reward management are practised.

There are **three core** themes in play that should be borne in mind when reading the descriptions which follow. The first is that of managerial interventions that reflect aspirations different to those nominally associated with applying the 'science' of JE as an objective technique to evaluate the relative worth of jobs. They will instead engaging specialist input to legitimize a different agenda; that of controlling the costs of paying employees under existing reward management policies. The second is around technical complexity and transparency issues such that understanding to facilitate the legitimacy of JE and related reward management was constrained. The third is problems where organizational 'culture' sits uneasily with senior managerial aspirations to update reward management arrangements so as to balance cost control and 'talent retention'.

CC1: A large UK-located property and retail organization

This stock-market-listed organization is the UK's largest operator in the hospitality and related property management sector. It employs over 30,000 people, mainly based in the UK. Established for over one hundred years, CC1 has been through a number of 'modernization' programmes, including redefinitions of its corporate values. Despite this, the organization operates without centralized consistent values driving all business arms, i.e., commercial, customer services, HRM. The result is a set of rather abstract guiding principles. The connection between 'values' and 'pay solutions' has not been articulated.

At the start of the project CC1 was in the process of structurally 'digesting' a merger with a smaller operator, a move intended to provide it with strategic competitive advantage in the sector. The group was also going through a large-scale process of digitalization of its distribution and internal management information flows intended to enable real-time 'retail benchmarking' to competitors. Organized along traditional lines, the HR department was composed of disconnected subgroups aligned to revenue streams and brands, with little information system mutualization or coordination. Two principal information systems were in use across two geographical sites. Around fifty individuals contributed to the HR efforts, primarily in recruitment and training. Significant unplanned staff turnover meant there was a lack of in-house expertise, and the remaining internal reward specialists were simply mentally exhausted from having to deal with a slew of management complaints, a sense of unfairness, and a need for clarity around why/how pay methods were rationalized across the group company.

A top layer of a dozen subject-specific experts, all contracted as temporary in-house consultants, lead the largest specialized projects (employee relations, communications, reward) designed to address some of the macro-organizational issues resulting from both post-merger integration efforts and digitalization. All reporting lines converged to an HR director with significant experience as a full-time contributor to the organization's long-term plans in previous years, working to the CEO to coordinate reporting on progress in enactment of the change programme. The reward management stream of activity was nominally to create from scratch job descriptions to inform evaluation, and to address issues around salary market benchmarking, while tackling the costs of operating an inherited bonus scheme.

Whilst the size and diversity of the internal HR resource provided a sense that 'business as usual' and 'project work' were under control, several challenges quickly appeared, challenging resources available, exhausting incumbents' motivation and determination simply to 'crack on' with the tasks assigned to them. Fatigue, long hours and systemic complexities meant that not only were teams unstable, but they were also often lacking capability to deliver projects according to plan. Plans were constantly reviewed and recalibrated under the pressure of mounting costs and decreasing available time. In this context, the with a year of experience within the organization the group remuneration director was struggling in covering day-to-day pay and benefits activities: problems included delayed salary benchmarking, delayed monthly salary payments, inaccurate bonus calculations, inappropriate communication channels used to inform incumbents, and incorrect reporting to the corporate board members.

Despite this challenging context, the organization embarked on a mission to match the value of bonus payments more accurately to financial targets. Publicly recognised for his experience, the group remuneration director faced huge internal time and other resource pressures and limited leeway to step back and come up with a feasible plan to address bonus cost reduction.

The organization's chosen narrative underpinning a 'quick solution with a reliable approach' was a move to create a clear cut-off point between individuals occupying the largest roles and other incumbents with lower positions. That was the basis on which a JE programme was initiated.

CC1 managers believed that, once properly 'sized', jobs would be easier to categorize for bonus entitlement. However, the starting point was not th of a complete consensus with no one receiving bonuses, but instead a large group of incumbents receiving hardly any bonuses (due to very demanding performance criteria) and therefore unwilling to abandon bonus entitlements. New appointees were also promised bonuses through the recruitment process; a process that used out-of-date salary packages and internal benchmarks out of synch with the corporate intent to contain bonuses.

The 'valuing work' project was, in fact, approached with the intention of 'selectively containing variable pay entitlements', under an internal comparative lens, rather than a genuine 'fair pay' measure. Another factor influencing the outcome of the JE exercise was the absence of any coherent and centrally held job documentation. HR practitioners' reluctance to contribute to a large exercise of 'writing down what everybody knew already anyway' created a further barrier to action: how could an external consultant operating in-house have a sufficient mandate to order such a documentation exercise when the primary reason for the consultant's presence within the organization was to value work using JE methods? It was as though the exercise would 'magically' allocate a job size score to each job. The implicit reasoning around 'valuing work' was to 'scientifically', yet without any coherent and consistent 'facts', legitimize a job size score so that objective comparisons would enable a group of incumbent employees to become ineligible for a generous simplified bonus payout under existing policy.

In summary, under the auspices of these entanglements, the in-house consultant's role was to confirm that: (1) 'valuing work' could be done without job documentation; (2) that job documentation could be completed afterwards, once resource availability permitted it; and (3) the consultant should indirectly translate, correlate and confidently connect both 'valuing work' and 'bonus reduction'. In other words, rather than following a standardized JE protocol, starting with job documentation, then evaluation and, in turn, designing externally benchmarked reward packages the process was reverse-engineered to match time imperatives driven by organizational desires.

On the face of it, CC1's managerial goals were reasonable in principle: to construct an acceptable narrative for applying bonus entitlements differentially between employee populations, applying judgement to evaluate levels of skill, problem solving, and responsibility for each role. Several HR professionals internally were trained in the application of JE techniques. In practice, however, what was observed was action ignoring some of the prerequisites (including adequate, clear and approved documentation); in effect, colluding with an overarching aim managerially to 'deliver a score quickly'. Rather than challenging this distortion of what is intended to be fair comparative work valuing, the group remuneration director was directed to delegate to the in-house consultant application of the technical expertise, but without sufficient mandate to situate the programme within an overall reward change management framework – involving stakeholders in job description and communication to build support for the programme among those impacted by it. Within months, the internal HR community became suspicious of the actual reasons behind the evaluation and documentation, and organized protests amongst senior management levels to contribute to the derailment of the project. The latter became so obstructed with refusal to cooperate internally that a 'quick and dirty' completion was pushed, ahead of schedule and lacking any methodological foundations, and the in-house consultant involvement was interrupted.

CC2: A large international consumer goods company

This large UK stock market-listed beverages multinational employs 33,000 employees. In 2015, it replaced its entire team of reward specialists in 2015 under the general premise that 'internal experts' were 'too close' to the schemes, including the one covering share-based long-term incentives for executives, to provide adequate technical flexibility for a 'full revamp' if it was demanded by business conditions. The company was under external scrutiny from shareholders very keen to achieved a detailed understanding of the mechanisms by which all shares granted to the top executive team were vested, exercised or lapsed. In respect of this group, the focus was not much around the value of the job held or job size, but the valuation of the output created and corresponding share awards.

CC2 set the following desired objectives for the project:

1   Share awards to be accompanied by a de-accelerated vesting and exercise timetable in order to allow more effective performance review matched to corporate financial outcomes;
2   Preparation of an annual report, called the 'Directors' Remuneration Report' (DRR), required to match the level of transparency demanded by shareholders. The production of the report had to be underpinned by accurate data, manipulated in such ways that could be used to set a benchmark for the following year's reporting cycle.

However, there were tensions between these objectives, shaped by shareholders' demands, and the capacity of CC2's reward expertise to deliver them given a majority of those involved in supporting operation of the reward management architecture had left the organization.

One concern was that the company's reward schemes had reached such a level of complexity that they were virtually impossible to communicate without becoming ensnared in historical award outcomes. A thick layer of synonyms was used to described essentially the same options for decisions made by executives before exercise; the accounting and public reporting in the DRR had more footnotes than actual clear figures. Two analysts contracted-in for the project were briefed on a weekly basis, but without receiving fully documented access to historical data. And interacting with a corporate audit body (two individuals) expected to receive the reporting conclusions for assessment despite privately confessing they could 'hardly dive into the details' due to limited understanding of past practices.

A total of seven individuals were involved in the process of writing the DRR yet fewer than half of them had participated in the previous year's cycle. On top of the internal team, a group representing shareholders (ten people) would review the share awards accounting figures, plus the senior remuneration team (three), the finance team (two people) plus the five executive leaders themselves (i.e., those receiving the awards). All groups could allegedly claim to support the transparency goal, yet each group had a different agenda: 'accuracy' for the auditors; 'financial consistency' for the finance team; 'simplicity and consistency with historical practices' for the reward contractors; 'manageability' for the senior remuneration directors; 'fairness' for the share-holder group; and 'maximization' for the share award recipients.

Corporate reward practitioners may well be familiar with such layers of complexity, which add more opacity than transparency. One might speculate, however, that such 'organizational politics' set the scene for strained relations between the specialists and some other stakeholders in valuing corporate executives. Once again corporate 'panic' may have set in during the finalization of the report's production. The process was then assumed by a senior director resourced by a temporary contracted team called in eight weeks earlier, then dismissed along with the corporate memory that might have been built up.

CC3: A not-for-profit/charitable organization focused on developing countries

This large international non-governmental organization has a presence in Africa, Asia and South America, employing 10,000 people, and has been growing following successful campaigns to secure donations. Its managerial structure has expanded in order to coordinate both at horizontal (operational) levels, which have been diversifying, and also vertical management of the organization reporting to a senior group of directors. One project deliverable was to report to the executive board, in turn reporting to trustees who represent donors. Transparency, in governance and uses of charitable funds, was expected across all layers of resource deployments to tackle social and health issues across countries during conflicts or hit by natural disasters, with limited forecasting being available given the nature of the activities the charity has to respond to in real time. With international experts being deployed on longer secondment contracts came the desire to selectively allocate limited relocation and 'hardship' allowances based on job levels, which were to be defined. The evaluation of targeted roles represented in itself an important departure from a traditional culture of 'service for the public good', to a much more 'performance-related' philosophy, serving both commercial governance imperatives, expertise retention and needs for governance transparency, equal treatment, and perceived as well as actual fairness in enabling staff rotations/replacements.

Internal conflicts emerged between the top executive group keen to protect existing reward packages awarded based on length of service, donors keen to explore in detail how resources were used, and lower managerial levels keen to award salary increases to recognise staff whose behaviour was seen to model service of the charity cause. Such ideological divisions (the organizational politics) had the effect of slowing down progress in consensus building around the most appropriate method to be used for job evaluation. The social factors in play in CC3 included historical recognition of exceptional individuals fighting for humanitarian causes who have slowly grown up within the organization, HR representatives keen to gain tools to exercise greater control over underperforming role incumbents internally, and donors seeing an opportunity through work evaluations to better comprehend the roles played by employees, their impact, and thus worth to external donor causes. The absence of relative comparators to assess roles fed the required opacity for internal groups to exercise counter-influence, under the guise of moral duty and fair recognition principles, to such an extent that any evaluation was quickly either questioned, ignored, or seen as 'dangerous' and reported to trade union representatives.

Various initiatives born in the charity sector may be regarded as meritorious for sensitivity to both equal pay and more socially conscious practices for general resource usage. And yet in a reality check derived from experience in this case the organization gives rise to a judgement that 'schizophrenic' definitions become evident as to balancing attempted objectivity in approaches to jobs being evaluated, and institutionalised expectations about the influence of, e.g., length of services or 'social meritocracy' in terms of perceived contribution to corporate mission. Parameters that traditionally are external to processes for measuring and scoring jobs in terms of relative organizational value.

One conclusion from the situation observed in CC3 is a need to sensitize the process contextualized to the sector: for work value/reward analysts to spend time in in-depth dialogue with key stakeholders. In this case, the key stakeholders included: a new CEO wishing to promote social justice whilst demonstrating internal transparency; a group HR director keen to insert a significant dose of 'performance management spirit' across the charity's workforce; and the most experienced managing director, publicly recognised for successfully conducting several complex, large-scale humanitarian campaigns across countries in desperate situations, yet anxious to protect the status quo regarding valuing work, for ideological and personal network reasons. Thus, the value of work roles may be understood as less than applying a pseudo-scientific template experientially derived from other sectors, and more making best efforts to work with the grain of socially constructing work roles and the basis by which consensus may be arrived at factoring-in multiple, sometimes completing aspirations – needing to arrive at a compromise that could none the less pass scrutiny in terms of meeting the spirit as well as the letter of the law in terms of equal pay for work of equal value, and encouraging the right balance between the efficient application of compassionate resources both in challenging circumstances in the field as well as in less environmentally demanding corporate settings with a suitable performance ethos.

In practice, in CC3 sufficient job documentation was gathered and a clear timescale for delivery was publicly negotiated across stakeholder groups, yet evaluations of top roles were never conducted. Which made the process of cascading evaluation scores vertically throughout the whole organization to say the least challenging for the project analysts.

Suggest influences from the social context for work valuation

At CC1, an unvarnished description of its approach to reward management is one of a combination of confusion, even panic – emerging as 'we will pay whatever is necessary in order for the problems to disappear'.

At CC2 a much more thorough approach was evident, with more methodical – even microscopic – analysis. The espoused aspiration was for transparent senior role valuations linking forward to share-based reward and accounting for it, but in practice only those expert in the nuances of reward management could understand the details of the DRR. The huge levels of complexity placed opacity in tension with espoused transparency aims to satisfy shareholder demands.

At CC3, senior management wanted to deal with practical employment issues: retention and motivation problems. These aims were compromised by the politics manifested in long meetings and group debates, but with little attention to methodical application of objective processes. Externally sourced expert input was regarded as a 'toolbox'; the process was emergent and negotiated rather than coherently planned. The 'performance-related pay' ambition was seen as a solution to retention, low morale and pay inequality issues, with JE meant to act as a foundation. But the prevailing 'charitable' or 'public service' organizational culture was likely to have frustrated implementation of any work value attribution method drawing on private sector ideology.

In terms of outcomes, CC1 ran out of budget for the exercise, resulting in the abandonment of the whole project despite the mechanics of JE having been completed. For CC2 the project was brought to an abrupt end, leaving consequential tasks redistributed internally among a group of senior insiders. At CC3, yet again, the project was interrupted due to political disagreements between the various stakeholders.

Conclusions and action pointers

'Reading between the lines': The mechanics and political environments in place to facilitate the valuation of roles is the central focus of this chapter. The contribution is based on an experiential and reflexive methodology to craft case cameos that contain lessons for academic research. Forces surfaced in the cameos are often hidden, covered, for example, by sophisticated linguistic usage under the guise of 'best practice' translated and retranslated several times by external sources of expert input motivated to achieve 'client satisfaction' as well as institutional norms and values that may in practice dilute or frustrate outcomes. It may also inform practitioners assessing how the process of valuing work may need to be approached mindful of organizational specificity.

Connections between academic commentary and the hiring-in of consultants: The academic world is regularly challenged to demonstrate 'impact' on delivery and the relevance of theory, and too often these do not translate visibly through JE processes and resulting reward management outcomes. The core message from the material presented in this chapter is that to navigate around real people in real organizational settings JE, or, more broadly, work value analysts need access not only to normative theories around the valuation of work and roles. But to theories to assist them, and the managements they strive to assist, in balancing corporate rhetoric that can insinuate unnecessary opacity into processes potentially frustrating the completion of JE projects with an understanding of the unique *social* circumstances needing to be included by professional 'facilitators' between the interested parties. Outcomes may fall short of normative 'perfection', but may achieve a better balance accounting for organizational culture and key actors.

Practical considerations: The normative approaches around following objective criteria to allocate an evaluation score to a job, for instance, are highly dependent on access to clear job documentation. Inadequate access to such documentation or time to secure it risks undermining legitimacy where stakeholders suspect 'political forces' have altered outcomes. For the practitioner undertaking JE, it is essential to have a careful assessment of the resources available. This includes bringing to the surface potential gaps between actual resources and what is needed for successful completion, as well as historical factors. Those entering an organization to undertake work valuation need to add to their technical armoury means by which swiftly to understand and mitigate for organizational politics, bearing in mind potential risks around group interactions within organizations, attempts to exercise influence and power, including to shape perceived problems, underpinned by the capacity to hire and fire the consultant. Questions to consider might include does the organization operate to a set of rules that might not be relevant for a sectoral comparator? Can indications around comparative staff subsets be collected to understand their likely organizational weight of influence and direct connectivity to issues at stake?

References

BEIS. (2017). *Corporate Governance Reform: Government Response.* Available at: www.gov.uk/government/consultations/corporate-governance-reform, accessed on November 20, 2017.

Berger, P. and Luckmann, T. (1966). *The Social Construction of Reality: A Treatise in the Sociology of Knowledge.* London: Penguin.

eReward. (2017). Job Evaluation in the UK – initial survey findings: eReward bites 427 (email distribution, 20 October 2017).

Gibbons, A. (2017). 'The amazing renaissance of job evaluation: how a 20th century millstone is transforming itself into the 21st century's most powerful business tool' – presentation to 11th e-reward annual conference. Available at: www.therewardpractice.com/news/amazing-renaissance-job-evaluation/, accessed on 8, November 2017.

Gupta, N. and Jenkins, G. D. (1991). Job evaluation: an overview. *Human Resources Management Review.* 1(1), 91–95.

HMSO. (2010). *Equality Act 2010.* London: Her Majesty's Stationery Office.

Perkins, S. J., White, G., and Jones, S. (2016) *Reward Management: Alternatives, Consequences and Contexts.* London: CIPD Publishing.

21

MINDING THE GAP IN REWARD MANAGEMENT

The academic–practitioner divide

Marie Bailey

Introduction

The case study presented in this chapter provides an empirical base upon which is developed a broader academic narrative, in support of embracing an evidence-based approach. The chapter looks more widely at the role practitioners and researchers play and the competing forces that restrict the use of an evidence-based approach. Consideration is also given to the ways in which both interested parties can take practical steps to ensure decision-making in reward management is embedded in scientific theory, rather than unjustified claims and assumptions.

Before advancing the case for evidence-based practice, it should be noted that, writing as both an HRM practitioner and academic, in parts the chapter takes on a more personal tone. For this I make little apology, since many of the frustrations born of working on both sides of the practitioner–academic divide have been personally witnessed. Indeed, it is through these experiences that the argument for taking an evidence-based approach in reward and HR management has become all the more compelling. To some extent, this chapter acts as a call to arms to fellow academics and practitioners, but before developing this argument, we begin with a summary of NetTech and their approach to reward interventions.

Tunnel vision at NetTech

It took three years to launch NetTech's new pay framework. Specialist reward teams were rounded up. Jobs were evaluated and regraded. Pay bands were recalculated. The purpose of the exercise was to create accountability and transparency across the pay framework and to create a simplified process for setting and determining pay progression.

The decision to design a more transparent and equal pay framework across this UK-based organization was long overdue. In some cases, postholders were paid in excess of £10,000 more per annum to undertake the same role in the same location. Pay bands across the group were not always aligned, causing a range of problems for both managers and employees, in what was meant to be a templated organizational structure. Justifying excesses in one part of the organization whilst providing explanations as to why expanding job roles elsewhere were apparently 'pay-neutral' was no easy task, and it did little to improve employee morale in an organization whose key message was "do more with less".

Pay restructuring is a difficult process in any organization, not least because of the controversies and sensitivities surrounding it. The monetary values placed upon someone's worth to an organization can provoke robust debate and argument both in the workplace (see Daste, this volume) and more widely amongst academics and philosophers. Employees will always view their pay as a reflection of their value, rather than that of their role. Most of us believe we are worth more. In the case of NetTech, the final restructure prompted a number of appeals – both individually and collectively – demonstrating that the real work of embedding a new pay system had only just begun.

Whilst the intention to create a fair and transparent pay structure was to be applauded, the process for assessing each role was perhaps less clear. Communication around the change and how pay grades had been arrived at was slow and patchy. Whilst top-end salaries were frozen in order to allow the lower end of the pay band to catch up, the results of the job evaluation exercise did not always accurately reflect the roles being undertaken. There seemed little justification for some of the decisions made and no sign of any evidence to support them. Predictably, employee 'buy-in' to the new model was not forthcoming and dialogue between the trade unions, individual workers and management dragged on long past the scheduled deadlines. Naturally, there were winners and losers.

As with many organizations, NetTech often took its lead from others in the field (see also Sahakiants and Festing, this volume). What appeared to work elsewhere seemed to provide all the necessary evidence required to adopt a similar strategy at home. What was deemed 'best practice' somewhere else was seen as a safe solution at NetTech.

At the same time, the new pay framework was rolled out, the reward team sought to design a new employee engagement survey. This biennial process for testing the temperature of staff attitudes had always produced mixed results, depending upon where in the company individuals were based. Generally speaking, those on the 'coalface' of NetTech were less satisfied than those based in either regional hubs or head office. Survey response rates were also far fewer amongst staff members located further away from NetTech's central offices. Previous surveys had taught NetTech that there was room for improvement in assessing staff attitudes and the forthcoming survey provided a good opportunity to review the existing approach.

As a member of the human resources team – qualified as both an academic and practitioner – I advised the reward team on the development of the new survey. This seemed like the perfect occasion to bring together colleagues from both quarters of the practitioner and researcher divide and apply theory to practice. The organization would benefit from delivering a survey that was underpinned by robust, evidence-based research. It would produce well-informed outcomes, strengthen trust in the process and not simply pay lip service to employee voice. It would not cause the same complexity of issues that the pay framework had received. Conversely, academic insights would directly inform and shape employee engagement practices.

Yet despite the initial enthusiasm from both sides to collaborate, the bid to design and launch the new employee engagement survey was eventually won by a consultancy firm familiar to the business. In the end, the evidence-based option was ruled out in favour of an 'off-the-shelf' solution. This was apparently the easiest and quickest option.

This felt hugely frustrating and a missed opportunity for all. NetTech had failed to see the benefit of engaging in a new approach and the academics involved had fallen short in convincing the organization of the benefits. Sadly, NetTech are not alone, since much of the academic and broader HRM debates demonstrate the persistence of the gap between academic research and professional practice (Rynes et al. 2007; Rousseau 2006). As Bevan (2006) points out, ad hoc, piecemeal decision-making is often the primary force in strategy and policy making. But the role of the academic also requires scrutiny if business and management research is to have an impact beyond higher education circles (Rynes et al. 2007). The responsibility of both practitioner and academic to work together to address these issues is considered further on in the chapter, but in the first instance we look at the role of evidence-based practice and the part it plays in creating better-informed managers and decision-making.

Providing a platform for evidence-based practice in management

Evidence-based practice emerged in the 1990s and quickly became well-established in medical science and the treatment of patients. Since then, the practice has been extended effectively to the fields of nursing and social policy (Briner et al. 2009). However, its use in management and HRM is less common, since its application in the business world has been a more recent development (Barends et al. 2017).

Briner et al. (2009:19) define evidence-based management as:

> making decisions through the conscientious, explicit and judicious use of four sources of information: practitioner expertise and judgement, evidence from the local context, a critical evaluation of the best research evidence and the perspectives of those people who might be affected by the decision.

From this, it is suggested that a more favourable solution will emerge. Embedding management practices in fact rather than fads should produce a more valid and satisfactory outcome. Rather than assuming something has worked, an evidence-based approach allows practitioners to understand better and to evaluate the true outcomes of their practices (Kearns 1995).

In an age of big data and analytics, embracing evidence-based practice to help provide the answers might seem a more logical option. Unfortunately, the literature suggests that managers rarely consult academic journals or take on board scientific evidence when making decisions (Bartunek and Rynes 2014; Gopinath and Hoffman 1995; Rousseau 2006). In his article on the role of academic research in HRM, Guest (2007) highlights that the UK's most widely read periodical for practitioners – *People Management* – which is distributed to the members of the professional body, the Chartered Institute of Personnel and Development (CIPD) – has moved towards a more magazine-style publication, rather than showcasing new research in the discipline. Whilst the more recent addition to the newsstand – *Work* – also published by the CIPD – has made some attempt to bridge this gap, its distribution only to the fellows of the Chartered Institute, means access is limited and therefore its impact is less widespread.

As Guest (2007) points out, communication between the academic and practice-led communities is an age-old problem that transcends the scientific disciplines. Rynes et al. (2007) remind us that the lack of research-supported practice within the wider HRM context is not a new phenomenon and that the recognition of these 'separate worlds' is well reported (Straus et al. 2005; Pfeffer and Sutton 2006).

On an anecdotal level, a recent discussion with a group of consultants underlined how frequently ad hoc business decision-making takes place in the workplace. Regular first-hand witnesses to the decision-making process believe that leaders are more likely to base their decisions on impulse or convenience, rather than on rational evidence and fact. Going with gut instinct over scientific evidence is, of course, well documented within the academic literature (Barends et al. 2017; Armstrong et al. 2011; Bevan 2006; Kearns 1995).

The use of evidence-based practice is particularly absent within reward management and a scan of the existing research field provides a limited number of empirical studies of evidence-based reward management (Armstrong et al. 2011; Rousseau 2006). However, in a prominent study of pay and grading frameworks carried out in the UK, it was concluded that limited evaluation of the process took place and decision-making was largely based on feeling rather than fact. As a result, managers were often unconvinced by the established practices and outcomes (Corby et al. 2006). In the US, similar research undertaken by Scott et al. (2006) found that there was limited evidence for the adoption of reward strategies, and practices were rarely evaluated once implemented.

Where investment in human capital and reward is so closely aligned to the overall performance and success of a business, it seems remarkable that an evidence-based approach to reward management remains so low. Armstrong et al.'s (2011) study of reward management found that just under half of organizations surveyed undertook a full evaluation of their pay policies. Those that did invest in this process did so because they recognised the importance in evaluating the value for money their reward strategies produced.

In short, whilst a minority of organizations are engaging in evidence-based practice, the majority are not. This suggests that there are barriers in place that are in need of removal. Some of these constraints are analysed below through the prism of both the practitioner and the researcher.

Barriers to practice: the practitioner

For NetTech, it was speed and convenience that were the deciding factors in their choice of consultancy firm to produce their staff engagement survey. These reasons are commonly cited throughout the existing debates (Sanders et al. 2008; Guest 2007, Guest and King 2004; Rynes et al. 2007). Pressures on managers to juggle deadlines and meet the demands of their team and senior management mean that many do not possess the luxury of time to give to analysing data. The 'off-the-shelf' approach provides a quick fix and a short circuit to delivering on time. In the case of NetTech, the priority was 'doing' instead of 'thinking' and unfortunately this meant that mistakes were often repeated.

There is also a tendency for practitioners to follow in the well-trodden footsteps of other organizations. Once again, the NetTech study demonstrates how influential existing pay strategies in operation elsewhere can be and how attractive the 'one-size-fits-all' approach really is to managers. Most students of HRM with a modest knowledge of strategic management are able to put forward a relatively robust argument for not always adopting a universal mechanism when it comes to crafting policies. However, the desire to adopt what others are doing often feels like the safer option. A good example of this is the HRM Business Partnering model (Ulrich 1997). Within NetTech, the adoption of this approach to structuring people management – some 25 years or more after its inception – was readily embraced. Yet, in practice, operating as an HR function head under the 'three-legged stool' framework felt at times more like a clumsily adapted 'three-and-a-half-legged' version of the model. In essence, the structure did not suit NetTech's organization because it did not take account of either the sector, or the history or culture of the company. The pieces in the jigsaw did not fit, but so-called 'best practice' won the day and the HR team muddled along.

Scepticism around the use of data can also act as a barrier to evidence-based practice. Within reward management, managers query the cause and effect of the variables tested. Will a particular input, such as a change in the pay framework, produce a desired outcome? And how can we isolate these variables and be sure that it is these that are taking effect? Studies by both Armstrong et al. (2011) and Kessler and Purcell (1992) underline the difficulties in separating out the data to directly link inputs with output. Of course, this issue appears to chime with the perennial debate on the impact of HR more generally. In 2015, KPMG reported that one in five C-suite executives still struggle to understand the value of the HR function (KPMG 2015). This report was written in collaboration with senior practitioners and academics and it demonstrates that making the business case for HR and showcasing its capabilities has never been more important. Whilst some level of scepticism could be regarded as healthy, ignoring the data could prevent strengthening the credibility and progress of HR.

Earlier in the chapter it was mentioned that only a few practitioners tend to read academic journals (Guest 2007; Rynes et al. 2007). Barends et al's (2017) study reinforces this, but also suggests that access goes beyond the physical possession and availability of journal articles. The stylistic presentation of papers can equally hinder the impact of research. Having already established that time often constrains a practitioner's opportunity to engage in research, the use of verbose language and the complex presentation of findings can also alienate readers. This was evident at NetTech, where practitioners often shied away from reading theoretical and lengthy research papers. Where there was appetite for accessing these kinds of studies, this tended to be amongst colleagues who were keen to progress or amongst co-workers who had recently undertaken postgraduate training in HRM.

Barriers to practice: the researcher

Of course, it would be unfair to lay the blame solely at the door of reward and HR practitioners. Whilst they may not readily seek out answers underpinned by evidence, the academic community also has its part to play in the success of promoting evidence-based practice. On more than one occasion during my own career there have been opportunities to bring researchers and practitioners together to collaborate and engage in applied research. However, the intended outcomes from such interactions have not always been mutually beneficial and it has been difficult to find common ground.

More often, the two parties follow parallel paths because their ambitions are not aligned. If practitioners feel the pressure of work deadlines, then academics are constrained by the pressures of the Research Excellence Framework (REF). Despite the growing importance of impact case studies within the REF, the necessity to play an active part in the research cycle and to put institutional priorities before wider knowledge exchange seems to remain entrenched within the system. It is perhaps unfair to point the finger at individual researchers, eager to make their way in the world, but it does bring into question on a broader scale how competing structural pressures can have an effect on the uptake of collaborative research and evidence-based practice.

Conversely, those who seek to remain impactful and relevant to the wider discipline run the risk of 'dumbing down' in order to influence management decision-making (Neil et al. 2001). By following the fads and fashions and attempting to engage with a wider audience, academics perhaps lose sight of the evidence-based approach. Popularity amongst practitioners must not come at the price of rigorous research. There has to be a balance between being relevant and being robust. This point also extends to how research is presented. Whilst journal articles may be hard for practitioners to translate, oversimplifying the research may mean that the essence of the data is lost and the outcomes overly reductive. Communication to a wider audience is key; but not at the expense of the quality of the research itself. It is unlikely a lifetime's work can be conveyed in a Tweet.

As Rousseau (2006) points out, it is in the classroom where most academics first come into contact with the future leaders of industry and it is here where first impressions are made and indeed count. How reward management and HRM is taught plays a large part in how research is perceived and how individuals respond to it. Those academics engaged in both the teaching and the researching of the subject act as ambassadors for evidence-based practice and the relative value placed on it by those students who eventually become decision-makers. It is therefore the role of academics to embrace this opportunity and effectively communicate the importance and use of data in this setting. Moreover, strong relationships built in the classroom will transport to the workplace and evolve over a lifetime, helping to overcome the issue of access to the field. [Editor's note: *As it happens, we have tried to model such behaviour in compiling this volume: several authors writing from a practitioner vantage point are former students of the editorial team.*]

The divergence between academic researcher and practitioner creates a 'lose–lose' situation for all – particularly for those on the receiving end of ill-conceived reward and HR strategies. When it comes to decision-making, practitioners may be guilty of choosing the most expedient and safe option, but academics are also guilty of keeping within the comfort zone of their own institutions. Newly built open-plan business schools may have replaced the ivory towers of academe, but they have not necessarily facilitated greater collaboration. Indeed, the competing forces at large have stifled a more applied, interdisciplinary approach. So how can evidence-based practice in reward and HR management be encouraged? What interventions can be staged to ensure both worlds collide to create a more powerful enabler in management decision-making? The next section puts forward some options worthy of consideration.

Bridging the gap between theory and practice

Having observed colleagues from across the divide in their natural habitat, it is evident that more can be done to ensure good research informs management decision-making. Both practitioners and researchers can be more proactive in bringing evidence-based practice to life in reward and HR management and making sure research shapes practice.

Firstly, education is key. Earlier in the chapter, the role academics play in the classroom was touched upon and this is one space where all tutors can promote the benefits of evidence-based practice. Not only does this feed enquiring minds and invite them in to the world of research, but it also demonstrates the relevance and impact of taking an evidence-based approach in achieving organizational success. In order for this to be effective, two-way interactive dialogue between the student and the tutor must be nurtured. Experience and expertise both play a critical part in shaping practice. Therefore, in order to achieve better outcomes, the research findings must be measured alongside the students' experiences of practice.

It is through this kind of dialogue that academics will begin to understand and unpack the types of challenges facing practitioners. This will then allow researchers to adapt their own research agendas and to focus on actual rather than presumed management issues. Practitioners (often students of HRM) must, of course, be willing to discuss and share information in order for this repositioning to take place. Greater openness will create stronger synergies and develop more effective, evidence-based solutions.

Indeed, gaps will only be bridged if greater effort is placed on filling them and for this to occur both partners must look to grow stronger and more complex networks. This means reaching out to existing platforms both physically and virtually, and learning to build new channels through which convergence can take place. Finding common ground is key to ensuring that these relationships evolve and create opportunities that are mutually beneficial. These networks should also extend to the wider business community and professional groups. It is this dynamic that will be the catalyst for greater collaboration and thus better understanding.

Having established that academic journals do not provide an effective cross-over from research into practice, rather than change the existing formula, there is scope for adopting a more multichannelled approach and expanding the routes through which research evidence is disseminated and recognised. Greater circulation of publications – such as the CIPD's *Work* – or better use of social media platforms to distribute new findings in a more user-friendly context – may increase engagement amongst practitioners. Understanding the identity of the key influencers, and where they exist in the virtual world, is vital if evidence-based practice is to be adopted.

Of course, many of these solutions have one theme in common – communication. For there to be a better use of evidence-based practice in reward and HR management, both parties need to communicate effectively and learn how to find a mutual language through which to engage. This requires researchers and practitioners to understand the priorities of each other and establish how – collaboratively – these outcomes can be achieved. If academic research is to play a much greater role in shaping reward practice, then academics and practitioners need to work towards shared end goals.

Within the academic community, this may require shifting the agenda – away from individual research outputs and embracing a more interdisciplinary approach. Of course, this also requires there to be further progress made in redefining research aims at an institutional level. In short, improvements in communication across interested stakeholders needs to be addressed – underpinned by a shift in cultures. The NetTech case study demonstrates how adopting a path-dependency culture can influence decision-making both in terms of the staff survey and in the construction of a new pay framework. Short-circuiting the process and sticking with tried-and-tested methods tends to produce the same sorts of outcomes and, in the end, undermines the effectiveness of decision-making and reward strategies (Armstrong et al. 2011).

Conclusion

The gap between theory and practice and the lack of an evidence-based approach in reward management and HRM more broadly considered, has been examined through the prism of NetTech. From the discussion, the parallel paths down which practitioners and academic researchers travel have been identified. Having established the void in evidence-based practice, the question remains whether – as practitioners and academics – we mind the gap in reward management. It is difficult to understand the benefits of bridging the gap if neither party has ever experienced the impact of evidence-based practice, but it feels safe to conclude that practitioners and researchers are missing out. More importantly, the health and effectiveness of reward management is much poorer for its lack of popularity.

Having outlined the competing agendas and priorities placed on both practitioners and academic researchers, it is clear that a varying number of constraints play their part in creating this divergence. Lack of time, understanding and information, along with a lack of mutual interests and common language, all combine to impede the positive impact evidence-based practice could have on reward practices and on improved decision-making.

Of course, as the chapter shows, there are ways in which both practitioners and researchers can play a more active part in ensuring the gap is narrowed and reward management practices are embedded in scientific fact rather than assumption. Communication across both groups needs to be effective and there must be a greater willingness to reach out and to develop mutual interests. Compromises must be made and collective ambitions must rise above individual gains. For evidence-based practice to really take effect, critical mass needs to gather momentum at both the local and institutional level.

As a practitioner and academic, I have witnessed – first-hand – the frustrations of being on both sides of the divide and observed the impact of not engaging in evidence-based practice. The choice to embrace or avoid it is not a binary one and the opportunity it provides to strengthen and improve reward and HRM frameworks is limitless. If we are prepared to open our minds – and our hearts – then we stand a much better chance of closing the gap and creating a powerful tool for improving practice.

References

Armstrong, M., Brown, D. and Reilly, D. (2011). Increasing the effectiveness of reward management: an evidence-based approach. *Employee Relations.* 33(2), 106–120.

Bartunek, J. M. and Rynes, S. L. (2014). Academics and practitioners are alike and unalike: the paradoxes of academic–practitioner relationships. *Journal of Management.* 40(5), 1181–1201.

Barends, E., Villanueva, J., Rousseau, D. M., Briner, R. B., Jepsen, D. M., Houghton, E. and Have, S. (2017). Managerial attitudes and perceived barriers regarding evidence-based practice: an international survey. *PLoS ONE.* 12(10), 1–15.

Bevan, S. (2006). *New Realism in Reward Strategy.* Stockport: e-reward.

Briner, R. B., Denyer, D. and Rousseau, D. M. (2009). Evidence-based management: concept clean-up time? *Academy of Management Perspectives.* 23(4), 19–32.

Corby, S. White, G. and Stanworth, C. (2006). No news is good news? Evaluating new pay systems. *Human Resource Management Journal.* 15(1), 4–24.

Gopinath, C., and Hoffman R. C. (1995). The relevance of strategy research: practitioner and academic viewpoints. *Journal of Management Studies.* 35(5), 575–594.

Guest, D. E. (2007). Don't shoot the messenger: a wake-up call for academics. *Academy of Management Journal.* 50(5), 1020–1026.

Guest, D. E. and King, Z. M. E. (2004). Power, innovation and problem-solving: The personnel managers' three steps to heaven? *Journal of Management Studies.* 41, 401–423.

Kearns, P. (1995). *Measuring Human Resources and the Impact on Bottom Line Improvements.* Hitchin: Technical Communications (Publishing). Ltd.

Kessler, I. and Purcell, J. (1992). Performance-related pay: objectives and application. *Human Resource Management Journal.* 2(3), 16–33.

KPMG (2015). *Evidence-based HR: The Bridge Between Your People and Delivering Business Strategy.* KPMG International.

Neil, A., Herriot, P. and Hodgkinson, G. P. (2001). The practitioner–researcher divide in industrial, work and organizational (IWO). psychology: where are we now, and where do we go from here?. *Journal of Occupational and Organizational Psychology.* 74, 391–411.

Pfeffer, J. and Sutton, R. I. (2006). Evidence-based management. *Harvard Business Review,* January, 62–74.

Rousseau, D. M. (2006). Is there such a thing as "evidence-based management"?. *Academy of Management Review.* 31(2), 256–269.

Rynes, S. L., Giluk, T. L. and Brown, K. G. (2007). The very separate worlds of academic and practitioner periodicals in human resource management: implications for evidence-based management. *Academy of Management Journal.* 50(5), 987–1008.

Sanders, K., van Riemsdijk, M. and Groen B. (2008). The gap between research and practice: a replication study on the HR professionals' beliefs about effective human resource practices. *The International Journal of Human Resource Management.* 19(10), 1976.

Scott, D., McMullen, T. D. and Sperling, R.S. (2006). Evaluating pay program effectiveness: a national survey of compensation professionals. *WorldatWork.* 15(3), 47–53.

Straus, S. E., Richardson, W. S., Glasziou, P. and Haynes, R. B. (2005). *Evidence-based Medicine: How to Practice and Teach EBM* (3rd ed.). Edinburgh: Elsevier.

Ulrich, D. (1997). *Human Resource Champions: the Next Agenda for Adding Value and Delivering Results.* Boston, MA: Harvard Business School Press.

22

THE RISKY BUSINESS OF REWARDING FOR PERFORMANCE[1]

Jonathan Trevor

Few managers in firms I work with are completely happy about how they reward their people. Attracting valuable talent, engaging staff and securing positive behaviour remains as challenging as ever. Worse still, reward is often blamed for misdirected employee effort, dysfunctional behaviour, disengagement and energy-sapping conflict. These firms, like the clear majority across industry, reward their people based on performance.

For decades, a plethora of books, articles and consultants' reports have espoused the bottom-line benefits of using reward for performance to align employees' financial interests with those of their employer. Firms have rushed to embrace the unitarist logic of reward for performance for all sections of the workforce, not just executives. A 2013 survey of more than 350 publicly traded companies in the US revealed that nearly all (99%) use some form of short-term incentive plan for their broad-based employee population (WorldatWork 2013). The proportion of UK organizations in 2013 operating performance-related reward, incentive and recognition schemes was 77% in private sector services, and as high as 92% in very large and multinational organizations (CIPD 2013). The consultancy, Towers Watson, puts the figure even higher, with 94% of organizations using some form of annual bonus or short-term cash incentive (Towers Watson 2014). Individual performance is the most important criterion for determining base pay progression for the majority (74%) of companies, and individual bonuses the most prevalent form of financial incentive (66%), in the latest survey of UK reward management practice by the Chartered Institute of Personnel and Development (CIPD 2017). Reward is no longer simply the cost of hiring necessary labour as it once was. It is a management tool for securing strategically valuable employee outcomes by attracting key talent, fostering desirable behaviour and maximizing performance. Reward for performance *is* the dominant logic of how firms remunerate their people in the contemporary workplace.

Armies of consultants and career remuneration managers are employed to ensure reward for performance does exactly what it says on the tin. But does it? Over the past decade reward for performance has become associated with *bad* business. Banking bonuses have been routinely blamed in the media for the excessive risk-taking that precipitated the global financial crisis. Investors and the public alike continue to heap scorn on dramatic increases in executive reward and the lack of commensurate growth in performance. In these austere times of shaky economic recovery, high-value bonus awards are instantly front-page news amidst cries of corporate greed. Governments and regulators have moved to place caps on the value of financial incentives awarded to staff to curb reckless behaviour, implying in the process that companies (especially banks) cannot be trusted to manage their own remuneration arrangements responsibly (Slater 2013). Within research literature, establishing a positive link between performance and reward remains elusive.[2] There is increasing criticism of rewarding performance (Culbert 2010). Many call for the complete decoupling of performance appraisals and reward decisions (DiDonato 2014). Rewarding performance, it seems, is a risky business – there are significant economic, social and reputation risks to getting it wrong. Why are attempts to reward for performance not delivering the expected results?

Reward is risky business

As we enter a period of relative economic stability following the global financial crisis of 2008, this chapter offers insights and guidance drawn from a multi-year study of global firms during the last period of economic confidence and stability (2002–2007). Controlling for industry effects, the study offered an in-depth exploration of how seven leading consumer perishable goods firms competing internationally managed reward for performance as part of a wider strategic human resource management agenda. At the time of the research (2003–2007), their combined annual global sales exceeded US$160 billion and they employed a collective worldwide staff of over 560,000 staff. In all cases, spend on employee reward constituted the largest single operating cost. All firms operated in multiple international locations, with one firm operating in over 120 locations throughout the world. All were large, established and well-resourced. All were household names, with their brands dominating the perishable goods marketplace.

Specifically, the research reviewed reward arrangements of all grades and occupations of employee below board level and above shopfloor level during the period 2002 to 2007. Over 150 interviews were conducted with senior executives, people managers and HR specialists across a diverse range of international functions and operations within the seven case companies. The interviews were supplemented by employee workshops, attitude surveys, documentary analysis and additional interviews with retained management consultants.

Rewarding performance

All seven firms used a variety of reward for performance schemes to reward the vast majority of their managerial, technical and professional employees – the bulk of their workforces. The degree of employee reward 'at risk' (based upon performance) differed across all seven firms for comparable roles, but increased drastically in all cases with employee seniority. All seven firms professed to view reward for performance as a strategic tool through which to leverage employee effort and secure strategically desirable behaviour. In all cases, concerns over performance influenced the choice to use reward for performance. It was viewed as a powerful tool in the management arsenal to secure positive performance outcomes that could not easily be achieved through other means. At considerable expense, all firms employed full-time and dedicated remuneration specialists within their human resources departments.

Reward failing to deliver, and worse

The multi-year research programme revealed that all seven case study firms struggled to manage reward for performance in line with their aspirations. In two of the seven cases, the gap between intended policy and operational reward practice was relatively small, because the management of reward for performance systems was largely devolved to line managers. Line managers were good at managing reward systems of their own design. In cases where reward for performance systems were corporately designed – by headquarters HR staff, for example – there was evidence of wide variation between espoused policy and what was implemented at the coalface. For a variety of reasons, line managers did not manage employee performance in line with corporate policy, or via the formal management process, thereby limiting the effectiveness of the linkage to corporately desired reward outcomes. Reward for performance schemes were not typically the driver of positive behaviour envisaged by headquarters staff. This was especially true in cases where incentives, for example, were corporately mandated but felt to be a poor fit for the culture of the local workplace. They were often adapted or rejected by line managers – frequently unbeknown to headquarters staff. Corporate-wide reward for performance cannot be effective if it is not being implemented as intended. We know what companies say they do, but they don't always do what they say.

Worse still, individual accounts of attempts to implement reward for performance across all seven case studies revealed numerous examples of unintended and negative consequences. Negative outcomes included misdirected staff effort and behaviour, high staff turnover, disengagement and elevated levels of workplace conflict. The negative impact of ineffective reward for performance schemes was often discreet, especially in cases with a high power-distance between those designing performance-based reward systems, such as the corporate human resources department, and line managers tasked with their implementation within operational business units. The consequences were all too real and all too immediate for those on the front line. Employee reward is an emotive subject – ask any manager and they will say it is easier to get it wrong than it is to get it right. When wrong, it is difficult to remedy the damage arising from the perceived unfairness of mismanaged reward. Why were many attempts to reward for performance failing to deliver, or worse?

Reward design involves complex trade-offs

The ability to design reward for performance systems that are fit for their purpose is key to their effectiveness. The dominant logic follows that, for reward for performance systems to produce strategically desirable employee outcomes, they, as an organizational *means*, should be closely aligned to strategic *ends* (Lawler 1984). However, choosing to reward for performance involved making tough choices with unpredictable outcomes. Decision-makers within the sample firms were routinely confronted by multiple and unavoidable dilemmas.

Individual and collective performance-based reward

One key dilemma was striking the right balance between using individual and collective performance measures to inform compensation awards. Rewarding individual employee performance was intended to create personal accountability for performance by establishing line of sight between the individual employee, their actions and their performance. There was a strong trend at the time of the research towards the greater use of individual performance-based bonuses. Concerns about diminishing performance drove sample companies to want to maximize the contribution of each individual employee. It was highly problematic, however, to define what good performance looked like for each role across the vast and complex operations.

So too was creating performance processes that consistently and accurately measured performance and differentiated fairly between employees. In all cases where individual incentives were used, employees were ranked and placed on a distribution curve along which, inevitably, there were winners and losers. Employees perceived the 'forced ranking'-style system of differentiating employee performance as highly divisive – with colleagues being pitched against each other for a zero-sum slice of the cake according to their rating on a scale of 1–5 or their positioning within a nine-box grid. The culture it engendered was one of being in competition for reward, job security and promotion with their peers. In individualistic work environments, this was perceived to matter less (indeed, competition may be healthy), but in teamworking environments, which depended upon collaboration for success in role, it was perceived to create a counterproductive conflict. This is a much-publicized negative feature of highly leveraged forced distribution systems, as this reported example from Microsoft illustrates: "The behaviour this engenders, people do everything they can to stay out of the bottom bucket [. . .] People responsible for features will openly sabotage other people's efforts. One of the most valuable things I learned was to give the appearance of being courteous while withholding just enough information from colleagues to ensure they didn't get ahead of me on the rankings" (*The Slate* 2013).

Aligning reward to corporate performance, and thereby not differentiating between individuals (or teams), was equally viewed as problematic. Where used, collective performance-based bonuses were perceived as potentially unfair, because they did not consider differences between individuals' contributions, and potentially allowed unproductive staff to 'freeload' off the efforts of their more productive colleagues. Equally, the degree to which individual employees could meaningfully influence overall company success was considered minimal, unless they occupied a senior position. Bonuses were limited in their motivational effect because of their unpredictability and/or lack of direct relation to the efforts of the individual:

> When people [staff] look at their variable reward, one of the big problems we've had with all the bonuses is how much can you predict, or influence, your bonus? And, you know, if there's a corporate element I can't predict it. One year it's very good, and I haven't a clue why, and the next year it's terrible and yet I thought we were doing all right. Very unpredictable.
>
> *(interview with business unit general manager)*

The most common way in which the individual and collective performance dilemma was overcome was to blend elements of both. Thus, individual performance was sacrificed at the expense of a collective performance focus, and vice versa. No one solution was felt to address performance concerns fully, so companies settled for a complicated blend of measures in which the 'line of sight' between individuals' and groups' performance and their reward was lost.

Short-term and long-term reward gearing

A second key dilemma was balancing the short-term performance needs of the business against long-term priorities for growth. Typically, short-term incentives – or bonuses – captured the former, whilst long-term incentives – including share options – attempted to generate a focus on the long term (especially for middle- to senior-ranking staff). The prevailing business performance climate was one of short-termism, however. Quarterly results drove a focus on performance for the short term – often it seemed at the expense of engaging in long-term and difficult-to-measure business-building activity. Indeed, long-term incentives were principally used to attract senior talent (i.e., at the point of recruitment). It is not obvious if they succeeded in creating a sense of ownership or alignment to corporate success over the long term.

Objective and subject performance measures

A third dilemma in reward for performance design was the appropriate degree of emphasis placed on objective and subjective measures to determine financial awards. Objective measures in the form of quantitative performance results were favoured, on balance, because they were perceived to be hard data against which the relative performance of staff and teams could be compared objectively. Subjective measures were treated with a degree of scepticism, and their influence within appraisals limited where possible. However, objective measures were often crude, capturing only measures of output, and not at all nuanced in reflecting the way in which staff performed. Subjective assessment relied upon the subjective judgement of line managers within the performance management process.

Overcoming subjectivity in financial reward for performance was a perennial source of tension, especially for those managing reward systems corporately and trying to ensure robust performance measurement across varied firm operations. Performance management for virtually all staff within the sample of seven firms incorporated a blend of hard and soft measures, as companies attempted to balance both. However, there was a significant difference between firms in the weighting attached to either hard or soft measures. North American firms tended to place a much greater emphasis on hard measures of performance, such as financial performance. European firms also incorporated financial measures within appraisals, but they moderated typically by assessment of performance against softer behavioural measures, e.g., teamworking, attitude and interpersonal behaviour.

Failing to align reward to strategic priorities

There are no easy or right answers to these complex trade-offs. Managing reward for performance is extremely technically challenging. Poor choices can easily produce unpredictable and damaging outcomes. Its sheer technical complexity and difficulty goes some way to explaining why reward for performance can fail to deliver strategically desired outcomes in the form of appropriate employee behaviour and enhanced performance. There are also other less obvious reasons.

Firms struggle to link reward to performance priorities

An additional major challenge to the effective management of reward for performance was an absence of understanding of the firm's strategic priorities. Decision-makers were often unclear about the strategic *function* of the reward systems they were designing and struggled to select the appropriate organisational *form* for implementation.

Conceptually, reward for performance is located within a value chain, which connects corporate strategy to employee outcomes in the form of resourcing requirements (attraction and retention of valuable talent), motivation (securing effort and productivity) and positive behaviours (necessary to implement the strategy) (Lawler 1990). For instance, firms seeking to outcompete their peers on the basis of innovation (e.g., new products) will seek to attract the best available talent according to their knowledge, creativity, long-term focus and the potential to work free from supervision (Schuler and Jackson 1987). Such discretionary effort would be highly undesirable for firms seeking to compete on the basis of cost minimization. Desirable employee outcomes in that context include error-minimizing behaviour, cost-consciousness, a short-term performance focus, diligence and compliance with highly routinized behaviours to maximize productivity. Irrespective of the strategy being pursued, it was apparent that reward for performance systems often failed to produce desirable employee outcomes because the strategic ends were not well understood by those responsible for reward system design and implementation. A lack of strategic direction, and too few parameters against which to balance the complex trade-offs already mentioned, resulted in high levels of uncertainty for all concerned – HR, managers and employees alike.

In the absence of understanding the strategic context, those with responsibility for reward decisions were understandably risk-averse in their choices. Very few attempts within the case firms to identify new or creative ways in which to reward their people in support of firm-strategic priorities were observed. Innovation was simply not on the agenda. On the contrary, given the potential negative consequences of poor reward decision-making (e.g., employee dissatisfaction), every attempt was made to avoid getting it wrong – including choosing the path of least resistance with regard to stakeholders or simply doing nothing new. It would be expected that as firm-strategic priorities shift in response to new competitive threats, changing customer preferences and regulation, so too should the firm's reward strategy if it is to remain aligned and capable of producing employee outcomes of strategic value. There was little evidence of creative attempts to introduce differentiated reward systems in step with strategic change, or anything that wasn't a known quantity:

> I used to have a joke where the marketing director used to rush into the managing director's office and say: 'I've got this brilliant new idea, nobody has ever thought of it before'. And the managing director says: 'go for it, yeah!'. And then the HR director tries the same thing and he [managing director] says: 'are you sure we should be doing this, if nobody else is doing it, is it right for us?'. Just because it is an HR initiative.
>
> *(interview with line HR director)*

Further in evidence was intense pressure to adopt reward for performance for reasons other than fulfilling strategic objectives. In some cases, it was simply to send signals to investors and markets about the commitment of the firm to improving their financial performance. For example, in one US-headquartered firm, linking reward and performance was an important element of instilling confidence in investors:

> For [Home Co.], the most important people are the Wall Street analysts. Humungous! [Reward for performance] messages primarily for the analysts, secondarily for everyone else.
>
> *(interview with remuneration director)*

The implication is that reward choices are informed primarily by factors other than purely a concern for strategic alignment (Trevor 2011).

Legitimacy is prioritized over strategy in reward choices

The desire for legitimacy amongst peers exerted a powerful influence over the choice to adopt reward for performance. Reward managers within each of the seven companies participated in an invitation-only 'industry Club' (the Club). Hosted by individual members on a rotating basis (and often at the host's offices), the Club met regularly (often quarterly) to review general trends within the industry, common challenges and new techniques. The Club allowed reward professionals from different companies to compare their thinking and current practice against their peers in a benign environment. More importantly, members of the Club sponsored and participated in a yearly salary survey to establish median and quartile market rates in a like-for-like comparison of key roles and occupations. Without knowing what specific peer companies paid – these often being direct competitors – these data provided external salary benchmark data on a role-by-role basis. An independent third party, always a remuneration consultancy during the term of the research, administered the salary survey. Consultancies gathered, analysed and disseminated the results supplemented by insights from their own experiences with clients (often individual members of the Club). As a valuable source of fees and a network for new business, there was intense competition between different consulting houses to serve the needs of the Club.[3]

These same consultancies also simultaneously advised several individual Club members on reward scheme design and governance. Both directly and indirectly, management consultancies exerted huge influence over the reward decision-making process of individual Club members and, by extension, the industry. Direct influence took the form of consulting services relating to reward design and workforce solutions. Indirect influence arose from the dissemination of research reports, opinion pieces and the hosting of themed conferences and networking events. These events were considered valuable marketing opportunities to promote new consulting services and build client relationships. Clients were not oblivious to the influence of consultancies on reward determination:

> They're [consultants] always looking for the next product to sell, they're no different from any other industry and they will leap onto a bonus scheme design, or have a share incentive scheme, or have something like that, that they can hawk round us, as often willing victims. Because, yeah, we are all looking for the Holy Grail! (laughs)
>
> *(interview with remuneration director)*

Nevertheless, in addition to valuable technical input, the use of external consultants brought additional legitimacy to proceedings, notionally as an independent expert third party. The more prestigious the consultancy house, the more legitimate the reward determination process, or so the logic seemed to go.

Such clubs are not limited to the industry under study. They exist for the purpose of sharing experiences with fellow professionals, finding support and establishing relative benchmarks with those considered to be peers (and therefore desirable comparators). Inevitably, it is not simply salary levels that are compared, but reward practices as well on the basis of 'You show me yours and I'll show you mine'. As a result, these clubs can act as a powerful mechanism for generating industry norms, or "best practices", as Club members commonly refer to them. These norms become institutionalized and highly influential as the industry standard (Meyer and Rowan 1991). Despite the absence of collective representation of employees' interests, the sample firms were voluntarily setting rates for reward in a way that was reminiscent of the co-ordinated industry-wide collective bargaining of the previous century. Reward norms were effectively binding for those wishing to be competitive within the labour market, both in respect of *what* they paid (i.e., how much) and *how* they paid (i.e., the mix of reward elements, including incentives). The effect was to produce conformity and standardization of reward practice at the industry level, and not managerial differentiation and distinctiveness at the enterprise level. Employers were choosing instead to *conform* to industry norms, perhaps because it was easier or less risky than genuinely attempting to align reward in support of their own business strategy.

Deviating from these 'legitimate' norms became increasingly difficult to justify as the competition for talent intensified or corporate performance declined. Moreover, conforming to legitimate norms served a very practical purpose for the reward professionals involved. By adopting what was considered industry 'best practice', it was easier to defend their choices to their superiors, irrespective of whether the outcomes were good or bad for the company. All these factors combined explain the startling conformity of reward practice observed across the seven firms. Companies throughout the period of the research exhibited strongly herd behaviour. They moved in co-ordinated formation as they carefully picked a path between volatile market forces, threatening regulation and the increasingly activist demands of institutional shareholders, using legitimate reward norms for shelter.

Failing to implement reward strategy as intended

It is well established that effective reward for performance requires robust performance management – the objective setting and appraisal processes through which performance reward outcomes are determined. The research revealed further a range of barriers to effective *implementation* that raise additional concerns over the manageability of rewarding for performance. It was standard practice within the case firms to devolve primary responsibility for managing performance (and, by extension, performance-related reward outcomes) to line managers, i.e., those with direct responsibility for managing people and their performance on a day-to-day basis. How line managers chose to approach their task had a profound impact on *how well* reward reinforced performance, and vice versa. Managers and employees alike generally viewed new attempts to introduce reward for performance with scepticism and apathy, especially if the business benefit was unclear.

One size does not fit all

Three broad approaches to implementing reward for performance were apparent within the participating case study firms. The first approach saw reward and performance management schemes determined corporately, on a 'one-size-fits-all' basis universally applied across the global operations of the business. The second was a regional focus; responsibility for reward determination was devolved geographically (e.g., North America) or divisionally (e.g., household products) with managements taking responsibility for determining reward in accordance with their specific concerns, albeit within global guidelines. The final level was highly decentralized, with determination occurring at the level of the individual business unit, country operation or workplace.

Each approach involved complex trade-offs. Universal 'global' schemes were perceived to be simpler (i.e., one system instead of many). They reinforced alignment behind a singular corporate culture and enabled labour mobility across international operations. Regional schemes were considered to be more responsive to operating market requirements, permitting managements to tailor their reward systems to the different needs of, say, mature markets and emerging markets. 'Local' reward for performance schemes were typically even more highly customized to local line business requirements, and considered highly fit for purpose, but only in that specific context. The perceived disadvantage of global systems was the lack of sensitivity to the local business environment and the imposition of reward systems that made sense corporately, but were a poor fit for divisional or local requirements. Equally, the disadvantage of local systems (regional too, to a lesser degree) was the absence of common standards and pan-organizational integration. A patchwork of different payment systems within each of these highly diversified (product and geography) settings made for a globally confusing picture, and the loss of potential economies of scale of management (e.g., shared services) and governance.

As noted by one senior manager within Home Co., there is no easy answer to the challenge of striking the right balance between global consistency *and* local flexibility of reward scheme and/or system:

> It's [centralisation versus decentralisation] a massive, massive issue which we are torturing ourselves with daily at the moment.
>
> *(interview with senior manager)*

Two of the sample firms, Confectionery Co. and Tobacco Co., adhered to a philosophy of locally aligned reward. Food Co., Candy Co., and Drink Co., had either regionally or divisionally aligned reward. The remaining firms, Home Co. and Grocery Co., by degree, subscribed to a global reward philosophy. In Grocery Co., globally consistent reward systems were prescribed top-down by HQ, with no option for line managers but to implement as desired by their corporate masters.

For a variety of reasons, the research indicated that 'one-size-fits-all' global reward for performance systems were typically the least well implemented (when measured against the original reward scheme design). Firstly, centrally located decision-makers, typically the corporate HR department, were perceived to be too far away to understand immediate business needs by those responsible for implementation:

> The rewards team sits in an HR department and has very, very little contact with the business. It's not 'out there'; it hasn't got a finger on the pulse; it's not, you know, day to day. It's not talking to the business leader; it's not out there seeing what the problems are.
> *(interview with line HR manager)*

Secondly, in all cases, line managers desired freedom to manage their people as they saw fit, and would resist or even rebel if they perceived corporate intervention as a threat to the local status quo or undermining their authority.

Managers will manage performance and reward their way

In Tobacco Co. and Confectionery Co., responsibility for managing reward and performance was largely decentralized, with local management free to choose the means and the method through which corporate reward principles were upheld. The principle behind this approach to implementation was that local management knew their business and people needs best and should be empowered to make choices, as long as they operated with corporately mandated minimum standards. The desire for autonomy resonated strongly among business leaders within operations, even if it presented its own challenges. As one senior line manager commented:

> I think being part of a management team where you're in a unique business environment, being able to tailor to that unique environment and reward the way you want to reward is an opportunity worth having, even if it does take more management time and there's more complexity and there's potential for it going wrong.
> *(interview with business unit manager)*

Where they had the freedom, few local managers (e.g., business unit general managers) in both companies used reward for performance aggressively to drive productivity. Rather, bonuses, when used, took the form of relatively small retroactive rewards, as opposed to incentives set a priori and tied to performance against hard targets and measures. Awards were recognition of performance and good behaviour already exhibited. Performance conversations were also more developmental in nature, being forward-focused on objectives and personal development potential. Thus, when given freedom, local managers interpreted the corporate reward for performance philosophy in myriad different ways, reflecting their idiosyncratic business circumstances, existing custom and practice, and personal preferences. A common finding was the 'light touch' use of reward for performance, merely to reinforce a positive working climate and harmonious workplace relations between team members. Financial reward was viewed typically as a hygiene factor – its absence would be demotivating, but it was not itself motivating except for a narrowly defined range of roles, such as sales. It was not viewed as the primary driver of employee engagement, motivation and performance at the level of workplace. Reward, as much as possible, was removed from the performance equation.

Not in my back yard!

Where the introduction of new reward for performance systems was corporately mandated, and line managers perceived they were a poor fit for their own operations, or a threat to workplace harmony, or simply perceived as ineffectual, extreme attempts by local managers, to limit the impact of changes to their people's remuneration arrangements were observed. Corporately mandated performance measures and related bonuses were considered in some cases entirely counterproductive, producing employee dissatisfaction and demotivation to the exasperation of their immediate superiors:

> I happen to believe that the objectives we've been set [centrally] are plain [expletive] stupid and unreasonable. Now how the hell do you mitigate against that?
>
> *(interview with business unit general manager)*

A common response regarding the effective use of reward for performance was:

> So, is someone's bonus that we reward out in September going to be influenced by what they do in March? Very unlikely. We just adapt and get on with it regardless.
>
> *(interview with line manager)*

Adaptation took two forms typically – adaptation of the centralized scheme to limit its impact on the local workplace or, simply, outright rejection. In such cases, there is an obvious tension between the 'corporate centre' and the 'business' – a binary that reflects competing managerial interests within the single firm's management structure. Remarkably, in several instances, interviews with headquarters staff revealed those operating corporately were unaware of the intension or the actions of the line managers upon whom they relied for the implementation of corporate reward principles and policies. Total compliance with the intended reward policy was assumed – wrongly. In the candid words of an HR manager embedded within an operational business unit:

> I mean I can tell you what the past . . . one of the real roles of [line based] HR was a little bit about trying to screw around with the system to come up with whatever your line manager had asked you to do . . . what we've ended up doing is . . . we've ended up being the people who've attempted to interpret the policy in a way which suited our boss.
>
> *(interview with line HR manager)*

It is a mistake to assume line managers always implement reward for performance system in ways intended by their corporate brethren or masters. In all cases, there was evidence of both innocent *and* wilful misinterpretation of binding centralized reward policies. Inevitably, the quality of implementation was highly variable across global operations within the sample of firms. The evidence indicates that line managers resist attempts to introduce reward for performance, either passively or actively, especially when they perceive it a threat to local workplace relations. Their resistance is sometimes obvious, but often not – occurring unbeknown to those corporately responsible for attempting to harness the perceived business benefits of reward for performance at the enterprise level.

Often either motivating nor manageable

Despite its prevalence and intuitive appeal, there is surprisingly little evidence that rewarding for performance results in superior employee outcomes: e.g., performance, desirable behaviour and engagement. On the contrary, there is growing evidence – including the evidence presented here – of its potential wastefulness and destructiveness. Reward for performance often fails to create expected value because it is not aligned to what is valued strategically, for myriad reasons, many of which are social and not economic in nature. Equally, the dominant logic of reward for performance, like other complex organizational systems, assumes a level of manageability that is not borne out in practice. The sheer complexity of reward for performance and numerous organizational barriers limit the ability of firms to design and implement reward for performance as an effective means to achieving strategic ends. If rewarding for performance is inherently risky, as the evidence would indicate, then a fundamental revision to how we reward people for value in future is required.

Firstly, the underlying assumptions of current approaches to reward for performance require revision. The original 'New Pay' (Schuster and Zingheim 1992) school of thought placed too great an emphasis on reward as a mechanistic system for aligning employees' financial interests to those of their employer. Employee motivation and engagement cannot be secured by using financial reward as a lever to be pulled whenever there are concerns over poor performance. Reward systems yield unpredictable results when used to direct employee effort and enhance performance – this is especially true in the long term. The research indicates the more complex the reward system, the more uncertain its outcome – both positive and negative. In place of the mechanistic approach to reward, a more nuanced appreciation of how reward is managed in large, complex and fast-moving organizations is required. This would require understanding the impact of reward at both the front line and at the enterprise level, and how the two connect as one organizational system that shapes the way in which employees experience their work and their employer. It also requires that reward be more than simply an economic exchange, but much more a part of the social and emotional fabric of the employment relationship overall.

Secondly, reward for performance cannot be made to work better simply by increasing the value of the financial reward involved – which is perhaps the temptation when confronted by lacklustre employee performance. More money does not translate directly to a more engaged employee or effective organization. The best-rewarding organizations are often not the best performing. Many organizations reward only competitively, but excel at leveraging the value of their human capital by active management of engaging their people in the vision and values of the organization. Reward has an important role to play in reinforcing organizational cultures that reflect what is behaviourally important to the firm. An appeal to the common purpose and values of the firm does not sit well with individualistic, short-term and transactional incentive systems.

Thirdly, the introduction of reward for performance is the single greatest reason why reward levels have increased so dramatically over the past twenty years for some occupations and levels of employee (senior executives, for example) when compared to the employee average. The unequal inflation of reward for some and not all, and especially if perceived for reasons other than merit (payment for failure, for example), can easily become a corrosive element in the workplace. Equally, the reputational risk that pay awards now pose within the public domain, whether it is perceived excessive payments, or self-serving and dysfunctional 'bonus behaviour', will persist and perhaps increase, attracting the ire of governments, main street and investors. Inequity has the potential to limit value creation by creating conflict in organizations between individuals, teams and between employer and employee.

Finally, reward for performance will continue to fail to deliver organizationally as a system for the management of people. Organizations invest a huge amount of time and treasure in managing their complex reward for performance systems. The research indicates they often do so for little perceived benefit. Reward is for many the largest single operating cost of doing business – it is a risk, and should be managed as such. Reducing the risks associated with paying for performance is more important than finding the 'holy grail' of the reward lever that directly and predictably impacts the bottom line. Reward, either as a carrot or a stick, is a blunt tool – especially when attempting to manage complex roles and occupations for which performance is neither tangible nor easily measurable. In the words of one senior reward professional: *"Pay can become a very good brake [on performance], but not a very good accelerator"* (interview with remuneration director).

Notes

1 An abridged version of this chapter appeared as an article in the September/October 2017 edition of the *European Business Review,* titled 'Why reward for performance fails to deliver'.
2 For a classic treatment see Steven Kerr's (1975) 'On the folly of rewarding A while hoping for B', published in the *Academy of Management Journal*, 18, 769–783.
3 Two remuneration consultancies were retained as the annual survey administrator during the term of the research. Both were large international firms headquartered in the United States.

References

CIPD. (2013). *Reward Management Survey*. London: Chartered Institute of Personnel and Development.
CIPD. (2017). *Reward Management Survey*. London: Chartered Institute of Personnel and Development.
Culbert, S. A. (2010). *Get Rid of the Performance Review! How Companies Can Stop Intimidating, Start Managing – and Focus on What Really Matters*. New York: Business Plus.
DiDonato, T. (2014). Stop basing pay on performance reviews. *Harvard Business* Available at: https://hbr.org/2014/01/stop-basing-pay-on-performance-reviews, accessed on August 19, 2017.
Lawler, E. E. (1984). The strategic design of reward systems. In Fombrun, C, Tichy, N & Devanna, MA, (eds.). *Strategic Human Resource Management* (pp. 127–147). New York: John Wiley & Sons.
Lawler, E. E. (1990). *Strategic Reward*. New York: Jossey-Bass.
Meyer, J. and Rowan, B. (1991). Institutionalized organizations: formal structure as myth and ceremony. In Powell, W. and DiMaggio, P. (eds.). *The New Institutionalism in Organizational Analysis*. Chicago: University of Chicago Press.
Schuler, R. and Jackson, S. (1987). Linking competitive strategies with HRM practices. *Academy of Management Executive*. 1(3), 209–13.
Schuster, J. and Zingheim, P. (1992). *The New Pay*. New York: Lexington Books.
Slater, S. (2013). Barclays rejigs pay to counter EU bonus clampdown. Reuters, November.
The Slate. (2013). Available at: http://www.slate.com/blogs/future_tense/2013/08/23.
Towers Watson. (2014). *UK HR Consultant's Survey*.
Trevor, J. (2011). *Can Pay Be Strategic?* London: Palgrave Macmillan.
WorldatWork and Deloitte Consulting LLP (2013). *Incentive Reward Practices Survey*.

PART III

Reward management in practice

In this segment attention is directed to what's going on in reward management, across its various constituent elements and as it is practised across different sectors and geographies.

Charles Cotton makes the case for investing more effort into looking at the potential and actual role played by employee benefits within the total rewards bundle. While areas such as executive reward management have seemingly attracted far more attention among academic commentators, the effect of investment (positive or misapplied) may have far more profound organizational impact. And in a research vacuum, the danger is that policy choices rely on 'best-practice' promises whose operational requirements and potential investment returns have not been fully scrutinized before the policy adoption die is cast.

Social exchange theory and the underlying notion of reciprocity in human interaction is adopted by **Charlotte Lucy Smith** to scrutinize the idea and practise of employee recognition. Sometimes confused in discussion of providing employees with incentives to perform, recognition initiatives need to be located within particular contexts for managing employee performance in ways organizational stakeholders intend should be more holistically grasped. While nominally 'a good thing', a critical review of 'recognition schemes' in practice suggests the risks of unintended consequences for social harmony and teamwork if mismanaged.

Extending the definition of reward to offering employees a direct stake in the business, financial participation in various forms has a lengthy, if often unsung history. **Andrew Pendleton** explains the ways in which employee financial participation can serve as one of the routes to involving workforce members in the organization that employs them building, and if well-managed sustaining, a collective sense of engagement beyond a transactional effort–reward deal. While exercising care before assuming its role as a 'high-performance driver', evidence suggests that HR and organizational outcomes can be strengthened if employee financial participation arrangements are administered authentically.

Practices across all sectors of the economy related to deferred reward, or occupationally aligned retirement pensions, are a source of considerable controversy and debate, especially when taken in concert with the changing demography of the advanced industrial nations: the 'aging population' problem. **Geoff White** traces the provenance of employer-administered pension schemes, describes the various trends at the state–employer interface, and provides theoretically informed argument to help understand advantages and disadvantages for employers and employees alike of initiatives rooted in 'welfare capitalist' principles.

Brian Dive offers a historical context to help grasp issues surrounding the highly controversial escalation of reward applied at senior executive levels. Based on myth-busting argument derived from some four decades operating internationally within large corporate settings, a corrective is offered to flawed logic informing corporate governance of 'top pay', paving the way for regulators (including remuneration committees) to address a problem that flies in the face of building a sense that 'we're all in this together' in securing organizational effectiveness, with reform initiatives enabled by a more effective basis on which to establish defensible differences in accountability across corporate environments and their recognition.

A theoretically informed account, derived from political economic principles, is offered by **Andreas Kornelakis and Howard Gospel** to address the problem of the CEO–average worker pay gap. Raising sights from micro to macro levels of analysis, the financialization of firms as it may be manifested across the varieties of capitalism that have been observed and codified in academic commentary offers a basis to comprehend comparative international trends. Accepting the premise of the argument presented, solutions follow that involve tying the assessment and reward of corporate leadership to a broader range of stakeholder, rather than just financial shareholder, interests.

While multinationals continue to have a significant gender imbalance among their expatriate populations, evidence shows that the success of women assigned internationally provides a competitive business asset. **Susan Shortland** makes up the deficit in relevant published literature by explaining issues organizational stakeholders may find instructive in taking progressive action in this field. She analyses the combination of organizational decision-making, institutional and sociocultural influences and women's choices themselves to help clarify the gender deficit in expatriation. She also explains for the benefit of practitioners and researchers alike the balance of factors influencing women's decisions on whether or not to accept international assignment postings of various durations and types.

Ian Kessler highlights the fact that despite the prevalence of work and employment in public services, and the level of 'politicized' scrutiny it attracts given funding from the 'public purse', it is rare to find dedicated focus providing a systematic overview of reward management in the sector in published commentary and research findings. He addresses this gap in the literature enabling enhanced comprehension of trends in managerial action and consequent outcomes. Questions surrounding importance, distinctiveness and change in public services reward management are used to organize the analysis thematically, with discussion further delineated to discuss remuneration levels, structures and systems.

James Allan offers a perspective on the controversial question of what bankers want from the employment relationship, benefitting from an insider's experience of the sector in the UK, and looking back to the fallout of the financial crisis that began in 2007-8. Informed by viewpoints assembled from a range of vantage points, including bankers themselves, attention is moved beyond 'toxic bonus culture' hyperbole to a position where decision makers of all shades may gain a better awareness of a more nuanced picture and what more holistic theory and practice may do to tap into aspirations among many in the sector to be good organizational citizens, and for this to be reflected in their effort–reward bargain.

Given the importance of the so-called pivot to Asia, with China's rise to economic prominence and increasing global reach, in-depth attention is paid to contemporary reward management observable within the People's Republic of China (PRC). In the first of these contributions, **Qi Wei** charts the evolution of the pay system environment, summarizes key themes that have been studied to date, and offers case study evidence illustrating the intentions and outcomes associated with focusing practice on pay for performance within a key area of the state's public services.

Mark Wickham and Tommy Wong use evidence from interviewing managers in the Chinese (privately-owned) hospitality sector, to build understanding of reward management issues when an American multinational seeks to achieve and maintain *employer-of-choice* status. A total rewards approach is investigated through this case to generate theoretical conclusions paying attention to how other aspiring private sector investors may weigh strategic choices they face when planning to arrive at an effort–reward bargain with individuals and groups of employees that meets corporate aspirations on the part of multinationals as well as those seeking careers within this dynamic political economy.

The third contribution grounded in developments within the PRC turns the focus to small business enterprises that operate as 'platforms' decentralized from larger corporate structures. **Jian Han and Jason D. Shaw** analyse the implications of these efforts to reduce the complexity of business organization in relation to employee incentive reward arrangements. Outcomes are found needing to balance aspirations to create agile, customer-centred and cost-conscious operations, generating potentially high financial returns, while overcoming the inherent risks to the sustainability of pay levels or even security of job tenure when a small enterprise platform fails to perform to corporately determined standards.

In a final PRC-evidenced contribution, **John Shields** uses a case study from a newly risen giant telecommunications company to examine the long-term interplay between reward management practices and corporate business development, taking account of the fact that the enterprise is majority employee-owned. While distinctive reward management appears to have been fit for purpose during its emergent phase building both its domestic and global presence, external and internal factors have given rise to the need for corporate management to examine the legitimacy of continuing with the same policies and practices looking ahead. Lessons learned may inform managerial and wider stakeholder reflections on how reward management strategy requires continuous evaluation and possible change under emerging and transforming economic conditions.

At this point in the volume, the focus geographically moves from East to West – to Mexico, where **Sergio M. Madero-Gómez and Miguel R. Olivas-Luján** locate reward management in that country in historical perspective. From being one where accounting and tax regulatory issues and an administrative orientation prevailed, they argue that organizational managements in Mexico have been paying attention to normative commentary travelling from north to south in the Americas which suggests the need for better integration between reward and HR management practices as a strategic opportunity to boost business competitive advantage. While engaging with this discourse critically given lessons learned from misapplication as well as success in the field, the argument is that systemic reward management needs to evolve in line with efforts to assure enterprise sustainability.

Transition states in Central and Eastern Europe provide the canvass on which **Ihar Sahakiants and Marion Festing** detail what they locate analytically as path-dependent reward management. These are practices that evolved as part of a common heritage among the former centrally planned economies in the region. The discussion leads into an evaluation of research into observable practices since the fall of state-socialist regimes, including the effects on different groups of employees of contextually influenced 'pay for performance' programmes and 'social benefits', for example. Peculiarities in corporate governance applicable to European transition states are surfaced to identify implications for executive rewards in particular, informing the basis for a distinctive future research agenda.

Shifting the spotlight towards Southern Europe as well as looking specifically at developments in small and medium-sized knowledge-intensive firms in Italy, **Daria Sarti and Teresina Torre** reveal the results of a survey-based investigation. The research was designed to evaluate the extent

to which using non-monetary reward management initiatives affected organizational performance outcomes, taking into account employee preferences. Findings suggest that, compared with
traditional employers, in Italian SMEs whose workforce members may be significantly characterized as 'knowledge' workers, there is a greater prevalence of non-monetary rewards. Caution is
needed to avoid the overuse of such provision within the effort–reward bargain, however, to
avoid the risk of adverse effects.

A short case study is drawn from the African continent, where the author is a long-standing
participant observer. **Adebabay Abay Gebrekidan** illustrates deficiencies in public services
reward management contributing to impediments to aspirations among federal leaders in
Ethiopia to build capacity so as to realize an aim of becoming a middle-income country by the
next mid-decade. Evidence from World Bank investigations shows that levels of remuneration
among professional grades in Ethiopia compare adversely with those enjoyed by similar public
service employees in other parts of the continent. Negative implications for motivation and
compensating agency by individuals flow through to service underperformance and concomitant
disquiet among the 'client' population at large.

This third segment of the volume concludes with a narrative in which **Natarajan Sundar**
describes the evolution of remuneration and its management in India, embracing both private and
public sector practice. Trends in levels and how remuneration is determined are described with an
analysis of the contemporary scene informed by bespoke qualitative research involving key actors
in senior roles – specialists and general management executives/NEDs in Indian companies – to
help build understanding of ways in which, while retaining contextual distinctiveness, reward
management in this dynamic and populous economy has begun to feature many characteristics
evident in 'the West'. The corporate governance and socially generated regulatory issues that tend
to accompany such developments are flagged.

23

WHAT IS THE CASE FOR OFFERING BENEFITS?

Charles Cotton

In 2013, the last time the Chartered Institute for Personnel and Development (CIPD – the professional body for HR and people development) explored the topic of employee benefits, it found a wide range of financial and non-financial perks on offer among the UK employers that had responded to its survey. Examples of financial benefits included such things as private medical insurance, employer contributions to a workplace pension, Christmas bonuses, and enhanced maternity and paternity pay. Non-financial benefits included such perks as allowing employees to have their internet purchases to be delivered at work, dress-down days for staff, on-site aerobics/Pilates and a workplace choir/band.

However, the UK is not alone in the richness of its employee benefit offering. In the USA, the survey of employee benefits by the Society for Human Resource Managers (2017) reveals a wide range of perks, such as an on-site nap room, paid time off to vote, the shipping of breast milk for those on business trips, indemnity theft protection and on-site haircuts.

Unusual examples of employee benefit provision can make the national media. For instance, it has been reported recently that a Scottish brewer has announced the launch of a new employee perk – one week's paid leave for all workers who adopt a puppy or a rescue dog.[1] Perhaps unsurprisingly, the media have also highlighted how some employers deal with pet bereavement. For instance, some units of Mars now offer one or more days to staff on the death of a pet, flexible hours and the ability to work from home when the animal dies.[2]

UK papers have also reported that some firms in the US have been offering their female employee the option to freeze their eggs. In fact, UK benefit provision can often follow in the wake of the US. Where the states has led, the UK has often followed, whether it is in terms of adopting such approaches as flexible benefits or providing employees with benefit statements, to such perks as dress-down days, bring your 'child/parent/pet to work' days, or financial education programmes. Similarly, it has been recently reported that British firms are talking to IVF clinics about offering "egg-freezing" as a perk for their female employees.[3]

Benefit provision can vary significantly by country, often in response to what employers are required, or not required, to do by law. For instance, in France, all firms employing more than 50 staff must offer them a share of the profits (see Pendleton on 'employee financial participation', this volume). By contrast, the US has the dubious honour of being the only industrialized country in the world that does not currently have statutory requirements on employers to provide paid holiday, with the average American enjoying a mere two weeks of annual leave. A quarter of the population get no paid holiday at all.

Similarly, benefits can vary by economic sector. For instance, prior to 2013 employees working for the UK Civil Service received 2.5 'privilege days' each year on top of their annual paid leave entitlement. The half-day was for the afternoon of Maundy Thursday; something that very few employers in the private sector offered to staff as annual leave.

The CIPD's reward management survey for 2013 finds that UK benefit provision varies by sector, employer size and type of employee (CIPD 2013a). While private sector firms can offer a wider range of benefits than voluntary or public sector employers, there can be also variation within sector. When it comes to employer size, smaller firms typically provide fewer benefits than larger employers, though a small professional service firm, such, for example, as an advertising agency, would be expected to provide more staff benefits than a small restaurant. By employee grade, the survey finds that many benefits are commonly dependent on grade/seniority, such as private medical insurance, coaching/mentoring programmes, relocation assistance and company car.

In addition, employee benefits can cost a lot of money. Our survey also finds that, overall, benefits can account for between 10% and 20% of the total reward spend. In some employers, the CIPD research finds that 40% of total reward expenditure goes on benefits. This begs the question: why offer staff perks in the first place?

Theories and explanations

The CIPD employee benefits factsheet points out that, for firms, there can be many advantages to simply offering cash, rather than a mixture of pay and perks. You offer employees a cash sum and they can then use it to buy those goods and services that are of most relevance to them, such as a pension, company car or a flu jab. This helps give employees a feeling that they are in control of the benefits they receive.

Similarly, employers don't spend time and money on creating a rewards package and then not communicating and educating employees about it, or waste their investment on offering benefits that employees don't want. Even those benefits that don't have a significant financial cost, such as allowing staff to run a charity fundraising day, can have the potential to become complex to administer.

This also raises the issue of how we should answer the question: what is an employee benefit? Some benefits bring a cash benefit to the employee, such as maternity pay or a pension. Other benefits do not involve cash, such as family-friendly working or being allowed to bring your pet to work with you, but they do involve a cost to the employer that offers such a benefit. For instance, if you want to let your employees bring their pets to work, you have to define what animals are to be classified as pets, work out how to accommodate those employees who may have allergies or phobias related to certain animals and whether or not you need additional insurance. Whilst the solutions are not insurmountable, there is a danger that they can take time and energy away from business purpose and performance.

Given the smorgasbord of benefits on offer, various reward academics and authors have tried to impose some order by attempting to bring together similar benefits. For instance, Hume (1995) has three groupings: security; goodwill; and performance; Wright (2004) has four broad categories, namely: personal security and health; job, status and seniority-related; family-friendly; and social, goodwill or lifestyle benefits; while Armstrong and Murlis have managed to come up with seven (2007).

Interestingly, Smith (2000) tries to organize the various benefits on offer to staff according to their supposed impact on the organization, namely contribution to: the HRM function;

performance/goodwill/security; and employee motivation. He suggests that certain benefits are provided to motivate staff such as status cars. By contrast, others, such as sick pay or life insurance, are a 'hygiene factor': they don't motivate, but their absence would demotivate employees. Unfortunately, this model is untested as there is little evidence to show that particular employee benefits motivate individuals, or help to attract or retain them, an issue addressed below.

Given the fact that so many UK employers offer a wide range of benefits to their staff, it is reasonable to hypothesize that they must perceive that there are advantages from doing so in terms of recruitment, retention and motivation and, in turn, that they assume a positive impact on performance, productivity and profits.

It should be recognized, however, that some employers provide certain staff benefits in response to cultural, social and legal forces. For instance, in the UK there are legal requirements regarding such aspects of the benefits package as paid leave, paid maternity leave and sick pay. Certain staff benefits are provided because they are tax attractive, such as employers' pension contributions. Similarly, some employers provide workplace benefits because of collective bargaining while others may offer them in order to avoid having to bargain with a union.

A waste of money?

Are employers wasting money on staff benefits that don't recruit, retain or motivate? As was mentioned in the CIPD's survey on strategy and staff benefits, a quick perusal of *Google Scholar* for recent academic research on the role that employee benefits bring and deliver to their organizations reveals thin pickings. When one compares the amount of money that employers spend on staff benefits compared with the amount of money they spend on their chief executives we would expect more research to have focused on staff benefits, but this is not the case.

As Dulebohn et al. (2008:16) note in their US-focused literature review: "Due to the general dearth of normative benefits management research, practitioners are making their way by trial and error. Prescriptive guidelines are developed through conventional wisdom and hard earned experience, but lack evidence-based research support or guidance." They go on to say: "Practitioners have not had the luxury to wait on HRM researchers to catch up, because the cost of not making decisions relative to potentially cost saving programs like consumer-driven health care or defined contribution retirement plans is too high. However, the other side of the coin is that the cost of making poor decisions in healthcare and retirement benefits because of the lack of supporting HRM research is also potentially high" (2008: 16). Despite their call that more academic research needs to be carried out on employee benefits (a conclusion that can also be applied to the UK), little has appeared since then.

A CIPD (2013b) study tried to investigate the role of employee benefits in supporting business strategy and impacting on HR outcomes. The research finds a relationship between an organization's strategy and the workplace benefits on offer to the workforce, indicating that employers are not adopting benefits in an arbitrary fashion but to meet perceived business needs. For instance, using the strategic type framework developed by Miles and Snow (1978), a firm exhibiting a 'prospector' strategy or one that focuses on product quality is statistically more likely to provide those benefits associated with employee development (such as coaching and mentoring) than a firm following a 'defender' strategy or one that focuses on cost minimization.

In terms of HR workforce outcomes, businesses that report having a positive employee relations climate are statistically more likely to offer development benefits. Similarly, those employers that tend to report employee absenteeism difficulties are statistically less likely to offer staff such benefits as free tea and coffee, a Christmas party, flexible working, and training and career development.

Finally, the research found a positive relationship between the amount of transparency around benefits and various HR outcomes, such as employee relations, labour productivity and employee absenteeism.

Obviously, this is just one survey and there is always the question of reverse causality: does increased benefit transparency help foster better employee relations or do good employee relations result in better benefit transparency? However, we didn't find the opposite, i.e., poor benefit transparency and good employee relations.

To a certain extent, these findings support Flanery et al.'s (1996) suggestion that benefits can be categorized according to the type of organizational culture in which they are found, namely: network-based; time-based; process-based and functional. For instance, they would expect that, in a network culture, where work is designed around alliances for specific projects, there would be relatively few benefits. However, those that are provided would be very flexible. The cost, risk and reward associated with these benefits would be mostly borne by the workers.

However, as Perkins et al. (2016) point out, this analysis is based on the US experience, where firms have more freedom in the design of benefits than in other parts of the world, because of the different tax regulations and legal requirements.

Of course, while organizations may have the 'right benefits' on offer, they may not necessarily communicate them to staff in the 'right way'. Poor benefit delivery can then reduce their impact on such employee decisions as those to join, stay or engage. In their examination of employee benefit communications, Frietag and Pichert-Duther (2004) find a difference between staff satisfaction with benefits and staff understanding of them. This can be due to reward professionals not knowing how to talk to staff about the benefits on offer or reluctance to be seen spending money on education and communication material. Frietag and Pichert-Duther (2004) conclude that PR managers need to get involved in how perks are communicated if employers are going to get the best from their expenditure on staff benefits.

Another focus for research is the level of employees – how do they react to benefits? As Dulebohn et al. (2008) point out, not a lot has changed since Gerhart and Milkovich (1992:541) said: "The state of knowledge about the influence of benefits on employee attitudes and behaviours is dismal . . ." Part of the challenge is that employee benefit preferences depend on a range of factors, such as location, the nature of work or life stage.

Even the academic research that has been carried out within the field of benefits is not necessarily spread as one would expect according to Dulebohn et al. (2008). They find that while the prevalence of work–family benefits is low in the US, academic research in this area is quite extensive, not least attempting to answer the question as to why the prevalence of work family benefits in the United States is so low.

Behavioural science and benefits

Another area of employee-focused research is in the area of behavioural science and the link to benefits. Lupton et al. (2015) find that this approach can be useful in exploring why employees may not react to the provision of staff benefits in the way that is expected. For instance, why don't employees value the money spent on benefits to recruit or retain them, and, more importantly, what can be done to boost employee appreciation?

As a consequence of declining pension membership, the UK has embarked on what can be argued is the biggest experiment in behavioural science. The government now requires employers to enrol all employees (subject to certain earnings and age requirements) into a workplace pension scheme – either an existing plan or one set up for the purpose of automatic enrolment. The assumption is that after employees have been placed into a workplace pension, most of them will 'go with the flow' and stay in the pension plan rather than making an active decision to opt out.

According to the Pension Regulator, as at 31 March 2017, 503,178 employers had enrolled their staff into a workplace pension. As a consequence, 7.6 million workers are now saving for their retirement. As a proportion of the workforce, the Office for National Statistics estimates that in 2016, 68% of the workforce was saving into a pension. By way of comparison, 47% of employees belonged to a workplace pension scheme in April 2012, prior to the implementation of workplace pension reforms.

But what are the benefits to employers from enrolling staff into a pension and giving pension members a contribution towards their retirement plan? Lupton et al. (2015) argue that there is little evidence to show that pensions attract staff to an employer. What evidence exists shows that there is some variation by age, with younger workers being less influenced by a pension scheme. This may be because they are less effected by the long-term deferral of reward, or that they simply do not appreciate the importance of being in a pension plan.

However, Lupton et al. (2015) find more evidence to suggest that pensions can boost staff retention. Similarly, there is little research evidence to suggest that providing a pension increases employee commitment or engagement. Interestingly, one potential benefit of providing a pension for employers is that it helps them facilitate older workers to retire from the organization. However, this aspect of pension scheme provision hasn't been explored by academics.

While Lupton et al. (2015) note that academic evidence suggests that pensions don't punch at their weight as an element of reward, behavioural science does indicate various ways that employers can improve the impact of pensions. For instance, the way in which communication is framed can be important – emphasizing to employees the losses incurred by not participating in a pension. Tests around loss aversion indicate that employees are more receptive to messages around potential losses rather than potential gains. This suggests that HR should 'sell' the benefits of belonging to a pension scheme by highlighting the value that staff are securing now in terms of employer contributions and government tax relief, that they might otherwise forego, rather than focusing on the potential benefits of belonging to a pension.

Similarly, gamification can be used to encourage workers to boost the amount they pay in when the employer offers to increase its pension contribution if the employee does likewise. A CIPD report (2016a) shows the positive impact of such employer pension contribution matching schemes on employee contribution levels.

What does behavioural science have to say about other benefits? One issue is how employees respond if they are offered some flexibility in the benefits they can select, such as with a 'flexible benefits' plan. Using Kahneman (2011), Lupton et al. (2015) suggest that this could potentially force people into 'System 2' deliberative thinking whereas their day-to-day use of the benefits would predominately be in the instinctive 'System 1'. In other words, under flexible benefits employees would think about what perks they should select rather than the ones they would actually use.

For instance, some workers may select gym membership from their flexible benefits plan because they think it will help them stay, or become, fit, i.e., they are adopting System 2 thinking (a more conscious thought process, triggered when making infrequent or important decisions). However, most of us tend to conduct day-to-day activities in System 1 (our everyday autopilot mental process), which is the mindset that is more prone to bias; in the case of gym membership, the self-control bias.

As Lupton et al. (2015:29) point out: "We can see how someone who takes a gym membership could potentially not use this benefit and get zero value from an employer contribution. This could furthermore be seen as a loss, as in effect the employee has paid for something they will not use, with the employer being a reminder of this loss and thus associated with it."

In effect, rather than choice being valued by employees, some of them could see such choice as a cost. This tendency can be countered by HR reducing the range of benefits offered and simplifying the process of choice. It can also be countered by recognising when employees are more likely to make everyday decisions (such as going to the gym) and when they are more likely to make conscious decisions (joining a pension scheme) and structuring benefit decisions around System 1 and 2 thinking.

However, there are limitations with behavioural science. As Lupton et al. (2015) note, much research in this area often relies upon experimental designs and is usually carried out in laboratory-type settings. Also, when it comes to neuroscience, trying to explain complex social behaviour by observing particular activated regions of the brain has obvious limitations, as it tells us little about the nature of wider contextual factors.

There is also ethical concern about how HR practitioners might use their insights to manipulate employees to make certain decisions and use communication to make subliminal messages to workers to nudge them in the right direction.

However, as Lupton et al. (2015:9) suggest: "the ethical implications surely depend on the use to which the science is put. If behavioural science were to be used to help employees make better provision for their retirement, or to encourage senior executives to behave sustainably, the ethical assessment would surely be different". For instance, enrolling workers into a pension scheme and then relying on their inertia not to opt out is probably a good way of helping them to save for their old age.

Summary

A recent joke at a reward conference was that the only thing growing faster than executive pay was academic research on executive pay. Unfortunately, as academic CEO reward research expands like a black hole, it sucks away academic time, energy and insight that could be better spent looking at other aspects of HR research, such as employee benefits. One area that may potentially have a far more profound impact on the organization.

As the CIPD has warned in a recent report (2016b), the danger is that in this knowledge vacuum, reward professionals rely overly on 'best practice' (what's said to have worked well for others in the past) to inform their decisions. Instead, they should be deciding on what's the best thing to do, in their unique circumstances, in order to help create sustainable and successful relationships between people and the organization.

While the amount of academic literature around staff perks is lacking, that doesn't mean that practitioners can't be evidence-based in their decision-making. As Barends et al. (2014) point out, in addition to scientific literature and empirical studies, there are three other forms of evidence that can be used to make evidence-based decisions, namely: practitioners' professional expertise; the internal data within the organization; and stakeholders' values and concerns.

To be effective, Barends et al. (2014) assert that evidence-based practice should be about making decisions through the conscious, explicit and judicious use of the best available evidence from multiple sources. This is done by asking, acquiring, appraising and aggregating the evidence and then applying this by taking action and ultimately assessing the outcome of the decision taken.

Hopefully, academics will see the importance of employee benefits both to organizations and individuals and we'll start to see more research in the coming years. However, in the meantime, there are actions that reward professionals can take to ensure that their benefits practices are aligned to the needs of employees and the business, integrated with other elements of people management, based upon multiple sources of evidence, and that their impact is regularly evaluated.

Notes

1 "'Pawternity' leave firms with unusual staff benefits", BBC, April 27, 2017.
2 "The challenge of grieving for a pet at work", *Wall Street Journal*, November 10, 2015.
3 "It's not a perk when big employers offer egg-freezing – it's a big bogus bribe", *The Guardian*, April 26, 2017.

References

Armstrong, M. and Murlis, H. (2007). *Reward Management: a Handbook of Remuneration and Strategy.* London: Kogan Page.

Barends, E., Rousseau, D. and Briner, R. (2014). *Evidence-based Management: the Basic Principles.* Amsterdam: Centre for Evidence Based Management.

Chartered Institute of Personnel and Development. (2013a). *Reward Management Survey.* London: CIPD.

Chartered Institute of Personnel and Development. (2013b). *Reward Management Survey* Supplemental Report *Aligning Strategy and Benefits.* London: CIPD.

Chartered Institute of Personnel and Development. (2016a). 'Focus on employee attitudes to pay and pensions'. *Employee Outlook, Winter 2015–16.* London: CIPD.

Chartered Institute of Personnel and Development (2016b). *In Search of the Best Available Evidence.* London: CIPD.

Dulebohn, J. H., Molloy, J. C., Pichler, S. M. and Murray, B. (2008). Employee benefits: literature review and emerging issues. *Human Resource Management Review.* 19(2), 86–103.

Flanery, T. P., Hoflrichter, D. A. and Platten, P. E. (1996). *People, Performance and Pay: Dynamic Compensation for Changing Organizations.* New York: Free Press.

Frietag, A. R. and Pichert-Duther G. (2004). Employee benefits communication: proposing a PR–HR cooperative approach. *Public Relations Review.* 30, 475–482.

Gerhart, B. A. and Milkovich, G. T. (1992). Employee compensation: research and practice. In M. D. Dunnette and L. M. Hough (eds.), *Handbook of Industrial and Employer Psychology* (2nd ed.) (pp. 481–569). Palo Alto, CA: Consulting Psychologists Press.

Hume, D. A. (1995). *Reward Management: Employee Performance, Motivation and Pay.* Oxford: Blackwell.

Kahneman, D. (2011). *Thinking, Fast and Slow.* London: Penguin.

Lupton, B., Rowe, A. and Whittle, R. (2015). *Show Me the Money! The Behavioural Science of Reward.* London: CIPD.

Miles, R. and Snow, C. (1978). *Organizational Strategy, Structure, and Process.* New York, NY: McGraw-Hill.

Perkins, S. J., White, G. and Jones, S. (2016). *Reward Management: Alternatives, Consequences and Contexts.* London: CIPD.

Smith, I. (2000). Benefits. In White, G. and Drucker, J. (eds.). *Reward Management a Critical Text* (pp. 152–177). London: Routledge,.

Society of Human Resource Managers. (2017). *Employee Benefits: Remaining Competitive in a Challenging Talent Marketplace.* Virginia: SHRM.

Wright, A. (2004). *Reward Management in Context.* London: CIPD.

24

EMPLOYEE RECOGNITION

Charlotte Lucy Smith

Introduction

Whilst few would dispute the motivational power of recognising exceptional performance in the workplace, it is unusual for texts on reward management to feature a chapter that focuses solely on employee recognition schemes, separate from the related constructs of non-financial reward and total reward (cf. Cotton, this volume). There exists a sense of ambiguity around the concept of employee recognition – its meaning, constitution and role – which is reflected in the lack of scholarly research or theory development in this area, compared to other components of the reward system.

This chapter is intended to extend thinking and practice around employee recognition and its management through detailed and focused consideration of its distinctive characteristics and role within contemporary organizations. In so doing, the chapter aims to stimulate empirical research into this increasingly widespread but underexplored area of reward management. Research which shows the effects of recognition on employees' engagement and well-being, motivation and performance is balanced against evidence that employee recognition may have unintended dysfunctional consequences. Whilst acknowledging the traditional theoretical foundation of needs-based motivation and reinforcement theory, there is a consideration of social exchange theory as an alternative lens through which to view the effects of recognition on individuals and organizations. The chapter concludes by offering practical advice on the effective design and management of programmes for recognising employee performance.

A neglected area of reward management

Recognition for performance is a form of intrinsic reward offered to employees in addition to pay and benefits as part of a complete or 'total' rewards package designed to recruit, retain and engage talented employees, as well as motivate them to high performance (CIPD 2016; World at Work 2015). Although informal recognition is by no means a new managerial practice, there has been a significant increase in the number of organizations implementing formal employee recognition schemes in recent years, driven in part by concerns about possible detrimental effects of monetary and other extrinsic rewards on intrinsic motivation (Long and Shields 2010). According to a 2015 survey conducted by World at Work, 89% of US organizations have some kind of employee recognition scheme in place. Of these, the most popular are for length of service (87%), above-and-beyond performance (76%), and schemes to motivate specific behaviours (51%). Employee recognition programmes are also gaining ground outside of the US, with 31% of UK organizations reporting that they operate some kind of individual non-monetary recognition scheme (CIPD 2015).

Unfortunately, unlike some other components in the reward system, employee recognition has attracted very little empirical research or development of theory. As Miller (1978:115) noted some years ago, recognition is "one of the most neglected, taken for granted, and poorly performed management functions". It has been argued that the concept of employee recognition is ambiguous, and research has been constrained by the lack of a clear conceptual definition (Long and Shields 2010). Neckermann and Frey (2013) add that the huge variety in the type, style and scope of employee recognition interventions within organizations makes it a difficult concept for researchers to study.

The lack of academic research targeted at employee recognition is particularly marked when compared with the volume of practitioner-oriented literature promoting its benefits. This literature advocates employee recognition as a cheaper and more effective motivational alternative to cash (Nelson 1996; McAdams 1991, 1995, 1999; Rose 2001, 2011), a tool of leadership (Luthans 2000), means of enhancing quality (Hale and Maehling 1992; Knouse 1995; La Motta 1995), improving health and safety compliance (Pardy 1999) and reducing absenteeism (Boyle 1995).

The importance of recognition is also acknowledged within the 'engagement' discourse which has gained traction among both academic and practitioner audiences, encouraged by David MacLeod and Nita Clarke's report to government (MacLeod and Clarke 2009). Employee engagement, defined here as "being positively present during the performance of work by willingly contributing intellectual effort, experiencing positive emotions and meaningful connections to others" (Alfes et al. 2010:5), is widely accepted as an important factor in achieving performance in the workplace. In turn, recognition has been found to be a critical component of engagement (Saks 2006; Gostick and Elton 2009). A global recognition study conducted in 2008 by Towers Watson showed that, in organizations with generally low levels of engagement, strong manager performance in recognising employee performance increased engagement from 33% to 52% (Towers Watson 2008). Indeed, the importance of recognition for engagement is acknowledged by the global performance-management consultancy, Gallup, which includes a survey item on recognition in its G12 survey ('In the last seven days, I have received recognition or praise for doing good work').

Recognition has also been found to promote employee well-being, which increases the likelihood of such engagement being sustainable (Robertson and Cooper 2009; Lewis et al. 2012). Grawitch et al. (2014) identify recognition as one of five categories of healthy workplace practices which can be used to establish a positive environment conducive to well-being, the others being employee involvement, work–life balance, health and safety, and growth and development. Of the five, recognition has received the least focused research attention, significantly limiting our understanding of how recognition schemes operate within organizations and their effects (Grawitch et al 2014; Tetrick and Haimann 2014).

Defining employee recognition

The most comprehensive definition of employee recognition to date is offered by Brun and Dugas (2008) following a review of the diverse literatures dealing with employee recognition and other related topics:

> Recognition is first and foremost a constructive response; it is also a judgement made
> about a person's contribution, reflecting not just work performance but also personal

dedication and engagement. Lastly, recognition is engaged in on a regular or ad hoc basis, and expressed formally or informally, individually or collectively, privately or publicly, and monetarily or non-monetarily.

(Brun and Dugas 2008:727)

This definition indicates a multidimensionality to employee recognition which is not often fully acknowledged in the discourse around non-financial reward. So much more than the practice of giving a reward for the achievement of a given objective, employee recognition has multiple objects, and may be expressed in a range of different ways and from a number of sources: including co-workers, subordinates, managers, the organization, external clients, and even the wider community (Brun and Dugas 2008).

Practitioners also provide further useful definitions of employee recognition, including UK reward management consultant Michael Rose, who defines recognition as:

A process of acknowledging or giving special attention to a high level of accomplishment or performance, such as customer care or support to colleagues, which is not dependent on achievement against a given target or objective. It can be day to day, informal or formal.

(Rose 2011:1)

An important distinction should be emphasized between 'recognition' and 'incentives' (Hansen et al. 2002). Rose (2011:1) defines an incentive as a "material tangible reward that is earned through achieving specific defined aims or objectives that are known in advance". For example, a parent might offer a treat to a child for tidying their room. The child tidies the room *in order to* obtain the treat. By contrast, recognition is not offered in advance but retrospectively, being given in special acknowledgement of an accomplishment or standard of performance, as when a parent rewards a child with a treat for good behaviour.

This distinction is similar to that made by US reward management writer Jerry McAdams (1999) between 'performance improvement plans' and 'recognition plans'. Performance improvement plans (or incentives) are "formula-driven and specify both performance expectations/targets/goals and potential reward outcomes *in advance* of actual performance" whereas recognition plans are "*retrospective* and usually discretionary in nature" (Shields 2006:3, my italics). Recognition plans are used to "honour outstanding performance after the fact and are designed for awareness, role modelling and retention of recipients" (McAdams 1999:242). Such plans "typically seek to recognise behaviours that fulfil overall values but are difficult, if not impossible, to record in terms of objectives – even if it were desirable to do so" (Rose 2001:37). Examples might include exceptional customer service, 'going the extra mile', dedication, innovation, suggestions and team work.

Although employee recognition is often characterized as 'non-financial' or 'non-monetary', as Silverman (2004:3) notes, this "does not necessarily mean that the recognition provided should have no financial value, it simply means that whatever is given, it should not be just money". Many so-called 'non-financial' or 'non-monetary' employee recognition awards, including merchandise and travel vouchers, have a financial value, a symbolic value (providing employees with a sense that their contributions are appreciated by the organization) and an informational value (providing them with feedback on their performance) (Long and Shields 2010). This is consistent with Brun and Dugas who observe that, for the recipient, "recognition represents a reward experienced primarily at the symbolic level, but may also take on emotional, practical or financial value" (2008:728).

In order to alleviate confusion, previous researchers have preferred to use the term 'non-cash recognition' (Long and Shields 2010; Rose 2011; Shields 2006). This term encompasses tangible and non-tangible rewards of varying economic value, including vouchers and gift cards (which are close to cash, but which place a limit on where the recipient can spend them). It also includes the five forms of non-cash award identified by McAdams (1999): social reinforcers (such as praise from the manager in the morning team meeting), merchandise awards, travel awards, symbolic awards (for example, certificates and trophies) and earned time off.

Theorizing employee recognition

The existing theoretical basis for employee recognition as a management technique is rooted in a combination of needs-based theories of motivation and reinforcement theory (Long and Shields 2010). For example, Maslow's (1943) 'hierarchy of needs' identifies social acceptance, self-esteem and recognition from others as key human needs which drive behaviour (see also Fish, this volume). Recognition schemes are directed at the satisfaction of these needs by providing external acknowledgement of an individual's worth and recognition of their achievements by others in the organization. Similarly, according to Herzberg's (1959) 'two-factor model', recognition is a key 'motivator' which can be used by managers to motivate employees to higher performance.

However, recognition may also be understood in the context of reinforcement theory (Skinner 1974) and its elaborated form 'organizational behaviour modification theory' (Bandura 1969, 1986; Luthans and Stajkovic 1999; Stajkovic and Luthans 1997). According to this perspective, specific types of behaviour are strengthened or weakened by the consequences of the behaviour. Individuals are motivated to perform behaviours for which they have been rewarded and recognised in the past and will avoid engaging in behaviours which have previously led to punishment. As such, recognition is an important way of motivating employees to continue engaging in organizationally desirable behaviours.

Empirical research provides substantial support for the reinforcing effect of employee recognition on behaviour, noting that it leads to performance improvement in both manufacturing and service settings. A meta-analysis conducted by Stajkovic and Luthans (2003) found that the use of social recognition programmes increased employee performance by an average of 17%. However, the largest performance improvement (45%) was produced when recognition was combined with monetary reinforcement and feedback, suggesting that employers wishing to maximize performance should seek to incorporate all three within their reward management system. Indeed, a recent survey of 349 Australian and Canadian organizations found a number of significant positive relationships between non-cash recognition and cash-based reward practices (Long and Shields 2010). This suggests that, contrary to the view of non-cash recognition advocate, Bob Nelson, that organizations should 'dump the cash' and 'load on the praise' (Nelson 1996:68), organizations are using recognition to complement rather than as a substitute for cash-based reward.

However, whilst financial reward is an important part of the effort–reward bargain, commentators have noted that the employment relationship must also be recognised as a social exchange relationship between employees and employing organizations, or the employee's immediate manager (Shore and Barksdale 1998; Wayne et al. 1997). Social exchange is regulated by the norm of reciprocity whereby individuals who have received benefits feel compelled to repay the favour (Gouldner 1960). The performance-enhancing effect of social exchange has been supported by research on perceived organizational support (POS; Eisenberger et al. 1986) and leader–member exchange relationships (LMX; Wayne et al. 1997). Employees who perceive high levels of organizational support feel that the organization values their contributions and cares about their well-being (Eisenberger et al. 1986). This perceived organizational support increases employees' felt obligation to reciprocate by engaging in behaviours which support the organization's goals. Since an employee's immediate manager is considered representative of the organization, employees are likely to view their manager's favourable or unfavourable treatment of them as indicative of the organization's support and respond accordingly (Eisenberger et al. 1986; Kottke and Sharafinski 1988; Levinson 1965).

Reward and recognition therefore play an important part in the development and maintenance of high-quality exchange relationships between managers and employees. Contemporary managers have access to a range of resources to help develop beneficial social exchange relationships with employees. These resources can be economic (i.e., money) or socio-emotional (Foa and Foa 1980). The latter resources are aimed at fulfilling employees' social and esteem needs and may include the manager giving the employee attention, showing an interest in their personal life, listening to their personal problems, paying them respect (Cropanzano and Mitchell 2005). Thus, when a manager praises or recognises an employee's performance or achievements, they provide socio-emotional resources which are valuable to the employee and costly to the manager.

As in social exchange relationships when one person does something beneficial for the other there is the expectation that the action will be reciprocated, employees may seek to return the favour by engaging in behaviours which are beneficial to the manager, such as demonstrating loyalty and increased work effort. Once such exchanges begin, they can develop into self-reinforcing cycles (Cropanzano and Mitchell 2005). Therefore, when managers show that they care for their employees through giving them attention, respect and recognition, social exchange relationships can develop which in turn produce positive employee attitudes and effective work behaviour.

This is consistent with Dur's (2009) signalling model of manager–employee relationships where employees care more for their manager when they are more convinced that their manager cares for them. Managers can signal how much they care about the well-being of their employees in two ways: by offering them a generous wage and by giving them attention. Dur argues that altruistic managers (managers who care about their profits and about the well-being of the employees that they hire) may offer lower wages and still build up better social exchange relationships with their employees than do egoistic managers (managers who care only about profits). According to this model, a low wage signals to employees that the manager has other socio-emotional resources to offer, which will induce the employee to offer the manager loyalty and exert high levels of effort.

Frey and Gallus (2014) further stress that, in order for the award to be perceived as an authentic signal, the number of awards given out must be limited, and the award must be consistent with other signals conveyed by the manager or organization (for instance, the award should not accompany a reduction in salary). This is supported by recent research by Smith (2014) which found that, in a public sector context characterized by high levels of disruption and uncertainty, employees were mistrustful of recognition awards which were perceived as conflicting with the other signals emitted by the organization towards them (e.g., reduced job security). The findings of this study suggest that the wider organizational context within which recognition schemes operate may mediate employees' perceptions of recognition and its effects on employee behaviour.

The 'dark side' of employee recognition

Continuing to draw attention towards the 'dark side' of reward management theme that is the focus of Angela Wright's chapter within this volume, this chapter now turns to further consider empirical evidence which suggests that employee recognition schemes may have unintended negative consequences which offset their intended performance benefits.

Johnson and Dickinson (2010) found that, in a simulated work setting, the employee of the month scheme failed to improve performance over time and, in some cases, the performance of recipients actually fell after they received their award. Another study by Gubler et al. (2013) found that an awards scheme designed to improve attendance did, on average, reduce tardiness and increase punctuality. However, productivity also fell by 1.4% and employees with previously high attendance suffered a 6–8% drop in productivity following the start of the scheme. The authors suggest that these employees were demotivated by the offer of awards for good behaviour which they already exhibited.

These findings are consistent with a body of literature which argues that extrinsic rewards undermine or 'crowd out' intrinsic motivation (Deci 1971; Deci et al. 1999; Kohn 1993; Lepper et al. 1973). The concern is that rewarding employees for organizationally desirable behaviours or activities may decrease their intrinsic motivation to perform the behaviour or activity. Usually, the notion of 'crowding out' applies to the behaviour which is being compensated; however, research has shown that offering a reward for one behaviour can lead to crowding out of another completely different behaviour.

One mechanism by which intrinsic motivation may be crowded out is perceived fairness. Research in the field of organizational justice has shown that perceptions of unfairness can motivate employees to 'get even' by reducing effort and productivity (Akerlof 1982; Ederer and Fehr 2007) and engaging in other dysfunctional behaviours (see Skarlicki and Folger 1997). Employees who perceive there to be a lack of procedural justice consider the procedures by which rewards are allocated to be unfair (Leventhal 1980). Perceptions of favouritism or bias in how recognition is given are likely to diminish trust in the recognition scheme, and, by extension, towards the organization, and could lead to the belief that promises associated with the fair treatment of employees have been breached (Shields 2007; see also Shortland and Perkins, this volume). This may have serious negative implications for social exchange relationships as psychological contract theory predicts that the failure of the organizational manager to meet their obligations to the employee may affect what that employee feels obligated to offer in return (Robinson et al. 1994).

In his book *Punished by Rewards* (1993), influential reward critic Alfie Kohn also expresses concerns regarding the effects of employee recognition on interpersonal relationships within the organization. Kohn argues that precisely because verbal rewards such as praise involve one individual making a value judgement about the behaviour or performance of another, praise may be interpreted by the recipient as an attempt by the giver to gain or maintain power. If a high-status individual is praised by someone of lower status, this may be seen as presumptuous or insulting. A manager praising the work of an employee may be perceived by the employee as a reminder of the higher status of the manager, whilst a colleague praising another colleague may be interpreted as an attempt to occupy a position of greater power over the other.

According to Kohn, through highlighting power disparities, rewards have adverse effects on relationships between the individuals giving the rewards and those receiving them. In an organizational context, the perception that the manager controls the distribution of rewards creates the feeling of being evaluated rather than supported. By forcing employees into a position of dependency on their manager for their rewards, employees are more likely to conceal problems, overstate their capabilities and focus on impressing or flattering the person who controls the rewards, thus potentially undermining the intended performance improvements of the rewards.

In addition to having negative effects on the relationship between manager and employee, Kohn also considers rewards to be detrimental to the development and maintenance of positive relationships between co-workers which benefit teamwork and the sharing of knowledge. He argues that, by explicitly pitting employees against one another in pursuit of a scarce reward, the message conveyed to employees is that their co-workers are a barrier to their own success. Consequently, employees are disinclined to help others with their work and instead are more likely to perceive their co-workers as rivals to be defeated.

Kohn's warnings about the potential negative side effects of rewards on relationships in the workplace are supported by the findings of several studies on recipients of teaching awards which revealed award winners who experienced hostility or resentment from co-workers upon receiving recognition (Carusetta 2001; Mackenzie 2007; Warren and Plumb 1999). In a study of award-winning estate agents, Henagan (2010) found that award recipients experienced feelings of guilt at having been recognised and feared negative reactions from their co-workers. This finding is in line with research on social comparison which has found that individuals often experience feelings of discomfort or a sense of guilt as a result of outperforming others (Exline and Lobel 1999; Exline et al. 2004; Rodriguez Mosquera et al. 2010). Research suggests that employees who are concerned that their achievements may pose a threat to others' self-esteem and self-worth may respond through attempting to redefine their individual successes as collective achievements and/or demonstrating sympathy for individuals who they have outperformed (Smith 2014). Outperformers have also been found to deliberately reduce their subsequent efforts in order to maintain their interpersonal relationships (White et al. 2002).

Finally, in a study investigating the impact of co-workers receiving recognition on their participants' emotions and behavioural intentions, Feys et al. (2013) found that participants' emotional responses to a co-worker receiving recognition were moderated by the quality of the relationship between the two. Where the quality of the relationship was low, recognition led to the highest amount of negative emotions towards the co-worker, whereas the highest amount of positive emotions towards the co-worker emerged when the relationship quality was high. The study also revealed that recognition of a co-worker may lead to harmful interpersonally targeted behaviours such as verbal or physical abuse or deliberately failing to help a co-worker. The findings of this study indicate that understanding how employees react to their co-workers receiving recognition requires consideration of the quality of the relationship which they share. Furthermore, although recognition can have a positive effect on the motivation of the recipient, if applied in settings where the quality of relationships between co-workers is low it also has the potential to undermine the motivation of co-workers and lead to behaviours which may be harmful to both individuals and the organization.

Conclusions and practical implications

The existing body of theoretical and empirical evidence on employee recognition also offers valuable advice for practitioners in the process of or considering implementing an employee recognition scheme. Firstly, there is no 'one-size-fits-all' approach to employee recognition. Practitioners responsible for designing employee recognition schemes should tailor each scheme to the needs and circumstances of the individual organization, including its culture and external environment. It is recommended that practitioners consult with employees through employee voice channels and incorporate the findings into their plans for the scheme to ensure alignment with cultural norms. Public sector organizations may respond to the unique public service ethos of its employees by designing practices and strategies which more easily allow for employees to be appreciated by service users (Wittmer 1991). Increased involvement from service users may also have the added benefit of avoiding the perception of bias in award allocation decisions and increasing employees' perceptions of the overall fairness of the scheme.

Whilst HR practitioners typically design employee recognition schemes, most rely on line manager involvement and support; therefore, employees' responses to such schemes are liable to be influenced by the manager's own attitudes and approach to recognition and the quality of the manager–employee relationship. As a result, it is important that the right people with the appropriate interpersonal and leadership skills are recruited into these crucial line management roles and that they are given access to the appropriate training and resources to support them in delivering recognition which is meaningful for each individual. This is of central importance since the quality of the manager–employee relationship contributes to employees' perceived organizational support and consequently influences employees' levels of organizational commitment and attitudes towards the organization (Purcell and Hutchinson 2007).

In order for recognition to be valued by the employee, it must not be perceived as an attempt to manipulate or control (Hansen et al. 2002). It should clearly communicate to the recipient what the donor values about them personally and be accompanied by specific feedback regarding why the individual has been chosen to receive an award (Smith 2014). Recognition which is informational and communicates how the recipient has made a difference to the donor personally is more likely to be experienced by the recipient as genuine and therefore rewarding (Blau 1964). It may also increase perceived self-determined competence and enhance intrinsic motivation (Deci et al. 1999). It is also important that recognition awards are allocated in a way which recipients (and other employees) see as fair and transparent, especially in organizations where levels of trust towards the organization are already diminished as a result of organizational change (Smith 2014).

Finally, practitioners should be prepared for employees to respond to employee recognition schemes in ways contrary to those expected and intended by the organization. Individuals may experience discomfort, embarrassment or guilt as a result of receiving recognition if they perceive that their achievements pose a threat to others' self-esteem and self-worth, and their interpersonal relationships, expressing this 'outperformance distress' through a range of different emotional and behavioural responses (Exline and Lobel 1999; Exline et al. 2004) which may disrupt the effective and efficient operation of the organization. Although many organizations like to publicly present recipients with recognition to encourage other employees to emulate their behaviour, they should be mindful that not everyone likes to be singled out in this way. Where there is a strong sense of solidarity between employees, there is an increased likelihood of award recipients experiencing feelings of discomfort when their superior performance is highlighted through receiving a public recognition award. Recognition which is delivered privately to recipients may allow organizations to recognise high-performing individuals and teams whilst avoiding the interpersonal risks of outperformance.

There is a wealth of practitioner literature providing further inspiration and advice for the effective design and implementation of recognition schemes, including Nelson's (1994) book *1001 Ways to Reward Employees*, which offers considerable anecdotal evidence and testimony on the effectiveness of recognition programmes in improving employee performance. However, it is clear that recognition schemes do not always work in the way they are expected or intended. Therefore, before employee recognition is unreservedly recommended as a motivational strategy, further empirical research is needed to investigate those aspects of the design and implementation of employee recognition schemes which may result in unintended negative consequences. This research would be of clear value to managers responsible for designing and implementing employee recognition schemes, as well as for researchers seeking to understand the underlying dynamics of employee recognition as a human resource management practice.

References

Akerlof, G. A. (1982). Labor contracts as partial gift exchange. *The Quarterly Journal of Economics*. 97(4), 543–569.

Alfes, K., Truss, C., Soane, E. C., Rees, C. and Gatenby, M. (2010). *Creating an Engaging Organization: Findings from the Kingston Employee Engagement Consortium Project*. Wimbledon: CIPD.

Bandura, A. (1969). *Principles of Behavior Modification*. New York: Holt, Rinehart & Winston.

Bandura, A. (1986). *Social Foundations of Thought and Action: a Social Cognitive Theory*. Englewood Cliffs, NJ: Prentice Hall.

Blau, P. M. (1964). *Exchange and Power in Social Life*. New York: John Wiley & Sons.

Boyle, D. C. (1995). *Secrets of a Successful Employee Recognition System: The 100 Club Solution*. Portland, OR: Productivity Press.

Brun, J.-P. and Dugas, N. (2008). An analysis of employee recognition: perspectives on human resources practices. *The International Journal of Human Resource Management*. 19(4), 716–730.

Carusetta, E. (2001). Evaluating teaching through teaching awards. *New Directions for Teaching and Learning*. 88, pp. 31–40.

Chartered Institute of Personnel and Development. (2015). *Reward Management 2014–2015*, CIPD (online). Available at: https://www.cipd.co.uk/Images/reward-management_2014-15_tcm18-11382.pdf [Accessed 01 February 2017].

Chartered Institute of Personnel and Development (2016). *Strategic Reward and Total Reward*, Factsheets (online). Available at: https://www.cipd.co.uk/knowledge/strategy/reward/strategic-total-factsheet [Accessed 01 February 2017].

Cropanzano, R. and Mitchell, M. S. (2005). Social exchange theory: an interdisciplinary review. *Journal of Management*. 31(6), 874–900.

Deci, E. L. (1971). The effects of externally mediated rewards on intrinsic motivation. *Journal of Personality and Social Psychology*. 18(1), 105–115.

Deci, E. L., Koestner, R. and Ryan, R. M. (1999). A meta-analytic review of experiments examining the effects of extrinsic rewards on intrinsic motivation. *Psychological Bulletin*. 125(6), 627–668.

Dur, R. (2009). Gift exchange in the workplace: money or attention? *Journal of the European Economic Association*. 7(2–3), 550–560.

Ederer, F. and Fehr, E. (2007). Deception and incentives: how dishonesty undermines effort provision. Discussion Paper Series, Institute for the Study of Labor (IZA), University of Bonn, No. 3200.

Eisenberger, R., Huntington, R., Hutchison, S. and Sowa, D. (1986). Perceived organizational support. *Journal of Applied Psychology*. 71(3), 500–507.

Exline, J. J. and Lobel, M. (1999). The perils of outperformance: Sensitivity about being the target of a threatening upward comparison. *Psychological Bulletin*. 125(3), 307–337.

Exline, J. J., Single, P. B., Lobel, M. and Geyer, A. L. (2004). Glowing praise and the envious gaze: social dilemmas surrounding the public recognition of achievement. *Basic and Applied Social Psychology*. 26(2–3), 119–130.

Feys, M., Anseel, F. and Wille, B. (2013) Responses to co-workers receiving recognition at work. *Journal of Managerial Psychology*. 28(5), 492–510.

Foa, U. G. and Foa, E. B. (1980). Resource theory: interpersonal behavior as exchange. In Gergen, K. J., Greenberg, M. S. and Willis, R. H. (eds.). *Social Exchange: Advances in Theory and Research*. New York: Plenum.

Frey, B. S. and Gallus, J. (2014). Awards are a special kind of signal. *CREMA Working Paper Number 2014-04*.

Gostick, A. and Elton, C. (2009). *The Carrot Principle*. London: Simon & Schuster.

Gouldner, A. W. (1960). The norm of reciprocity: a preliminary statement. *American Sociological Review*. 25(2), 161–178.

Grawitch, M. J., Ballard, D. W. and Erb, K. R. (2014). To be or not to be (stressed): the critical role of a psychologically healthy workplace in effective health management. *Stress Health*. 31(4), 264–273.

Gubler, T., Larkin, I. and Pierce, L. (2013). The Dirty Laundry of Employee Award Programs: Evidence from the Field. Working Paper Series, Harvard Business School, No. 13–069.

Hale, R. L. and Maehling, R. F. (1992). *Recognition Redefined: Building Self-Esteem at Work*. Minneapolis, MN: Tennant Company.

Hansen, F., Smith, M. and Hansen, R. B. (2002). Rewards and recognition in employee motivation. *Compensation & Benefits Review*. 34(5), 64–72.

Henagan, S. (2010). The perils of workplace recognition: antecedents to discomfort associated with being the target of upward comparisons. *Basic and Applied Social Psychology*. 32(1), 57–68.

Herzberg, F. (1959). *The Motivation to Work*. New York: Wiley.

Johnson, D. A. and Dickinson, A. M. (2010). Employee-of-the-month programs: do they really work? *Journal of Organizational Behavior Management*. 30(4), 308–324.

Knouse, S. B. (1995). *The Reward and Recognition Process in Total Quality Management*. Milwaukee, WI: ASQC Quality Press.

Kohn, A. (1993). *Punished by Rewards: the Trouble with Gold Stars, Incentive Plans, A's, Praise and Other Bribes*. New York: Houghton Mifflin Company.

Kottke, J. L. and Sharafinski, C. E. (1988). Measuring perceived supervisory and organizational support. *Educational and Psychological Measurement*. 48 (4), 1075–1079.

La Motta, T. (1995). *Recognition: the Quality Way*. New York: Quality Resources.

Lepper, M. R., Greene, D. and Nisbett, R. E. (1973). Undermining children's intrinsic interest with extrinsic reward: a test of the 'overjustification' hypothesis. *Journal of Personality and Social Psychology*. 28 (1), 129–137.

Leventhal, G. S. (1980). What should be done with equity theory? New approaches to the study of fairness in social relationships. In Gergen, K., Greenberg, M. and Willis, R. (eds.). *Social Exchange: Advances in Theory and Research*. New York: Plenum Press, pp. 27–55.

Levinson, H. (1965). Reciprocation: the relationship between man and organization. *Administrative Science Quarterly*. 9(4), 370–390.

Lewis, R., Donaldson-Feilder, E. and Tharani, T. (2012). *Managing for Sustainable Employee Engagement: Developing a Behavioural Framework*. London: Chartered Institute of Personnel and Development.

Long, R. J. and Shields, J. L. (2010). From pay to praise? Non-cash employee recognition in Canadian and Australian firms. *The International Journal of Human Resource Management*. 21(8), 1145–1172.

Luthans, F. and Stajkovic, A. D. (1999). Reinforce for performance: the need to go beyond pay and even rewards. *Academy of Management Executive*. 13(2), 49–57.

Luthans, K. (2000). Recognition: a powerful, but often overlooked, leadership tool to improve employee performance. *Journal of Leadership & Organizational Studies*. 7(1), 31–39.

Mackenzie, N. (2007). Teaching excellence awards: an apple for the teacher? *Australian Journal of Education*. 51(2), 190–204.

MacLeod, D. and Clarke, N. (2009). *Engaging for Success: Enhancing Performance Through Employee Engagement*. London: Department for Business Innovation and Skills.

Maslow, A. H. (1943). A theory of human motivation. *Psychological Review*. 50(4), 370–396.

McAdams, J. L. (1991). Nonmonetary rewards. In Rock, M. and Berger, L. (eds.). *The Compensation Handbook* (3rd ed., pp. 218–235). New York: McGraw-Hill.

McAdams, J. L. (1995). Rewarding special performance: low-cost, high-impact awards. In Risher, H. and Fay, C. (eds.). *The Performance Imperative: Strategies for Enhancing Workforce Effectiveness* (pp. 361–388). San Francisco: Jossey-Bass.

McAdams, J. L. (1999). Nonmonetary rewards: cash equivalents and tangible awards. In Berger, L. A. and Berger, D. R. (eds.). *The Compensation Handbook* (4th ed., pp. 241–260). New York: McGraw-Hill.

Miller, L. M. (1978). *Behavior Management: The New Science of Managing People at Work*. New York: Wiley.

Neckermann, S. and Frey, B. S. (2013). And the winner is . . .? The motivating power of employee awards. *The Journal of Socio-Economics*. 46, pp. 66–77.

Nelson, B. (1994). *1001 Ways to Reward Employees*. New York: Workman Publishing.

Nelson, R. B. (1996). Dump the cash, load on the praise. *Personnel Journal*. 75(7), 65–70.

Pardy, W. G. (1999). *Safety Incentives: the Pros and Cons of Award and Recognition Programs*. Greenbrier, TN: Moran Associates.

Purcell, J. and Hutchinson, S. (2007). Front-line managers as agents in the HRM-performance causal chain: theory, analysis and evidence. *Human Resource Management Journal*. 17(1), 3–20.

Robertson, I. and Cooper, C. L. (2009). Full engagement: the integration of employee engagement and psychological well-being. *Leadership and Organization Development Journal*. 31(4), 324–336.

Robinson, S. L., Kraatz, M. S. and Rousseau, D. M. (1994). Changing obligations and the psychological contract: a longitudinal study. *Academy of Management Journal*. 37(1), 137–152.

Rodriguez Mosquera, P. M., Parrott, W. G. and Hurtado de Mendoza, A. (2010). I fear your envy, I rejoice in your coveting: on the ambivalent experience of being envied by others. *Journal of Personality and Social Psychology*. 99(5), 842–854.

Rose, M. (2001). *Recognising Performance: Non-Cash Rewards*. London: CIPD.

Rose, M. (2011). *A Guide to Non-Cash Reward*. London: Kogan Page.

Saks, A. M. (2006) Antecedents and consequences of employee engagement. *Journal of Managerial Psychology*. 21(7), 600–619.

Shields, J. L. (2006). *The cashless turn in performance and reward management: evidence from the colonies*. Performance and Reward Conference, Manchester Metropolitan University.

Shields, J. L. (2007). *Managing Employee Performance and Reward: Concepts, Practices, Strategies*. Cambridge: Cambridge University Press.

Shore, L. M. and Barksdale, K. (1998). Examining degree of balance and level of obligation in the employment relationship: a social exchange approach. *Journal of Organizational Behavior*. 19(7), 731–744.

Silverman, M. (2004). *Non-Financial Recognition: the Most Effective of Rewards?* London: Institute for Employment Studies.

Skarlicki, D. P. and Folger, R. (1997). Retaliation in the workplace: the roles of distributive, procedural, and interactional justice. *Journal of Applied Psychology*. 82(3), 434–443.

Skinner, B. F. (1974). *About Behaviorism*. New York: Random House.

Smith, C. L. (2014). *Employee Recognition at Work: a Study of Employee Experiences* (unpublished doctoral thesis). University of York, UK.

Stajkovic, A. D. and Luthans, F. (1997). A meta-analysis of the effects of organizational behavior modification on task performance, 1975–1995. *Academy of Management Journal*. 40(5), 1122–1149.

Stajkovic, A. D. and Luthans, F. (2003). Behavioral management and task performance in organizations: conceptual background, meta-analysis, and test of alternative models. *Personnel Psychology*. 56(1), 155–194.

Tetrick, L. E. and Haimann, C. R. (2014). Employee recognition. In Day, A., Kelloway, E.K. and Hurrell, J. (eds.). *Workplace Wellbeing: How to Build Psychologically Healthy Workplace* (pp. 161–174). Chichester: Wiley.

Towers Watson. (2008). *Turbocharging Employee Engagement: The Power of Recognition from Managers*. Available at: https://www.towerswatson.com/en-GB/Insights/IC-Types/Survey-Research-Results/2009/12/Turbocharging-Employee-Engagement-The-Power-of-Recognition-From-Managers-Part-1, accessed on February 1, 2017.

Wayne, S. J., Shore, L. M. and Liden, R. C. (1997). Perceived organizational support and leader–member exchange: a social exchange perspective. *Academy of Management Journal*. 40(1), 82–111.

World at Work. (2015). *Trends in Employee Recognition*. Available at: https://www.worldatwork.org/adimLink?id=78679, accessed on February 1, 2017.

Warren, R. and Plumb, E. (1999). Survey of distinguished teacher award schemes in higher education. *Journal of Further and Higher Education*. 23(2), 245–255.

White, P. H., Sanbonmatsu, D. M., Croyle, R. T. and Smittipatana, S. (2002). Test of socially motivated underachievement: "Letting up" for others. *Journal of Experimental Social Psychology*. 38(2), 162–169.

Wittmer, D. (1991). Serving the people or serving for pay: reward preferences among government, hybrid sector, and business managers. *Public Productivity & Management Review*. 14(4), 369–383.

25

FINANCIAL PARTICIPATION

Andrew Pendleton

Employee financial participation has become a common component of reward management, especially in larger firms, in many countries. It is generally understood to involve the participation of employees in the financial returns (profit sharing) or the ownership (employee share ownership) of the company. It can be seen as a financial complement to employee participation, which generally refers to employee involvement in decisions within the company. The novelty of financial participation is that it provides rewards to labour which are generally seen as returns to capital. Some refer to financial participation as 'shared capitalism' (Kruse et al. 2010). In the case of employee share ownership labour actually assumes partial ownership, i.e., becomes part of capital. For these reasons, in the reward management literature employee financial participation tends to be seen as separate from group incentives, even though profit sharing and some forms of share ownership scheme are clearly group incentive schemes.

Instances of employee financial participation can be traced back to the early years of industrialization, but in many countries widespread financial participation is a relatively recent phenomenon. In the US and the UK, the use of financial participation took off from the late 1970s, though France has had widespread profit sharing for rather longer. In many European countries, the use of financial participation has been more hesitant, though there has been a growth in incidence in the last few years, alongside greater support from policy makers. Analysis of the nature and effects of financial participation has developed in tandem with its development in policy and practice: in the US and the UK research into financial participation flowered from the early 1980s. We aim to provide a flavour of the main currents of this research in the chapter.

This chapter provides an outline of the various forms of financial participation, noting that the boundaries between the various forms and with other types of employee reward are often blurred. Information on variations in national incidence of financial participation is presented, along with analysis of the types of firms that tend to use it. The main reasons for using financial participation are discussed, drawing attention to key theories and empirical evidence. Finally, the chapter considers the main outcomes of financial participation considered in the literature.

Financial participation: the various forms

Two main forms of financial participation can be identified: profit sharing and employee share ownership (see Poutsma 2001). However, the picture is complicated by the presence of hybrid arrangements combining elements of both profit sharing and employee share ownership. Financial participation may also overlap with other elements of reward management such as group incentive plans and pensions.

Profit sharing is the sharing of profits involving, in addition to the fixed wage, a variable income component linked directly to profits or some other measure of enterprise results. Some definitions of profit sharing emphasize that it should be based on a formula that is used from year to year, to distinguish it from one-off or irregular bonuses awarded when the company is doing well. In practice, profit sharing can take various forms. At the enterprise level, it can provide employees with immediate or deferred benefits; it can be paid in cash, enterprise shares or other securities; or it can be allocated to specific funds invested for the benefit of employees. At higher levels, profit sharing takes the form of economy-wide, sectoral or regional wage-earners' funds. Profit sharing may be paid to all or most employees or just selected employees: our interest is primarily in broad-based schemes.

The simplest form of profit sharing is *cash-based profit sharing* (CPS), whereby employees receive a one-off cash payment based on the profits of the previous financial year. *Deferred profit sharing* (DPS) is a form of deferred compensation under which the allocated profit share is not immediately released to the employee. In the meantime, the profit shares may be held in a collective fund or invested on behalf of the employee in a savings or investment plan. The deferred nature of the profit share differentiates this payment from wages and salaries, and hence can provide the basis for more favourable tax treatment. Where there are tax and social security concessions, profit-sharing plans usually have to be approved by the tax authority. Some deferred profit-sharing arrangements grant employees shares in the company paid for by the profit share. These shares are usually subject to a holding period before employees are allowed to sell them.

There is often a close relationship between profit sharing and workplace asset accumulation/savings plans, as exemplified by the French case. In some instances, employee contributions into these plans from profit sharing are matched by further employer contributions. Whilst the link between profit sharing and these savings plans has often been assessed over the medium term, changes in pensions regimes have recently encouraged more long-term linkages between profit sharing and employee savings in some countries.

Within the reward management literature, gain sharing is usually seen as distinct from profit sharing and is not usually viewed as financial participation. However, it is conceptually similar to profit sharing in so far as employees benefit from reductions in costs, and hence increases in surplus. Gain sharing might therefore be seen as an alternative form of financial participation suitable for non-profit and public sector organizations.

Employee share ownership provides for employee participation in enterprise results in an indirect way by enabling employees to participate in the ownership of the company. Share ownership then gives them access to dividend payments based on profits and to appreciation in the market value of share capital. Employee share ownership plans are usually underwritten by regulatory and fiscal supports: typically, this takes the form of capital gains rather than income tax on the benefit accruing to employees from increases in share price.

There are several main types of employee share ownership plan. The first is the award of free shares to employees. Here there is an obvious overlap with profit-sharing schemes in so far as the distribution of shares might be financed out of profits. A second involves the purchase of shares by employees, typically on advantageous terms (e.g., a discount on prevailing market prices). In some plans, employers match the purchases made by employees. Since the onus is on the employee to opt into buying shares, actual participation rates in share purchase plans tend to be lower than eligibility rates. A third form is the stock option plan, whereby employees are granted rights, possibly at a discount on market rates, to acquire shares in the future, typically between three and ten years. The rationale here is that employees will benefit from any growth in share value between grant and exercise. At exercise, employees may choose not to exercise, to exercise and sell, or to exercise and retain the shares thereby acquired.

Employee share ownership can be both individual and collective. In some cases, shares are held collectively for employees, and are not distributed to individuals. In this instance, the dividends received by the collective body may be distributed to employees as a profit share. Alternatively, shares may be initially held collectively but then distributed to individual employees over time. This is typically what occurs in Employee Share Ownership Plans (ESOPs). The chief difference between ESOPs and other apparently similar share ownership plans is that ESOPs typically enable a higher proportion of the firm to be owned by employees. Most 'conventional' employee share ownership plans, coming under the label of 'financial participation', involve only a small proportion of the firm (typically less than 5%) becoming owned by employees. Although employees may acquire voting rights through share ownership, they do not usually gain significant control rights in practice.

Who does it?

There are pronounced inter-country differences between countries in the incidence of financial participation (Poutsma and Nijs 2003). International comparisons show that broad-based ESOPs are more widespread in liberal market economies such as the UK, the US and Ireland than in many Western, and especially Southern, European countries (see Ligthart et al. 2018). Share ownership plans are also widely used by listed companies in Japan (Jones and Kato 1993). Profit sharing tends to be more widespread than share ownership because it is less costly to set up and administer. Notable users of broad-based profit sharing are France, where it is usually compulsory for firms with more than 50 employees, and Finland, where there is a tradition of industry-wide personnel funds. Employee-level data provide a more conservative picture of the incidence of financial participation. Drawing on the European Working Conditions Survey, Welz and Fernández-Macías (2008) find that around 12% of European employees receive income from some form of profit sharing and just 2.3% from company shares.

In some countries, there is extensive statutory and fiscal support for financial participation; in others, there is little or none. Several surveys have shown (Uvalic 1991; Poutsma 2001; Pendleton et al. 2001, 2003) that statutory and fiscal support for employee financial participation is the most important influence on variations in incidence between countries. Within the European Union, there has been periodic interest in promoting financial participation amongst Member States, as reflected in a series of so-called PEPPER Reports (Promotion of Employee Participation in Profits and Enterprise Results) since 1991 (Uvalic 1991; Poutsma 2001; Lowitzsch 2006; Lowitzsch et al. 2008) and EU policy initiatives. Since the turn of the century, this has been reflected in legislative reform in several European countries, such as Germany, to facilitate or promote financial participation. A deeper question is why some countries have legislated to support financial participation whereas others have not. The answer may lie in deep-rooted differences in national business systems and between 'varieties of capitalism'. Croucher et al. (2010) find that share-based financial participation tends to be most common and supported in liberal market economies, such as the US and the UK, where equity markets are large and liquid, and where economic activity tends to rely more on markets than long-term relationships between stakeholders.

Within countries, the evidence consistently indicates that some types of firm and workplace are more likely to use financial participation than others. The British Workplace Employment Relations Survey (WERS) indicates that the probability of having a share ownership scheme is significantly greater in listed companies, larger workplaces, larger organizations, and those in the finance sector. These findings are replicated in the CRANET cross-national surveys (Pendleton et al. 2003; Croucher et al. 2010), and also in studies of individual countries such as Australia (Landau et al. 2013). The picture is less clear cut for profit sharing, though there are some indications that it is more likely to be found in finance than other sectors. Studies of multinationals find that country of origin is an important influence: MNC subsidiaries with head offices in the US are more likely to have financial participation (Poutsma et al. 2005) whilst those with head offices in Germany are less likely to (Lavelle et al. 2012).

And why do they do it?

Why do some firms, but not others, operate financial participation? Kruse (1996) identifies four main sets of reasons, relating to productivity, flexibility, trade unionism, and tax and social security concessions. We consider the first three of these, having already highlighted the role of legislative and fiscal support. In doing so, we highlight relevant theory, empirical predictions and observed findings.

Productivity. The most common explanation for the use of financial participation is that it provides an incentive for employees to work more productively. The theoretical basis for this resides in principal–agent theory, the main theoretical approach to the analysis of financial participation over the years. Starting from the basis that the interests of employees and firms are likely to diverge, it is argued that linking employee remuneration to company results will provide an incentive for employees to pursue the interests of the company. In other words, employees' interests will become aligned with those of the firm. Financial participation may mitigate *moral hazard,* whereby firms have inadequate information to monitor workers' actions, and *adverse selection,* whereby firms have inadequate information about worker quality. Financial participation may, as with other incentives, help to attract better quality workers as well as motivate them to work harder (Lazear 2000). Given the assumption of rational self-interest and utility maximization in agency theory, it is assumed that employees' attitudes and behaviour change 'automatically'.

The key claim is that financial participation mitigates monitoring costs arising from deficiencies of information about worker quality and job performance. On this basis it has been predicted that financial participation is more likely to be used where monitoring costs are especially high, such as where job tasks are complex and interdependent or involve a high mental component or where work environments are capital intensive. The evidence on this is, however, mixed. Whilst some find that employee share ownership is more common in 'hard-to-monitor' environments (Jones et al. 2006), other research has found that profit sharing is not significantly more prevalent where there is a high proportion of white-collar staff, high capital intensity, or advanced technology (Heywood et al. 1997). An alternative perspective suggests that financial participation may be used to mitigate 'hard' monitoring: its apparent capacity to enhance employee cooperation and commitment may help to mitigate the dysfunctional effects of stronger incentives and monitoring such as individual incentive pay (Pendleton and Robinson 2015) or 'hard-nosed' 'calculative HRM' (Croucher et al. 2010).

Another challenge for the agency perspective is the capacity of employees to 'free ride' on the efforts of other employees. Since this 'free-rider' or '1/n' problem grows with organizational size, it follows that financial participation should be more effective in smaller companies, and hence more likely to be used in these. Unfortunately, the evidence is not at all supportive of this prediction about incidence. Larger firms are much more likely to use employee share ownership, in part because of the high set-up costs of implementing employee share ownership. Large firms are also more likely to be listed on stock markets, which is also a strong predictor of share plan usage. The evidence is more mixed in relation to profit sharing. In the UK, the use of profit sharing appears to be unrelated to organizational and workplace size, though in other countries, such as Germany, there is a clearer association between size and profit sharing (Andrews et al. 2010).

The fact that employee share ownership is used in cases where incentive effects are likely to be weakest has presented a conundrum for principal–agent perspectives (Oyer 2004). The financial participation literature has attempted to resolve this by drawing attention to complementarities between financial participation and employee involvement in work and company decisions (Kaarsemaker and Poutsma 2006). It is argued that participative work environments stimulate 'repeated games', whereby employees come to see the benefits of working harder (Weitzman and Kruse 1990), and peer pressure on 'free riders' (Freeman et al. 2010). Although there is evidence of this relationship in the US, elsewhere there is mixed evidence of the coexistence of financial participation and other forms of employee participation (see Pendleton and Robinson 2010; Kalmi et al. 2006).

An alternative perspective draws on transaction costs economics and property rights theory, highlighting the capacity of financial participation to encourage long-term employment relationships. Because the financial benefits of financial participation are usually deferred, they serve to 'lock-in' employees to the company. There is some evidence that quit rates are lower in firms and workplaces with financial participation (Wilson and Peel 1991). This has been described as 'golden handcuffs' (Sengupta et al. 2007). Furthermore, the offer of financial participation by firms signals to employees that it is worthwhile developing their human capital within the firm rather than elsewhere because employees will share in the success of the company. Another perspective derived from economics suggests that financial participation provides 'efficiency wages' (remuneration above market-clearing levels) and hence discourages quits and shirking. Financial participation is therefore likely to enhance productivity by discouraging employee quits and hence building up the stock of human capital in the firm. In turn, this is likely to promote employer-provided training within the firm. Evidence from the UK, Finland, France and Germany finds that high levels of employer-provided training are significantly associated with the use of share ownership (Jones et al. 2012; Pendleton and Robinson 2011; Guery and Pendleton 2016) and profit sharing (if most of the workforce receive profit shares) (Kraft and Lang 2013).

Flexibility

Another potential reason for using financial participation is that it provides firms with greater remuneration flexibility. In principle, total labour costs, including financial participation, vary with the financial fortunes of the firm. If a profit share is paid as a fixed percentage of profits, then clearly there will be a lower payout when profits are smaller. Some firms have a trigger point by which profit shares are only paid out if profits exceed a certain level, proportion of turnover, or growth from the previous year. A theoretical basis for this use of financial participation was provided by Weitzman (1984). He argued that flexible wages linked to profits could boost employment by combatting wage 'stickiness' – the tendency of wages to remain unchanged at the cost of higher unemployment during economic downturns. If firms could adjust wages downwards by having profit sharing as a component of remuneration, they would be less likely to lay off workers when times are bad. Thus, financial participation could stabilize employment and might even increase employment (by lowering the marginal cost of labour). Some support was provided for the Weitzman thesis in the 1980s and 1990s (Kruse 1991), but it seems less appropriate since the 2007 financial crisis since wage stickiness appears to be less in evidence than before. However, financial participation may contribute to employment stability by enhancing the potential for company survival during recessions (Kurtulus and Kruse 2017), though recent German evidence suggests otherwise (Bellman and Moller 2016).

One problem with the Weitzman thesis is that the compensation risk assumed by employees is potentially costly to firms: risk-averse employees may require risk premia in return for substitution of base pay, and this may wipe out the cost advantage of financial participation. In fact, contrary to the Weitzman thesis, financial participation generally complements rather than substitutes for base wages. Recent French studies find that financial participation increases both base and total wages, suggesting that it is not used to transfer risk to workers and therefore contradicting the Weitzman thesis (Baghdadi et al. 2013; Floquet et al. 2016). A recent Canadian study finds that wages grow more in firms that have adopted profit sharing (Long and Fang 2012).

An interesting perspective on the contribution of employee share schemes to flexibility notes that shares, and options in particular, become more valuable when the economy is doing well (see Oyer 2004). Share prices tend to rise because of general market movements as well as in response to the particular performance of the individual firm. Since this is the time that labour turnover may well be highest, because of higher alternative employment opportunities, share schemes can function as an employee retention device. Employees do not want to miss out on the value of their shares or options, which may well be forfeited if they leave the firm. It is difficult to test this prediction because of the need to consider counterfactuals, but it nevertheless seems highly plausible.

Countering trade unionism

Firms may use financial participation to weaken the role of trade unions. Financial participation might have this effect because linking an element of remuneration to profits can weaken union influence over pay outcomes. In so far as financial participation may encourage a sense of identity between employees and firms, it may weaken employee attachment to trade unions. Some unions have been wary of financial participation because of suspicions that employers may use it for this purpose (see Pendleton and Poutsma 2004 for some European evidence).

The theoretical background to this claim is Marxian theory highlighting a fundamental conflict of interests between labour and capital. Its main expression in the literature has been the 'cycles of control' thesis, developed by Harvie Ramsay (1977). He argued that firms are more likely to use financial participation when unions are powerful, typically when economies are doing well and labour markets are buoyant. Financial participation is a device to counter the strength of labour. There is some historical evidence to support this, with waves of adoption of profit sharing corresponding to economic upturns. It also has some purchase in the US where union certification has traditionally given unions substantial power over labour utilization, and hence many employers have been strongly motivated to find ways of reducing union influence. However, the rise in the use of financial participation in Europe and elsewhere over the past two decades has followed a long period of union decline. It is more likely that a decline in union power has led to increases in the use of financial participation rather than vice versa.

Although it is unlikely that financial participation has been widely used as a weapon by employers to counter trade unionism, it is more likely that it has been used to assist in modifying collective bargaining arrangements in some countries. Where collective bargaining over pay is highly centralized (at industry or national level), as in countries such as Italy and Germany, financial participation has been used to provide greater flexibility at firm level so as to link remuneration more closely to the performance of individual firms (Kalmi et al. 2012: Croucher et al. 2010). On the whole, cash profit sharing is a more suitable instrument than employee share ownership in this respect because it can be more closely related to salary payments.

Outcomes

The most common justification for financial participation is that it leads to improved performance, especially productivity, by companies. This claim typically involves a three-stage argument (see Pendleton et al. 1998). First, it is claimed that financial participation will lead to the development of employee attitudes that are more favourably inclined to the firm. Employees may feel greater commitment to and identification with the firm due to the alignment of interests, as in agency perspectives, or the gift made by the company, as in gift exchange perspectives (Cappelli and Conyon 2011; Bryson and Freeman 2014). Second, attitudinal change will lead to behavioural change, as manifested by greater work effort, co-operation with management, lower absenteeism, and the reduced likelihood of quitting. Third, these behavioural changes will lead to changes in collective performance.

There has been a large number of studies concerned with each of these three stages, though rarely two or more due to methodological reasons, over the last 35 years. The literature has to be treated with a degree of caution because many studies do not distinguish clearly between employee ownership, where there may be fundamental changes in how the company is run, and financial participation.

Employee attitudes

There are far more studies of the attitudinal effects of employee share ownership than profit sharing. Research typically compares shareholders and non-shareholders within the same company, employees in share ownership companies and those in companies without share ownership, and employers before and after a share scheme is implemented. The evidence tends to be mixed. Some studies have found attitudinal differences between shareholders and non-shareholders, as shown by differing levels of organizational commitment, but others have not. A methodological problem here is that those who choose to become employee shareholders, where participation is discretionary, may well be more committed to the firm in the first place. This may account for a similar finding in before and after studies that employee attitudes do not seem to change very much over time (Dunn et al. 1991). On balance, the evidence is more positive than negative, but the conditions under which financial participation affects employee attitudes is not fully clear. There is some evidence that participation in decision-making and other forms of employee involvement may be important, but equally the financial pay-off of financial participation may by influential (Buchko 1992).

The most comprehensive attempt to develop theory relating to employee attitudes in the context of ownership is that by Pierce and colleagues in their notion of 'psychological ownership' (Pierce et al. 1991). Broadly, this refers to how strongly employees feel like owners. This concept does not apply uniquely to company ownership, but is especially relevant to employee ownership (though less so financial participation). It is possible that psychological ownership mediates ownership and attitudes such as commitment: Pendleton et al. (1998) find that the extent of attitudinal change in employee-owned firms is dependent on the extent to which employees feel like owners.

Behaviour

Central to the justification for employee ownership provided by principal–agent and other theories is that financial participation will lead to behavioural change. The literature has taken two main approaches to the consideration of this. One involves comparison of behavioural indicators, such as employee turnover and absenteeism rates, across workplaces and firms. The other involves employee perceptions of how their behaviour has changed. As ever, there are methodological challenges: employees are unwilling to report unauthorized absences whilst quit rates are subject to a variety of other influences. Early versions of the British WERS did find lower quit rates in firms with employee share ownership plans (Sengupta et al. 2007), but this effect has been absent from the last two surveys (Sengupta et al. 2017). The largest-scale recent investigation of employee perceptions of behaviour has been conducted by Kruse et al. in the US (2010). They find that turnover is lower, workers work harder, and employees monitor fellow workers more when there is more 'shared capitalism'.

Company performance outcomes

Notwithstanding the shortcomings of and mixed results of investigations of employee attitudes and behaviour, there is a large body of evidence indicating positive performance effects of financial participation. A recent meta-analysis of 102 samples finds a small, but significant relationship (an average of around 4%) between employee ownership and firm performance (Boyle et al. 2016). There is also a body of evidence indicating that profit sharing has positive effects (Perotin and Robinson 2003). However, there is some evidence that the two forms of financial participation may effect performance outcomes via different routes, reflecting the different work environments the two systems are often found in Robinson and Wilson (2006). A common argument in the literature is that financial participation and other forms of employee involvement have a complementary relationship, but the evidence for this is not that strong (Kalmi et al. 2005; Pendleton and Robinson 2010).

An issue with many studies is reverse causality. Does financial participation lead to improved performance or does any relationship operate in the other direction? The latter is entirely plausible since better-performing firms, especially those with better financial performance, may have more to share with employees. A recent study of profit sharing by Kraft and Lang (2016) is notable for controlling for selection bias. They indeed find that profit-sharing firms are more productive before they implement profit sharing. However, they become more productive still after introducing it.

Conclusion

In this chapter we have sketched the development of employee financial participation, covering where, by whom and why it occurs. Various theoretical perspectives are offered that aim to explain the rationale for employers to adopt financial participation arrangements, and to predict the outcomes of doing so. On the whole, empirical evidence suggests that, although needing to be cautious due to methodological considerations, organizations do gain in terms of enhanced employee attitudes and behaviours. And that these can lead to better HR outcomes and, in turn, enhanced organizational performance outcomes; though the question of reverse causality lingers, prompting resistance to overgeneralization.

References

Andrews, M., Bellman, L., Schank, T. and Upward, R. (2010). The impact of financial participation on workers' compensation. *Journal for Labour Market Research*. 43, 72–89.

Baghdadi, L., Bellakhal, R., and Diaye, M. (2013). Financial participation: does the risk transfer story hold in France? *British Journal of Industrial Relations*. 54(1), 3–29.

Bellman, L. and Moller, I. (2016). Are firms with financial participation of employees better off in a crisis? Evidence from the IAB Establishment Panel Survey. *Management Revue*. 27(6), 304–320.

Boyle, E., Patel, P., and Gonzalez-Mule (2016). Employee ownership and firm performance: a meta-analysis. *Human Resource Management Journal.*

Bryson, A. and Freeman, R. (2014). Employee stock purchase plans: gift or incentive? Evidence from a multinational corporation. IZA Discussion Paper No. 8537. Bonn: IZA – Institute of Labour Economics.

Buchko, A. (1992). Effects of employee ownership on employee attitudes: a test of three theoretical perspectives. *Work and Occupations.* 19 (1), 59–78

Cappelli, P. and Conyon, M. (2011). Stock option exercise and gift exchange relationships: evidence for a large US company. NBER Working Paper No. w16814. Cambridge, MA: NBER.

Croucher, R., Brookes, M., Wood, G., and Brewster, C. (2010). Context, strategy and financial participation: a comparative analysis. *Human Relations.* 63(6), 835–855.

Dunn, S., Richardson, R., and Dewe, P. (1991). The impact of employee share ownership on worker attitudes: a longitudinal case study. *Human Resource Management Journal.* 1(3): 1–17.

Floquet, M., Guery, L., Guillot-Soulez, C., Laroche, P. and Stevenot, A. (2016). The relationship between profit sharing schemes and wages: evidence from French firms. *Management Revue.* 27 (6), 219–233.

Freeman, R., Kruse, D. and Blasi, J. (2010). Worker responses to shirking under shared capitalism. In Kruse, D., Freeman, R. and Blasi, J. (eds.). *Shared Capitalism at Work: Employee Ownership, Profit and Gain Sharing, and Broad-based Stock Options.* Chicago: University of Chicago Press.

Guery, L. and Pendleton, A. (2016). Do investments in human capital lead to employee share ownership: evidence from French firms. *Economic and Industrial Democracy.* 37, 567–591.

Heywood, J., Siebert, W., and Wei, X. (1997) Payment by results systems: British evidence. *British Journal of Industrial Relations.* 35(1), 1–22.

Jones, D., Kalmi, P. and Kato, T. (2012). Financial participation in Finland: incidence and determinants. *International Journal of Human Resource Management.* 23, 1570–1589.

Jones, D., Kalmi, P. and Makinen, M. (2006). The determinants of stock option compensation: evidence from Finland. *Industrial Relations.* 45(3), 437–468.

Jones, D. and Kato, T. (1993). The scope, nature, and effects of employee stock ownership plans in Japan. *Industrial and Labor Relations Review.* 46(2), 352–367.

Kaarsemaker, E., and Poutsma, E. (2006). The fit of employee ownership with other human resource management practices: theoretical and empirical suggestions regarding the existence of an ownership high-performance work system, or Theory O. *Economic and Industrial Democracy.* 27(2), 669–685.

Kalmi, P., Pendleton, A. and Poutsma, E. 2006. The relationship between financial participation and other forms of employee participation: new survey evidence from Europe. *Economic and Industrial Democracy.* 27, 637–667.

Kalmi, P., Pendleton, A. and Poutsma, E. 2005. Financial participation and performance in Europe. *Human Resource Management Journal.* 15(4), 54–67

Kalmi, P., Pendleton, A. and Poutsma, E. (2012). Bargaining regimes, variable pay and financial participation: some survey evidence on pay determination. *The International Journal of Human Resource Management.* 23(8), 1643–1659.

Kraft, K. and Lang, J. (2013). Profit sharing and training. *Oxford Bulletin of Economics and Statistics.* 75(6), 940–961.

Kraft, K. and Lang, J. (2016). Just a question of selection? The causal effect of profit sharing on a firm's performance. *Industrial Relations.* 55(3), 444–466.

Kruse, D. (1991). Profit sharing and employment variability: microeconomic evidence on the Weitzman theory. *Industrial and Labor Relations Review.* 44(3), 437–453.

Kruse, D. L. (1996). Why do firms adopt profit-sharing and employee ownership plans? *British Journal of Industrial Relations.* 34, 515–538.

Kruse, D., Blasi, J. and Park, R. (2010). Shared capitalism in the US economy: prevalence, characteristics, and employee views of financial participation in enterprises. In Kruse, D., Freeman, R. and Blasi, J. (eds.). *Shared Capitalism at Work: Employee Ownership, Profit and Gain Sharing, and Broad–based Stock Options.* Chicago: University of Chicago Press.

Kruse, D., Freeman, R. and Blasi, J. (2010). *Shared Capitalism at Work: Employee Ownership, Profit and Gain Sharing, and Broad-based Stock Options.* Chicago: University of Chicago Press.

Kurtulus, F. and Kruse, D. (2017). *How did Employee Ownership Firms Weather the Last Recession? Employee Ownership, Employment Stability, and Firm Survival in the US 1999–2011.* Kalamazoo, MI: Upjohn Institute.

Landau, I., O'Connell, A. and Ramsay, I. (2013). *Incentivising Employees: The Theory, Policy and Practice of Employee Share Ownership Plans in Australia.* Melbourne: Melbourne University Press.

Lavelle, J., Turner, T., Gunnigle, P. and McDonnell, A. (2012). The determinants of financial participation schemes within multinational companies in Ireland. *International Journal of Human Resource Management.* 23 (8), 1590–1610.

Lazear, E. (2000). Performance pay and productivity. *American Economic Review*. 90, 1346–1361.

Ligthart, P., Pendleton, A. and Poutsma, E. (2018). Financial participation: the nature and cause of national variation. In Brewster, C., Farndale, E. and Mayrhofer, W. (eds.). *Handbook of Comparative HRM* (2nd ed.). Cheltenham: Edward Elgar.

Long, R. and Fang, T. (2012). Do employees profit from profit sharing? Evidence from Canadian panel data *Industrial and Labor Relations Review*. 65 (4), 899–927.

Lowitzsch, J. (2006). *The PEPPER III Report: Promotion of Employee Participation in Profits and Enterprise Results in the new Member and Candidate Countries of the European Union*. Berlin: Free University, Inter-University Centre at the Institute for Eastern European Studies.

Lowitzsch, J., Hashi, I. and Woodward, R. (2008). *The PEPPER IV Report: Benchmarking of Employee Participation in Profits and Enterprise Results in the Member and Candidate Countries of the European Union*. Berlin: Free University, Inter-University Centre at the Institute for Eastern European Studies.

Oyer, P. (2004). Why do firms use incentives that have no incentive effects? *Journal of Finance*. 59 (4), 1619–1650.

Pendleton, A., Poutsma, E., Brewster, C., and Van Ommeren, J. (2001). *Employee Share Ownership and Profit Sharing in the European Union*. Dublin: European Foundation for the Improvement of Living and Working Conditions.

Pendleton, A., Poutsma, E., Van Ommeren, J., and Brewster, C. (2003). The incidence and determinants of employee share ownership and profit sharing in Europe. In Kato, T. and Pliskin, J. (eds.). *The Determinants of the Incidence and the Effects of Participatory Organizations*. Amsterdam: JAI Press.

Pendleton, A. and Poutsma, E (2004). *The Policies and Views of Peak Organizations Towards Financial Participation (synthesis report)*. Dublin: European Foundation for the Improvement of Living and Working Conditions.

Pendleton, A. and Robinson, A. (2010). Employee stock ownership, involvement and productivity: an interaction-based approach. *Industrial and Labor Relations Review*. 64 (1), 746–772.

Pendleton, A. and Robinson, A. (2011). Employee share ownership and human capital development: complementarity in theory and practice. *Economic and Industrial Democracy*. 32 (3), 439–457.

Pendleton, A. and Robinson, A. (2015). The productivity effects of mixed incentives. *Economic and Industrial Democracy*. 38(4), 588–608.

Pendleton, A., Wilson, N. and Wright, M. (1998). The perception and effects of share ownership: empirical evidence from employee buy-outs. *British Journal of Industrial Relations*. 36 (1), 99–124.

Perotin, V. and Robinson, A. (2003). 'Employee Participation in Ownership and Profit. A Review of the Issues and Evidence', (with V. Perotin). *European Parliament Working Paper, No. SOCI109EN*, Social Affairs Series, Directorate-General for Research. 2002.

Pierce, J., Rubenfeld, S., and Morgan, S. (1991). Employee ownership: a conceptual model of process and effects. *Academy of Management Review*. 16(1), 121–144.

Poutsma, E. (2001). *Recent Trends in Employee Financial Participation in the European Union*. Luxembourg: Office for Official Publications of the European Communities.

Poutsma, E., Ligthart, P., and Schouteten, R. (2005). Employee share ownership in Europe: The influence of US multinationals. *Management Revue*. 16(1), 99–122.

Poutsma, F., and Nijs, W. F. de. (2003). Broad-based employee financial participation in the European Union. *International Journal of Human Resource Management*. 14(6), 863–893.

Ramsay, H. (1977). Cycles of control: worker participation in sociological and historical perspective. *Sociology*. 11, 481–506.

Robinson, A. and Wilson, N. (2006). Employee financial participation and productivity: an empirical reappraisal. *British Journal of Industrial Relations*. 44(1), 31–50.

Sengupta, S., Whitfield, K. and McNabb, R. (2007). Employee share ownership and performance: golden path or golden handcuffs? *International Journal of Human Resource Management*. 18(8), 1507–1538.

Sengupta, S., Pendleton, A., Whitfield, K. and Huxley, K. (2017). Employee share ownership and organizational performance: a tentative opening of the black box. *Personnel Review early view*.

Uvalic, M. (1991). *The Promotion of Employee Participation in Profits and Enterprise Results. Social Europe, Supplement 3/91*. Luxembourg: Office for Official Publications of the European Communities.

Weitzman, M. (1984). *The Share Economy*. Cambridge, MA: Harvard University Press

Weitzman, M. L. and Kruse, D. L. (1990). Profit sharing and productivity. In Blinder, Alan S. (ed.), *Paying for Productivity: A Look at the Evidence* (pp. 95–142). Washington, DC: The Brookings Institution.

Welz, C., and Fernández-Macías, E. (2008). Financial participation of employees in the European Union: much ado about nothing? *European Journal of Industrial Relations*. 14(4), 479–496.

Wilson, N. and Peel, M. (1991). The impact on absenteeism and quits of profit sharing and other forms of employee participation. *Industrial and Labor Relations Review*. 44(3), 454–468.

26

PENSIONS/RETIREMENT BENEFITS

Geoff White

Introduction

The provision of an income for employees in their retirement has a long history. The earliest forms of pension scheme were created for public servants in the UK in the late seventeenth century and these were followed by some major private sector schemes in the nineteenth century. The first pension scheme in the USA was established for Presbyterian Ministers' widows and children in 1759 (Milkovich et al. 2017). It was only in the twentieth century, however, that the state began to provide some minimum retirement income for citizens. In the UK the first, non-contributory, state scheme was established in 1908.

The balance of responsibility for retirement income has always varied between the individual, the state and the employer and this complex picture is obvious once one looks at pensions from a comparative perspective. Pensions provided by employers are termed 'occupational pensions' to distinguish them from those provided on an individual basis (private pensions) and those provided by the state. In most European countries, the major source of retirement income is from the state, not the employer, although Ireland and the Netherlands have schemes similar to the UK. In many Asian, Latin American and African countries retirement income is very limited and, where provided, may be through provident funds which pay out a cash sum on retirement. The country most similar to the UK system is the USA, where there is a minimum state provision alongside employer funded schemes. In Australia, there is a means-tested state pension but from the 1990s compulsory private sector pensions have been required for everyone earning more than a fixed monthly figure and employers are obliged to pay into these private pensions. Most pension schemes in Australia are run on an industry basis, rather than at the company level (Schifferes 2005).

While the provision of pension schemes by employers requires specialist professional advice, because they form part of many organizations' benefits packages they are a key area of knowledge and skills for the reward manager. All those working in the field of reward management will be expected to have some basic knowledge of how pension schemes operate and the advantages and disadvantages of different forms of pension provision.

In this chapter we consider: (1) the rationale for employers providing a retirement income to their employees as part of their reward systems; (2) the various and changing forms that these schemes exhibit; and (3) the major challenges facing employers (and employees) in providing such benefits. In general, the academic research literature on pensions is limited and much of the literature is government-sourced material. Over the last three decades, occupational pensions have become a major issue for employers, not least because of their escalating costs, and in some large organizations where trade unions are present there has been increasing industrial conflict over changes to the existing schemes. Pensions remain a major part of the reward system in many countries, not least those where employers are required to provide some minimum level of cover. Given the wide range of practice in retirement income provision between countries, this chapter concentrates on the UK situation but reference is also made to other systems.

Employer rationale for pension schemes provision

The growth of employer-run occupational pension schemes is closely linked to the growth of welfare capitalism and the development of personnel management policies in the twentieth century. The first private employer pension schemes in the UK were developed in organizations associated with government, such as the Bank of England scheme in 1739 and from the mid-nineteenth century the emerging railway companies began establishing schemes for their employees. These were followed by large private sector firms such as Reuters (1882), W.H. Smith (1894) and Colmans (1899). Public sector schemes for schoolteachers and police officers began in 1890 and 1922, respectively. These early private employer schemes varied in form from simple flat cash amounts on retirement to pensions based on career average and final salary. Covering mainly managers and white-collar staff, these schemes did not cover the majority of the workforce and hence both friendly societies and trade unions began to introduce their own retirement benefits for members. These schemes were significant players in the past – for example, in 1901 the Northumberland and Durham Miners' Permanent Relief Society was paying significant pensions to 4000 members (Hewitt Associates 1991). From the twentieth century large private corporations began to introduce pension schemes as a useful aid to reward employee loyalty and retain those staff they wished to keep. Pensions developed alongside the growth of the 'internal labour market', in which employers sought to protect themselves from competition for their labour by providing a range of human resource practices which emphasized fair treatment (such as job evaluation) and paternalistic benefits (such as paid holidays and pensions).

A number of theoretical positions might explain the popularity of the provision of employee benefits and especially pensions. Robinson and Hudson (2008) suggest that such schemes may encourage and safeguard employers' investments in human capital and create employee commitment and loyalty to the organization. They might also be seen as a form of 'efficiency wage', which increases the total reward value above the market clearing rate to retain valuable labour. In such a way, employee benefits may encourage alignment of goals between the employer and employee, motivating employees to volunteer additional effort and provide private information useful to production. This may be especially the case where "workers' actions are unobservable or not easily measured and consequently the potential for opportunism is high" (Robinson and Hudson 2008:213). Where benefits levels are linked to hierarchical levels in the organization, employees may also be motivated by the prospect of promotion to a higher level. In contrast, where the provision of benefits is on a 'single status' basis, employees may be motivated by the sense of equity. US evidence indicates that there is a linkage between the provision of benefits and employee retention (Mitchell 1982; Schiller and Weiss 1979), but on closer examination the impact on mobility was found to be largely down to pensions and health care provision (Evan and Macpherson 1996; Mitchell 1982).

Forms of pension scheme

Apart from the issue of who provides the pension scheme – the state, the employer or the individual – there are also two major forms of financing the pension. These have become known as 'defined contribution' (DC) or 'defined benefit' (DB). In the former, also known as 'money purchase' schemes, the individual (and often the individual's employer) pay regular contributions into the scheme, but the amount of the final pension amount is not known until retirement age is reached. At that stage the total pension contributions in the individual's 'pot' are valued and a decision made about how much the fund will provide as a regular pension payment. The size of the final pension will therefore depend on both the size of the individual's fund, the investment performance of the fund over the individual's working life and the charges levied by the pension provider. In contrast, a 'defined benefit' scheme provides a pension on retirement based on a known formula and where the benefit does not depend on how much money is in the fund (i.e., the pension is guaranteed whether the fund is in surplus or deficit). Contributions are normally made to a DB scheme by the individual and their employer (although in some case schemes may be non-contributory for the individual) and the contributions are paid into a fund which, like DC schemes, is invested for growth. The formula used to calculate the pension is normally based on years of membership of the scheme and traditionally was based on the final salary of the individual at retirement (number of years x an agreed proportion of the final salary).

In recent years, however, these 'final salary' schemes have become unacceptably expensive for many employers and there has been a shift towards 'career average re-valued earnings' (CARE), where the pension is based on years of service x an agreed proportion of the average earnings re-valued over the working life. Where salaries increase in line with inflation, final salary and CARE schemes produce similar results in terms of the annual pension amount. CARE may therefore benefit those on lower incomes and those whose earnings peak in mid-career. Conversely, those whose salaries peak at the end of their careers benefit more from final salary. CARE is also fairer for women who may have career breaks. In some cases, public sector employees may be in schemes established by statute and based on a 'pay as you go' basis (there is no fund and the contributions of those in work pay the pensions of those in retirement) under which the government guarantees the cost of the scheme. These public sector schemes are governed by their own regulations and traditionally have been DB schemes.

There are advantages and disadvantages for both types of pension scheme (DC and DB) for both employers and employees. For employers, the advantage of a DC scheme is that contributions are capped (although contribution levels may rise with service). In general, employer contribution levels to DC schemes are much lower than to DB schemes. Research by the Office for National Statistics in the UK indicated that 69% of employer contributions to DC schemes were below 4%. Because there is no guaranteed level of pension for employees, the fund does not need to be topped up by the employer if it declines in value. For employees, the benefits of DC schemes are less clear as there is no guaranteed pension amount. However, if employees move between employers on a regular basis, the great advantage of DC schemes is the portability provided (i.e., the invested fund can be moved). Another advantage of DC schemes is the flexibility available in how the final fund can be drawn upon – from taking the whole amount in cash to buying an annuity.

In the case of DB schemes, the advantage to employers used to be that they helped recruitment and retention (and this is still seen as an advantage by some employers). DB schemes also had the benefit of setting a retirement age for employees which encouraged them to remain until retirement but no longer. In the UK, this is no longer the case since the default retirement age was removed in 2011. The big disadvantage for a DB employer, however, is that they have to bear the ultimate financial risk of the scheme and ensure that there is sufficient money in the fund to meet the scheme liabilities. The liabilities of a DB scheme may exceed its assets if salaries grow faster than expected, the age at which pensioners die increases (so the pension has to last longer) or the fund investment strategy does not meet expectations. Of course, in the past, when schemes were in surplus employers could cease making contributions (which many did in the 1980s and 1990s). For the employee, the advantages of a DB schemes are clearer. The final pension amount is guaranteed and hence there is some degree of financial security in old age. Portability is more of a problem with DB schemes, however, because moving between DB schemes is complex and expensive.

Because of the escalating cost of DB schemes, there has been a dramatic decline in their use. While overall membership of pension schemes in the UK has risen significantly – between 2008 and 2013 membership increased by 200,000 and between 2013 and 2015 by 2.5 million – membership of DB open private sector schemes (those still open to new members) fell to 0.6 million in 2014 from 1.4 million in 2006 (ONS 2015). The large increase in membership of DC schemes has been driven primarily by the new legal requirement for employers to automatically enrol employees into an occupational pension scheme.

The range of benefits available from a pension scheme to the pensioner will vary between schemes but some of the most common are: (a) an income in retirement; (b) the facility to draw down a tax-free lump sum; (c) dependents' benefits; and (d) benefits on death in service and death in retirement. In addition, DB schemes often include the ability to enhance the value of the pension through the employee making additional voluntary contributions (AVCs), the ability to purchase 'added years' to enhance the final pension, benefits on leaving the employer before normal retirement age (early retirement), and benefits on serious ill health.

Major challenges

Pension schemes face a number of challenges. As suggested above, the escalating cost of DB pension schemes has recently led to major changes in the provision of such schemes. A number of reasons might explain the decline in DB schemes and the rise of alternative DC arrangements.

- The cost of having to provide deferred pensions to those who have left the scheme and statutory increases to deferred pensions and pensions in payment, which deters employers from providing such schemes.
- The fact that pensioners are now living much longer in retirement, which means the pension has to last for a much longer period than had been funded for.
- The removal of the ability of employers to make occupational pension scheme membership compulsory for employees and the introduction of personal pensions, which reduced membership participation levels.
- The return on investment for pension funds has reduced significantly, given the low interest rates pertaining since the recession of 2008–10.
- The increased regulation of pension schemes, following the mis-selling scandals of the 1980s, has deterred employers from providing schemes (although from 2015 there is now a legal requirement for all employees to be automatically enrolled into a scheme providing minimum levels of benefit).
- A decision of the UK Accounting Standards Board in 2005 changed the way organizations are required to value pension fund assets and liabilities in annual accounts on a market-related basis, meaning that they can affect the company balance sheet and the perceived value of the company among investors.

- The size of the pensioner population is projected to grow significantly, leading to an imbalance between the total amount of pensions being paid out and the amount of employees' contributions to the fund. This can lead to funds having to sell assets to pay the guaranteed pensions, which, in turn, reduces the returns on assets, driving up cost further.

The Pensions Commission, chaired by Lord Adair Turner, was established in 2004 to analyse the problems faced in providing adequate pensions. Turner proposed four options:

- Pensioners will have to expect to be poorer in future.
- A greater share of taxation will need to be allocated to pensions.
- People will have to save more for their retirement.
- People will have to work longer.

Turner (2004) pointed out that the UK state pension scheme had been the least generous among developed countries, but that this had been compensated for by the voluntary privately funded pensions, so that the overall level of GDP transferred to pensioners was about the same as other countries. Given that the state was intending to reduce its spending on state pensions, and the trend in private pension provision had been towards less generous provision rather than greater, meant that the overall level of pension saving was falling. In the medium to long term, this would lead to many workers facing a bleak retirement. To avoid this crisis in pensions provision, Turner suggested three possible options – a major revamping of the voluntary system; significant changes to the state system; or an increased level of compulsory private pension saving. In his second report (2005), Turner laid out four recommendations. The state scheme was to be reformed to deliver a more generous, more universal, less means-tested and simpler state pension. Individuals would be strongly encouraged to save for their retirement through automatic enrolment in a scheme by the employer. Employers would be required to provide a minimum compulsory level of contribution for each employee. Turner also suggested the creation of a national Pension Savings Scheme. Following the Turner Report, the UK government produced new legislation, the Pensions Act 2007, which led to major reforms of the state scheme. This was followed by the Pensions Act 2008 which introduced automatic enrolment and led to the creation of the National Employment Savings Trust (NEST).

References

Evan, W. and MacPherson, D. (1996). Employer size and labor turnover: the role of pensions. *Industrial Relations and Labor Review*. 49(4), 707–729.

Milkovich, G., Newman, J. and Gerhart, B. (2017). *Compensation* (11 ed.). New York: McGraw-Hill Irwin.

Mitchell, O. (1982). Fringe benefits and labor mobility. *Journal of Human Resources*. 17(92), 286–298.

ONS. (2015). *Occupational Pension Schemes Survey 2014*. London: Office for National Statistics.

Robinson, A. and Hudson, R. (2008). From fringe to mainstream? A portrait of employee benefit provision in Britain. In Vartianien, M., Antoni, C., Baeten, X., Hakonen, N., Lucas, R. and Thierry, H. (eds.). *Reward Management – Facts and Trends in Europe*. Lengerich, Germany: Pabst Science Publishers.

Schifferes, S. (2005). *Pension reform: what other countries do*. BBC News. November 24. Available at: http://news.bbc.co.uk/go/pr/fr/1/hi/business/4462404.stm

Schiller, B. and Weiss, R. (1979). The impact of private pensions on firm attachment. *Review of Economics and Statistics*. 61 (3), 369–380.

Turner, A. (2004). *Pensions: Challenges and Choices: The First Report of the Pensions Commission*. London: The Stationery Office.

Turner, A. (2005). *A New Pension Settlement for the Twenty-First Century: the Second Report of the Pensions Commission*. London: The Stationery Office.

27

THE MARKET – WHAT MARKET? LONDON'S BIG BANG REWARD CONSEQUENCES, MYTHS AND MORALITY

Brian J. Dive

Introduction: the morality of 'enough'

It is a truth universally acknowledged that a well-run organization has an effective leader. Good CEOs deserve to be well rewarded. Forty years ago, a consensus was emerging in Europe that pay differentials should be around 5:1 (gross) from top to bottom in any organization. While that was shown to be unworkable, today we have more like 500:1, and climbing. How did this happen?

In the late 1990s, the self-styled social philosopher Charles Handy wrote:

> A society that does not recognise the morality of 'enough' will see excesses arise which verge on the obscene, as those who have the first choice of society's riches appropriate them for themselves. Democracy will not tolerate such an abuse of the market . . . When senior executives of companies earn fifty, sometimes even one hundred, times the pay of their own workers, it is hard not to feel that is an affront to those workers.
>
> *(Handy 1997)*

Yet it seems our moral sensitivity has been so bludgeoned by the pillage and plunder at the top of both private and public sector organizations that, twenty years later, Handy's admonition on the danger and extent of 'excess' seems almost quaint.

Across the Atlantic, US 'reward guru' Ed Lawler wrote: "The core reward principles that an organization develops should represent a standard for the organization – that is, the organization should always test its behavior against them." And, more recently, American philosopher Michael Sandel (2012:6) continued Handy (1997) and Lawler's (1990) theme: "Markets have become detached from morals and we need somehow to reconnect them." Rather obvious, of course, but try telling self-serving investment bankers that.

When did today's escalation in pay start and what caused it?

As good a place as any to start is 1974, when the Diamond Commission was set up in the UK by the Labour government to examine the distribution of wealth of those earning £10,000 or more whether employed or in self-employment. It was felt then that a ratio of 5:1 gross from the top earner to the lowest employee should be the norm.[1] Similar ideas were canvassed in the French Sudreau report published during the same period (Sudreau 1975) and were also gaining favour in The Netherlands, Denmark and Sweden. The only social democratic group out of step was in Germany where Willy Brandt referred to these ideas as "Kindergarten economics."

I was involved in preparing the Unilever submission to the Commission in 1975. We showed the objective was unworkable by focusing on the net lifetime earnings of a manager in a large factory compared to the that of the lowest-paid worker in the same factory: the unskilled cleaner.[2] The figures demonstrated that the final average lifetime earnings of the factory manager compared to the cleaner were 1.8:1 gross and 1.6:1 net. Added to which the company's submission showed that the cleaner's earnings, indexed at 100 in 1965, had risen to 118 by 1975, while that of the manager had fallen to 96 on the same basis.[3] Bear in mind that inflation in the UK in the mid-1970s reached 26% and that the government then froze salaries over £8500, which triggered substantial distortion in the market. This was the reality of working under a high-tax, socialist government with a philosophy that eroded all incentive for a young person to go to university and work up to a top role at the end of a long career. My experience of the recent Hutton Commission on fair pay (2011) demonstrated that some of this thinking about a desire for narrow differentials is alive and well.

Developments post-Diamond

The erosion of the importance of performance pay

One impact of Diamond and the Labour government's executive pay freeze in the 1970s was the beginning of the erosion of the importance of pay for performance. Rocketing inflation saw managers' standard of living falling very quickly. Little ingenuity was required to introduce a raft of tax-effective fringe benefits to protect living standards. During this period the incidence of the car benefit increased rapidly in the UK and it reached much further down into management layers than was the case, for example, in Germany. Education allowances were introduced, travel subsidies, 'working clothes' (suits) and so on. If, as was the case, benefits are given to all management, irrespective of their performance, it is self-evident that this undermines the philosophy of 'pay for performance', which was a fundamental principle stated in the management remuneration policies of the day.

The undermining of the need for market measurement

It also led to the first subtle undermining of the need for accurate assessment of the market since this was becoming irrelevant in an era when fringe benefits ruled and cost of living payments outreached merit percentages as the inflation rate reached 26%. Since performance was not the key factor influencing the level of individual reward, market measurement to establish competitiveness was less critical. This only began to be reversed when the Thatcher (Conservative) government started to tax individual benefits in line with their income tax level. This change encouraged the payment of salaries rather than the extensive awarding of benefits which, in turn, made the collection of taxes more straightforward for the government and in theory put greater focus on merit. But just as life was returning to 'normal' with less dramatic levels of inflation another tremor hit the London and UK executive pay markets.

The 'Big Bang' in London

The 'Big Bang' refers to the day of deregulation for the securities market in London on October 27, 1986, a day on which the London Stock Exchange (LSE) became a private limited company.

The Big Bang witnessed many changes in the financial markets, including the removal of fixed commission charges, the removal of the distinction between stockbrokers and stockjobbers, and the switch from open-outcry to electronic trading. The changes led to large banks taking over old firms. It was part of the UK government's reform programme aimed at the elimination of the City's major problems: overregulation and the widespread influence of 'old boy' networks and was predicated on the doctrines of free market competition and meritocracy.

The consequences of the Big Bang

Although the Big Bang triggered some beneficial changes, it also had some negative effects. Due to the deregulation of the markets, the concentration of power was focused on the big companies that took over long-standing small, often family-run, firms. This same change created by the Big Bang trickled throughout the financial systems around the world. Now, financial cities are dominated by companies that are 'too big to fail', trends which led to the Great Recession that began in 2008. More relevant to this topic, however, Big Bang started to erode further the disciplines underpinning the measurement of market pay for individuals. During this period for the first time, I encountered reward managers in those large banks that had gobbled up the small family firms in the late 1980s, on recruitment drives talking of 'the need to pay the market rate'. One group in short supply at this time was accountants, whose pay started to reflect the increased levels of competition. Yet beyond this simplistic belief that every job or person had a specific 'market rate', I was shocked to notice that the 'science' behind this talk of the market was a reality that said, in effect: 'We have to pay that because this is what he (then, still invariably 'he') wants. So, that is what he is worth. That is his market rate.' When I asked 'What is the margin of error in your assessment?', I was lucky to get so much as a blank stare.

It was sloppy work by the reward profession, which helped unleash the start of a 'free for all' in financial services that has continued to accelerate since then. There was allegedly a shortage of 'talent', rarely defined or rigorously assessed, which contributed to an erosion of market measurement disciplines. In short, Big Bang fuelled a spurious unshackling of reward constraints, unleashing a scramble for the highest 'market rate' under the misnomer of 'competition for talent' (cf. Greenbury 1995), which has continued unchecked into the twenty-first century.

The erosion of skill and techniques needed to reliably assess the market

My mentor in the 1970s, Philip Clemow, a qualified actuary and mathematician, taught me the basics concerning the statistical validity needed to measure a particular executive reward market reliably. If one was attempting to measure a national market, such as the UK, the critical foundation was the composition of the panel of comparator enterprises. It was important to have at least one 'leading player' from all of the key industries, with each being of comparable size, complexity and taking a professional approach to assessing the accountability of roles and their consequent reward levels. It was also a requirement to change a couple of companies within the panel each year to protect the reliability of the sample. Following the Big Bang, financial institutions first broke this fundamental rule of statistical reliability by setting up a club of similar companies in the one single industry, which measured only a small part of the executive market in the UK. This led predictably to gross pay distortions, as will be shown below.

The effective approach was to survey a wide cross-section of job types ('families') *and* at different layers across the company. Thus, one could establish Table 27.1, which illustrates the known degree of statistical error of varying samples.

Table 27.1 Maximum error of market position as a % of the comparator company's salary level

No. of companies in different industries	No. of jobs per company			
	5	*10*	*20*	*30*
5	6.9	4.5	3.1	2.5
10	4.8	3.1	2.1	1.7
20	3.3	2.2	1.5	1.2
30	2.7	1.8	1.2	1.0

For example, as set out in Table 27.1, a sample of five jobs from five banks could at best yield a result that was either 7% above the market rate or 7% below it. Such a spread (14%) is worse than useless. The trouble is that many reward managers seem oblivious to this.

Table 27.1 also shows that a mix of 30 jobs across at least 20 *different companies in different industries*: a totally reliable measure of a national market since the error rate is well within the acceptable statistical error, at 1.2. The next critical variable is the number and mix of jobs, across different levels which, after a certain point, provides greater significance than the number of companies. Thus, for example, a sample limited to 15 companies with at least 20 jobs per company would give a result within +/-2%, which is statistically acceptable.

In recent years, probably the worst example of this breakdown in statistical orthodoxy has been in financial services, where a favoured consultant's survey panel consisted of *only companies such as banks*. This was in fact a club spiralling upwards without any valid connection to the actual UK executive remuneration market. This provided docile (or statistically illiterate) remuneration committees (remcos) with 'evidence' needed to award ever more grotesque pay increases, which spiralled upwards. The people talking about 'measuring the market rate' were only approximating a measurement of the market, because their method, taking a reading of only a small slice of the total market, was unsound. History and statistical theory suggests that such a club quickly becomes a separate rogue market. In this way, the 'submarket' exists as a separate segment and drives 'club' remuneration levels up (they could, in theory, fall, but that tends not to happen given the objective of the 'club') and then takes on a life of its own. This submarket continues to ratchet rates upwards as an executive in that it now expects a certain amount for his/her job – more than job family peers in other industries – and has the option to move to a 'club' competitor if not paid according to that expectation. The inflationary genie is then out of the bottle of statistical rectitude. Pressure for better rewards is nothing new. Professional ineptitude is.

In 2009, I undertook a survey of management base pay in the UK for a client that aimed to be (and was) at or near the top of its industry, but which suspected financial companies were paying well above the UK executive management market. I had a sample of pay from over 20,000 jobs in the financial sector covering Work Levels 1 to 5.[4] This revealed that the median of the financial services market base pay was indeed around 30% higher than my client and the trend line indicated the rate of progression was ever upwards. Just imagine the effect of that on the multipliers used for bonus payments, long-term 'incentives' and the other rewards paid by these banks. This example illustrates just how quickly unprofessional statistical surveys can distort the reading of a given market, whether intentional or otherwise, where 'damn lies' become the norm.

Within twenty years, the banking market had risen well ahead of other companies in the UK, primarily because of the unprofessional way it was measured. Was this justified? What was so special about banking jobs? In truth, very little; certainly not enough to justify the market gap. Most jobs in a bank across, for example, Finance, HR, IT, Market Research, Tax, Treasury, to name but a few, clearly do not warrant a premium. They are common to the national market. And candidates were not really in short supply, despite the so-called 'war for talent'. Added to which the few jobs that were specific to the industry were exposed by the 2008–9 financial crisis selling bundles of securities they did not understand. One cannot envisage the management of an oil, consumer goods, pharmaceutical or car company being so ignorant of their own products. Finally, my field-work since 2003 has revealed UK banks as the most consistently overmanaged, excessively layered, bureaucratic and wasteful organizations in the private sector (see Dive 2016, for the evidence). The logic for any sort of premium based on performance or shortage of talent in the sector has been wafer-thin at best (Dive 2009). The banking pay bubble is real, but artificial and unjustified.

The onset of variable pay for executives

The next significant development accelerating the climb to steeple-high differentials was the onset of variable pay, which started to come into Europe via the UK in the 1990s, although the US market had been awash with variable pay and long-term awards for some considerable time prior to that. This was probably another trickle-down result of Big Bang coupled with more international companies coming into London and thereby increasing the mobility of management it encouraged, as Herwig Kressler has argued.[5] Thus 'the bonus' initially began to become established in London headquartered companies, especially those in financial services. At broadly the same time, companies started to identify international cadres of, usually, top managers who increasingly argued they were in an international market and therefore should have rewards based on international relativity. For example, in 2002 BP, then the second-largest company in the UK, announced that its CEO had been given a rise of 72%. His workers had been offered increases of 3% during the same period, at a time when 1,000 jobs were cut. His salary and bonuses rose from £1.8 million to £3.1 million. Leaving aside share options of another £2.6 million, his earnings were already more than 100 times the national average. When asked to justify such an increase, the company explained this decision that was based on a comparison with the largest oil company in the world, ExxonMobil, which had paid its CEO £22 million the previous year – a figure that included non-salary items! This was a highly questionable benchmark, since ExxonMobil was a much larger and more complex organization than BP. BP also pointed out that their CEO was a long way behind Britain's top earner at Vodafone (ranked at number 3 in the UK), meaning that the increase was 'justified' by market relativities. This was a classic case of an inability to identify relevant and accurate benchmarks. This was *not* an international market at the time: was it credible to anticipate that Exxon would have looked inside BP for a successor to its CEO? This stardust logic was apparently accepted and swallowed whole by shareholders at the time, however. Corporate governance initiatives and remco roles are discussed further below.

The history of variable pay

Variable pay originally applied to blue-collar work in the early twentieth century, where quantity and quality of work was easily and immediately measurable. It was the child of industrial mass production and the insights of so-called 'Scientific Management', with its time and motion studies calling for subordination and conformity to the machine, not individuality and innovation. Workers in factories and offices had no impact on the design of the processes underpinning their work. Time and motion studies gave way in time to systems analysis, operations research, process engineering and latterly cybernetics and the digital economy (see Vartianinen, this volume). Thus, well into the second half of the twentieth century variable pay was a feature of both unskilled and semi-skilled work. By the mid-1980s, however, variable pay for management roles that emerged in the US in the 1970s had migrated to Europe. It was underpinned by three myths, the entrepreneurial myth, the incentive myth and the market myth, discussed in turn below. Initially, the bonus element in Europe represented 10% or perhaps as much as 20% of salary, but by the end of the twentieth/beginning of the twenty-first century the levels were already being expressed in multiples of salary.

The entrepreneurial myth

Large businesses tend to be run not by entrepreneurs or owner-managers, but by individuals with employment contracts. A need and desire for a new 'dynamism' after the difficult 1970s and 1980s, following the growth years of the 1960s, gave rise to so-called 'entrepreneurial' pay policies. It was then argued that the earlier practice of a fixed salary and key perquisites such as a company car was not the kind of guaranteed reward an entrepreneur would expect. Rather, if entrepreneurial behaviour was sought then manager-employees should have part of their income at risk, as had traditionally been the case with salesmen. This reinforced thinking about paying a bonus in addition to the management salary, since that part of the reward package would be 'at risk' and would therefore drive higher performance, achievement and innovation. Within a decade, this logic saw the emergence of share schemes and options based on the logic of 'variableness is a good thing' if the aim is entrepreneurial leadership and innovation. Gifford Pinchot even invented the term 'intrapreneur' for an entrepreneur inside an organization (Macrae 1982). For others, however, this was an oxymoron. The desire for money can father many illegitimate offspring.

The incentive myth

The next myth that increasingly flourished in this 'gung-ho' environment was the labelling of variable pay as 'incentive pay'. Another misnomer, although 'inventive pay' may have been nearer the mark. The word 'incentivise' seems to have landed around 1990. Since then its usage has soared by 1,400 per cent (cited by Sandel 2012:87); a Lexis-Nexis search of newspapers' use of 'incentivise' reveals a similar trend. Kressler (2003:43) is also very sceptical:

> Incentive systems do not motivate because they cannot. Instead they do other things, such as encourage certain levels of performance [I would rephrase as 'behaviours'] independent of the degree of motivation in the short term.

He argues persuasively that motivation and incentive cannot be lumped together. But, of course, most reward specialists and remcos seem to do just that. In short, he plays out the powerful argument started by Herzberg (1968) that money does not (of itself) motivate, although Gellerman (1963) implied it could steer behaviour if paid in very large dollops (see also Fish, this volume).

The consolidated market-performance myth

Kressler (op. cit.) insightfully refers to the 'market-performance paradox'. In all my years of surveying executive remuneration around the world, I almost never encountered a situation where 'variable' pay levels went down. Variability was only upwards, with one exception, which was the Ford Motor Company, whose bonuses could fall in a year when sales targets were missed. The logic behind this mentality has now been stitched into the so-called market argument: i.e., 'we must pay the market rate'. The original 'entrepreneurial' argument about some reward being 'at risk' has atrophied. It has been replaced by one riddled with self-interest and more than a little hypocrisy. This was illustrated by the CEOs of banks such as Varley and Hester when challenged about the rates of pay they were offering to new recruits in the midst of the Financial Crisis. According to John Varley, then Barclays CEO, writing in the *Telegraph* in 2009:

> On the one hand, we must be sensitive to the views of many stakeholders that bankers are paid too much. On the other, we have to recognise that talent is not a commodity, and that our shareholders and customers expect Barclays to field the best people we can across all of our businesses. . . . We compete in global markets, and labour has, in my experience, never been more mobile. Our objective is to pay the minimum compensation consistent with competitiveness and performance.
>
> *(cited by Ahmed and Aldrick 2009)*

Citing his own circumstances at RBS following adverse reaction to bonus payments in 2012, Stephen Hester declared to the *Guardian*: "I attempt to be commercial in the results I get, and I want to be commercial in the way I'm treated . . . albeit in a societal debate I can't win" (Treanor 2012).

By the end of the twentieth century, the favoured pattern and stated logic for reward that emerged was:

- Pay for performance – salary.
- Pay for results – bonus, shares, options, long-term incentive plans.
- Pay competitively – according to the market.

But with the market-performance paradox operating, rather than being but one valid factor 'market rate' becomes the sole determinant of pay levels, undermining equitable reward given the deficiencies in market measurement already highlighted. And administration of 'bonus' awards degenerates into an expectation. Not the espoused logic of those advocating 'entrepreneurial reward policies'. Worse than that, if the bonus is not paid for performance it has to be paid for spurious 'market reasons' – 'otherwise I am underpaid!'.

Quis custodiet ipsos custodes?[6]

Regulatory influence seems to be muted. I was once replacing a job-grading system, implementing levels of accountability in a bank that was told by the sector's Regulator that a job evaluation scheme was mandatory. The Regulator seemed to be oblivious, however, to the overlayering and ineffective leadership development these schemes were causing. And where is the influence on this sorry state of affairs of the professional body as custodian of best practice and standards in reward management and general HRM? Perhaps, latterly, the CIPD is attempting to influence debate. In early 2018, on what has become known as 'Fat Cat Thursday', the Institute's Chief Executive called for ". . . a significant re-think on how and why we reward CEOs" (CIPD press release 2018).

In theory that leaves corporate shareholders, subject in the UK to The Stewardship Code, referred to by the Financial Reporting Council in December 2017 when distributing proposed revisions to the Corporate Governance Code (FRC 2017). The FRC (op. cit.: 1) call for "responsible engaged investors to work alongside company executives to achieve . . . long-term success". The problem is that shareholders too are rarely entrepreneurs these days, instead being invariably another layer of 'professional management'. For example, as I write this the Investors arm of the Aviva Insurance company are lobbying other investors to break out Openreach from its mothership, BT. These are managers simply responsible for handling a pile of other people's funds available for investment. They have no 'skin in the game' and are not noticeably motivated by what is best for BT, its customers, its employees or its pensioners, let alone the health of Openreach. They are simply trying to up the return on Aviva's investments, which, if positive, will do no harm to the Aviva managers' bonuses.

Governance issues and Remuneration Committees

Robert Maxwell's pillaging of Mirror Group pension funds in 1988 gave rise to a number of committees and reports on governance. Cadbury in 1992 which "begat Greenbury's (1995) unhappy and unsuccessful attempt to tackle the then heated argument on executive directors' pay which in turn begat the Hampel Report (1998)" (Garratt 2003). Garratt (op. cit.) was rightly critical of Greenbury, since his committee was made up of chairmen and CEOs of boards whose unhelpful 'conclusions' could have been written up in advance. Although these initiatives led to much-needed improved governance overall, their contributions to executive reward have simply stoked the fires of greed or at best cognitive dissonance.

One outcome of these reports was the establishment of Remuneration Committees and the publication of executive remuneration outcomes as part of quoted companies' annual reporting cycle. Remcos are a fine idea on paper, but it seems little thought was given by the great and good chiselling their various governance reports as to how they would work in practice and, more importantly, who should sit on them and what would be their level of relevant competence. It would be interesting, and I suspect revealing, to study how many remco members in the UK have any experience in the field of reward management, let alone conducting executive remuneration surveys. Their collective performance has not been a noticeable success since most of those serving on remcos are 'remuneration experts' based on a sample of one: their own salary. If you wish to question this assertion, simply ask a remco: "What is the statistical reliability of the data on which you are basing your decisions?"

I will limit myself to just one example to illustrate the last two paragraphs. The Northern Rock[7] remco decided they should align their directors' rewards to 'the market' and chose as their working benchmark HSBC in London, whose public remuneration details they could access in the remuneration report of their annual report and accounts. They noted that the London bank was 'a bit bigger' (by a factor of about ten although, as far as I know, this was not acknowledged in any Northern Rock annual report and accounts) so felt a relationship of about 80% between their respective banks was 'about right' . . . The pay premium of the London market was ignored or perhaps not understood. I had worked in Northern Rock at the time of its turnaround and assessed the bank as *Work Level 5* – i.e., having five discrete levels of accountability. NR was a small, regional bank while HSBC was a very large international bank. Although I have not worked in HSBC it would seem the CEO's job could be *Work Level 8*. This is a huge chasm in size and complexity that no job evaluation expert worth his or her salt would seriously countenance as the basis for any meaningful comparison, let alone a decision. This approach reveals naivety and ignorance of the basics on how to assess market-comparative data by the remco in question. Unless, of course, the aim was more self-serving. It meant the NR executives were obscenely overpaid. Add to that their incompetent performance in achieving the first run on a British bank in over a century and you have to wonder about the value of the remco. And, taking the counterfactual position, if the HSBC reward details had not been public would the NR project have been so readily fed?

The influence of pay consultants

Remco executives might defend themselves by claiming they are advised by pay consultants who, after all, are 'the experts in the specialism' and, of course, using third-party advisors 'guarantees objectivity'. Pay consultants are another reward gift from the US. Anti-trust law precluded companies from sharing information as this was deemed anti-competitive. This included management compensation, as it is called in America, which in turn spawned the need for consultants in this field. In due course, these spread to other countries that did not need them since there was already a practice in other parts of the world for in-house top reward specialists to exchange this information as required – although with a necessary caveat regarding hermetically sealed 'pay clubs' as discussed earlier in the chapter.

Reviewing the collective performance of reward consultants over the last thirty years reveals some basic flaws in their various approaches. As I conducted surveys around the world, it was noticeable that their interpretation of their own job evaluation systems was applied inconsistently from country to country and even from industry to industry within a country by different consultants. Again, an example from the UK may illustrate the point: not so long ago I assessed two key jobs in two different organizations. One was in a bank and the other in one of the UK's largest local authorities. Both jobs were given the same points by the same consultant company. The trouble was that, based on their discrete decision rights, the role in the bank was Level 4 and the other was Level 6. Although consultants vigorously deny this, it was further proof that their systems are driven by their sizing factors that fail validly to assess relative decision-making accountability. Banks wallow in other people's cash which is given to them; local authorities do not.

The other major flaw relates to pay consultants' guidance on target positions in the market. The standard advice is to position the company at the upper quartile of the relevant market. Now it is self-evident that if everyone is aiming to be at the upper quartile, then that becomes the average of the market. No problem for the consultant, as this simply triggers a flurry of leap-frogging as each company strives to correct its 'slippage' in the market when the consultant survey illustrates it has dipped below its target position. Ditto for every other company in the panel. Great business for the consultant company, which is the perennial winner in this game. So, pity the remcos. Most do not seem to know how to reliably measure the market and are advised by consultants who are muddying the water. But, you might say, isn't this all really irrelevant as the financial services sector is simply awash with greed and this will nullify any attempts to establish fair reward? Let's turn to that by way of a conclusion to the chapter.

Summing up: cognitive dissonance or immorality?

There are no doubt people in banking and elsewhere whose god is mammon and who are obsessed with money. It also helps explain the industry's great resistance to properly splitting retail banking from the 'casino' investment banks. But it would be simplistic to ascribe *all* these distortions, including the explosion of differentials, to greed and moral or ethical deficiencies (see Allan, this volume).

Kressler (2003) points out that pay has two sides: one rational, the other emotional. Purchasing power represents the rational side – although anyone who has dealt with expatriates arguing about their respective standards of living would wish it was so simple! The emotional aspect is more about relativities. How well am I doing compared to: last year, others, my expectations? This he describes as the 'diabolical side' of money. It tends to leave us dissatisfied, aggrieved, disappointed as soon as we discover disharmonies to any one of these or other relativities. This, he says, is not greed but 'cognitive dissonance', i.e., the state of having inconsistent thoughts, beliefs, or attitudes, especially as relating to behavioural decisions and the capacity to change them. A phenomenon which has been aggravated by well-meaning, but clumsy governance efforts in the field of executive reward.

Consider for a moment the following. If CEO A takes home a salary of £2 million, but CEO B is now known from public information to earn £3.5 million, the former may be forgiven for thinking that he or she is underpaid, not because he or she has not earned "enough" to make a decent living but probably because of a belief they have been undervalued and 'exploited' since they cannot be worth less than a peer. So, the leapfrogging discussion begins. . .

Based on current Anglo-American executive reward management practice, the answer to the 'What market?' question posed at the chapter's outset seems to be: 'any market will do; the higher the better'. Pseudo-professionalism, cognitive dissonance and greed prevail. Such shortcomings in the institutional architecture of executive pay ought to be redressed.

Notes

1 It is worth recalling the marginal tax rate then reached 80% and could go higher in some cases. It was a gross ratio in more ways than one.
2 The calculations in both cases assumed a married man with two children (one under 11 and one over 16) and no other sources of income and no other deductions other than National Insurance and a contribution to the company pension fund.
3 Unilever's evidence to the Diamond Commission (1975), table 3, p. 11.
4 For a description of levels of accountability (Work Levels), see chapter 8 of Dive (2016).
5 Personal lecture notes on H. W. Kressler, 'Management Pay between Promise and False Trails', University of Vienna 2009/2010.
6 "Who guards the guards themselves?", Juvenal, *Satire VI*, lines 347–348.
7 Any discussion of specific pay is fraught with confidentiality issues, but this does not apply in this case since Northern Rock no longer exists and the information is now over ten years out of date.

References

Ahmed, K. and Aldrick, P. (2009). Barclay's John Varley admits banks have 'much to be sorry for'. Available at: www.telegraph.co.uk/finance/newsbysector/banksandfinance/6570677/Barclays-John-Varley-admits-banks-have-much-to-be-sorry-for.html, accessed January 9, 2018.
CIPD. (2018). Press release: *Fat Cat Thursday 2018*. Available at: www.cipd.co.uk/about/media/press/040118-fat-cat-thursday, accessed on January 9, 2018.
Dive, B. J. (2009). Why do banks continue to waste talent? *Industrial & Commercial Training*. 40(1), 15–19.
Dive, B. J. (2016). *Mission Mastery: Revealing a 100-Year-Old Leadership Secret*. Gewerbestrasse, CH: Springer.
FRC. (2017). *Proposed Revisions to the UK Corporate Governance Code*. London: Financial Reporting Council.
Garratt, B. (2003). *Thin on Top*. London: Nicholas Brealey.
Greenbury, R. (1995). *Directors' Remuneration: Report of the Study Group Chaired by Sir Richard Greenbury*. London: Gee Publishing.
Gellerman, S. W. (1963). *Management and Productivity*. New York, NY: American Management Association.
Handy, C. (1997). *The Hungry Spirit*. London: Hutchinson.
Herzberg, F. (1968). One more time: how do you motivate employees? *Harvard Business Review*. 46(1), 53–62.
Kressler, H. W. (2003). *Motivate and Reward*. London: Palgrave Macmillan.
Lawler, E. E., III. (1990). *Strategic Pay Aligning Organizational Strategies and Pay Systems*. San Francisco: Jossey-Bass.
Macrae, N. (1982). Intrapreneurial now: big goes bust. *The Economist*. 283, 47–52.
Sandel, M. J. (2012). *What Money Can't Buy*. London: Allen Lane.
Sudreau, P. (1975). *The Reform of the Enterprise in France*. Paris: Documentation Française.
Treanor, J. (2012). RBS boss Stephen Hester speaks out after bonus row. Available at: www.theguardian.com/business/2012/feb/08/rbs-stephen-hester-bonus-row, accessed on January 9, 2018.

28

CEO PAY AND CORPORATE FINANCIALIZATION

The UK in comparative perspective

Andreas Kornelakis and Howard Gospel

Introduction

In 1965 the pay of the average US Chief Executive Officer (CEO) pay was times higher than that of the average worker pay; thereafter it has massively increased, to 123 times higher in 1995 and 303 times higher in 2014 (Mishel and Davis 2015:3). In all countries, executive pay has attracted considerable attention with the public, in the media, and among policy makers and it has spurred debates across many countries. In the UK, the controversy around executive remuneration has focused on four key issues: (i) the relatively high level of pay; (ii) the lack of transparency in determining reward; (iii) the opaque relationship between pay and corporate performance; and (iv) the growing use of incentives and bonuses which may have prompted 'dysfunctional' behaviour (Kessler 2013:260). This chapter will focus on the following questions, dealing with the UK in particular: How can we account for the widening of the CEO-to-worker pay gap over recent years and how can we explain its cross-national variation? What are the possible means to arrest this trend and what are the implications for reward management practice?

The chapter is structured as follows. The next section will consider theoretical perspectives which we argue may explain the high levels of CEO pay. In particular, it will draw on concepts and models derived from so-called Personnel Economics and from Political Economy. As the recent trends cannot be fully explained by either approach, the chapter will add an alternative explanation relating to the financialization of the economy and companies, in both the financial and the non-financial sectors. The chapter then briefly considers the different regulatory approaches towards curbing CEO pay in the US, Continental Europe and the UK. The final section concludes with some implications for reward management practice.

Theoretical perspectives on CEO pay: between economics and political economy

CEO pay: an economics perspective

Traditionally, economics had seen pay setting in terms of supply and demand factors in the labour market and had suggested that people were paid according the value of their production, or their so-called marginal productivity. Workers would also be rewarded for the nature of the job – how much responsibility they had to take on or how dirty or dangerous the job was. Workers could not be paid consistently above or below the going rate: if they were paid above, the employer would go out of business; if they were paid below, workers would leave. There were many criticisms of such theories – that they ignored power relations, the forces of comparison, customary notions in pay setting; moreover, the empirical reality was that the actual structure of wages did not match the theory and some individuals doing the same job were paid very different wages in different firms. Moreover, the theory did not tell one about the magnitudes of differences in pay, nor how these might move over time (Boyer and Smith 2001). In recent years, two influential bodies of theory have been elaborated within economics, which have sought to add to these theories and to analyse in particular top management pay. The first of these is 'principal–agent' theory and the second 'tournament' theory. We pay more attention to each of these.

Principal–agent theory sees owners or shareholders as 'principals', while it sees CEOs and top managers as 'agents'. It is argued that the interests of the latter need to be aligned with the interests of the former, given risks in terms of: (i) moral hazard; (ii) transaction costs; and (iii) asymmetric information. Because of the presence of these risks, the theory suggests that aligning the incentives of managerial agents with those of owner principals is best served by the link of pay to company performance, in particular to the share price of the company, and binding them into the company by high pay (Lazear 1998:122).

First, moral hazard is present in a situation in which a person has little incentive to act honestly or with due prudence in the absence of penalties or corrective incentives. For example, CEOs may be inclined to seek excessive 'perks', which will increase their own utility, but may decrease the wealth of the company and therefore contradict shareholders' interests. Second, transaction costs include the costs of negotiating contracts with CEOs and also 'monitoring' costs used to assess and evaluate performance. These transaction costs, it is argued, can be reduced if there is a close link to performance. Third, asymmetric information suggests that CEOs have superior information compared to shareholders, regarding the state of the shareholders' investment, and therefore again the use of this should be mitigated by financial incentives.

Jensen and Murphy (1990:139–142) argued that a combination of three basic principles will create the 'right' monetary incentives: (i) CEOs should become owners of stock; (ii) compensation systems should provide big rewards for superior performance and big penalties for poor performance; and (iii) the threat of penalties and dismissal for poor performance should be real. The argument was that the advantages of these principles are that they align shareholders' interests and discourage opportunistic behaviour.

But these principles also have disadvantages; they may encourage short-termism (e.g., cuts in difficult to observe investments, such as training); they may make CEOs risk-averse in some areas (e.g., reluctant to spend on risky R&D); conversely, they may encourage CEOs to take risky initiatives in other areas (e.g., news that may increase share price); and they may discourage the sense of the company as a team. While there is some evidence suggesting a positive relationship between performance-related pay schemes and firm productivity (Kornelakis et al. 2016), there is inconclusive evidence suggesting a strong relationship between CEO pay and company performance. In an early article in this area, Gregg et al. (1993) found a weak link between CEO pay and performance, while they also found evidence of empire-building behaviour from CEOs. More recent evidence suggests that the link between CEO pay and performance is conditional: for instance, it is strong when institutional owners (e.g., pension funds) have a large equity share (see Bell and Van Reenen 2013). These inconclusive empirical findings have quite strong theoretical underpinnings.

The so-called '*tournament*' theory, deriving from Personnel Economics, is another way to analyse the pay gap between CEOs and average workers (Lazear 1998:225–227). The theory conceptualizes the position of CEO as the 'prize' in the final stage of a notional tournament.

One of the assumptions is that there is a 'demonstration effect' attached to the process and this provides the incentive for people lower down in the organizational hierarchy to expend more effort and work harder to climb the career ladder. The greater the wage gap, the more effort they are incentivized to expend. What matters for promotion in the tournament is *relative* performance between competing colleagues at each stage, and the tournament *ranks* employees according to their productivity. At the final stage of the tournament there is no further career advancement, hence the value of the prize should be a very high reward. Although the principal–agent theory justifies why CEO pay needs to be linked with performance and the tournament perspective seeks to explain the pay gap between CEO and average worker, neither would seem to explain why CEO pay has increased so much over time. Presumably, historically there have always been principal–agent problems and tournaments have always taken place.

Other recent arguments to explain increases in the level of CEO pay shift the attention to 'efficient contracting' (Murphy 2013). The literature harks back to an older tradition and suggests that the observed level and composition of compensation reflects a competitive equilibrium in the market for managerial talent (Murphy 2013). In other words, as there are no perfect substitutes for scarce CEO 'talent', this argument suggests that markets for talented CEOs operate as auctions and therefore the most talented CEOs go to the highest bidder. Even further, in an increasingly competitive world, the premium on the pay for talent has increased. By contrast, others have argued that 'managerial power' is more important, suggesting that CEOs extract economic rents from shareholders in a number of ways: by seeking share options and timing, the exercise of options to occur just before the release of good news; by insider trading; through lucrative severance provisions; and by consuming excessive perquisites (Bebchuk and Fried 2004). In sum, theories drawn from economics provide a frame to start to understand the pay gap between CEO and average worker pay; they are inadequate in terms of explaining why the gap has increased over the past few decades, and why it differs across countries.

CEO pay in comparative perspective: a political economy perspective

This section introduces insights from institutionalist Political Economy and approaches based on so-called 'national business systems' (Whitley 1999, 2007) or 'varieties of capitalism' (Hall and Soskice 2001). These emphasize an interlock between finance, the control and governance of firms, and employment systems in so-called shareholder and stakeholder models (Gospel and Pendleton 2006). In this perspective, there are two main variants of political economy, the shareholder-value system in Liberal Market Economies (LMEs) (usually seen to include the US, the UK, Australia and Canada) and the stakeholder systems in Coordinated Market Economies (CMEs) (usually seen to include Germany, Austria, Sweden, Netherlands and Japan).

Under the shareholder model, the firm's primary goal is "the maximization of shareholder value" and "only shareholders enjoy strong formalized links with top management" (Vitols 2001:337). Payment systems, in a firm following the shareholder model, should address the principal–agent problem, the possibility of a fundamental conflict of interest between shareholders and top management (Vitols 2001:340). The payment of top management should, therefore, be linked directly to shareholder value in order to align the interests of the shareholders to the CEO. Performance-related pay (PRP) systems such as bonuses and stock options are deemed as most appropriate.

On the other hand, the stakeholder model of governance is more prevalent in CMEs. In such systems, CEOs are constrained to take into account a variety of stakeholders – including employees, suppliers, customers, and the communities where companies are located. Long-term organizational effectiveness is more important than short-term profits; firms are interested in market share and long-term incremental growth, as purportedly in Japan (Dore 2000:27) and in Germany (Vitols 2001:352). Payment systems may be partly linked to merit and performance. But they also have two other elements which are very important, viz.: (i) seniority or tenure within the firm; and (ii) qualifications or skills. They thus reward employee loyalty and competence.

Extrapolating these stylized pictures to expectations for CEO-to-worker pay gaps, this approach suggests that the pay gap should be higher in LMEs and lower in CMEs, reflecting different historical and institutional configurations in the different countries. More specifically, it is expected that CEO-to-worker pay gaps will vary according to: (i) the relative importance of skills-based or seniority-based promotion criteria; (ii) the extent of 'poaching' practices; and (iii) the strength of employee voice such as unionization and employee representation on company boards.

In countries such as Germany and Japan, where promotion is linked to attainment of qualifications (skills-based) and often tenure within the company, the CEO-to-worker wage gap is expected to be smaller. The argument is that, if promotion is linked to skill and/or seniority, it resembles less of a 'tournament', and competition between employees is tempered. By contrast, in countries such as the US and the UK, where promotion is linked more to performance and does resemble more of a tournament, the CEO-to-worker wage gap is expected to be larger.

A variation of this argument looks at the inter-firm relations and the skill-formation system. In countries where 'poaching' is constrained and companies take a long-term view and invest in skills, a highly competitive market for CEOs is less likely to develop. In this case, the CEO-to-worker pay gap is expected to be smaller. By contrast, if 'poaching' is common, the market for CEOs is likely to develop and operate as an auction. Therefore, in LMEs the CEO-to-worker pay gap is expected to be larger.

In terms of employee voice, we refer to levels of unionization and the presence or absence of employee representatives on the boards of companies. Over time, the decline in unionization is an important factor, accounting for the increasing pay inequality, as unions have helped to institutionalize norms of equity even in non-union workplaces (Western and Rosenfeld 2011). According to Hall and Soskice (2001), in CMEs the unionization is higher and the wage structure is more compressed, and therefore the CEO-to-worker pay gap is expected to be smaller. By contrast, in LMEs, unionization is lower and the wage structure more dispersed; therefore, the CEO-to-worker pay gap is expected to be larger. In CMEs such as Germany, where workers are legally represented on company boards or in Japan where boards are largely made up of long-term promoted employees, the responsibility and power is more diffused between company boards and CEOs. In these cases, the CEO-to-worker pay gap is expected to be smaller. By contrast, in LMEs, the CEO is 'king' and boards are relatively weaker and therefore the greater the CEO-to-worker pay gap is expected to be.

We next present some international data on CEO-to-worker pay ratios around the world to see whether these arguments hold in practice. Figure 28.1 represents some LME and CME countries according to their CEO-to-worker pay ratios. It confirms that two LMEs are at the top of the table, viz. the US and Canada. However, note that the US appears as an outlier, since its pay ratio is 1.7 times the ratio of its next-door neighbour. How can this be explained? Murphy (2013) suggests that half of the cross-sectional variation in the US may be explained by company size and sector. Hence, we may assume that since the US is the home of some of the largest and most high-tech companies in the world, this may partly explain the large difference with other countries.

Interestingly, though, two CMEs, Switzerland and Germany, are third and fourth. As far as Switzerland is concerned, this is perhaps unsurprising as it has been suggested that the corporate governance system in Switzerland has increasingly moved in a liberal market direction (Schnyder 2012:1442). However, Austria, Norway, Denmark and the Netherlands are ranked as expected,

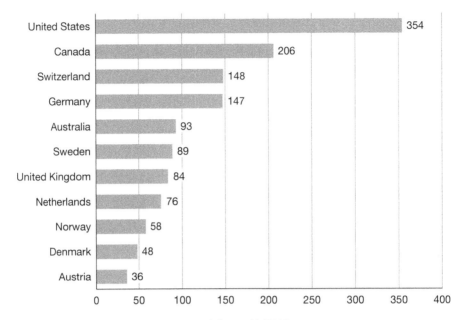

Figure 28.1   CEO-to-worker pay ratios around the world (2012)

Note: Original Data come from OECD and S&P Capital IQ, Figure is the authors' elaboration.

Source: AFL-CIO (2014).

towards the bottom. Still, Germany has a higher CEO-to-worker wage ratio than Australia and the UK, while Sweden (both a CME and also a Nordic so-called solidaristic model) has a higher ratio than the UK. This ranking is puzzling and casts doubt on the predictions of varieties of capitalism regarding LMEs and CMEs.

Figure 28.2 is informative on the structure of executive pay in Europe. Note that bonuses and long-term incentive plans are the highest over the two periods in the UK. If the US was included, we would see that even higher. But note that Switzerland and Benelux are catching up. In fact, all but the Nordic countries show an increase. Given this background and these complications, we now turn to an alternative explanation which has affected many countries, with increasing pressure, though to differing degrees.

A complementary explanation: corporate financialization

A further explanation of the increase in earnings inequality broadly, and the CEO-to-worker pay ratio in particular, draws on the recent theoretical perspectives suggesting an overall trend towards financialization in contemporary capitalism (Dore 2008; Epstein 2005; Freeman 2010; Lapavitsas 2011). To begin with, Lapavitsas (2011:611–612) broadly defines financialization as a systemic transformation of capitalist economies and identifies a number of fundamental elements: (i) the growth of the financial sector; (ii) large non-financial corporations have acquired financial capacities; (iii) banks and other financial institutions have expanded their mediating activities in financial markets; (iv) households have become increasingly involved in the realm of finance both as debtors and as asset holders. Dore (2008:1097–98) defines financialization as: "the increasing role of financial motives, financial markets, financial actors, and financial institutions in the operation of the domestic and international economies". According to Dore (2008:1098), there

CEO average pay mix by country
Incentive pay is most significant in the German, UK and Swiss companies.

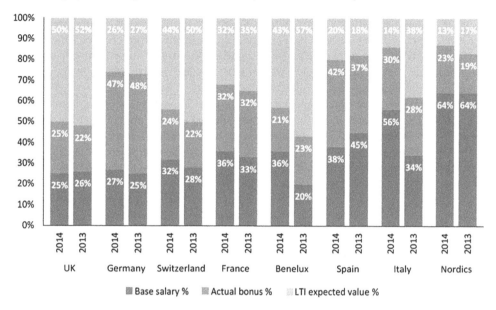

Figure 28.2   Structure of executive pay in Europe

are three key elements attached to this process: (i) the growth and increasing complexity of speculative intermediating activities; (ii) the increasing assertion of the property rights of owners as transcending other forms of social accountability; and (iii) the increasing efforts on the part of governments to promote an 'equity culture' in the name of competitiveness.

The link with pay may be elaborated as follows. On the one hand, CEOs and top managers have come to be more and more motivated by higher levels of pay and bonus and share options. With control over these systems, they have pushed up their wages. On the other hand, workers' wages in most advanced industrialized countries have stagnated since the 1980s. The demand-led growth models of the Fordist era that rewarded productive activities and increased workers' wages in line with the creation of wealth have given way to financialization of the economy which has been credit-based, short-termist, and speculative. This has progressively shifted the focus from productive value creation in the long term to the reward of short-term profits that increase shareholder value, even if they come from speculative activities. Overall, this perspective suggests that the virtuous circle has been replaced by a more vicious cycle, which led ultimately to the global financial crisis of 2007/08.

This broad conception of the process of financialization and the move to a post-Fordist regime has been empirically supported by Vidal (2013), who provides a historical examination of the evolution of profit rates, wage shares and debt in the US, the UK and Germany. He argues that a model of post-Fordist financialization fits all three countries, effectively cutting across LMEs and CMEs. Nonetheless, Vidal (2013:467) identifies differences in the forms of post-Fordism, with a declining profit rate and falling wage share being a characteristic of all three countries, while the expansion of household debt and debt-led growth is manifested mainly in the US and the UK. A debt-led growth model is manifested with an immense growth of the banking and finance sector, the profitability coming from speculative non-productive activities, the skyrocketing of top pay in finance, and the exposure to financial products for borrowing or use as collateral that have diffused to non-financial firms.

Connecting the macro-level analysis to the micro-level analysis, a useful link is provided by what Thompson (2013:478) calls the "financialization of organizational structures". This suggests the interplay between large-scale structural shifts and micro-level changes. This entails a strengthening of the powers of CEOs, Chief Financial Officers, and others in the top management team and a weakening of other stakeholders. This has led, in turn, to the support for speculative behaviours and short-termism of corporate agents at senior executive level. The latter has been increasingly secured through practices such as stock options. In other words, the tight link of CEO pay to bonuses, in the form of shares and share options, exacerbated those perverse incentives, which have cumulatively contributed to exacerbating pre-existing inequalities. Lazonick (2014) emphasizes another device that leads to profits without prosperity: share buybacks. He suggests that many companies have cut capital expenditure and even increased debt to boost dividends and increase share buybacks (Lazonick 2014:48).

The intensifying financialization of the economy has not only been strengthened by these managerial practices but has been encouraged by the appearance of actors who favour a focus on shareholder value. New investment funds, such as private equity and hedge funds, exemplify this process of financialization, which have altered corporate governance regimes (Gospel et al. 2014). Firms which operate in typical CMEs such as Germany and Sweden are increasingly less able to adhere to the principles of stakeholder models, if their main owners are private equity funds, or if they are subject to pressure from hedge funds (Lippert et al. 2014). Even so, in these countries, national laws and trade unions reduce the effect of financialization (Vitols 2014).

Some others have gone further. Freeman (2010), for instance, attributes the advent of the global financial crisis in 2007/08 partly to regulatory failure and partly to the perverse monetary incentives that led to greedy decisions. He suggests that in order to receive large bonuses and to cash in on options, CEOs had to report financial statistics in ways that raised share prices, for example, either redistributing from workers or consumers to the firm (e.g., squeezing wages or inflating prices) or by finding ways of reporting high profits and boosting share prices (e.g., downsizing) (2010:175). All in all, these strategies have inflated stock prices (and therefore CEO pay), with the possibility that this will be at the expense of the average worker.

Curbing CEO pay? The UK in comparative perspective

This section examines the debate on how to curb CEO pay and looks at the case of the UK in comparative perspective. We have seen attempts in both the US and Europe to curb the pay gap, for instance, by the requirement to publicize CEO-to-worker ratios. Such policies alone are not likely to go a long way towards reversing the trend. What is required instead is a reform of regulatory and institutional frameworks and putting in place appropriate incentives and disincentives to encourage or discourage certain practices. So far one may discern three types of possible remedies in response to the widening pay gap: (i) a voluntary 'light touch' approach; (ii) empowering shareholders; and (iii) empowering stakeholders.

In the United Kingdom, we may observe a widening gap between the income of the top 1% and median income (Figure 28.3) since the early 2000s. Even more, we observe the same trend, when we look at the gap between CEO pay (FTSE100) and average employee pay during the same period (Figure 28.4). This undoubtedly remarkable increase in inequality has prompted regulatory responses. Under new rules introduced in 2013, shareholders/investors in the UK were given two votes: a binding vote on pay policy every three years and an advisory vote every year on the previous year's pay level. More recent proposals on corporate governance reform

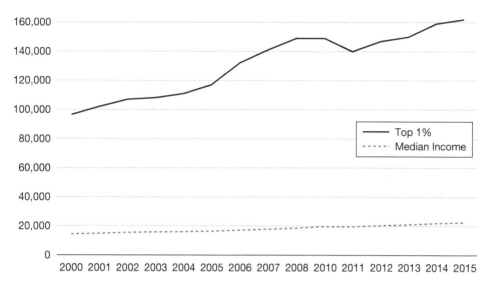

Figure 28.3 Total income (£) before tax, UK 2000-2015

Note: Top 1% is 99th percentile and Median Income is 50th percentile.

Source: Original Data from HMRC, Survey of Personal Incomes 2014-15 available at: https://www.gov.uk/ government/statistics/percentile-points-from-1-to-99-for-total-income-before-and-after-tax (Accessed: 25/ 04/2017), Figure is author's elaboration.

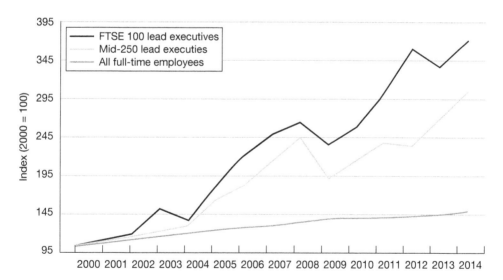

Figure 28.4 Executive pay against employee pay

suggest that a more watered-down version of the initial proposals should be expected (House of Commons 2017).

The US has adopted a voluntary 'light touch' approach. In 2015, the Securities and Exchange Commission issued a rule requiring disclosure of the ratio of CEO pay to that of the median employee, under Section 953(b) of the Dodd–Frank Act. Even where firms have complied, there is some leeway about how these ratios are calculated. For instance, if additional items, such as company-paid healthcare, are used to calculate total compensation for the median employee, such amounts must be included in the CEO's annual total compensation, and the inclusion of benefits in the calculation of total compensation, may drastically decrease the pay ratio (*CFO Journal* 2016). In Switzerland, in a referendum held in March of 2013, Swiss citizens voted to impose some controls on executive pay, forcing public companies to give shareholders a binding vote on compensation (*Reuters* 2013). The trade unions campaigned in favour of a proposal to legislate a cap on executive pay at 12 times the wage of a firm's lowest earner. However, Swiss voters rejected the proposal in a subsequent referendum held in November 2013. Rather than imposing a legislated cap, which might be thought to be arbitrary or might alternatively be circumvented, it might be more effective to convince shareholders that it goes against their long-term interests and let them monitor the excess of CEO pay. Following the Swiss lead, the European Commission drafted a proposal for EU law, requiring that the EU's 10,000 listed companies reveal their pay ratios and allow shareholders to vote on whether or not they are appropriate (*Financial Times* 2014).

However, empowering shareholders through a binding vote to put limits on CEO pay may halt the trend of an increasing pay gap, but further solutions would be required to reverse the trend. There are two possible forms this may take; either *directly*, through some sort of shared ownership (so that employees become in fact shareholders), or *indirectly*, through representation on company boards. Reducing the CEO-to-worker pay gap can take two main forms – either reducing the numerator or increasing the denominator. On the one hand, putting a lid on CEO pay might be following the relaxation of the link with financial performance, and the inclusion of other performance criteria such as sustainability indicators and social performance indicators. On the other hand, increasing the average worker's pay may require tightening the link with profitability, by making employees participants in share ownership or through a greater share of wages in overall profitability. More generally, reversing the inequality in pay requires a reconfiguration of the shareholder-value model of financialized capitalism. To achieve these aims, this would necessitate changes in the broader regulatory and institutional frameworks, but also changes in current reward management practice.

Implications and conclusions

The chapter concludes by arguing that what is required is a reforming of reward at the top and the bottom of organizations, through altering incentives in the regulatory and institutional frameworks. At the bottom of organizations, this might include broader adoption of innovative models of 'shared capitalism' that link average worker pay to profitability (Freeman et al. 2010). Hence, average worker pay would increase in tandem with CEO pay. Incentives to diffuse such broad-based shared ownership schemes may take the forms of tax breaks and tax discounts. At the top, CEO compensation may be linked with a wider set of performance indicators, including social and environmental measures. For instance, consider one of the recommendations of the 2013 report of the High Pay Centre (2013:6–7), namely that non-financial performance measures should constitute at least 50% of performance-related executive pay.

Such a shift in reward practice requires moving away from narrow indicators of performance, i.e., profits and share price. It requires taking a broader perspective on top performance and might also include performance criteria such as employees' well-being at work, customer service ratings, and social/environmental impacts. This would shift the attention from shareholders to a wider set of stakeholders, while tilting the game away from short-termism towards longer-term success and impact on society. Specific indicators to measure this performance could include: net tax contributions; employee security; pay differentials within the company and across a sector; and gender pay differences. The key message here is that there are several measurable indicators that may feed into the calculation for CEOs' performance-related pay.

The government may also use a variety of tools, especially preferential tax rates and tendering/procurement policies, to promote compliance with social reporting requirements. Regulation could also be revised with respect to the duties and responsibilities of pension fund trustees, investment managers and commercial pension providers. For instance, a "revised fiduciary duty" would recognise that the interests of pension fund beneficiaries are bound with those of society as a whole (High Pay Centre 2013:7). Finally, as suggested above, employee representatives on boards would introduce a broader definition of success and challenge decisions based on short-term financial considerations, which may come to jeopardize the company in the long term.

We make one final point about reward systems and pay structure. Managers create pay systems to motivate and control those below them. In the case of top pay, CEOs and senior managers largely design their own pay systems, albeit to varying degrees, with checks and balances by boards of directors. However, as a long tradition of research has shown, pay systems tend to get out of control. This is very much what has happened with CEO and top pay. Pay structure is a broader question of differentials within the economy. Over time, these differentials have seen long-term trends in terms of narrowing and widening. Broad factors have brought this about: the financialization of the economy; regulatory changes; the growth and decline of trade unions; the changing nature of the business enterprise. Over the last three decades or so, there has been a widening of top-to-average or -bottom pay. But there are concrete ways that may help to halt or reverse the widening and in this chapter we considered some of them. Taken together, these policies would represent a genuine shift away from the 'financialized' business models. They would ensure that company performance is judged in terms of a company's value to its stakeholders as a whole and to broader society, rather than narrowly to just shareholders.

References

AFL-CIO. (2014). *CEO-to-Worker Pay Ratios Around the World*. Available at: www.aflcio.org/Corporate-Watch/Paywatch-Archive/CEO-Pay-and-You/CEO-to-Worker-Pay-Gap-in-the-United-States/Pay-Gaps-in-the-World, accessed on March 27, 2017.

Bebchuk, L. and Fried J. (2004). *Pay Without Performance*. Boston, MA: Harvard University Press.

Bell, B. and J. Van Reenen (2013) Extreme wage inequality: pay at the very top. *American Economic Review, Papers and Proceedings*. 103(3), 153–157.

Boyer, G. and Smith, R. (2001) The development of the neo-Classical tradition in labor economics. *Industrial & Labor Relations Review*. 54(2), 199–223.

CFO Journal. (2016) Preparing for the new CEO pay ratio disclosure requirement, November 30, 2016 by Deloitte at *The Wall Street Journal:* Available at: www.deloitte.wsj.com/cfo/2016/11/30/the-boards-agenda-preparing-for-the-new-ceo-pay-ratio-disclosure-requirement/, accessed on, February 26, 2017.

Dore, R. (2000). *Stock Market Capitalism: Welfare Capitalism. Japan and Germany versus the Anglo-Saxons*. Oxford: Oxford University Press.

Dore, R. (2008). Financialization of the global economy. *Industrial and Corporate Change*. 17(6), 1097–1112.

Epstein, G. (ed.) (2005) *Financialization and the World Economy*. Aldershot: Edward Elgar.

Financial Times. (2014) 'Brussels plans fresh rules on executive pay' *Financial Times*, 7 March 2014, Available at: www.ft.com/content/4f4edc90-a542-11e3-8988-00144feab7de, accessed on February 26, 2017.

Freeman, R (2010). It's financialization! *International Labour Review*. 149(2), 163–183.

Freeman, R., Blasi, J. and Kruse, D. (2010). Introduction. In D. Kruse, R. Freeman and J. Blasi (eds.), *Shared Capitalism at Work: Employee Ownership, Profit and Gain Sharing, and Broad-based Stock Options* (pp. 1–37). Chicago: University of Chicago Press.

Gospel, H. and Pendleton, A. (2006). Corporate governance and labour management: an international comparison'. In Gospel, H. and Pendletone, A. (eds.). *Corporate Governance and Labour Management* (pp. 1–32). Oxford: Oxford University Press.

Gospel, H., Pendleton, A. and Vitols, S. (eds.) (2014). *Financialization, New Investment Funds, and Labour: an International Comparison*. Oxford: Oxford University Press.

Gregg, P., Machin, S. and Szymanski, S. (1993). The disappearing relationship between directors' pay and corporate performance. *British Journal of Industrial Relations*. 31, 1–9.

Hall, P. and Soskice, D. (2001) (eds.). *Varieties of Capitalism: Institutional Foundations of Comparative Advantage*. Oxford: Oxford University Press.

High Pay Centre. (2013). *Paid to Perform? What Do We Want Our Business Leaders to Achieve?* London: High Pay Centre. Available at: www.highpaycentre.org/files/HPC_11_Paid_to_perform_06.pdf, accessed on, August 20, 2016.

House of Commons. (2017). *Green Paper on Corporate Governance*, Energy and Industrial Strategy Committee, 3rd Report of Session 2016–17. Available at: www.publications.parliament.uk/pa/cm201617/cmselect/cmbeis/702/702.pdf, accessed on, April 12, 2017.

Jensen, M. and Murphy, K. (1990) CEO incentives – it's not how much you pay, but how. *Harvard Business Review*. 68(3), 138–149.

Kessler, I. (2013). Remuneration systems. In Bach, S. and Edwards, M. (eds.). *Managing Human Resources* (pp. 243–267). New York: Wiley.

Kornelakis, A. Veliziotis, M. and Voskeritsian, H. (2016). How can competitiveness be achieved in post-crisis Europe: deregulating employment relations or enhancing high performance work practices? *The International Journal of Human Resource Management*.

Lapavitsas, C. (2011). Theorizing financialization. *Work, Employment & Society*. 25(4), 611–626.

Lazear, P. (1998). *Personnel Economics for Managers*. New York: Wiley.

Lazonick, W. (2014). Profits without prosperity. *Harvard Business Review*. 92(9), 46–55.

Lippert, I., Huzzard, T., Jurgens, U. and Lazonick, W. (2014). *Corporate Governance: Employee Voice, and Work Organization*. Oxford: Oxford University Press.

Mishel, L. and Davis, A. (2015). Top CEOs make 300 times more than typical workers. *Economic Policy Institute, Issue Brief No. 399* (21 June 2015).

Murphy, K. J. (2013). Executive compensation: where we are, and how we got there. In Constantinides, G., Harris, M., and Stulz, R. (eds.). *Handbook of the Economics of Finance* (pp. 211–356). North Holland: Elsevier.

Reuters. (2013) Swiss back executive pay curbs in referendum. *Reuters*, 3 March 2013. Available at: www.reuters.com/article/us-swiss-regulation-pay-idUSBRE92204N20130303, accessed on, February 26, 2017.

Schnyder, G. (2012). Varieties of insider corporate governance: the determinants of business preferences and governance reform in the Netherlands, Sweden and Switzerland. *Journal of European Public Policy*. 19(9), 1434–1451.

Thompson, P. (2013). Financialization and the workplace: extending and applying the disconnected capitalism thesis. *Work, Employment and Society*. 27(3), 472–488.

Vidal, M. (2013). Postfordism as a dysfunctional accumulation regime: a comparative analysis of the US, UK, and Germany. *Work, Employment and Society*. 27(3), 451–471.

Vitols, S. (2001). Varieties of corporate governance: comparing Germany and the UK. In: Hall, P. and Soskice, D. (eds.), *Varieties of Capitalism: Institutional Foundations of Comparative Advantage* (pp. 337–360). Oxford: Oxford University Press.

Vitols, S. (2014). New investment funds and labour impacts: implications for theories of corporate financialization and comparative capitalism. In Gospel, H., Pendleton, A. and Vitols, S. (eds.). *Financialization, New Investment Funds, and Labour: an International Comparison*. Oxford: Oxford University Press.

Western, B. and Rosenfeld, J. (2011) Unions, norms, and the rise in US wage inequality. *American Sociological Review* 76(4), 513–537.

Whitley, R. (1999). *Divergent Capitalisms*. Oxford: Oxford University Press.

Whitley, R., (2007). *Business Systems and Organizational Capabilities*. Oxford: Oxford University Press.

29

INTERNATIONAL ASSIGNMENT REWARD POLICIES

The importance of compensation and benefits to women's expatriate participation

Susan Shortland

Introduction

Since the first studies on expatriate gender diversity were conducted, men have comprised the majority of expatriates (Altman and Shortland 2008). Although around one-quarter of expatriate roles are held by women today (Brookfield 2016), the male-dominated picture of expatriate gender diversity looks set to continue. Gender diversity in expatriation is regarded as an asset to business given women's success in their international assignments (Shortland 2016) and, as such, various studies have explored why women's expatriation remains low in comparison to men's. Issues identified as having some bearing include: women's choices and family constraints; organizational decision-making (for example in selection, and in relation to their human and social capital); societal cultural explanations; and institutional effects, such as gendered labour market structures (Shortland 2014). Yet there is currently little published research on the effects of international reward and how this might affect the gendered nature of expatriation (Shortland and Perkins 2016). This chapter therefore sets out to address this issue. It examines which elements of international assignment reward policy and practice have the strongest influence on women's acceptance of international assignments, and of different lengths and patterns of expatriation.

Reflecting its exploratory nature, this research employs a case study design (Eisenhardt 1989; Yin 2009). It is set in the oil and gas exploration and production sector, which has been selected because it uses large and increasing numbers of expatriates (Air Inc. 2016, 2017), is known for its relatively attractive provision of expatriate compensation and benefits (IDS 2002), and yet has low expatriate gender diversity (ORC Worldwide 2007). This study sets out to identify the main reward policy items that women regard as critical preconditions to assignment acceptance and to outline recommendations to employers where policy and practice improvements might make a difference to increasing expatriate gender diversity across a range of assignment types. In this way it contributes both to our knowledge of expatriate reward and to our understanding of women's expatriate representation. The study sets out to address the following research question:

> To what extent and how do the elements of international assignment reward policy support women's expatriation in different assignment lengths and patterns?

Method

The research was set within two medium-sized oil and gas exploration and production organizations, identified through convenience sampling (Saunders et al. 2009). The case study firms had operations across 30 countries worldwide; these were not considered to be unique or extreme cases (Yin 2009). In total, they employed 93 female expatriates (between 8% and 11% of their total expatriate populations). The research approach involved: analysis of the international assignment reward policies applicable to different lengths and patterns of international mobility; interviews being conducted with 14 Human Resource (HR) professionals with responsibility for these policies to discuss their implementation in practice; a survey (conducted by e-mail) of all of the 93 women assignees who were policy recipients; and interviews being conducted with 26 of the survey respondents, selected using stratified sampling (Collis and Hussey 2009) to ensure appropriate representation by assignment length and pattern.

First, the international relocation policies were read and summarized descriptively, with any differences in approach by company identified. Using these data, an e-mail questionnaire was designed so that each female respondent could record which of the specific financial and non-financial elements identified she had received in relation to her current assignment type, and record and comment on the importance of each element in supporting her expatriate participation. Of the 93 women, 71 replied to the survey (response rate of 76%): 51 long-term assignees, 12 short-term and graduate placement assignees; five on rotational assignments; and three undertaking extended international transfers. The importance ratings data (from not important to very important) were analysed using SPSS but, given the skewed nature of the assignment types undertaken by the respondents (with the majority being on long-term assignments) and the small size of the populations represented by each of the other policy types, these factors prevented tests of association and strength of relationship from being undertaken. Nonetheless, descriptive statistics were produced to highlight which reward policy elements were deemed to be very important (i.e., they were rated the most highly) to women's assignment participation, recorded by assignment length/pattern.

The interviews addressed how written policy was implemented in practice. These were semi-structured and conducted confidentially either face-to-face or by telephone: the HR interviews lasted between 30 and 90 minutes; those with the female assignees between 60 and 90 minutes. The interviews were taped with participant agreement, transcribed, read systematically and coded via NVivo 8. Comments recorded in the survey were also coded. A thematic analysis was conducted (Braun and Clarke 2006) to identify the financial and non-financial elements within international assignment reward policy that were of particular relevance to women's assignment participation.

Findings

Analysis of the policy documentation and discussions with the HR personnel in each firm revealed that the two firms had very similar policy provision supporting their expatriate workforces and so the policy elements that were offered under their reward policies were combined, as shown in Table 29.1. The main policy items covered were grouped under the following headings: remuneration and allowances; housing and related issues; travel, transport and leave; medical and emergency assistance; visa and tax support; and financial payments relating to partner and family issues. The following sections examine these elements as made available under expatriate reward policy linked to assignment type (length/pattern), highlighting those of greatest importance to women's assignment participation decisions.

Table 29.1 Reward policy elements by assignment type received by female assignees

Reward policy elements included in international assignments reward policy and received by female assignees (✓)	Long-term assignments	Short-term assignments	Rotational assignments	Extended international transfers*
Remuneration and allowances				
Pension continuity	✓	✓	✓	✓
Bonus	✓	✓	✓	✓
Cost of living (COLA)	✓	✓	✓	
Foreign service premium (FSP)	✓	✓	✓	
Mobility premium	✓	✓		✓
Rest and recreation allowance (R&R)	✓	✓		
Disturbance allowance	✓	✓		
Rotation allowance			✓	
Graduate placement allowance (graduates only)		✓		
Car/allowance/local transport	✓	✓	✓	✓
Housing and related issues				
Housing	✓	✓	✓	
Temporary accommodation	✓	✓		✓
Home search	✓	✓		✓
Utilities payment	✓	✓	✓	
Telephone payment	✓	✓	✓	
Shipment of household goods	✓	✓		✓
Meals payment			✓	
Travel, transport and leave				
Transport to and from host location	✓	✓	✓	✓
Home leave travel costs	✓	✓		
Vacation allowance	✓	✓		
Flights to reunite family	✓	✓		
Medical and emergency assistance				
Medical insurance	✓	✓	✓	
Family emergency assistance in host location	✓			
Visa and tax support				
Work permit/visa assistance	✓	✓	✓	✓
Tax preparation/assistance	✓	✓	✓	✓
Partner and family issues				
Children's education allowance	✓			
School search in host location	✓			
Education assistance for children on repatriation	✓			
Spouse/partner allowance	✓			
Work permit/visa assistance for spouse/partner	✓	✓		✓

*One company only had a specific policy for transfers exceeding five years' duration.

Long-term assignees

Long-term assignments were defined as being over a year in length; on average, these were typically around three years' duration in both firms. The majority of the assignees (51 women) were undertaking this assignment type. The most important elements of remuneration/allowances were identified from the survey as being pension continuity, the foreign service premium (FSP), the cost of living allowance (COLA) and the provision of a car with over 85% of the respondents rating these policy items as very important to their assignment participation. The provision of a disturbance allowance, paid in recognition of the need to replace various goods on relocation, was considered as very important by 80%. Approximately 70–75% of the long-term assignees rated the assignment bonus, the mobility premium (paid in recognition of being mobile) and payments that supported rest and recreation (R&R) in hardship locations as very important.

The interview data confirmed that the "financial rewards are a big driver" for assignees. These data indicated that the key issue was the FSP, which acted as a significant "uplift" to base salary. It was paid as a percentage of salary, determined by the hardship nature of the host location, and this frequently made a substantial difference to assignees' wealth. The HR personnel reported that the FSP could raise salaries by some 50–60% in certain hardship locations. The assignees interviewed agreed: "Uplift on salary in terms of hardship locations, yes, that's probably the number one really" and that "it makes you feel a little bit better about being here". Even in less difficult locations, such as Australasia, where FSPs were around 10%, this still acted as an incentive for assignees to go, being seen as "a prize". The COLA was especially important to those relocating to high-cost locations. As such, concern was raised by those interviewed that the allowances were sufficient and reviewed regularly so that standards of living could be maintained. Cars – although standard in policy – were considered of greatest importance in "car culture" locations (North America, in particular).

The housing allowance (or provision of company housing as appropriate) was considered to be very important to assignment acceptance by all of the long-term assignees ("having the housing . . . and all that, paid for by the company . . . that is nice, and I wouldn't want to have to maintain my own housing"). Around 90% said that the provision of temporary accommodation, home search assistance and payments for shipment of household goods were also very important to them. Utilities and telephone payments were considered to be very important by over half of the assignees ("Getting your bills paid is enormously useful . . .").

Allowances related to home leave travel costs, transport to and from the host location, flights to reunite families and vacation were valued very highly by around 90% of the long-term assignees. For example, as one interviewee explained: ". . . the elements that are straight off that the company arranges for you . . . like for example . . . you get your flights out and you don't have to worry about and you get your home leave back and you get your travel days, it makes the whole decision a lot easier".

Over 90% of long-term assignees reported that medical insurance and family emergency assistance were very important to their assignment acceptance ("we have a very good benefits package, but the medical insurance, the personal accident insurance, just for the supporting framework . . ."). Around 80% of the women said that tax preparation and work permit/visa assistance were very important to them ("The tax briefing. . . was important because I have got a house that I rent out and you need to understand the tax implications of going abroad . . .").

Turning to family assistance, support for children's education applied only to long-term assignees. Nine women had received education allowances for their children's schooling in the host location and three were eligible for education assistance for their children on repatriation (due to the ages of their children). All regarded these items as being very important to them in being able to take up their assignments ("allowances are set to pay for decent schools"). Seven of these women had received support to pay for a school search consultant and five said that this was very important.

Nineteen women had received work visa support for their spouses with 17 reporting this as being very important to their assignment participation (". . . anything . . . to assist spouses in getting work visas or accommodating them to work . . . is beneficial in accommodating women expatriates").

Long-term assignees were eligible for limited spouse/partner financial allowances in recognition of spouses giving up work on relocation. Twelve women had received this support and half regarded it as very important when accepting their assignments. ("The partner gets . . . the partner support programme. So they try and encourage and provide financial support if partners want to do any studying or take courses that will enable them to work whilst overseas . . . So that has been very good.")

Short-term assignees and graduate scheme trainees

Short-term assignees undertook assignments that were typically between six and 12 months in duration. Graduate trainees undertook a series of four six-month placements, one of which was guaranteed to be an expatriate assignment. Twelve women were on short-term/graduate placements. The majority reported the FSP as the most important financial element supporting their assignment participation. Around two-thirds said that the mobility premium, bonus, pension continuity and car were very important while around half rated the COLA as very important. Only one woman was based in a location which attracted R&R, but she rated this as very important to her decision to accept her assignment. The graduates received a graduate placement allowance – and all viewed this as very important to assignment acceptance.

The provision of company housing (or a housing allowance if this was appropriate) was rated as very important by around 80% of the short-term/graduate assignees ("just because it takes so much of the hassle out of it"). Around 60% rated home search assistance and temporary accommodation as very important. Payments for utilities and telephone expenses were only rated as very important by around half of the assignees.

Given the relatively short timescale that assignees were away from home, only two-thirds noted that vacation allowances were very important to them; nonetheless, over 80% said that home leave travel costs, flights to reunite families and transport to and from the host location were very important to their assignment acceptance. Family emergency assistance did not apply in the host location as assignments were typically unaccompanied but medical insurance was covered. However, the assignees explained that should an emergency take place with family members at home then their company did address this ("the transporting you back, if something happens to a family member is very important"). Around two-thirds reported that medical insurance was very important to their assignment decision. Over 70% said that work permit/visa assistance was very important to their assignment participation ("the main area that is difficult to handle is things to do with visas and changing over your visa"), but, reflecting the short length of time that they were away, only 45% said that tax preparation was very important.

Rotational assignees

Five women were undertaking rotational assignments. These involved working 28 days on assignment, followed by 28 days off-shift at home. Certain allowances were not applicable (R&R, mobility, disturbance), but all received a rotation allowance and this was rated as very important by four of the five women. All rated the FSP as very important to their assignment participation; three placed high importance on pension continuity, the car and the bonus. COLA was only applicable to one assignee, who rated it as important to her assignment take-up. Assignees said that rotation locations were usually remote and challenging, sometimes dangerous. They acknowledged that the money was good ("the bonus I would say is excellent"), but said that if rotation, with additional allowances paid as compensation for challenging location factors, was to be replaced with long-term in-country postings, very high salaries would be needed to encourage assignment participation.

Rotational assignees lived in company housing with paid utilities; no temporary accommodation, home search assistance or shipment of household goods applied to these transfers. Assignees' telephone expenses were paid and meals provided. Approximately two-thirds of the respondents rated these issues as very important to their assignment acceptance.

With respect to travel, transport and leave, company policy only addressed transport costs to and from the home location; four women said that this was very important to their assignment participation. Family emergency assistance did not apply in the host location as the assignments were unaccompanied, but if an emergency arose at home, assignees' transport home was covered ("The hardest thing when you work on rotation is not to be at home in case of an emergency. There is . . . a very good emergency response plan in place and it is very important to me to know that I can go home very quickly if need be . . ."). Medical insurance was covered in policy and four women reported this as being very important. Three women reported that tax preparation and two said that work permit/visa assistance were very important to their assignment participation ("they get you your work permit. So that was fairly easy").

Extended international transfers

One of the firms had a policy that specifically addressed extended international transfers (over five years' duration). This was a modified form of the policy that applied to long-term assignees, and it included some local terms. Thus, certain allowances were not applicable (COLA, FSP, R&R, and disturbance). Only three women were undertaking such assignments. Assignees noted that allowances were considerably limited. Thus, all rated those that they did receive – mobility premiums and bonuses – as very important to their assignment participation; two placed high importance on pension continuity and one on the provision of a car.

Assignees on extended transfers did not receive support with housing, utilities or telephone expenses under policy as they were expected to manage their own costs similar to locally hired employees. However, assistance with home search, the provision of temporary accommodation and the shipment of household goods were all company-funded and all assignees regarded these to be very important to their assignment acceptance.

Company policy only addressed transport costs to and from the home location; all assignees said this was very important. Medical insurance and family emergency assistance were not provided under policy as local terms applied. Tax preparation and work permit/visa assistance were supported under policy; the women all regarded these items as very important to them being able to undertake their assignments. Two women had received work visa support for their spouses and both said this was very important to them in their assignment decision.

Discussion

While it is widely accepted that money is not the main driver for international assignment acceptance (Pate and Scullion 2010; McNulty 2014), if the reward package is not considered sufficient or equitable, it can act as a reason for assignment refusal (Suutari et al. 2012; Warneke and Schneider 2011; Welch 1994). Hence, even though career development and family circumstances are recognised as the most crucial factors influencing expatriation decision-making (Dickmann et al. 2008; Hippler 2009), we cannot discount the relevance of reward policy as a factor in the decision to undertake a global career (Suutari et al. 2012).

Disentangling the various influences that affect women's assignment acceptance is notoriously difficult as potential posts are weighed up in terms of the balance between career, family and financial outcomes (Shortland 2016). To attempt to address this, this research study examined the reward elements that women assignees reported as being the most important in their decision to go, having evaluated career and family assignment outcomes as favourable. This section discusses these findings in the context of relevant theoretical frames presented in Chapter 17 entitled "Segmenting International Assignments: Theorizing Expatriate Reward" – compensating differentials (Rosen 1986) in terms of the sufficiency of the package; and equity theory (Adams 1963) in relation to its fairness.

As Rosen (1986) proposes, compensating wage differentials relate to extra payment(s) necessary to encourage workers to undertake jobs that are viewed as less desirable relative to others that the person could do. While expatriate assignments typically offer desirable career benefits, the provision of additional rewards addresses factors such as the disruption to family and friendship relationships as a direct result of being globally mobile, working in challenging locations and living in unfamiliar cultures, to name but a few. Expatriate reward policy design does not differentiate by gender, with policy elements applying both to men and women. The various additions to salary given in the form of expatriate allowances and benefits in the two case studies acted as a significant compensating differential for undertaking an international assignment, making the financial aspect of expatriation very attractive to anyone offered such a posting.

Turning to women's expatriation, it is helpful to examine compensating differentials specifically from a gender perspective. In relation to women's work, Anker (2001) theorizes that women 'prefer' good working conditions and fringe benefits (supporting their family responsibilities) over high monetary rewards. It would therefore be expected that women assignees would focus their attention on elements in the reward package, particularly fringe benefits, which address family issues. In contrast to this prediction, however, it was clear from this research study that financial reward elements stood out as being of the greatest importance to women in their assignment acceptance decision. In the main, the women assignees placed the highest importance on pension continuity, the FSP, COLA, bonuses, mobility premiums, housing allowances, cars, and, for mothers, payments to support children's education. Nonetheless, Anker's (2001) gendered interpretation of compensating differentials did have some relevance as the female assignees in this study did value certain fringe benefits linked to their family concerns, especially work visa assistance to address partner employment, and support with moving home (including home search and household goods shipments). Home leave travel supporting family reunion and to help them address family emergencies was also particularly relevant to their assignment participation.

With respect to equity, this research identified differences in reward policy content applying to different lengths and patterns of assignments. While policy segmentation is becoming increasingly popular as a means of differentiating between assignment types and in facilitating cost control (Air Inc. 2016, 2017), this leads to different levels of financial and practical support being made available depending on the assignment type undertaken. This research identified that women primarily undertook long-term assignments. These were best supported financially and in practice by organizations through international assignment reward policy. Short-term and rotational assignments did attract a wide range of allowances and benefits demonstrating significant compensating differentials, but the generosity of provision was more limited, typically linked to the single-status nature of these assignments. Extended transfer assignments also demonstrated that compensating differentials had been applied, but the range of allowances and benefits was much lower, with local terms in operation for some elements.

While equity was preserved within a policy type (such that all moving under the umbrella of a particular assignment type were treated equitably under policy), differential treatment was in evidence between the terms and conditions of policies designed to address different mobility requirements. This has implications linked to equity theory (Adams 1963). Assignees can compare the elements of their reward packages with those offered to individuals undertaking different types of assignments. If the roles performed are similar in the assignment location, but the assignees undertaking these are on different assignment types with different reward packages applied, inequity can be perceived. When this takes place, Adams (1963) suggests such perceived inequity leads to tension flowing from potential dissatisfaction and, as a result, this affects individuals' effort. With respect to expatriation, it can affect decisions to engage in particular activities (such as assignment acceptance) as well as dissatisfaction once involved in the posting. Potentially, this might also have ramifications for expatriate adjustment (Zhu et al. 2016). For example, in this research women placed considerable emphasis on fringe benefits connected to home-making. While long-term and extended transfer assignees received support to find a home and furnish it with their own belongings, this fringe benefit was limited for short-term assignees who were mostly offered company housing, and was not afforded to those on rotation who lived in furnished camp accommodation.

Accompanied short-term assignments were permissible in both firms, but the supporting reward package reflected, in the main, the assumption that these assignments would typically be undertaken solo. As such, only limited assistance was given with family issues for this type of assignment. Yet this research study shows that the women assignees were concerned about family unity and the policy elements that maintained this when making their assignment participation decision. This suggests that women would be less willing to endure fairly lengthy periods of family separation necessitated by single-status short-term assignments and, for mothers in particular, the month away from home on rotational working patterns. As assignments become shorter and more flexible in terms of the deployment patterns used (Brookfield 2016), equity theory (Adams 1963) and gendered predictions in relation to compensating differentials (Anker 2001) would indicate that the lower levels of family support provided for short-term and rotational assignments could reduce women's willingness to engage in these types of assignments, reinforcing the gendered nature of expatriation.

Implications for organizational practice

These research findings are of value because they can assist organizations to increase expatriate gender diversity through the inclusion of policy elements that are of particular relevance to women, helping to support their decision to accept an assignment. In particular, the importance of practical support should not be ignored. There was clear evidence in this study that women looked to their employers to assist with family-related fringe benefits, especially in relation to spousal employment, finding and setting up home, and assisting them in maintaining family unity and in responding to family emergencies. Without these aspects being included in the international reward policy, women's willingness to accept assignments could be compromised. Of course, it is important to be mindful of any 'decoupling' of what may be articulated in policy from what is offered/received in practice; policy intent and implementation can differ substantially – with potentially negative implications for perceived equity.

With respect to policy segmentation, while employers will be mindful of cost constraints and the need to tailor reward policy to ensure that it is 'fit-for-purpose', care must be taken not to make particular assignment types unattractive by removing highly appreciated elements of family support. Thus, regarding women's assignment participation, action to address spousal and family concerns across the range of assignment lengths and patterns is necessary.

Limitations and call for further research

This cross-sectional case study research addressed female expatriation in two medium-sized firms in the oil and gas exploration and production sectors. It would be helpful to further our understanding of the influence of reward policy on female expatriation across a wider spectrum of industries. In addition, we need to learn how trends are developing in relation to the effects of policy segmentation on gender diversity as assignment lengths shorten and deployment patterns become more flexible. Longitudinal research would therefore be especially useful. As international reward policy and practice is designed to address both male and female mobility, research that examines any differences in the importance that men and women place on particular policy elements would be valuable. Such information would help to identify not only how gender diversity can be facilitated but also how all assignees can best be supported across a range of assignments. The potential relationship between reward practices and expatriate adjustment would also prove to be a valuable line of enquiry.

Concluding remarks

Expatriate reward policy demonstrates the application of significant compensating differentials, making international assignments financially attractive. Female assignees do look to the expatriate reward package to provide financial enhancement via premiums and allowances that raise their base salaries substantially when making their expatriate assignment acceptance decisions. However, besides financial incentives, they also focus on home-making and family support/unity and the policy elements that address these factors. Segmentation of expatriate reward policy results in long-term assignments being especially well-rewarded both financially and via the provision of fringe benefits that address the key issues that women wish to see in place when making their assignment acceptance decisions. Potential disincentives to women undertaking alternative assignments need to be recognised and remedial action taken. Hence, appropriate benefits should be included within international reward policy across the spectrum of alternative assignment types if organizations are to increase expatriate gender diversity.

References

Adams, S. J. (1963). Towards an understanding of inequity. *Journal of Abnormal and Social Psychology*. 67(5), 422–436.

Air Inc. (2016). *Mobility Outlook Survey*. Cambridge, MA: Air Inc.

Air Inc. (2017). *Mobility Outlook Survey*. Cambridge, MA: Air Inc.

Altman, Y. and Shortland, S. (2008). Women and international assignments: taking stock – a 25-year review. *Human Resource Management*. 47(2), 199–216.

Anker, R. (2001). Theories of occupational segregation by sex: an overview. In Loutfi, M. F. (ed.). *Women, Gender and Work: What is Equality and How Do We Get There?* (pp. 129–155). Geneva: International Labour Organization.

Braun, V. and Clarke, V. (2006). Using thematic analysis in psychology. *Qualitative Research in Psychology*. 3(2), 77–101.

Brookfield Global Relocation Services (Brookfield). (2016). *Breakthrough to the Future of Global Talent Mobility: 2016 Global Mobility Trends Survey*. Chicago, IL: Brookfield Global Relocation Services.

Collis, J. and Hussey, R. (2009). *Business Research: a Practical Guide for Undergraduate and Postgraduate Students*. Basingstoke, UK: Palgrave Macmillan.

Dickmann, M., Doherty, N., Mills, T. and Brewster, C. (2008). Why do they go? Individual and corporate perspectives on the factors influencing the decision to accept an international assignment. *The International Journal of Human Resource Management*. 19(4), 731–751.

Eisenhardt, K. M. (1989). Building theories from case study research. *Academy of Management Review.* 14(4), 532–550.

Hippler, T. (2009). Why do they go? Empirical evidence of employees' motives for seeking or accepting relocation. *The International Journal of Human Resource Management.* 20(6), 1381–1401.

IDS. (2002). *International Assignments.* IDS Studies, 728(May). London: Incomes Data Services Ltd.

McNulty, Y. (2014). Modern expatriation through the lens of global careers, psychological contracts, and individual return on investment. *Global Business and Organizational Excellence.* 33(3), 6–22.

ORC Worldwide. (2007). *2006 Worldwide Survey of International Assignment Policies and Practices.* New York, NY: ORC Worldwide.

Pate, J. and Scullion, H. (2010). The changing nature of the traditional expatriate psychological contract. *Employee Relations.* 32(1), 56–73.

Rosen, S. (1986). The theory of equalizing differences. In Ashenfelter, O. and Layard, R. (eds.). *Handbook of Labor Economics* (Vol. 1, pp. 641–692). Amsterdam: Elsevier Science Publishers B.V.

Saunders, M., Lewis, P. and Thornhill, A. (2009). *Research Methods for Business Students.* Harlow, UK: Pearson Education.

Shortland, S. (2014). Women expatriates: a research history. In Hutchings, K. and Michailova, S. (eds.). *Research Handbook on Women in International Management* (pp. 18–44). Cheltenham, UK: Edward Elgar.

Shortland, S. (2016). The purpose of expatriation: why women undertake international assignments. *Human Resource Management.* 55(4), 655–678.

Shortland, S. and Perkins, S. J. (2016). Long-term assignment reward (dis)satisfaction outcomes: hearing women's voices. *Journal of Global Mobility.* 4(2), 225–250.

Suutari, V., Tornikoski, C. and Mäkelä, L. (2012). Career decision making of global careerists. *The International Journal of Human Resource Management.* 23(16), 3455–3478.

Warneke, D. and Schneider, M. (2011). Expatriate compensation packages: what do employees prefer? *Cross Cultural Management: An International Journal.* 18(2), 236–256.

Welch, D. (1994). Determinants of international human resource management approaches and activities: a suggested framework. *Journal of Management Studies.* 31(2), 139–164.

Yin, R. K. (2009). *Case Study Research: Design and Methods.* Thousand Oaks, CA: Sage.

Zhu, J., Wanberg, C. R., Harrison, D. A. and Diehn, E. W. (2016). Ups and downs of the expatriate experience? Understanding work adjustment trajectories and career outcomes. *Journal of Applied Psychology.* 101(4), 549–568.

30

REWARD MANAGEMENT IN THE PUBLIC SERVICES

Continuity and change

Ian Kessler

A dedicated focus on reward management in the public services by researchers and commentators is rare. There are significant research literatures on aspects of reward in the sector (Berman et al. 2010; Pynes 2013), but few systematic overviews of pay and non-pay benefits in the public services. This absence of overview pieces might be linked to difficulties in defining the public sector and, as a consequence, the scope of reward management. Thus, the public services can be defined in various ways: as any valued community 'good', whether privately, publicly or independently funded or delivered; as an activity funded by the state, but open to delivery by *any* private, independent and public sector organization; or as a service funded by the state and *exclusively* delivered by publicly owned organizations.

At the same time, it is unusual for any mainstream text to consider reward policies and practices by industrial sector. So why the interest in the public services reward in this edited volume? The answer to this question centres on three issues: importance, distinctiveness and change.

In considering each in turn, the discussion takes the public service sector to include activities directly funded *and* principally delivered by publicly owned organizations. The focus is mainly, but not exclusively, on the UK, where the main parts of public services are the Civil Service, healthcare, and local government, including education and social care.

Importance

Reward management in the public services derives its importance from the labour-intensive nature of the sector (Pynes 2013). Despite ongoing technological advances, public service delivery is still rooted in the unmediated relationship between the frontline worker and the service user – the schoolteacher in the classroom, the nurse at the bedside, and the social care assistant in the home. This typically renders wage costs the lion's share of total costs in the public services. For example, in healthcare systems across most developed countries wage costs constitute around two-thirds of total healthcare costs (Dubois et al. 2006:13). The scale of expenditure on staff in the public services renders the management of reward of significance, not only to the nature and quality of worker–user interaction, but to broader policy developments and outcomes. In the UK, this is reflected in Treasury pay guidance to Civil Service departments, 2016–17 (Treasury 2016) which reads:

> Given that public sector pay bill makes up over half of departmental resource spending, managing public sector pay within agreed departmental baselines and performance targets continues to be central to the government's plans for fiscal consolidation and will help protect jobs and services.

Distinctiveness

Stakeholders

The importance of pay to public policy makers points to the distinctiveness of reward management in the public services. Reward management in the sector is influenced by a unique set of stakeholders and interests. Often directly employed by politicians, public sector workers are subject to a set of shifting values-driven prescriptions on reward management. Funded by the public, reward management in the sector is additionally subject to taxpayer scrutiny. This necessitates not only publicly acceptable criteria for setting reward, but also processes which are transparent and ensure accountability. For Hutton (2011:9), a 'fair' reward management process is essential to the broader legitimacy of the public services:

> Public trust in public services requires that public pay is fair and seen to be fair, and that public services stand up to high standards of scrutiny.

Workforce

The distinctiveness of reward management can also be related to features of the public service workforce, particularly its diversity in terms of gender, ethnicity and occupation. Such diversity raises questions about the capacity of reward systems and structures in the public services to capture difference and deal judiciously with it. In the public services, women form a much higher proportion of the workforce than in most other sectors of the economy. While there are national variations, women make up on average 58% of the public sector workforce in OECD (2015:86) countries. In the UK, where much care work falls within the public services, this figure is much higher: around two-thirds of the public sector workforce are women, compared with just over half in the private sector (Institute of Fiscal Studies (IFS) 2014:18).

Ethnic diversity is reflected in black and minority ethnic groups often making up a relatively high proportion of health and social care workforces. In the UK, labour from these communities is particularly drawn to this type of work. Thus, it is noteworthy that one in four black workers is employed in the National Health Service (NHS) (McGregor-Smith 2017:66). The diversity of the public service workforce is further apparent in the sector's wide variety of occupational groups, ranging from routine job roles to the most expert and technical. In the UK NHS alone, there are over 300 different available careers (www.jobs.nhs.uk/about_nhs.html).

The public services are additionally distinctive in having highly professionalised workforces, including doctors, nurses, teachers and social workers. In the UK, this is reflected in the fact that well over half of public sector employees have a higher education qualification, compared to a third of employees in the private sector (IFS 2014:18). The professional character of the work-force ensures a well-articulated collective employee voice regarding reward management in the sector. While overall trade union density varies by country, it is almost invariably higher in the public than in the private sector (Visser 2006). The contrast is often stark: in the UK, 55% of public sector workers are in a union, compared to 14% in the private sector (Department for Business, Innovation and Skills (BIS) 2016). This difference is explained by various factors: for example, public sector workplaces are relatively large and union density is typically higher in larger organizations. But high union density in the public sector also derives from the alacrity with which professionals join their associations, partly as a means of strengthening occupational identity and securing career development opportunities, but also to protect their pay interests.

The free expression of this strong collective voice in determining reward is tempered by the nature of the work performed by public service professionals – and indeed other workers in the sector. Workers in health, education, transport and, in some countries, electricity, water and gas generation and distribution, are essential both to the efficient and effective running of the economy and to individual well-being, often amongst the most vulnerable community members. Against this backdrop, any breakdown in reward management, leading, for example, to industrial action, can be highly disruptive.

Across most developed countries, the combination of a strong collective voice amongst workers often performing essential services has resulted in the tight regulation of reward management in the public sector (ILO 2015). There has, however, been variation in the national arrangements put in place to deal with these distinctive workforce characteristics. Some governments have cut through any uncertainty or risk flowing from a strong collective worker voice in essential services by unilaterally determining pay and conditions. This 'sovereign employer' approach in the public services (Beaumont 1992) has been most apparent in Germany, where the pay of the *Beamte* strata of civil servants is set down in laws. This contrasts with the 'model employer' approach in the UK, where governments have sought to set an example to other sectors by traditionally supporting free collective bargaining as the preferred means of determining pay in the public services. British governments have, nonetheless, acknowledged the broader sensitivities raised by reward in the sector, with the establishment of pay review bodies, which cover the main service groups – NHS staff, teachers, prison officers, the Armed Forces and senior civil servants – and make annual recommendations to government on the pay increase (White 2000).

Workings

Finally, the distinctiveness of reward management lies in the workings of the public sector – in particular, the regulated nature of labour and product markets which shape and control aspects of reward management. For example, product or service markets in the sector, traditionally sheltered from the full force of competition, have been less fertile ground for the use of reward as a strategic resource. Within the context of the 'New Pay' agenda (Schuster and Zingheim 1992), what scope or incentive do not-for-profit public service organizations with limited control over the size of their pay bill have to align their reward practices with competitive business objectives? Indeed, in some parts of the public services, wage fixing might be seen to depend less on the free interplay between the forces of labour demand and supply than on government decisions about pay bill funding and the number of training places funded by government in key professions such as nursing and medicine.

A fuller consideration of how the distinctiveness of the public services influences reward needs to drill down to the key elements of this management domain: remuneration levels; reward structures; and reward systems. In doing so, it will become clear that, while the sector's distinctiveness has had an enduring influence on reward management, this influence has assumed different forms and impacted in various ways over the years. Subject to shifting socio-economic and political circumstances, there have been important changes in public service reward management policies and practices.

Remuneration levels

Pay criteria

A number of change narratives can be associated with rates of remuneration in the public services. The first relates to the criteria used by governments to uprate pay in the sector. This connects to process issues and the state's search for legitimacy in the pay increases awarded to its employees. In the UK, there have been significant shifts in the emphasis given to pay criteria in the context of changing economic conditions and political priorities. The post-1945 decades were characterized by the privileging of comparability in public service pay determination: in a period of economic growth, it could plausibly be argued by governments that public servants 'deserved' pay rates similar to those paid to private sector workers. The approach was most formalized in the Civil Service, where a Pay Research Unit (PRU) made wage recommendations on this basis from the mid-1950s to the late 1970s (albeit with short periods of suspension in times of pay restraint) (Fry 1993).

With the arrival of the 'New Right' Thatcher government in 1979, seeking to reduce public expenditure and with an ideological antipathy to the public sector workforce, comparability gave way to a standard managerial mantra of pay rates designed to 'recruit, retain and motivate'. This shift was signalled by the abolition of the PRU, although it is noteworthy that the government continued to rely on, and indeed extend, the coverage of the pay review bodies. Across UK governments of different party political complexions, the remit of the review bodies has continued to centre on 'recruitment, retention and motivation', although with periodic 'nudges' towards other criteria, such as regional labour market conditions. Thus, individual employers in health and local government have occasionally bridled against the perceived rigidity of national pay rates in the context of different local labour market conditions, a concern bolstered by research suggesting that such rates might lead to the suboptimal distribution of the public service workforce (Wolf 2010), with negative consequences for service quality (Propper and Van Reenen 2010). In most cases, however, an interest in regional pay has been countered by the capacity of national agreements to 'flex' pay to deal with such issues.

The financial crisis, which began in 2008, had a more significant impact on pay criteria, deepening the emphasis on affordability. Given the scale of the pay bill, reducing wage costs increasingly became seen as means of reducing government spending deficits. In part, this reduction has been achieved by workforce cuts: in the UK, the public sector workforce has fallen by over a million between 2009 and 2015. It has also been addressed by limiting pay increases: pay in the sector was frozen between 2011 and 2014 and limited to an annual 1% rise between 2014 and 2016. Britain has not been alone in this respect, with similar government-imposed wage freezes in, for example, Italy, Finland and Portugal and Hungary. At the same time, variation in the impact of the financial crisis has led to some differences in practice, with some of the less-affected countries, such as Denmark, Germany and the Netherlands, still awarding moderate pay increases (Glassner 2010; Leisink and Bach 2014).

Public–private differentials

The financial crisis has had a ripple effect, impacting on other aspects of pay rates. Thus, a second change narrative has centred on differential public–private sector pay rates, which, despite recent government attempts to control pay increases, have continued to favour the public sector. In short, across most developed countries, public sector workers receive a higher average rate of pay than those in the private sector (Giordana et al. 2011). In times of austerity, this difference has attracted attention, particularly from commentators arguing that it is indicative of the uneven distribution of hardships associated with the financial crisis.

Such a debate obscures the long-standing nature of the public–private differential, explained less by the uneven impact of austerity than by differences in the background composition of the respective sector workforces. In general, human capital in the public sector has a higher value than in the private, given its levels of training, qualifications and experience. Once these factors are controlled for the public sector pay premium is much reduced. In Britain, for example, 2009 figures indicate that, in crude terms, men in the public sector had weekly earnings 11.0% higher than those in the private. Controlling for human capital, this difference is reversed with private sector men earning 1.7% more. For women, the public sector differential does remains after controlling for human capital, but falls from 21.4% to just 3.9% (Dolton and Makepeace 2011).

Debate on the public–private sector differential has not been limited to pay, however, with considerable attention also devoted to the perceived preferential treatment received by public sector workers in relation to the non-pay element of remuneration. Most striking in this respect are differences in pension rights. In the UK, for example, 87% of employees in the public sector have a workplace pension, compared with 55% of private sector employees. Moreover almost 95% of public sector employees have an occupational defined benefit pension, compared to only 15% in the private sector (Senior Salaries Pay Review Body 2016). Governments have been keen to draw the attention of public sector workers to the benefits associated with these pension schemes, which are often felt to be overlooked by employees. This has encouraged the introduction of total reward statements (cf. Cotton, this volume), highlighting the ongoing value of their pension, particularly in times of wage restraint.

Top pay

Another change narrative affected by austerity relates to the pay of senior managers in the public sector. These managers have increasingly been drawn into more general debates about 'excessive' top pay across the economy, especially given widespread evidence of organizational under-performance and failure, not least in the financial services sector in the context of the 2008 crisis. In the UK, the critical gaze on the pay of chief executives in the private sector has been mirrored in talk of 'fat cat' public sector managers, with interest groups such as the Taxpayers' Alliance regularly publishing a public sector 'rich list' of senior managers. This rhetoric has prompted government inquiries, such as that chaired by Will Hutton in 2011 and based on looking across the public sector and another three years later, which had a narrower focus on chief executive pay in local government. Both inquiries sought to bring perspective to comparisons between top pay on the private and public sectors. The latter inquiry, for example, published data showing a 6:1 ratio between the highest- and lowest-paid workers in local government, compared to a 228:1 ratio in the private sector (House of Commons 2014:16). Indeed, the Hutton inquiry (2011) rejected calls for a cap on senior manager pay in the public sector, raising concerns about likely gaming around it.

Both inquires, however, recognised the need for greater transparency in pay determination, and a plausible public rationale for senior manager pay in the public sector. Resisting the critical literature on performance pay in the public sector (see below), the Hutton inquiry proposed an 'earn back' scheme linking part of the individual senior managers' pay to the achievement of organizational objectives. Aligning with the government's localism agenda, Hutton's call for greater transparency in public sector senior management pay arrangements was received more positively: all local authorities are now required to publish an annual pay statement setting out such arrangements.

Pay structures

Pay structures in the public sector have traditionally been characterized by a number of features, but they are also subject to recent pressures for change. The first of these characteristics is the wide variety of occupational groups embraced by many of these pay structures. Indeed, in Britain occupational coverage of such structures has broadened over recent years: for example, in local government a single-status agreement in 1997 covering 1.4 million workers brought together myriad manual and non-manual occupations under a single pay structure, while in the NHS an agreement, Agenda for Change, 2005, covering 1.3 million workers, was rooted in grading structure which integrated most NHS occupations (Perkins and White 2010).

Second, public sector pay structures have been founded on job evaluation, placing particular emphasis on internal relative job worth. Notably, in Britain an emphasis on internal equity is reflected in a Chartered Institute of Personnel and Development (CIPD) (2003) survey highlighting that almost two-thirds of public sector employers (60%) included 'internal equity' as a 'strategic reward goal' compared to well under a third of private sector employers (30%).

Third, public service pay structures have typically comprised long pay scales providing scope for annual service-based incremental progression. Again, the contrast with the private sector is striking: another CIPD (2015) survey indicated that while close to two-thirds of public service employers (63%) had a service-related pay spine, this was the case for only for a fifth of private service employers (20%).

Over recent years, the predominant change narrative associated with pay structures in the public services has centred on gender pay equality (Stewart 2014). The gender pay gap is engrained across industries in most developed countries (Eurostat, 2017), but the public sector has a particular story to tell revolving around the size of this gap, and its causes and consequences. In terms of size, there are noteworthy national variations in the public sector gender pay gap, ranging from 22.5% in Bulgaria to 2.9% in Italy. Nonetheless Eurostat (2017) data indicate that in most countries the gap is narrower in the public than the private sector, suggesting a sector effect. The Eurostat data, however, do need to be treated with some caution. They are based on raw figures which fail to control for the coverage of the public sector. Moreover, they are based on gross *average* earnings for *all employees*, with much debate on how the gender gap should be measured. In Britain, for example, the headline measure is based *median* earnings of *full-time* employees producing public/private sector gender gaps of 9.2%/18.4% (TUC 2012). The gender gap amongst part-time workers is also a crucial element of the story. Thus, in the UK the gap is much wider for part-time workers, at 36.3% in the public and 42.8% in the private sectors (TUC 2012).

Notwithstanding technical debates on measurement, there remains a public sector gender pay gap to be explained. As in the private sector, the gap might be related to occupational segregation, with women workers in the public sector disproportionately concentrated in lower-graded work roles. In the English NHS, for example, around 80% of healthcare support workers (https://www.gov.uk/government/organisations/health-and-social-care-information-centre) and in English schools over 90% of teaching assistants (2016 DfE School Workforce in England) are women. Indeed, there is evidence to suggest that the mainly female care workforce is subject to a wage penalty. In the United States, research has revealed that after controlling for various personal characteristics, those in care work earned 5–6% less those in non-care work (England et al. 2002). Barron and West (2013) confirm this wage gap in a British context, particularly amongst lower-graded workers. Amongst nursing assistants there is an annual earnings deficit of £800, while for childcare and welfare the gap is closer to £4,000.

The gender pay gap in the public sector can also be related to the discriminatory workings of pay structures. This has increasingly come to light in the context of various statutory developments designed to address gender bias (Kirton and Greene 2015). In the UK, for example, long incremental scales, seen to indirectly discriminate against women, who are more likely than men to take a career break, have gradually been shortened across the public services. Most significant, however, has been a gender bias deeply embedded in pay structures, which has undermined the capacity of women workers to earn equal pay for jobs which are very different to those performed by men, but of equal value to the public sector organization.

From the late 1990s onwards, stakeholder attempts to ensure women receive equal pay for work of equal value in the public sector have often been incremental and disordered (Bach and Kessler 2012). Equal pay claims have emerged in an ad hoc and opportunistic way, on a hospital-by-hospital and a local authority-by-local authority basis. 'No-win-no fee' lawyers' prepared to take up the cause added to the disorder, threatening trade unions' credibility in protecting their members' interests. The single-status agreement in local government and the Agenda for Change agreement in the NHS can, in large part, be seen as a union and management attempt to regain control over and address this equal pay issue. The new pay structures established by these agreements were based on 'equality-proofed' job evaluation schemes, sensitive to the distinctive features of female job roles. The financial consequences of these steps should not be underestimated, however; perhaps a reflection of the scale of gender inequality in the public sector. In 2008, the cost of introducing single status in local government was put at £2.8 billion (Bach and Kessler 2012:70), with half of the local authorities still to complete their re-evaluation of work roles. In the NHS, the value of Agenda for Change was put at £1.3 billion, flowing in part from increased worker productivity, but also from a 'reduction in equal pay claims' assured by the new grading structure (House of Commons 2009:1).

Pay systems

Over the last thirty years or so, debate on public service pay systems has been dominated by an interest in individual performance-related pay (PRP). This is perhaps a surprising preoccupation given that reviews of the evidence have typically cast doubt on the efficacy of PRP in the public sector and the take-up of PRP has been patchy. Nonetheless, as an approach to pay in the sector, whether in determining incremental progression within grade, establishing consolidated increases to pay rates or setting non-consolidated bonus payments, PRP has retained a seductive hold over the sector's policy makers and practitioners, which is worth exploring.

Of all the developments in reward management, the interest in PRP is most indicative of broader changes in models of public service delivery across OECD countries. Post-1945 welfare state bureaucracies lent themselves to hierarchical grading structures and service-based progression and promotion. Delivering services according to standard operating procedures, these bureaucracies were founded on the assumption of limited variance in employee performance, negating the need for pay schemes which rewarded on this basis. From the late 1970s, however, state bureaucracies came under pressure as the principal vehicle for public service provision in ways which brought performance-based rewards to the fore. These pressures were associated with the 'new public management' (NPM) (Pollitt 2011), an approach informed by public choice theory's critique of public services as vulnerable to 'producers' capture' (Buchanan and Tollison 1984), but also by the values of emerging 'New Right' governments, particularly in the UK and the US. Such values promoted the exposure of public services to market forces and encouraged a set of policy prescriptions to facilitate this process. PRP was often totemic to the NPM approach: a private sector practice designed to reward those individuals 'best equipped' to perform in the new competitive environment of public service provision.

The diffusion of NPM practices across developed countries should not be overstated (Pollitt 2011). However, the emergence of NPM also coincided with a broader government interest in the tighter control of organizational performance amongst public service providers, particularly in the context of growing resource constraints and increasing service demand. An interest in organizational performance encouraged a focus on PRP. As the OECD (2005:12) noted:

> PRP fits within the wider performance budgeting and management developments in vogue over the past two decades, which emerged against the background of the economic and budgetary difficulties in OECD member countries.

Indeed, the take-up of PRP in the national civil services covered by the OECD (2005:35) report was marked:

> Twenty years ago, nearly all civil servants in the central government of OECD member countries were paid according to service-incremental salary scales . . . By the turn of the millennium, significant numbers of civil servants were covered by performance-related pay (PRP) schemes in most OECD member countries.

The relatively high take-up of PRP in civil services might well reflect the fact that as the direct employer, governments were well placed to adopt their 'preferred' reward practice. The diffusion of PRP to other parts of the public services, particularly health and local government, with the government often funding service rather than directly employing staff, was much patchier. In the UK, for example, a recent CIPD (2015) survey revealed that only around a half of public sector employers used individual performance as the basis of pay progression, compared to well over 80% in the private sector. Indeed, despite strong encouragement from central government in Britain over the years, PRP has made limited headway, even at senior management levels, in health and local government (House of Commons 2014).

The uneven diffusion of PRP in the public services might well be indicative of the concerns raised about its efficacy in the sector, as regularly highlighted by reviews of the evidence. Any attempt to assess efficacy is dependent on the managerial goals underpinning PRP, whether they relate to: increased motivation; changes in employee behaviour; or improved service outcomes. However, an extensive range of studies has challenged the capacity of PRP in the public services to achieve any of these goals. Reviewing such studies, Perry et al. (2009:41) delivered a stark conclusion:

> Performance related pay in the public sector consistently fails to deliver on its promise.

Other reviews of the evidence have come to somewhat more nuanced conclusions, but still informed by scepticism on PRP's efficacy. Prentice et al (2007) found a 'small worker response' to financial incentive, although mainly limited the education sector, and tempered by evidence of manipulative behaviours in the setting and assessing of performance objectives for pay purposes. A follow-up review (Ray 2014:6) suggested that the impact of PRP was contingent on scheme design and service area, and similarly noted the difficulty of unpacking positive outcomes:

> . . . findings are mixed and context- or outcomes-specific, making it difficult to draw overall conclusions about the effectiveness of PRP for particular public services.

The doubts raised about the efficacy of individual PRP in the public services are well rehearsed and include:

- *Multiple stakeholders:* With the delivery of public services involving multiple stakeholders – policy makers, practitioners, service users – driven by very different values and interests – setting, assessing and then rewarding individual performance objectives becomes a highly problematic process. In such a context, the assumption that principal–agent interests can straightforwardly be aligned through the controlling influence of performance incentives emerges as a somewhat oversimplified view (Dixit 2002).
- *Teamworking:* The collective nature of much public service work creates difficulties in distinguishing the contribution of individuals to outcomes, essential to many PRP schemes. For example, is the teacher who sorts out the behavioural problems of a class any less entitled to a performance payment for pupil test results than the teacher in the succeeding year, who is then better able to prepare these students for the exams?
- *Intrinsic motivation:* Deriving intrinsic reward from their work, public service employees have often been viewed as not particularly susceptible to performance-based extrinsic rewards. Indeed, a well-developed literature has argued that the extrinsic reward underpinning PRP and closely tied to a task and outcome might well 'crowd out' the public servants' intrinsic rewards (Deci 1971; Frey et al. 1997). The managerial consequences are likely to be reflected not only in an undermining of employee job satisfaction and possibly well-being, but more prosaically in higher pay costs, as organizations are required to pay for behaviours infused by a public service ethos (Le Grand 2003) or a public service motivation (Perry and Wise 1990) and volunteered by the employee as a 'gift' to their employer.
- *Funding constraints:* Given the state's concern to control public sector staff costs, especially in periods of austerity, questions are raised as to whether the scale of funding for PRP is high enough to prompt significant shifts in employee attitude and behaviour. Large performance pay increases are often required to incentivize employees, with employees always likely to make a cognitive calculation as to whether or not the (limited) pay at stake is worth the (additional) effort needed to secure it.

These repeatedly articulated concerns about the effective implementation of individual performance-related pay in the public services have, over the years, prompted some policy refinements. For example, in the early 2000s the 'New Labour' government in Britain moved from individual to team-based performance pay in a number of civil service agencies, prompted by the Makinson (2000:12) report, which noted that:

> Public sector employees take pride in collective achievement and collective progress is generally easier to measure and benchmark than individual achievement.

Yet despite these policy modifications, individual performance pay has retained a strong hold over national policy makers. Indeed, as recently as September 2013 the UK government introduced a new individual PRP system for primary and secondary teachers, in the wake of a School Teachers Review Body report (STRB, 2012:7), quoting a 37-country OECD (2012) study which had "found no relationship between pupil performance and the use of pay systems with performance-based elements".

The sustained disconnect between research evidence and government policy on PRP in the public services has encouraged speculation on its cause, with a number of suggested answers put forward (Kellough and Li 1993; Marsden 2009; Bowman 2010). Some commentators suggest that PRP has acquired a symbolic status which establishes resilience to evidence-based analysis. As Bowman (2010:78) argues:

> Performance pay is a titanic cultural icon. Merit is simply too oceanic a social myth to reject outright: to do so would imply that individuals do not make a difference.

It is an icon with particular potency in the political arena, with PRP for public service workers having an intuitive appeal to a range of stakeholders. Thus, there is evidence to suggest that public service workers tend to support the principle of pay for performance, although they are far less sanguine about PRP in practice (Makinson 2000). Moreover, pay for performance has been used to send out a strong signal to the electorate of the government's modernization of pay systems (Perkins and White 2010). Indeed, there are instances where PRP has been used as a means of legitimizing public sector pay increases to the benefit of employees. For example, the introduction of an upper pay scale (UPS) for British teachers in 2000 was explicitly trailed by the New Labour government as the introduction of performance pay to the profession. However, it might better be seen as a means of justifying a pay increase for such workers: 80% of 200,000 eligible teachers applied, with 96% of these applicants allowed to move onto the UPS (Bach and Kessler 2012:61).

For others, the disconnect between policy and evidence reflects the narrow set of criteria often used to assess the efficacy of PRP in the public services. Researchers have tended to concentrate on PRP's capacity to motivate and contribute to the achievement of various 'hard' service outcomes (Perry 1986). However, PRP might more usefully be viewed as a means of achieving tighter managerial control. For example, Marsden (2009), drawing on evidence from the British Inland Revenue, suggests that the cycle of setting, evaluating and then re-setting individual performance objectives binds the employee into a tight work agreement which can be regularly renegotiated on management's terms. More prosaically, PRP might also be seen as a means of controlling the pay bill. Thus, PRP allows government greater discretion over the award of pay increases and provides an opportunity to drive out other bases for pay increases, such as those reflecting length of service or cost of living.

Conclusions

In exploring reward management in the public services, this chapter has sought to strike a balance. On the one hand, it has outlined the procedural and substantive distinctiveness of reward management in the sector, stressing enduring differences with reward policy and practice in the private sector. In the labour-intensive public services, reward management has remained a major element of public expenditure and consequentially a particularly important tool of government macro-economic policy. Moreover, reward management in the sector has been exposed to the interests of a wide range of stakeholders, not least party politicians keen to use reward as a means of expressing and furthering ideological values. The sector's reward management has also been shaped by the diversity of the workforce in terms of gender, ethnicity and occupation. Such features, along with the particular structure and operation of the public services, have combined to produce heavily regulated forms of reward management, reflected in institutions for pay determination which provide for an especially strong collective employee voice.

On the other hand, the chapter has examined how these distinctive features have been sensitive to broader socio-economic and political influences and manifested themselves in different ways over the post-1945 period. In setting rates of reward, attention has been drawn to the move from the use of comparability in determining public sector pay, through to a reliance on 'recruitment, retention and motivation' to an emphasis on affordability and constraint, particularly in times of austerity. Pay structures covering a multiplicity of very different occupations have been seen as gradually exposed as discriminatory in failing to provide women equal pay for undertaking work of equal value to men. Attention has been drawn, in particular, to the reconstitution of pay structures on the basis of more gender-sensitive forms of job evaluation. Finally, debate on pay systems has been presented as increasingly dominated by an interest in individual performance-related pay, an approach associated with the shift from bureaucratic to market forms of public service delivery. Adopting a symbolic significance in this context and providing a means of tighter control of employee performance and costs, public policy interest in PRP has remained buoyant.

References

Bach, S. and Kessler, I. (2012). *The Modernisation of the Public Services and Employee Relations*. London: Palgrave.

Barron, D. and West, E. (2013). The financial cost of caring in the British labour market: Is there a wage penalty for workers in caring occupations? *British Journal of Industrial Relations*. 51(1), 104–123.

Beaumont, P. (1992). *Public Sector Industrial Relations*. London: Routledge.

Berman, E., Bowman, J., West, J. and Van Wart, M. (2010). *Human Resource Management in Public Service*. London: Sage.

Bowman, J. (2010). The success of failure: the paradox of performance pay. *Review of Public Personnel Administration*. 30(1), 70–88.

Buchanan, J. and Tollison, R. (eds.). (1984). *The Theory of Public Choice*. Ann Arbor, MI: University of Michigan Press.

CIPD (2003). *Reward Management Survey*, 2003. London: CIPD.

CIPD (2015). *Reward Management Survey*, 2015. London: CIPD.

Deci, E. (1971). Effects of externally mediated rewards on intrinsic motivation. *Journal of Personality and Social Psychology*. 18(1), 105–115.

Department for Business, Innovation and Skills (2016). *Trade Union Membership. 2016*, London: BIS.

Dixit, A. (2002). Incentives and organization in the public sector. *The Journal of Human Resources*. 37(4), 696–727.

Dolton, P. and Makepeace, G. (2011). Public and private sector labour markets. In Gregg, P. and Wadsworth, J. (eds.). *The Labour Market in Winter*. Oxford: Oxford University Press.

Dubois, C., McKee and Nolte, E. (2006). *Human Resources for Health in Europe*. Maidenhead: Open University Press.

England, P., Budig, M. and Folbre, B. (2002). Wages of virtue: the relative pay of care work, *Social Problems*. 49(4), 455–473.

Eurostat. (2017). *Report on Equality between Men and Women in the European Union*. Brussels: European Union.

Frey, B. and Oberholzer-Gee, F. (1997). The cost of price incentives: an empirical analysis of motivation and crowding put, *American Economic Review*. 87(4), 746–755.

Fry, G. (1993). Development in civil service pay since the Megaw Report. *Public Policy and Administration*. 8(3), 4–18.

Giordana, R., Domenico, D., Coutinho, M., Eugene, B., Papapetrou, E., Perez, J., Reiss, L. and Roter, M. (2011). *The Public Sector Pay Gap of Euro Asia Countries*. Frankfurt: European Central Bank.

Glassner, V. (2010). *The Public Sector in Crisis*. July. Brussels: ETUI.

House of Commons. (2009). *NHS Pay Modernisation: Agenda for Changes*, Public Accounts Committee. London: House of Commons.

House of Commons. (2014). *Local Government Chief Officers' Remuneration*. London: House of Commons.

Hutton, W. (2011) *Review of Fair Pay in the Public Sector*. London: HMSO.

IFS (2014). *The Public Sector Workforce: Past, Present and Future*. London: IFS.

ILO (2015). *Collective Bargaining in the Pubic Services in the European Union*. Geneva: ILO.

Kellough, J. and Lu, H. (1993). The paradox of merit pay in the public sector. *Review of Public Personnel Administration*. 16(2), 45–64.

Kirton, G. and Greene, A.-M. (2015). *The Dynamics of Managing Diversity*. London: Routledge.

Le Grand, J. (2003). *Motivation, Agency and Public Policy*. Oxford: Oxford University Press.

Leisink, P. and Bach, S. (2014). Economic crisis and municipal public service employment: Comparing development on seven EU member states. *Transfer*. 20(3), 227–342.

Makinson, J. (2000). *Incentives for Change*. London: Cabinet Office.

Marsden, D. (2009). *The Paradox of PRP Systems*. London: Centre or Economic Performance. LSE.

McGregor-Smith, R. (2017). *Race in the Workplace*. London: Department of Business, Energy and Industrial Strategy.

OECD (2005). *Performance-related Pay Policies for Government Employees*. Paris: OECD.

OECD (2012). *PISA in Focus 16: Does Performance Based Pay Improve Teaching?* Paris: OECD.

OECD (2015). *Government at a Glance*. Paris: OECD.

Perkins, S. J. and White, G. (2010). Modernising pay in the UK public services: trends and implications. *Human Resource Management Journal*. 20(3), 244–257.

Perry, J. (1986). Merit pay in the public sector: the case for a failure of theory. *Review of Public Personnel Administration*. 7(1), 57–69.

Perry, J., Engbers, T. and Yun Jun, S. (2009). Back to the future? PRP: Empirical research and the perils of persistence. *Public Administration* 69: 39–51.

Perry, J. and Wise, R. (1990). The motivational bases of public service. *Public Administration Review*. 50, 367–373.

Pollitt, C. (2011). *Public Management Reform: A Comparative Analysis*. Oxford: Oxford University Press.

Prentices, G. Burgess, S. and Propper, C. (2007). *Performance Pay in the Public Sector: a Review of Issues and Evidence*. London: OME.

Propper, C. and Van Reenen, J. (2010). Can pay regulation kill? Panel data evidence on the effect of labor markets on hospital performance. *Journal of Political Economy*. 118(2), 222–273.

Pynes, J. (2013). *Human Resources Management for Public and Non Profit Organizations*. San Francisco: Josey-Bass.

Ray, K. (2014). *A Review of the Evidence on the Impact, Effectiveness, and Value for Money of Performance Pay in the Public Sector*. London: Work Foundation.

Schuster, J. and Zingheim, P. (1992). *The New Pay: Linking Employee and Organizational Performance*. New York: Lexington.

Senior Salaries Pay Review Body (2016). *38th Annual Report*. London: Senior Salaries Pay Review Body.

Stewart, M. (2014). *Why is the Gender Pay Gap Higher in the Private Sector?* Warwick: University of Warwick.

Treasury. (2016). *Civil Service Pay Guidance 2016 to 2017*. London: HM Treasury.

TUC. (2012). *Women's Pay and Employment Update: A Public–Private Sector Comparison*. London: TUC.

Visser, J. (2006). Union membership statistics in 24 countries. *Monthly Labor Review*. 129(1), 38–49.

White, G. (2000). The pay review body system: Its development and impact. *Historical Studies in Industrial Relations*. 9, 71–100.

Wolf, A. (2010). *More Than We Bargained For: The Social and Economic Costs of National Wage Bargaining*. London: CentreForum.

31

REWARD MANAGEMENT AND ORGANIZATIONAL CITIZENSHIP BEHAVIOURS IN UK BANKS

James Allan

Introduction

In public statements over the past decade or so, UK banking leaders have set out intentions to align their businesses with certain core values. The sentiment is that it is only when people in organizations work as a team and 'act with integrity' that the trust of clients, shareholders and other key stakeholders can be secured and maintained.

Against that backdrop, drawing on primary interview data collected in 2011 while the author was undertaking an Executive MBA programme, this chapter analyses questions surrounding the role of bankers' rewards. The consensus at the time was that the way the banks behaved and reacted to the financial crisis in terms of reward was not good enough. Hindsight on issues below the surface helps understand the extent to which declared aspirations to create conditions that encourage integrity and teamwork among those in banking are helped or hindered. The phenomena are theorized using the term 'organizational citizenship behaviours' (OCBs), namely increased engagement, loyalty and extra-role performance. The purpose of this chapter is to take a measured view on the question: for Britain's bankers, is it 'all about the pay'?

The chapter concludes that senior banking management have to balance encouraging OCBs while satisfying the demands of regulators and the UK public. In determining bankers' rewards, consultants, HR specialists and senior managers need to take adequate account of the complexity of the contextual environment. An overemphasis on financial reward in attempts to control banker behaviour neglects the importance to bankers of non-financial rewards. OCBs are fostered through non-financial reward. In common with other employees, bankers seek a long-term, relational contract with their employers. This can be undermined by perceived unfairness in reward management linked with perceptions of an autocratic organizational culture. An overly short-term focus in managing the employment relationship leaves bankers feeling disempowered by the process. A 'black box' approach offers little transparency to individuals on how reward management decisions are made.

Defining key terms

Employee reward represents one of the key themes supporting the employment relationship (Kessler 2005). For the purpose of this chapter, reward is differentiated between financial and non-financial reward factors. Perkins and White (2016) define financial or *extrinsic* reward as the tangible or transactional reward for undertaking work in employment and non-financial or *intrinsic* reward derived from work and employment. Financial reward can be offered in the form of salary, incentive pay and non-cash benefits, and directly recognises the value of employee contribution. Non-cash benefits include pensions, health insurance, flexible holiday allowances and childcare vouchers (Silverman 2004). But taking a wider definitional stance, non-financial reward is applied in support of employee learning and development, in the form of praise and recognition, and helps the employee gain feelings of accomplishment (Milkovich and Newman 2004).

Remuneration reports reviewed in the course of this research indicate that financial reward at UK banks is made up of base pay and variable financial incentives. Base pay is the fixed cash element of employee compensation and reflects both the value of employee skills and the market valuation of the role. Financial incentives can be either short or long term in nature and are based on firm, business unit and individual employee performance. Variable financial reward can include cash or direct equity grants in the firm, or a mix of both, and typically represent 60% of employee compensation in the UK banks studied.

Milkovich and Newman (2008) argue the interest in pay is unsurprising given the importance of this to employees, but there is an underestimate of the value of non-financial reward in driving employee motivation and behaviours. Significant research has been carried out to determine the drivers of employee motivation (e.g., Herzberg (1966), Lawler et al. (1975), and Maslow (1954)). In more detailed consideration of employee behaviours, Organ (1988) defined the concept of Organizational Citizenship Behaviour (OCB) as "individual behaviour that is discretionary, not directly or explicitly recognised by the formal reward system, and that in aggregate promotes the effective functioning of the organization".

Bankers' rewards, the 2007–2009 financial crisis and its aftermath

Over the years since the 2007–2009 financial crisis, the UK media has carried considerable reporting on the subject of bankers' pay – in particular so-called 'incentive rewards' or bonuses. This commentary has questioned bankers' motives and behaviours. Bankers have been portrayed as greedy and motivated by self-interest, reinforcing a sense widely shared among the UK public that banks were responsible for the crisis. Academics Bebchuk et al. (2009) argue, in their paper *Wages of Failure,* that reward systems in banks, heavily focused on performance-based rewards, encourage excessive risk-taking: behaviour that caused the collapse of investment banks such as Bear Stearns and Lehman Brothers. Despite those banks failing in 2008, their top bankers were paid and cashed-in $2.4bn in compensation over the period 2000–2008.

The Turner Review published by the UK Financial Services Authority (FSA 2009a) found that the primary cause of the crisis lay in inappropriate levels of risk-taking by bankers, who were incentivized by high levels of short-term variable pay. The conclusion was that bank reward systems needed to be overhauled. The Turner Review was followed in November 2009 by the Walker Review on corporate and risk governance in UK banks, also published by the FSA. Walker commented: "it is clear governance failures contributed materially to excessive risk taking in the lead up to the financial crisis" (FSA 2009b). Walker proposed changes to financial reward systems in UK banks to improve the future stability of the financial services industry. Key proposals focus on the need for transparency around the pay of "high-end" employees (those defined as having total remuneration in excess of the executive board median).

Incorporating these various proposals, following a period of consultation, the FSA published an updated Remuneration Code (FSA 2010), incorporating also the requirements of the EU

Capital Requirements Directive (CRD3). All Tier 1 UK banks (those with capital resources over £1 billion) were required to comply with the new requirements of regulation from January 2011. The FSA requires that remuneration policy must not encourage risk-taking in firms and should support the firm's business strategy. A firm's employees must not use personal hedging strategies that undermine remuneration policy. Including financial and non-financial criteria, performance management must be set in a multi-year framework with employee assessment based on long-term performance. Finally, variable pay must be deferred over a period of three to five-years, contain at least 50% in company shares, and include a "claw-back" for *malus* (discovery of defective performance in terms of corporate impact).

Research into banker behaviours informing the chapter focuses specifically on Corporate and Investment Banking. A range of views was gathered from thirty individuals and interviews were held with four reward consultants, five corporate HR professionals, 12 senior banking managers, the head of a PR and communications company specializing in financial services and seven mid-level corporate bankers. And input was obtained in a written communication with a representative of the FSA. The aim of the investigation was to understand comparative perceptions of the motivational inputs informing banker behaviour and to assess the relative importance of financial as well as non-financial reward factors in employee performance outcomes. Further, the chapter examine how perceptions of fairness of a bank's performance management and reward processes may improve trust and encourage bankers to demonstrate OCBs. In turn, to align bankers with corporately espoused values and to rebuild trust with society.

In line with the FSA's requirement for increased transparency on bankers' pay, Tier 1 UK banks publish remuneration reports as supplements to annual reports. The content of reports of the main UK banks Barclays, HSBC, Lloyds Banking Group, RBS and Standard Chartered (StanChart) published between 2009 and 2011 was examined (Barclays PLC 2010; HSBC PLC 2010; Lloyds Banking Group 2010; RBS 2010; Standard Chartered Bank 2010). The purpose was to determine the character of bank reward systems post-2007–2009 crisis and to assess how successfully banks publicly communicate their approach to reward.

While space precludes detailed description of findings, UK banks' reward practices since the financial crisis had mostly responded in a largely reactive way to the FSA (2010) Remuneration Code, only observing its core requirements. Notably incentive pay was now deferred, although only over a three-year period, and this was common to all banks. The banks, despite their objective to link performance to reward, had failed to deliver positive shareholder returns over the period, with the exception of HSBC and StanChart. This said, HSBC, Barclays and StanChart offered a stronger level of transparency in reporting and Barclays had taken the lead in moving the demonstration of long-run firm performance from purely 'Total Shareholder Return' to Return on Equity and capital adequacy. StanChart provided the clearest evidence of all banks on the importance of non-financial reward factors in performance management. Here, employee behaviours were aligned with firm culture to focus on the long-term interests of clients, shareholders and other key stakeholder groups.

Perspectives on bankers' reward and recognition

In the next section, findings are summarized from the 35 interviews, organised across the four stakeholder groupings: Reward Consultants (RCs), HR Professionals (HRs), Senior Management in banks (SMs), and Bankers (Bs). The stakeholder groups have been given codes and the names of interview participants removed to ensure anonymity. This was a requirement of the interview participants in order to provide open and comprehensive views and opinions. Direct quotations are attributed to participants by their reference code. Each participant was chosen based on their specialist knowledge of the topic, seniority of position in the bank or length of experience in banking, making them well qualified to discuss the topic of reward systems and OCBs.

Views of Reward Consultants

For reward consultants, the purpose of regulatory change is unclear and regulators do not understand reward. Increased transparency on pay, required by the regulator and provided through industry benchmarking used by banks, is driving up salaries for bankers, particularly for senior management. The press focuses disproportionately on coverage of top management pay. Banks should take the lead on regulation and emphasize its importance to creating a safe and sustainable financial system.

R egarding financial rewards, UK banks are "following the herd" (RC1) – no bank wants to differentiate their approach to reward, particularly on compensation. The market drives pay decisions in banks and artificially low basic pay, coupled with increased value of short-term variable pay through cash bonuses, drives short-term focus and excessive risk-taking by bankers. This said, moving short-term variable pay into a higher basic without maintaining a direct link to performance, so that in effect bankers are paid "come what may", is a "totally flawed concept" (RC1). Annual compensation still remains backward-looking and, although the use of deferred pay has increased in recent years, 'clawbacks' for *malus* are not practical and do not drive long-term behaviour. Banks have adopted a 'one-size-fits-all' approach. Indeed, the purpose of reward in banks needs to be reassessed at a fundamental level:

> Reward systems are asymmetric – it's all about avoiding banker dissatisfaction, not to reward and satisfy.
>
> (RC2)

Communication on and distribution of financial reward needs to be improved. Line manager discretion should be limited to increase bankers' perception of organizational justice. Bankers want to be treated fairly and to understand what they are being rewarded for, relative to others. In addition to attracting and retaining talent, reward should be used to motivate outperformance whilst also ensuring a more risk-focused approach from bankers. The importance of non-financial reward should be emphasized in performance management. Further, HR has a poor image in banks and is seen to have failed in either improving employee engagement among bankers or to ensure that risk management frames the award of compensation.

The culture within banks, mediated through reward management, should be based on fairness and on values shared by both banker and the firm. Bankers are not "guns for hire" (RC2) motivated purely by financial reward. While pay is a 'hygiene factor' for bankers, it is nonetheless important they have "skin in the game" (RC3) through reward of deferred compensation heavily weighted by stock. Finally, engagement is driven not by pay but by non-financial factors such as career progression and role challenge.

Views of (Banking) HR Professionals

HR Professionals believe that the principles of regulation are good, but the application of changes to financial reward structures has been poor. The regulator has prescribed rules that are incompletely thought out and inconsistent. Regulators have also become "pernicious" (HR5) in their sense of duty regarding reward. The regulator has reacted to media pressure and negative public opinion and neither the media nor regulators understand reward. Society does not trust banks and communication from banks on reward systems has been poor. As one interviewee put it, on balance, the Bank has "played a smart game with the cards dealt" (HR2) and the flawed "one-size-fits-all" approach prescribed by the regulator. Further, "clawbacks" are completely impractical.

Increased transparency through industry benchmarking has driven pay decisions in banks. HR Professionals are divided on financial reward as a driver of behaviour in bankers. The majority of interviewees felt it is "all about the pay" for bankers, financial reward being a "way to keep score with colleagues" and a "measurement of ego and importance" (HR2):

> Man is an economic beast – financial incentives can moderate behaviour.
>
> (HR1)

Others felt that both financial and non-financial reward factors were important to bankers and that bankers want reward and recognition to be linked. The use of deferrals dilutes the impact of reward. The link between performance and reward must be clear and deferred payments do not match the performance period. This said, the use of conditionality in financial reward is considered bad as this would make the system more complicated. Recent changes to financial reward, including higher base pay and increased use of deferred compensation for bankers, have not increased loyalty and have negatively impacted the link between performance and reward:

> The move to higher basic pay and additional fixed payments (non-pensionable guaranteed pay) has been applied without reason or relationship to performance.
>
> (HR5)

This said, the use of guaranteed pay was considered to reduce risk-taking by bankers in the firm.

Unanimously, HR Professionals felt that bankers compare their pay/reward ratio with others. A reward system perceived as just by bankers is crucial to driving improved employee engagement, therefore. Further, both loyalty and engagement are driven by strong and transparent performance management with a long-term focus.

There was, however, further evidence of inconsistency in HR opinion. Interviewees were divided on whether or not the banker should be in 'economic exchange' with the bank:

> Bankers are employed to make money for shareholders only.
>
> (HR2)

Certain interviewees believed banks value employee engagement and loyalty more than transactional relationships. This opinion was driven more by whether the interviewee believed that bankers are more motivated by financial incentives or by career progression and other non-financial reward factors. However, one participant argued any 'psychological contract' the banker had with the firm was broken by the sudden introduction in 2009 of deferred compensation, even at more junior levels. This damaged the relationship between bankers and the firm. There appears to be an internal issue of trust in banks which prevents creation of covenantal relationships in the firm:

> Banks have a big issue here – there is a lack of trust between bankers and the firm – a transactional relationship dominates.
>
> (HR3)

The majority of HR Professionals interviewed believed that that financial reward dominates the culture of banks. Compensation should be used as a lever to drive banker behaviours:

> Compensation has become a tool of organizational socialisation especially for senior bankers.
>
> (HR5)

Views of Senior (Banking) Management

Senior management interviewee views focused externally on regulators and internally on the needs of bankers. In common with reward consultants, senior management perceive regulators to have responded poorly to the credit crisis and not to understand reward. The regulator was well-intentioned; however, their actions have driven up base pay. This takes away the incentive to perform and drives less entrepreneurial behaviour in bankers. The press is seen to have "tarred all bankers with the same brush" (SM10) and has misreported and sensationalized the issue of bankers' pay. Society has a low regard for bankers, believing banks have "privatised gains and socialised losses" (SM7). Moreover, senior management has failed to communicate effectively how compensation works and have thus been forced by the regulator into a reward structure they do not want.

Indeed, even senior managers believe that top management pay in banks is excessive, arguing that bankers have become cynical about pay at top management level. Reward systems are considered poorly designed, being short-term in focus and not taking adequate account of risk. Their objective is to pay the least possible to retain talent. Financial reward is also market- rather than target-driven. Financial reward in banks has created a "dog-eat-dog" (SM8) culture, conditioning "robotic" (SM3) behaviours in bankers who are ultimately driven by self-interest and short-term gain:

> Banks use financial reward childishly – the annual bonus is a gift from the boss like "Santa at Christmas" once a year – bankers do not perceive this a pay for performance; creating an obligation to firm but not loyalty.
>
> (SM3)

Deferrals are considered a way of smoothing the volatility in bankers' pay, but bankers discount their value and dislike any conditionality in financial reward. Short-term variable pay drives short-term focus and higher base salaries drive a more risk-focused, long-term approach from bankers. Banks should continue to pay for performance, but a 'one-size-fits-all' approach' to financial reward is ill-conceived. Senior management should be paid differently, be subject to longer periods of compensation deferral and hold a minimum level of stock in the firm.

To be trusted, financial reward must be perceived fair and just by bankers. Increased transparency on the percentage of bonus pool awarded to top performers, it is argued, will drive fairness in the system. Moreover, performance and reward must have a clear link. The bank's performance management system is too subjective with objectives set too late in the year to achieve senior management aims to drive bankers' performance. A one-year view creates a transactional contract with bankers and, therefore, does not encourage employee engagement.

Excessive compensation "crowds out" (SM5) the importance of non-financial reward. Non-financial rewards are seen to drive OCBs. While deferrals achieve a "lock-in" of bankers, non-financial reward and recognition influences increased participation of bankers, long-term behaviour and loyalty:

> [The Bank] pays lip-service to non-financial reward and makes only a passing effort to celebrate success.
>
> (SM7)

Reward systems significantly impact firm culture. StanChart, it is argued, has set itself apart from other UK banks in emphasizing the importance of non-financial reward in driving banker behaviours and actively rewards citizenship behaviour. Financial objectives are balanced by hard measures of how targets are achieved:

> Citizenship is very important at StanChart – culture and firm identity focus on the importance of citizenship.
>
> (SM10)

At another bank, there is a lack of trust between management and bankers. It is "top-heavy and centralised" (SM12). Senior management do not trust line managers to make decisions and senior bankers lack autonomy. Being dominated by a bonus culture makes bankers "mercenary and focused on self-preservation" (SM9). There is "little trust in management as there has been significant management churn and bankers fear regime change" (SM3).

Employee engagement is seen to be driven through non-financial reward and firm culture. This must teach values and align bankers with the firm's strategy.

> OCBs must be reflected in the culture of the firm – shared vision, shared journey, shared success – we must improve communications to bankers and provide unity of purpose.
>
> (SM7)

Views of Bankers

For the Bankers interviewed, regulation neither prevented the financial crisis nor works because the regulator does not understand reward. Public pressure has driven changes in reward systems at banks and communication on compensation from banks to the press has been poor.

Bankers feel that reward has had too short-term a focus and pay has, in general, been too high.

> The role reward systems have played in banks over the last 3–4 years is a disgrace – if you stood on principle you'd have walked away.
>
> (B1)

Reward can incentivize behaviour, but has to be balanced between financial and non-financial reward factors. Financial reward drove bad behaviours pre-2007–2009 crisis and should now be structured to drive a long-term focus. Deferrals are seen as a "rational response to the financial crisis" (B5), are not discounted by bankers, and are seen to align bankers with shareholder interest. Deferrals retain bankers on a coercive basis, but only non-financial reward factors such as career development, teamwork, recognition and working environment drive banker loyalty. Bankers discount complexity in reward and, while pay is very important, financial reward can "crowd out" (B2) the importance of non-financial reward. On average, the balance in importance of financial to non-financial reward is 60:40. Lower job security increases banker sensitivity to financial reward and job challenge is of key importance in helping banker "self-determine at work" (B5).

Bankers were generally critical of the reward system. The Bank "pays enough to keep you" (B7) and has a "black box approach to reward" (B6) where it is unclear how reward decisions are made. Bankers agreed reward must be just and fair, pay for performance is a good methodology, but without transparency on how reward decisions are made it is undermined. The pay differential between corporate banking and the rest of banking groups is unfair and pay is not linked to performance. Reward also has too short-term a focus and does not adequately account for risk-taking:

> [The Bank] has an asymmetric reward system. It only looks at improving performance and drives damaging behaviour with a focus on short-term profits.
>
> (B3)

Indeed, nearly all Banker interviewees commented that the link between performance and reward was unclear and should be improved. There is a high degree of line manager subjectivity in reward decisions and communication regarding rewards was also seen as unfair. At one bank, while the firm has introduced a system of deferred bonuses under which financial reward is paid out over a longer term, for roles which take more risk:

> The Bank still views bankers like sportsmen and pay the most to the person who scores the most goals this year – very short-term approach rewarding the "what" and not the "how".
>
> (B4)

Bankers also feel disempowered by the performance management process. Targets are given without discussion and are based on one-year cycles. This creates a transactional relationship with the firm based on economic exchange only:

> [The Bank] performance manage in March each year with a financial target you don't agree and no clear link on how reward links with success.
>
> (B5)

> Reward comes down to a 30 minute conversation once a year.
>
> (B5)

For Bankers, the culture of the firm is "all about the money" (B1) and undermines potential for a relational contract between the firm and banker. Citizenship is important to Bankers but banking culture is considered "autocratic, invasive and controlling" (B5) which discourages Bankers from increased OCBs. A lack of trust and autonomy for Bankers was also cited:

> [The Bank] is highly centralised and there is a mistrust of the business by senior management – the command and control culture is disempowering.
>
> (B3)

In line with senior management, Bankers felt their firm's culture should become more trusting of bankers and allow greater business ownership. Bankers like the partnership model and to have "skin in the game" created through stock ownership. Perceived organization support is also crucial in promoting OCBs. Bankers want to know they are in the "DNA of banks" (B4); loyalty will be increased by an employer that values, trusts, and engages bankers over the long term.

Bankers want to feel they have rights to take decisions and to participate in strategy. Loyalty, employee engagement and extra-role behaviour are driven by non-financial reward factors and being part of a successful firm. The firm in return must be loyal, consistent and fair in its treatment of and in its relationship with bankers.

Discussion

In this section findings reported in the above section are confronted by commentary distilled from relevant academic literature to draw out theoretically informed conclusions with practical implications for policy makers and managers.

Regulation and society

The challenge is for bank senior management to instigate cultural change to encourage OCBs from bankers while satisfying the demands of regulators and the UK public. Since 2007, the FSA has made substantial changes to the requirements of UK bank reward systems. Baiman (1990) believes an agent (i.e., an employee) may act to maximize outcomes at the expense of the firm, Bebchuk (2010) furthers this in arguing bankers take more risk than is *socially desirable*. In its 2010 Remuneration Code, the FSA aimed to reduce this potential *moral hazard* and to ensure bank reward strategies underpin the future stability of the UK's financial system. However, nearly all interviewees felt that the FSA has reacted too strongly to public opinion and does not understand reward. And although banks are mandated to adhere to new regulations, the principle-based style of the FSA's requirements has allowed banks to implement changes in different ways, only really enacting the minimum, as evidenced in bank remuneration reports. Banks were generally perceived to have been reactive in their approach to dealing with the regulator and the press and communication on reward systems has been poor. The findings have also evidenced that bankers resent being held solely accountable for the credit crisis. There is mistrust both within banks and between banks and different stakeholder groups.

Thus, the context of reward systems is complicated by varying stakeholder interests and by information asymmetry. This influences both how banks have chosen to structure their reward systems and emphasises the need for an evolution in the culture of UK banks, particularly if trust with society is to be rebuilt.

Reward and recognition

The research established that assumptions used by reward consultants, HR professionals and decision-makers to determine bankers' reward appear not to take adequate account of the complexity of institutional settings. Senior management believe a bonus–inclined culture drives individualistic behaviour (Deci and Ryan 1980; Weibel et al. 2007) and, for the bankers interviewed, the bank 'makes it all about the pay'.

This research confirmed compensation is used in an attempt to control behaviour (Gagné and Forest 2008). Senior management believe bankers are socially conditioned (Ferster and Skinner 1957) through short-term variable pay and agree with reward consultants that it creates obligation but not loyalty. Contrary to the view that deferred compensation devalues the impact of reward (Gosling 2011), bankers interviewed dislike deferrals; they give 'skin in the game', although this is achieved on a coerced basis. Findings suggest that money represents a 'lower-order need' for bankers and non-financial reward factors support self-actualization (Maslow 1954; McClelland 1961; Deci and Ryan 1985).

Furthermore, both senior management and bankers agree that extrinsic financial reward, particularly high levels of short-term variable pay, 'crowd out' non-financial reward factors (Frey and Jergen 2001). The feeling is that transparency and industry benchmarking is driving up pay, particularly for banking senior management. Although certain interviewees support the argument that higher base pay would reduce risk-taking by bankers and drive better firm performance (Levine 1993), pay increases have been driven by benchmarking rather than by a desire to improve behaviours. Senior management disagree with Baiman (1990), arguing that instead of creating more sustainable performance, higher base pay actually makes bankers 'lazy' as bankers are paid 'come what may'.

Low engagement has been shown to inhibit OCBs (Deckop et al. 1999). Driven by fear of attrition, no UK bank wants to differentiate in reward strategy, even though a 'one-size-fits-all' approach particularly to financial reward is argued, both by senior management and by reward consultants, to be ill-conceived.

Organizational justice

Bankers interviewed seek a relational contract with their employer based on trust (Rousseau and McLean Parks 1993; Kramer and Tyler 1996). This is undermined, however, by perceived unfairness in banks' reward systems and by adoption of an autocratic culture. Organizational justice is considered an antecedent to the relationship between firm and employee (Blau 1964; Gouldner 1960). Among HR professionals, interviews evidenced differing views on whether bankers should be in a relationship of economic or *social* exchange with the firm (Blau 1964; Gouldner 1960). While recognising the value of longer-term, more loyal and engaged behaviours, bankers are considered by certain HR professionals to be producers of shareholder value only. This orientation reinforces the sense of a monolithic, transactional relationship.

Gratton (2004) argues employees are affected by the *distribution* of rewards and not the absolute amount. In line with this, bankers are critical of the perceived unfair distribution of rewards between a bank's divisions. Furthermore, bankers argue the bank has a 'black box' approach to reward and there is little transparency on how reward is allocated (Pearce et al. 1985). The level of interactional and procedural justice is also considered low by bankers as communication on reward in some firms is inconsistent and poorly delivered. These findings were consistent with studies by Bies and Moag (1986) and Leventhal (1976) which found that, for perceptions of organizational justice to increase, reward decisions and communication must be clear, consistent and fair.

Like Organ's (1990) argument, the perception of unfairness in a bank's reward system further drives an economic-centred relationship between bankers and their employer. The findings also extend those of Rhoades and Eisenberger's (2002) study where low interactional justice and the lack of trust between senior management and bankers undermines bankers' feeling of 'Perceived Organizational Support' (POS). This issue is of critical importance as trust (Kramer and Tyler 1996) is argued to be the basis for a relational contract as well as for improved loyalty and organizational commitment (Cohen-Charash and Spector 2001; Organ 1988; Rousseau and McLean Parks 1993; Shore and Shore 1995).

To improve perceptions of organizational justice, reward consultants and bankers believe line manager discretion should be limited in allocation of rewards (Leventhal 1976) and perceptions of distributive, procedural and interactional justice enhanced through better communication on the procedures and rationale for reward decisions and distribution. Enhanced perceptions of fairness and POS will encourage bankers to reciprocate through OCBs (Fasolo 1995; Organ and Konovsky 1989).

Performance management and goal setting

Strong performance management (PM) is key to formalizing the link between performance and reward (Liccione 2007) and in driving perceptions of organizational justice (Gagné et al. 2007). Senior management interviewees felt banks fail in the objective to align firm with employee goals in setting PM expectations too late in the year. Interviewees also believed PM should be within a multi-year framework. Drucker (1974) found PM must be two-way and participative to have impact, although bankers generally feel disempowered by their bank's PM process. They were highly critical of one-year PM cycles which force a short-term view. Goals are unclear and targets are not mutually agreed. Furthermore, the *pay for performance* link is not clear. This further reinforces the transactional relationship between bankers and their firm. Reward consultants believe hard metrics for non-financial reward should be built-in to performance expectations for bankers in order to promote citizenship behaviours. Unusually, StanChart has implemented this and evidence of OCB is formally assessed and rewarded by the bank.

OCB and organizational commitment

In line with research by Bienstock et al. (2003) and Graham (1991), reward consultants agree that OCB enhances organizational commitment and performance. A focus on *pay for performance* in banks actually inhibits OCB and loyalty cannot be fostered through maintaining an economic exchange relationship between bankers and the firm. Contrastingly, HR interviewees feel banker behaviour is most effectively driven through financial reward (Lawler et al. 1975) and reward consultants support this view in promoting use of deferred compensation the form of company shares. The argument is that long-term incentives align firm and employee interests (Bloom and Milkovich 1998) and that increased feelings of possession and firm ownership can both increase performance and improve behaviours (Etzioni 1991; Pierce and Dyne 2004).

Senior management and bankers all agreed that employee engagement, extra-role performance and loyalty are fostered more through non-financial reward than pay (Hackman and Oldham 1980). Senior management observe that OCBs must be embedded in the firm's culture to have relevance; however, bankers believe that when a bank's culture is autocratic, OCBs are inhibited. This reduces their level of POS as they want to be part of a more trusting culture where they feel they have rights in firm decisions. Bankers favoured a 'partnership model' under which increased share ownership granted and held over the long term is linked with autonomy and participation in defining the firm's strategy (Davidoff 2008).

Conclusion

This chapter has synthesized findings from primary research using interviews with key actors in the field of interest with those derived from relevant literature. While limited to the opinions of a sample of bankers and professionals working with banks in the UK Corporate and Investment Banking industry, the data confirm themes emerging from the literature. Notably, the research extended previous findings as it was set in the contemporary banking context.

The investigation found that in banks' excessive focus on financial reward, HR and senior management both misinterpret the drivers of banker behaviour and reinforce negative public opinion. The form of *pay for performance* approach adopted by UK banks may inhibit citizenship behaviours and banks underestimate the role of non-financial reward as an influence on long-term banker behaviour. Performance management often fails to link performance with reward and, in so doing, underpins perceptions of injustice in the firm.

To foster a culture of organizational citizenship in UK banks, reward arrangements should include a balance of financial and non-financial rewards. Reward management should be 'open' and be supported by effective performance management which is perceived fair by bankers. Finally, an accent on OCBs should be embedded to align bankers with firm values and to increase bankers' positive extra-role behaviour.

References

Baiman, S. (1990). Agency research in managerial accounting: a second look. *Accounting, Organizations and Society*. 15(4), 341–371.

Barclays PLC. (2010). *Remuneration Report*. Available at: www.barclays.com.

Bebchuk, L. (2010). *How to Fix Bankers' Pay*. Discussion Paper No. 677, John M. Olin Center for Law, Economics and Business. Harvard Law School.

Bebchuk, L., Cohen, A. and Spamann, H. (2009). *The Wages of Failure: Executive Compensation at Bear Stearns and Lehman 2000–2008*. Discussion Paper No. 657, John M. Olin Center for Law, Economics and Business, Harvard Law School.

Bienstock, C., DeMoranville, C. and Smith, R. (2003). Organizational citizenship behavior and service quality. *Journal of Services Marketing*. 17(4), 357–378.

Bies, R. and Moag, J. (1986). Interactional justice: communication criteria of fairness. In Lewicki, R., Sheppard, B. and Bazerman, M. (eds.). *Research on Negotiations in Organizations* (Vol. 1, pp. 43–55).

Blau, P. (1964). *Exchange and Power in Social Life*. New York: Wiley.

Bloom, M. and Milkovich, G. (1998). Relationships among risk, incentive pay and organizational performance. *Academy of Management Journal*. 41(3), 283–297.

Cohen-Charash, Y. and Spector, P. (2001). The role of justice in organizations: a meta-analysis. *Organizational Behavior and Human Decision Processes*. 86, 278–321.

Davidoff, S. (2008). *A Partnership Solution for Investment Banks?* Available at: www.dealbook.nytimes.com/2008/08/20/a-partnership-solution-for-investment-banks/.

Deci, E. and Ryan, R. (1980). The empirical exploration or intrinsic motivational processes. In Berkowitz, L. (ed.). *Advances in Experimental Social Psychology* (Vol. 13). New York: Academic Press.

Deci, E. and Ryan, R. (1985). *Intrinsic Motivation and Self–determination in Human Behavior*. New York: Plenum Press.

Deckop, J., Mangel, R. and Cirka, C. (1999). Research notes. Getting more than you pay for: organizational citizenship behavior and pay-for-performance plans. *Academy of Management Journal*. 42(4), 420–428.

Drucker, P. (1974). *Management: Tasks, Responsibilities, Practices*. New York: Harper and Row.

Etzioni, A. (1991). The socio-economics of property. In Rudmin, F. (ed.). *To Have Possessions: A Handbook on Ownership and Property* (Vol. 6, pp. 465–468). *Journal of Social Behavior and Personality*.

Fasolo, P. (1995). Procedural justice and perceived organizational support: hypothesized effects on job performance. In Cropanzano, R. and Kacmar, K. (eds.). *Organizational Politics, Justice, and Support*. Westport, CT: Quorum.

Ferster, C. and Skinner, B. (1957). *Schedules of Reinforcement*. New York: Appleton-Century-Crofts.

FSA. (2009a). *The Turner Review*. London: Financial Services Authority. Available at: www.fsa.gov.uk.

FSA. (2009b). *The Walker Review*. London: Financial Services Authority. Available at: www.fsa.gov.uk.

FSA. (2010). *Remuneration Code*. London: Financial Services Authority. Available at: www.fsa.gov.uk.

Frey, B. and Jergen, R. (2001). Motivation crowding theory. *Journal of Economic Theories*. 15, 591–611.

Gagné, M., Bérubé, N. and Donia, M. (2007). *Relationships between Different Forms of Organizational Justice and Different Motivational Orientations*. New York: Society for Industrial and Organizational Psychology.

Gagné, M. and Forest, J. (2008). The study of compensation systems through the lens of self-determination theory: reconciling 35 years of debate. *Canadian Psychology*. 49(3), 225–232.

Gosling, T. (2011). *If Executive Pay is Broken, Making it More Complex is Not the Answer: The Psychology of Incentives*. Available at: www.pwc.com.

Gouldner, P. (1960). The norm of reciprocity. *American Sociological Review*. 25, 165–167.

Graham, J. (1991). An essay on organizational citizenship behavior. *Employee Responsibilities and Rights Journal*. 4, 249–278.

Gratton, L. (2004). More than money. *People Management*. 10(2), 23–24.

Hackman, J. and Oldham, G. (1980). *Work Redesign*. Reading, MA: Addison-Wesley.

Herzberg, F. (1966). *Work and the Nature of Man.* Cleveland, OH: World.

HSBC PLC. (2010). *Remuneration Report.* Available at: www.hsbc.com.

Kessler, I. (2005). Remuneration systems. In Bach, S. (ed.). *Managing Human Resources: Personnel Management in Transition.* Oxford: Blackwell Publishing.

Kramer, R. and Tyler, T. (1996). *Trust in Organizations: Frontiers of Theory and Research.* Thousand Oaks, CA: Sage Publications.

Lawler, E., Porter, L. and Hackman, J.R. (1975). *Behaviour in Organizations.* New York: McGraw-Hill.

Leventhal, G. (1976). The distribution of rewards and resources in groups and organizations. In Berkowitz, L. and Walster, W. (eds.). *Advances in Experimental Psychology* (Vol. 9, pp. 91–131).

Levine, D. (1993). What do wages buy? *Administrative Science Quarterly.* 38, 462–483.

Liccione, W. (2007). A framework for compensation plans with incentive value. *Performance Improvement.* 46(2), 16–21.

Lloyds Banking Group. (2010). *Remuneration Report.* Available at: www.lloydsbankinggroup.com.

Maslow, A. (1954). *Motivation and Personality.* New York: Harper & Row.

McClelland, D. C. (1961). *The Achieving Society.* Princeton, NJ: Van Nostrand.

Milkovich, G. and Newman, J. M. (2004). *Compensation* (8th ed.). New York: McGraw-Hill.

Milkovich, G. and Newman, J. M. (2008). *Compensation* (9th ed.). Boston: McGraw-Hill.

Organ, D. (1988). *Organizational Citizenship Behaviour: The Good Soldier Syndrome.* Lexington, MA: Lexington Books.

Organ, D. (1990). The motivational basis for organizational citizenship behavior. In Cummings, L. and Shaw, B. (eds.). *Research in Organizational Behavior* (Vol. 12). Greenwich, CT: JAI Press.

Organ, D. and Konovsky, M. (1989). Cognitive versus affective determinants of organizational citizenship behaviour. *Journal of Applied Psychology.* 74, 157–164.

Pearce, J., Stevenson, W. and Perry, J. (1985). Managerial compensation based on organizational performance: A time series analysis of the effects of merit pay. *Academy of Management Journal.* 28, 261–278.

Perkins, S. and White, G. (2016). *Reward Management: Alternatives, Consequences and Contexts.* London: CIPD.

Pierce, J. and Dyne, L. (2004). Psychological ownership and feelings of possession: three field studies predicting employee attitudes and organizational citizenship behavior. *Journal of Organizational Behavior.* 25, 439–459.

RBS. (2010). *Remuneration Report.* Available at: www.rbs.com.

Rhoades, L. and Eisenberger, R. (2002). Perceived organizational support: a review of the literature. *Journal of Applied Psychology.* 87, 698–714.

Rousseau, D. and McLean Parks, J. (1993). The contracts of individuals in organizations. In Cummings, L. and Shaw, B. (eds.). *Research in Organizational Behavior* (Vol. 15, pp. 1–43).

Shore, L. and Shore, M. (1995). Perceived organizational support and organizational justice. In Cropanzano, R. and Kacmar, K. (eds.). *Organizational Politics, Justice and Support: Managing the Social Climate of the Workplace.* Westport, CT: Quorum.

Silverman, M. (2004). *Non-Financial Recognition: The Most Effective of Rewards?* Brighton, UK: Institute for Employment Studies.

Standard Chartered Bank. (2010). *Remuneration Report.* Available at: www.standardchartered.com.

Weibel, A., Rost, K. and Osterloh, M. (2007). *Crowding-Out of Intrinsic Motivation: Opening the Black Box.* IOU Institute for Organizational and Administrative Science, University of Zurich.

32

CHANGING PATTERNS OF PAY SYSTEMS IN CHINA

Qi Wei

Introduction: development of pay components and determination in China

The pre-reform pay system (1949–1978)

After the PRC was founded in 1949, the highly centralized economy with central planning and public ownership as the two prominent characteristics was developed and maintained until the economic reforms in 1978 (Pu 1990; Riskin 1987). Central planning involved the central government distributing materials and finance to enterprises through setting priorities for them and taking orders of output from them. Public ownership reflected the control of state institutions over enterprises, including state-owned enterprises (SOEs) and collective-owned enterprises (COEs). Under this command economy, the 'Three-Irons' polices can be used to best describe the key features of people-management in China, consisting of the 'Iron rice-bowl' ('tie fanwan'), 'Iron Wages' ('tie gongzi'), and 'Iron Armchair' ('tie jiaoyi') (Ding et al. 2001; Zhao 2005). The 'Iron rice-bowl' refers to the employment system with lifelong guaranteed job security, as well as steady income and benefits, which led to a surplus of unproductive personnel. The 'Iron Wages' describes the state-led national reward system, in which pay distribution had very little to do with individual and organizational performance. 'The iron Armchair' describes the permanent job system for managing technicians and executives. Under the 'Three Iron' model, employee rewards usually consisted of three major components: monetary wages (provided in the forms of pay, bonuses and various allowances), social wages (provided in the forms of labour insurance and collective welfare), and non-material incentives (provided in the forms of recognition and honour etc.) (Chow 1992; Shenkar and Chow 1989) (see Table 32.1).

A nationwide Soviet-style wage grading system was formally implemented in 1956 (Cooke 2004), including eight wage grades for skilled production workers, 15 wage grades for operatives who worked in selected industries, 24 wage grades which covered white-collar workers and staff (Jackson and Littler 1991) as well as ten wage grades and above for teachers and scientists in education sector (see Table 32.2).

Some main characteristics of this pre-reformed Chinese state pay system can be described as below. First, the pay components included low take-home monetary wage but high subsidies with an emphasis on moral encouragement rather than 'bourgeois materialism' incentives; as well

Table 32.1 Pay components in the Chinese public sector (1949–1978)

Monetary wages	
Basic wage	Virtually fixed across the country by the state and relatively stable over time except for adjustments to match the reginal cost of living.
Seniority wage	Based on years of service
Position wage	Determined by a worker's position on the industry ladder and his/her current position
Bonuses	Payments based on such criteria as above-quota output, superior product quality, cost reduction, waste elimination, on- or before-schedule completion, improved safety and technical innovation.
Allowances	Allowance for overtime, shift work, difficult or hazardous working conditions, cost of living adjustments, and fuel in some cold regions.
Social wages	
Labour insurance	Paid sick leave, disability pay,
Collective welfare	Subsidies paid by SOEs included work insurance, medical coverage, public welfare, non-staple food, winter heating fee and home-leave travelling allowances. Subsidies paid by the central government were housing, education and medicine, transportation and staple foods.
Non-material incentives	
Model workers	Recognition offered at various levels, from the work unit up to the national level. Model workers were publicly praised and presented as role models for other employees to follow.
Participatory management	Allowed employees to participate in decision-making, but was frequently a ritual, orchestrated from above.
Job enrichment	Various job enrichment strategies, e.g., rotation
Election of directors	Election of top workers to management positions

Source: Adapted from Shenkar and Chow (1989) and Chow (1992).

Table 32.2 Pay grades in China (1949–1978)

Wage system	*Grades*	*Coverage*
National workers' wage system	8 wage grades, skill-based, to be linked to bonus system	Production workers
Occupational wage system ("gangwei gongzizhi")	15 wage grades; output based, to be linked to piecework	Selected industries such as textiles, chemicals, iron and steel, railways and other transport
Cadre wage system ("zhiwu gongzizhi")	24 wage grades; responsibility-based; to be linked to the bonus system	White-collar workers and staff
Teachers' wage system	10 wage grades	Schoolteachers
	12 wage grades	College teachers
	13 wage grades	Scientists in research institutes and teaching members in higher education

Source: Adapted from Jackson and Littler (1991) and Cooke (2004).

as seniority-based wage promotion rather than performance-related pay (PRP) increments (De Cieri et al. 1998). The pay and benefit system was strictly controlled by the state and helped to further form the 'Iron rice bowl'. During the Cultural Revolution (1966–1976), the wage level was fundamentally frozen (Cooke 2004).

Second, pay variation within a collective was rigid, highly centralized and influenced by the Soviet system. The vertical pay differentials, which refer to pay variation across jobs, were based on the grades set by the state for skilled production workers, operatives, white-collar workers and staff (Takahara 1992; Ding and Warner 2001). The horizontal pay differentials, which refer to pay variation among people holding the same job, were minimal and largely based on time-rate, seniority, political background and connections (Knight and Song 1991; Shenkar and Chow 1989; Walder 1986). Enterprises had no right to set up or change any pay scale, and had a wage fund fully supplied by the government (Harding 1987). Even though all SOEs had trade unions, no wage bargaining mechanism effectively existed for employees in China. Unions served as workers' clubs only due to the social ideology that believed there should be no conflict of interests between employers and employees under the 'Three-iron' model (Henley and Nyaw 1987; Jackson 1992; Takahara 1992).

Third, several norms governed reward management within the pre-reformed model (Cooke 2003; Yu 1998). The egalitarian norm was regarded as the most significant and 'taken-for-granted' assumption of fairness and equity. Employees' working experience accumulated in the past year was the important norm to measure their contribution, which means seniority pay still exists in the present pay components in the public sector. Employee work attitude, political loyalty to the Communist Party, integrity of personality, and diligence at work played as significant indicators in promotion and bonus allocation.

The post-reform pay system (1978 to present)

At the end of 1978, China entered a transformation stage from a centrally-planned economy to "market socialism" with Chinese characteristics (Zhu and Warner 2000). Since then, the traditional pay system had become a major target because of its basic deficiencies, which were criticized as 'eating from the big iron rice bowl (life-tenure employment)'. The primary socialist principle of "to each according to one's work" was stated as the only practicable approach to distributing wealth to accelerate productivity and economic growth (Glover and Trivedi 2007). Following this, diversified pay reforms were implemented in the 1980s, 1990s and 2000s that played a vital role in China's economic transformation.

The 1984 pay reform consisted of two forms: floating and structural wage systems (Ding et al. 2001; Zhao and Nichols 1996). The 'floating wage system' (*fudong gongzi*) was intended to partially replace bonuses which failed to link pay directly to individual and/or organizational performance. The enterprise's wage fund by the government was adjusted according to organizational performance indicators such as profits, sales and measures for other outputs. The individual wage would vary according to production, types of responsibility, workload and enterprise profit level for managerial and non-production workers (Child 1994; Cooke 2005). In order to abolish the previous rigid pay grading system (see Table 32.2), the structural wage system (*jiegou gongsi*) was introduced to the state sectors, including education, healthcare and civil servants, under which, pay components consisted of base pay (about 30–40% of total cash income), positional pay (about 30% of total cash income) seniority pay (up to one-third of total cash income), and variable pay (around 20–30% of total cash income) (Cooke 2005; Jackson and Littler 1991).

The 1993 pay reform focused on separating the pay system in the public sector from that in governmental organizations, which was the first step to establish a differentiated management system for the public sector. Organizations in the state sector involved five categories, each of which had its own pay system: these included a pay system based on technical position levels such as education and health, a pay system based on technical positions such as ocean research, a pay system for the performing arts sector, and pay systems for both the sports and the financial sectors (Cooke 2004, 2005; Warner 1998).

Although the overall pay level was increased and PRP elements were implemented in the Chinese public sector during the 1993 pay reform, still seniority-based pay as well as unjustified bonuses and subsidies remained as the key pay components in most state organizations. Thus, the central government launched another pay reform in 2006 aimed to closely linking earnings to both individual and organizational performances across the public sector, especially the Public service units (PSUs) (Ge 2003). This was also part of the PSUs reform in China's economic transition, targeted to re-define the size and role of government as well as its funding mechanisms (OECD 2005).

The major changes through the pay reforms after 1978 were as follows. First, the egalitarian pay ideology was transformed to non-egalitarian; i.e., 'a person's grade on the pay scale is determined mainly by individual performance on the job, technical level and actual contribution' (Child 1994). The "Iron-wage" system based on job rank and seniority in the state sector was phased out gradually, and replaced by a market-based model which encouraged the link between worker performance and efficiency and income polarization rather than equal distribution (Ding et al. 2000; Warner 1996a). Second, diversified pay systems emerged and the proportion of each pay component within the pay systems varies according to the industry types as well as the nature of the business. As a result of this initiative, China began to move away from the Soviet-style grading system and to establish greater pay flexibility (Ding et al. 2000). Moreover, since the early 1990s SOEs as the dominant ownership type were permitted to build their internal pay structures under the overall pay budget determined by the government (Yueh 2004). The third major change happened in foreign-invested enterprises (FIEs). A radical reform of the ownership system occurred after the introduction of China's economic reform in 1978, which allowed the establishment of private and collective enterprises and also foreign direct investment (FDI). FIEs, including Sino-foreign joint ventures (JVs) and wholly foreign-owned multinational corporations (MNCs), were granted legal status in 1988 (Tung 1991) and soon flourished (Chui et al. 2007). Compared with SOEs, FIEs were subject to much less stringent government regulations. In 1980 bottom and top pay levels were set up by the government for JVs, although this system was eliminated in 1986 in order to promote productivity (Horsley 1988). After 1994, FIEs became free to set their own wage scale and only needed to adhere to minimum wage regulations.

Review of studies on pay in China

Since there has still been limited understanding about the pay practices and their effectiveness in the context of China compared to research in the USA and other countries (Wang et al. 2009), this section reviews major empirical studies on pay systems in China over the past two decades and highlights the main topic areas discussed, as well as some reflections on the changes to the pay system.

Pay system transformation

The pre-reform and post-reform pay systems in China have received considerable attention over the past two decades. There is a cluster of studies that focused on the general pay system evolution (Child 1994; Cooke 2004; Jackson and Littler 1991; Peng 1992; Shenkar and Chow 1989; Takahara 1992; Warner 1996b, 1997; Yueh 2004). Since ownership is an important aspect in research on HRM in China (Zhu et al. 2008), some other studies discussed pay reforms and practices in specific ownership types such as SOEs (Child 1995; Cooke 2004), FIEs (Hickey 2003), international JVs (Giacobbe-Miller et al. 1997, 2003), and township and village enterprises (TVEs) (Chow and Fu 2000; Dong 1998). There have been very limited systematic firm-level data provided to explain the variation of pay structures across ownerships (Ding et al. 2006; Huang 2016; Zhu et al. 1998). More studies are needed to explore whether organizations with different ownership types adopt different pay systems and how firms' management interpret contextual factors that influence their pay systems and make pay decisions.

Employee pay preferences

What motivates employees in China? During the pre-reform period, basic pay, bonus and housing prevision were the most important motivational factors (Henley and Nyaw 1987; Yu et al. 1989). During the post-reform period, base salary, individual and year-end bonuses, merit pay, housing provision and cash allowances became the most significant factors to retain and motivate employees (Chui and Luk 2002), and a differentiated income system based on ability, skills and performance was mostly favoured by employees (Chow 1992). In reward decision-making by Chinese managers, work performance was less emphasized when making bonus decisions, the relationship with co-workers received more emphasis when non-monetary decisions were being made. More emphasis was placed on relationship with managers when making non-monetary award decisions and more emphasis on personal needs applied when making bonus decisions (Zhou and Martocchio 2001). Apart from the ownership reform and individuals' collectivist values on rewards allocation (He et al. 2004), both past and future interactions and relationship closeness between co-workers had significant influence on reward-allocation decisions (Zhang 2001). Moreover, the study by Chiang and Birtch (2006) further investigated employee pay preferences in a cross-national context (Finland and Hong Kong) and signalled that Hofstede's typology (1984) should not be overestimated when studying reward preferences. Employee characteristics and other contextual factors beyond culture should be considered at the same time.

Performance-related pay

PRP in China has been the subject of continuous attention from academics. The literature shows that the acceptance and adoption of PRP in the non-state sector seemed to be much smoother (Shen 2004; Wei and Rowley 2009) than that in SOEs. Zhu and Dowling (1994:7) indicated that with 'increased autonomy and decision-making power it is becoming possible for managers in SOEs to select differential monetary rewards to motivate the workforce according to individual performance'. But Easterby-Smith et al. (1995) and Warner (1995b) discovered that bonus levels did not reflect individual performance, and Chen (1995) and Korzec (1992) identified the egalitarian distribution of bonuses turned it into simply another type of base pay. After PRP in SOEs was strengthened through pay reforms in the 1990s, the results in later studies were much more positive. For instance, Bodmer (2003) found the significant sensitivity of wages through linking profit to bonuses. Baruch et al. (2004) confirmed the importance of instrumentality of performance for implementing PRP in Chinese professional sports. The sources of dissatisfaction were mainly the determination of wage and the performance evaluation process (Bozionelos and Wang 2007), which were affected by personal relationships (Guanxi).

The Chinese central government reinforced PRP implementation in the PSUs such as the education sector after 2009 (see the discussion in section 2.2). However, studies on PRP in the

PSUs in China have been extremely limited. Wang et al. (2014) examined teacher professionalism under performance pay in public schools. There was an increase in teachers' workload, but only those teachers whose PRP indicators were highly ranked were given opportunities for pay progression and professional development. The findings suggested that teaching innovation and teachers' autonomy needed to be the focus in order to achieve the goal of improving the quality of education. The case study in section 5 further illustrates PRP practices in Chinese public schools.

Employees' attitudes towards PRP have been an interesting topic in China. It was argued that PRP would be generally inappropriate for Chinese organizations because PRP was less likely to be associated with cultures having higher levels of collectivism such as that in China as opposed to individualism (Schuler and Rogovsky, 1998). Warner (1993, 1995a) further suggested the values of employees lagged behind organizational changes towards PRP in the early stage of pay reforms. However, more recent studies such as Wu et al. (2011) indicated that in fact employees in SOEs have become more receptive to the meritocratic compensation criteria when economic transition progressed in China. The influence might have come from both meritocracy values from the West as well as the Confucian emphasis on hard work and striving. Moreover, Du and Choi (2010) investigated how non-Western employees reacted to Western HR practices such as PRP. It was found that employees were motivated by PRP to work conscientiously at both the individual and organization levels. In current emerging markets such as China, where financial rewards with fairness in place are highly valued, PRP may be positively recognised as a channel for equity and greater income (Du and Choi 2010; Wu et al. 2011). Some new employee attitudes and behaviours in transition economies have been confirmed. Employee values and preferences may be directly influenced by transformation at the societal level. It is likely that, when the managerial norms and practices of an organization are in the minority in society, employees may endorse mainstream societal values and regard management practices in their organizations as outdated. Following this, employee negative reactions to rewards may be caused in part by the general gaps between their preferences towards these criteria in the SOE sector and the criteria used in the organization.

Pay disparity

Since PRP increased in importance as a form of pay in China, associated gender differences have been reported. Xiu and Gunderson (2013) found that, relative to men, women had a 6% lower probability of receiving PRP because women were more likely to be employed by ownership types and occupations that do not provide PRP. And on a total reward basis, men earned about 30% more than women with the gender gap in PRP being 35% and in other forms of pay, 28%. Xiu and Gunderson (2015) further highlighted that the male–female pay gap was almost completely explained by wage discrimination, which is defined as females being paid less than males within the occupation groups, even when they had the same endowments of pay-determining characteristics. Occupational segregation explains virtually none of the overall male–female pay gap. This relative unimportance of occupational segregation is consistent with other Chinese studies which are restricted to using broad occupational groups, although the evidence is often mixed.

Pay disparity between locals and expatriates has received substantial attention in research after many FIEs entered China in the form of JVs in the 1980s and as wholly owned subsidiaries in the 1990s. The major focus in the literature has been on how local employees in JVs perceived disparity between their pay and foreign expatriates' pay from a social justice per-spective. Chen et al. (2002) revealed that less fairness was perceived by Chinese locals when their pay was compared with expatriates than when it was compared with other locals. Furthermore, the effect of disparity on perceived fairness was reduced by expatriates' interpersonal sensitivity towards locals. Leung et al. (2009) also confirmed that the negative effect of perceived distributive injustice on evaluation of expatriates was moderated by perceived trustworthiness of expatriates by locals, whereas the relationships between perceived distributive injustice and job satisfaction as well as organizational commitment were moderated by perceived reward.

Moreover, Leung et al. (2011) examined the antecedents and consequences of pay disparity associated with expatriate managers and with Chinese managers recruited from distant geographical areas (outside managers). Leung et al. (2014) extended the above study on moderating the impact of pay parity between locals and expatriates by exploring how pro-disparity norms at the personal and organizational levels are formed. The findings show that the trust climate can mediate the moderating effects of organizational pro-disparity norms. One policy implication is for FIEs to try to strengthen the trust climate, such as through including Chinese locals in decision-making.

CEO pay and performance link

CEO pay determinants in China have also received lots of attention from researchers (Shengli and Yanling 2005). The factors that were found to be positively associated with CEO pay were firm size, board size, firm value, institution ownership and CEO ownership; the factors negatively associated with CEO rewards were firm age, research and development expenditure rates and firms' risk profile (Lee and Chen 2011). Moreover, the use of accounting versus stock market performance measures determined Chinese top managers' rewards (Cordeiro et al. 2013). The intra-firm pay structure also affected managerial incentives (Su 2011). The first study examining organizational differences in managerial pay systems in Chinese SOEs revealed that young firms, firms in high-tech industries and service industries, tended to pay their managers higher salary. The coverage of health insurance, pension fund and unemployment fund for CEOs was significantly influenced by firms' location and industry (Ding et al. 2006).

Many other studies have concentrated on whether Chinese CEO pay relates to firm performance (Cheng and Firth 2005; Conyon and He 2012; Firth et al. 2007). The pay reforms in 1986 and 1995 proposed high income (up to three times as high income as that of average workers) and annual pay system for top managers in SOEs in order to increase productivity (Wang 2008). Yet, CEO pay-performance sensitivity increased only marginally (Mengistae and Xu 2004). More specifically, in younger firms, the CEO pay and firm performance link was weaker. In smaller SOEs and SOEs with more complex technology, managerial discretion was greater (Bai and Bennington 2005). A positive relationship between CEO pay and performance was found in China's listed firms because the state is the dominant shareholder and many of the listed firms were former SOEs (Firth et al. 2007). More recently, CEO pay was found to be also associated with firms' environmental performance in the Chinese context (Zou et al. 2015a, 2015b).

Another interesting focus in some very recent studies has been whether CEOs in China utilize their power to advance their private interests. It was found that CEOs in listed companies in China would use their power to increase their own salary. CEOs in private-owned listed companies were more likely to use their power to increase their own pay and other benefits (Zhang et al. 2016). And politically connected boards of directors may weaken the top executive pay-performance link (Chizema et al. 2015).

Case study: Performance-related pay in Chinese Public Schools

The following case study research evidence is offered as a practical illustration of changing patterns of pay systems in China. Pay reforms in the PSUs were carried out through the national pay reforms in 1953, 1985 and 1993. However, the traditional emphasis on seniority and the weak pay–performance link had not really been improved. Pay reform in the PSUs since 2006, with PRP as its main theme, has been part of the organizational reform of SOEs and core government, aimed at transforming the organizational efficiency of the public sector into one that is of great assistance to the socialist market economy.

It is important to bear in mind the precise characteristics of the national educational system in China before examining PRP for public schoolteachers. The education system in China consists of pre-school education/kindergartens (3–5 years old), primary schools (6–12 years old), secondary schools (12–18 years old, including middle and high schools) and higher education. China is also guaranteeing nine years of compulsory education for children from 6 to 15 years of age (six years in primary and three years in middle schools). All general policies and guidelines are decided by the nation's Ministry of Education. The educational laws and policies are implemented within the jurisdiction of provincial-level educational evaluation agencies and the education bureaus at the district level are responsible for the actual evaluation of local schools (Liu & Onwuegbuzie, 2012).

Since 1985, the Chinese education system has experienced a series of interventions which aim to transform it from the traditional examination-oriented to a quality-oriented system. Eight years after the latest full-scale National Curriculum Reform (NCR) had come into force, the government announced "*The Guidelines on Performance Related Pay in Compulsory Education Schools*", which were to be implemented in all public primary and junior high schools from January 1, 2009, due to the limited changes observed after the pay reform in 2006 in the PSUs. The primary aim of this guideline was to reinforce PRP in the education sector, with the average total income of schoolteachers to be no less than the average pay of civil servants in the local area. The secondary aim was to close the pay gap between public schools in rural and urban areas in order to retain good performers especially in the rural area.

To inform the case study, teachers and headmasters in Yingzhou, one of the top junior secondary schools in Ningbo City, Zhejiang province (east coast China), were interviewed in 2017. Before the 2009 Guidelines, teachers' pay consisted of basic salary, seniority pay, allowances and bonuses (see Table 32.3). Allowances were associated with both local and country-based funding. Bonuses were funded from local/regional and school-based provision, from which school managers had autonomy over bonus allocation. After the publication of the 2009 Guidelines, 70% of teachers' income was from their basic salary, seniority pay and 'basic performance pay' (BPP), and 30% from 'encouraging performance pay' (EPP) (see Table 32.3). All allowances and performance pay were allocated from the country-based public fund. All performance pay schemes, and plans for their application, had to be approved by the teacher representatives' congress in each school on an annual basis and their PRP implementation was subject to monitoring by Ningbo City Education Bureau.

All interviewees agreed that, overall, the aims of the Guidelines had been fulfilled. Seniority pay was a small part of teachers' fixed salary to reward and encourage loyalty. After the Guidelines, the country-wide standardization of basic salary and BPP was established to eliminate unjustified regional/local fund-based allowances or performance pay, which had also improved the overall income level of all public-school teachers. Pay for teaching in rural areas was included in basic salary to close the gap between teachers in rural and city areas. However, interviewees reported that some major issues in PRP implementation had occurred.

Table 32.3 Components of pay for public schoolteachers before and after the PRP reform in 2009

Pay components	Before	After
Basic salary	• Position pay • Benchmark pay • 10% of basic salary	• Position pay • Benchmark pay • 10% of basic salary • Pay for teaching in rural areas
Seniority pay Allowance/PRP	Pay based on years of teaching Allowance • Country-based position allowance • City/province-based position allowance • Welfare allowance • Cost of living allowance • Headteacher allowance • Allowance for special-grade teachers • Allowance for teaching in special need schools	Pay based on years of teaching Basic performance pay (BPP) • Pay for cost of living • Pay for position • Headteacher allowance • Allowance for special-grade teacher • Allowance for teaching in special need schools
Bonus/PRP	Bonus • Monthly bonus • Annual bonus • Bonus for target achievement Others • Overtime working compensation • Over workload compensation	Encouraging performance pay (EPP) • Pay for attendance • Pay for performance review • Pay for over workload • Pay for outstanding achievement in teaching and overtime working.

Source: Internal report from Education Bureau of Ningbo city Zhejiang province, 2017.

First, the new pay system is still egalitarian-orientated. In principle, BPP should be an incremental increase in addition to base salary which recognises past performance. EPP should be a lump-sum cash payment used to recognise past performance. And each of these rewards past performance and sets future expectations. Yet the major incremental increase in BPP is based on seniority – i.e., the number of years of teaching. The pay–performance link in EPP has somehow become insensitive too, as pointed out by Weidong Qin, Yingzhou's headteacher: "The EPP scheme will not be approved by the annual teacher representatives congress when the individual EPP differentiation seems to be big to some teachers. Because lots of my colleagues feel their money has been taken by others." The school principal also mentioned that "I had to compromise while differentiating individual EPP because if the proposal is not approved, I will be criticised by the local Education Bureau for not implementing PRP properly, which will then affect my annual performance review. So teachers' pay preferences have made egalitarian distribution the only choice, which I believe is a serious issue happening in lots of other local public schools."

Second, the pay gap between teachers in rural areas across provinces has not been closed, which discourages teachers from staying in poor rural areas. The pay gap between teaching in rural and city areas has been reduced, but this reduction only occurs within the same province. The gap among rural teachers' overall income across provinces is still rather obvious because of inequality in regional economic development. Xueyan Jiang, the senior officer in Ningbo City Education Bureau, explained that "EPP comes from the public finance of every city, region and province. However, there are obvious gaps between the amount of public funding provided by rich and poor areas. In other words, teachers in rural areas are less likely to be paid as much as those in cities, even with outstanding performance."

Third, stimulating teachers' initiatives and creativity has been neglected. The 2009 Guidelines require that EPP be based on the combination of appraisal methods by the local education bureau as well as the school. Due to the non-linear nature of the relationship between teaching activities and student performance, the most important performance indicators adopted by many schools have been student exam results, student/teacher awards in external competitions, and the proportion of students entering senior secondary schools with a higher grade. The whole performance appraisal has become grades- or exam-orientated. Peizheng Yan, the headteacher, observed that: "I understand the reasons why quantifiable methods were used for appraisal. But I'm highly under pressure to get good overall class results in so many national/regional examinations and delivering open classes. The school lacks necessary teaching facilities and materials in my subject, Physics, which made our teaching innovation rather difficult."

Fourth, PRP has caused conflicts among teachers with the appraisal mechanism used being criticized for not being fully reasonable and scientific. "Teaching is a complex process, and should not be assessed using quantification indicators only. Colleagues who teach music and sports do not usually have external competitions for students to join, so we feel our money has been taken by others", said Jun Zheng, the music teacher. Some internal resistance to PRP from teachers was also observed. The amount of additional pay that can be achieved through increased employee effort was mentioned by the headteacher, Weidong Shi: "I'm not interested in having higher EPP because I earn a lot more money than EPP from taking more private tutees after work. Small individual differentiation is better. Otherwise I have to work with quite a few colleagues in the team who are uncooperative due to receiving lower EPP than mine."

It has been observed that the major issues in implementing PRP after the Guidelines have been relating to 'scientific' appraisal mechanisms, supervising mechanisms by local/regional education bureaus and school distribution systems. Although PRP is problematic in Chinese public schools, there is evidence to suggest that researchers, management and practitioners should pay more attention to understanding how it works, rather than whether it works (Nyberg et al. 2016).

Conclusion

This chapter provides an understanding of pay system changes in China since the establishment of the PRC in 1949. The evolution of pay components, pay determinants and performance–pay link have been examined in various periods, key characteristics of the pay system reforms summarized, and there has been a review of relevant empirical studies that reflect on the changes. In general, changes in pay systems have been sweeping through all types of organizational ownership types in China. This chapter has illustrated the evolutionary nature of change in pay systems in China, which has been shown to be complex and ongoing. While new pay components and determinants have been introduced, the full adoption of performance-based pay in the public sector is far from widespread. Research on the new PRP reform in the PSUs is still lacking. The case study in this chapter indicates that the content of PRP practices cannot not be treated as discrete activities, and nor should practices be considered in isolation from the context in which change has taken place. The complexity of the transitional Chinese economy can involve change forces operating in pay systems across different types of firms and at different time periods and for different pay elements.

References

Bai, X. and Bennington, L. 2005. Performance appraisal in the Chinese state-owned coal industry. *International Journal of Business Performance Management.* 7(3), 275–287.

Baruch, Y., Wheeler, K. and Zhao, X. 2004. Performance-related pay in Chinese professional sports. *International Journal of Human Resource Management.* 15(1), 245–259.

Bodmer, F. 2003. On the use of incentive pay in Chinese state-owned enterprises: the role of hierarchy. *Labour.* 17(2), 299–314.

Bozionelos, N. and Wang, L. 2007. An investigation on the attitudes of Chinese workers towards individually based performance-related reward systems. *International journal of Human Resource Management.* 18(2), 284–302.

Chen, D. C., Choi, J. and Chi, S. C. 2002. Making justice sense of local–expatriate compensation disparity: mitigation by local referents, ideological explanations, and interpersonal sensitivity in China-Foreign joint ventures. *Academy of Management Journal.* 45(4), 807–817.

Chen, K. (Ed.). 1995. *The Chinese Economy in Transition: Micro Changes and Macro Implications.* Singapore: Singapore University Press.

Cheng, S. and Firth, M. 2005. Ownership, corporate governance and top management pay in Hong Kong. *Corporate Governance: An international Review.* 13(2), 291–302.

Chiang, F. F. T. and Birtch, T. A. 2006. An empirical examination of reward preferences within and across national settings. *Management International Review.* 46(5), 573–596.

Child, J. 1994. *Management in China during the Age of Reform.* Cambridge: Cambridge University Press.

Child, J. 1995. Changes in the structure and prediction of earnings in Chinese state enterprises during the economic reform. *International Journal of Human Resource Management.* 2(1), 1–30.

Chizema, A., Liu, X., Lu, J. and Gao, L. 2015. Politically connected boards and top executive pay in Chinese listed firms. *Strategic Management Journal.* 36(6), 890–906.

Chow, I. H. S. 1992. Chinese workers' attitudes towards compensation practices in the People's Republic of China. *Employee Relations.* 14(3), 41–55.

Chow, I. H. S. and Fu, P. P. 2000. Change and development in pluralistic settings: an exploration of HR practices in Chinese township and village enterprises. *International Journal of Human Resource Management.* 11(4), 822–836.

Chui, R. K. and Luk, V. W.-M. 2002. Retaining and motivating employees: compensation preferences in Hong Kong and China. *Personnel Review.* 31(4), 402–431.

Chui, W. C. K., Hui, C. H. and Lai, G. W. F. 2007. Psychological ownership and organisational optimism amid China's corporate transformation: effects of an employee ownership scheme and a management-dominated board. *International Journal of Human Resource Management.* 18(2), 303–320.

Conyon, M. J. and He, L. 2012. CEO compensation and corporate governance in China. *Corporate Governance: An International Review.* 20(6), 575–592.

Cooke, F. L. 2003. Seven reforms in five decades: civil service reform and its human resource implications in China. *Journal of Asia Pacific Economy.* 8(3), 895–916.

Cooke, F. L. 2004. Public-sector pay in China: 1949–2001. *International Journal of Human Resource Management.* 15(4), 895–916.

Cooke, F. L. 2005. *HRM, Work and Employment in China.* Abingdon, Oxon: Routledge.

Cordeiro, J. J., He, L., Conyon, M. J. and Shaw, T. S. 2013. Informativeness of performance measures and Chinese executive compensation. *Asia Pacific Journal of Management.* 30(4), 1031–1058.

De Cieri, H., Zhu, C. J. and Dowling, P. L. 1998. The reform of employee compensation in China's industrial enterprises. *Center for Advanced Human Resource Studies (CAHRS), Working Paper Series* 98–05.

Ding, D. Z., Akhtar, S. and Ge, G. L. 2006. Organisational differences in managerial compensation and benefits in Chinese firms. *International Journal of Human Resource Management.* 17(4), 693–715.

Ding, D. Z., Goodall, K. and Warner, M. 2000. The end of the 'iron rice-bowl': whither Chinese human resource management? *International Journal of Human Resource Management.* 11(2), 217–236.

Ding, D. Z., Lan, G. and Warner, M. 2001. A new form of Chinese human resource management? Personnel and labour–management relations in Chinese TVEs. *Industrial Relations Journal.* 32(4), 328–343.

Ding, D. Z. and Warner, M. 2001. China's labour-management system reforms: breaking the 'three old irons' (1978–1999). *Asia Pacific Journal of Management.* 18, 315–334.

Dong, X.-y. 1998. Employment and wage determination in Chin's rural industry: investigation using 1984–1990 panel data. *Journal of Comparative Economics.* 26(3), 485–501.

Du, J. and Choi, J. N. 2010. Pay for performance in emerging markets: insights from China. *Journal of International Business Studies*. 41(4), 671–689.

Easterby-Smith, M., Malina, D. and Yuan, L. 1995. How culture-sensitive is HRM? A comparative analysis of practice in Chinese and UK companies. *International Journal of Human Resource Management*. 6(1), 31–59.

Firth, M., Fung, P. M. and Rui, O. M. 2007. How ownership and corporate governance influence chief executive pay in China's listed firms. *Journal of Business Research*. 60(7), 776–785.

Ge, Y. 2003. Principles of the PSU reform. *Management World (guanli shijie)*. 1, 71–77 (in Chinese).

Giacobbe-Miller, J., Miller, D., Zhang, W. and Victorov, V. I. 2003. Country and organizational-level adaptation to foreign workplace ideologies: a comparative study of distributive justice values in China, Russia and the United States. *Journal of International Business Studies*. 34(4), 389–406.

Giacobbe-Miller, J. K., Miller, D. J. and Zhang, W. 1997. Equity, equality and need as determinants of pay allocations: a comparative study of Chinese and US managers. *Employee Relations*. 19(4), 309–320.

Glover, L. and Trivedi, A. 2007. Human resource management in China and India. In Beardwell, J. and Claydon, T. (eds.). *Human Resource Management: A Contemporary Approach* (5th ed). Essex: FT Prentice Hall.

Harding, H. 1987. *China's Second Revolution, Reform after Mao*. Washington, DC: The Brookings Institution.

He, W., Chen, C. C. and Zhang, L. H. 2004. Reward-allocation preferences of Chinese employees in the new Millennium: the effects of ownership reform, collectivism, and goal priority. *Organization Science*. 15(2), 221–231.

Henley, J. S. and Nyaw, M. K. 1987. The development of work - incentives in Chinese industrial enterprises: material versus non-material incentives. In Warner, M. (ed.). *Management Reforms in China*. London: Frances Pinter.

Hickey, W. 2003. MNC pharmaceutical compensation in China: a predictor for human capital trends. *Journal of General Management*. 29(1), 32–46.

Hofstede, G. 1984. *Culture's Consequences: International Differences in Eork-related Values* (Abridged ed.). London: SAGE.

Horsley, J. P. 1988. The Chinese workforce: reform in the domestic labour system complement innovations at foreign invested enterprises. *The China Business Review*. May-June, 50–55.

Huang, W. 2016. Responsible pay: managing compliance, organizational efficiency and fairness in the choice of pay systems in China's automotive companies. *International Journal of Human Resource Management*. 27(18), 2161–2181.

Jackson, S. 1992. *Chinese Enterprise Management Reforms in Economic Perspective*. Berlin: De Gruyter.

Jackson, S. and Littler, C. R. 1991. Wage trends and policies in China: dynamics and contradictions. *Industrial Relations Journal*. 22(1), 5–19.

Knight, J. and Song, L. 1991. The determinants of urban income inequality in China. *Oxford Bulletin of Economics and Statistics*. 53(2), 123–154.

Korzec, M. 1992. *Labour and the Failure of Reform in China*. New York, NY: St Martin's Press.

Lee, S.-P. and Chen, H.-J. 2011. Corporate governance and firm value as determinants of CEO compensation in Taiwan: 2SLS for panel data model. *Management Research Review*. 34(3), 252–265.

Leung, K., Lin, X. and Lu, L. 2014. Compensation disparity between locals and expatriates in China: a multilevel analysis of the influence of norms. *Management International Review*. 54(1), 107–128.

Leung, K., Wang, Z., Zhou, F. and Chan, D. K. S. 2011. Pay disparity in multinational and domestic firms in China: the role of pro-disparity norm. *International Journal of Human Resource Management*. 22(12), 2575–2592.

Leung, K., Zhu, Y. and Ge, G. 2009. Compensation disparity between locals and expatriates: moderating the effects of perceived injustice in foreign multinationals in China. *Juornal of World Business*. 54(1), 85–93.

Liu, S. and Onwuegbuzie, A. J. 2012. Chinese teachers' work stress and their turnover intention. *International Journal of Educational Research*. 53, 160–170.

Mengistae, T. and Xu, L. C. 2004. Agency theory and executive compensation: the case of Chinese state-owned enterprises. *Journal of Labour Economics*. 22(3), 615–637.

Nyberg, A. J., Pieper, J. R. and Trevor, C. O. 2016. Pay-for-performance's effect on future employee performance: integrating psychological and economic principles toward a contingency perspective. *Journal of Management*. 42(7), 17531783.

OECD. 2005. *Governance in China*. Available at: http://www.oecd.org/gov/governanceinchina.htm, accessed on December 29, 2017.

Peng, Y. 1992. Wage determination in rural and urban China: a comparison of public and private industrial sectors. *American Sociological Review*. 57(2), 198–213.

Pu, S. 1990. Comment: Planning and the market. In Dorn, J. A. and Xi, W. (eds.). *Economic Reform in China: Problems and Prospects* (pp. 17–20). Chicago, IL: University of Chicago Press.

Riskin, C. 1987. *China's Political Economy: The Quest for Development Since 1949*. Oxford: Oxford University Press.

Schuler, R. S. and Rogovsky, N. 1998. Understanding compensation practice variations across firms: the impact of national culture. *Journal of International Business Studies*. 29(1).

Shen, J. 2004. Compensation in Chinese multinationals. *Compensation and Benefits Review*. 15–25.

Shengli, D. and Yanling, Z. 2005. An empirical study of the determinants of executive compensation – a case study on China's listed company. *Management World*. 143(8), 14–20.

Shenkar, O. and Chow, I. H. 1989. From political praise to stock options: reforming compensation systems in the People's Republic of China. *Human Resource Management*. 28(1), 65–85.

Su, L. 2011. Managerial compensation structure and firm performance in Chinese PLCs. *Asian Business and Management*. 11(2), 171–193.

Takahara, A. 1992. *The Politics of Wage Policy in Post-Revolutionary China*. London: Macmillan.

Tung, R. L. 1991. Motivation in Chinese industrial enterprises. In Steers, R. M. and Peter, L. W. (eds.). *Motivation and Work Behaviour* (pp. 342–351). New York: McGraw-Hill.

Walder, A. G. 1986. *Communist Neo-traditionalism: Work and Authority in Chinese Industry*: Berkeley: University of California Press.

Wang, L., Lai, M. and Lo, L. N.-K. 2014. Teacher professionalism under the recent reform of performance pay in Mainland China. *Prospects: Quarterly Review of Comparative Education*. 44(3), 429–443.

Wang, L., Nicholson, J. and Zhu, J. 2009. Pay systems in Chinese state-owned enterprises: a review. *Chinese Management Studies*. 3(4), 328–355.

Wang, W. 2008. *Gongzi Chabie de Xingcheng Jizhi (The Mechanisms of Wage Differences among Firms with Different Ownership)*. Beijing: China Economic Publishing House.

Warner, M. 1993. Human Resource Management 'with Chinese Characteristics'. *International Journal of Human Resource Management*. 4(1), 45–65.

Warner, M. 1995a. *The Management of Human Resource in Chinese Industry*. London: Macmillan.

Warner, M. 1995b. Managing China's human resources. *Human Resource Management*. 14(3), 239–248.

Warner, M. 1996a. Chinese enterprise reform, human resources and the 1994 Labour Law. *International Journal of Human Resource Management*. 7(4), 769–796.

Warner, M. 1996b. Human resources in the People's Republic of China: the "Three Systems' reforms. *Human Resource Management Journal*. 6(2), 32–42.

Warner, M. 1997. Management–labour relations in the new Chinese economy. *Human Resource Management Journal*. 7(4), 30–43.

Warner, M. 1998. China's HRM in transition: towards relative convergence? In Rowley, C. (ed.). *Human Resource Management in the Asia Pacific Region: Convergence Questioned* (pp. 19–33). London: Frank Cass.

Wei, Q. and Rowley, C. 2009. Pay for performance in China's non-public sector enterprises. *Asia–Pacific Journal of Business Administration*. 1(2), 119–143.

Wu, P., Chen, T. and Leung, K. 2011. Toward performance-based compensation: a study of the gaps between organizational practices and employee preferences with regard to compensation criteria in the state-owned sector in China. *International Journal of Human Resource Management*. 22(9), 1986–2010.

Xiu, L. and Gunderson, M. 2013. Performance pay in China: gender aspects. *British Journal of Industrial Relations*. 51(1), 124–147.

Xiu, L. and Gunderson, M. 2015. Occupational segregation and the gender earnings gap in China: devils in the details *International Journal of Manpower*. 36(5), 711–732.

Yu, K. C. 1998. Chinese employees' perceptions of distributive fairness. In Francesco, A. M. and Gold, B. A. (eds.). *International Organisational Behaviour*. Englewood Cliffs, NJ.: Prentice Hall.

Yu, K. C., Bunker, D. R. and Wilderom, C. P. M. 1989. *Employee values related to rewards and the operation of reward systems in contemporary Chinese enterprises*. Paper presented at the Proceedings of the 3rd International Conference, Managing in a Global Economy III, Eastern Academy of Management.

Yueh, L. Y. 2004. Wage reforms in China during the 1990s. *Asia Economic Journal*. 18(2), 149–164.

Zhang, X., Tang, G. and Lin, Z. 2016. Managerial power, agency cost and executive compensation – an empirical study from China. *Chinese Management Studies*. 10(1), 119–137.

Zhang, Z.-x. 2001. The effects of frequency of social interaction and relationship closeness on reward allocation. *Journal of Psychology*. 135(2), 154–164.

Zhao, M. H. and Nichols, T. 1996. Management control of labour in state-owned enterprises: cases from the textile industry. *China Journal*. 36, 1–21.

Zhao, S. 2005. Changing structure of Chinese enterprises and human resource management practices in China. In Smyth, R., Tam, O. K., Warner, M. and Zhu, C. J. (eds.) *China's Business Reform: Institutional Challenges in a Globalised Economy.* London: RoutledgeCurzon.

Zhou, J. and Martocchio, J. J. 2001. Chinese and American managers' compensation award decisions: a comparative policy-capturing study. *Personnel Psychology.* 54(1), 115–145.

Zhu, C. J., De Cieri, H. and Dowling, P. J. 1998. The reform of employee compensation in China's industrial enterprises. *Management International Review.* 38(2), 65–87.

Zhu, C. J. and Dowling, P. J. 1994. The impact of the economic system upon human resource management practice in China. *Human Resource Planning.* 17, 1–21.

Zhu, C. J., Thomson, S. B. and De Cieri, H. 2008. A retrospective and prospective analysis of HRM research in Chinese firms: implications and directions for future study. *Human Resource Management.* 47(1), 133–156.

Zhu, Y. and Warner, M. 2000. An emerging model of employment relations in China: a divergent path from the Japanese. *International Business Review.* 9, 354–361.

Zou, H. L., Zeng, S. X. and Lin, H. 2015a. Top executives' compensation, industrial competition, and corporate environmental performance: evidence from China. *Management Decisions.* 53(9), 2036–2059.

Zou, H. L., Zeng, S. X. and Zeng, R. C. 2015b. Are top executives rewarded for environmental performance? The role of the board of directors in the context of China. *Human and Ecological Risk Assessment: An International Journal.* 21(6), 1542–1565.

33

EXPLORING THE STRATEGIES UNDERPINNING MARRIOTT'S REWARDS PRACTICES IN THE EMERGING CHINESE HOTEL INDUSTRY

Mark Wickham and Tommy Wong

Introduction

The shift away from the traditional HRM view of remuneration (i.e., one focused on the motivational aspects of 'total compensation and benefits' packages) towards that of the strategic HRM view (i.e., focused on 'Total Rewards Management' (TRM) and its link to mutual employee/organizational satisfaction) has been increasingly evident in the academic and practitioner literature over the past decade (see CIPD Website 2017; Kang and Shen 2015; Marx et al. 2016; Sayim 2010; World at Work Website 2017). Driving this shift has been recognition that, unlike the 'traditional' approach, the TRM view provides a more holistic alignment of 'business with people strategy' and seeks to encompass all of the workplace elements that are simultaneously valued by both employees and the organization (e.g., compensation and benefits, career development, the work environment, organizational culture, etc.) (Jiang et al. 2009; Kaplan 2007; Kastrati 2014; Manas and Graham 2002). Recently, and coinciding with increasing competition for skilled labour and viable market positions in emerging Asian markets (Cavusgil and Cavusgil 2012; London and Hart 2004; Johnson and Tellis 2008; Wei and Rowley 2009; Yaprak 2011), academics and practitioners alike have taken an interest in determining the extent to which extant Western-based TRM practices provide an effective basis for competition in that context (Bonache and Zárraga-Oberty 2017; Fenton-O'Creevy and Gooderham 2003).

One stream of international business research that has enjoyed growing attention in this area is that concerning 'convergence' (i.e., the extent to which Western-based management practices are able to be effectively adopted/adapted to non-Western contexts) (Gooderham and Brewster 2003; Vanhala et al. 2006; White 2005). At its most basic, the concept is used to detect the level of similarity apparent in the HRM policies of two separate entities at a certain point in time; more complex applications attempt to detect 'directional-'/'majority-convergence' – i.e., the extent to which Western-based HRM practices are present and effective across national boundaries (e.g., see Kang and Shen 2015). At its most complex, research has sought to gain a finer-grained comprehension of 'final convergence', which explicitly focuses on what constitutes sustainable HRM practices that are effective across national boundaries (e.g., see Brewster and Tregaskis 2003; Mayerhofer et al. 2011; Tregaskis and Brewster 2006). Common to the more complex convergence research is recognition that national/cultural differences (e.g., additional layers of national and international law, different and sometimes clashing cultural norms, different social priorities, different technological and logistical capacity, etc.) require some form of adaptation to TRM practices for them to deliver the 'final convergence' benefits sought by organizations operating in emerging market contexts (Bonache and Zárraga-Oberty 2017; Cavusgil and Cavusgil 2012; Crook et al. 2011; Gupta and Govindarajan 2000). As such, the broad research opportunity to be addressed in this chapter is to explore what strategies underpin the transfer of TRM 'best practice' in organizations operating in an emerging economic context.

Literature review

In order to explore the strategies that might underpinned the final convergence of TRM best practices, it is important to first define the component parts that differentiate it from the traditional 'total compensation and benefits' view. According to Jiang et al.'s (2009) definition, traditional 'total compensation and benefits' specifically comprises a range net cash payments, non-cash benefits, flexible schedules, education assistance, training courses and workplace opportunities that assist the employee to achieve a functional work–life balance. In contrast, the TRM view incorporates all of the elements that employees might consider valuable in their employment relationship, and emphasizes additional intrinsic value propositions such as work–life effectiveness, recognition and awards, performance management practices, talent and career development opportunities, and rewards for behaviours consistent with the organization's desired culture (see Kaplan 2007; Kastrati 2014; Kwon and Hein 2013; World at Work Website 2017). Critically, extant literature indicates that the design and delivery of TRM best practices appears grounded in three core principles (see Kwon and Hein 2013; Marx et al. 2016; Sayim 2010): firstly, that they align with the organization's overall strategy and associated workforce goals. Secondly, that there be capital allocations made to the total reward programmes, and that measures are put into place to accurately measure the returns of these investment. Lastly, that the TRM programme be communicated clearly throughout the organization, and enacted in such a way that the desired employee behaviours are reinforced consistently. As noted, however, the complicating factors associated with effective human resources management in international business contexts requires ongoing research to account for their impact in the HRM/convergence debate; despite extant empirical research confirming the organizational benefits of the TRM approach generally, there remain calls to explore the principles and strategies that underpin the transfer of TRM best practices by Western firms in emerging market contexts (see Kwon and Hein 2013; Marx et al. 2016; Sayim 2010; Wasti 1998; Wei and Rowley 2009).

Research opportunity

One international hotel organization that has replicated their employer-of-choice status in the emerging Chinese economy is Marriott International Inc. (hereafter 'Marriott'); in 1997, Marriott expanded into China through multiple acquisitions and management contract takeovers of established domestic hotel chains. By the end of 2016 (i.e., after twenty years of operation), Marriott had grown from one hotel operating in Hong Kong to 92 hotels operating across mainland China (Marriott Website 2017a). Through its commitments to employee development and reported satisfaction levels, Marriott has been awarded employer-of-choice status in China for the four consecutive years ending in 2015 by the European-based Top Employers Institute (Marriott Website 2017b; Top Employers Website 2015). According to the European-based institute, the basis for Marriott's awards were an effective mix of reward management practices, comprising: innovative compensation and benefits packages (e.g., the evolution of yearly bonus structures, subsidized medical care etc.), flexible working conditions, networking opportunities (e.g., seasonal social events, Alumni), on-boarding activities (e.g., mentoring programmes), career management practices, well-being programmes, and training and development opportunities (for details, see Top Employers Website 2015). Given its success in achieving employer-of-choice status in the emerging Chinese hospitality industry, the Marriott case represents an opportunity to explore the following research question: *What reward management strategies underpinned Marriott's employer-of-choice status in the Chinese hotel industry?*

Method

In order to address this research question, this study comprised a series of semi-structured interviews with senior managers in the Marriott Group's Chinese operation (that is, those comprising the Marriott and Courtyard brands). Two major factors influenced the selection of Marriott for this study: as noted above, Marriott represents a case of an internationally renowned organization which has been awarded 'employer-of-choice' status for its rewards practices in the Chinese hotel industry. Secondly, its operations represent a revelatory case in which its senior management have the ability to reflect upon the factors underpinning its award-winning rewards processes as they relate to their domestic Chinese employees. In total, 12 Marriott senior managers were recruited to provide primary data relating to the organization's reward management processes. Of the 12 senior managers, three were General Managers (of Marriott hotels), three were Marketing Directors (that had been working with Marriott since its entry into China in the mid-1990s), three were Human Resource Directors, and three were Sales Directors (see Table 33.1 for a summary).

Given the inherent complexity of the topic, we decided to interview the respondents on four occasions over a four-year period (i.e., 2009–2012 – fortuitously during the years leading up to Marriott's Top Employer awards); this longitudinal approach to primary data collection was chosen for two main reasons: firstly, it allowed time for the respondents to reflect on the HRM strategies developed and implemented in the Chinese hotel industry (i.e., we provided the interview questions in advance so that the respondents could prepare their responses more fully). Secondly, it allowed the researchers to focus their interviews on specific elements of the research opportunity (i.e., compensation and benefit schemes, flexible working conditions, networking opportunities, on-boarding activities, career management practices, well-being programmes, and training and development). The semi-structured interview questions posed to the respondents (see Box 33.1) were designed to cover the necessary issues, but were framed in an open-ended manner, to allow the respondents sufficient latitude for introspection and open reporting of their own

Table 33.1 Summary of the senior managers interviewed at Marriott

Title	Interviews (n =)
General managers	10
Marketing directors	12
Human resources directors	12
Sales directors	12

Box 33.1   Semi-structured interview questions posed to the respondents

- Please describe Marriott's core business activities in the Chinese hotel industry.
- How would you describe Marriott's employer brand in China? What key attributes do you believe it possesses?
- Please identify and describe Marriott's major competitors in the Chinese hotel industry.
- What advantages do you perceive Marriott has over their competitors in the Chinese labour market? What strategies did Marriott implement in order to protect their advantages in the Chinese labour market?
- What disadvantages you perceive Marriott has against their competitors in the Chinese labour market? What strategies did Marriott implement in order to overcome the disadvantages they experienced in the Chinese labour market?
- What strategies did Marriott implement in order to protect and develop their employee relationships?
- What strategies did Marriott implement to develop and protect its employer brand in China?
- What do you believe are the most challenging employment issues faced by Marriott in China in the next five years?

---

perspectives. As a result, the respondents were free to pursue those matters that they considered important. In total, 46 semi-structured interviews were conducted, each of which lasted between 60 and 120 minutes. Secondary data were also collected from local and international newspaper archives, historical publications of China's economic and hospitality industry development, Chinese government agency publications, and the annual reports of the Marriott group.

Each of the primary interview transcripts and secondary data sources were subject to a rigorous content analysis process that followed the five-stage protocol forwarded by Finn et al. (2000), Hodson (1999) and Neumann (2003). The content analysis and the verification of the conclusions drawn were facilitated by the use of the NVIVO (version 10) software package. Computer software programs such as NVIVO are of significant value in qualitative analysis and any subsequent theory building (Kelle 1995; Richards and Richards 1995). During Stage One of the content analysis, the aims and objectives of the research were identified, and the first-round coding rules were developed (NB: this research used the literature review as a guide to initially organize the data by the variables listed in Table 33.2). In Stage Two, all of the interview transcripts and secondary data were entered into a codified NVIVO database. In Stage Three, the coded data were further interrogated to detect any significant themes that emerged in terms of HRM strategies; the trends and emerging themes detected in the analysis formed the basis for establishing the second round of data coding categories. In Stage Four, the second round of coding rules were developed prior (to maintain a consistent approach between researchers), and to provide a protocol for others to follow should they wish to replicate the analysis. In the final stage of the content analysis, the results of the second-round coding were refined and the research findings finalized.

In order to generate the necessary empirical knowledge, memos were maintained about the data, the first- and second-round coding categories, and the relationships between them as they emerged (Wilson 1985). Utilizing the memo capability within the NVIVO package, memo reports were generated by the software; from these reports, the trends and emerging themes became clearer. The themes emanating from the 'second round' of coding form the basis of the results section that follows.

Table 33.2 First-round coding variables and definitions

Node	Definition
Compensation	This node seeks to identify any reward strategies or philosophies relating to the base compensation practices adopted by Marriott in its Chinese hotel operations
Benefits	This node seeks to identify any reward strategies or philosophies relating to programmes that supplement the base compensation adopted by Marriott in its Chinese hotel operations
Work–life effectiveness	This node seeks to identify any reward strategies and philosophies relating to organizational policies and programmes that supports employees achieve satisfaction in both their home and work environments
Recognition/organizational culture	This node seeks to identify any reward strategies and philosophies relating to the formal or informal programmes that acknowledge or given special attention to employee behaviour or efforts that contribute to the organization's culture
Performance management	This node seeks to identify any reward strategies and philosophies relating to the alignment of organizational, team and individual efforts to the achievement of broad organizational goals
Training and development	This node seeks to identify any reward strategies and philosophies relating to the opportunities afforded to employees to advance their skills and competencies in the short, medium and long term
Organizational culture	This node seeks to identify any reward strategies and philosophies relating to the support of the organization's desired culture
Organizational strategy	This node seeks to identify any reward strategies and philosophies relating to specific organizational goals (e.g., customer satisfaction, customer loyalty, profitability, cost minimisation, etc.)

Results

Analysis of the primary and secondary data indicated that there were five critical TRM strategies underpinning Marriot's 'employer-of-choice' status in China: the faithful transfer of an employee-centric corporate philosophy to the developing Chinese economy; generating a detailed understanding of China's labour market constraints; generating a detailed understanding of the Chinese government's labour market objectives; offering strategic training and development opportunities as *de facto* rewards for domestic employees; and guarding against the head-hunting of domestic employees. Each of these strategies will be discussed in turn in the following sections.

Faithful transfer of an employee-centric corporate philosophy to the domestic Chinese economy

The data indicated that despite the opportunity for Marriott to exploit the relatively lower wage levels and working conditions prevalent in the emergent Chinese labour market, the organization chose instead to faithfully transfer its extant corporate philosophy and human resource management strategies to inform its HRM in this new market. In terms of its extant corporate philosophy, respondents noted that in order to establish and maintain its leading labour market presence in the Chinese hotel industry, Marriott's credo of "people first" was maintained:

> At Marriott, everything we do is built on our culture of "people first" . . . We are committed to providing an environment where employees have the opportunity to achieve their potential . . . We are proud that our inclusive culture is the main ingredient that sets us apart from other companies. We know that when our employees feel valued and respected, they'll help make our guests feel that way too.
>
> *(Marriott website 2012d)*

In addition to this, Marriott's senior management reported that the corporate philosophy (which they term the "Marriott's Way") served as the basis for their competitive advantage in China:

> Our competitive advantage is that we care about our people, our associates [employees] . . . the "Marriott's Way" is the core capability to our success for over eighty years, which is based on the philosophy of if you treat your associates well, and in turn they will treat your customers well.
>
> *(General Manager 2, Personal Interview, 2011)*

> As part of Marriott's "Spirit to Serve" value, we invest in our people and knowledge to provide our guests with high quality products, services and experiences.
>
> *(General Manager 1, Personal Interview, 2010)*

Almost immediately, Marriott's philosophy concerning the treatment of domestic workers became a point of differentiation in the Chinese hotel labour market, which, in accordance with its stated competitive advantage, gave the organization first access to an increasingly highly trained and educated labour market:

> . . . in the 1990s and even in the early 2000s investing in your employees and treating them well were not common management practices in China . . . Marriott is perceived as a very good employer in the Chinese market . . . it shows as Marriott was awarded the top employer in China by the Corporate Research Foundation (CRF) Institute in 2012.
>
> *(Human Resources Director 1, Personal Interview, 2012)*

> Our growth has been fast in emerging markets like China, but we have to do things differently to succeed. Manpower is an issue. Finding experienced associates is difficult . . .
>
> *(Senior Vice President of International Marketing of Marriott International in Babitch and Chen 2005)*

Detailed understanding of China's labour market constraints

The data also indicated that Marriott's senior management took marketing research measures to inform their understanding of the labour market constraints in the Chinese hotel industry. In particular, the labour market research focused on gathering information about two specific issues: domestic labour market skill deficiencies, and attitudes towards employment. In terms of labour market skill deficiencies, Marriott was able to determine the extant level of skill and ability in the target labour force and was therefore able to forecast the level of training and development required to get their staff performing at the minimum levels required:

> The country [China] and its cities can build the world's most outstanding or tallest buildings in the world, but the skills level is still very much behind most of the developed markets.
>
> *(General Manager 5, Personal Interview, 2011)*

> . . . in the early 1990s, hotel employees had no clue and no ideas of how to handle their own grooming and personal hygiene, not to mention providing quality service to the guests . . . we started with very basic training to get them up to our minimal standards, then slowly introduced our SOP [Standards of Operation] . . . The employees are very different today, they now emulate western lifestyles while enjoying materialism and consumerism.
>
> *(Marriott General Manager 1, Personal Interview, 2009)*

> . . . the one child policy has contributed to the current skill-shortage situation in China. However, hotels are also competing with the domestic government departments for skilled employees, as the domestic governments are now providing benefits such as welfare, less hours and higher salaries to attract talent.
>
> *(Human Resources Director 3, Personal Interview, 2009)*

In terms of employment attitudes, Marriott was able to determine the extent of the disconnect that existed between the target labour markets' extant beliefs, feelings, and behaviour towards the workplace environment, and the minimum requirements of the "Marriot's Way" organizational culture. In doing so, the organization was similarly able to forecast the level of training and development investment required to integrate domestic Chinese employees into the desired organizational culture:

> International hotels are struggling to implement autonomous workplace conditions, or empowerment process in China due to its "fear to get into trouble" culture and the extremely tough employment regulations . . . we have dedicated human resources officers to deal with the various domestic government departments for all our domestic employment issues.
>
> *(Marriott General Manager 3, Personal Interview, 2011)*

> . . . in the early days, our domestic associates needed to be shown how to perform tasks and to be reminded how to work within the boundaries of procedures and processes.
>
> *(Marriott Human Resources Director 2, Personal Interview, 2010)*

Detailed understanding of the Chinese government's labour market objectives

Similarly, the data indicated that Marriott's senior managers took measures to gather information regarding the Chinese government's labour market policies and objectives. In particular, the organization sought to understand the level of protectionism that still existed in the labour market (despite the "open door" policy espoused by the Chinese government) and the bases of negotiation that were possible in this context. In terms of the level of protectionism, Marriott's senior managers were particularly interested in the legal safeguards offered to domestic employees in the termination process:

> . . . we constantly have to keep an eye on our associates and to let them know that they are being watched to protect our profits. For example, we caught two associates stealing from us, but we could not sack them due to various domestic employment protection regulations . . . we ended up paying them compensation to get them out of our hotel.
>
> *(Human Resources Director 2, Personal Interview, 2009)*

> . . . [the Chinese] hotel industry is one of the big employers in the market . . . the domestic governments still closely monitor our employment practices . . . they are turning the private sector into the modern iron rice bowl to look after the local Chinese workers.
>
> *(General Manager 6, Personal Interview, 2011)*

In terms of the bases of negotiation that were possible the Chinese context, Marriott senior managers were specifically interested in the range of governmental authorities that existed in the country, and a clear understanding of their specific spheres of influence and control. This understanding provided the organization with cost advantages that allowed them to optimize their negotiated outcomes with the Chinese authorities:

> We have a better understanding of domestic employment regulations and what governments are trying to achieve in the labour market . . . we are in a much better position to negotiate with all relevant authorities regarding employment terms and conditions.
>
> *(Human Director 1, Personal Interview, 2010)*

> We [Marriott] work very closely with the domestic hospitality training schools in China . . . we get good students from some of these schools . . . our in-house training programs help the students to get up to our standards pretty quickly once they have started with us.
>
> *(Human Resources Director 3, Personal Interview, 2011)*

Training and development opportunities as de facto rewards for domestic employees

Consistent with the principles of strategic HRM (i.e., to advance organizational goal attainment whilst simultaneously contributing to the domestic employees' career potential – cf. Jackson et al. 2014), analysis of the data demonstrated Marriott's commitment offering training and developing opportunities as *de facto* rewards for is domestic employees. In particular, the data demonstrated significant commitment to employee development through on-the-job training practices, placement opportunities, and internship opportunities. In terms of the organization's commitment to employee development through on-the-job training practices, the data demonstrated that the organization provided centralized investment support for its domestic Chinese employees. The investment support tended to take the form of infrastructural training for its front-line staff, and capital allocations to staff promoted to managerial positions within the organization:

> . . . with good support and training from Marriott's international office, we were able to achieve good results from some of the newly implemented processes and systems in areas such as hotel operation standards, overall food and beverage offerings and management and

general customer service . . . up-skilling our [domestic Chinese employees] took longer
. . . training and development of [domestic Chinese employees] is a continuous process.
(Marriott General Manager 1, Personal Interview, 2010)

Marriott is very good with their in-house training programmes . . . we were spending
around US$800.00 per manager per year in training expense back in the early 2000s. . . we
value our skilled associates and in China where hospitality skills are very hard to find, we use
our in-house training programs to increase our available pool of skilled human resources.
(General Manager 1, Personal Interview, 2011)

In addition to this, the Marriott's Way philosophy (and related corporate culture) also sought to
ensure that employees engaging in the desired behaviours were provided ongoing access to
experienced managers willing and able to assist in their development:

. . . Marriott's General Managers are hands-on operators. We invest in our people, and
we set examples for our young managers, so they can follow. . . this is very important in
this domestic market.
(General Manager 3, Personal Interview, 2010)

We always have a pool of well-trained and experienced managers ready to be posted
anywhere in the world. The combination of this pool of foreign managers supported by
our selected domestic managers is one of Marriott's strengths.
(Marriott Human Resources Director 3, Personal Interview, 2010)

In terms of placement opportunities, the data demonstrated: (a) that the organization maintained
regular audits of the human resource skills and abilities under their control; and (b) took measures to
allocate these skills and abilities to areas within the organization where they would bring most benefit:

A fluent Mandarin speaking expatriate manager is still a rare resource in today's market,
but we commonly transfer them across our hotels internally for training. . . one of our
immediate issues is [training] enough English speaking associates . . . English language
skills are still considered to be low in China and that causes us concern with regard to
our service quality level.
(Marriott Human Resources Director 1, Personal Interview, 2011)

Human capital capabilities are becoming more important than having a Western
manager . . . Western management strategy no longer requires a certain number of
foreigners working as staff to operate in China. . . Foreign managers no longer have the
monopoly of first pick of all the good positions.
(Marriott Human Resources Director 3, Personal Interview, 2012)

In terms of internship opportunities, the data demonstrated that Marriott underpinned its
selection process via a probationary path that enabled the organization to screen potential
employees/managers in terms of their fit with the corporate culture:

Marriott's internship programme works very well as a screening process . . . we often
have a number of domestic and international interns working at our hotels and we filter
out the potential interns and offer them positions in the hotels. Many of them ended up
being one of our functional managers . . . our internship programme is an important
source of talents. . . there are many workers in the market, but to find suitable workers

that speak English with good customer skills is very difficult . . . we are not only competing with other hotels, we are competing with all industries including the domestic government departments for talents.

(General Manager 3, Personal Interview, 2012)

Guarding against the headhunting of domestic employees

The final theme to emanate from the data analysis was Marriott's commitment to guarding against the headhunting of its domestic employees once their skills and abilities became valuable commodities in the labour market:

It is becoming more difficult to employ and retain younger, quality staff because there are so many opportunities now open to young people in China.

(Director of User Experience of Marriott International
in Babitch and Chen 2005)

Overall, good experienced managers are still looked upon as the person who set the brand standards in a country where human capital is still at a development stage and the "Marriott's Way" is still very effective in associates' training and development. Hopefully, we can keep them for as long as possible before our competitors poach them away.

(General Manager 1, Personal Interview, 2012)

In particular, the data demonstrated that: (a) Marriott remained sensitive to evidence of headhunting by competitors (and indeed organizations in other industries); and (b) invested heavily to protect its store of HR skills and abilities:

. . . if you see some strangers talking to your top managers, you can be certain that your top managers are being poached by your competitors.

(General Manager 4, Personal Interview, 2011)

Marriott is perceived as a very good employer in the Chinese market . . . it [is important to] show [that] Marriott was awarded the top employer in China by the Corporate Research Foundation (CRF) Institute . . .

(Marriott Human Resources Director 1, Personal Interview, 2012)

Discussion

The research question posed in this study sought to explore the strategies underpinning Marriott's TRM/employer-of-choice status in the emerging Chinese hotel industry. Whilst the results reported here are idiosyncratic to the Marriott case, we do believe that the strategies detected in this research can be applied to guide the transfer of TRM best practices by similar organizations seeking to operate in China (and, arguably, other emerging markets as well). Fundamentally, this research suggests that the transfer of TRM best practices (depicted in Figure 33.1) requires a range of management and investment support for the five strategies identified in our thematic analysis of the data, commensurate with an organization's desired labour market position.

Accordingly, we recommend that organizations seeking to transfer/generate TRM- (and indeed HRM-) best practices in an emerging economy context should consider: (a) taking action to define their corporate philosophy and its relationship to TRM practices, and benchmark these against employers-of-choice in the domestic setting and/or in the emerging market setting;

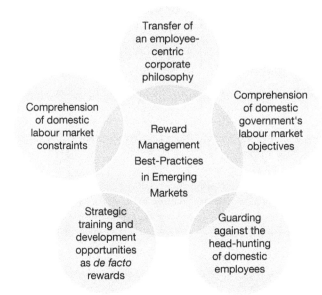

Figure 33.1 Rewards management strategies underpinning Marriot's employer-of-choice status in the Chinese hotel industry

(b) taking measures to audit their corporate philosophy and accurately compare it against these employer-of-choice benchmarks; (c) undertaking market research in order to gain a comprehensive understanding of the constraints inherent to the target economy's labour market; (d) undertaking market research in order to gain a comprehensive understanding of the domestic government's labour market objectives; (e) faithfully transferring the corporate philosophy (along with the necessary managerial and capital support for the related TRM) to the emerging market context; (f) taking measures to offer training and developmental opportunities to employees in the emerging economy as de facto rewards (ensuring that they are also aligned with the strategic imperatives of the organization); and (g) implementing safeguards against the headhunting of domestic employees as their skills and abilities become valuable commodities in the domestic labour market. In terms of the convergence literature, this research supports the contention that the transfer of Western-conceived HRM practices into emerging-economy contexts requires specific consideration of national/cultural differences, and an understanding of their likely impact on the international transfer process. In particular, our analysis demonstrated the critical importance of Marriott's employee-centric organizational culture in 'setting the scene' for its boundary-spanning activities (e.g., its labours market and government-policy research agenda) prior to its entry into the emerging Chinese hotel industry. Relatedly, the organization developed its culture and reputation within the industry to position its training and development opportunities as rewards in their own right, thereby insulating its HRM investments against the headhunting practices/high attrition rates for skilled employees that characterize labour markets in this context.

Conclusion

The findings of this research need to be assessed in relation to the limitations of the selected research methodology and case organization. The qualitative methodology adopted in this research does not allow for generalizations of Marriott's employer-of-choice success in its China operations to explain or predict how similar organizations might achieve the same outcome in the emerging market context. Similarly, the accuracy of the historical data gathered here may be characterized by contextual misinterpretation of the critical decisions under review, especially where the researchers are unable to directly ascertain the motivations of the actors involved (Andrew 1985; Breisach 1994). In terms of the chosen case organization, it is important to recognise that the Marriott chain of hotels possesses a significant array of resources and capabilities which are matched by only a few major competitors in the global hospitality sector, and would not be representative of the majority of hotel organizations seeking to expand internationally. It is, therefore, a recommendation that additional research be undertaken into three key areas to further advance research in this field: firstly, the extent to which the strategies not only presented here are transferable to organizations in different hospitality industry segments (e.g., hostels, resorts, restaurants, etc.) and in other international emerging markets would help to validate the findings of this study, but also explore any potential moderating impacts (e.g., organizational size, industry, location, etc.). Secondly, the impact that the different stages of an organization's operation in a given emerging market (e.g., using the Product/Industry Life Cycle, or the Uppsala Stages Model) may present a finer-grained understanding of the correctional/majority/final convergence issues as they apply to the international transference of best-TRM practices. This research, for example, was able to broadly analyse Marriott's 'introduction', 'growth' and 'early-maturity' stages of its operations in the emerging Chinese hotel industry, but was unable to consider, inter alia, more advanced stages of the internationalization process (i.e., the 'late-maturity' 'decline' and 'divestment' stages). Finally, we recommend that quantitative research be undertaken to determine the relative importance/statistical significance each of the strategic factors in relation to the desired employee and organizational outcomes commonly associated with best-TRM practices.

References

Andrew, A. (1985). In pursuit of the past some problems in the collection, analysis and use of historical documents. In Burgess, R. (ed.). *Strategies in Educational Research*. Sussex: Falmer Press.

Babitch, S. and Chen, J. (2005). *Design for the Emerging Markets: Interview with Marriott International*. Chicago: Institute of Design.

Bonache, J. and Zárraga-Oberty, C. (2017). The traditional approach to compensating global mobility: criticisms and alternatives. *The International Journal of Human Resource Management*. 28(1), 149–169.

Breisach, E. (1994). *Historiography Ancient, Medieval and Modern*. Chicago: University of Chicago Press.

Brewster, C. and Tregaskis, O. (2003). Convergence or divergence of contingent employment practices? Evidence of the role of MNCs in Europe. In Cooke, W. (ed.). *Multinational Companies and Global Human Resource Strategies* (pp. 143–166). Greenwood, IL: Quorum Books.

Cavusgil, S. T. and Cavusgil, E. (2012). Reflections on international marketing destructive regeneration and multinational firms. *Academy of Marketing Science*. 40, 202–217.

CIPD Website. (2017). *Strategic Reward and Total Reward*. Available at: https://www.cipd.co.uk/knowledge/strategy/reward/strategic-total-factsheet#7366, accessed on January 23, 2017.

Crook, T. R., Todd, S., Combs, J., Woehr, D. and Ketchen, D. Jr. (2011). Does human capital matter? A meta-analysis of the relationship between human capital and firm performance. *Journal of Applied Psychology*. 96(3), 443–456.

Fenton-O'Creevy, M. and Gooderham, P. N. (2003). International management of human resources. *Scandinavian Journal of Business Research*. 17(1), 2–5.

Finn, M., Elliott-White, E. M. and Walton, M. (2000). The analysis of qualitative data: content analysis and semiological analysis. In *Tourism and Leisure Research Methods: Data Collection, Analysis and Interpretation*. Harlow: Pearson Education.

Gooderham, P. N. and Brewster, C. (2003). Convergence, stasis or divergence? Personnel management in Europe. *Scandinavian Journal of Business Research*. 17(1), 6–18.

Gupta, A. K. and Govindarajan, V. (2000). Knowledge flows within multinational corporations. *Strategic Management Journal*. 21, 473–496.

Hodson, R. (1999). *Analyzing Documentary Accounts*. Thousand Oaks, CA: Sage Publications.

Jackson, S. E., Schuler, R. S. and Jiang, K. (2014). An aspirational framework for strategic human resource management. *The Academy of Management Annals*. 8(1), 1–56.

Jiang, Z., Xiao, Q. and Qi, H. (2009). Total reward strategy: a human resource management strategy. *International Journal of Business and Management*. 4(11), 177–183.

Johnson, J. and Tellis, G. (2008). Drivers of success for market entry into China and India. *American Marketing Association*. 72, 1–13.

Kang, H. and Shen, J. (2015). Transfer or localize? International reward and compensation practices of South Korean multinational enterprises in China. *Asia Pacific Business Review*. 21(2), 211–227.

Kaplan, S. L. (2007). Business strategy, people strategy and total rewards. *Benefits and Compensation Digest*. 44(9), 12–19.

Kastrati, I. (2014). The total rewards strategy transformation through time and trends in accordance with human resource strategy. *Journal of Human Resource Management*. 17(2), 25–30.

Kelle, U. (1995). *Computer-Aided Qualitative Data Analysis: Theory, Methods, and Practice*. London: Sage Publications.

Kwon, J. and Hein, P. (2013). Employee benefits in a total rewards framework. *Benefits Quarterly*. 2013(1), 32–38.

London, T. and Hart, S. (2004). Reinventing strategies for emerging markets: beyond the transnational model. *Journal of International Business Studies*. 35, 350–370.

Manas, T. M. and Graham, M. D. (2002). *Creating a Total Rewards Strategy: a Toolkit for Designing Business-Based Plans*. AMACOM Division of the American Management Association, USA.

Marriott Website. (2017a). *About Marriott International – Find Your World*. Available at: http://www.marriott.com/marriott/aboutmarriott.mi, accessed on January 16, 2017.

Marriott Website (2017b). *Awards and Recognition*. Available at: http://news.marriott.com/p/awards-and-recognition, accessed on January 16, 2017.

Marx, R., Soares, J. P. R. F. and da Silva Barros, L. S. (2016). Organizational context variables to be considered in the reward system design oriented to product innovation. *Review of Business Management*. 18(60), 267–289.

Mayerhofer, W., Brewster, C., Morley, M. and Ledolter, J. (2011). Hearing a different drummer? Evidence of convergence in European HRM. *Human Resource Management Review*. 21(1), 50–67.

Neumann, W. L. (2003). *Social Research Methods* (5th ed.). Upper Saddle River: Prentice Hall.

Richards, T. and Richards, L. (1995). Using computers in qualitative research. In Denzin, N. and Lincoln, Y. (eds.). *Handbook of Qualitative Research* (pp. 445–462). Upper Saddle River: Sage Publishers.

Sayim, K. Z. (2010). Pushed or pulled? Transfer of reward management policies in MNCs. *The International Journal of Human Resource Management*. 21(14), 2631–2658.

Top Employers Website. (2015). *Marriott International*. Available at: http://www.top-employers.com/companyprofiles/cn/Marriott-International/, accessed on January 16, 2017.

Tregaskis, O. and Brewster, C. (2006). Converging or diverging? A comparative analysis of trends in contingent employment practice in Europe over a decade. *Journal of International Business Studies*. 1, 111–126.

Vanhala, S., Kaarelson, T. and Alas, R. (2006). Converging human resource management: a comparison between Estonian and Finnish HRM. *Baltic Journal of Management*. 1(1), 82–101.

Wasti, S. A. (1998). Cultural barriers in the transferability of Japanese and American human resource practices to developing countries: the Turkish case. *The International Journal of Human Resource Management*. 9(4), 608–631.

Wei, Q. and Rowley, C. (2009). Changing patterns of rewards in Asia: a literature review. *Asia Pacific Business Review*. 15(4), 489–506.

White, R. (2005). A strategic approach to building a consistent global rewards program. *Compensation and Benefits Review*. 37(4), 23–40.

Wilson, H. S. (1985). *Research in Nursing*. Boston: Addison-Wesley.

World at Work Website. (2017). *What is Total Rewards?* Available at: https://www.worldatwork.org/aboutus/html/aboutus-whatis.jsp, accessed on January 23, 2017.

Yaprak, A. (2011). Market entry barriers in China: a commentary essay. *Journal of Business Research*. 64, 1216–1218.

34

MANAGING SMALL ENTERPRISES IN CHINA'S DECENTRALIZED ORGANIZATIONS

The platform function and employee incentives

Jian Han and Jason D. Shaw

Introduction

Organizational design trends change in increasingly complex ways. In 2016, BCG and Ali Research conducted a joint study of more than 100 European and American listed companies and found that, over the preceding 15 years, the number of vertical levels, number of coordination parties, and complexity of decision approval procedures had increased by some 50% (Candelon et al. 2016). In theory, integrated firms can become too large, leading to a decline in performance levels. In response, organizations may split into smaller business divisions (Chandler 1962; Williamson 1975). One option for splitting is through 'platform' or networked structures (Ciborra 1996; Siggelkow and Levinthal 2003), which are becoming increasingly popular in China. Concomitantly, as structures change and evolve, organizations may need to adjust their employee reward and incentive systems to align with new work, information and strategy.

Typically, platform organizations comprise a multifunctional platform and many independent small enterprises (SEs). Figure 34.1 illustrates a typical organizational platform in which the platform is at the centre of the network and is surrounded by many small and independent business units. These SEs are fully or partially self-contained and account for their own target performance, they operate independently, and have split financial statements (Meyer et al. 2017). Companies have various names for decentralized SEs. For example, the Japanese Kyocera Corporation has an SE operating under the name *Amoeba* (Inamori 2013) and the Haier Corporation calls its SE *Micro Enterprise*. Similarly, the Handu Group names its SE *Small Groups*, and Vanke has *Project Teams*. According to their business or organizational needs, the teams employed within the SEs range from three to a dozen employees.

Firms leverage the decentralized structures to expand their search for novel opportunities and rapid responses to competitive demands, but the question arises as to the adaptation of their management and incentive systems to support such responses (Siggelkow and Levinthal 2003). The decentralized structure brings with it the managerial challenge of balancing the independence of SEs while securing integration and coordination through the platform, with consequences for the way in which employees in these SEs are compensated and incentivized. To better understand decentralized structures and their corresponding incentive systems, we studied

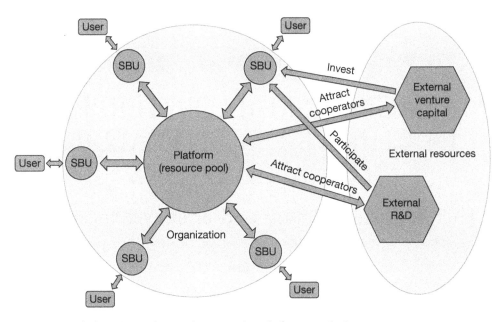

Figure 34.1 Platform, SEs, and external resources in a platform organization

SE design applications in Haier, Handu, and Vanke by way of examples from three Chinese companies in different industries. All are leaders in their field who have been experimenting with decentralization, and each one faces industry-specific challenges: technological transformation pressure (Haier); diversified customer demand and homogeneous competition (Handu); or high market risk because of turbulent regulatory changes (Vanke). Their transformations have lasted for more than three years, enabling observation of the impacts of organizational change. Our data came from interviews with company leaders and SE employees, established business cases, and archival company data. Table 34.1 provides a summary of the case company profiles.

How do companies coordinate their SEs?

Each company has different strategic objectives and operational styles, but we found several commonalities with regard to how they manage and incentivize people in their SEs. Our interviews revealed that organizations are motivated to decentralize and authorize SEs by the need to respond quickly to customer demand, reduce trial-and-error costs, and innovate rapidly. The companies we observed grant greater authority to SEs than most bureaucratic or matrix organizations give to their subordinate teams. For example, SEs in all three companies make autonomous daily operational

Table 34.1 Description of cases

Firm	Industry	Product	Year founded	Employees in 2015
Haier	Manufacture	Household appliances; consumer electronic goods	1984	63,802
Handu Group	Retail	Apparel	2006	1979
Vanke	Real estate	House property; property services	1984	42,295

decisions to promote or demote staff and distribute profits. In addition, Haier's and Handu's SEs can make independent decisions about products and designs.

To achieve their organizational goals, these firms implement mechanisms that coordinate SE initiatives and control their performance within the company's strategic context. Control and coordination functions are carried out through three interrelated methods: *direction, support and internal market*. The direction efforts include setting strategic directions, instituting incentive rules, and conducting audit and risk control. For example, Haier organizes all SEs according to the principle of self-initiation and self-organization, but they must submit proper business plans in order to obtain approval by Haier's strategy and investment committees (Hwang et al. 2017). In Handu, SEs accept goals at the beginning of the year and the SEs compete on monthly, quarterly, annual, and other assessment indicators. In Vanke, the platform and the SE co-initiate new projects and attract investment, and the platform performs risk control with regard to SE operations.

The extensiveness of the support granted to SEs depends on business strategies. Haier has an open innovation strategy and open organization boundary, so the platform is responsible for steering the SEs into new ventures to devise innovative products and services. In their early stages, SEs usually encounter difficulty in accessing resources, so the platform will help them coordinate and integrate resources within and beyond Haier. Such incubating efforts include organizing roadshows, providing incubation funds, and offering training. Handu's strategy, by contrast, is to devise multiple products and brands. Therefore, the platform is dedicated to organizing production, customer service, marketing, logistics, photography for online promotion, finance, human resources and administration. The platform also supplies cross-SE coordination when multiple teams compete for limited resources. To nurture more brands, the platform even established a brand planning team to help their SEs raise new brands, conduct pre-market research, apply for trademarks and protect intellectual property.

Another method for managing SEs is through internal competition and transactions. SEs operating in similar categories usually compete for platform resources, such as human resources, financial services, logistics, and supplies. In principle, the platform allocates resources according to the SE performance and therefore must establish an assessment system to allocate resources. We observed varying levels of competition among the SEs, perhaps because of industry-distinct product and investment cycles. For instance, Handu Group is in the fast-moving fashion and retail industry; thus, the competition between Handu's SEs is more intense because of the short cycles from design to sales and high levels of product homogeneity. The company implements daily sales rankings and a 'hot–popular–mediocre–unsalable' evaluation mechanism among the SEs, adding impetus to the competitions. In Haier, it often takes at least six months from idea development to product sales. With the platform's coordination of resources and the SE's efforts to differentiate the user values, the products meet different needs of various user groups. Therefore, Haier's SEs experience less-fierce direct competition. Vanke, which is in the real estate industry, features vast capital investments in the early stages, rare customer overlaps, and significant geographical differentiations. Consequently, its SEs have much less direct competition.

Differing from conventional hierarchical or matrix organizations, SEs often use internal transactions to promote goal congruence between the platform and the SEs. In Haier, based on customer needs, the SE devoted to sales will purchase product solutions from the SE devoted to production and R&D. Each SE is an independent accounting unit, and therefore they have an incentive to improve their profits and reduce purchasing costs. Similarly, the production SE must attain repeated orders from the sales SE by providing products of quality and timeliness. Members of the R&D SE must be effective innovators, able to meet the needs of the production team and thus compete for the next project. The HR SE must deliver good results in recruitment, training and incentive solutions if they are to receive repeat service requests from the other SEs. Haier's internal information platform records all SE orders. The records also include user comments that are then considered during performance appraisals.

Like Haier, Handu is divided into product and functional SEs. The product team includes one designer, one web media specialist and one production and orders specialist, integrating R&D, sales, and purchasing functions. The company uses an internal bidding system regarding support services such as photography and logistics. For example, when a product SE needs photos to promote a product online, photographic SEs compete for the assignment. The product SE will then select the best bid according to cost performance and internal settlement formalities. Members of functional SEs are paid according to the quantity and quality of their service to the product SE, thereby strengthening their service orientation.

Incentive plans and performance assessment for SEs in platform organizations

Under these business strategy and management system frameworks, SEs in platform organizations enjoy higher autonomy and incentives than do traditional organizations, but they also face high risks. More important, incentive systems work only when the corresponding assessment is effective. SEs' principles of assessment must reflect and align with the company's overall strategy.

Haier uses a two-dimensional lattice assessment of SE market performance. The horizontal dimension measures short-term competitiveness, using indicators such as sales revenue, profits, and market shares. The vertical dimension measures user value with indicators such as the amount of interaction with external users and partners through the Internet or mobile networks, indicating behaviours that lead to long-term business transformation. Interviews with Haier's executives revealed that Haier considers interaction with external users and partners to be an essential strategic path if they are to transform from traditional manufacturing operations and become an industry leader able to form an intelligent home applicant ecosystem.

Compensation at each SE depends on pre-set goals and performance. SE employees compete for SE leadership by establishing aggressive goals and budget programmes. At the time of SE establishment, SE leaders sign compensation adjustment agreements with the platform. The SE account and funds raised by SE leaders may be used to pay basic living expenses to SE members. When value created exceeds pre-set goals and profits, SE members can share profits and purchase phantom stock in the SE. When the SE creates value that leads in the industry and attracts external investment, Haier gives SE members shares according to their contribution. Furthermore, the SEs can become independent companies, and members can benefit from shares and increased stock value. The platform assesses SE market performance according to pre-agreed indicators. SEs showing good market performance can obtain more resources and support, while underperforming SEs may be eliminated.

Based on the two dimensions, the platforms measure SE performance as fitting into *red*, *yellow*, *blue* and *green* zones. If current SE performance deteriorates from the same period in the previous year, the SE is marked as *red* and may be disbanded. If SE performance improves but still misses the pre-set goal, the SE moves to the *yellow* zone. The platform then must pay for its resource allocation mistakes or personnel misplacement, but the SE is given a deadline to rectify the situation. SEs that reach their targets are labelled *blue*. Members can then share benefits with the company. If SEs exceed their optimal market performance goals, they are labelled *green*, and members share the excess profits, sometimes doubled according to the predetermined adjustment mechanism. In addition, the platform will allocate more resources to green SEs to foster greater competitive advantages.

In Handu, SEs can obtain direct bonuses through sales, gross profit ratios and commission coefficients. Thus, they can directly calculate increased revenue from products sold. For each SE, the next month's working capital is 70% of the current month's sales, and teams with high growth receive additional investment. SEs showing good performance will get more marketing resources. In addition, daily sales rankings are an honour incentive for SEs with good market performance. Handu adopted a four-category evaluation mechanism: *hot–popular–mediocre–unsalable*. The system is designed to motivate SEs to aggressively promote their designs and reduce inventory. After products are posted online for 14 days; they are categorized based on sales. Hot and popular styles are quickly reordered to meet consumer demand; mediocre and unsalable styles are discounted and cleaned. All SEs are ranked daily, based on their task accomplishment ratio, gross profit ratio and inventory turnover ratio.

Vanke differs from manufacturing and retail companies. As a national leader in the real estate industry, Vanke has been decentralized into many SEs by regions, each naturally formed from a residential community. Vanke initiated the co-investment system to drive the SEs to be responsible for profits and losses and to motivate employees to work harder to achieve higher income and co-investment returns. SE leaders and regional leaders are required to co-invest in projects and sign value adjustment agreements in advance. The company sets hurdle rates and expected rates of return according to the regional market environment and relevant policies, average regional income and the historical income of the project team.

In Vanke, SE incomes are based on performance categories. If the co-invested project fails to reach the internal hurdle rate of return (IRR), the company takes the income at the hurdle rate, and then distributes any remaining income among SE investors. If the IRR of the co-invested project is higher than the hurdle rate but not higher than the excess rate of return, the co-investors distribute the income according to the proportion of investment. If the IRR of the co-invested project is higher than the excess rate of return, the co-investors distribute the excess return according to the proportion of investment. They then distribute the income exceeding the excess return according to 1.2 times the income they get proportional to the investment. In addition, like most players in China's real estate industry, Vanke makes large investments in advance and must wait a long time before realizing profits, so the agreed exit mechanism is that they will withdraw the principal and distribute dividends after development loans are available, cash flows back, and 70% of mortgage loans and sales are achieved.

Discussion and conclusion

Haier, Handu and Vanke have engaged in platform transformation for several years. All three companies demonstrated overall healthy product development and financial performance during their transformations (see Table 34.2). Despite their financial performance gains, however, the companies face several challenges. First, platform organizations decentralize employee decisions by giving SEs high autonomy and flexibility in daily operation. Although platform organizations provide SEs with functional support and resource coordination, the SEs' incentive systems feature potentially high returns but also high risks, especially low pay or even jeopardized job security when SEs fail to perform satisfactorily. Indeed, during Haier's organizational transformation, their employee population decreased by 8%, from 86,000 at the beginning of 2013 to 70,000 at the end of 2013, and they decreased by a further 5000 in May 2014 (*Caijing Report on Haier Layoffs* 2014). Thus, internal competition and subsequent downsizing may decrease organizational loyalty and commitment (e.g., Spiegelaere et al. 2014).

Furthermore, internal pricing systems between SEs may increase internal conflict and reduce trust across the entire corporate structure. Pricing is a key component in the internal purchase

Table 34.2 Revenues and profits for three companies before and after their transformation

Firm	Year of transformation	Revenue (year before transformation) (in US dollars)	Profit (in US dollars)	Revenue (year) (in US dollars)	Profit (in US dollars)	Revenue (year after transformation) (in US dollars)	Profit (in US dollars)
Haier	2014	26.5B(2013)	1.6B	29.5B (2014)	2.2B	27.8B (2015)	2.6B
Handu Group	2008	0.44M (2008)	N/A	1.76M(2009)	N/A	12.8M (2010)	N/A
Vanke	2014	19.9B(2013)	2.2B	21.5B (2014)	2.3B	28.7 (2015)	2.7B

* Exchange rate: 1 USD = 6.8012 RMB.

market (Adler and Hiromoto 2012), with the external market price providing references for transaction prices. In platform organizations, however, transactions between SEs differ from contracts among economic entities in the market. Repeated price-based transactions are efficient for clearly divided projects and responsibilities, but it is difficult to achieve market price bases in unfinished and uncertain transactions. In theory, the purchase price among SEs should be based on the value negotiated among SE leaders. However, in large organizations with complex internal value chains, such as Haier, the various nodes find it almost impossible to agree on internal pricing. Thus, higher-level platform owners must often make subjective and sometimes biased coordination decisions. The seemingly objective pricing system and the subjective nature of the leadership decision may send mixed signals to SE managers and other employees, affecting perceptions of fairness and, in turn, motivation. Therefore, internal pricing systems are similar to bureaucratic and matrix organizations in that they must be compatible with incentives and congruent with goals to motivate performance and organizational effectiveness (Hart and Holmström 1987; Paolillo et al. 1986; Witt 1998).

In this chapter, we use examples from three Chinese companies to discuss observations regarding the transformation to platform organizations through which organizations use decentralized SEs to improve their organizational agility and speed. The platforms manage the SEs by directing, supporting and building internal markets. In addition, during the change process, they build incentive and performance assessment systems that reflect their unique business strategies, organization design and competitive context. Although these companies have demonstrated healthy financial performance to date, further research attention should be paid to platform transformation and effects on sustainability factors like SE employee commitment and trust.

References

Adler, R. W. and Hiromoto, T. (2012). Amoeba management: lessons from Japan's Kyocera. *MIT Sloan Management Review.* 54(1), 83.

Caijing Report on Haier Layoffs. (2014, June 26). Haier's radical transformation resulted in layoffs of more than ten thousands of employees: employees don't understand what the boss is doing. *Finance and Economy Website (Chinese)*. Available at: http://tech.caijing.com.cn/2014-06-26/114292167.html, accessed on March 22, 2017.

Candelon, F., Kaufman, E., Morieux, Y., Li, S., Ruan, F., Cao, Y., Song, F., Alamusi, Cui, H. (2016). Platform organizations: "Prefaces" of the frontiers of organizational transformation. Joint research report by BCG and Ali Research (published in Chinese).

Chandler, A. D. Jr. (1962). *Strategy and Structure: Chapters in the History of the American Industrial Enterprise.* Cambridge, MA: MIT Press.

Ciborra, C. U. (1996). The platform organization: recombining strategies, structures, and surprises. *Organization Science.* 7(2), 103–118.

Hart, O. and Holmström, B. (1987). The theory of contracts. In Bewley, T. (ed.). *Advances in Economic Theory: Fifth World Congress.* Cambridge: Cambridge University Press.

Hwang, Y., Han, J., Xu, D., and Yu, F. (2017). *Breaking up from within: management control system design in transforming organization into a platform-oriented strategy.* Conference paper accepted for presentation at the AAA 2018 Management Accounting Section Midyear Meeting, Scottsdale, Arizona.

Inamori, K. (2013). *Amoeba Management: The Dynamic Management System for Rapid Market Response.* Boca Raton, FL: CRC Press.

Meyer, M. W., Lu, L., Peng, J. and Tsui, A. S. (2017). Microdivisionalization: using teams for competitive advantage. *Academy of Management Discoveries.* 3(1), 3–20.

Paolillo, J. G., Jackson, J. H. and Lorenzi, P. (1986). Fusing goal integration. *Human Relations.* 39(5), 385–397.

Siggelkow, N. and Levinthal, D. A. (2003). Temporarily divide to conquer: centralized, decentralized, and reintegrated organizational approaches to exploration and adaptation. *Organization Science.* 14(6), 650–669.

Spiegelaere, S. D., Gyes, G. V., Witte, H. D., Niesen, W. and Hootegem, G. V. (2014). On the relation of job insecurity, job autonomy, innovative work behaviour and the mediating effect of work engagement. *Creativity and Innovation Management.* 23(3), 318–330.

Williamson, O. E. (1975). *Markets and Hierarchies: Analysis and Antitrust Implications.* New York: Free Press.

Witt, L. A. (1998). Enhancing organizational goal congruence: a solution to organizational politics. *Journal of Applied Psychology.* 83(4), 666–674.

35

REWARD MANAGEMENT AT HUAWEI, CHINA'S LEADING GLOBAL ENTERPRISE[1]

John Shields

The rise of a new telecommunications giant

Telecommunications giant Huawei is one of China's most successful businesses. It also remains one of China's few truly globalized corporations. Further, Huawei is unusual in that it is neither a private or family business, nor a public listed company. It is an employee-owned firm, with the founder and CEO, Mr Ren Zhengfei, owning less than 2% of the company's share. The remaining equity is owned (as at 2014) by over 82,000 employees under an employee stock ownership plan designed by Mr Ren at Huawei's inception in 1987 (De Cremer and Tao 2015a). The management philosophy applied by its founder is a combination of Confucian values, military discipline, entrepreneurial verve and global aspiration (De Cremer and Tao 2015b; Tao et al. 2016).

Huawei's initial success involved trading private branch exchanges (PBX) into mainland China with a Hong Kong-based telecommunications company. Two years later, its founder decided to invest in research and development of its own telecommunications products. In 1994, the launch of 'C&C08', Huawei's own milestone product, took the local market by storm and by 1996 Huawei had become the No. 1 telecoms equipment vendor in China. The firm's emphasis on telecoms equipment that combined high quality and low cost meant that, by the late 1990s, a rapidly growing number of Chinese families were able to afford to install a home telephone. In line with its founding mission – *To improve quality of life through communication* – Huawei transformed domestic communication in China and enriched the country's quality of life, in the process effectively combatting one of the blights of domestic telecoms at the time in rural and remote China – plagues of rats that played havoc with telecoms connections (De Cremer and Tao 2015b). Mr Ren's acumen as a strategist and logistician had undoubtedly been deepened by his years of ervice in the People's Liberation Army. His political and military connections stood Huawei in good stead within China's changing political economy. The firm's rapid emergence also owed a great deal to timely strategic repositioning, while its signature reward practices have been instrumental in its continued growth and development (De Cremer and Tao 2015b). As might be expected in a majority employee-owned enterprise, the firm does offer employees a degree of consultation and voice in reward decisions (De Cremer and Tao 2015b). However, as we shall see, there are indications that Huawei may now have to modify its approach to reward management at both domestic and global scales if it is to maintain a positive ratio of payroll costs to performance benefit.

The success of C&C08 reinforced Huawei's commitment to R&D as the key ingredient for future success and sustainability. Over the past two decades, the firm has routinely invested at least 10% of annual revenue into R&D, and R&D engineers have consistently comprised more than 40% of the firm's workforce, of which 98% hold a bachelor's degree or a higher degree qualification. Huawei now also has a far wider range of telecoms products; a range that gives it commanding presence in the global marketplace.

A further impetus to Huawei's success has been its willingness to globalize. Its first overseas operation, in Bangalore, India, came in 1998 – with R&D as its chief focus. At this point, the strategic aim was to take advantage of the software development capability of Indian engineers rather than to establish a local market presence. Soon afterwards, however, Huawei began exploring international sales prospects, with Russia the initial country of interest for market expansion primarily because the firm saw considerable potential in the country's underdeveloped telecoms market and prevailing economic circumstances. Although this assessment soon proved to be overly optimistic, Huawei soon shifted its focus to the European market where it was able to achieve a market breakthrough and consolidate its reputation as a high-quality supplier.

The 'tech-wreck' of 2000–2001 forced Huawei to accelerate its globalization activities due to the downturn in China's domestic market. In 2005, its inclusion in the short-list of suppliers for the "21st CN", an ambitious transformation network plan of the established telecoms company British Telecom signalled the firm's emergence as a major global player in the high-standard, developed telecoms market. In the same year, Huawei's overseas sales exceeded its domestic China sales for the first time, signifying its emergence as a truly global enterprise.

Huawei's expansion into the global telecoms market, coupled with the global economic crisis of 2008–2010, set the stage for a major shake-up of existing western telcos, with Nortel being acquired by Ericsson following bankruptcy, and mergers occurring between Nokia and Siemens, and between Alcatel and Lucent. By 2014, Huawei's telecoms sales had outstripped those of the previous market leader, Ericsson, giving it the No. 1 position in the global telecoms market and symbolizing its transition from a traditional follower to that of global leader. At the same time, Huawei has moved to transform itself into an even more broadly-based IT firm. In 2011, it established two new business groups: Device BG, producing smartphones and tablets for terminal consumers; and Enterprise BG, providing telecoms solutions and services to all types of organizations, including government and private companies.

By 2015, Huawei had around 170,000 employees worldwide, including over 40,000 non-Chinese, with 75% of its international employees being hired locally. The firm now has offices in 140 countries, with its largest international operations in Europe, and a worldwide customer base of three billion. Huawei's footprint now extends from the snow of Siberia and the plains of Africa to the sun and sand of the South Pacific. On flights to African countries, Chinese passengers are commonly asked by locals: "Are you from Huawei?" It is at the time of writing the only Chinese firm that generates greater revenue internationally (67%) than domestically (De Cremer and Tao 2015a).

Huawei's reward strategy

As its founder and CEO remarked recently in an internal speech to Huawei employees: "to a certain extent, Huawei's success is the success of its human resources strategy" (Anon. 1). As the core of its approach to people management, its reward strategy and practices play a key role in the success of its drive for diversification and globalization.

Management's key message to employees regarding the firm's approach to reward management is that those who contribute can expect to share in the fruits of success. CEO Mr Ren believes in "gathering people by scattering the wealth, while people scatter when the wealth gathers to one" (Anon. 1). Management's intention is to use reward management practices to encourage employees to have a deep affinity with the company, an abiding commitment to its mission and a strong sense of shared ownership and enterprise.

Long-term incentives for a global workforce: the Time-Based Unit Plan (TUP)

Huawei's main vehicle for employee stock holding and profit sharing globally is its Time-Based Unit Plan (TUP). This was introduced in 2014 in recognition of the limitations of the firm's pre-existing employee share ownership plan, in which non-Chinese staff were ineligible to participate. Available to Huawei employees worldwide, the TUP is essentially a combined profit-sharing and phantom share plan, with employees whose performance is rated as good (that is, achieving at least two 'Bs' in annual performance review) being eligible to receive a quantum of phantom shares based on five years of company profitability. TUP shares are granted free of cost to eligible employees, which entitles recipients to receive an annual dividend in the form of cash incentive payments based on an annual profit-sharing pool and a cumulative end-of-term gain amount (De Cremer and Tao 2015a). However, the number of shares granted to each employee also varies according to the individual's prior year performance assessment. A cap is also applied for each job level such that once an employee's TUP share quantum reaches the top amount specified for their job level, they do not receive new shares until they are elevated to a higher job level with a higher cap (Anon. 1). Even so, Huawei's strong financial performance means that the TUP has delivered considerable additional income to many of its employees.

The TUP is a broadly-based global plan, covering around 80% of all company employees. As such, it is also a long-term incentive plan to retain valued employees. TUP thus serves to align employees' long-term personal interests and corporate performance and profitability. This long-term incentive programme appears to have made a significant contribution to Huawei's growth and expansion, with employees being rewarded directly for the firm's business success.

The promise of long-term profit sharing also serves as a powerful staff retention device, Since competitors find it difficult to match the extra income afforded by TUP. As such the workforce of Huawei is very stable, with a voluntary turnover rate averaging just 5–8% organization-wide – and lower still for managerial staff (Anon. 1).

Short-term incentives

To complement TUP, Huawei also uses a variety of short-term incentive plans. The annual bonus is the major part of the firm's value proposition to employees, comprising 20% to 40% of the total annual income of an employee with acceptable performance. The firm uses special short-term incentives to reinforce particular strategic priorities from time to time. These include a special performance bonus which is paid out when business unit performance exceeds its target, a lump-sum payment to all employees based on the company's success in combatting business bribery and commercial corruption (as revealed by auditing and legal recourse), and a bonus payment linked to the success of the company's efforts to achieve cost savings to encourage employees' awareness of cost-saving activities, including travel bookings.

Although the nomenclature applied to these plans varies, the message employees receive is clear: the company is willing to share the profits earned with employees providing they act with propriety and aligning with the management purposes.

Reward equity

The fairness and equity of reward outcomes is also an important consideration at Huawei. One key principle in company thinking here is the importance of widening the reward premium for outstanding staff.

In a highly competitive global market for professional skills, attracting, motivating and retaining outstanding staff is a vital consideration. Huawei seeks to address this through a general compensation and benefits programme incorporating a broadbanded salary structure, individual incentive bonuses, and a targeted approach to staff welfare and benefits.

Huawei positions its base salary at the 75th percentile for each country in which it operates (Anon. 1). While this is not a particularly competitive position for high-tech industry, Huawei also uses its broadbanded salary structure to allow fast and flexible salary adjustment. This allows base salaries for consistently high performers to be increased significantly within a relatively short period – say, one or two years.

Huawei's annual bonus system is based on the year-end performance of the business, instead of being determined by the finance budgeting at each year start. This reflects Huawei management's view that the bonus should be determined by the profit actually earned by employees and business units, not merely a device for motivating future performance. On this basis, the bonuses of the front-line managers and customer-facing staff in revenue-generating roles, such as sales and pre-sales staff, can be many times above that received by staff working in the functional areas, such as Finance and Human Resources. Management believes that since staff working directly with customers make a major contribution to revenue generation, they should receive a greater share of earnings.

In recent years, Huawei has promoted a project-based approach to its global operations with a view to enhancing organizational agility and efficiency. Project managers, who are viewed as the business CEO of the relevant project, are authorized to distribute discretionary bonuses to team members based on their contributions to the project. The delegation of bonus pay allocation to project leads has certainly motivated ambitious employees to look to front-line projects in international operations. At the same time, however, it has served to demotivate employees remaining behind in home-country operations, notwithstanding the attractions of the TUP.

Global rewards

In line with its long-term objectives, another key consideration in Huawei's reward system is supporting global business operations, especially by recognising the additional demands of operating in 'hardship' countries. In a very real sense, Huawei's approach to rewarding expatiates and host-country employees presages the approach to international reward management that China's multinational firms will adopt in future years.

To address the language and cultural challenges arising from its growing global operations, along with the lack of management and professional talent in many spheres of operation, employees expatriated from China play an important role in maintaining the firm's global activities. In 2017, there were some 16,800 Chinese expatriates on short- and long-term assignment with Huawei. These employees are viewed as a floating human resource to meet the company's business needs in any country.

In designing its international assignment compensation and allowance programme Huawei adopts a 'balance sheet' approach, with the intention of preserving the expatriate's standard of living as far as is possible via provision of special benefits (cf. Shortland and Perkins, this volume). The structure of relocation benefits for Chinese assignees is summarised in Table 35.1.

Table 35.1 Relocation benefits for Huawei's Chinese expatriates

Allowance	Purpose	Rates set for long-term international assignment	Rates set short-term international assignment
Home leave	Compensation for long-term leave from the homeland and inconvenience of living in foreign countries.	Fixed Renminbi [RMB] value based on job level of the assignees	Fixed RMB value based on assignment time-long accrued.
Hardship	Compensation for working and living in hardship countries and areas	The level of payment for each country/city is determined using data provided by consulting companies benchmarked against internal investigations of HR and assignees. The hardship benchmark is China.	
Meals	Subsidiary to ensure assignees have a nutritious and adequate food supply	1 The standard amount is 15 USD/day; for a minority of countries like Northern EU countries it is 25 USD/day plus. 2 In most countries, Huawei sets up canteens with Chinese cuisine. The allowance is paid directly to the canteen managed by the company administration department and the international assignees receive free means, while their accompanying family members receive a 50% subsidy. Where there is no company canteen, meal allowances to assignees are issued in non-cash form (food card/restaurant coupons).	
Home–visit air-ticket	Subsidiary for assignees to return to China to meet families or invite families to meet in host countries.	1 Offered in quota manner. One each four months, three annually. Each quota is valid for two years during the assignment, with unused travel entitlements expiring once the term of expatriation ends. 2 Can be used by assignees themselves, the parents of single assignees, and spouses and dependent children of married assignees.	

Source: Anon. 1 (2017). Information on Huawei's business strategy and global rewards practices, Huawei senior HR professional.

Huawei's management pays particular attention to compensation for placement in hardship countries. This derives from its need to maintain global business competitiveness. It also aligns with Huawei's corporate core values. Western competitors such as Ericsson, Nokia Siemens and Alcatel-Lucent are very strong in developed countries, while they have less presence in developing countries in Africa, the Middle East and South-East Asia. In many such countries, Huawei's competitive advantage lies in the fact that it is frequently the best available choice among limited options for local telecoms carriers. At the same time, in these hardship countries, local talent in high-tech roles is relatively scarce and skilled Chinese employees are indispensable, at least during the start-up phase. As such, the company invests heavily in encouraging Chinese employees to accept placement in hardship countries, particularly in Africa and the Middle East. The company reviews the hardship allowance rate for expatriates each year in the light of changing economic, social and political circumstances. In 2015, due to the deteriorating situation in some countries, the top hardship allowance rate was increased from US$60 per day to US$80 per day. In addition, when there is conflict or natural catastrophe in a country, the company pays a temporary higher allowance of up to US$100 per day for the assignees involved (Anon. 1).

Employee benefits

In contrast to its approach to incentive plans and tailored expatriate allowances, Huawei prefers an egalitarian and low-level approach to benefits. In most countries, Huawei applies the minimum standards of statutory benefits legally required by the country, including compulsory pension plans, medical insurance and the like. Huawei's management views benefits in terms of basic employee welfare rather than as a means of attracting, retaining and motivating high-performing employees. As such, benefits provision does not reflect the company's overall reward strategy of widening the gap between high performers and the rest of the workforce.

This approach has both benefits and disadvantages. On the one hand, benefits costs are stable and predictable. On the other, they are also largely fixed and inflexible. While Huawei realizes it operates in an industry that is subject to rapid technological change, the rigidity of its benefits provision means that, in contrast to incentive payments, related costs cannot be adjusted readily to accommodate downturns in business revenue. Overall, however, its strong accent on incentive pay, coupled with the lighter burden of employees' fixed benefits, leaves Huawei better placed to adjust payroll costs than many of its western competitors. Thus far, unlike many other high-tech firms, Huawei has not had to undertake large-scale layoffs during downturns in the business cycle.

The twin challenges of rising compensation costs and home country staffing

While Huawei's reward management strategy has served it well until now, the firm's accelerated pace of growth and diversification means that it needs to rethink its approach. There are some clear indications of the scale of this emerging challenge.

Firstly, TUP-related payroll costs are outstripping growth in revenue. According to an internal analysis), over the triennium 2013–15, Huawei's payroll costs rose by 34% and compensation per employee by 26%, compared to a 27% increase in revenue (Anon. 2) (Table 35.2).

Table 35.2 ICT companies: compensation per employee and growth in revenue and payroll cost, 2013–2015 (USD)

	Compensation per employee (US$)			Compound growth rate, 2013–2015		
	2013	2014	2015	Revenue (%)	Compensation cost (%)	Compensation per employee (%)
Huawei	59,000	68,000	93,000	27	34	26
Ericsson	89,038	88,266	81,158	− 8	− 2	− 5
Nokia	72,248	89,479	73,175	− 8	− 4	1
ZTZ	25,580	27,860	30,811	15	15	10
Tencent	65,787	90,323	100,880	29	53	24

Note: Tencent is the biggest Internet communication company in China, known as China's Facebook.

Source: Anon. 2 (2017). Internal analysis by Huawei Finance expert published on Huawei business management website forum, April.

According to data extracted from SalaryList (2017), and summarised in Figure 35.1, as at 2016, Huawei's compensation per employee was in the top bracket of global ICT firms: US$113,000 compared to US$93,000 for Microsoft and US$78,000 for Ericsson. In the context of declining profit margins in the telecoms industry, this signals difficulty ahead for reward management at Huawei. Left unchecked, this blowout in compensation costs threatens to reduce Huawei's competitive position, particularly relative to major western firms.

Since salary and benefits are relatively fixed and account for only a fraction of Huawei's total compensation costs, the growth in costs comes chiefly from its long-term and short-term incentive plans. The TUP's five-year payment timeframe heightens Huawei's compensation liability. Due to its long-term cumulative effect, the longer the employee stays with the company, the larger the payout generated from the TUP: for some high-level long-service employees, TUP's payout is 50% or an even higher percentage of an individual's total income. This also gives rise to the possibility that employees may come to see TUP compensation as an entitlement rather than a reward for contribution. Likewise, the desire to retain individual bonuses may lead employees to seek to ingratiate themselves with managers, or to engage in office politics, nepotism and misconduct.

The second factor contributing to the blowout in payroll costs is Huawei's high level of allowances for Chinese expatriates. Even after more than ten years of global expansion, Huawei still favours the use of home-country nationals (i.e., Chinese citizens) for leadership roles. The percentage of local managers is very small – less than 10% (Anon. 1) – while the number of Chinese assignees continues to rise. This not only inflates payroll costs, but also inhibits the localization of Huawei's overseas business, the use of local labour at local rates and the development of host-country talent. Many of the firm's current expatriates were born in the early 1970s, when China's English-language education was very weak, and the proficiency in English of this generation is generally poor. These employees are attracted by the relatively generous reward packages available for hardship placements and tend to monopolize jobs to the exclusion of host-country nationals.

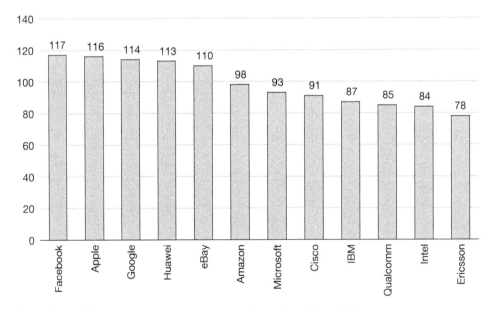

Figure 35.1 ICT companies: compensation per employee, 2016 (USD '000s)

Source: Data from SalaryList.com. http://www.salarylist.com/ (2017).

While, in developed countries, even though the relocation package is less generous, expatriates look to such placements to afford themselves and their family improved life opportunities and have little motivation to develop and use local talents as well.

Huawei has made an aggressive push into the consumer business in smartphones and the enterprise business market. In both areas, awareness of local consumer values, needs and expectations is key to successful market penetration. Host-country nationals are better placed to understand the local market, how to deal with local customers and how to engage with potential business partners. Huawei's current approach to expatriate reward and its reliance on home-country expatriates now threatens to impede localization of its overseas operations and its transition to new business areas. In response, the firm is looking to offer non-Chinese staff salaries higher than those made available to Chinese employees in similar roles (De Cremer and Tao 2015a).

Conclusion

In its early growth and initial globalization, Huawei made effective use of domestic political and military connections and innovative reward practices to support and reinforce its business model and strategy. The challenges it now faces in employee reward and global talent management warrant a review of existing practices and a substantial change to its approach to reward management for both home and host-country nationals. At the same time, on the political front, Huawei global expansion is encountering growing resistance in some host countries where concerns have been raised about its connection with the Chinese military and Communist party elite and the perceived/potential threat to host-country national security. It remains to be seen how and how effectively Huawei will rise to these particular challenges, and others that may await it in its quest for global influence and impact.

Note

1 This case has been written with input from a senior professional knowledgeable on Huawei's history, business strategy and human resource practices and the author particularly wishes to acknowledge this invaluable assistance.

References

Anon. 1 (2017). Information on Huawei's business strategy and global rewards practices. Huawei senior HR professional.

Anon. 2 (2017). Internal analysis by Huawei Finance expert published on Huawei business management website forum. April.

De Cremer, David and Tao, Tian (2015a). Huawei: a case study of when profit sharing works. *Harvard Business Review.* Available at: www.hbr.org/2015/09/huawei-a-case-study-of-when-profit-sharing-works

De Cremer, David and Tao, Tian (2015b). 'Leading Huawei: Seven Leadership Lessons of Ren Zhengfei'. Available at: www.europeanbusinessreview.com/leading-huawei-seven-leadership-lessons-of-ren-zhengfei/

SalaryList.com (2017). Comparative salary data on IT businesses. Available at: www.salarylist.com/

Tao, Tian, De Cremer, David, and Wu, Chunbo (2016). *Huawei: Leadership, Culture, and Connectivity.* Thousand Oaks, CA: Sage Publications.

36

MANAGING EMPLOYEE REWARDS IN MEXICO

In search of competitive advantage

Sergio M. Madero-Gómez and Miguel R. Olivas-Luján

Introduction

According to the Global Competitiveness Report 2015–2016 (World Economic Forum 2016), the 7th pillar for competitiveness is related to efficiency in the labour market, which is ultimately related to human resources processes in companies. In Mexico, Central America and the Caribbean, the item that appears with the best indicator for this 7th pillar is related to the purported flexibility for determining and setting wages, an aspect that from a business perspective is very interesting to analyse. It demands reflection on the importance of the human resources area in the country, mainly for job creation and the economic development of the region. However, there is another point of view that should be taken into account for the determination of wages, the ethical and moral perspective. If the employer does not want to, or is not able to provide decent, fair and competitive wages, this can be regarded as short-term abuse and a lack of respect from superiors for the worker, which is what happens in most of the countries in the region.

Trends in Mexico's labour market

Flores (2015) argues that the changes being made under labour reform in relation to employment and wages in Mexico should be deep, because in recent years (2006–2014), the minimum wage has increased 28.06%, while the weighted price of the basic food basket was 125%. He also says that it is necessary to strengthen labour law to circumstances that it will face in the coming years as a nation, in order to combat poverty, strengthening the purchasing power of wages and reducing the gaps between the top earners and those who receive less.

Flores (2015) and Pérez (2014) indicate that the labour reform of 2012 being implemented in Mexico aims to improve productivity and competitiveness through the increased number of jobs, opening the door to work for young people, labour flexibility for recruitment, and modernity for everyone (Curiel 2013), but the need to achieve greater equity protection, and worker safety is ever more pressing.

Mexico's Federal Labor Law (FLL), in particular, imposes a number of obligations on business owners when an employment relationship with others is established. Among the mandatory compensation for the private sector (article 132) are aspects that include a Christmas (or year-end) bonus payment, social security (art. 472), mandated vacation periods (art. 76) and timely salary payments (art. 82).

The financial situation in Mexico remains quite difficult; there are currently a number of barriers to significant increases in salary, fringe benefits, or in the allocation of monetary bonuses for achieving results. This adds to complexity in terms of the healthy administration of employee rewards (Galetic and Nacinovic 2006; Scott et al. 2006).

In many Mexican organizations, managements have decided to use alternative payment schemes or 'payment differentiators', in order to maintain and achieve retention of a low-cost workforce. Among relatively inexpensive but innovative features are, for example, activities such as raffles and sweepstakes tickets that are included through social media for employees to attend concerts or special events focusing mainly on young people as well as custom design benefits for single or married employees, or benefits such as scholarships for children or recognition schemes for achieving some personal or professional goal. While nonmonetary in nature, these rewards, broadly defined, can have high impact on employee morale, retention and similar outcomes.

Generational change and competition for talented workers

Meister (2012) says that by 2020 more than 50% of people working in companies will be from "Generation Y", meaning those born between 1980 and 2000. By 2030, they will reach a total of 75% of the workforce; so it is important that companies know the characteristics of the new generations to achieve greater competitiveness in the labour market, to create offers and work environments suitable to achieve better attraction and retention (Golik 2013; Milkovich et al. 2014; Mulvey et al. 2002; Ng et al. 2010). In Mexico, the main challenge is to transform the old and obsolete businesses into attractive organizations for young talent.

Notable characteristics among young workers are that: (1) they were born in a digital age; and (2) their life does not revolve mainly around work; they demand time to engage in other activities (Gonzáles, 2011). Moreover, Boschma and Groen (2006) argue that authenticity, respect, personal development and honour are among the values that represent greater importance in the lives of this generation, besides being smarter, faster and more sociable, but, above all, interconnected in social networks.

It is essential to identify when designing compensation systems factors that have an effect on employees when making their decision to join or stay with an organization. HR managers need actionable information that helps them restructure their management plans and reduce important employment metrics such as levels of voluntary employee turnover (or 'quit rate'). A sample of 642 university students in Mexico[1] indicated that the expectations they have to work in a company are growth opportunities (mean = 4.54, SD = 0.81), salary (mean = 4.53, SD = 0.81), quality of work life (mean = 4.51, DS = 0.80), work environment (mean = 4.45, SD = 0.86) and challenging projects at work (mean = 4.44, SD = 0.81).

Increasingly, changes in the business environment and the speed with which information is disseminated are a major source of problems for the HR department. If HR fails to identify the characteristics and preferences of Millennials in the workplace, mainly because of inadequate processes, employees who meet a job search profile will simply go to a new employer (e.g., Boschma and Groen 2006; Ferri-Reed 2014; Golik 2013; Gonzáles 2011; Karsten et al. 2012; Meister 2012; Thompson and Gregory 2012). Madero et al. (2012) show that the reward mix (for definition see Chapman, this volume) in a sample of Mexican family businesses is made up of 74% base salary, 12% variable compensation, 9% benefits and 1% in stock options. A survey of 642 Mexican university students about their preferences and expectations of their reward mix produced the following results: 61% base salary, 15% variable compensation, 13% benefits and, finally, 11% in payment of stock options.

Balancing reward technical design and strategic aspiration

Like all organizational techniques, elements of employee reward were created to meet specific objectives (Scott et al. 2006; Scott et al. 2004; Galetic and Nacinovic 2006; Mulvey et al. 2000). However, if managers are to secure the investment in such initiatives it is logical to link them strategically: to the HRM and to the overall business goals of the employer. A host of writers, including Snell and Bohlander (2010), Bohlander et al (2018), Ellig (2002), Mulvey et al. (2002), Fay and Thompson (2001), Lawler (1995), Newman and Krystofiak (1998), Murray and Gerhart (1998), Milkovich and Milkovich (1992), and Werther et al. (2014), argue that the design of reward systems should have specific – strategically aligned – objectives. While historically in Mexico reward management was seen as an administrative function whose only purpose was transactional, paying people to work under the purview of corporate accounting systems, and to comply with labour and tax laws, there is evidence of change and not only in terms of the economic labour system reform changes being promoted by government. A recent study conducted in Mexico (Madero 2016) found that the main objective of reward management is to improve the results of the company (mean = 4.25, SD = 1.17). Promoting the effectiveness of the company (mean = 4.06, SD = 1.16) and motivating the performance of people (mean = 4.02, SD = 1.22) are the next main objectives. The findings indicate a reward management environment in which greater importance, in the perception of respondents who participated in the research, is being given to what may be counted as strategic considerations. Ensuring equality (mean = 3.53, SD = 1.17), retention of staff (mean = 3.89, SD = 1.13) and the acquisition of qualified candidates (mean = 3.90, SD = 1.15) are given less importance in that research, suggesting that change is somewhat narrowly directional than complete.

Wage inequality or gaps caused by the lack of emphasis on reward issues in organizations may be viewed as a source for many employee relations conflicts and related problems that arise in Mexican companies. Issues including, but not limited to turnover, absenteeism, distractions and accidents. Correlation between these and direct reward issues may be hypothesized because they are directly related to extrinsic motivation and employee satisfaction (Kopelman et al. 2008; Schwarz 1989), factors which in turn impact on the workplace environment.

Concern for the better utilization of resources, the need for greater social equality and the pursuit of economic growth have been increasing steadily. Various business practices have been adjusted in response to this trend, as indicated in commentary by Henriques and Sadorsky (2006), referring specifically to action in countries with emerging economies. The relevance of sustainability impacts a large number of sectors around the world (Henriques and Sadorsky, 1999). There are lessons here for Mexican employers, as well as a need for further systematic academic research to expose what is happening and what remains to be tackled.

Conclusion

Analysis from the World Economic Forum (2016), highlights the demand for Mexican organizations to increase their interest in human resources management, to enhance the treatment of workers as human beings, sensitized to the importance of justice, equality, dignity and respect for people, and so operate in ways that have implications for the whole of society.

One of the main strengths of sustainability in human resources is the alliance (engagement) that can be created between workers and their employer mainly due to the consistency of ideals and values (Kramar 2014; Albrecht 2012; Cañibano 2013; Jose and Mampilly 2012; Jackson et al. 2011). Organizations' image and reputation before society plays an important role in human processes. Companies conducting sustainable practices are more likely to generate feelings of identification among employees, and pride to be employed within a particular organization.

From this perspective, reward management means achieving organizational sustainability through the development of human resources policies, strategies and practices which also support the three pillars of sustainable development (Boxall 2003; Hsi-An et al. 2006; Theriou and Chatzoglou 2009). Regarding the evolution of human resource management, Freitas et al. (2011) and Gupta (2014), promote the need to be more strategic and give relevance to the human factor within the organization, helping people to achieve corporate objectives through integration between all areas of the organization, combining success through innovation, diversity and good environmental stewardship (Reihaneh et al. 2013) and development of sustainable behaviour and capacities.

Note

1 Using a survey with a 1–5 Likert scale, 1 is not important and 5 is very important.

References

Albrecht, S. L. (2012). The influence of job, team and organizational level resources on employee well-being, engagement, commitment and extra-role performance. *International Journal of Manpower.* 33(7), 840–853.

Bohlander, G., Snell, S., and Morris, S. (2018). *Administración de Recursos Humanos.* (17ª edición). México: D.F. Cengage Learning Editores.

Boschma J., and Groen, I. (2006). Generación Einstein: más listos, más rápidos y más sociables. Comunicarse con los jóvenes del siglo XXI, 89–112.   Available at: http://anele.org/jornadas_tecnicas/generatie_einsteinspaans_jeroen.pdf, accessed on June 29, 2018.

Boxall, P. (2003). HR strategy and competitive advantage in the service sector. *Human Resource Management Journal.* 13(3), 5–20.

Cañibano, A. (2013). Implementing innovative HRM: trade-off effects on employee well-being. *Management Decision*, 51(3), 643–660.

Curiel, S. V. (2013). La reforma a la Ley Federal del Trabajo en materia de subcontratación en México. *Alegatos.* 83. Enero–Abril.

Ellig, B. (2002). Executive compensation 101: considering the many elements. *WorldatWork Journal.* 11(1), 11–20.

Fay, C. H., and Thompson, M. A. (2001). Contextual determinants of reward systems' success: an exploratory study. *Human Resource Management.* 40(3), 213–226.

Ferri-Reed, J. (2014). Are millennial employees changing how managers manage? *The Journal for Quality & Participation.* 37(2), 15–35.

Flores, P. (2015). Reforma Laboral. *El Cotidiano.* 190. Marzo–Abril.

Freitas, W. R. D. S., Jabbour, C. J. C., and Santos, F. C. A. (2011). Continuing the evolution: towards sustainable HRM and sustainable organizations. *Business Strategy Series*, 12(5), 226–234.

Galetic, L., and Nacinovic, I. (2006). Compensation management in Croatian enterprises: an empirical study. *The Business Review.* 5(2), 204–212.

Golik, M. (2013). Las expectativas de equilibrio entre vida laboral y vida privada y las elecciones laborales de la nueva generación. *Cuadernos de Administración.* 26(46), 107–133.

Gonzáles, R. S. (2011). La incorporación de la Generación Y al mercado laboral. *Palermo Business Review.* 5, 67–93.

Gupta, S. (2014). Sustainability as a competitive advantage: An outcome of strategic HRM. *Review of HRM.* 3, 129–139.

Henriques, I., and Sadorsky, P. (2006). The adoption of environmental management practices in a transition economy. *Comparative Economic Studies.* 48, 641–661.

Henriques, I., and Sadorsky, P. (1999). The relationship between environmental commitment and managerial perceptions of stakeholders importance. *Academy of Management Journal.* 42(1), 87–99.

Hsi-An Shih, Yun-Hwa Chiang, and Chu-Chun, H. (2006). Can high performance work systems really lead to better performance? *International Journal of Manpower.* 27(8), 741–763.

Jackson, S., Renwick, D., Jabbour, C., and Muller-Camen, M. (2011). State-of-the-art and future directions for green human resource management: introduction to the Special Issue. *German Journal of Research in Human Resource Management.* 25(2), 99–116.

Jose, G., and Mampilly, S. R. (2012). Satisfaction with HR practices and employee engagement: a social exchange perspective. *Journal of Economics and Behavioral Studies.* 4(7), 423–430.

Karsten, J., Stephanie, W., and Rafael, M. (2012). Cómo gestionar a los nativos digitales. *Capital Humano.* 266, 60–65.

Kopelman, R. E., Prottas, D. J., and Davis, A. L. (2008). Douglas McGregor's Theory X and Y: toward a construct-valid measure. *Journal of Managerial Issues.* 20(2), 255–271.

Kramar, R. (2014). Beyond strategic human resource management: is sustainable human resource management the next approach?. . . *International Journal of Human Resource Management.* 25(February 2015), 1069–1089.

Lawler, E. (1995). The new pay: a strategic approach. *Compensation and Benefits Review.* 27(4), 14–22.

Lawler, E., and Mohrman, S. A. (2003). HR as a strategic partner: what does it take to make it happen? *HR. Human Resource Planning.* 26(3).

Madero, S. M. (2016). Impacto de los objetivos de la administración de compensaciones en los elementos de la compensación monetaria y no monetaria. *Investigación Administrativa.* 45(117), 38–51.

Madero, S.M., Trevinyo, R.N. and Avendaño, J. (2012). Compensaciones en la empresa familiar Mexicana: sus componentes, herramientas de apoyo y criterios de efectividad. *Revista Internacional Administración & Finanzas.* 5(5), 41–56.

Meister, J. (2012). *Three Reasons You Need To Adopt A Millennial Mindset Regardless Of Your Age.* Available at: http://www.forbes.com/sites/jeannemeister/2012/10/05/millennialmindse/, accessed on June 28, 2018.

Milkovich, G. T., Newman, J. and Gerhart, B. (2014). *Compensation* (11ª edición). New York: McGraw Hill.

Milkovich, G., and Milkovich, C. (1992). Strengthening the pay–performance relationship: the research. *Compensation and Benefits Review.* 24(6), 53–62.

Mulvey, P. W., LeBlanc, P. V., Heneman, R. L., and McInerney, M. (2002). Study finds that knowledge of pay process can beat out amount of pay in employee retention, organizational effectiveness. *Journal of Organizational Excellence.* 21(4), 29–42.

Mulvey, P. W., Ledford Jr., G. E., and LeBlanc, P. V. (2000). Rewards of work: how they drive performance, retention and satisfaction. *WorldatWork Journal.* 9(3), 6.

Murray, B., and Gerhart, B. (1998). An empirical analysis of a skill-based pay program and plant performance outcome. *Academy of Management Journal.* 41(1), 68–78.

Newman, J. M., and Krystofiak, F. J. (1998). Value-chain compensation. *Compensation and Benefits Review.* 30(3), 60–66.

Ng, E.S.W., Schweitzer, L. and Lyons, S.T. (2010). New generation, great expectations: a field study of the millennial generation. *Journal of Business Psychology.* 25, 281–292.

Pérez, P. G. (2014). La Ley Federal del Trabajo: crónica de una reforma anunciada. *El Cotidiano.* 184. Marzo–Abril.

Reihaneh, M. S., Rosmini, O., Kunio, I., and de Sao Pedro, F. F. (2013), Embracing green technology innovation through strategic human resource management: a case of an automotive company. *American Journal of Economics and Business Administration.* 5(2), 65–73.

Scott, D., McMullen, T. D., and Sperling R. S. (2006). Evaluating pay program effectiveness: a national survey of compensation professionals. *WorldatWork Journal.* 15(3), 47–53.

Scott, D., McMullen, T. D., Wallace, M., and Morajda, D. (2004). Annual cash incentives for managerial and professional employees. *Worldatwork Journal.* 13(4), 6–15.

Schwarz, R. (1989). Participative decision making. Comparing union-management and management designed incentive pay programs. *Group & Organization Management.* 14(1), 104–122.

Snell, S. and Bohlander, G. (2010). *Principles of Human Resource Management.* Canada: Cengage Learning.

Theriou, G. N., and Chatzoglou, P. D. (2009). Exploring the best HRM practices–performance relationship: An empirical approach. *Journal of Workplace Learning.* 21(8), 614–646.

Thompson, C., and Gregory, J. B. (2012). Managing millennials: a framework for improving attraction, motivation and retention. *The Psychologist-Manager Journal.* 15(4), 237–246.

Ulrich, D. (2007). The new HR organization. *Workforce Management.* 86(21), 40–42, 44.

Ulrich, D., Younger, J., Brockbank, W., and Ulrich, M. (2012). HR talent and the new HR competencies. *Strategic HR Review.* 11(4), 217–222.

Vosburgh, R. (2007). The evolution of HR as an internal consulting organization. *Human Resource Planning.* 30(3), 11–16, 18–23.

Werther, W., Davis, K., and Guzmán, P. (2014). *Administración de Recursos Humanos.* (7ª edición) Mexico: McGraw Hill.

World Economic Forum. (2016). *Global Competitiveness Report 2015–2016* Available at: www.reports. weforum.org/global-competitiveness-report2015-2016/, accessed on March 14, 2016.

37

REWARDS IN EUROPEAN TRANSITION STATES

Ihar Sahakiants and Marion Festing

Introduction

Since the fall of state-socialist regimes more than two decades ago, European transition states have been at the centre of investigations by scholars in various fields of economics and management (Flanagan 1998; Peng and Heath 1996, to name a few). Especially important in the context of the ongoing institutional transformation in the region (Flanagan 1998; Newman 2000) is the issue of the development of industrial and employment relations (Aguilera and Dabu 2005; Martin and Cristescu-Martin 2006) and – more specifically – human resource management (HRM) practices in these countries (Morley et al. 2009; Ross 2006; Zupan and Kaše 2005). Here, hardly any other HRM activity has undergone such a deep transformation during the transition period than rewards and, even more precisely, compensation and benefits. While the latter include monetary incentives such as base pay, short- and long-term variable compensation and benefits, the notion of rewards also points to the importance of other non-cash elements, including intrinsic incentives (Sahakiants et al. 2018).

The rewards provided to employees in this region are nowadays guided by market logic as opposed to the predominant[1] central planning and welfare philosophy in state-socialist economies (Festing and Sahakiants 2010, 2013; Sahakiants et al. 2016), and local enterprises often adopt pay configurations which are novel for their institutional environments (Festing and Sahakiants 2011; Sahakiants and Festing forthcoming). The historically determined idiosyncrasies of local compensation and benefits systems become especially obvious when multinationals from developed countries design reward practices in subsidiaries operating in post-state-socialist countries (Festing and Sahakiants 2013; Grill et al. 2016).

This chapter provides an overview of the extant research on the history and current developments related to rewards in European transition states, as well as some projections about possible future advances. We start with a discussion on pre-transformation reward systems by focusing on the theoretical concept of path dependence, which explains the historical embeddedness of organizational practices, policies and systems. This view is instrumental in understanding the specifics of the current reward configurations in firms operating in this region, which we present in the next section. Thereafter, by linking our discussion to the evolution of corporate governance in European transition states, we analyse the current state and trends related to executive compensation in the region. This is followed by a conclusion outlining avenues for future research.

Historical development of rewards in the region

The academic interest in organizational practices, including rewards, in today's European transition states (see, for instance, Prasad 1966; Richman 1963, for examples of discussions of employment practices in Czechoslovakia and the Soviet Union) dates back to long before economic, political and social reforms in the Soviet Union were introduced in the mid-1980s. According to Pridham and Vanhanen (1994), these reforms, which are often referred to by using the Russian word *Perestroika*, served as a catalyst of change in the state-socialist countries of that time. These and later pieces of research (Adam 1984, 1987; Altmann 1987; Fallenbuchl 1987; Gramatzki 1988) provided valuable overviews of the particular organization of enterprises, employment relations and incentive systems in European transition economies. According to the terminology used by the International Monetary Fund (Roaf et al. 2014), this region is referred to as Central and Eastern Europe (CEE) and includes post-state-socialist Central European countries, the former republics of the Soviet Union (including the Baltic states) and Southeastern European countries such as Bulgaria, Romania and Albania as well as the states created after the dissolution of Yugoslavia.

One of the central features of the pre-transformation economies of European transition states, albeit with some exceptions (e.g., the former Yugoslavia as mentioned above), was the central planning system built following the example of the Soviet Union (Adam 1984). This system included central wage planning, whereby company-level labour and wage departments administered compensation in accordance with nationwide rules and tariffs, while personnel departments were responsible mainly for personnel records and any remaining administrative functions (Koubek and Brewster 1995; Shulzhenko 2012). Such a system was a strong constraint to rewarding individual effort and using pay as a means to attract and retain employees in line with the sorting effects of pay (Milkovich et al. 2014). As a result, a number of additional incentives on top of centrally planned wages were offered to employees, above all promotion opportunities, regular bonuses and various perquisites and benefits (Adam 1984; Flanagan 1998; Pearce et al. 1994; Poór 2009), which Gramatzki (1988) described in his overview on employment policies in the USSR as "ways to decentralize wage policy" (p. 254). These incentives and benefits, such as housing, were used by enterprise managers to attract and retain a skilled workforce, which resulted in low employee mobility – a feature still observed in CEE countries (Festing and Sahakiants 2013; Shulzhenko 2012). An important role in the distribution of benefits was played in centrally planned economies by socialist trade unions, which in fact did not participate in collective bargaining and thus wage determination (Aguilera and Dabu 2005; Flanagan 1998; Trif 2007).

In the 1990s, after the fall of the state-socialist regimes, there was increased interest in employment practices in European transition states. This was motivated by the necessity to reorganize former or current state-owned enterprises, the growth of the private sector and foreign direct investment in countries in the region in view of the deep political, social and economic transformation of local institutions (Flanagan 1998; Hegewisch et al. 1996; Koubek and Brewster 1995; Pearce et al. 1994). Following the logic of those studies, in order to understand the specifics of rewards in European transition states, it is necessary to consider the unique historical developments in these countries in their evolution from state-socialist regimes to political democracies and capitalist economies (Morley et al. 2016). One of the important features of the emerging business systems was their segmented character, as suggested by Martin (2008), who, based on the example of Hungary, identified four groups of companies – state, privatized, de novo (private companies established during the transformation period) and international. As suggested by Festing and Sahakiants (2010), these enterprises differ from each other with respect to their embeddedness in former state-socialist organizational systems.

While discussing change processes in European transition states, some researchers have described the transformation in these countries as 'path-dependent', in order to underscore their embeddedness in pre-transformation systems, policies and practices (Czaban et al. 2003; Whitley and Czaban 1998). Applied to compensation and benefits systems in European transition state companies, Festing and Sahakiants (2010, 2013) suggested that the concept of organizational path dependence, defined by Sydow et al. (2009:696) as a "rigidified, potentially inefficient action pattern built up by the unintended consequences of former decisions and positive feedback processes", is a useful tool with which to analyse reasons behind the continuity of pre-transformation practices and to design ways of overcoming organizational inertia. In our subsequent discussion on current developments with respect to compensation and benefits in European transition states, we will refer to this theoretical perspective as one of the explanations for the described specifics.

Current developments

Currently, two main issues dominate the reward-related discussions in European transition states: the development of wage levels, including the question of the convergence of the analysed countries with developed European economies, and the specifics of reward packages provided by organizations in the region.

The issue of pay level convergence has been discussed often, mainly with respect to European transition states that are currently members of the European Union (EU). There are significant differences in economic conditions (Festing and Sahakiants 2010) and pay levels within member states. Recent data show that although wages in the majority of post-state-socialist countries are lower than in many developed EU economies, median gross hourly earnings in states such as Slovenia, Estonia or the Czech Republic are roughly comparable or exceed those in some older EU members nations such as Portugal, for example (Eurostat 2017). Wage increases in European transition states have been stimulated, to a large extent, by increases in mandatory minimum wages, which have grown faster in the majority of cases than the average wage in these countries (International Monetary Fund 2016). Furthermore, between 2010 and 2017, minimum wages in new EU member states increased faster in real terms than in older EU member nations, with real minimum wage increases in Bulgaria and Romania amounting up to around 80% (Eurofound 2017). Thus, if this trend continues, a further convergence of wage levels within the European Union could be expected.

To date, one specificity of reward systems in European transition states has been the frequent use of benefits, ranging from additional paid days of leave to private pension schemes (Berber and Štangl-Šušnjar 2013; Festing and Sahakiants 2013), with meal vouchers being amongst the most frequently used examples (Aldea 2015). Although fringe benefits are quite widespread in many other countries, such as Belgium or France, benefits in a good number of European transition states, in many cases, are quite specific to the region and resemble pre-transformation practices, such as giving employees gift baskets for Christmas or tickets for cultural events (Eurofound 2016). In their study of remuneration systems in the subsidiaries of a multinational enterprise (MNE) in Poland, Hungary and the Czech Republic, Festing and Sahakiants (2013) showed that benefits provided in former state-owned companies could be seen as good examples of organizational path dependence. This path dependence is sustained by the persistent role of trade unions as distributors of social benefits and statutory regulations, as in the example of enterprise social benefits funds in Poland (see also Eurofound 2016), which are mandatory in Polish companies employing more than twenty persons. Although benefits provided to employees from social funds during the state-socialist period were different from those offered today, this feature can be seen as an example of organizational continuity in the region (Festing and Sahakiants 2013).

Evidence on the use of pay-for-performance (PfP) schemes in European transition states is mixed. On the one hand, European comparisons of reward systems show a relatively high prevalence of PfP in European transition states, especially in Lithuania, the Czech Republic and Estonia (Eurofound 2014, 2016). According to these statistics, organizations operating in CEE often implement variable pay schemes, and many countries in the region lead Europe with respect to the percentage of companies implementing team-based PfP (Estonia), variable pay schemes based on individual performance (the Czech Republic) or profit-sharing schemes (Slovenia). While these data may seem surprising in view of the state-socialist past of the abovementioned countries, Sahakiants et al. (2016) suggested that this could also be regarded as an indicator of the path dependence of compensation practices. In particular, the frequent use of pay-for-performance schemes in European transition states could be related to the tradition of piece-rate pay systems, used frequently during the pre-transformation period by manufacturing enterprises, and the reliance on bonuses to increase the state-controlled tariffs mentioned above. Indeed, Festing and Sahakiants (2013) showed that there are still instances where variable pay is perceived by employees as a form of guaranteed pay, though in some cases it acts as a reverse incentive (i.e., when guaranteed bonuses are decreased or not provided, due to underperformance). Shulzhenko (2012) showed that a bonus system based on so-called 'coefficient of labour partici-pation', used by enterprises under central planning, was still utilized frequently by contemporary Russian companies. Within such a system, bonuses are allocated to the whole team, and the individual performance of team members is rewarded according to preset coefficients, including a zero coefficient in the case of underperformance, which normally results in no bonus. This suggested path dependence, in some cases, implies a lack of effectiveness of such compensation schemes. For instance, extant research on European transition states indicates a lack of alignment between incentive schemes provided by companies operating in the region and existing per-formance management systems (Rejc Buhovac and Zaman Groff 2012), which can also be explained by a lack of experience in this field prior to transformation (Morley et al. 2016).

At present, there is a lack of concrete evidence on the use of share-based compensation schemes in European transition states. Overall, European surveys indicate large variations between the EU member states in the percentages of companies implementing share ownership schemes (Lowitzsch and Hashi 2014). However, although Festing and Sahakiants (2011) showed that share-based pay is a quite frequently used type of executive reward in major publicly traded companies in a number of European transition states, evidence of providing such compensation schemes to employees below top and middle managerial level is still scarce. One of the most challenging issues is the development of executive compensation in CEE countries in light of current discussions and legislative initiatives in large industrialized countries, which are, for instance, related to prohibiting certain compensation elements – as in the case of Switzerland (Sahakiants and Festing 2014) – or to strengthening further shareholders' roles in shaping executive remuneration policy (for a discussion in the UK, see The Department for Business 2016). In the subsequent section, we discuss the issue of directors' remuneration, including share-based pay, in European transition states in light of corporate governance specificities in these countries.

Corporate governance and executive pay in European transition states

The topic of executive compensation in European transition states has seen relatively low interest, especially compared to intensive discussions about excessive top managers' pay in developed countries in the wake of the recent financial crisis. A possible reason for this may be that executive pay levels in the CEE countries are still much lower than in the USA and other world-leading economies. For instance, according to a recent international ranking of CEO compensation conducted by Bloomberg (Lu and Melin 2016), executive pay level in Poland, the only European post-state-socialist country included in the list, was much lower than in the analysed developed economies and well below the average. Even within this country, as shown by Słomka-Gołębiowska and Urbanek (2016) in their study of CEO pay in Polish banks, host-country executives were paid less than their foreign counterparts employed by banks operating in Poland.

Corporate governance systems in European transition states were created after the fall of state-socialist regimes based on different models. Some countries chose the one-tier corporate governance model similar to US-American boards of directors, while other states implemented a two-tier board system similar to that in Germany or Austria, where supervisory boards oversee the activities of management boards (Festing et al. 2011). However, previous research has provided evidence that CEE countries display common challenges related to the weak protection of shareholders' rights or highly concentrated ownership (Berglöf and Pajuste 2003), which are also common features of a wider range of so-called 'emerging' markets (Young et al. 2008). In line with these insights, Sahakiants and Festing (forthcoming) proposed in their study of executive share-based pay in Polish publicly traded companies that when analysing CEO compensation in European transition states, it is useful to consider the dominance of principal–principal conflicts (Young et al. 2008), which take place between controlling and minority shareholders. The authors argued that due to the control exerted by majority shareholders over senior managers in this case, controlling principals (shareholders) rely to a lesser extent on financial incentives, including share-based compensation, than suggested by the standard principal–agent theory (Jensen and Meckling 1976; Jensen and Murphy 1990).

The impact of EU legislation

An important barrier to research on executive pay in European transition countries is the lack of transparency in directors' compensation, even though Central and Eastern EU member states are affected to a large extent by EU acts promoting the disclosure of CEO compensation, such as the *Recommendation of 14 December 2004 on fostering an appropriate regime for the remuneration of directors of listed companies (2004/913/EC)* or the *Commission Recommendation of 30 April 2009 as regards the regime for the remuneration of directors of listed companies (2009/385/EC)*. For instance, Festing et al. (2011) showed that executive remuneration disclosure standards among European transition states differed to a significant extent, with the highest level of transparency among analysed countries provided by Polish enterprises.

However, the impact of EU legislation on compensation schemes implemented in EU member states is not limited to acts promoting the transparency of directors' pay. At the time of preparing this chapter, on March 14, 2017, the European Parliament approved the *Proposal for a Directive of the European Parliament and of the Council amending Directive 2007/36/EC as regards the encouragement of long-term shareholder engagement and Directive 2013/34/EU as regards certain elements of the corporate governance statement* (EUR-Lex 2017; European Parliament 2017). This directive should strengthen so-called 'say-on-pay' rights, i.e., voting on a remuneration policy for company directors.

The impact of national legislation – the case of Poland

The relatively high disclosure standards in Polish listed enterprises were probably one reason why executive pay in this country has been studied quite extensively recently. One of the specificities of CEO pay administration in Poland is the existence of pay limitations for executives in companies predominantly owned by the state. For instance, the consolidated annual report for 2016 for Lotos Group, a leading Polish oil company, 53.19% of whose shares were owned as of December 22, 2016 by the state, stated that the compensation of the management board in 2016 was governed by a number of laws: The "Act on Remunerating Persons Who Manage Certain Legal Entities, dated April 10th 2000" and the "Act on Rules of Remunerating Persons Who Manage Certain Companies, dated June 9th 2016" (Grupa Lotos, 2017:133). Pursuant to the above regulations, "the monthly remuneration of Members of the Management Board of Grupa LOTOS S.A. was computed as six times the average monthly salary in the business sector, net of annual bonuses. . . [and] Members of the Management Board of Grupa LOTOS S.A. may be awarded an annual bonus for the previous year of not more than threefold their average monthly salary in the preceding year" (ibid., pp. 133–134).

A further example of laws in Poland related to executive pay configurations is the *Polish Financial Supervision Authority Resolution No. 258/2011* of October 4, 2011, according to which 50%, or a larger part, of variable pay should be provided in the form of long-term incentives, such as company shares (Polish Financial Supervision Authority, n.d.). For instance, the Capital Adequacy, Risk and Remuneration Policy Report of Bank Millennium Capital Group for 2016 specifically mentions this resolution as the act governing its compensation policy (Bank Millennium Capital Group 2017).

The impact of MNEs

Executive remuneration in CEE is also shaped by MNEs that may set higher pay rates for their executives in European transition states and transfer their parent-country pay models to subsidiaries operating in countries in the region. For instance, in their study of executive remuneration in Polish banks, Słomka-Gołębiowska and Urbanek (2016) showed that executives in Polish subsidiaries of foreign banks, especially stemming from Southern and Northern Europe, receive higher compensation than those employed in the remaining banking institutions. This can be interpreted as an indicator of the segmented character of post-state-socialist capitalism discussed above (Martin 2006, 2008). The influence of foreign parent companies on CEO compensation schemes in their subsidiaries in European transition states was also discussed by Festing and Sahakiants (2011), who showed that MNCs often transfer their parent-country equity-based compensation schemes to their companies operating in Poland, Hungary and the Czech Republic.

Conclusion

Whilst in this chapter we have discussed a number of common features related to the developmental paths and current status of rewards in European transition states, we also acknowledge the existence of differences between the countries determined by individual, organizational or environmental factors. Examples of such differences are the historical distinction between the decentralized economic system in the former Yugoslavia and the central planning system of the Soviet Union and its satellite states (Bandelj 2008). Furthermore, there is evidence of a particular remuneration system in contemporary Russia, where wages and salaries in many cases are increased or decreased at will by company managers or owners, and where the related phenomenon of wage arrears has often happened at the times of economic instability or crisis (for an overview, see Shulzhenko 2012). Another example of differences concerns illegal pay practices, or so-called 'envelope wages', in post-state-socialist countries (Shulzhenko 2012;

Williams 2008), depending on the stance of local governments on this issue or the perceived legitimacy of the state (Festing and Sahakiants 2010).

Overall, given the increased level of integration of European transition states into the global economy, the impact of international standards and regulations on compensation and benefits configurations, especially in the form of the EU acts discussed above, it is expected that pay systems and practices in post-state-socialist states will gradually lose their historically determined specifics and rather reflect regional or global trends.

To conclude, the currently available research and knowledge about rewards in European transition states is still scarce and fragmented, which provides important and wide-ranging opportunities for future research. In terms of country-specific information, we have shown that a lot of research is available for some countries in the region (e.g., with respect to executive compensation in Poland), but less so on rewards in other European transition states. We lack both descriptive data on and explanations for the specificities of reward systems in these countries. For example, it would be interesting to know more about the corporate governance systems in these states and their impact on pay elements provided for different target groups of employees (of various hierarchical levels and in different industries). Pointing towards comparative research, it would be important to investigate systematically not only the common features of reward systems in the CEE region, but also their differences, especially as compared to other emerging countries and to more developed states. With respect to the various reward practices, it seems that non-cash rewards as elements of total reward systems are particularly under-researched. Based on further knowledge in these areas, studies about the behavioural and performance impacts of reward practices could be conducted. Overall, the abovementioned potential areas of study are just a few of the many fruitful avenues for future research on rewards in European transition states which can further contribute to the understanding of this field from both practitioner and academic standpoints.

Note

1 The former Yugoslavia did not follow the central planning system typical of the Soviet Union, but adopted a decentralized economic model, with workers' self-management as its particular feature (Bandelj 2008).

References

Adam, J. (1984). *Employment and Wage Policies in Poland, Czechoslovakia and Hungary since 1950*. London: Macmillan.

Adam, J. (1987). Similarities and differences in the treatment of labour shortages. In Adam, J. (ed.). *Employment Policies in the Soviet Union and Eastern Europe* (pp. 127–148). London and Basingstoke: Macmillan.

Aguilera, R. V. and Dabu, A. (2005). Transformation of employment relations systems in central and Eastern Europe. *Journal of Industrial Relations*. 47(1), 16–42.

Aldea, B. (2015). The compensation and benefits system: private companies vs. budgetary system. *European Review Of Applied Sociology*. 8(11), 31–39.

Altmann, F.-L. (1987). Employment policies in Czechoslovakia. In Adam, J. (ed.). *Employment Policies in the Soviet Union and Eastern Europe* (pp. 78–102). London and Basingstoke: Macmillan.

Bandelj, N. (2008). *From Communists to Foreign Capitalists: The Social Foundations of Foreign Direct Investment in Postsocialist Europe*. Princeton: Princeton University Press.

Bank Millennium Capital Group. (2017). *Capital Adequacy, Risk, Remuneration Policy Report of Bank Millennium Capital Group as at 31 December 2016*. Available at: www.bankmillennium.pl/documents/10184/ 25852145/Information+on+risk%2C+capital+and+remuneration+policy+of+Bank+Millennium +in+2016.pdf/8922d426-768e-4a43-9c6a-6425134f3a99, accessed on March 4, 2017.

Berber, N. and Štangl-Šušnjar, G. (2013). Comparative analysis of workers' compensations in Serbia and Central-Eastern Europe countries. *Managerial Challenges of the Contemporary Society*. 5, 25–30.

Berglöf, E. and Pajuste, A. (2003). Emerging owners, eclipsing markets? Corporate Governance in Central and Eastern Europe. In Cornelius, P. K. and Kogut, B. (eds.). *Corporate Governance and Capital Flows in a Global Economy* (pp. 267–302). Oxford: Oxford University Press.

Czaban, L., Hocevar, M., Jaklic, M. and Whitley, R. (2003). Path dependence and contractual relations in emergent capitalism: contrasting state socialist legacies and inter-firm cooperation in Hungary and Slovenia. *Organization Studies*. 24(1), 7–28.

EUR-Lex. (2017). *Procedure 2014/0121/COD*. Available at: www.eur-lex.europa.eu/legal-content/EN/HIS/?uri=COM:2014:213:FIN#2017-03-14_OPI_R1_byEP, accessed on March 17, 2017.

Eurofound. (2014). *European Company Survey 2013*. Available at: www.eurofound.europa.eu/surveys/ecs/2013/, accessed on June 23, 2014.

Eurofound. (2016). *Changes in Remuneration and Reward Systems*. Luxembourg: Publications Office of the European Union.

Eurofound. (2017). *Statutory Minimum Wages in the EU 2017*. Available at: https://www.eurofound.europa.eu/sites/default/files/ef1703en.pdf, accessed on March 10, 2017.

European Parliament. (2017). *Stronger Rights for Shareholders in EU Companies*. Available at: www.europarl.europa.eu/news/en/news-room/20170308IPR65673/stronger-rights-for-shareholders-in-eu-companies, accessed on March 14, 2017.

Eurostat. (2017). *Wages and Labour Costs*. Available at: www.ec.europa.eu/eurostat/statistics-explained/index.php/Wages_and_labour_costs, accessed on March 11, 2017.

Fallenbuchl, Z. M. (1987). Employment policies in Poland. In Adam, J. (ed.). *Employment Policies in the Soviet Union and Eastern Europe* (pp. 27–54). London and Basingstoke: Macmillan.

Festing, M. and Sahakiants, I. (2010). Compensation practices in central and Eastern European EU member states – an analytical framework based on institutional perspectives, path dependencies, and efficiency considerations. *Thunderbird International Business Review*. 52(3), 203–216.

Festing, M. and Sahakiants, I. (2011). Determinants of share-based compensation plans in Central and Eastern European public companies: an institutional analysis. *Journal for East European Management Studies*. 16(4), 338–357.

Festing, M. and Sahakiants, I. (2013). Path-dependent evolution of compensation systems in Central and Eastern Europe: a case study of multinational corporation subsidiaries in the Czech Republic, Poland and Hungary. *European Management Journal*. 31(4), 373–389.

Festing, M., Sahakiants, I., von Preen, A. and Smid, M. (2011). *Directors' Remuneration in the Czech Republic, Hungary, Poland, Romania, Russia and Slovakia. Companies Composing Major Stock Exchange Indices*. Gummersbach: Kienbaum Management Consultants GmbH.

Flanagan, R. J. (1998). Institutional reformation in Eastern Europe. *Industrial Relations*. 37(3), 337–357.

Gramatzki, H.-E. (1988). Employment policy in the USSR. In Dlugos, G., Dorow, W. and Weiermair, K. (eds.), *Management Under Differing Labour Market and Employment Systems*. Berlin: Walter de Gruyter.

Grill, T. V., Maharjan, M. P. and Sekiguchi, T. (2016). Human resource management of Japanese companies in Hungary: how do Japanese and Hungarian styles blend? *Journal of East–West Business*. 22(3), 145–167.

Grupa Lotos S. A. (2017). *Consolidated Annual Report of LOTOS Group 2016*. Available at: www.inwestor.lotos.pl/repository/48674/en/, accessed on March 13, 2017.

Hegewisch, A., Brewster, C. and Koubek, J. (1996). Different roads: changes in industrial and employee relations in the Czech Republic and East Germany since 1989. *Industrial Relations Journal*. 27(1), 50.

International Monetary Fund. (2016). Central, Eastern, and Southeastern Europe: How to Get Back on the Fast Track. Available at: www.imf.org/external/pubs/ft/reo/2016/eur/eng/pdf/rei0516.pdf, accessed on March 10, 2017.

Jensen, M. C. and Meckling, W. H. (1976). Theory of the firm: managerial behavior, agency costs and ownership structure. *Journal of Financial Economics*. 3(4), 305–360.

Jensen, M. C. and Murphy, K. J. (1990). CEO incentives – it's not how much you pay, but how. *Harvard Business Review*. 68(3), 138–149.

Koubek, J. and Brewster, C. (1995). Human resource management in turbulent times: HRM in the Czech Republic. *International Journal of Human Resource Management*. 6(2), 223–247.

Lowitzsch, J. and Hashi, I. (2014). *The Promotion of Employee Ownership and Participation*. Available at: www.ec.europa.eu/internal_market/company/docs/modern/141028-study-for-dg-markt_en.pdf, accessed on March 11, 2017.

Lu, W. and Melin, A. (2016). *The Best and Worst Countries to Be a Rich CEO.* Available at: www.bloomberg.com/news/articles/2016-11-16/ranking-where-to-work-to-be-a-rich-ceo-or-richer-than-neighbors, accessed on March 12, 2017.

Martin, R. (2006). Segmented employment relations: post-socialist managerial capitalism and employment relations in Central and Eastern Europe. *International Journal of Human Resource Management.* 17(8), 1353–1365.

Martin, R. (2008). Post-socialist segmented capitalism: the case of Hungary: developing business systems theory. *Human Relations.* 61(1), 131–159.

Martin, R. and Cristescu-Martin, A. M. (2006). Industrial relations in Central and Eastern Europe. In Morley, M. J., Gunnigle, P. and Collings, D. G. (eds.). *Global Industrial Relations.* London: Routledge.

Milkovich, G. T., Newman, J. M. and Gerhart, B. (2014). *Compensation* (11th ed.). New York: McGraw-Hill.

Morley, M., Heraty, N. and Michailova, S. (2009). *Managing Human Resources in Central and Eastern Europe.* London: Routledge.

Morley, M., Poór, J., Heraty, N., Alas, R. and Pocztowski, A. (2016). Developments in Human Resource Management in Central and Eastern Europe in Comparative Perspective. In Dickmann, M., Brewster, C. and Sparrow, P. (eds.). *International Human Resource Management: Contemporary Human Resource Issues in Europe* (3rd ed., pp. 73–99). New York and London: Routledge.

Newman, K. L. (2000). Organizational transformation during institutional upheaval. *Academy of Management Review.* 25(3), 602–619.

Pearce, J. L., Branyiczki, I. and Bakacsi, G. (1994). Person-based reward systems: a theory of organizational reward practices in reform-communist organizations. *Journal of Organizational Behavior.* 15(3), 261–282.

Peng, M. W. and Heath, P. S. (1996). The growth of the firm in planned economies in transition: institutions, organizations, and strategic choice. *Academy of Management Review.* 21(2), 492–528.

Poór, J. (2009). Managing Human Resources in Hungary. In Morley, M. J., Heraty, N. and Michailova, S. (eds.). *Managing Human Resources in Central and Eastern Europe* (pp. 188–218). London: Routledge.

Prasad, S. B. (1966). New managerialism in Czechoslovakia and the Soviet Union. *The Academy of Management Journal.* 9(4), 328–336.

Pridham, G. and Vanhanen, T. (1994). *Democratization in Eastern Europe: Domestic and International Perspectives.* London; New York: Routledge.

Rejc Buhovac, A. and Zaman Groff, M. (2012). Contemporary performance measurement systems in Central and Eastern Europe: a synthesis of the empirical literature. *Journal for East European Management Studies.* 17(1), 68–103.

Richman, B. M. (1963). I. Managerial motivation in Soviet and Czechoslovak industries: a comparison. *The Academy of Management Journal.* 6(2), 107–128.

Roaf, J., Atoyan, R., Joshi, B., Krogulski, K. and an IMF Staff Team. (2014). *25 Years of Transition: Post-communist Europe and the IMF.* Washington, DC: International Monetary Fund.

Ross, P. (2006). Management strategies in transitional economies: organizational restructuring and employment relations (ER) at Cesky Telecom. *Employee Relations.* 28(2), 184–200.

Sahakiants, I. and Festing, M. (2014). *The Minder Initiative and Executive Pay Narratives in Germany and Russia: Cases of Path Dependence?* (ESCP Europe Working Paper No. 64). Berlin: ESCP Europe.

Sahakiants, I. and Festing, M. (forthcoming). The use of executive share-based compensation in Poland: investigating institutional and agency-based determinants in an emerging market. *The International Journal of Human Resource Management.*

Sahakiants, I., Festing, M., Engle, A. D. and Dowling, P. J. (2018). Comparative total rewards policies and practices. In Brewster, C., Mayrhofer, W. and Farndale, E. (eds.). *Handbook of Research on Comparative Human Resource Management* (2nd ed. pp. 143–163). Cheltenham: Edward Elgar Publishing.

Sahakiants, I., Festing, M. and Perkins, S. (2016). Pay-for-performance in Europe. In Dickmann, M., Brewster, C. and Sparrow, P. (eds.). *International Human Resource Management: A European Perspective* (3rd ed., pp. 354–374). London: Routledge.

Shulzhenko, E. (2012). Human resource management and industrial relations in post-transitional Russia. In Jürgens, U. (ed.). *Human Resource Management and Industrial Relations in the BRICs: a Review of the Research Literature* (pp. 63–102). Berlin: Logos Verlag.

Słomka-Gołębiowska, A. and Urbanek, P. (2016). Corporate boards, large blockholders and executive compensation in banks: evidence from Poland. *Emerging Markets Review.* 28, 203–220.

Sydow, J., Schreyögg, G. and Koch, J. (2009). Organizational path dependence: opening the black box. *Academy of Management Review.* 34(4), 689–709.

The Department for Business, Energy and Industrial Strategy (BEIS). (2016). Corporate Governance Reform. Green Paper. Available at: www.gov.uk/government/uploads/system/uploads/attachment_data/file/584013/corporate-governance-reform-green-paper.pdf, accessed on January 3, 2017.

Trif, A. (2007). Collective bargaining in Eastern Europe: case study evidence from Romania. *European Journal of Industrial Relations.* 13(2), 237–256.

Whitley, R. and Czaban, L. (1998). Institutional transformation and enterprise change in an emergent capitalist economy: the case of Hungary. *Organization Studies.* 19(2), 259–280.

Williams, C. C. (2008). Illegitimate wage practices in Eastern Europe: the case of 'envelope wages'. *Journal for East European Management Studies.* 13(3), 253–270.

Young, M. N., Peng, M. W., Ahlstrom, D., Bruton, G. D. and Jiang, Y. (2008). Corporate governance in emerging economies: a review of the principal–principal perspective. *Journal of Management Studies.* 45(1), 196–220.

Zupan, N. and Kaše, R. (2005). Strategic human resource management in European transition economies: building a conceptual model on the case of Slovenia. *International Journal of Human Resource Management.* 16(6), 882–906.

38

REWARD MANAGEMENT IN SMALL–MEDIUM KNOWLEDGE-INTENSIVE FIRMS

Evidence from Italy

Daria Sarti and Teresina Torre

Introduction

The aim of this chapter is to consider reward management in small and medium-sized enterprises (SMEs) with a specific focus on knowledge-intensive firms (KISs). Our interest towards SMEs with knowledge orientation is motivated by some reasons. One of them is, of course, the important role SMEs play in many countries (Acs et al. 1997). It is true that SMEs play an important role in economic development. Enterprises belonging to this dimensional class are relevant everywhere in terms of economic activity, employment, innovation and wealth creation (Acs et al. 1997; Katsikeas et al. 1998) and, in general, it underscores the belief that attention towards the small business sector embodies an important policy priority (Bell et al. 2004). Recent data indicate that in OECD economies, SMEs comprise 95% of private companies and, among them, 76% are working in the services industry (OECD 2014). Other estimates also suggest that SMEs account for 98.9% of the total number of businesses in China (Singh et al. 2009) and the trend is similar in many other countries of the world. With regard to Italy, we have to remember that there is a long tradition of studies on this group of enterprises (Ciambotti and Palazzi 2015; Corbetta and Montemerlo 1999; Corbetta 2000: Cortesi et al. 2012), which constitutes a large part of the national productive system. According to recent data, SMEs in Italy constitute 99.8% of the national productivity (ISTAT 2015).

Two main issues are critical and under-investigated in the current literature on SMEs. One is the importance of a qualified workforce for SMEs and of those organizational practices favouring the motivation of workers. Despite the significance of human capital and its engagement in SMEs, hardly any empirical research has been done on them (Behrends 2007; Bacon and Hoque 2005; Heneman et al. 2000; Michiels 2017). The other gap highlighted in the debate on SMEs is the prevailing focus on 'traditional' firms, while literature on 'knowledge-intensive' firms is scarce and the topic needs to be further investigated (Bell et al. 2004).

KIFs are firms in which the workforce is largely composed of well-educated and qualified employees and most work is intellectual in nature (Swart and Kinnie 2003; Alvesson 2000). Since the increasing relevance of knowledge in the present economy, KIFs are emerging as dominant and highly successful (Barney 1991; Grant 1997; Kogut and Zander 1992; Teece 2000;

Wright et al. 1994). This research is therefore aimed at investigating how small and medium-sized KIFs manage their human resources, since they constitute an important resource for their organizational success (Behrends 2007).

In an attempt to respond to the above calls, the elements that may favour the contribution of the workforce to the overall performance of both traditional and KIFs firms will be analysed. In this sense, this chapter investigates monetary and non-monetary rewards and their specific motivational roles in affecting employee behaviour. Research on reward management, applied mainly among large firms, stresses on the importance of non-monetary aspects of remuneration and suggests that knowledge workers are driven mainly by an intrinsic motivation (Frey and Stutzer 2006). At the same time, in managerial practice, non-monetary schemes are becoming increasingly popular while the efficacy of this kind of rewarding scheme has not yet been proven.

The purpose of this chapter is twofold: firstly, to understand if non-monetary reward practices prevail in KI-SMEs, and, secondly, to verify whether they are effective in spurring organizational performance or risk being a 'dangerous' fad.

To support our reasoning at the theoretical level, we provide evidence from a survey conducted on a sample of 95 SMEs in different industries in Italy. Results of a regression analysis show greater use of non-monetary incentives for firms with higher levels of knowledge intensity, compared to non-knowledge-intensive ones. Moreover, our results demonstrate that the overuse of non-monetary rewards may produce adverse effects. Some managerial actions are being proposed considering this outcome.

Rewarding practices in SMEs: exploring 'traditional' and 'knowledge-intensive' firms

Contributions in managerial literature highlight the peculiarities of SMEs when compared to large companies. It is suggested that SMEs are more flexible and innovative than larger ones and this is supposed to be attractive for workers in the dynamic context. At the same time, they are less inclined to adopt sophisticated and formal HR practices (Bacon and Hoque 2005; Michiels 2017) and are considered less appealing considering the difficulty they face in attracting and retaining talent (Carlson et al. 2006).

Further, it has been argued that 'because of their comparatively lesser endowment with material or financial resources, smaller businesses are often dependent on highly motivated and qualified workforce' (Behrends 2007). In this perspective, human resource management (HRM) is recognized as an important issue for SMEs (Bacon and Hoque 2005; Heneman et al. 2000). Several studies find, for example, that a skilled workforce represents an important source of innovation in SMEs (De Jong and Vermeulen 2006) and determines a firm's performance (e.g., Guest 1997; Gratton et al. 1999; Wood 1999; Becker et al. 2001).

The absence of a formal HRM approach in SMEs (Behrends 2007) is the result of insufficient knowledge. It can be claimed that 'relatively, little is understood regarding the HR-related needs, practices, behaviours and outcomes of smaller firms' (Hornsby and Kuratko 2003:74). Thus, further research is needed in this field (Bacon and Hoque 2005) not only in terms of overall HR practices but also for specific HR practices, such as compensation (Michiels 2017), which is traditionally considered the way 'to attract, motivate and retain people'. This is significant for SMEs (Cardon and Stevens 2004; Rutherford et al. 2003; Astrachan 2010; Heneman et al. 2000; Sels et al. 2006). Earlier literature (Behrends 2007) says that studies are often focused on SMEs operating in the so-called 'traditional' industries, while exploration of 'knowledge-intensive' industries is considered a relevant topic to be further investigated (Bell et al. 2004). This interest is also supported by the view that, for SMEs operating in knowledge-intensive sectors, human resource constitutes an important prerequisite for organizational success (Behrends 2007). So, it can be of interest, from academic, managerial and public policy perspectives, to deepen the experiences of 'knowledge-intensive' firms and of 'traditional' ones, to understand how their way of retaining such a critical workforce is appropriate (Lawler 2011; Markova and Ford 2011).

Despite the relevance, there has been relatively little research on HRM practices in these types of enterprises. The current study investigates the role of incentives in reward policies in an attempt to throw more light on such a relevant issue.

Monetary and non-monetary incentives: what are the implications in KI-SMEs?

The fundamental objectives of reward systems are to boost the achievement of goals owing to high performance and to attract and retain talent (Armstrong 2015). It is also to increase the amount of effort that employees put in to work in order to obtain a set of effective behaviours (Katz 1964; Weiner 1980) as desired by the organization. The most important of these are commitment, cooperation and performance.

According to the theory of 'organizational balance' (Barnard 1938; Simon 1947; March and Simon 1958), the decision of individuals to 'actively participate' in the organization is connected to "their activities in the organization contribute, directly or indirectly, to their individual purposes" (Simon 1947:181), which are different from one person to another. In order to understand Simon's indication, we need to focus on the popular taxonomy, introduced by Lawler (1973) and Deci (1975), who distinguish between extrinsic (i.e., monetary) and intrinsic (i.e., non-monetary) incentives. When individuals seek their reward in their external environment, using the work as an instrument (Dyer and Parker 1975), they appreciate extrinsic incentives. By contrast, the intrinsic incentives are associated with the contents of the task: So to say, the work is itself a 'reward'.

First, in the 1930s Barnard underlines the role of non-material incentives, referring to their importance in the fulfilment of a cooperative action in the organization (Barnard 1938). Later, in the 1990s, Pfeffer (1998) suggests that 'People do work for money — but they work even more for meaning in their lives . . . Companies that ignore this fact are essentially bribing their employees and will pay the price for lack of loyalty and commitment' (112).

Notwithstanding this position, many concerns have been expressed about the dominant role of money among reward schemes (Torre 2011). In fact, 'money has come to play an overly important role in our thinking about the causes of behaviour. In most companies, very limited time and effort are spent on considering non-monetary sources of motivation' (Gratton 2004:33).

In literature, there is a general agreement on the importance of total reward systems designed in order to facilitate the processes of knowledge diffusion and team-based work (Despres and Hiltrop 1995). Scholars widely recognize the importance of non-monetary incentives as facilitators of employees' engagement (Hulkko-Nyman et al. 2012), innovation (Freeman 1988) and as critical factors in firms with a high percentage of knowledge workers (Despres and Hiltrop 1995; Alvesson 2004).

Moreover, increasing interest in the intrinsic meaning of work was seen during a debate on the 'economics of happiness and well-being' (Frey and Stutzer 2006). According to these studies, all workers, especially those with higher educational qualifications, place a greater emphasis on aspects other than money (Frey 2005). Companies and practitioners acknowledge the importance of the different ways people are rewarded at work in the knowledge-intensive context, especially related to non-monetary schemes.

Following previous assumptions, we can say that firms with a high degree of knowledge intensity are likely to use non-monetary incentive schemes more than firms in which the intensity of knowledge is low. Thus, we posit that:

HP1. There is a positive and significant relationship between knowledge intensity and non-monetary incentives, so that higher the knowledge intensity of the firm, higher is the use of non-monetary incentives and lower the knowledge intensity, lower is the amount of non-monetary incentives.

Furthermore, since this massive (and relatively unique) interest in non-monetary aspects of innovation and performance, we think that no relationship exists between knowledge intensity and monetary incentives. This means that difference does not exist in the use of the lever of monetary reward in 'traditional' firms and KIFs. Therefore, our hypothesis is that:

HP2. There is no relation between firms' knowledge intensity and monetary incentives.

In his work, Deci (1971) demonstrated the effects of intrinsic and extrinsic 'motivators' and the negative effects of contingent rewards on intrinsic motivation. Frey (1997) also stated that 'an intrinsically-motivated person is denied the chance to display his or her own interest and involvement in an activity, when someone else offers a reward' (Frey 1997:47) and hence his propensity to 'active participation'. This phenomenon was defined by the author as a crowding-out effect. So, according to Deci (1975) and Kruglanski (1978), the emphasis on compensation based on contingent reward would increase the orientation to extrinsic reward and choke the orientation to intrinsic reward. Furthermore, it could feed a 'vicious circle' in which the use of monetary incentives could, in time, lead to their devaluation in the perspective of individual motivation (Tyagi and Block 1983).

Current research on reward management stresses the importance of non-monetary aspects of remuneration (Aguinis et al. 2013) and their role as antecedents of a firm's performance (Güngör 2011). It also suggests that knowledge workers are driven by an intrinsic motivation (Frey and Stutzer 2006; Despres and Hiltrop 1995). In managerial practice, non-monetary schemes are becoming increasingly popular while academic research is needed to prove their efficacy. However, these aspects are rarely studied in the context of SMEs, with particular attention to knowledge-intensive ones.

We suggest that the overuse of non-monetary rewards may have adverse effects. There are some studies which cast doubts on the effectiveness of non-financial rewards in specific economic environments and among technical workers. One of these, Tahmincioglu (2004), suggests that the external economic environment may have an impact on the effectiveness of non-monetary incentives. For example, in times of crisis, non-monetary incentives may be ineffective in motivating employees, since they may potentially be seen by employees as the employer's attempts to appease them.

Other authors, while trying to develop a social identity for KIFs (Alvesson 2000) and stressing the risk related to high turnover for technical employees, propose that 'technical employees behave as individual contractors, willing to change jobs with little remorse if their needs are not met by their current company' (Gomez-Mejia et al. 1990:62).

For these reasons, we think that an increase in the use of non-monetary incentive schemes may have a counterproductive effect on performance in companies with high knowledge intensity compared to those with low knowledge intensity. Thus, we wish to verify:

HP3: The intensity of knowledge will moderate the relationship between non-monetary incentive schemes and performance such that the relationship between non-monetary incentives and performance will be stronger at lower levels of knowledge intensity and weaker for higher levels of knowledge intensity.

On the other hand, the crowding-out effect suggested by Frey (1997) increases the use of monetary incentive schemes and may have a counterproductive effect on performance of KIFs compared to those with low-knowledge intensity, as with the traditional ones. So, we posit that:

> HP4: The intensity of knowledge will moderate the relationship between monetary incentive schemes and performance such that the relationship between monetary incentives and performance will be stronger at lower levels of knowledge intensity and weaker for higher levels of knowledge intensity.

Empirical research in the Italian context

To deepen our questions, we administered an online questionnaire to representatives of a sample (N= 95) of Italian SMEs. The data were built using the Italian database AIDA[1]. We considered enterprises with the number of employees below 250 and belonging to different industries such as information technology, consulting, furniture making, mechanical engineering and textiles. Questions about the general data of the firm (e.g., age, sector, number of employees and the number of employees with higher levels of education, etc.) were included along with the specific demands on necessary variables of the analysis we wished to develop such as performance, monetary and non-monetary incentives. Data were then analysed with the statistical package SPSS (Version 20.0).

Performance was assessed as the dependent variable of this study on a three-item scale: trends in turnover, profit and number of employees. All items were scored on a five-point frequency rating scale, ranging from 1 ('dramatically decreased') to 5 ('extremely increased'). The scale's reliability was 0.84. *Knowledge intensity* was measured on the basis of the proportion of knowledge workers in the total workforce in each organization. Despite the substantial debate on the nature of knowledge-intensive firms and the difficulties in finding a measure for this variable (Alvesson 1993), we decided to follow the author's suggestion in considering knowledge-intensive firms as companies where the majority of employees are well qualified (Alvesson 2001). Finally, *monetary incentives* and *non-monetary incentives* in this study, which were considered as the moderating variables, were measured with one question each focused on the manager/entrepreneur perception about their effectiveness. The two questions were marked on a five-point frequency rating scale, ranging from 1 ('very poor') to 5 ('very good').

Findings

The use of non-monetary incentives and monetary incentives in KIS and traditional firms

According to the results of a correlations analysis among the main variables of this study (see Table 38.1), a positive and significant relationship is found between non-monetary incentives and firms' knowledge intensity ($r = .345$; $p < .01$). It demonstrated the first hypothesis suggesting that where knowledge intensity is higher, there is also a higher recourse to non-monetary incentives. Where the proportion of the skilled workforce is lower, there is a fall in the use of non-monetary incentives.

Table 38.1 Descriptive statistics and correlation among the variables of the study

	M	SD	1	2	3	4
1. Performance	2.804	.857	–			
2. Knowledge intensity	55.161	33.906	.458**	–		
3. Monetary incentives	3.200	.929	.250*	.097	–	
4. Non-monetary incentives	3.442	1.008	.270**	.345**	.507**	–

Note: Significance ** $p < .01$.

Further, results show that there is no relationship between the degree of monetary incentives and a firm's knowledge intensity ($r = .097$; $p > .05$). Therefore, there is no clear distinction in terms of monetary incentives between firms that we may categorize as knowledge-intensive and the more traditional ones, thereby supporting our second hypothesis.

In Table 38.1, the descriptive statistics and correlation among all variables are shown.

The moderating effect of monetary and non-monetary incentives

In order to investigate the other aspect, the moderating effect of non-monetary and monetary incentives was used to determine the relationship between knowledge intensity and performance. For this, a regression analysis was used. Centred scores were used to solve the problem of multicollinearity (Tabachnick et al. 2001).

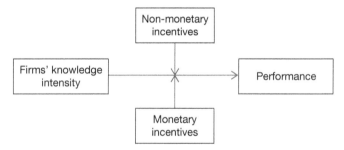

Figure 38.1 The moderating effect of non-monetary and monetary incentives on the relationship between knowledge intensity and performance

The overall model explains 35% of the total variance. According to the results, the relation between knowledge intensity and performance is positive and significant (=.19; $p < .05$) and it is moderated by both interacting factors: the level of non-monetary incentives (=-.17; $p < .05$) and monetary incentives (=-.19; $p < .05$).

In the first case, the higher the degree of non-monetary incentives, the weaker is the relationship between knowledge intensity and performance. At the same time, the lower the level of non-monetary incentives, the stronger the link. Graphical representation (see Figure 38.1) helps to clarify the nature of the interaction effect. In this case, we need to read this result together with higher recourse to non-monetary incentives among knowledge-intensive firms, as demonstrated earlier.

In the second situation, which is related to the role of monetary incentives, the higher the degree of monetary incentives, the weaker the relationship between knowledge intensity and performance. At the same time, the lower the level of monetary incentives, stronger is the

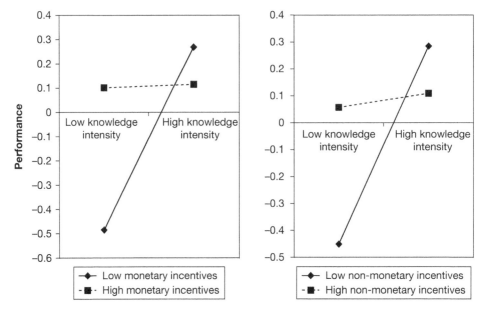

Figure 38.2 (a) and (b): Graphical representation of the moderating role of non-monetary incentives and monetary incentives on performance

relationship. A graphical representation (see Figure 38.2) shows the nature of interaction. As demonstrated for non-monetary incentives for low and middle levels of knowledge intensity, performance is higher in the case of greater levels of monetary incentives. For very high levels of knowledge intensity, a high recourse to monetary incentives seems to have an adverse effect compared to lower levels of monetary incentives in predicting performance.

These findings seem to suggest that the frequent use of both non-monetary and monetary packages may tend to level out the preferences of all workers, both low- and high-skilled, in a sort of crowding-out effect in which neither monetary nor non-monetary incentives offer higher performance. Rather, a lack of both kinds of such incentives may have a detrimental effect on workers who are low on skills.

Also, from the graphical representations, it is shown that if high levels of monetary and non-monetary incentives are provided, their effects on performance growth from low knowledge-intensive firms to KIFs is very weak. Monetary incentives have almost a 'null' effect on performance.

Conclusions and managerial implications

The findings of our empirical research demonstrate that SM-KIFs are characterized by the use of non-monetary incentive schemes. This makes us conclude that this specific rewarding approach is particularly diffused among these enterprises, which is not the case among low-knowledge intensive firms. In addition, we find no statistical difference between high and low KIFs in relation to the use of monetary incentives.

It is interesting to see that further investigation of data proves that the role of non-monetary incentives is upper-evaluated. In fact, when knowledge intensity is considered in the relationship between non-monetary incentives and performance, it is seen that the link becomes negative, suggesting that an increase in non-monetary rewards in firms with a higher presence of knowledge workforce would see a decrease in the overall organizational performance.

So, our final result establishes that the overuse of non-monetary rewards in the context of SMEs with knowledge orientation may produce adverse effects. This outcome offers the opportunity to consider a generalized opinion which prefers non-monetary incentives as it allows the proposing of some managerial implication with regard the role of rewards systems for pursuing organizational success in knowledge-intensive firms.

Also, consistent with our expectations, the results demonstrate that the overuse of monetary rewards in the context of SMEs with knowledge orientation may also produce adverse effects.

The results may have two main implications for managerial practice in SMEs.

Firstly, it seems that knowledge workers are interested in a mix of the two components, the balance of which has to be built through personal relationship with each worker to understand his/her orientation. In this way, the role of the team leader is crucial in understanding where intrinsic motivation and external rewards play better and which composition between these two components is best for a worker. At the same time, the HR department has to intervene with a set of tools and bring about a culture of dialogue between the leader and employees.

Secondly, attention to monetary incentives in this context may be given. Such systems of management by objectives — and evaluation of their achievement — need to be implemented, keeping in mind that, in times of crisis such as we living in at present, the definition of goals is important, probably more than the definition of the amount of money connected with them. In other words, stimulating goals and explicating the recognition of their achievement is the true motivating element. In fact, the misalignment of wages (compared to the level of education) may be a reason for these findings, since it could negatively affect overall performance and not bring about work satisfaction.

Our analysis also gives some stimuli, even from a theoretical perspective. As a preliminary point, we investigate KIFs, giving some empirical evidence on rewarding the mix's efficacy. Moreover, it gives support to the importance of knowledge workers that deserves more attention from scholars.

In this sense, practitioners should be aware of knowledge workers' specificities when the rewarding mix for this category is designed. It has already been proved in earlier studies that the degree of loyalty with reference to KIFs makes social identification and loyalty a critical theme for these kinds of firms and workers (Alvesson 2000).

Several limitations of this study need to be acknowledged, even if we believe that these limitations do not invalidate the results but can rather represent suggestions to empirical advancement and refinement. We point out some of these. Firstly, the measure of knowledge intensity was long disputed (Alvesson 2001), while other variables may play a critical role in these findings. Therefore, new areas of investigation could also cover aspects related to internal equity in terms of distribution of financial rewards. In addition, other methodological limits need to be recognized: the cross-sectional nature of the data does not allow us to test the direction of relationships hypothesized. Future longitudinal studies may shed light on whether reverse or reciprocal relationships exist. Secondly, our sample is specifically related to the firms' dimension and sector, even though it is quite small. At the same time, our narrow focus did not allow us to control country -specific effects. Future studies may be conducted in other countries as well by using larger samples to see whether our results can be generalized. Thirdly, the answers came only from one entrepreneur or owner-manager in each firm. In order to broaden the focus there is a need for more than one owner-manager from each firm to answer.

Note

1 AIDA is a Bureau van Dijk database containing economic data on firms operating in Italy. This database is similar to AMADEUS 200 (Europe) and OSIRIS (World).

References

Acs, Z. J., Morck, R., Shaver, J. M. and Yeung, B. (1997). The internationalisation of small and medium-sized enterprises: a policy perspective. *Small Business Economics.* 9(1), 7–20.

Aguinis, H., Joo, H. and Gottfredson, R. K. (2013). What monetary rewards can and cannot do: how to show employees the money. *Business Horizons.* 56(2), 241–249.

Alvesson, M. (1993). Organizations as rhetoric: Knowledge-intensive firms and the struggle with ambiguity. *Journal of Management Studies.* 30(6), 997–1015.

Alvesson, M. (2000). Social identity and the problem of loyalty in knowledge-intensive companies. *Journal of Management Studies.* 37(8), 1101–1124.

Alvesson, M. (2001). Knowledge work: ambiguity, image and identity. *Human Relations.* 54(7), 863–886.

Alvesson, M. (2004). *Knowledge Workers and Knowledge-Intensive Firms.* Oxford: Oxford University Press.

Armstrong, M. (2015). *Armstrong's Handbook of Reward Management Practice.* London: Kogan Page.

Astrachan, J. H. (2010). Strategy in family business: toward a multidimensional research agenda. *Journal of Family Business Strategy.* 1(1), 6–14.

Bacon, N. and Hoque, K. (2005). HRM in the SME sector: valuable employees and coercive networks. *The International Journal of Human Resource Management.* 16(11), 1976–1999.

Barnard, C. I. (1938). *The Functions of the Executive.* Cambridge, MA: Harvard University Press.

Barney, J. B. (1991). Firm resources and sustained competitive advantage. *Journal of Management.* 17(1), 99–120.

Becker, B. E., Huselid, M. A. and Ulrich, D. (2001). *The HR Scorecard: Linking People, Strategy, and Performance.* Boston, MA: Harvard Business Press.

Behrends, T. (2007). Recruitment practices in small and medium-sized enterprises. An empirical study among knowledge-intensive professional service firms. *Management Revue.* 18(1), 55–74.

Bell, J., Crick, D. and Young, S. (2004). Small firm internationalization and business strategy an exploratory study of 'knowledge-intensive' and 'traditional' manufacturing firms in the UK. *International Small Business Journal.* 22(1), 23–56.

Cardon, M. S. and Stevens, C. E. (2004). Managing human resources in small organizations: What do we know? *Human Resource Management Review.* 14(3), 295–323.

Carlson, D. S., Upton, N. and Seaman, S. (2006). The impact of human resource practices and compensation design on performance: an analysis of family-owned SMEs. *Journal of Small Business Management.* 44(4), 531–543.

Ciambotti, M. and Palazzi, F. (2015). Medie imprese italiane: un'indagine sui valori d'impresa. *Piccola Impresa/Small Business.* 1, 10–31.

Corbetta, G. (2000). *Le medie impresa: Alla ricerca della loro identità.* Milano: Egea.

Corbetta, G. and Montemerlo, D. (1999). Ownership, governance, and management issues in small and medium-size family businesses: a comparison of Italy and the United States. *Family Business Review.* 12(4), 361–374.

Cortesi, A., Alberti F. and Salvato, C. (2012). *Le piccole imprese. Struttura, gestione, percorsi evolutivi.* Roma: Carocci.

De Jong, J. P. and Vermeulen, P. A. (2006). Determinants of product innovation in small firms: a comparison across industries. *International Small Business Journal.* 24(6), 587–609.

Deci, E. L. (1971). Effects of externally mediated rewards on intrinsic motivation. *Journal of Personality and Social Psychology*, 18(1), 105–115.

Deci, E. L. (1975). *Intrinsic Motivation.* New York: Plenum.

Despres, C. and Hiltrop, J. M. (1995). Human resource management in the knowledge age: current practice and perspectives on the future. *Employee Relations.* 17(1), 9–23.

Dyer, L. and Parker, D. (1975). Classifying outcomes in work motivation research: examination of intrinsic–extrinsic dichotomy. *Journal of Applied Psychology.* 60(4), 455–458.

Freeman, C. (1988). 1–8. In Dosi, G. *et al.* (eds.). *Technical Change and Economic Theory.* London: Pinter Publishers.

Frey, B. (1997). *Not Just for The Money: An Economic Theory of Personal Motivation.* Cheltenham: Edward Elgar.

Frey, B. S. (2005). *Non solo per denaro: le motivazioni disinteressate dell'agire economico.* Milano: B. Mondadori.

Frey, B. and A. Stutzer (2006). *Economia e Felicità.* Milano: Il Sole 24 Ore.

Gomez-Mejia, L. R., Balkin, D. B. and Milkovich, G. T. (1990). Rethinking rewards for technical employees. *Organizational Dynamics.* 18(4), 62–75.

Grant, R. M. (1997). The knowledge-based view of the firm: implications for management practice. *Long Range Planning*. 30, 450–454.

Gratton, L. (2004). More than money. *People Management*. 10(2), 23–24.

Gratton, L., Hope-Hailey, V., Stiles, P. and Truss, C. (1999). Linking individual performance to business strategy: the people process model. *Human Resource Management*. 38(1), 17–31.

Güngör, P. (2011). The relationship between reward management system and employee performance with the mediating role of motivation: A quantitative study on global banks. *Procedia-Social and Behavioral Sciences*. 24, 1510–1520.

Guest, D. E. (1997). Human resource management and performance: a review and research agenda. *International Journal of Human Resource Management*. 8(3), 263–276.

Heneman, R. L., Tansky, J. W., and Camp, S. M. (2000). Human resource management practices in small and medium-sized enterprises: Unanswered questions and future research perspectives. *Entrepreneurship Theory and Practice*. 25(1), 11–26.

Hornsby, J. S. and Kuratko, D. F. (2003). Human resource management in US small businesses: a replication and extension. *Journal of Developmental Entrepreneurship*. 8(1), 73–92.

Hulkko-Nyman, K., Sarti, D., Hakonen, A. and Sweins, C. (2012). Total rewards perceptions and work engagement in elder-care organizations: findings from Finland and Italy. *International Studies of Management & Organization*. 42(1), 24–49.

ISTAT. (2015). *Struttura e competitività delle imprese industriali e dei servizi*. Roma: ISTAT.

Katsikeas, C. S., Bell, J. and Morgan, R. E. (1998). Editorial: advances in export marketing theory and practice. *International Marketing Review*. 15(5), 322–332.

Katz, D. (1964). The motivational basis of organizational behaviour. *Behavioural Science*. 9, 131–136.

Kogut, B. and Zander, U. (1992). Knowledge of the firm, combinative capabilities, and the replication of technology. *Organization Science*. 3, 383–397.

Kruglanski, A. (1978). Issues in cognitive social psychology. In Lepper, M. R. and Greene, D. (eds.). *The Hidden Costs of Reward: New Perspectives in the Psychology of Human Motivation*. Hillsdale, NJ: Lawrence Erlbaum Associates, John Wiley and Sons.

Lawler, E. E. (1973). *Motivation in Work Organizations*. Pacific Grove, CA: Brooks/Cole Publishing Company.

Lawler, E. E. III (2011). Creating a new employment deal: total rewards and the new workforce. *Organizational Dynamics*. 40(4), 302–309.

March, J. G. and Simon, H. A. (1958). *Organization*. New York: Wiley.

Markova, G. and Ford, C. (2011). Is money the panacea? Rewards for knowledge workers. *International Journal of Productivity and Performance Management*. 60(8), 813–823.

Michiels, A. (2017). Formal compensation practices in family SMEs. *Journal of Small Business and Enterprise Development*. 24(1), 88–104.

OECD. (2014). *Entrepreneurship at a Glance 2014*. Paris: OECD Publishing.

Pfeffer, J. (1998). Six dangerous myths about pay. *Harvard Business Review*. 76(3), 109–119.

Rutherford, M. W., Buller, P. F. and McMullen, P. R. (2003). Human resource management problems over the life cycle of small to medium-sized firms. *Human Resource Management*. 42(4), 321–335.

Sels, L., De Winne, S., Delmotte, J., Maes, J., Faems, D. and Forrier, A. (2006). Linking HRM and small business performance: an examination of the impact of HRM intensity on the productivity and financial performance of small businesses. *Small Business Economics*. 26(1), 83–101.

Simon, H. A. (1947). *Administrative Behaviour*. New York: Macmillan.

Singh, R. K., Garg, S. K. and Deshmukh, S. G. (2009). The competitiveness of SMEs in a globalized economy: observations from China and India. *Management Research Review*. 33(1), 54–65.

Swart, J. and Kinnie, N. (2003). Sharing knowledge in knowledge-intensive firms. *Human Resource Management Journal*. 13(2), 60–75.

Tabachnick, B. G., Fidell, L. S. and Osterlind, S. J. (2001). *Using Multivariate Statistics*. New York: HarperCollins.

Tahmincioglu E. (2004). Gifts that gall. *Workforce Magazine*, April Issue, 43–46.

Teece, D. J. (2000). Strategies for managing knowledge assets: the role of firm structure and industrial context. *Long Range Planning*. 33, 35–54.

Torre, T. (2011). *Verso logiche di Total Reward. Una ricerca su incentivazione e dintorni*. Roma: Aracne.

Tyagi, P. and Block, C. (1983). Monetary incentives and salesman performance. *Industrial Marketing Management*. 12(4), 263–269.

Weiner, N. (1980). Determinants and behavioral consequences of pay satisfaction: a comparison of two models. *Personnel Psychology.* 33, 741–757.

Wood, S. (1999). Human resource management and performance. *International Journal of Management Reviews.* 1(4), 367–413.

Wright, P. M., McMahan, G. C. and McWilliams, A. (1994). Human resources and sustained competitive advantage: a resource-based perspective. *International Journal of Human Resource Management.* 5(2), 301–326.

39

POOR REMUNERATION MANAGEMENT AND ITS CONSEQUENCES IN THE ETHIOPIAN CIVIL SERVICE

Adebabay Abay Gebrekidan

Introduction

The chapter offers a short case study, written from an *insider's* perspective, to illustrate problems arising from inadequacies in employee remuneration which can be viewed as undermining efficiency and governance in the Ethiopian civil service. Remuneration here means, in particular, monthly payment in Ethiopian birr to those employed full-time in the service. The currency exchange rate is 30 birr to one pound sterling.

The Ethiopian civil service consists of four layers of government: Federal; Regional; Zonal; and Woreda (the lowest tier of government). The country is governed in accordance with a bicameral (i.e., upper- and lower-chamber) parliamentary system, with legislators elected to form the government supported by a professional civil (public) service. The Ethiopian government has been pursuing a public service reform agenda, including a donor-supported component: the Public-Sector Capacity Building Program (Rogger 2017).

Issues in the character of Ethiopian Civil Service employment conditions

The following list outlines the basis on which civil servants are employed at each tier of government:

- There are more than one million civil servants for the country's one hundred million population, deployed to serve an 85% rural population and 15% urban population.
- There is low basic pay, eroded by an 8% monthly inflation rate.
- Fringe benefits are poor. In fact, there is only one benefit available to all civil servants: free transportation.
- When deployed on fieldwork assignments to rural areas the daily allowances are so low as to make it almost impossible for individuals to sustain themselves.
- There is no effective system in place to enable structured career progression: unless a position is vacant, promotion to a higher role in the next level is impossible.
- Working methods remain manually intensive with the consequence that less knowledge and skill is built up to fulfil individual duties and responsibilities.

- Linked to the remuneration problem and in the absence of a comprehensive performance management system, team working culture is low.
- Accountability and transparency is poor, undermining civil servants' trust in the employment system, discouraging talented people from applying to join and stay, and creating a lack of enthusiasm and motivation among the workforce.

Perceived consequences of low remuneration: undermining national transformation

Remuneration levels across the Ethiopian civil service compare poorly with those in other African nations. Currently, for civil servants to meet basic living needs, engaging in part-time additional work is a must. In some cases, to top up income levels, civil servants rent out their home while renting another residence at a lower price to live in. Some people build service quarters for themselves and use them as a means of securing additional income. Others work part-time in recruitment services to get additional income. And those with professional skills use their spare time to undertake training and consultancy assignments to raise the additional income necessary to maintain a reasonable lifestyle.

A World Bank report (Rogger 2017) cites, among other factors, poor remuneration as impacting on turnover in the number of professionals employed, undermining efficiency and limiting capacity building across the Ethiopian civil service. One practical effect is that parts of the service lack 'corporate memory' accumulated from lessons learned from past practice; thus, they remain 'always the beginner' in policy studies. As a service undergoing a process of reform, there is significant demand for high calibre professionals to innovate or to recreate the service itself. But poor remuneration means that high calibre professionals are not being attracted to, or retained by, the service. This undermines any efforts at transformation promoted by legislators; accordingly, as required changes are not feeding through to match promised enhanced service delivery over time, public dissatisfaction has increased, leading to public resistance and, in some cases, open conflict.

In an organization with poor remuneration, the momentum of change is low. And, lacking any sense that performance will be recognised, apathy sets in. The Ethiopian civil service is a typical expression of low remuneration and the absence of performance-based rewards. Many specific change initiatives, such as Business Process Re-engineering (BPR), the Balanced Score Card, high performance team building, and efforts to modernize HRM fail to meet expectations. This means the change initiatives do not fulfil the ambition for them to improve good governance, again undermining public confidence with the consequences noted earlier.

Consequences of poor remuneration include increases vertical hierarchy and horizontal 'branching', as gradations of employee are created to artificially inflate pay levels, blurring accountability and undermining organizational effectiveness aspirations. Given its reported benefits of creating the conditions for vertical compression, flattening organizational hierarchies (Hammer and Champy 2001), since 2004 all government-owned institutions in Ethiopia, including the public financial institutions, have embarked on large-scale change projects in which BPR is a central element (Kuhil 2014).

Empirical research by Kuhil (2014) reported improvements such as introducing a single customer contact point through employee empowerment to make all the necessary decisions at that point of contact, with potential enhancement of satisfaction levels among employees and customers alike, and also introduction of information and communication technology services (e.g., e-banking). Kuhil's findings report that the challenge was resistance from employees, and some managers (who labelled the initiative 'blood pressure raiser), due to assumptions on their part that BPR will result in layoffs for some and increased workloads for the remaining employees, without compatible rewards following the process redesign.

So, while in the early stages of the re-engineering era in Ethiopia, horizontal compression and limiting the proliferation of public services departments was evident, in later phases the contrary has happened. Most civil service organizations become more hierarchical and, with many departments, horizontally expanded. The driver for this incorrect implementation of BPR has been to address inadequacies in job grades and concomitant salary levels; in other words, a consequence of poor remuneration management. In practice, under the guise of service reform, one perverse outcome has been that remuneration has led to organizational structure and grading, rather than the other way around. And, in turn, hierarchical organization is accompanied by inefficient decision-making in government-run services, with the public dissatisfaction that follows from it.

A further perceived problem derived from the poor remuneration of public services employees is the risk of it driving corruption. In present-day Ethiopia, rent-seeking behaviour (manipulating policy or economic conditions for personal gain) stands as a clear and present danger within the nation's political economy. Using the trappings of public office to seek bribes and embezzle public funds appears endemic, standing in stark contrast to democratic aspirations to create the conditions for Ethiopia to transform into a middle-income country. According to a recent briefing by the country's ruling party, and seen by the author, a large number of government officials have a strong belief that power is a source of wealth rather than a means to serve the public. It is not unreasonable to infer that poor remuneration packages associated with civil service employment are a contributing factor to corruption in public life. It is ironic to conclude that the amounts subject to embezzlement are much higher than what would be the cost to government payroll if legitimate levels of remuneration were enhanced across the civil service. And calculating hidden costs in terms of open conflict and adverse public appraisal the problem is further compounded.

Undermining aspirations to break the macro-level negative cycle, criticism can be laid at the door of poor remuneration as inhibiting high-performance teambuilding and thus, due to a lack of resource capacity, to the poor implementation of the national strategic transformation programmes. As noted already, poor remuneration is a driver for high turnover among professionals: the shorter the service or 'experience profile' of team members, the more likely it is that high-performance teambuilding in Ethiopia will be hampered.

Ethiopia is envisioning middle-income democratic nation status by 2025. Even though it had achieved many developmental targets in the government's first growth and development plan (2010–2014), overall achievement in the quality of programme implementation has fallen short of expectations. As a result, many projects are lagging behind deadlines. Now the country is embarked on the second growth and transformational plan (2016–2020), which is expected to herald the country's transformation to industrialization. But success depends heavily on civil service performance, and forecast outcomes against lead measures are presently unsatisfactory. Furthermore, the recent conflict in the country reduces confidence among infrastructure capital investors. While Ethiopian civil servants remain negatively motivated by public sector remuneration management, economic strategy and policy implementation will be hampered. In short, looking at the problem in context, on the ground, as a participant observer, one reasonable inference is that poor-quality policy, strategy and programme delivery is a consequence of poor remuneration. Further systematic empirical research is needed to help in elevating understanding, and building resolve to do something about it, among policy makers.

Conclusion

There are, of course, limitations to generalization from an impressionistic inquiry – albeit with the authenticity of an embedded point of view. However, there is evidence enough to state that, unless the government fixes the long-standing problem of poor remuneration in the Ethiopian civil service, policy makers' goals of good governance will not be realized as expected. Improving remuneration among the civil service workforce would, it is argued, bring about a decrease unwarranted personnel costs, such as artificially constituted grading structures and the costs of 'field allowances' and, through reduced scope for corruption, public procurement and property administration costs. To achieve overall cost reductions, it is important to 'right size' the civil service. As is investment in technology such as making the civil service a 'paperless' organization to minimize information management costs. Applying efficient and effective remuneration management systems, based on paying appropriately for employee contributions – skills and performance – would be a route to curbing rent seeking in the sector.

References

Hammer, M. and Champy, J. (2001). *Reengineering the Corporation: a Manifesto for Business Revolution.* Boston, MA: Nicholas Brealey Publishing.

Kuhil, A. M. (2014). Business Process Reengineering and organizational performance: a case of the Ethiopian banking sector. University of South Africa, Pretoria. Available at: www.hdl.handle.net/10500/13265.

Rogger, D. (2017). *Who Serves the Poor? Surveying Civil Servants in the Developing World.* World Bank Group Policy Research Working Paper 8051.

40

THE STORY OF INDIAN REMUNERATION

Natarajan Sundar

Story of public sector pay

More than the total workforce of a country like Germany, Italy or the UK are employed in India's 'public sector' – 40 to 50 million in state and central Government and public institutions – all governed by a common pay policy framework. Their pay evolution is important not just because of their sheer numbers, but because of its influence on pay in the private sector.

Public sector pay is substantially a political matter. For a period of ninety years, from 1857, India was the so-called 'Jewel in the Crown' of the British Empire. In 1911, King George V made the only visit to India by a reigning monarch of the colonial period. Maharajas paid obeisance to the emperor in the Delhi Darbar and the commoner subjects had the Royals' darshan (i.e., beholding of a revered object) when they appeared on the balcony of the Red Fort.

The sharp distinction between the rulers and the ruled was reflected in a top-to-bottom pay ratio of 1000:1. Philip Mason appropriately titled his classic on the Indian Civil Service (ICS), staffed almost exclusively by Brits, *The Men Who Ruled India*. The rulers, essentially the one thousand-strong ICS, were covenanted in Britain and paid enough in pounds sterling to make attractive enough for them to serve in the colony. Even their guaranteed monthly pension of £1000, when they retired and returned to the UK, was a princely sum. As for the Indians, there were enough takers, even if they were paid a pittance, especially at the bottom. The only change was during the Second World War, when prices rose sharply, and the lowest-paid ones received, ostensibly for a temporary period, a Dearness Allowance (DA).

In 1947, India achieved independence. Jawaharlal Nehru, India's first prime minister, was a Fabian Socialist. His goal was to establish a 'Socialistic pattern of society; planned economic development; heavily controlled by, and the commanding heights occupied by, the State; and equitable distribution of wealth and income'. This philosophy was reflected in the recommendations of the First Pay Commission in 1947: to increase the minimum government pay from Rs 10 per month to Rs 30, with top pay left untouched. During this period, the top-to-bottom pay ratio fell to 100:1. Successive Pay Commissions did much to further this progress.

In 1966, twenty months after the death of Nehru, his daughter Indira Gandhi – no relation to Mahatma Gandhi – became the prime minister. Her political slogan *'garibhi hatao'* ('abolish poverty') did no harm to her hold on power. The march towards socialism became increasingly strident, including the nationalization of all major banks, announced by her without even the direct involvement of her finance minister. By 1973, when annual inflation was close to 30%, DA for lower-level employees had gone up so much that even with some increase in the top salaries, the top-to-bottom ratio was down to less than 10:1. In 1975, the monthly salary of the chairman of a large public sector bank was Rs 3000, and that of a branch department manager Rs 2000. The country was moving towards the Soviet Union socialistic pay model of 'need-based and not responsibility-based pay'.

In 1984, Indira Gandhi was succeeded by her son, Rajiv Gandhi. In his 40s, he was the then 'next generation'. It was clear to him that during three-and-a-half decades of independence, despite starting at a low base, the Indian economy had grown at the so-called 'Hindu rate of growth', an annual figure of 3%, vastly inferior to that of the 'tiger economies' of the Far East. He decided to take a U-turn to 'a judicious combination of liberalisation, import substitution and access to foreign technology'.

The 4th Pay Commission around that time made two huge changes: Cost of Living increases to be automatically reflected in DA; and it to be given to even the most senior civil servants: The extent of 'neutralization' ranged from 100% for the lowest to 65% for the highest. This pattern has continued since then: The latest (7th) Pay Commission, in 2017, has set the minimum salary at Rs 18000 per month and the top salary at Rs 250,000 per month. Adjusted for the fringe benefits applicable at the top, the top-to-bottom ratio now stands at around 20:1. The salaries of all government functionaries, ministers, members of parliament, and, others, have all risen dramatically.

The story of private sector pay

Until the mid-1980s

For the first 37 years of independence, India's GDP growth remained feeble and there was little demand for talent. The country's huge population meant that average talent was in huge supply. The five Indian Institutes of Technology, the Indian Institutes of Management and a few other institutions produced enough world-class professionals, net of emigrations to America. There was, therefore, little reason for professionals' pay levels to rise.

During the colonial days, managers in the (mostly UK) multinationals were covenanted in their home country and, like the ICS, received pretty generous pay; and so were the few Indians appointed as covenanted managers. After independence, however, their pay did not keep pace with inflation; and by the mid-1970s they were paid well, but not outrageously. Professional managers in Indian domestic businesses were paid even less.

There was a ceiling on the salary of directors of Rs 90,000 per annum (about $9000, at the 1980s exchange rate) plus half the amount as fringe benefits. Taxes during this period were usurious – there was a marginal income tax rate of up to 97.5%, plus wealth tax in the mid-70s. Chill penury was not, of course, freezing the noble souls at the top since Indian companies found ways of taking care of them. When Russi Modi, the chairman of Tata Steel, was asked to retire in his 70s, his benefits included luxurious houses in Calcutta, Delhi and Mumbai. Similarly, foreign companies could legally make remittances to their top management. Such special arrangements could, however, be done only for a select few, and not in the case of all companies.

Remuneration as a managerial function, as understood in the West, was simply unnecessary. Companies adopted the public sector model of pay scales linked to 'grades' of management. You joined at the bottom of the grade and moved up slowly. There was little performance-based differentiation and no variable pay for managers. Given that inflation was eroding the real value of remuneration received year on year, and the high tax rates, the focus was on finding ways of paying additional 'cash' reimbursements.

Through the 1970s and up to the mid-1980s, at all levels of management, the remuneration saga – how much was paid, and how – left a bad taste in the mouth. There was no transparency and pay integrity was questionable even in the most genuinely responsible companies.

Mid-1980s to mid-1990s

In the mid-1980s, Rajiv Gandhi took tentative steps towards increasing economic liberalization in the country: the top income tax rate reduced to 50% and select foreign investments became permissible. Foreign banks such as Citibank eyed opportunities for expansion. In 1986, the Indian government started talking to Pepsi about an agro project in Punjab. These companies needed to quickly appoint trained managers at all levels, and companies like Unilever's subsidiary, Hindustan Lever Ltd (HLL), which were well regarded for their management talent, began to lose managers, drawn by noticeably higher pay levels. In 1986, HLL and Citibank became the first companies to appoint senior-level remuneration managers. For gamekeeping as well as poaching, it helps to know the territory!

Throughout the previous period, there was really no need to mark the market, which did not move much in any case. In the mid-1980s, for the first time, meaningful salary surveys, the kind done in the West, covering properly benchmarked jobs in relevant companies that compete for talent began to be conducted, resulting in double-digit average salary increases. With inflation in low single digits, this meant significant real salary increases that could be sharply differentiated: even 30% or 40% for high-potential top performers. Variable pay for senior managers trickled in and target-setting and performance management processes began to become more robust.

Rajiv Gandhi was the prime minister for a period of only four years. He was not permitted to take really giant steps, but the genie of liberalization was now out of the bottle. Professionalism in remuneration, double-digit and differentiated increases in pay and improved performance management had all started to appear.

Post-1991 liberalization

The biggest push towards the liberalization of the Indian economy came in 1991. Rajiv Gandhi had been assassinated and the country was now on the brink of defaulting on its international loan repayments. Partly as a result of the bailout conditions and partly out of genuine conviction, the new prime minister, P.V. Narasimha Rao, and his Oxford and Cambridge alumnus finance minister, Dr Manmohan Singh, dismantled the old economic order. Import restrictions were removed and replaced by relatively modest tariffs; the licence-raj with regard to industry jettisoned; and foreign investment permitted. Income tax rates were reduced sharply. The ceiling on directors' remuneration was doubled and later abolished. At once, both liberalization and globalization were in the air.

The net result was a sustained growth rate of more than 6% in the economy during the 1990s which altered the dynamics of the talent and remuneration markets. One large multinational carried out an empirical study on the impact of liberalization and growth on management salaries in countries using data from countries like Indonesia and Thailand. Typically, the western countries were in an equilibrium state: GDP growth and inflation of 2–3% per annum and real salary growth of 1 or 2%. If a country grew at a significantly higher rate, however, say 6 or 7% per annum, it amplified the demand for talent and remuneration rose depending on supply of talent and the 'global–local' remuneration differential. The message was clear. With the kind of growth likely and resultant demand for talent, the low level of Indian remuneration, and annual inflation of 5%-plus, double-digit pay increases would continue for several years to come.

Companies now had a simple choice: follow the remuneration market, with attendant consequences on talent acquisition and retention, or lead the market, take a remuneration stance at market median plus, or even 75th percentile for their best talent, and grab the opportunities for growth in a liberalizing India.

The new Millennium

This was the dawn of a new era for India, thanks to Y2K. Huge remedial recoding work had to be done across the world and only India had the technically qualified manpower to do it. The fortuitous exposure to the global companies meant even after Y2K they were asked to do other IT work. The IT majors, TCS, Infosys, IBM, Wipro and others, took off, each recruiting in tens of thousands every year.

Two other major developments took place around turn of the millennia. New industries rose up, such as Bharti Airtel in the Telecom industry. And some of the biggest Indian companies became more global, with the overseas acquisitions by Aditya Birla Group, Tata Motors, Tata Steel and others. Parts of the western corporate world was being ruled from India and heads of huge businesses in the UK, USA and other countries reported to their bosses sitting in Delhi, Mumbai or Bangalore.

Growth in remuneration over the preceding four decades

The growth in remuneration in India over the past four decades is illustrated by the pay levels in a leading benchmark company, as shown in Table 40.1.

These are market median plus figures for global quality talent in India. Table 40.2 shows the growth rates that these represent.

These rates reflect the movement in the total remuneration for global quality talent working in India, although the actual levels and the movement over time differs from industry to industry and company to company. Some conclusions emerge:

- The 1970s represented the low point in Indian remuneration. What little growth there was until the late 1980s hardly made up for inflation. India remained a very low-paying market in the world.
- The decade 1987–97, when the liberalization took place, saw a sea change at all levels of management. Remuneration at the middle levels grew four times, at the senior level six times, and at the top eight times, meaning annual growth of 15%, 20% and 24% respectively. Dramatic though these increases sound, having started at a very low base, Indian remuneration levels were still a long way below equivalent levels in the West.
- Remuneration growth has continued through the past twenty years. In the last decade or so the growth rate has averaged around 10%.
- The growth in senior management and CXO pay in the past decade is actually understated as a significant component of their pay is stock-based pay and not included in these figures.

During the four decades reported above, the Rupee has weakened, from about Rs 10 to a US dollar in the 1970s to Rs 65 now. Despite that, even in dollar terms, the remuneration has risen significantly. This is shown in Figure 40.1.

Table 40.1 Total remuneration (i.e., base plus variable) in Rs 000 per annum

	1977	*1987*	*1997*	*2007*	*2017*
Middle manager	54	86	323	1020	2470
Senior manager	160	272	1710	5800	14300
Chief executive (CXO)	310	528	4484	16000	45500

Table 40.2 Annual growth rate in total remuneration

	1977–1987	*1987–1997*	*1997–2007*	*2007–2017*
Middle Managers	5%	15%	12%	9%
Senior Managers	6%	20%	13%	10%
CXO	6%	24%	14%	11%

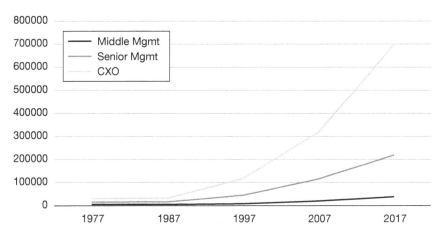

Figure 40.1 Total remuneration in India in US$ per annum

In sum, expressed in US dollars, Indian remuneration levels, which were low throughout the 1980s, began to rise in the 1990s, and have sharply increased in the preceding twenty years:

- At middle and senior management levels, pay is now comparable to the West, especially for global quality talent and adjusted for cost of living, perhaps at par.
- At the top management level, pay is at the global level; indeed, adjusted for the cost of living, it is probably better.

Trends and challenges in Indian remuneration

According to the IMF and other reports, the Indian economy is doing rather well. Riding on an exports uplift and benefiting from various structural reforms and the liberalization of Foreign Direct Investment (FDI) policy, the IMF estimates that GDP will grow annually at 7.5% to 8% during 2017–20, making India the fastest-growing large economy in the world. On various other parameters such as inflation, foreign exchange reserves, stock market performance and higher tax base, the performance is impressive.

Against this background, several heads of remuneration, global as well as national CHROs and chairmen of companies and remuneration committees were interviewed specifically to inform the chapter; with findings described qualitatively in the following paragraphs.

Blue- and white-collar and unskilled workers

The analytical focus of this chapter is not the blue- or low-paid white-collar workers. Two challenges, however, are being mentioned, as they have a bearing on the economy as a whole and the remuneration of everyone employed in a company:

- Tens of millions are employed in the unorganized and non-unionized sectors and are paid very low wages. In a democracy, each political party tries to outdo the others in extending them state-funded welfare benefits and 'freebees', with mounting cost to the exchequer.
- The second challenge is that posed by the tens of millions employed in public sector and traditional industries in the private sector. DA that started as a temporary hardship compensation for the very low-paid during the Second World War has been institutionalized as guaranteed inflation neutralization for everyone, to a greater or lesser degree. In addition, either through Pay Commission or union negotiations with their companies, pay gets revised periodically. This is resulting in uncontrollable, mounting costs. The defence services 2018–19 budget of US$62 billion highlights this. In the past seven years, the expenditure has doubled, but been mostly eaten up by salary and pensions, which have risen from 44% of the total budget to 56%.

Junior management, including IT professionals

This is the category with the high employment growth in the past two decades. The IT industry alone currently provides three million direct and 10 million indirect employees.

- The demand for the 'traditional' skills in this sector is coming down, especially because of Artificial Intelligence and Robotics. It is estimated that private sector corporate jobs that grew at 4% per annum during 2006–2009 grew at 1% or even less in the past three years.
- Supply of talent in India is quite abundant, thanks to tightening immigration and visa grants in several developed countries, including the USA, the UK and Australia. This is also an industry with high manpower cost, typically 60% of revenue. Reduced demand and the improved supply of talent means the salaries in this sector are unlikely to sustain the growth levels of the past two decades. Much the same is the situation with regard to engineers in the traditional manufacturing industries. With restrictions on employment after obtaining a qualification in countries like the UK, the 'brain drain' is coming down.

The result is, to quote the CHRO of a US$10 billion company, 'the remuneration for entry level IT or traditional engineering jobs is certainly cooling off', but skills in the Internet of Things (IoT), are, however, at a 'tremendous premium'. These include skills in Artificial Intelligence, Machine Learning (so that data from connected devices can be harvested and analytics wrung out), Cyber Security, Data Visualisation, Data Science, GPS development for wearables, etc. London and the US's Silicon Valley are the global centres of IoT excellence and two of the highest pay markets in the world. To get someone with these skills to come and work in India, 'we not only have to pay the going international rate upwards of US $100,000, but a premium to make up for the pollution of Delhi or the traffic chaos of Bengaluru. Even persons of Indian ethnicity will come only for a Global plus pay.'

Middle and senior managers

The pay levels of middle and senior managers vary from industry to industry. Some organiz-ations in the FMCG and Banking industries want the best talent for their operations in India, especially as their management costs are only a small part of their revenue. Their stated remuneration policy is to 'gain competitive advantage through pay in the calibre of their managers'. In addition, they look at India to provide a stream of their global cadre of managers. Their campus recruitment pay for the really top trainees is upwards of Rs 2,000,000 per year. Adjusted for inflation, this is at West European levels. Companies' policy stance at the middle-management level tends to flow through to the senior management. The only caveat is that with regard to campus salaries, companies have little choice other than move with the market. So, the practice of sign-on bonuses, which do not have to be paid to those already in the company, is catching up.

According to one leading remuneration survey, over 90% of the big companies offer variable pay at middle- and senior-management level. The payout is typically 15 to 20%, heavily dependent on individual performance. Mostly carried out annually, some do performance reviews more frequently. Half of these companies also offer long-term Incentives for their senior managers, both stock options and restricted stocks. Key challenges in managing remuneration at these levels is performance management systems which ensure variable pay and pay differentiations are credible.

During the early years of economic liberalization, the demand for really good managers at the middle and senior levels was very high, as new companies that came into the country did not have the time to develop their own talent. This type of demand is no longer there. Mergers and consolidations are now taking place: e.g., the merger of Vodafone and Idea Cellular in telecom, Flipkart and eBay India, or, Aditya Birla Nuvo and Grasim, making corporate- and middle-level jobs redundant. As the global reward head of a conglomerate expects, "some cooling off in the pay growth at these levels will happen".

Top management

It is at the level of top management, CXOs and executive directors of the big corporates, one has seen dramatic change over the years. The situation until the 1980s was absurd, with top man-agement being paid only pennies. Some – not all of them – did manage to live like maharajas, however, thanks not so much to 'fringe' benefits, or foreign remittances, as to the fact that pay below top management levels was suppressed to unrealistic levels.

This began to change in the 1990s once the legal limits on executive pay were first relaxed and then removed. The growth in the past decade is very dramatic, as shown in Figure 40.2.

Figure 40.2 is based on analysis of published data from some of the leading Sensex 30 com-panies, turnover US $5 billion plus, across industries like FMCG, IT, Telecoms and Engineering. The CEO total pay has risen from US$1 million to US$4 million in the past decade. These total remuneration figures exclude the value of Long-Term Incentive Plans (LTIPs). The pay mix of total pay of CXOs is typically 50% fixed pay, 20 to 30% short-term incentives paid as cash, and 20 to 30% long-term incentives, mostly stock options and restricted stocks. To arrive at the total

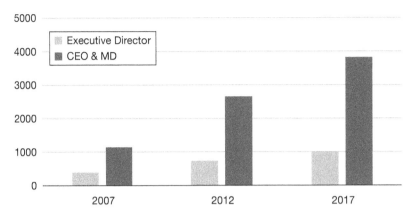

Figure 40.2   Top management total remuneration excluding LTIP values (US$000 per annum)

compensation including LTIPs, one should apply a plus 25% to plus 40% factor to the figures in Figure 40.2.

What are the key trends and challenges?

- According to a leading CEO coach: "The reward philosophy varies across different levels of management. At the lower level, cost and productivity are the drivers. At the top, it is about acknowledging their distinctiveness in contributing to the success of the company." The reward in its totality has to recognise their value to the company. Roles incorporating regional or global responsibilities have therefore to be tailor-made and reflected in their pay in a global context. "In places like Delhi, Mumbai and Bangalore, multi-million-dollar, exclusive, by invitation-only, apartments are coming up, and, you want to tell the world, you belong there!" Visible 'asset creation' is something sought by many top managers in India.

- As in the West a clearly tiered top management pay market linked to company size and global reach has emerged. As the CFO of a Telecoms giant says: "There is a well-defined market for the Sensex 30 Company Managing Directors and Executive Directors." Pay packages are no longer perquisites-heavy. Cash is king – along with stocks.

- According to a leading remuneration consultant: "The pay levels and increases have been justified, as elsewhere in the world, on competitive market pressures and the need for remuneration levels to attract and retain top global talent, and align their pay with company performance, and indeed reinforce top performance culture: you pay top dollars, you get top performer."

- Headhunters routinely tap top Indian executives working abroad; to lure them back to India, they have to be paid at 'global' levels. Many multinational company roles in India are regional roles with responsibility for parts of or the whole of the rest of Asia, and their pay does not depend on their location: Delhi, Mumbai or Singapore. And some are global CXOs or directors, with MDs or senior managers in their subsidiaries in Europe or USA reporting to them and paid according to those markets. For all these reasons, top pay levels in India are 'global'.

- Regulations on governance have been tightened and institutional investors, foreign and Indian, are a major force. Boards of directors, therefore, take the task of target setting and the performance evaluation of their top management very seriously. 'Alpha' and 'Delta', in particular, are important considerations: 'Alpha', as the financial analysts use it, is how much better your performance is relative to the benchmark; 'Delta' is all about growth, i.e., how your business is growing.

- There are extensive disclosure requirements. Not only does top management have to be explained and justified, but information on parity with other employees, both on the level of pay and increase in pay, also has to be disclosed. Reported remuneration differentials, CXO to the median remuneration of all employees, varies from 100:1 to 300:1. To date, criticism on top pay and such huge pay differentials has been muted. Some CXOs are careful: Mukesh Ambani, India's richest person, operates a self-imposed ceiling of Rs 150 million on his remuneration, although not exactly the $1 salary of Mark Zuckerberg of Facebook, or, Larry Page of Google. There are others like Sunil Mittal, another billionaire and CXO of Bharti Airtel, who has sought approval for increasing the ceiling on his remuneration to Rs 700 million!

- According to the chairman of a major company, who also sits on several other Remuneration Committees, there are thus three key challenges. First, while global bench-marking is accepted, the question is – What is global: UK levels, US levels? Second, how do we justify the pay and the top-to-bottom pay differential to the shareholders and other stakeholders? Third, how do we assess performance and, given the volatile market conditions, should factors beyond one's control be taken into account? Boards are no longer willing to listen to reasons – such as demonetization, or a ban on alcohol sales in shops near motorways, if targets are missed.

Epilogue

In the past hundred years, India has gone on a substantial journey: from *Pax Britannica*, to an archetypal socialist economy, to being increasingly liberalized in a globalizing economy. Pay levels and pay practices which atrophied for forty years since India's independence have caught up with the developing world. India's unique combination of sheer numbers, 1.3 billion and counting, history and traditions, diversity and differences, and democracy, means any prediction could turn out to be completely wrong. With that caveat, here are some predictions to draw the chapter to a conclusion:

- With management pay in India at or close to global levels, especially when adjusted for cost of living, big, sustained, across-the-board, pay increases of the kind witnessed in the past two decades will not continue; if India continues to be the top of the pack in economic growth rate, however, pay levels will go up in pockets where there are supply–demand gaps, especially for global quality and new skills.
- New models of employment will become more prevalent and remuneration will be for tasks or projects delivered as contract employees or third-party associates.
- At senior and top management levels, the focus will be on performance metrics and measurement and justifying their pay. At all levels, cost control will be important.
- The search will continue for truly meaningful long-term performance measures and claw-back provisions if achievements turn out to be mirages.
- It is a moot point how long the current huge disparity between the top and median pay in Indian companies will be acceptable. Sooner or later, some interest group or a political party will focus on the issue and everyone else will jump on to the bandwagon.

'Watch the Space!'

INDEX

Note: Page locators in italics refer to figures; those in bold refer to tables.